Corporate Information Strategy and Management

Text and Cases

Corporate Information Strategy and Management

Text and Cases

Eighth Edition

Lynda M. Applegate
Harvard Business School

Robert D. Austin
Copenhagen Business School
Harvard Business School

Deborah L. Soule
Harvard Business School

McGraw Hill Education (India) Private Limited
NEW DELHI

McGraw Hill Education Offices

New Delhi New York St Louis San Francisco Auckland Bogotá Caracas
Kuala Lumpur Lisbon London Madrid Mexico City Milan Montreal
San Juan Santiago Singapore Sydney Tokyo Toronto

McGraw Hill Education (India) Private Limited

CORPORATE INFORMATION STRATEGY AND MANAGEMENT: TEXT AND CASES

McGraw Hill Education (India) Edition 2014

Third reprint 2014
RLQYYDLURYYXQ

Reprinted in India by arrangement with The McGraw-Hill Companies, Inc., New York

Sales territories: India, Pakistan, Nepal, Bangladesh, Sri Lanka and Bhutan

Library of Congress Cataloging-in-Publication Data

Applegate, Lynda M.
Corporate information strategy and management: text and cases / Lynda M. Applegate, Robert D. Austin, Deborah L. Soule.—8th ed.
p. cm.
Includes index.
ISBN-13: 978-0-07-340293-2 (alk. paper)
ISBN-10: 0-07-340293-1 (alk. paper)
1. Information technology—Management. 2. Management information systems. 3. Information resources management. 4. Information technology—Management—Case studies. I. Austin, Robert D. (Robert Daniel), 1962-II. Soule, Deborah L. III. Title.
HD30.2A65 2009
658.4'038011—dc22 2008047906

ISBN-13: 978-93-392-0580-5
ISBN-10: 93-392-0580-4

Published by McGraw Hill Education (India) Private Limited,
P-24, Green Park Extension, New Delhi 110 016, and printed at
Pashupati Printers Pvt. Ltd., Delhi 110 095

Dedicated to our colleagues and mentors of many years,
James L. McKenney and F. Warren McFarlan.

About the Authors

LYNDA M. APPLEGATE is the Martin Marshall Professor of Business Administration at Harvard Business School and is chair of the Entrepreneurial Management Unit and Faculty Chair of HBS' Owner Management Executive Programs. Prior to joining the HBS faculty, she held various faculty and administrative positions. Dr. Applegate's research and recent publications focus on the impact of information technology on industries, markets, and organizations. In 1999, she was awarded Harvard Business School's prestigious Apgar Award for Innovation in Teaching and, in 1992, the School's Berol Award for research excellence.

Dr. Applegate is an active international consultant and is on the board of directors and advisory boards for both publicly-traded and venture-backed companies. She has served on the advisory board for NASDAQ, the World Bank's Global Development Gateway, and is on the board of trustees of the Massachusetts Technology Leadership Council. During the late 1990s, she participated on a Blue-Ribbon Panel to define a National Research Agenda on the Information Age economy and participated in a roundtable of advisors to President Clinton's Commission on Critical Infrastructure Protection.

ROBERT D. AUSTIN is a professor of managing creativity and innovation at Copenhagen Business School and an associate professor of technology and operations management at Harvard Business School (HBS). He chairs the HBS executive program for chief information officers and has written more than one hundred published papers, articles, and cases, some of which have received international awards. He is also author, co-author, or co-editor of several books, most recently *The Adventures of an IT Leader,* a novel about IT management. Before becoming a professor, he was an IT manager at a major international corporation. He is active on editorial and advisory boards for numerous academic organizations and companies.

DEBORAH L. SOULE is an independent consultant and a research associate at Harvard Business School. Prior to working at Harvard University as Research Manager of an executive-level learning consortium, she worked internationally as a management consultant, specializing in information systems (IS) issues, and as an IS professional in the chemical industry.

Dr. Soule's research and consulting focuses on the design, practice, and management of collaborative and innovative work in organizations, with particular attention to the roles of information technology, leadership, diverse knowledge, and dispersed settings. She has designed and taught graduate level management courses in the fields of information technology management and product development, and has facilitated collaborative learning experiences for management practitioners on innovation, change, and knowledge management.

Preface

Corporate Information Strategy and Management examines how information technology (IT) enables organizations to conduct business in radically different and more effective ways. The commercialization of the Internet and the steady stream of innovations have created a seismic change in the business environment. New channels of supply and distribution are emerging. New electronic marketplaces and exchanges are being created. The infrastructures of firms and the industries within which they operate have been permanently altered.

This is a fast-moving and global phenomenon. For established companies, the resulting challenges have been deep and pervasive. In many cases, the changes have threatened not just a firm's competitiveness but also its survival. Executives bear an enormous burden as they attempt to understand the challenges, keep abreast of events, and make intelligent decisions and plans.

The objective of this book is to provide readers with a better understanding of the influence of twenty-first-century technologies on business decisions. The book discusses today's challenges from the point of view of the executives who are grappling with them. It recounts stories of success and failure, focusing on the issues faced and the decisions made by executives in companies around the world.

The cases and readings presented here are organized in an Introduction, three modules, and a Conclusion. The first module is aimed at understanding the impact of IT on industries, markets, and organizations. It discusses issues of business model design, and strategic positioning and explains how twenty-first-century IT provides opportunities to alter market/industry structure, power, and relationships. The first module also discusses the impact of IT on organizational capabilities leadership. The first module ends with a discussion of how to frame the business case for IT and measure business value and governance. The second module turns the reader's attention to operational issues at the interface of business and technology as it examines approaches to designing and managing open-standard, networked technology infrastructures. The third module concentrates on leadership and management of IT activities, focusing on the issues that arise at the boundary as four key constituents—business executives, IT executives, users, and IT partners—work together to leverage technology to create a sustainable advantage. The Conclusion summarizes key frameworks, insights, and themes. Case studies are provided at the end of each module to enable discussion of the issues that twenty-first-century executives must address.

The material presented here is the outgrowth of field-based research we have conducted at the Harvard Business School since the early 1970s. To Deans John McArthur, Kim Clark, and Jay Light we express our appreciation for making the time and resources available for us to complete this work.

We are particularly indebted to the executives who provided so much time and insight during the course of our research. All the cases in this book are based on observations of strategic decision making and action in real organizations. Without the cooperation of many executives, the preparation of this book would not have been possible.

We are grateful as well for the many valuable suggestions and insights provided by our Harvard Business School colleagues, especially Jim Cash, Alan MacCormack, Andrew McAfee, Jim McKenney, F. Warren McFarlan, Richard Nolan, Kash Rangan, and David Upton. In addition, we acknowledge the valued work of our doctoral students, fellows, and research assistants. Our heartfelt thanks go to Nancy Bartlett, Alastair Brown, Elizabeth Collins, Mark Cotteleer, Melissa Dailey, Brian Delacey, LeGrand Elebash, Cedric Escalle, David Lane, Marc Mandel, Felipe Monteiro, Beth Rochefort, Tom Rodd, Mary Rotelli, Frederick Soule, Erin Sullivan, George Westerman, and Fred Young. We also acknowledge the support of the directors of Harvard Business School research centers, including Christina Darwall of the California Research Center; Gustavo Herrero, Director of the Latin America Research Center; Camille Tang Yeh, Director of the Asia Pacific Center; and Carin Knoop, Executive Director of Global Research. Thanks go to Alan Murray, a superlative friend and former colleague, who provided important reviews of technical details, especially in the chapter on computer security. Finally, we express our appreciation to our editor, Tom Cameron, and to Jennifer Chalfin, Maureen Donovan, Zoya Omartian, Brooke Spangler, Isaac Ugbabe, and Maurie SuDock, who provided administrative support.

Lynda M. Applegate
Robert D. Austin
Deborah L. Soule

Contents

MODULE TWO
THE BUSINESS OF IT 233

MODULE THREE
IT LEADERSHIP 401

Chapter 9
Governance of the IT Function 403

Chapter 10
Leadership of the IT Function 423

Concluding Thoughts 475

Introduction: Corporate Information Strategy and Management

Information technology (IT) has always been a wildcard in business, a source of opportunity and uncertainty, of advantage and risk. Business executives have often viewed the IT function with apprehension, as the province of technocrats primarily interested in new features that may have little relevance to real-world business problems. Technology executives have often considered business managers to be short-sighted, lacking the vision to exploit all that technology has to offer. Both struggle as they attempt to implement increasingly complex systems in the face of rapid change in business and technology.

And yet we have, since the inception of business computing, tightened our embrace of IT—and for good reason. Despite exasperating moments, technology has become embedded in the way we define and execute strategy, in how we organize and lead businesses, and how we define a unique value proposition.

Indeed, the pace of IT evolution has been both dramatic and disconcerting. The co-evolution of technology, work, and the workforce over the past 40 years has dramatically influenced our concept of organizations and the industries within which they compete. No longer simply a tool to support "back-office" transactions, IT has become a strategic part of most businesses, enabling the redefinition of markets and industries and the strategies and designs of firms competing within them. Today's global communication networks carry information around the world in seconds. Distance and time have become much less significant as limitations on our ability to define and execute business strategy.[1] Moreover, information has become a major economic good, frequently exchanged in concert with, or even in place of, tangible goods and services.

The events of recent years have added considerably to the mystique and the magic of IT. Something dramatic happened to technology in the 1990s, although it is probably too early to discern the full impact. Many of us remember the first time we opened

[1] T. Friedman, *The World Is Flat 3.0: A Brief History of the 21st Century*, Picador Publishing, 2007.

a browser and gained access to the World Wide Web (WWW). For some executives who had lived their lives avoiding technology, a light went on, and they glimpsed the potential of what previously had lain deep within the silicon switches that processed data in the basement of the organization. Others ventured forth only to become mired in a sea of useless information and broken links that convinced them that, although the technology was more appealing to the eye, the same old flaws remained.

Then came the boom of the late 1990s, when the capital markets caught the fever. Stories of "20-something" billionaires who only a few years earlier had plotted their business ideas on napkins grabbed our attention. Stories of investors who pushed entrepreneurs to take more money and spend it more quickly challenged our view of the blood, sweat, and tears that used to define how a new business was built from the ground up. Stories of newly public firms with market capitalizations in the billions of dollars, yet with no discernible path to profitability, caused us to question the fundamental economic principles that guided how we built and managed companies.

As the new century dawned, the "bubble" burst. The tech-heavy Nasdaq lost more than half its value within months and spending for IT equipment and services dropped. The world economy headed into a downward spiral.

Some young executives began their careers during the boom, and for a time it seemed they would have an advantage. When the dot-com bubble burst, executives young and old found themselves in pretty much the same situation as they attempted to make sense of which opportunities were real and which were nothing more than the hype that surrounds all new inventions. The years since have been characterized by gradual recovery from the collapse of tech stocks during 2000–2003, and the return of a more carefully reasoned approach to the use of IT practice—until very recently, that is. As we write, a global economic crisis has emerged that resulted in a dramatic collapse of worldwide stock markets.

But, even during these times of uncertainty, some things are clear. The world is forever changed. IT has burst forth from its safe containment in the basements of corporations. Business executives have begun to wrest control from IT executives who have failed to step up to the challenge of entering the boardroom. Technology has become a core enabler and, in some cases, the primary channel through which business is done. The world is smaller and the "global village" is quickly becoming a reality. Physical location matters less than it did. Borders and boundaries, ownership and control have become less rigid. The last decade has offered examples of IT-enabled "virtual" organizations in which many small, independent firms band together as nodes on an information network to achieve dramatic increases in scope and scale. Such arrangements challenge both our legal and social definitions of an organization as business practice outpaces legal and regulatory policy—especially in areas like international competitiveness and trade, intellectual property, privacy, security, family, community, education, and culture. And, yet, there are still new frontiers to explore, new challenges to meet, and new magic in store.

Because so much has changed so quickly, because the ups and downs have come in such a short interval, now is a difficult time to engage in sense-making. Yet that is precisely what we are doing in this book. We're attempting to relate what we know from decades of study to what we are learning from those who are creating the future. The last decade has been the richest vein of potential learning we have ever been positioned to mine. It has been a period of intense experimentation. Many new models were tried. Many of them failed. We would be remiss if we did not attempt to understand it all—the successes and the failures.

Our objective is to help business executives recognize the tremendous potential of technology in creating business advantage and to help them assume a leadership role in IT-enabled business transformation. At the same time, we wish to help IT executives assume leadership positions, not just in defining and executing technology strategy and managing the IT function, but also in defining and executing business strategy. As we work toward these dual objectives, we draw on years of research and experience, much of it in the field with executives who have accepted the challenge and are venturing forward into uncharted waters. This book is filled with their stories, captured in short examples throughout the text and in full-length case studies at the end of each of three modules.

- ***Module 1: IT and Business Advantage*** addresses the approaches executives use, decisions they make, and issues they face as they attempt to leverage IT to create business advantage. The module introduces the concept of a business model as a key framework that guides executive decision making and action. It then discusses the impact of twenty-first century IT on the three key components of a business model—strategy, capabilities, and value. The objective of Module 1 is to provide key frameworks and tools for understanding the impact of IT on business advantage.
- ***Module 2: The Business of IT*** shifts the focus from the impact of IT on business to the business of IT. The module examines the changing technology infrastructure and its impact on front-line operations. The chapters in this module examine how emerging technologies influence approaches to managing IT assets, projects, and risks. The objective of Module 2 is to provide key frameworks and tools for understanding how to manage the business of IT.
- ***Module 3: IT Leadership*** enables exploration of the responsibilities, obligations, and expectations of IT leaders as they exploit today's IT solutions and services to drive business advantage. The module discusses general IT governance matters, including strategic alignment, compliance and risk management, and relates these to more tactical IT management activities. The objective of Module 3 is to address issues facing twenty-first century IT leaders.

Before you turn to Module 1, take a moment to answer the following questions. Jot down your answers and use the insights from this book to address areas for improvement.

1. How important is IT to our success and survival? Are we missing opportunities that, if properly executed, would enable us to transform our company or industry?
2. Are we prioritizing IT investments and targeting our development efforts in the right areas? Are we spending money efficiently and effectively?
3. Are our IT and business leaders capable of defining and executing IT-enabled strategies? Have we opened an effective dialogue among business executives, IT executives, users, and partners?
4. Does our IT platform enable our business to be both lean and agile? What percentage of our IT-related activities are devoted to operating and maintaining outdated "legacy" applications versus enabling business growth and strategy execution?

5. Are we managing IT assets and infrastructure efficiently and effectively? Is leadership of IT activities at the right level? Do we have the right business and IT leaders given our goals for its use?
6. Are we organized to identify, evaluate, and assimilate IT-enabled business innovations? Are we missing windows of opportunity to exploit emerging technologies and business models?
7. Is our IT infrastructure sufficiently insulated against the risks of a major operational disaster? Are the appropriate security, privacy, and risk management systems in place to ensure "always on" and "always up" service?

We hope you enjoy the book and find it useful as you attempt to leverage the opportunities and address the challenges of using IT to drive business advantage.

IBM's Decade of Transformation: Turnaround to Growth

The story of IBM's rise to greatness, its abrupt fall, and the executives who led the company through one of the most spectacular turnarounds in history makes the IBM case a leadership classic. But the insights from the case extend well beyond the company's successful turnaround enabling discussion of the challenges large established firms face as they attempt to simultaneously manage disciplined execution, high growth, and emerging opportunities. As you read the case, consider the following questions: What factors led to IBM's problems? What actions did Gerstner take when he assumed the role of CEO in April 1993? How well did he perform as a turnaround manager? What challenges did Gerstner and his successor, Sam Palmisano, face as they attempted to position IBM for growth and innovation? Why do large established companies like IBM find it so difficult to innovate? What made IBM a "great company" during the 1960s and 1970s? Can the company become a great company again, and what is your definition of greatness?

Case I-1

IBM's Decade of Transformation: Turnaround to Growth

> This is my last annual letter to you. By the time you read this, Sam Palmisano will be our new chief executive officer, the eighth in IBM's history. He will be responsible for shaping our strategic direction as well as leading our operations. . . . I want to use this occasion to offer my perspective on what lies ahead for our industry. To many observers today, its future is unclear, following perhaps the worst year in its history. A lot of people chalk that up to the recession and the "dot-com bubble." They seem to believe that when the economies of the world recover, life in the information technology industry will get back to normal. In my view, nothing could be further from the truth.
>
> *Lou Gerstner, IBM Annual Report, 2001*

In 1990, IBM was the second-most-profitable company in the world, with net income of $6 billion on revenues of $69 billion, and it was completing a transformation designed to position it for success in the next decade. For the world leader in an industry that expected to keep growing spectacularly, the future looked promising. But all was not well within IBM, and its senior executives realized it. "In 1990, we were feeling pretty good because things seemed to be getting better," one executive remarked. "But we weren't feeling great because we knew there were deep structural problems." Those structural problems revealed themselves sooner than anyone expected and more terribly than anyone feared. Beginning in the first quarter of 1991, IBM began posting substantial losses. Between 1991 and 1993, IBM lost a staggering $16 billion. In April 1992, John Akers, IBM CEO from 1985 to 1993, vented his frustrations during a company training program. His comment, "People don't realize how much trouble we're in," made its way from company bulletin boards to the press, shaking employee and investor confidence.

In April 1993, Gerstner took charge. While many wondered how an executive with no technology background could rescue IBM, insiders knew that Gerstner was brought in not to rescue the company

Professors Lynda M. Applegate and Robert D. Austin and Research Associate Elizabeth Collins prepared this case as the basis for class discussion rather than to illustrate effective or ineffective management.

Reprinted by permission of Harvard Business School.

but to break it up for sale. In no time, however, Gerstner learned from customers, analysts, and employees that IBM's value was not in its pieces. Reversing direction, he rallied support for saving IBM.

By 1995, the company was back on solid financial footing. Catalyzed by the Internet boom and the massive technology spending needed to ready businesses for the new millennium, IBM began growing again—but at a slower rate than the information technology (IT) industry as a whole. While the press hailed the turnaround, executives inside IBM knew that the company had not yet found what they had begun to call "The Next Big Thing."

In March 2002, Gerstner passed the reins of power to Sam Palmisano, a 31-year company veteran, to complete the transformation. Palmisano and the senior executive team were committed to returning the company to greatness. "[Our problems in the late 1980s and early 1990s] were our own fault," Nick Donofrio, senior vice president, Technology and Manufacturing, explained. "We are driven by a passion that says: 'Never again.'"[1] IBM visionary Irving Wladawsky-Berger was reminded of the 1950s, when a "series of technology asteroids" had created seismic shifts in the computer industry, opening the way for the IBM System/360 to become the dominant design for the next 40 years. The launch of the S/360 catalyzed a period of IT-enabled business innovation that created new industries even as it transformed established industries and the organizations that competed with them. During that period IBM was viewed as the "greatest company in the world," Palmisano explained. Palmisano, Wladawsky-Berger, and the executive team at IBM believed that the Internet and associated network technologies had catalyzed a period of technological revolution that would usher in a new era of IT-enabled business innovation that would be even more profound. IBM, they reasoned, was positioned to lead this revolution. "Before they retire, people want to remember that old feeling."[2] A *Fortune* article commented on what would be required:

> The criteria for genuine greatness are daunting. "What is a great company?" asks management writer Jim Collins. "No. 1 is performance. Not just relative to your past but such that an investment in your company is substantially superior to an investment in the general market. And, no discounts for being in a tough industry. Second you need a unique impact. Are you doing something of such excellence that if your company went away it would leave an unfillable hole?" Collins says that any company that can stage a rebound like IBM's in the past decade is surely capable of meeting his tests. "But will they?" he asks. "That's up to them."[3]

Company Background

> IBM made a big bet on the 360 series [of mainframe computers] in the 1960s and by the end of it, people were talking about "IBM and the seven dwarfs." If they get this right, we could have the same thing all over again.
>
> *Charles O'Reilly, Professor, Stanford Business School, 2003*[4]

IBM was founded in 1911 through the merger of three companies that dated to 1890. Three years later, Thomas J. Watson joined the company and began instituting many of the principles and practices for which IBM would become known: dark-suited salespeople, a strong culture of corporate pride and loyalty, implied lifetime employment, and a work ethic expressed in the slogan "THINK." Watson led the company through almost 40 years of success. At the threshold of the computer era in 1952, he turned leadership over to his son, Thomas Watson, Jr.

[1] D. Kirkpatrick, "Inside Sam's $100 Billion Growth Machine," *Fortune*, June 21, 2004, p. 98.

[2] Ibid.

[3] Ibid.

[4] As quoted in Simon London, "IBM's New Chief Executive Is Betting That the Company's Future Lies in the Acquisition of a Consulting Firm," *The Financial Times*, October 10, 2003.

EXHIBIT 1 Timeline

Source: Author, based on IBM company documents and Web site; images downloaded from IBM Web site, July 2004.

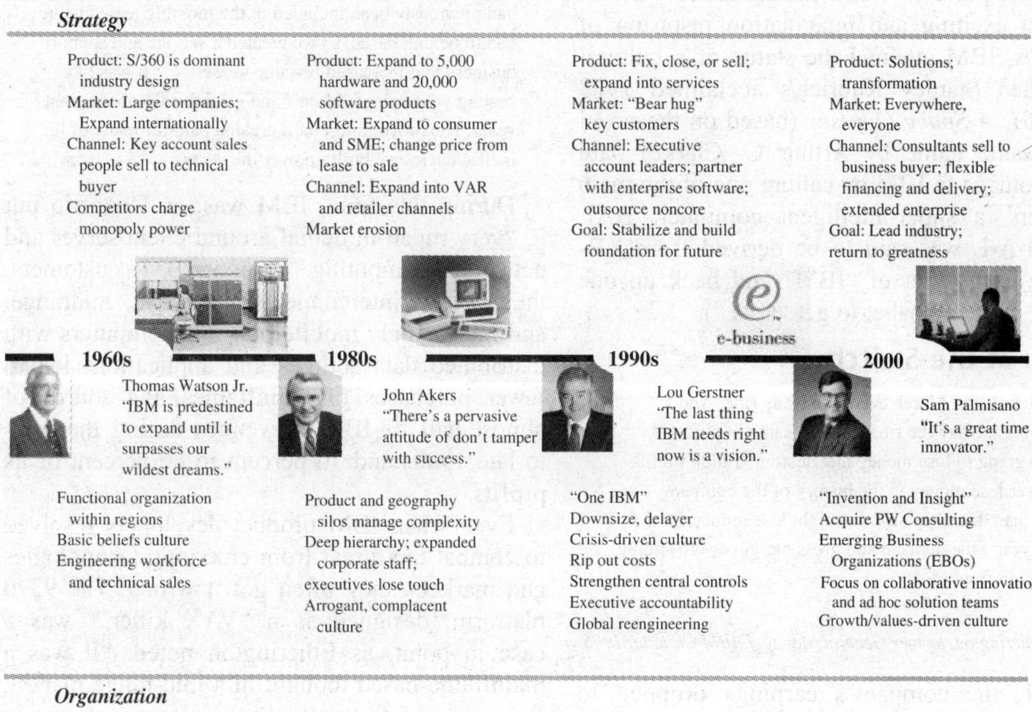

Note: SME = Small to medium-sized enterprises.

Under Watson, Jr., IBM became the world's dominant player in the growing IT industry. In a bold move, Watson Jr. invested $5 billion to develop the System/360 computer, the first family of products based on an integrated semiconductor chip and offering interchangeability of components. The System/360 was the "biggest privately financed commercial project ever."[5] This radical departure from the incremental innovation that characterized early vacuum tube computers transformed the industry and set the dominant design for decades to come. In the same time period, the company produced a series of related IT innovations, including one of the first English-like computer languages (FORTRAN), the hard disk, the floppy disk, the IBM supermarket checkout station, and an early version of the automatic teller machine. So dominant was IBM by the late 1960s that it became the target of an unsuccessful 13-year-long antitrust action by the U.S. Justice Department. (See Exhibit 1 for a timeline of the company.)

With its on-time launch in 1981, the IBM PC became the most successful technology introduction of its time; its sales of 241,683 units *in a single month* exceeded the five-year forecast. While successful, however, the PC was always considered a "stepchild" of the real money-making machine—the mainframe. Rather than push low-margin PCs through IBM's traditional field sales force, IBM for the first time marketed and sold it through third-party retailers, distributors, and value-added resellers (VARs).

By the mid-1980s, IBM's products were universally regarded as sound solutions to a range of business problems, as was apparent from the

[5] Spencer Ante, "The New Blue," *BusinessWeek*, March 17, 2003.

oft-repeated dictum that "nobody ever got fired for buying IBM." The company was also known as *the* best place to work. Sitting astride one of the most exciting and imagination inspiring of industries, IBM attained the status of a cultural icon when Stanley Kubrick's acclaimed 1968 film *2001: A Space Odyssey* (based on the novel of the same name by Arthur C. Clarke) paid subtle homage to IBM by calling one of the main characters, a super-intelligent computer, HAL 2000. H-A-L was said to be derived from I-B-M (take each letter of "IBM" and back up one position in the alphabet to get "HAL").

Asleep at the Switch

> From January to March everything was fine. And I remember the day the finance guys came in and said, "We're going to lose money this quarter." I didn't think we'd ever lose money in the history of the company. Worse than that, they said we might lose money for a whole year—the demand and gross margins were sliding that fast in front of us.
>
> *Bill Etherington, former General Manager, IBM Canada, 1995*[6]

In 1991, the company's earnings dropped to negative $2.8 billion—a plummet of 146 percent. As revenues continued to slide by more than 60 percent for each of the next two years, the "most admired" company in the world was tagged a "dinosaur" and a "has-been." (See Exhibit 2 for company financials.) Critics recited a litany of problems: The company was blinded by hubris, out of touch with its customers, and distracted by internal turf battles. "The money tree stopped growing," explained Donofrio.

Early signs of trouble had appeared in 1984 as returns on sales, assets, and equity began to decline. That weakening was, in part, the aftermath of converting a leasing-oriented business for mainframes into a sales-oriented business. John M. Thompson, former vice chairman, explained:

> It had a huge effect on revenue because we not only recorded sales from the new shipments, but we could also book one-time gains from selling installed rental machines that had been mostly written off the balance sheet. Once you sold a mainframe, the maintenance that had previously been included in the monthly lease charge had to be purchased, so we created a service and support business that increased revenue as well. . . . It was like "eating your own children," and we did it for about eight years. The profit umbrella it created paid for many of the inefficiencies we built up over the years.[7]

During this time, IBM was, as Donofrio put it, "very much in denial around client/server and networked computing."[8] Among IBM's customers, the need to interconnect mainframe, midrange, and increasingly mobile personal computers with distributed data sources and applications led to fewer purchases of mainframes, the source of almost half of IBM's revenues during the mid- to late 1980s and 70 percent to 80 percent of its profits.

Even when IBM product developers resolved to combat the threat from emerging technologies and markets, they often got it wrong. The 9370 platform, designed as a "VAX killer,"[9] was a case in point, as Etherington noted: "It was a mainframe-based thought in a mid-range market. We used mainframe thinking, in terms of pricing and cost structures, and tried to launch it in the middle market—and it bombed."[10] That same mainframe thinking also blinded IBM to the much faster evolutionary path of the PC. In addition, IBM's marketing efforts for PCs missed the mark. "Just about every vendor [did] a better job of marketing PCs than IBM [did]," said the CEO of one IBM customer. "No one ever looked at the IBM PC as being inferior, but IBM [did] nothing to sell it. Meanwhile, in the early '90s, Compaq

[6] R. Austin and R. Nolan, "IBM Corporation: Turnaround 1991–1995," HBS Case No. 600-098 (Boston: Harvard Business School Publishing, 2000), p. 4.

[7] Ibid., p. 3.

[8] Ibid., p. 4.

[9] The VAX was a Digital Equipment Company midrange computer that gained wide popularity in the 1980s; platforms in the VAX family, from high to low end, were based on the same architecture and interoperated well. This degree of interoperability was unusual at the time the VAX was introduced, and it provided a flexible and cost-effective alternative to mainframes for many applications.

[10] R. Austin and R. Nolan, "IBM Corporation: Turnaround 1991–1995," HBS Case No. 600-098, p. 5.

EXHIBIT 2 IBM Corporation Financial History

Source: Company documents and annual reports.

Consolidated Statement of Earnings for the Years Ended December 31 (US$ millions)	1980	1985	1990	1992	1994	1996	1998	2000	2001	2002
Revenue:										
Services	4,425	11,536	11,322	14,987	16,936	22,310	28,916	33,152	34,956	36,360
Hardware	21,788	38,520	43,959	33,755	32,344	36,634	35,419	34,470	30,593	27,456
Software			9,952	11,103	11,346	11,426	11,863	12,598	12,939	13,074
Financing			3,785	4,678	3,425	3,054	2,877	3,465	3,426	3,232
Enterprise investments/other						2,523	2,592	1,404	1,153	1,064
Total Revenue	**26,213**	**50,056**	**69,018**	**64,523**	**64,051**	**75,947**	**81,667**	**85,089**	**83,067**	**81,186**
Cost:										
Services	2,181	4,689	6,617	9,481	11,404	16,270	21,125	24,309	25,355	26,812
Hardware	7,968	14,911	19,401	19,698	21,300	22,888	24,214	24,207	21,231	20,020
Software			3,126	3,924	4,680	2,946	2,260	2,283	2,265	2,043
Financing		1,503	1,579	1,966	1,384	1,481	1,494	1,965	1,693	1,416
Enterprise investments/other						1,823	1,702	747	634	611
Total Cost	**10,149**	**21,103**	**30,723**	**35,069**	**38,768**	**45,408**	**50,795**	**53,511**	**51,178**	**50,902**
Gross Profit	**16,064**	**28,953**	**38,295**	**29,454**	**25,283**	**30,539**	**30,872**	**31,578**	**31,889**	**30,284**
Operating Expenses:										
Selling, general & administrative	10,324	13,000	20,709	19,526	15,916	16,854	16,662	17,393	17,048	18,738
Research, development & engineering		4,723	6,554	6,522	4,363	5,089	5,046	5,084	4,986	4,750
Restructuring charges				11,645						
Interest expense	273	443	1,324	1,360	1,227	716	713	344	234	145
Intellectual property and custom development income								(1,664)	(1,476)	(1,100)
Other (income) and expense	(430)	(832)	(495)	(573)	(1,377)	(707)	(589)	(990)	(353)	(227)
Total Expense and Other Income	**10,167**	**17,334**	**26,434**	**38,440**	**20,129**	**21,952**	**21,832**	**20,167**	**20,439**	**22,760**

(continued)

EXHIBIT 2 **IBM Corporation Financial History (*Continued*)**

Consolidated Statement of Earnings for the Years Ended December 31 (US$ millions)

	1980	1985	1990	1992	1994	1996	1998	2000	2001	2002
Operating Income (Loss)	5,897	11,619	10,203	(8,986)	5,154	8,587	9,040	11,411	11,450	7,524
(Provision) benefit for income taxes	(2,335)	(5,064)	(4,183)	2,161	(2,134)	(3,158)	(2,712)	(3,537)	(3,304)	(2,190)
Income (loss) from discontinued operations:								219	(423)	(1,755)
Net earnings (loss) before changes in accounting principles				(6,825)						
Effect of changes in accounting principles				1,900						
Net Income	3,562	6,555	6,020	(4,925)	3,020	5,429	6,328	8,093	7,723	3,579

Balance Sheet for the Years Ended December 31 (US$ millions)

	1980	1985	1990	1992	1994	1996	1998	2000	2001	2002
Assets:										
Cash and cash equivalents	281	896	3,853	4,446	7,922	7,687	5,375	3,563	6,330	5,382
Marketable securities	1,831	4,726	698	1,203	2,632	450	393	159	63	593
Notes and accounts receivable	4,877	10,566	16,962	14,199	15,182	17,446	20,271	12,021	10,362	11,362
Leasing/short-term financing receivables			5,682	7,405	6,351	5,721	6,510	18,705	16,656	15,996
Inventories	2,293	8,579	10,108	8,385	6,334	5,870	5,200	4,765	4,304	3,148
Other	643	1,303	1,617	4,054	2,917	3,521	4,611	4,667	4,746	5,171
Total Current Assets	**9,925**	**26,070**	**38,920**	**39,692**	**41,338**	**40,695**	**42,360**	**43,880**	**42,461**	**41,652**
Plant, rental machines, other property	26,370	34,483	53,659	52,786	44,820	41,893	44,870	38,455	38,375	36,083
Less: accumulated depreciation	11,353	14,803	26,418	31,191	28,156	24,486	25,239	21,741	21,871	21,643
	15,017	19,680	27,241	21,595	16,664	17,407	19,631	16,714	16,504	14,440
Deferred charges/investments and other assets	1,761	6,884	17,308	21,299	20,126	21,595	23,510	14,447	6,417	8,834
Software, less accumulated amortization			4,099	4,119	2,963	1,435	599			
Long-term financing receivables								13,308	12,246	11,440
Prepaid pension assets									11,397	16,003
Goodwill									1,278	4,115
Total Assets	**26,703**	**52,634**	**87,568**	**86,705**	**81,091**	**81,132**	**86,100**	**88,349**	**90,303**	**96,484**

Current Liabilities:										
Taxes	2,369	3,089	3,159	979	1,771	3,029	3,125	4,827	4,644	5,476
Loans payable	591	1,293	7,602	16,467	9,570	12,957	13,905	10,205	11,188	6,031
Accounts payable	721	1,823	3,367	3,147	3,778	4,767	6,252	8,192	7,047	7,630
Compensation and benefits	1,404	2,460	3,014	3,476	2,702	2,950	3,530	3,801	3,796	3,724
Deferred income	305	391	2,506	3,316	3,475	3,640	4,115	4,516	4,223	5,276
Other accrued expenses and liabilities	1,136	2,377	5,628	9,352	7,930	6,657	5,900	4,865	4,221	6,413
Total Current Liabilities	**6,526**	**11,433**	**25,276**	**36,737**	**29,226**	**34,000**	**36,827**	**36,406**	**35,119**	**34,550**
Deferred income taxes	182	3,650	3,861	2,030	1,881	1,627	1,514			
Reserves for employees' indemnities and retirement plans	1,443									
Retirement and nonpension postretirement benefit obligations									10,308	13,215
Long-term debt	2,099	3,955	11,943	12,853	12,548	9,872	15,508	18,371	15,963	19,986
Other liabilities		1,606	3,656	7,461	14,023	14,005	12,818	12,948	5,465	5,951
Total Liabilities	**10,250**	**9,211**	**44,736**	**22,344**	**57,678**	**59,504**	**66,667**	**67,725**	**66,855**	**73,702**
Stockholders' Equity:										
Common stock	3,992	6,267	6,357	6,563	7,342	7,752	10,121	12,400	14,248	14,858
Preferred stock					1,081	253	247	247		
Retained earnings	12,491	27,234	33,234	19,124	12,352	11,189	10,141	23,784	30,142	31,555
Translation adjustments		−1,466	3,266	1,962	2,672	2,401				
Less: treasury stock, at cost	30	45	25	25	34	135	133	13,800	20,114	20,213
Net unrealized gain on marketable securities						168				
Employee benefits trust							−1,854	−1,712		
Accumulated gains and losses not affecting retained earnings							911	−295	−828	−3,418
Total Stockholders' Equity	16,453	31,990	42,832	27,624	23,413	21,628	19,433	20,624	23,448	22,782
Total Liabilities and Stockholders' Equity	**26,703**	**52,634**	**87,568**	**86,705**	**81,091**	**81,132**	**86,100**	**88,349**	**90,303**	**96,484**

(continued)

EXHIBIT 2 **IBM Corporation Financial History (*Continued*)**

	Cash Flow Statement for the Years Ended December 31 (US$ millions)									
	1980	**1985**	**1990**	**1992**	**1994**	**1996**	**1998**	**2000**	**2001**	**2002**
Cash Flow from Operating Activities										
Income from continuing operations	3,562	6,555	6,020	−4,965	3,021	5,429	6,328	7,874	8,146	5,334
Operating activities:										
Depreciation and amortization	2,362	3,476	5,303	6,259	6,295	5,012	4,992	4,706	4,506	4,379
Deferred income taxes	0	0	0	0	825	11	−606	44	664	−67
Net gain on assets sales and other	1,009	867	32	54	−11	−300	−261	−751	−340	−343
Effect of changes in accounting principles	0	0	0	−1,900	0	0	0	0	0	0
Effect of restructuring charges	0	0	0	8,312	−2,772	−1,491	−355	0	0	0
Funds from operations	90	0	0	0	0	0	0	0	405	1,408
Change in operating assets and liabilities, net of acquisitions/divestitures:										
Receivables	0	0	−2,077	1,052	653	−650	−2,736	−4,692	2,837	4,125
Inventories	0	0	17	704	1,518	196	73	−22	287	793
Pension assets	0	0	0	0	0	0	0	−1,333	−1,758	−4,227
Other assets	0	0	−3,136	−3,396	187	−545	880	673	1,244	70
Accounts payable	0	0	293	−311	305	319	362	2,134	−918	−55
Pension liabilities	0	0	0	0	0	0	596	−237	−69	83
Other liabilities	0	1,880	1,020	465	1,772	2,294	0	441	−1,038	2,288
Net Cash Provided by Operating Activities	**7,023**	**12,778**	**7,472**	**6,274**	**11,793**	**10,275**	**9,273**	**8,837**	**13,966**	**13,788**
Cash Flow from Investing Activities										
Payments for plant, rental machines and other property	−6,195	−6,430	−6,509	−4,751	−3,078	−5,883	−6,520	−5,319	−5,400	−4,753
Proceeds from disposition of plant, rental machines and other property	0	−3,101	804	633	900	1,314	905	1,569	1,149	775
Investment in software	0	−785	−1,892	−1,752	−1,361	−295	−250	−565	−655	−597
Purchases of marketable securities and other investments	−275	−454	−1,234	−3,284	−3,866	−1,613	−4,211	−750	−778	−1,582

Proceeds from disposition of marketable securities and other investments	−1,659	0	1,687	3,276	2,476	1,470	3,945	1,393	738	1,185
Divestiture of businesses	0	0	0	0	1,503	0	0	0	0	1,233
Acquisition of businesses	0	0	0	0	0	−716	0	−329	−916	−3,158
Net Cash Used in Investing Activities	**−8,129**	**−10,770**	**−7,144**	**−5,878**	**−3,426**	**−5,723**	**−6,131**	**−4,001**	**−5,862**	**−6,897**
Translation effects	0	677	0	0	0	0	0	0	0	0
Net Provided from Operations	**−1,106**	**2,685**	**328**	**396**	**8,367**	**4,552**	**3,142**	**4,836**	**8,104**	**6,891**
Cash Flow from Financing Activities										
Net change in long-term debt	510	−686	4,676	10,045	5,335	7,670	7,567	9,604	4,535	6,726
Short-term (repayments)/ borrowings less than 90 days—net	0	−459	1,966	4,199	−1,948	−919	499	−1,400	2,926	−4,087
Payments to settle debt	0	0	−3,683	−10,735	−9,445	−4,992	−5,942	−7,561	−7,898	−5,812
Preferred stock transactions—net	0	0	0	0	−10	0	−5	0	−254	0
Common stock transactions—net	−62	−133	−491	−90	318	−5,005	−6,278	−6,073	−3,652	−3,087
Cash dividends paid	−2,008	−2,703	−2,774	−2,765	−662	−706	−834	−929	−966	−1,005
Net Cash Used in Financing Activities	**−1,560**	**−3,981**	**−306**	**654**	**−6,412**	**−3,952**	**−4,993**	**−6,359**	**−5,309**	**−7,265**
Effect of exchange rate changes on cash and cash equivalents	0	0	131	−549	106	−172	120	−147	−83	148
Net cash (used in)/provided by discontinued operations	0	0	0	0	0	0	0	190	55	−722
Net change in cash and cash equivalents	−1,007	1,260	153	501	2,061	428	−1,731	−1,480	2,767	−948
Cash and Cash Equivalents at Jan. 1	**4,406**	**4,362**	**3,700**	**3,945**	**5,861**	**7,259**	**7,106**	**5,043**	**3,563**	**6,330**
Cash and Cash Equivalents at Dec. 31	**3,399**	**5,622**	**3,853**	**4,446**	**7,922**	**7,687**	**5,375**	**3,563**	**6,330**	**5,382**

stole IBM's PC market with the right price and the right message. Now it's Dell. IBM [was] a sleeping giant losing its golden egg."[11]

Turf battles between autonomous divisions often absorbed more energy than marketplace battles. According to Fran O'Sullivan, general manager of IBM's Personal Computing Division: "At first, the PC group wanted nothing to do with the rest of IBM. We were the mavericks. We saw them as outdated and irrelevant. Then as our business matured, we got into trouble. We couldn't leverage the sales and global services strengths of the company. We came hat in hand for help, but they viewed us as if our ten minutes of fame were up."[12]

While revenues softened, fixed costs burgeoned. Parts of the company were still operating in growth mode. New buildings were being constructed. Warranty costs reached record levels, and customers became more vocal about quality problems. At the heart of the company's problems were its evolved product complexity and the organizational silos that had developed to manage it. (See Exhibit 3 for IBM organization charts in 1993 and 1995.) IBM had 20 separate business units, which collectively sold 5,000 hardware products and 20,000 software products. There were different designs for components that served exactly the same purpose in different products. Different business processes were used in different parts of the company for accomplishing the same thing. Where commonality did exist in products or processes, it was not fully exploited. Most telling was IBM's poor performance in the area in which it should have been most expert—internal IT management. The company had 125 separate data centers worldwide and 128 CIOs. There were 31 private and separate networks and literally hundreds of different configurations of PC installations. Data processing costs were a dramatic three times the industry average.

Executives were isolated from the growing problems by deep levels of hierarchy, a heavy reliance on an army of corporate staff, and a consensus-driven decision-making culture. Decisions "made by committee" took an exceedingly long time and a "nonconcur" from any one member could overrule general agreement on a course of action. Executives had large staffs and little direct involvement in writing their own reports. They delivered presentations prepared by staff members during numerous "pre-meetings" in which the staff worked to align positions and eliminate surprises. Armies of staff members attended executive meetings, lingering in hallways or—in the case of very senior staff—seated close behind their executive in the meeting room, armed with volumes of backup material. Prepared presentations dominated even informal meetings, and most executives had projectors built into their office furniture.

In 1991, Akers began cost cutting. Employee perks such as fitness center memberships were cut back. Some shared services within IBM were subjected to external competition. A $3.7 billion restructuring charge was posted, and a series of personnel reductions began as senior executives offered voluntary retirement packages to their personnel, with the threat of involuntary retirements on less generous terms if targets were not met. The targets were not met, and the first round of forced layoffs shook IBM's culture to the core. While the jobs of some were saved by the creation in May 1991 of the Integrated Systems Solution Corporation (ISSC), which later became IBM Global Services (IGS), layoffs accelerated in 1992. By early 1993, the total number of eliminated jobs exceeded 40,000. Donofrio, whose mainframe business was in freefall, recalled the anguish he felt during this time:

> We had to implement large-scale layoffs affecting the majority of employees at several mid-Hudson Valley sites. The mid-Hudson Valley was where I grew up. I had to lay off friends and former classmates, people I considered family. Many lives were affected by these difficult but necessary actions. It was a very tough, emotional time. Nothing I've experienced has been worse than that.

When late 1992 forecasts suggested continued losses, the board began looking for a replacement to preside over the breakup and sale of the once-proud

[11] J. Stafford, "IBM's Plan to Win VAR 2000," *VarBusiness*, May 24, 1999.

[12] Author interview, April 2004.

EXHIBIT 3 IBM Organization, February 1993

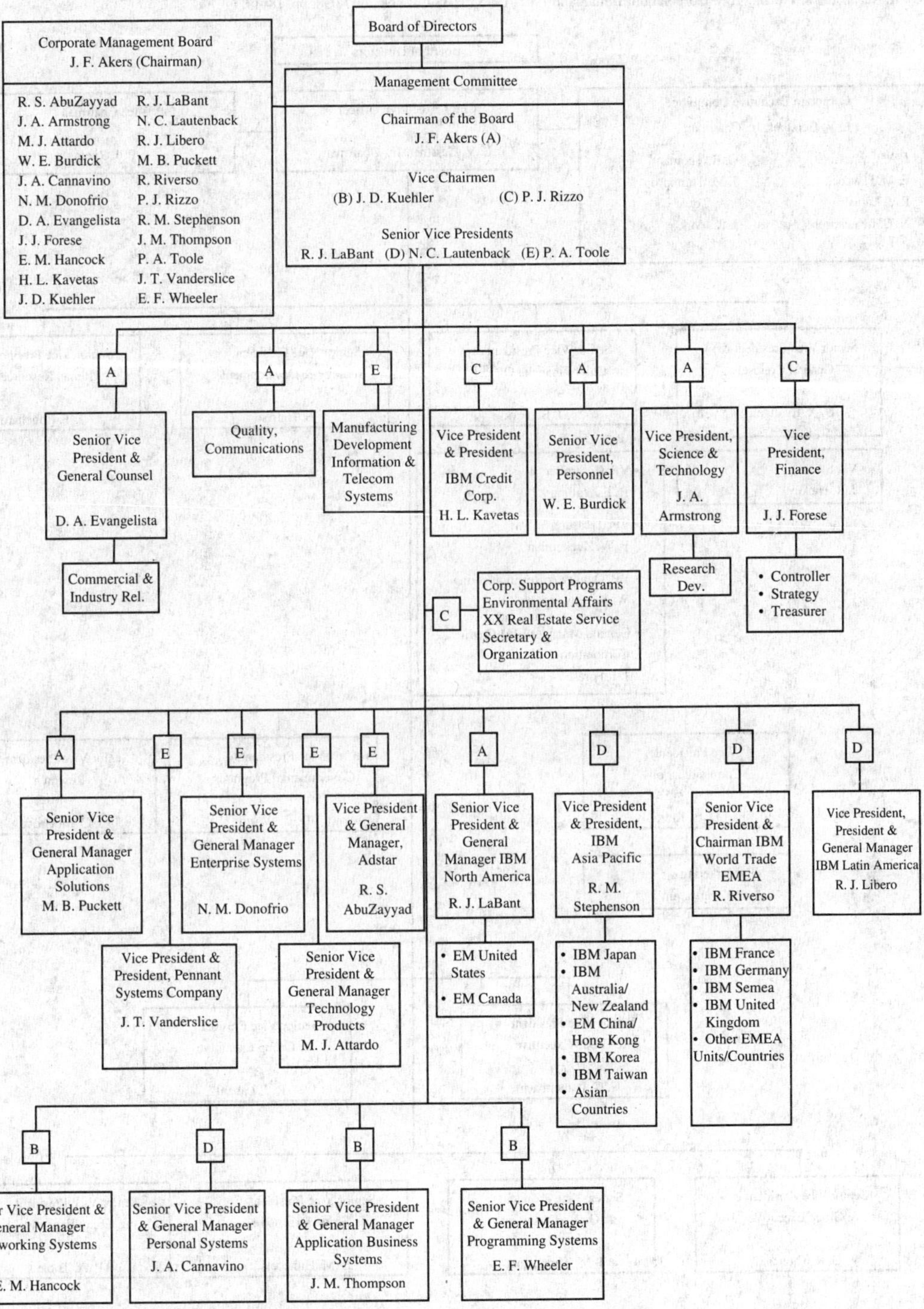

Note: The Letters represent the member of the Management Committee to whom each business unit head reports.

EXHIBIT 3 IBM Organization, February 1995 (*Continued*)

Source: R. Austin and R. Nolan, "IBM Corporation: Tumaround 1991–1995," HBS Case No. 600-098, pp. 18–19.

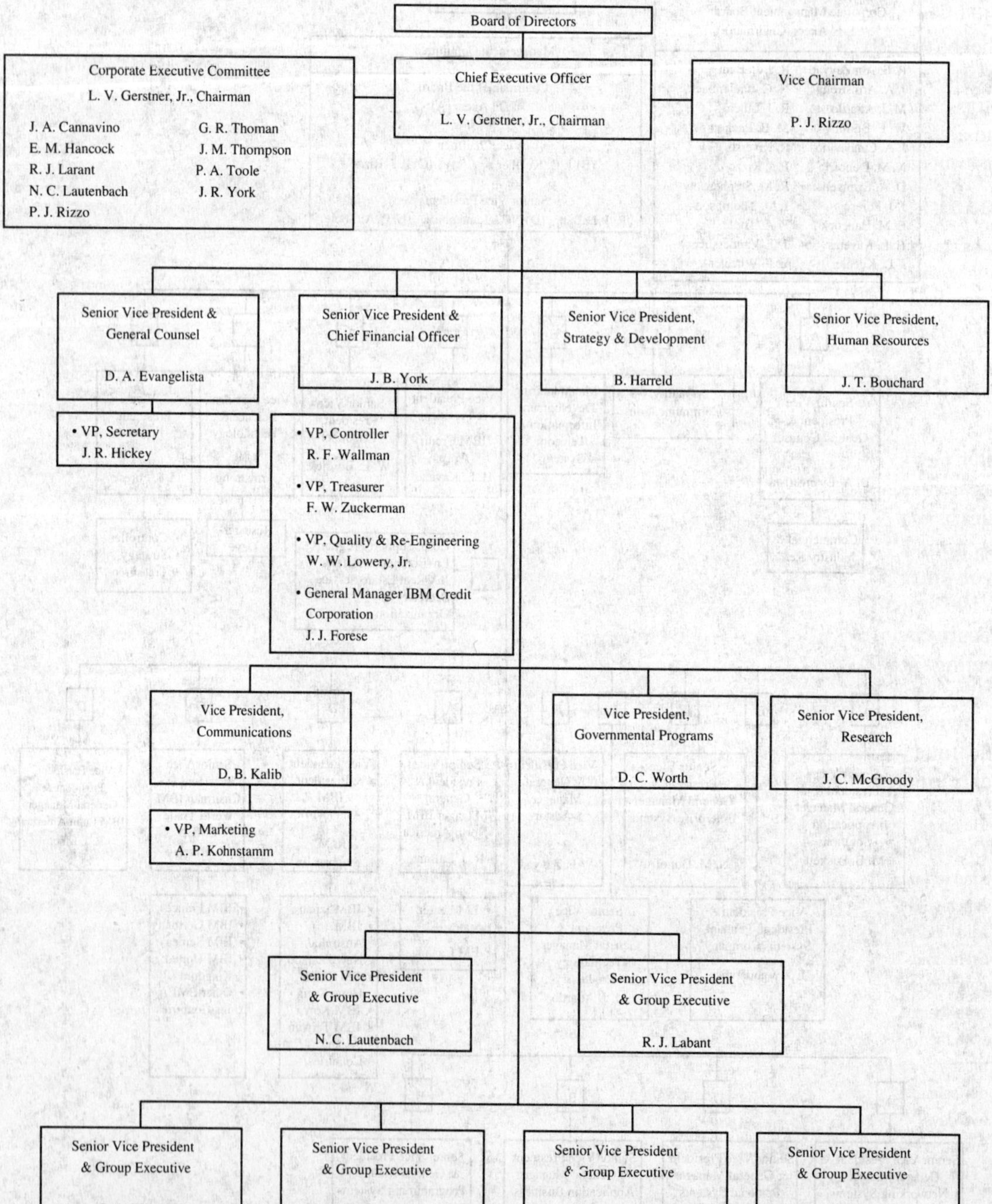

company. High-profile candidates such as Jack Welch (General Electric), Larry Bossidy (Allied Signal), George Fisher (Motorola), and John Young (Hewlett-Packard) declined to be considered. The board's choice, Louis V. Gerstner, had been chairman and CEO of RJR Nabisco for four years, a top executive at American Express for 11 years, and a consultant with McKinsey & Co. He was the first outsider CEO in the history of the company.

Leading through Crisis

> I start with the view that the customer drives everything the enterprise does. A lot of people say, "We put customers first," but it's a slogan for many companies. In my view, it is absolutely the thing you live by every day in a successful enterprise.
>
> *Lou Gerstner*[13]

After Gerstner took charge in April 1993, IBM's senior executives, employees, and customers quickly realized that "putting the customer first" was no mere slogan for Gerstner. The new CEO's involvement in a sales meeting in the spring of 1993 put executives on notice. In fact, IBM executives almost failed to invite Gerstner to the meeting, not wanting to inconvenience him when he was busy settling into his new position. When the invitation finally went out, it emphasized how little time Gerstner would need to spend at the event. Etherington explained Gerstner's reaction:

> He asked, "Who's there?" [We answered,] "About 300 CIOs in North America. Big banks, General Motors, that kind of thing." "Well," he said, "shouldn't I stay and have lunch with them?" "No, execs don't stay," we said. He said, "I don't understand. These are your best customers." So he said, and I remember this: "I'm going to the whole conference. I'll be there the first night. I'll have dinner with them. I'll have breakfast with them. I'll have lunch with them. And any IBM executive who wants to attend must stay for the whole two days." We were all erasing our calendars, saying, "I was always going to be there two days." At the meeting he opened a dialogue with the customers and he started to single IBM executives out. "This executive will fix that and get back to you this afternoon." It was unheard of—" The CEO's siding with the customers!" That was like a rocket through the company.[14]

During his first few months on the job, Gerstner logged thousands of miles visiting customers, analysts, and industry experts. He summarized the message he heard from customers in this way: "They said repeatedly, 'We don't need one more disk drive company, we don't need one more database company or one more PC company. The one thing that you guys do that no one else can do is help us integrate and create solutions.' They also saw the global nature of the company. . . . 'I use you guys all over the world.'"[15]

By late 1993, Gerstner realized that rather than break up the company, he could turn it around by going to market as "one IBM." To prevent customers from leaving in droves before he completed the turnaround, Gerstner called on each senior executive to go out to a group of customers and "bear-hug" them. He made the executives personally responsible for their assigned customer accounts and accountable for any problems that arose. At the same time, he asked each of the executives to write two papers, one on the executive's business and the other on key issues and recommendations for solving problems and pursuing opportunities. These papers became the basis for day-long discussions with Gerstner—without PowerPoint slides or support staff.

To prevent "brain drain" to competitors, Gerstner sought to "bear-hug" key employees as well; for example, he went to the board to change key employees' options, enabling them to exchange those that were "under water" for a smaller number that were not. Gerstner pointedly did not include the 23 most senior executives in the option repricing, sending a message to investors (and others) regarding his attitude about pay for performance. As one executive put it, "Lou is plenty collegial, but it's clear that has nothing to do with the business."[16]

[13] "The Customer Drives Everything," *Maclean's* magazine, December 16, 2002.

[14] R. Austin and R. Nolan, "IBM Corporation: Turnaround 1991–1995," HBS Case No. 600-098, p. 7.

[15] Ibid., p. 9.

[16] Ibid., p. 8.

After he decided to fight to save the company, Gerstner hired Jerry York, a former Chrysler CFO. Known for wearing Harley-Davidson tee shirts with a cigarette pack rolled up in a sleeve, York, whom employees called a "pit bull," was charged with getting costs under control. York launched a benchmarking study to determine how IBM's costs in each of its businesses compared with those of competitors. The results were daunting: The ratio of expense to revenue (42 percent in 1993) needed to be reduced by 9 percent. Overall, the company was too expensive by at least $7 billion. Opting for the single swing of the scythe rather than the slow and traumatic reductions of the previous few years, York and Gerstner approved layoffs of over 75,000 employees in early 1993. Business unit managers were charged with "fixing, closing, or selling" underperforming parts of the business.

The PC division exemplified the changes made within business units. In January 1994, Gerstner hired Rick Thoman, a former colleague from Nabisco, American Express, and McKinsey, to head the troubled PC division. Thoman killed nearly all of the PC company brands, saving only the eventually very successful ThinkPad brand for the laptop computer business. "We would still target individuals," O'Sullivan explained, "but we were after individuals who wanted a high-quality, reliable productivity tool, not the best gaming machine." Recognizing that PC manufacturing was not a core competency and that IBM's dedicated PC factories came with high fixed costs, the company outsourced PC manufacturing. Finally, by capitalizing on the successful ThinkPad brand and moving all products under that brand, the PC organization was able to move forward with one marketing team, one development team, shared synergies, and an executive team slimmed by 25 percent.

IBM's internal IT organization contributed to the $7 billion cost reduction. Between 1994 and 1997, the cost of operating and running IT operations was cut in half, generating over $2 billion in cost savings. Key savings came from reducing the number of data centers from 155 to 3 regional "megacenters" fed by 11 "server farms" and a 60 percent reduction in headcount. IT leadership was centralized; 128 CIOs were reduced to 1. Networks were converted to one common protocol (TCP/IP).[17] The systems development process was also reengineered; internal applications decreased from 16,000 to 5,200, and component reuse increased by 34 percent.

By the fourth quarter of 1993, IBM posted a small profit of $382 million. A similarly sized profit followed in the first quarter of 1994 ($392 million). By the third quarter of 1993, the company's stock price had doubled as investors voted with confidence in the decision to fix—rather than break up and sell—IBM. By year-end 1994, profits had risen to $5 billion on revenues of $64 billion.

Reorganizing as One IBM

> Gerstner saw the SBU [strategic business unit] as fatally flawed for IBM. SBUs had been created around products. We're not GE with SBUs around different products and customers. We need to integrate while preserving our strong product focus and leadership. How do you do that?
>
> *Bruce Harreld*[18]

"One IBM" became the impetus for reorganizing the company (refer back to Exhibit 3 for a comparison of the IBM organization chart in 1993 and in 1995). Gerstner pulled divisions into larger business groups and formed the Corporate Executive Committee (CEC), about a dozen senior executives who met every two weeks to focus on corporate strategy and the turnaround. Another group, the Worldwide Management Council (WMC), composed of the top 35 people including geographic leaders and division presidents, met monthly to define and execute global tactical strategy and operations.

The sales organization, which had been organized by geography and product, was reorganized into

[17] TCP/IP (Transport Control Protocol/Internet Protocol) is the standard used to communicate and share information on the Internet.

[18] Author interview, January 2004.

global sales teams. In response to numerous customer complaints, a customer relationship manager and a dedicated sales and service team were appointed for each key customer account. These teams were grouped within larger vertical industry teams, and product specialists were assigned to each. The product specialists served as boundary spanners, moving back and forth between focused product groups and key account teams, taking product knowledge to the field and customer input back to the product groups. Product specialists reported to the product organization, but incentives rewarded increased sales of their products through industry sales teams.

Changing Culture

In early 1994, Gerstner, writing at his kitchen table, set out eight operating principles for doing business as one company. He made no attempt to incorporate the "Basic Beliefs," developed by Watson. (See Exhibit 4 for Gerstner's eight principles and a comparison to IBM's original Basic Beliefs and the three core values developed by IBM Employees during a "Values Jam" in 2003.) The break with the past was apparent to IBMers. As Gerstner traveled to different company sites, he met with employees to explain the principles and how to put them into action. He wrote frequent "Dear Colleague" notes directly to the employees when he wanted to convey important information. As one executive noted, "We had no idea when he was going to send them; we got them when everybody else got them." There was inevitable resistance, as Harreld described:

> At the top of the organization was a leadership team that really wanted to speed up the pace of change. The customer-facing parts of the organization were ready for change and agreed with the direction the company was taking. But there was a group of people in the middle who didn't want to have anything to do with it. They just wanted it to go away. They wanted it to be the way it used to always be.[19]

One group of managers—those who ran IBM's country organizations—found the move to "One IBM" especially difficult. They believed global managers could not be relied upon to make the right choices for local markets and that initiatives and instructions from IBM corporate needed to be "customized" for particular countries. The differences came to a head when Gerstner found out that his notes to employees were being rewritten by country managers to "better fit their environment." The senior executive responsible for the country managers was fired, and many country managers resigned. Those who stayed were rapidly elevated to key positions. Despite pockets of resistance, Gerstner was impressed by employees' capacity to absorb change:

> [We had to change] the view that IBM was a group of fiefdoms. We needed to have a sense that we were going to operate as a team, as a global entity, and that was totally foreign to the culture. It took massive change to get people to do that. Compensation changes, organization changes, lots of things. To me it's a credit to the inherent strength of the people who were in IBM that so many of them were able to make the transition. It's one of the most remarkable things that happened.[20]

Reengineering Global Functions and Processes

As cost cutting got underway, Gerstner also focused the organization on becoming "One IBM" in terms of how the company operated. In late 2003, Gerstner assigned each member of the Corporate Executive Committee (CEC) responsibility for a functional reengineering project (e.g., procurement, product development, sales). He set two priorities for these projects: (1) Get cost out as quickly as possible; and (2) "clean-sheet" the process and redesign it for global use. The redesigned processes would form the foundation for sustained cost competitiveness and best-in-class operations as the company embarked on the growth phase of its transformation. Unwieldy executive governance structures and processes were removed, and Gerstner made it emphatically clear that senior executives were *unambiguously accountable* for making sizable and sustainable improvements in their assigned processes.

[19] Author interview, January 2004.

[20] "The Customer Drives Everything," *Maclean's*, December 16, 2002.

EXHIBIT 4 IBM Corporate Values

Source: Company documents.

1969 to 1993

IBM Basic Beliefs developed by Thomas J. Watson, Jr.

An organization, like an individual, must build on a bedrock of sound beliefs if it is to survive and succeed. It must stand by these beliefs in conducting its business. Every manager must live by these beliefs in the actions he (or she) takes and in the decisions he (or she) makes. The beliefs that guide IBM activities are expressed as IBM Principles.

Respect for the Individual

Our basic belief is respect for the individual, for his (or her) rights and dignity. It follows from this principle that IBM should:

- Help each employee to develop his (or her) potential and make the best use of his abilities.
- Pay and promote on merit.
- Maintain two-way communications between manager and employee, with opportunity for a fair hearing and equitable settlement of disagreements.

Service to the Customer

We are dedicated to giving our customers the best possible service. Our products and services bring profits only to the degree that they serve the customer and satisfy his (or her) needs. This demands that we:

- Know our customers needs and help them anticipate future needs.
- Help customers use our products and services in the best possible way.
- Provide superior equipment maintenance and supporting services.

Excellence Must Be a Way of Life

We want IBM to be known for its excellence. Therefore, we believe that every task, in every part of the business, should be performed in a superior manner and to the best of our ability. Nothing should be left to chance in our pursuit of excellence. For example, we must:

- Lead in new developments.
- Be aware of advances made by others, better them when we can, or be willing to adopt them whenever they fit our needs.
- Produce quality products of the most advanced design and at the lowest possible cost.

Managers Must Lead Effectively

Our success depends on intelligent and aggressive management which is sensitive to the need for making an enthusiastic partner of every individual in the organization. This requires that managers:

- Provide the kind of leadership that will motivate employees to do their jobs in a superior way.
- Meet frequently with all their people.
- Have the courage to question decisions and policies; have the vision to see the needs of the company as well as the division and department.
- Plan for the future by keeping an open mind to new ideas, whatever the source.

Obligations to Stockholders

IBM has obligations to its stockholders whose capital has created our jobs. These require us to:

- Take care of the property our stockholders have entrusted to us.
- Provide an attractive return on invested capital.
- Exploit opportunities for continuing profitable growth.

EXHIBIT 4 **IBM Corporate Values (*Continued*)**

Fair Deal for the Supplier

We want to deal fairly and impartially with suppliers of goods and services. We should:

- Select suppliers according to the quality of their products or services, their general reliability, and competitiveness of prices.
- Recognize the legitimate interests of both supplier and IBM when negotiating a contract; administer such contracts in good faith.
- Avoid suppliers becoming unduly dependent on IBM.

IBM Should Be a Good Corporate Citizen

We accept our responsibilities as a corporate citizen in community, national, and world affairs; we serve our interests best when we serve the public interest. We believe that the immediate and long-term public interest is best served by a system of competing enterprises. Therefore, we believe we should compete vigorously, but in a spirit of fair play, with respect for our competitors, and with respect for the law. In communities where IBM facilities are located, we do our utmost to help create an environment in which people want to work and live. We acknowledge our obligation as a business institution to help improve the quality of the society we are part of. We want to be in the forefront of those companies which are working to make our world a better place.

Source: Company documents; and R. D. Austin and R. L. Nolan, *IBM Turnaround* (HBS No. 600-098).

1993 to 2002

Gerstner's Eight Operating Principles

- The marketplace is the driving force behind everything that we do.
- At our core, we are a technology company with an overriding commitment to quality.
- Our primary measures of success are customer satisfaction and shareholder value.
- We operate as an entrepreneurial organization with a minimum of bureaucracy and never-ending focus on productivity.
- We never lose sight of our strategic vision.
- We think and act with a sense of urgency.
- Outstanding dedicated people make it all happen, particularly when they work together as a team.
- We are sensitive to the needs of all employees and to the communities in which we operate.

Source: Company documents; and L. M. Applegate, et al., *IBM's Decade of Transformation: Uniting Vision and Values* (HBS No. 805-132).

2003 to Present

IBM Values Developed by IBM Employees during "Values Jam"

IBMers Value: Dedication to every client's success.

IBMers are passionate about building strong, long-lasting client relationships. This dedication spurs us to go "above and beyond" on our clients' behalf.

IBMers are focused on outcomes. We sell products, services, and solutions, but all with the goal of helping our clients succeed, however they measure success.

IBMers demonstrate this personal dedication to every client, from the largest corporation and government agency to the startup and neighborhood market.

Every IBMer, no matter where he or she works, has a role in client success. It requires the full spectrum of IBM expertise.

(*continued*)

EXHIBIT 4 IBM Corporate Values (*Continued*)

IBMers Value: Innovations that matter for our company and the world.
IBMers are forward thinkers. We believe in progress, believe that the application of intelligence, reason, and science can improve business, society, and the human condition.
IBMers love grand challenges, as well as everyday improvements. Whatever the problem or the context, every IBMer seeks ways to tackle it creatively—to be an innovator.
IBMers strive to be first—in technology, in business, in responsible policy.
IBMers take informed risks and champion new (sometimes unpopular) ideas.

IBMers Value: Trust and personal responsibility in all relationships.
IBMers actively build relationships with all the constituencies of our business—including clients, partners, communities, investors, and fellow IBMers.
IBMers build trust by listening, following through, and keeping their word.
IBMers rely on our colleagues to do the right thing.
IBMers preserve trust even when formal relationships end.

Initial efforts were targeted at core processes such as procurement, manufacturing, new-product development, information technology, research, human resource management, and finance. Donofrio, the CEC executive responsible for reengineering new product development and manufacturing, explained:

> The first step in our financial, cultural, and business transformation was to drive common processes across all of our businesses. In our hardware businesses, we looked across all of our projects and found that our time to market was much longer than that of our competitors; in fact, in over 30% of our projects, we were more than twice as slow in getting our products to market and our costs were over twice as high. To address these problems, we developed a standardized "event-driven" product development process that we applied to all of our new product development activities across the corporation. The process specified a standard approach to product development and a staged investment model that was linked to performance within and across stages. As a result of the new process and standards, we cut development expense by over 50 percent and decreased new product development time by 67 percent. Even as new product quality improved, total costs per year were reduced by over $1.6 billion.[21]

Similar reengineering activities were also taking place in other portions of the supply chain. Kathy Colucci, who in the early 2000s was vice president of Finance, Integrated Supply Chain, explained how procurement, logistics, and fulfillment processes were standardized and streamlined to enable IBM to go to market as "One IBM":

> In 1995, each of our key brands handled its own procurement, logistics, and fulfillment activities. As a result, we had silos of these activities all over the company. During 1994 and 1995, we began to reengineer and standardize these activities. If there was someone on the outside that could perform the activity better, faster, and cheaper than us, we outsourced the physical activity and kept the strategy, planning, and management. For example, in logistics, we now handle all of the planning and management centrally, but we outsource all of the warehousing and distribution to a third-party partner. In addition, given our decision to move away from competing with enterprise application software vendors [explained later in the case], we decided to partner with SAP, PeopleSoft, and Siebel and use the same software internally as our customers used.[22]

Within one year of reengineering procurement processes, costs were down 20 percent and the time needed to complete and confirm supply orders had decreased from an average of 48 hours to 2.5 hours. By 2000, 94 percent of goods and services, representing $4.3 billion, were procured online from 24,000 worldwide suppliers at a cost savings of over $370 million annually. And even

[21] Author interviews, August 2003 and December 2004.

[22] Author interview, January 2004.

as year-over-year growth in procurement volume increased by 60 percent between 1999 and 2000, no new staff were added. (See Appendix for a summary of benefits due to cost-cutting and reengineering efforts.)

Waking Up to the Internet

> By the end of 1998, about a quarter of [IBM's] $82 billion in revenues was Net related. How did a company that had lagged behind every computer trend since the mainframe catch the Internet wave?
>
> *Gary Hamel, 2001*[23]

As IBM's cost structure improved, Gerstner and the senior team sought a unifying strategic vision to serve as a platform to reignite growth and industry leadership. As part of an early effort to rebuild the IBM brand around the "One IBM" theme, in June 1993, Gerstner hired Abby Kohnstamm as senior vice president of marketing. One of the first programs that she oversaw was IBM's sponsorship of the 1994 Winter Olympics in Lillehammer, Norway.[24] Intended to demonstrate IBM's renewed technology leadership, IBM's Olympic Web site also drew internal attention to the fact that the Internet promised much more than marketing. A grassroots Web movement within the company was soon channeled into a corporate strategy. (See Exhibit 5 for a description of how a bottom-up groundswell launched a strategy revolution in IBM.)

In November 1995 Gerstner announced "e-business" as IBM's strategic vision. His message, which in the early days of the Internet was considered revolutionary, was that the Internet is not just about browsing the Web and marketing to consumers. The killer application, Gerstner argued, would be business-to-business e-commerce in which the Internet and its associated technologies would become embedded within the way companies conduct business. The Internet was not about personal computers, either, he said. It was about a shift to network computing that would require increasingly powerful computers—called servers—that were capable of handling massive analytical and information processing tasks (see Exhibit 6).

While the decision to focus IBM's future strategy on the Internet went contrary to conventional industry wisdom at the time, "e-business" was a rallying cry that resonated with IBMers. In his autobiography, Gerstner commented:

> The concept of e-business galvanized our workforce and created a coherent context for our hundreds of products and services. The vast new challenges of networked computing reenergized IBM research and triggered a new golden age of technical achievement for the company. Most important, the investment did what we wanted to do at the outset—reestablish IBM's leadership in the industry.[25]

The e-business strategy triggered a cascade of decisions through the remainder of Gerstner's watch with regard to which products and businesses to exit, what to enhance, and what to acquire. Gerstner made enormous investments in Internet products and services at a time when few executives of major companies had put the words "Internet" and "strategy" together. (See Exhibit 7 for a summary of key acquisitions and divestitures between 1994 and 2003.)

One implication of this new focus was the increased importance of "middleware," which provided the tools and technology that served as the interconnections—the glue—between disparate and distributed data sources, applications, and computers. The shift from software applications to middleware prompted the major acquisition of Lotus Development Corporation for $3.5 billion in

[23] Gary Hamel, "Waking Up IBM: How a Gang of Unlikely Rebels Transformed Big Blue," *Harvard Business Review OnPoint*, 2001, p. 6. This section draws on the information in this article.

[24] In May 1994, Kohnstamm, who had worked with Gerstner at American Express, in what *The New York Times* called "the largest shift in advertising history," reallocated all of IBM's advertising budget of approximately one-half billion dollars from an assortment of 40 different agencies to a single agency, Ogilvy and Mather Worldwide. By the end of 1994, the team had launched the award-winning "Solutions for a Small Planet" campaign, which captured the One IBM theme.

[25] Lou Gerstner, *Who Says Elephants Can't Dance? Inside IBM's Historic Turnaround* (New York: Harper Business, 2002).

EXHIBIT 5 Gary Hamel's Summary of How a "Gang of Unlikely Rebels Woke Up IBM"

Source: G. Hamel, "Waking Up IBM: How a Gang of Unlikely Rebels Transformed Big Blue," *Harvard Business Review*, July–August 2000.

Establish a point of view. In a world of people who stand for nothing more than more of the same, a sharply articulated point of view (POV) is your greatest asset. It's a sword that lets you slay the dragons of precedent. It's a rudder that lets you steer a steady course when others are blown about by fad and whim. And it's a beacon that attracts those who are looking for something worthy of their allegiance. A powerful POV is credible, coherent, compelling, and commercial. To be credible, it must be founded on unimpeachable data. To be compelling, it must speak to people's emotions, telling them why your cause will make a difference in *their* world. To be commercial, it must have a clear link to the bottom line.

Write a manifesto. It's not enough to have a POV; you have to be able to pass it on, to infect others with your ideas. Like Thomas Paine, whose *Common Sense* became the inspiration for the American Revolution, you have to write a manifesto. It doesn't have to be long, but it must capture people's imaginations. It must paint a picture of what is and what is coming that causes discomfort. And it must provide a vision that inspires others.

Create a coalition. You can't change the direction of your company all by yourself. You need to build a coalition, a group of colleagues who share your vision and passion. It's easy to dismiss corporate rebels when they are fragmented and isolated. But when they present themselves as a coordinated group, speaking in a single voice, they cannot be ignored. And remember, as you struggle to attract recruits to your cause, you will have an advantage over top management. Your army will be made up of volunteers; theirs will be composed of conscripts. Conscripts fight to stay alive; volunteers fight to win.

Pick your targets. Sooner or later, a manifesto has to become a mandate if it's going to make a difference. The movement has to get the blessing of "the suits." That's why activists always identify and target a potential champion—an individual or a group of people that can yank the real levers of power. Ultimately, the support of senior management is the object of your crusade. Make an effort to understand them—the pressures they face, the objectives they have to fulfill. Find some who are searching for help and ideas, and go after them. If necessary, bend your ideals a bit to fit their goals. And don't forget that leaders are often more receptive to new thinking than are the minions who serve them.

Co-opt and neutralize. Some activists further their causes by confronting and embarrassing their adversaries. Such tactics may work in the public sphere, but in a business setting they'll probably get you fired. You need to disarm and co-opt, not demean and humiliate. To win over IBM's feudal lords, John Patrick constructed a set of win-win propositions for them: Lend me some talent, and I'll build a showcase for your products. Let me borrow a few of your top people, and I'll send them back with prototypes of cool new products. Reciprocity wins converts; ranting leaves you isolated and powerless.

Find a translator. Imagine how a buttoned-down dad looks at a daughter who comes home with green hair and an eyebrow ring. That's the way top management is likely to view you and your co-conspirators. And that's why you need a translator, someone who can build a bridge between you and the people with the power. At IBM, John Patrick was a translator for Dave Grossman. He helped the top brass understand the connection between the apparent chaos of the Web and the disciplined world of large-scale corporate computing. Senior staffers and newly appointed executives are often good translator candidates—they're usually hungry for an agenda to call their own.

Win small, win early, win often. None of your organizing efforts is worth anything if you can't demonstrate that your ideas actually work. You need results. Start small. Unless you harbor kamikaze instincts, search for demonstration projects that won't sink you or your cause if they should fail—for some of them will fail. You may have to put together a string of successful projects before top management starts throwing money your way. You have to help your company feel its way toward revolutionary opportunities, step by step. And as your record of wins gets longer, you'll find it much easier to make the transition from an isolated initiative to an integral part of the business. Not only will you have won the battles; you will have won the war.

EXHIBIT 6 IBM's Network Computing Vision

Source: Author. Pictures in this exhibit were downloaded from Photo.com (owned by ArtToday, a subsidiary of Jupiter Images, Inc.), July 15, 2004.

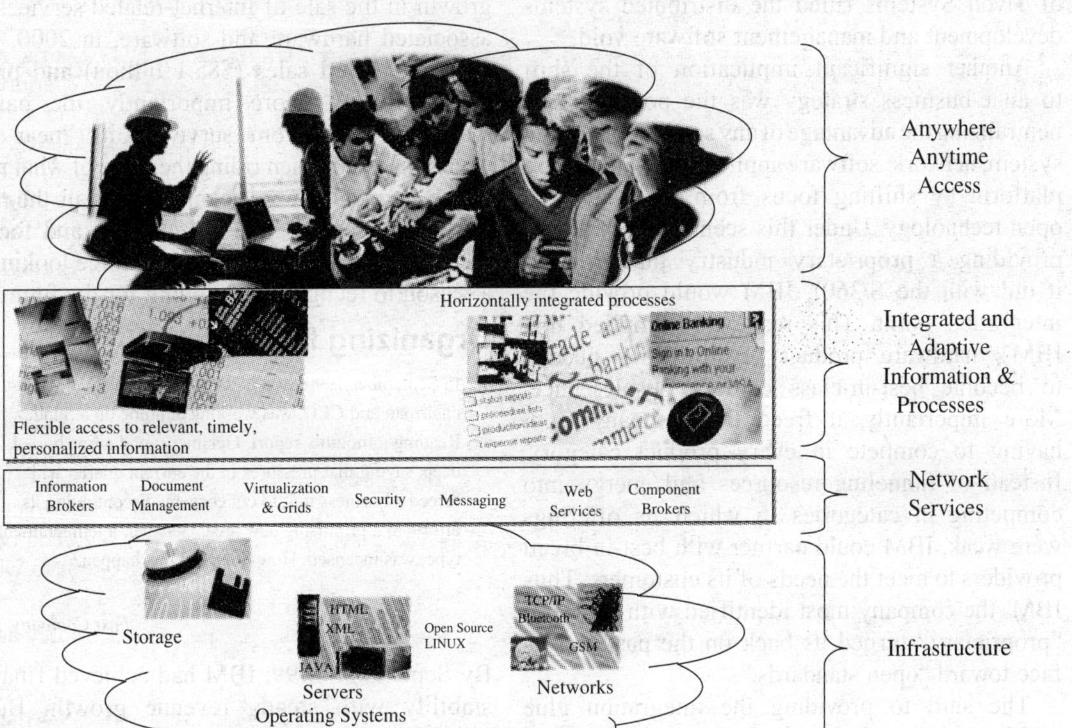

EXHIBIT 7 Acquisitions and Divestitures (1994–2003)

Source: Company documents.

Divestitures	**1994**	**1995**	**1996**	**1997**	**1998**	**1999**	**2000**	**2001**	**2002**	**2003**
Hardware	1	3	1	3	3	12	7	5	9	7
Software	0	0	0	1	4	0	2	1	1	0
Services	0	0	2	2	9	6	9	4	4	4
Financing	1							1		
Acquisitions	**1994**	**1995**	**1996**	**1997**	**1998**	**1999**	**2000**	**2001**	**2002**	**2003**
Hardware	0	0	2	0	2	2	2	0	0	0
Software	0	4	9	4	4	4	4	1	6	5
Services	0	5	7	8	9	12	7	4	4	1

1995, which provided a collaborative messaging/middleware platform. The $700 million acquisition of Tivoli Systems filled the distributed systems development and management software void.

Another significant implication of the shift to an e-business strategy was the possibility of neutralizing the advantage of any specific operating system, network, software application, or hardware platform by shifting focus from proprietary to open technology. Under this scenario, rather than providing a proprietary industry platform (as it did with the S/360), IBM would provide the integration point. This realization implied that IBM's hardware product organizations needed to become best-in-class or risk obsolescence. More importantly, it freed the company from having to compete in every product category. Instead of funneling resources and energy into competing in categories in which its offerings were weak, IBM could partner with best-in-breed providers to meet the needs of its customers. Thus IBM, the company most identified with the word "proprietary," turned its back on the past and its face toward "open standards."

The shift to providing the integration glue within an open networked platform also had implications for the importance of IBM's services units. By shifting resources and attention to services, by 2000, IBM Global Services (IGS) had grown to be the world's largest IT consulting and Web services organization, providing 38 percent of IBM's $88.4 billion revenue, compared with only 16 percent less than 10 years before.[26]

"Fifty percent of the $1 trillion opportunity [from the Internet] comes from services," Gerstner explained in 2000. "It dwarfs the other categories, and in that business we lead across the world."[27] While vendor independence was sometimes an issue for customers, IBM's technical expertise was also a strong drawing card. Fueled by record growth in the sale of Internet-related services and associated hardware and software, in 2000, IBM reported record sales ($85.1 billion) and profits ($8.1 billion). More importantly, the passion that had come from surviving its "near-death experience" and then riding the wave of what many in the company were beginning to call the "next big thing" captured the imagination and focused the energy of a demoralized workforce looking for a reason to reengage in building for the future.

Organizing for Growth[28]

> In September 1999, Lou Gerstner, who was then IBM's chairman and CEO, was working at home on a Sunday. Reading a monthly report, Gerstner found a line buried deep, saying that pressures in the current quarter had forced a business unit to cut costs by discontinuing its efforts in a promising new area. Gerstner, a temperamental type, was incensed. How often did this happen?
>
> *Fast Company, 2005*[29]

By September 1999, IBM had achieved financial stability with steady revenue growth. But at only 5.7 percent, this growth was well below the red-hot technology industry average. When Gerstner learned that funding for one of his key new-business initiatives in Life Sciences had been cancelled by line management in order to contain short-term costs, he "blew his stack." As head of corporate strategy, Harreld was given the task of looking into whether other promising new growth businesses were being abandoned. "I found a similar pattern across the board," he said,[30] and then Harreld set about documenting the problem with detailed case studies. While IBM had plenty of great ideas and inventions—in fact, IBM Research was granted more patents each year than any other company in the world—Harreld found

[26] Gerstner picked Sam Palmisano to run IGS from 1996 to 1999. "Services is the part of the business that saved Gerstner's job. Palmisano is the guy who made it work," said *The Wall Street Journal* reporter William Bulkeley. "IBM's Next CEO May Be the One to Bring Change." *The Wall Street Journal Europe*, May 22, 2001.

[27] Fuscaldo, "IBM Chairman Gerstner Calls 2000 a Good Year for Big Blue," IBM press release, 2000.

[28] This section draws on D. Garvin and L. Levesque, "Emerging Business Opportunities at IBM (A)," HBS Case No. 304-075.

[29] A. Deutschman, "Building a Better Skunk Works," *Fast Company*, March 2005, p. 68.

[30] Ibid.

that managers had a difficult time launching and growing new businesses that would commercialize these inventions and exploit growth opportunities arising in the marketplace.

Harreld's research showed that the majority of IBM employees focused on selling *current* products, serving *current* customers, and executing *current* operations. In fact, the focus on flawless execution and short-term results had intensified under the ruthless cost cutting necessary to survive during the 1990s. In addition, while common operating processes were enabling improvements in achieving the goal of "One IBM" in its current businesses, the innovation process continued to be focused within the silos of existing lines of business. "If we attempted to start a potential business and it didn't fall within a natural line of business, it was hard to develop," Paul Horn, senior vice president of Research, recalled.[31]

A corporate venture fund that had been established to support internal growth opportunities had also proved problematic. "We called it bowling for dollars," Harreld said, "because managers from [lines of business] tried to fund ideas with loose, back-of-the-envelope business plans."[32] The lack of experienced entrepreneurial leadership and processes caused most of these new IBM businesses to fail. (See Exhibit 8 for a summary of the study findings on causes of new-business failure at IBM.)

As part of his research on best practices for commercializing innovation, Harreld came across a book entitled *The Alchemy of Growth,*[33] which advocated dividing a company's portfolio of business initiatives into three "horizons." Horizon 1 (H1) businesses were mature and well established and accounted for the bulk of profits and cash flow; Horizon 2 (H2) businesses were on the rise and experiencing rapid, accelerating growth; and Horizon 3 (H3) businesses were emerging and represented the "seeds of a company's future strategy." Each horizon required different leadership and governance, a different approach to defining and executing strategy, a different way of organizing and managing, different types of people, culture, and incentives, and a different approach to financing (see Exhibit 9). Harreld and his colleagues concluded that IBM's difficulties were largely the result of trying, unsuccessfully, to apply a single approach to organizing and leading—one that was designed for large established businesses—to its high-growth and start-up businesses.

[31] D. Garvin and L. Levesque, "Emerging Business Opportunities at IBM (A)," HBS Case No. 304-075, p. 2.

[32] Ibid.

[33] M. Baghai et al., *The Alchemy of Growth* (Reading, MA: Perseus Press, 1999).,

Defining a New Approach to Innovation at IBM

Over the next few months, Harreld worked with the IBM business leaders to categorize IBM's businesses as H1, H2, and H3. While it was fairly straightforward to identify current businesses and then categorize them as either mature or high growth based on historical revenue trends and industry forecasts, executives recognized that, in the turbulent high-tech industry, the assumptions behind these forecasts could be wrong and would need to be continuously monitored. This job fell to the Corporate Strategy group.

Even more problematic, however, was the selection of H3 businesses, which would be designated as Emerging Business Opportunities (EBOs) and the decision of where in the organization to allocate leadership and authority for these EBOs. On the one hand, many argued that EBOs should represent cross-business initiatives and should be managed at the corporate level under the watchful eye of the Corporate Executive Committee (CEC). But others, like John Thompson—a 34-year veteran of IBM—believed that a fully centralized EBO model would make it tough to transition EBOs back into the divisions once they reached the growth stage and would also make it tough to gain the cooperation of business unit line managers—especially when pursuing opportunities that crossed lines of business. "Just when you need cooperation," he explained, "the white corpuscles from the existing businesses come out to protect their resources and try to kill the new effort."[34] After much debate, the CEC

[34] D. Garvin and L. Levesque, "Emerging Business Opportunities at IBM (A)," HBS Case No. 304-075, p. 5.

EXHIBIT 8 IBM Root Cause Analysis of New Business Failure during Late 1990s at IBM

Source: Adapted from D. Garvin and L. Levesque, "Emerging Business Opportunities at IBM (A)," HBS Case No. 304-075, pp. 3 and 4.

1. Our management system rewards execution directed at short-term results and does not place enough value on strategic business building.
2. We are preoccupied with our current markets and existing offerings.
3. Our business model emphasizes sustained profit and earnings per share improvement rather than actions to move into higher-growth/higher-price-to-earnings-ratio businesses.
4. Our approach to gathering and using market insights is inadequate for emerging markets, technologies, and businesses.
5. We lack established disciplines and processes for selecting, experimenting, funding, and terminating new business growth.
6. Once identified and funded, many IBM ventures fail due to poor execution.

decided that a centralized model would perpetuate the organizational silos that they had been working so hard to break down. Rallying behind the "One IBM" vision and values that had helped pull together the company during crisis, the CEC decided to organize EBOs to ensure corporate guidance and oversight while maintaining business unit line manager authority and accountability. In doing so, IBM sought to build innovation capabilities where they were needed in the divisions, focus business leaders on managing different business horizons, and ensure a smooth transition for successful EBOs into their ultimate business "home." More importantly, when EBOs required cross-business unit cooperation, CEC oversight would shine a spotlight on critical areas of need and would enable IBM's senior executives to work with business unit leaders to solve the organizational problems that made cooperation difficult.

Recognizing that strong corporate leadership would be required to ensure "corporate guidance and oversight," in July 2000, Gerstner promoted Thompson from SVP and Group Executive of the Software Division to vice chairman and "EBO czar." Gerstner also moved the Corporate Strategy group (led by Harreld) and the Corporate Technology and Manufacturing group (led by Donofrio) to report to Thompson. The appointment of Thompson, a respected strategist and operating executive who deeply understood IBM and its technology, signaled to everyone in the company that Gerstner meant business. Not only had Thompson led many of IBM's core software, hardware, and services businesses, he had also led various cross-business initiatives and was currently responsible for its Life Sciences business—which had been selected as one of the initial EBOs. While Thompson was the only IBM executive devoted full-time to the EBO initiative, both Harreld and Donofrio and their respective units devoted a percentage of their time to ensuring the success of the EBOs.

Initially, seven key business opportunities were designated as EBOs. The criteria for selecting these opportunities included: the need for cross-business cooperation and resources; the maturity of the business plan and strategy (e.g., key market and technology risks appeared manageable and expertise was available to build the first offering and take it to market); the forecasted size of the market; and the potential for generating over $1 billion in three to five years.[35] By 2003, the number of EBOs had grown to 18 and they addressed both new technology products (e.g., grid computing, blade servers, Linux, pervasive computing) and new markets (e.g., life sciences, digital media). (See Exhibit 10.)

Under Thompson, the corporate EBO process functioned effectively but relatively informally for its first two years. In addition to "evangelizing" the need for a commitment to innovation and growth and for developing different management

[35] Author interview, February 2004.

EXHIBIT 9 Three Business Horizons Require Different Organizational and Leadership Models

Source: Author. Adapted from D. Garvin and L. Levesque, "Emerging Business Opportunities at IBM (A)," HBS Case No. 304-075, p. 22 and from M. Baghai et al., *Alchemy of Growth: Practical Insights for Building Enduring Enterprises* (New York: Perseus Books Group, 2000).

	Horizon		
Issue	**H1 Mature Businesses**	**H2 Rapidly Growing Businesses**	**H3 Emerging Businesses**
Time Horizon	• Short term	• Medium term	• Long term
Focus	• Extend and defend core business • Increase productivity and profit contribution • Low uncertainty/risk	• Build emerging businesses • Scale businesses, increase market share • Expand into new products and markets to leverage opportunity • Medium uncertainty/risk	• Identify disruptors and industry trends • Analyze opportunities and prioritize investments in promising new ventures • Experiment to reduce risk and uncertainty • High uncertainty/risk
Profit Impact	• Invest to reduce costs and generate immediate-term cash flow • High profit margins will eventually flatten out and decline	• Investment to accelerate and sustain growth • Substantial profits may be 4–5 years in the future • Evaluate potential to replace or complement mature business core	• Invest to create future high-growth businesses • IBM invests in emerging businesses that have the potential to grow to $1B or more in revenues within 3–5 years
Key Challenge	• Revenue and profit growth through incremental sales, line extensions, and operating efficiencies • Spot and respond to disruptors	• Build the business and scale quickly • Manage double- and triple-digit growth and increased complexity • Scale organization as business scales	• Managing uncertainty in technology/product development, market adoption, access to resources (e.g., people, partners, cash, materials), and implementation • Assembling resources and deploying effectively • Managing targets and milestones that cannot be set with precision
Planning Output and Timing	• Annual budgets and plans • Short-term tactical plans • Annual budgets with quarterly or monthly reviews of tactical plans	• Business-building strategies • Business plans for scaling existing businesses and expanding into adjacent products and markets • Annual budgets with quarterly reviews and updates	• Decisions on opportunities to explore • New venture financing (staged commitments based on uncertainty) • Project-based metrics and timelines • Quarterly budgets with weekly reviews and updates

EXHIBIT 9 **Three Business Horizons Require Different Organizational and Leadership Models (*Continued*)**

Issue	Horizon: H1 Mature Businesses	Horizon: H2 Rapidly Growing Businesses	Horizon: H3 Emerging Businesses
Type of People	*Operators* • Deep functional and/or industry expertise • Strong drive to consistently meet short-term plans • Disciplined execution	*Business Builders* • General management expertise • Motivated to grow and scale • Top line focused • Execute to short- and medium-term plans	*Entrepreneurs* • Expertise in turning ideas into opportunities into businesses • Motivated to create new businesses • Able to manage risk and ambiguity • Creativity with discipline
Talent Approach	• Create personal consequences for near-term performance including clear penalties for underperformance • Impose "no excuses" management style	• Provide accountability and authority; reward growth and risk management • Provide opportunity to participate in upside (e.g., equity, cash bonuses) and to build and leave a legacy	• Provide psychological rewards: recognition of ideas, freedom to experiment and explore • Provide career advantage: opportunity to satisfy intellectual curiosity while also providing the option to become Horizon 2 business builders
Measures	• Traditional budgets and controls • Profit • Return on invested capital • Costs • Productivity or efficiency	• Capital efficient profitable growth • Market share gains • New customer acquisitions • Capital investment efficiency • Expected net present value	• Project-based milestones • Future options value • Success in moving through innovation stages: Idea to Opportunity; Product Development to Launch; Launch to Sustainability: Growth and Evolution
Corporate Behaviors	• Review, monitor • Set and monitor targets • Provide budget based on plans	• Invest in business growth • Address problems in scaling and exploiting opportunities to expand products and markets • Closely monitor viability and risk	• Identify opportunities, build teams and provide funding; support experiments and learning • Support transition to H2 • Develop innovation culture and capability

EXHIBIT 10 **Evolution of IBM Emerging Business Opportunities (EBOs) between 1999 and 2005**

Source: Author based on data supplied by IBM.

Original H3 Emerging Business Opportunities (Launched between 1999 and 2001) (by 2003, all except those marked with an ** had transitioned to H2 and been integrated into IBM lines of business)		
EBO	**IBM Business Unit**	**Comments**
Business Transformation Consulting	IBM Global Services	<$1 billion in revenues by 2005
Digital Media	Sales, Marketing, and Distribution	<$1 billion in revenues by 2005
Life Sciences	Sales, Marketing, and Distribution	<$1 billion in revenues by 2005
Linux	Systems and Technology Group	<$2 billion in revenues by 2005
Pervasive Computing	Software Group	<$2 billion in revenues by 2005
Autonomic Computing	Software Group	In H2 but not yet $1B in revenues
Blade Servers	Systems and Technology Group	In H2 but not yet $1B in revenues
Business Process Integration	Software Group	In H2 but not yet $1B in revenues
Dynamic Workplace	Software Group	In H2 but not yet $1B in revenues
Engineering and Technical Services	Systems and Technology Group	In H2 but not yet $1B in revenues
Flexible Hosting Services	IBM Global Services	In H2 but not yet $1B in revenues
Grid Computing	Systems and Technology Group	In H2 but not yet $1B in revenues
Learning Solutions	IBM Global Services	In H2 but not yet $1B in revenues
STI Cell	Systems and Technology Group	In H2 but not yet $1B in revenues
Storage Software	Systems and Technology Group	In H2 but not yet $1B in revenues
**eMarkets	IBM Global Services	Dropped
**Network Processes	Systems and Technology Group	Dropped
**Product Lifecycle Management	Sales, Marketing, and Distribution	Dropped
New H3 Emerging Business Opportunities (Launched between 2001–2005)		
Brazil, Russia (+ Eastern/ Central Europe), India, China	Emerging Geographies	BRIC nations grew 50 percent during 2003 and contributed over $3 billion in revenues
Retail on demand	Sales and Distribution	
Information-based Medicine	Sales and Distribution	Outgrowth of Life Sciences
Sensors and Actuators	Software Group	Outgrowth of Pervasive Computing

processes, the core activity was a monthly review of each EBO. Fashioned on the company's traditional business review process, each EBO leader, accompanied by his or her division head, met with Thompson, Harreld, and Donofrio to report progress, discuss plans, and solve problems. But unlike traditional IBM reviews, which focused on financial performance versus plan, these sessions were intended to verify and refine business plans and to measure the progress made as the EBO moved through the innovation process. Although efforts were made to identify expenses and revenues for each EBO, most questions during the meeting—and most of an EBO leader's compensation—revolved around clarifying assumptions and risks and assessing progress against key *project-based* milestones. Success against these project-based milestones could include clarifying market demand and willingness to pay by interviewing key customers or reducing technology risk by completing a key phase of the product development process. (See Exhibit 11 for a summary of key categories of risk and uncertainty during early phases of the innovation process and approaches and project-based metrics for managing them.)

With Thompson's retirement in 2002, Harreld and the Corporate Strategy group assumed formal responsibility for the EBO process. Harreld added staff to his group to provide expertise and leadership in project management, marketing, strategy, and analytics, and began to formalize systems and processes. Monthly and quarterly reports to senior management were refined and EBO leader forums for sharing best practices were established. At the same time, Donofrio redefined IBM's product-development process to accommodate the more uncertain and experimental approach required to launch and grow EBOs. By 2003, IBM had developed a new management system that clarified how businesses transitioned from EBO through high growth and maturity.

EBO Progress

In 2002, Harreld promised the board that EBOs would add two points in incremental revenue growth by year-end 2003 and, as 2003 results came in, he kept his promise. Of the original 18 EBOs, Life Sciences and Business Transformation Services had become $1 billion businesses with the latter growing over 30 percent during 2003, Digital Media grew 60 percent to $1.7 billion in revenue, Linux grew to over $2 billion in revenue and Pervasive Computing generated more than $2.4 billion in revenues. Three additional EBOs (blade servers, flexible hosting services, and storage software) doubled their revenues. Along the way, new EBOs were being developed—many of them around emerging markets and, during 2003, China, India, Russia, and Brazil had generated $3 billion in revenue, which represented double-digit annual growth.

As the number of EBOs requiring corporate oversight and guidance grew to 18 and, at one point, topped 25, Corporate Strategy resources became strained. Three EBOs were dropped because early results suggested that the business models were not sustainable. Given that 15 of the EBOs had entered or were entering the high-growth phase, Harreld considered whether it was time to transition them into an H2 management system and to integrate them fully into the business divisions. He was concerned, however, because some of the EBOs, which were growing revenues, still faced execution issues and still required investment. Harreld was also concerned about the strategy he should employ for restocking the pipeline of EBOs:[36]

> Basically, we're out there exploring all the time, listening, trolling for ideas, trying to find out what the next big thing is. . . . Not every well you drill yields oil. We're going to place a lot of bets and be in a position to capitalize early, or get out early. It was really hard to teach ourselves to focus, but we said, "We've only got so much energy, people, and money. . . ." Believe me, it takes a rare mix of expertise, guts, and discipline to place your bet on only a few things—not everything—and then to make it work and build from there. But that's the only way to grow a new business—one play at a time. Otherwise, you end up chasing everything and wind up with nothing. One thing we have done to help maintain

[36] Author interview, January 2004.

EXHIBIT 11 **Dealing with Risk and Uncertainty**

Source: Author. For further information see Govindarajan and Trimble, "Strategic Innovation and Learning," *MIT Sloan Management Review,* Winter 2004.

Categories of Risk and Uncertainty	Sample Approaches and Project-Based Metrics
Market/User Adoption Risk and Uncertainty • How many customers/users will adopt and how much will they pay? • How long/how hard will it be to adopt and use? • How much time/cost to penetrate? • How effectively (and how soon) will competitors respond? • Do we have effective strategic controls?	• Conduct market research and focus groups • Talk with industry experts and analysts • Review market research reports • Identify early adopters and work with them on developing new offerings • Develop education and training that will be needed to ensure adoption and use *Sample Project-Based Metrics* • Report on market size, growth, and segmentation • Decisions on entry target markets • Letters of agreement with early adopter customers
Technology/Product Risk and Uncertainty • Can we design/build products and operating processes? • Do we have effective operating controls? • How long will it take and how much will it cost to build the products or deliver the service offerings? • Can we attract, motivate, and retain reliable and affordable suppliers?	• Identify the level of uncertainty in different activities involved in developing the product • Experiment to reduce uncertainty and add time to enable experimentation • Develop project plans and milestones that take into account levels of uncertainty and the need to cycle back or even drop the product • Develop operating processes and controls required to launch and grow the business *Sample Project-Based Metrics* • Report on technology development process and success in reducing uncertainties
Resource Risk and Uncertainty • Can we attract, motivate, and retain reliable and affordable employees and partners? • Do we have the information/expertise we need when and where we need it? • Do we have the support/sponsorship/leadership we need? • Do we have the time we need and the capacity to implement? • Do we have the money we need when we need it?	• Attract key product and market development experts and partners • Identify information needs and find sources of information needed to reduce uncertainty • Attract and gain commitment from project leaders and sponsors • Identify window of opportunity and translate into a project timeline that reflects market and technology timing while also providing slack based on uncertainty • Attract financing *Sample Project-Based Metrics* • Number of recruits interviewed for each hire, recruitment, and development budgets • Level of financing secured and plans for use of financing
Implementation Risk and Uncertainty • Do I understand at the beginning of the project the implementation process and deliverables? • How complex is the project? If high levels of complexity, can I break the project into modules that can be implemented separately without high coordination costs? • How well do we understand the technology/business model? Is the technology and business model new to us or new to the world?	• Develop phased project plans, implementation activities, and deliverables and identify the level of uncertainty and complexity at each stage • Experiment to reduce key areas of uncertainty • Work with customers to define new business models *Sample Project-Based Metrics* • Progress on completing project milestones and deliverables • Project cost by activity • Cash flow forecasts and updates

> our focus is to work with the top venture capital firms and refer to them promising ideas that don't seem to be in our direct line of sight. Of course, we encourage them to use IBM technology to ensure that we seed our technologies into their products, and we also will serve as advisors or maybe invest a little money in the development.

The Next Big Thing

> As we began to recognize what it would mean to fully embrace the Internet and its associated emerging business opportunities, the answer to the question, "What is the next big thing?" began to come into focus.
>
> *Irving Wladawsky-Berger, 2001*[37]

In 2001, Wladawsky-Berger—well regarded as a technology visionary within IBM—gave an important speech that became a rallying cry for IBM executives searching for the platform upon which to build IBM's future vision. In a speech that he called the "Next Big Thing Speech," Wladawsky-Berger stated that the industry had reached the limits of what could be done to make traditional technology "behave as if it was a network":[38]

> The last decade has been a period of tremendous technological innovation . . . it's like a series of asteroids have been hitting the planet all at once. While many believe that this technological revolution was confined to the dot-com bubble, the more significant advancements have come during the last few years. . . . We are in the very early stages, as [we search for] the next big thing that will propel us forward.
>
> From a technology perspective, making the Internet into a "virtual computer" is the next big thing for the industry and for IBM. This is the grandest challenge that the industry has faced since the design of the System/360, and we are committed to leading the industry in defining—not just the new platform—but also the range of possibilities that it opens up.

Gerstner agreed that the business opportunities were staggering in their scope and scale. IBM's experience in attempting to transform to "One IBM" provided a glimpse of both the opportunities and challenges that IBM's customers would face. Gerstner believed that, while the technology platform was a critical catalyst, value creation would demand business innovation on a scale that most enterprises were ill-equipped to handle.

IBM had faced these challenges head on and had made a commitment to nurturing innovation and growth while also creating the foundation for flawless execution of its established businesses. Executives at IBM believed that these capabilities would keep the company from spinning out of control as it had in the early 1990s. Indeed, as Palmisano took the reins of the company, the dot-com collapse and subsequent economic recession caused the IT industry's rapid growth to screech to a halt. A *Fortune* article stressed the challenges Palmisano faced: "In early 2000, as Gerstner began handing him the reins by making him president and COO, the dot-com bubble burst. By the time Palmisano became CEO, revenues were down a whopping $5 billion and still declining. Palmisano found himself steering a technology company in the worst tech downturn in history."[39] By 2003, however, both revenues and profits, which had declined during 2001 and 2002, bounced back despite continued industry malaise. By year-end 2003, IBM revenues had risen 10 percent to $89.1 billion (a company record) and net income was up from $3.6 billion in 2002 to $7.6 billion. In addition, IBM had capitalized on the backlash on the accounting industry from scandals at Enron, WorldCom, and other firms to purchase PwC Consulting from PricewaterhouseCoopers. PwC consultants had assisted IBM on their path to becoming "One IBM," and it was hoped that the combined business and technology capabilities could assist IBM's customers on their path to transformation. Indeed, integrating PwC Consulting into IBM's Global Services organization had enabled the company to transition their Business Transformation Consulting EBO to High Growth, which helped drive IBM Global Service revenues to $31.9 billion (from $26.8 billion in 2002 and from $15 billion in 2002).

[37] Speech given at the IBM Academy, October 2001.

[38] Author interview, December 2004, and speech given at the IBM Academy, October 2001.

[39] D. Kirkpatrick, "Inside Sam's $100 Billion Growth Machine," *Fortune*, June 21, 2004, p. 98.

As Palmisano considered the opportunities and threats that IBM faced in the decade ahead, he recalled the dark days of the early 1990s, and he was committed to not just define strategic direction for the company but to set a course that would enable IBM to return to its former "greatness." Palmisano summed up his vision:[40]

> History suggests that a sustained period of growth is about to begin for the $1.4 trillion information technology industry. At the same time, new markets are opening up on its borders. But the rewards will not be shared equally. . . . Over most of our nearly 100-year history, IBM was consistently a company that outperformed others in our markets and generated superior returns. And that was because we were singularly focused on leading, and most often creating and defining, the high-value spaces in our industry . . . But it's also apparent that, somewhere along the line, we became more focused on defending our existing leadership position than on creating the next one. We weren't particularly bold or imaginative in getting into new markets or developing new businesses, products and services, even when our strategic analyses indicated that something new was coming. And, just as important, we hesitated to reinvent or get out of businesses that no longer represented high value for either clients or shareholders. In a word, we lost sight of IBM's mission, of what had always set us apart. Well, we've regained our focus now. IBM is an innovator—in every dimension of that word. We know that IBM and IBMers are at their best when they create value that our clients cannot get from anyone else. That means we will provide leading-edge technology, services, expertise and intellectual capital, and will integrate these capabilities for each client to provide them with competitive advantage. We commit to that. We commit to innovating to deliver client success.

[40] S. Palmisano, "Letter to Shareholders, *IBM Annual Report*, 2003.

Appendix

IBM Transformation (1993–2001): Summary of Benefits

IBM Turnaround: Sample Projects and Metrics

IBM Sample Projects and Operating Metrics	Sample Financial Metrics
Leverage Infrastructure: IT Operations	
• Decreased data centers from 155 to 11, which feed into three "mega centers"; developed single global Internet network to replace 31 incompatible networks • Shifted to "open source," common standards for information processing (Linux) and enterprise applications (SAP, PeopleSoft, Siebel) • Redesigned system development process to enable modular design and reuse • Decreased number of global applications from 16,000 to 5,200 • 60% reduction in IT professional headcount • 128 CIOs to 1	• 50% reduction in total cost of ownership for data center and network operations and internal enterprise application development and maintenance • Direct cost savings in internal IT expenses of over $2 billion per year beginning in 1997 • Return on invested capital ($100 million between 1994 and 1996 = less than 1 year)
Leverage Infrastructure: Enterprise Support Processes	
• Streamlined, integrated, and centralized IT-enabled enterprise processes (e.g., procurement, enterprise resource planning, human resources, payroll, finance) • Selectively outsourced activities and processes where IBM was not best-in-class (e.g., HR, physical warehouse, inventory management, and selected logistics) • Decreased the number of financial centers from 67 to 8 and financial applications from 145 to 55 • Decreased the cycle time for accounting close from 187 to 7 days • eEnabled then decreased the number of suppliers to 33,000; electronic purchases reached 95% • Centralized and integrated the supply chain and outsourced to IBM Global Services; 19,000 employees manage procurement, inventory, and logistics for over $47 billion in parts, equipment, and services • Decreased maverick buying from >35% to <0.2% • Supplier quality increased from <85% to >99% • Purchase order processing time decreased from >30 days to <1 day	• $7 billion in direct savings +$2 billion in cost avoidance per year from supply chain improvements • Cash generation increased by $8 billion from supply chain cost savings • HR, payroll, finance process costs reduced over 50%, representing almost $1 billion in direct cost savings per year • Purchasing expense/revenue ratio decreased from 3.2% to 1.5%

IBM Turnaround: Sample Projects and Metrics (*Continued*)

IBM Sample Projects and Operating Metrics	Sample Financial Metrics
Leverage Infrastructure: Enterprise Support Processes (*Continued*)	
• Ability to "sense and respond" to customer demand enables IBM to quickly meet unexpected rise or fall in demand for products • Supplier, employee, and partner satisfaction scores doubled • Winner, MIT Process Improvement Award and *Purchasing Magazine* Medal of Excellence	
Create Options	
• Transferred internal IBM-shared services and centralized process reengineering infrastructure and expertise to IBM Global Services, where it became the basis for new service offerings, including business transformation outsourcing • Leveraged end-to-end IT-enabled processes to deliver real-time, actionable information to internal IBM decision makers and to customers, suppliers, and business partners • Enabled continuous improvement and organizational learning	• See metrics associated with profitable growth and proprietary advantage
Drive Profitable Growth: Revenue-Generating Capabilities	
• Benchmarked new-product development process and found slow time to market (85% of projects at least 1.25X longer than best-in-class) and development expense ratio that was over 2X higher than best-in-class • Redesigned hardware/software research and new product development processes to reduce time to market and lower development costs	• Abandoned-project expense decreased by over 90% • Warranty expense to revenue decreased by 25% • New-product development cycle time: 67% faster time to market • Decreased product development expense ratio by 50%, generating cost savings of over $1.6 billion annually
Drive Profitable Growth: Actionable Information and Business Analytics	
• Developed knowledge management, content collaboration, and Web portal infrastructure and tools to enable knowledge workers to develop personalized knowledge sharing and business analytics • IBM Global Services developed a Web-based knowledge-sharing portal to leverage its consultants' expertise during period of rapid growth. • Partnered with Siebel to reengineer customer relationship management (CRM) processes then transferred demand generation process management to IBM Global Services • 68% of employees rank the intranet as preferred channel for doing business	• Consultant intranet led to decreased consulting engagement time by 40% to 80%, increased revenues per consultant by 20%, and improved consulting margins by 400% • eLearning saves $350 million per year on employee education (12% YOY savings) • Websphere, content management, and collaboration tools generate double-digit revenue growth in 2003 • Internal demand generation process and Siebel partnership become the foundation for IBM Global Services to launch a new business process outsourcing service offering

IBM Turnaround: Sample Projects and Metrics (*Continued*)

IBM Sample Projects and Operating Metrics	Sample Financial Metrics
Drive Profitable Growth: IT-Enabled Product/Service Offerings	
• Leveraged shared services infrastructure and expertise to deliver services to internal IBM customers and to offer significant enhancements to its data center outsourcing business • Launched new offerings related to business process outsourcing, e–business, and Web services • By 2003, 22 of 25 new emerging business opportunity (EBO) businesses had transitioned from new ventures to high-growth businesses	• IBM Global Services revenues exceeded $36 billion in 2002, up from $15 billion in 1992 • Linux-based (open standard) server market revenues growing at 35% per year • Server revenues grew at 32% and contribution margin increased to 31% • Software revenue increased to $14.2 billion in 2003, up from $11.1 billion in 1992 • Four new EBO product offerings were each generating over $1 billion in profitable high-margin revenues annually and three additional new businesses doubled their revenues

Source: Author.

Module 1

IT and Business Advantage

Lynda M. Applegate

Information technology (IT) spending worldwide exceeded US$ 2 trillion in 2007—a substantial increase over the preceding year and, despite a struggling economy, analysts projected that worldwide IT spending would grow 8 percent in 2008.[1] Confirming the truly global nature of IT, over one-third of IT spending occurred outside North America, Western Europe, and Japan. Indeed, IT spending has grown at a rapid pace in many developing countries over the past decade. This spending includes both the search for opportunity and the avoidance of operational risk that accompanies our ever-increasing dependence on and the impact of IT. Exploiting opportunities while avoiding risk requires vision, sound execution, and the ability to respond quickly. It also requires a deep understanding of how industries, markets, and organizations are built and managed for optimal performance.

The chapters in this module enable discussion of approaches executives use, decisions they make, and issues they face as they attempt to leverage IT to create business advantage. The module includes four chapters. Chapter 1 introduces the basic organizing framework for the module. It begins with a short overview that provides the definition of a business model; it then identifies an approach to conducting a business model audit. Chapters 2, 3, and 4 provide a detailed examination of the impact of IT on the three key components of a business model—strategy, capabilities, and value. Two articles and four cases are available at the end of the module to deepen your understanding of the impact of IT on business value.

[1] Barrels, A., "Global IT Market Outlook," *Forrester Research Services,* March 6, 2006.

Chapter 1

Understanding Business Models[1]

"Business model" was one of the great buzzwords of the Internet boom, routinely invoked, as the writer Michael Lewis put it, "to glorify all manner of half-baked plans. . . ." Many people—investors, entrepreneurs, and executives alike—bought the fantasy and got burned. And as the inevitable counter-reaction played out, the concept of a business model fell out of fashion. . . . That's a shame. For while it's true that a lot of capital was raised to fund flawed business models, the fault lies, not with the concept of a business model, but with its distortion and use. A good business model remains essential to every successful business.

Joan Magretta[2]

During the late 1990s, "dot-com" executives and Wall Street analysts routinely justified high valuations by claiming the superiority of emerging Internet business models. They maintained that new business metrics should be applied to calculate economic value and that these business metrics would eventually drive profitability—but only after huge amounts of capital had been invested to "get big fast." Yet few Internet entrepreneurs could trace the path between the new metrics they had chosen—our personal favorite was "eyeballs"—and the tangible economic returns investors would eventually demand. The irrational exuberance for Internet stocks reached its peak during 1999, when the number of Internet initial public offerings (IPOs) surged. During this 12-month period, hundreds of Internet companies went public, and with these IPOs came a flood of public data that highlighted the fatal flaws in many dot-com business models. By early 2000, concerns about the sustainability of these newly public, and not yet profitable, Internet businesses caused stock markets to plummet.

[1] This chapter is based on material developed by Professor Lynda M. Applegate for her online tutorial, Crafting Business Modules, available from Harvard Business School Publishing. Permission to reprint must be obtained from the author.

[2] J. Magretta, "Why Business Models Matter," *Harvard Business Review*, May 2002.

The resulting backlash caused many to question whether the concept of a business model had been invented simply to justify get-rich-quick Internet schemes. But this is far from accurate. While many still believe that business models emerged with the Internet, in fact, the concept can be traced to early management thinking. Published in the 1960s, Chandler's *Strategy and Structure* provided an important foundation for defining the underlying economic model upon which businesses were constructed.[3] This path-breaking book highlighted how alignment of strategy and organizational structure enables efficient coordination and execution while, at the same time, allowing the flexibility necessary to respond quickly and effectively to a changing environment. It also defined how strategy and organization drove capital efficient profitable growth and sustainable competitive advantage. Chandler's work, combined with a large body of increasingly sophisticated twentieth century management research, laid out the theory of the industrial economy business models that guided management practice through much of the twentieth century.[4] By the late 1990s, industrial economy business models had become so well defined that the approach to their analysis was fairly straightforward. Executives familiar with an industry understood the roles various firms played and the mechanisms through which each player created and captured value or, conversely, destroyed it.

In today's global network economy, however, new business models are emerging that are radically changing how firms create value within an industry and across industry boundaries. Indeed, as new technologies provide opportunities to radically change business and industry economics, the need to define strategy and its execution within the framework of a business model has become an increasingly important management tool—especially for executives and entrepreneurs who are searching for opportunities to create and exploit game-changing innovations.

This chapter introduces the basic organizing framework for Module 1 of this book. It begins with a short overview that provides the definition of a business model and then identifies an approach for conducting a business model audit. Chapter 1 also discusses business model analysis from a general business perspective. The remaining chapters in this module provide a more detailed examination of the impact of IT on the three key components of a business model—strategy, capabilities, and value—and the role of IT in transforming business models.

Overview

Few concepts in business today are as widely discussed—and seldom systematically studied—as business models.

Tom Malone et al.[5]

[3] A. Chandler, *Strategy and Structure: Chapters in the History of the American Industrial Enterprise* (Cambridge: MIT Press, reprint edition August 1969).

[4] For a summary of the strategy research that formed the backbone of business model research, see H. Chesbrough, and R. Rosenbloom, "The Role of the Business Model in Capturing Value from Innovation," *Industrial and Corporate Change,* June 2002.

[5] T. Malone, et al., "Do Some Business Models Perform Better Than Others?" MIT Sloan Working Paper, 4615-06, May 2006. ©2006, Thomas Malone, Peter Weill, Richard Lai, Victoria D'Urso, George Herman, Thomas Apel, Stephanie Woerner.

FIGURE 1.1
Business Model Framework and Definition

Business Model Definition
A business model defines how an organization interacts with its environment to define a unique *strategy*, attract the resources and build the *capabilities* required to execute the strategy, and create *value* for all stakeholders.

Have you ever watched young children play football (or soccer as we refer to it in the United States)? The referee blows the whistle to start the game and, immediately, all the players on both teams jump on the ball. Similarly, executives often use this "jump–on-the-ball" approach to formulate strategy. Michael Porter stresses that this approach is particularly common during the emergence of a new business phenomenon or a novel technology. While it is common to look to the marketplace for guidance, he cautions, market signals can be unreliable. "New technologies trigger rampant experimentation by companies and their customers, and the experimentation is often economically unsustainable. As a result, market behavior is distorted and must be interpreted with caution."[6]

The "jumping-on-the-ball" approach was popular during the "dot-com" era of the late 1990s, when many lost sight of the fundamental principles for how to build sustainable businesses. The results were predictable. Few of these businesses survived. How do you distinguish "hair-brained schemes" from "strategic coups"? In stable times, executives often rely on the intuition that comes from experience. When the rules of the game are changing, however, this experience may steer you wrong and new logic has yet to be developed. Renowned management theorist and consultant Peter Drucker cautioned that:

> In turbulent times, an enterprise has to be able to withstand sudden blows and avail itself of unexpected opportunities. This means that, in turbulent times, the fundamentals must be managed and managed well.[7]

An enterprise's business model frames these "fundamentals" and can be used to guide strategic analysis and decision making. As discussed in the remaining chapters in Module 1, the business model framework can also be used to assess IT impacts. The definition of a business model used in this book is presented in Figure 1.1.

A business model—whether it is for a publicly traded company, a new venture, a government agency, or an educational institution—forms the foundation for how executives make decisions about opportunities to pursue, businesses to launch or buy, activities to perform, talent to hire, and ways to organize to deliver value to stakeholders. For a new venture, the business model becomes a predictive forecasting tool that frames the development of a business plan and the assumptions used to forecast future financial returns.

The remaining sections of this chapter provide a more detailed examination of each component of a business model. The key steps in a business model audit are presented in Appendix 1A.

[6] M. Porter, "Strategy and the Internet," *Harvard Business Review*, March 2001.
[7] P. Drucker, *Managing in Turbulent Times* (New York: Harper & Row, 1980).

Analyzing Strategy

Competitive strategy is about being different. It is about deliberately choosing a different position and set of activities that enable you to deliver unique value.

Michael Porter, 1996[8]

Strategy is a series of choices that determine the opportunities you pursue and the market potential of those opportunities. It involves choices concerning products to sell, markets to enter, and ways a company differentiates its offerings from other alternatives. From a business model perspective, decisions concerning a company's strategy define the revenue drivers of the business and its potential for growth over time. These decisions also determine proprietary assets to be kept inside the walls of the firm and those that will be leveraged on the outside. These choices define strategic positioning along four key dimensions:

- *Market positioning* determines the choice of customers to serve, the needs and expectations that will be met, and the channels that will be used to reach those customers.
- *Product positioning* determines the choice of products and services to offer, the features of those offerings, and the price that will be charged.
- *Business network positioning* determines the role an organization plays and the activities it performs within an extended network of suppliers, producers, distributors, and partners.
- *Boundary positioning* determines markets, products, and businesses that will NOT be pursued.

In his best-selling article, Michael Porter stresses that successful strategies define how a company plans to achieve a distinctive and unique position that "woos customers from established players or draws new customers into the market."[9] But successful strategic positions often attract imitation. *Sustainable advantage* occurs when barriers exist that make it difficult for competitors to imitate your actions or for customers to switch. A business model *strategy audit* includes analysis in the four areas discussed below. The role of IT in transforming business model strategy is discussed in Chapter 2 of this module.

Assess business context. Begin by asking: "What business are we in?" Examine industry and competitive dynamics and consider relevant demographic, economic, political, regulatory, and societal factors that influence (or could influence) the business. Identify key trends that will either positively or negatively impact the industry and any disruptors—for example, technologies, globalization, new business models, or regulatory changes—that could be a source of opportunity or threat. Identify specific opportunities to pursue and, most importantly, those opportunities that will NOT be pursued. Analysis of the business context defines industry trends and disruptors. It also defines what opportunities can be pursued and their associated risks. This

[8] M. Porter, "What Is Strategy?" *Harvard Business Review*, November–December 1996, p. 64.
[9] Ibid. p. 65.

analysis helps frame choices concerning a company's boundary positioning. IT trends, disruptors, opportunities, and risks can also be identified.

Analyze customers. Armed with a high level of understanding of the industry, attention can now turn to an analysis of current (and future) customers. Identify pressing problems customers face and evaluate how a company's current products and services, as well as those under development address those problems. While both market research and internal customer information are critical to customer analysis, it is also important to get a first-hand perspective by talking with and observing customers. Watch them work and consider how easy or hard it is for them to use a company's offerings. Whenever possible, involve them in designing and developing products and services. This analysis helps frame choices concerning a company's market positioning. The ability to use IT to collect and analyze real-time and historical market information and to interact with current and future customers provides an important foundation for market positioning decisions.

Analyze competitors and substitutes. At this point, it is helpful to analyze alternatives customers have for meeting their needs. Which firms provide those alternatives? What makes one company's product or service offerings different from other offerings? Do these differences matter to customers? How much are customers willing to pay? How do prices differ from one competitor to another? Do competitors possess proprietary knowledge, assets, or intellectual property that serve as barriers to entry? What market share do different competitors have and how are these shares changing over time? Are there new entrants that offer radically different business models or offerings? This analysis helps frame choices concerning a company's product positioning. For many firms, IT serves as an important source of differentiation and proprietary advantage.

Assess the business network. Complete the business model strategy audit by analyzing the network of suppliers, distributors, and other partners needed to execute strategy. What activities do different players perform and what are the relationships among the various players? How powerful are individuals and organizations that control key activities, resources, or capabilities required to execute strategy? How is the network organized?

Traditionally, the activities of various players in a business network were organized as a sequential chain of inputs and outputs, which Michael Porter termed a "value chain" since it described the steps through which the inputs from one player were transformed into outputs that enabled various players to create and claim value.[10] Today, open standard networks enable companies like Google and Amazon.com to organize into densely connected "value networks" within which value is created and claimed through a complex set of interactions among multiple participants.[11]

Analysis of a company's business network helps frame more choices concerning the role a firm plays and its positioning within a business network. A more detailed discussion of approaches to organizing business networks is available in Appendix 1-B. The analysis of a company's business network serves as an excellent transition to a business model capability audit.

[10] M. Porter *Competitive Strategy: Creating and Sustaining Superior Performance* (NY: Free Press, 1985).

[11] P. B. Evans and T. S. Wurster, "Strategy and the New Economics of Information," *HBR OnPoint* (#4517), Boston: Harvard Business School Publishing, 2000.

Analyzing Capabilities

The fundamental purpose of organizations is to [enable the] attainment of goals that require coordinated efforts. Interdependence and uncertainty make goal attainment more difficult and create the need for organizational solutions.

McEvily et. al., 1998[12]

Once strategic positioning and direction have been defined and strategic goals have been set, the next step is to assemble the resources and build the capabilities required to achieve those goals. Capabilities enable a company to execute current strategy while also providing a platform for future growth. They define the resources needed to execute strategy and, in doing so, define the cost model of an organization. Capabilities also define the assets of a firm and the efficiency with which those assets are used. A business model *capability audit* frames analysis in the four areas discussed below (refer back to Appendix 1A). The role of IT in transforming business model capabilities is discussed in Chapter 3 of this module.

Analyze processes and infrastructure. It is helpful to begin the capability audit by extending the analysis of a company's business network through a more in-depth evaluation of core processes. This analysis should address core processes required to produce products; deliver services; acquire and serve customers; manage relationships with key stakeholders; and deliver a continuous stream of new products, services, and innovations. In addition, the analysis should include activities performed by a company and its suppliers, customers, and business partners. Once core operating processes have been analyzed, end-to-end support processes (e.g., payroll, finance, human resources management, and data center management) should be examined. Do these processes enable efficient and effective strategy execution? Do people and partners at all levels have the information needed to coordinate and control end-to-end processes and the infrastructure required to support them? Are operations best in class in terms of speed, quality, cost, and productivity?

Just as today's open standard IT networks and systems form the foundation for sharing information and transacting business among members of a business network, so too does IT form the foundation for the processes and infrastructure within a firm. Indeed, streamlined, synchronized processes are one of the most powerful sources of IT-enabled proprietary advantage. Not only does IT enable companies to coordinate activities and share information inside the organization and across an extended network of suppliers, customers, and partners; but IT also provides real-time information that enables executives and employees at all levels to make decisions and take actions that create value today and position the company for delivering increasing returns over time.

Evaluate people and partners. Armed with an understanding of end-to-end processes, evaluate whether the company has the expertise needed to carry out the required activities and processes. How easy or difficult is it (or will it be) to attract, develop, motivate, and retain the expertise needed to carry out activities

[12] B. McEvily, V. Perrone, and A. Zaheer, "Trust as an Organizing Principle," *Organization Science* 14, No. 1: 91–103 (1998).

and coordinate and control operations? Does the company have the reputation and image required to attract and retain top talent? Do culture and incentives enable leaders to engage and inspire? Have leaders developed clear performance targets, measurement systems, rewards, and punishments that ensure transparency and fairness? Keep in mind that performance measures for people and partners are often specific to the roles they have been hired to perform. For example, sales force quality and productivity are often measured in terms of sales per employee, customer retention per employee, and customer profitability per employee while manufacturing employees may be measured using production quality and efficiency measures. Once again, IT is a powerful tool for defining, organizing, and building knowledge assets within a firm and a business network. In fact, in 2007, an increasing percentage of the IT investments within firms were directed toward improving business intelligence.

Assess organization and culture. Once processes and people have been evaluated, assess whether the organization design makes it easier or harder for people to make decisions and get work done. Have people been grouped into work units and do they have the accountability and decision-making authority needed to do their work, make decisions, and meet performance targets? Are roles, responsibilities, and authority clear and are mechanisms in place for coordinating work across units? These coordinating mechanisms may include formal reporting relationships, steering committees, and liaison positions. They may also include information and communication systems. Does the informal culture support or hinder individuals and groups as they attempt to fulfill their roles and responsibilities? Do shared vision and values enable people and partners to work together to achieve shared goals? Does everyone understand the boundaries for decision making and action beyond which they must not cross? The ability to use IT to share relevant information and closely monitor decisions and actions made in the field enables companies to organize to achieve the speed and flexibility of a small firm while also leveraging the power, resources, and control of a big company.

Evaluate leadership and governance. Success over time demands strong leadership. Effective leaders use governance structures and systems to balance the creativity and vision needed to set goals and prioritize investments with the discipline needed to execute and deliver results. Governance systems include strategic controls (scanning the environment, defining strategic position, setting goals, and prioritizing projects and investments); operating controls (defining short-term objectives and controlling current business operations and projects); effective risk management (identification and management of key risks); and effective development and management of the shared values and culture that guide decisions and actions. Have leaders communicated a compelling and clear vision for the future that unites people and partners around common goals? Do leaders at all levels balance creativity and innovation with disciplined execution? Can they set goals and deliver results? Are leaders well connected and have they demonstrated a track record of success? Are there a high-performing board of directors and an executive team that closely monitor strategic and operating performance? Do the board and executive team have systems in place to identify and manage risks while also ensuring that the organization's culture and values guide decisions and behavior at all levels?

Analyzing Value Created for All Stakeholders

Behind every major resource allocation decision a company makes lies some calculation of what that move is worth.

Tim Luehrman[13]

The final component of a business model identifies value delivered to all stakeholders. Most executives of publicly traded for-profit firms begin their analysis of business value by looking at company financials.[14] These measures of economic value define the financial returns for business owners and investors, which, in turn, influence stock price and market value. Below we discuss how the business model strategy and capability audits define the drivers of economic value and financial return. The role of IT in driving financial returns and the implications for defining the business case for IT investments are discussed in Chapter 4 of this module.

Given that financial analysis often involves comparisons with other companies or with historical performance over time, *financial ratios* are often used. While specific financial ratios provide answers to questions about the economics of a business model, multiple ratios and measures are often required to understand the impact of strategic decisions or investments on economic value. For example, the decision to acquire a company or enter a new international market may involve new revenue streams and costs that change a company's profit margin while also decreasing cash, increasing debt, or increasing the value of assets on the balance sheet. Executives must be able to analyze the interaction of these financial metrics to make sound business decisions.

The DuPont Formula, created by financial analysts at E.I. du Pont de Nemours and Company in the 1920s, enables comparison of multiple ratios to assist in strategic decision making. This financial metric (see Figure 1.2) relates three different ratios—profit margin, asset efficiency, and leverage—that combine to determine return on equity (ROE).

While ROE is important for understanding business model performance, simply looking at financial returns is not enough. This is especially true when the business is growing quickly or an entrepreneurial executive is launching a new business where financial returns are speculative at best. When the business environment is rapidly changing and highly uncertain, understanding the drivers of value creation is essential. These drivers are identified during the strategy and capability audit. For example, during a strategy audit, an executive may learn that a company's current market is mature and does not provide sufficient revenue growth potential to enable the company to meet its growth goals. Given this analysis, the ability to offer value-added services to customers in the current market may be a key driver for revenue growth. But the decisions to invest in building and launching these value-added services would need to factor in the potential revenues that could be generated, the estimated cost and time

[13] T. Luehrman, "What's It Worth?: A General Manager's Guide to Valuation," *Harvard Business Review* (No. 97305), May–June 1997.

[14] See W. Bruns, "Financial Ratio and Financial Statement Analysis," Harvard Business School Publishing (No. 193-029).

FIGURE 1.2
Using the DuPont Formula to Deconstruct ROE

Profit Margin | Asset Efficiency | Leverage

$$\text{ROE} = \frac{\text{Net Income}}{\text{Revenue}} \times \frac{\text{Revenue}}{\text{Assets}} \times \frac{\text{Assets}}{\text{Shareholders' Equity}}$$

needed to achieve expected returns, the ability to differentiate the service over time, the opportunity cost of not pursuing other opportunities, and a host of other factors. A business model *value audit* frames analysis in the three areas discussed below.

Identify internal and external stakeholders. Begin the value audit by identifying internal and external stakeholders. Assess their interests and expectations. What do they require and what are they able (and willing) to provide? Can the company attract, retain, and motivate key customers and are these customers willing and able to pay? How do the interests of other stakeholder groups (e.g., employees, partners, government, society) influence a company's ability to attract and serve customers? What are the objective and subjective benefits that each of the key stakeholders (or stakeholder groups) receive from doing business with the company?

Identify business model drivers and alignment. When the analysis of each key component of the business model is complete, take a moment to review the insights gained. What are the key opportunities and threats identified during the strategy audit? What are the key strengths and weaknesses identified during the capability audit? From this "SWOT analysis,"[15] identify key revenue, cost, and asset efficiency drivers and develop a business model dashboard that reflects linkages and alignment among the various components. Identify how IT enables each of the key drivers of economic value. For example, does IT enable the company to reach new markets, which, in turn, drives revenue growth? Does IT enable the company to improve quality or streamline processes, which drives cost reductions?

Develop the financial model and determine financing needs. Once business model drivers and the value delivered (or to be delivered) to key stakeholders is understood, develop the financial model for the company. What assumptions have been made about the drivers of revenue, costs, and asset efficiency? How much uncertainty is there in these assumptions? How do changes in these assumptions based on best-case/worst-case scenarios change the economics of the business? In for-profit firms, translate the financial model into the three components of shareholder returns—profit margin, asset efficiency, and leverage—and calculate ROE. (Note: Other measures of shareholder value, such as return on invested capital (ROIC), may also be used.) How does the economic value delivered by a business relate to the market value expectations of shareholders? Are there any fatal flaws in the business model? If so, how should these problems be addressed?

[15] The term SWOT analysis refers to "**S**trengths, **W**eaknesses, **O**pportunities, and **T**hreats." An example of the SWOT analysis that resulted from the business model analysis of Amazon.com in 2001 is available in Appendix 1A.

Description of the Three Components of ROE

Profit margin is a measure of a company's success at turning revenues into profits. It answers the question: For every dollar of revenue that we generate, how much of that dollar goes to net income (also called profit)? In its most basic form, net income is calculated by subtracting expenses from revenues. As a result, anything that lowers expenses and increases revenues improves profit margin.

Asset efficiency measures the efficiency with which an organization utilizes its assets by answering the question: How many dollars of revenue do we generate for each dollar of assets on our books? Of course, traditional financial measures of asset efficiency often don't reflect the value of intangible assets such as the skills and knowledge of employees, the value of information and know-how captured in databases and computer applications, the value of a company's brand and reputation, or the value of its network of business partners and customers. In today's global network economy, these "intangible assets" become even more important as sources of asset value. As a result, forward-thinking executives are expanding the way they calculate the value of their assets to include financial surrogates for intangible assets.

Leverage measures the percentage of a company's assets that would be available to shareholders if the company was sold after first subtracting how much of its assets would be needed to pay off creditors. Understanding a company's leverage enables executives to answer the question: For every dollar of value that I create, how much goes to increasing shareholder value?

In summary, the power of the business model audit does not come from collecting and analyzing independent "buckets" of data. Instead, a business model defines the linkages among key strategy, capability, and value drivers of business performance. Figure 1.3 illustrates these linkages. Refer to Appendix 1A for key questions you can ask to identify the drivers of business model performance. In addition to the role of IT in transforming business models, IT can also be used to develop a business model dashboard and to monitor performance over time.

FIGURE 1.3
Analyzing Business Models

Source: L. M. Applegate, *Crafting Business Models*, Harvard Business School Publishing #808705, 2008.

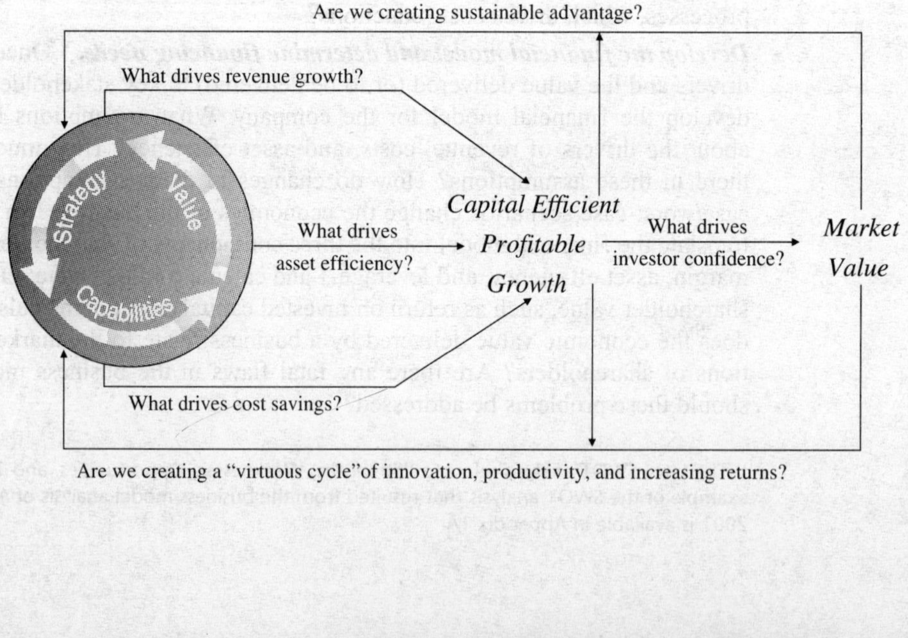

FIGURE 1.4
Evolving the Amazon.com Business Model (1995–2000)

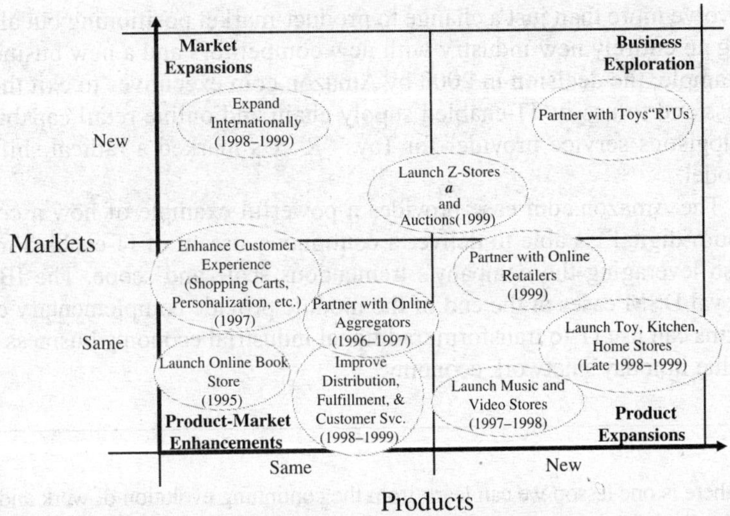

Evolving Business Models

Building a successful business is a journey—not a destination. As such, business models, like the businesses they represent, don't stay static. Instead, they evolve over time as executives exploit opportunities, respond to threats, and build capabilities. There are four key approaches to evolving a business model.

Enhance: Incremental improvements to an existing strategy or capability.

Expand: Launch new product categories, enter new markets, or expand capabilities.

Explore: Launch new businesses and build new capabilities.

Exit: Exit a product or market or outsource a capability.

Figure 1.4 shows how these four approaches to business model evolution can be framed within familiar strategic positioning choices. The figure illustrates the evolution of the Amazon.com business model and the choices made by CEO and founder, Jeff Bezos, as he built the company from its first product in 1995 through 2006.[16] More detail on the Amazon.com's IT-enabled business model is available in the case at the end of Module 1.

As can be seen in the figure, many business model shifts—for example, the decision to enhance a product or improve a process—represent incremental adjustments to a company's business model. At times, however, executives decide to follow a more revolutionary path and choose to launch—not just a new product, market, or channel—but a new business. These radical business model innovations often

[16] L. M. Applegate, *Amazon.com: The Brink of Bankruptcy*, available from Harvard Business School Publishing in the Crafting Business Models online tutorial. The case covers events in the company's evolution from 1994–2000. An update is also available that describes events from 2001–2006.

involve more than just a change to product-market positioning but also require entering an entirely new industry with new competitors and a new business network. For example, the decision in 2000 by Amazon.com executives to exit the retail toy business and to use its IT-enabled supply chain and online retail capabilities to become a logistics service provider for Toys "R" Us marked a radical shift in its business model.

The Amazon.com case provides a powerful example of how a company that was "born digital" is able to deliver a continuous stream of IT-enabled innovations while also leveraging the company's tremendous scale and scope. The IBM, Boeing, and Royal DSM cases at the end of the module provide complementary examples of how firms can use IT to transform traditional industrial economy business models to create value in today's network economy.

Summary

> If there is one lesson we can learn from the continuing evolution of work and competition in the new economy, it's this . . . Change the question and you change the game. . . . The old question was "What business am I in?" The new question is "What is my business model?"
>
> *Adrian Slywotzky and David Morrison, 1999*[17]

It's tough to build a business when the world is changing at warp speeds. We knew how to identify opportunities, launch new ventures, and build them into successful companies during the industrial economy but are just beginning to rewrite the rules for success in the network economy. While many long for more stability, savvy entrepreneurs and executives know that it is in just such times of turbulence that opportunities for creating value can be identified and exploited.

Building successful businesses in these challenging times requires that executives understand how to define and execute strategy, develop and leverage capabilities, and create value for all stakeholders. An enterprise's business model frames these decisions. But each component of the business model is not created in a vacuum. When strategy, capabilities, and value are aligned with each other and with the external environment, a business model creates what economists call a "virtuous cycle" of innovation, productivity, and increasing returns.[18] In contrast, a poorly aligned business model creates a "vicious cycle" that can quickly spin out of control, destroying value. And the more turbulent the business environment, the faster a vicious cycle can destroy your business.

The problem, however, is that tightly aligned business models are tough to change. In today's turbulent times, business models must be aligned, yet flexible, requiring even more skill and deep understanding of—not just the components of a business model—but also the linkages among those components as a business evolves and grows over time.

[17] A. Slywotzky and D. Morrison, *Profit Patterns* (New York: NY Times Business, 1999).

[18] A summary of the theory of "virtuous" and "vicious" cycles can be found in C. Shapiro and H. Varian, *Information Rules: A Guide to the Network Economy* (Boston: Harvard Business School Press, 1998).

During the last decade IT has dramatically transformed business models in most of the major industries within which firms operate. These transformative impacts have jumpstarted innovation and entrepreneurship in countries around the world, dramatically altering global economics. The remaining chapters in Module 1 provide multiple examples of firms such as Medtronic, IBM, Amazon.com, Boeing, and Global Healthcare Exchange that have embedded IT in the strategy and capabilities of the companies and their respective business networks to transform product, market, and business network strategic positioning and set the innovation agenda in their industries. The Amazon.com and IBM cases also show how these two companies used IT to build lean, yet agile, processes and capabilities that have enabled them to flexibly change strategy in response to crisis and drive increasing returns in good times and bad. A more detailed analysis of the impact of IT on driving economic value can be found in Chapter 4.

The questions below can be used to analyze business model performance.

1. What business are we in? Which opportunities will we pursue and which will we NOT pursue?
2. Who are our customers, suppliers, and business partners? What value do we provide to these key stakeholders? What value do we provide to employees and owners?
3. What are the competitive dynamics and balance of power within the industry? Who are our biggest competitors today? Who will they be in the future?
4. What differentiates us from competitors and substitutes? How easy (or difficult) is it for new players to enter our markets, offering a unique value proposition and/or substitute products and services? How easy (or difficult) would it be for customers, suppliers, or partners to switch?
5. How efficient and effective are our core operating activities and processes? How easy (or difficult) is it for customers, suppliers, and partners to do business with us? How easy (or difficult) is it for us to evolve our product-market positioning, to explore new businesses?
6. What are the capabilities and resources needed to execute strategy? Do we have, or can we build, the capabilities required?
7. What are the key business model drivers of capital efficient profitable growth and market value? What role does IT play in enabling the business model drivers of economic value? Can we use IT to develop a business model dashboard and monitor business model performance?

Appendix 1A

Analyzing Business Models

Business Model Strategy Audit

Business Model Capability Audit

Source: Author.

Business Model Strategy Audit: Suggested Approach and Sample Questions

Business Context Analysis	Sample Questions
• Identify relevant regulatory, societal, and industry trends and disruptors that signal opportunities and threats • Determine approaches to exploiting opportunities and managing risks • Determine which opportunities you will pursue in the future and which you will not pursue. • Answer the fundamental question: What business are we in today and should we be in?	• How favorable (or unfavorable) is the business context within which we operate today and what changes do we anticipate? • Are there disruptive changes on the horizon that would signal entry opportunities or threats to our existing strategy? Can we disrupt the industry and create new opportunities? • Which factors in the business environment help/hinder us in achieving our goals? • What must we do well to succeed? What are the key "failure factors"? • What are the key opportunities and threats? How quickly do we need to respond? • Have we clearly communicated to employees the range of opportunities that they should pursue and, most importantly, which opportunities they should NOT pursue? • Have we clearly identified future opportunities ("growth options")?

Customer Analysis	Sample Questions
• Talk with current and potential customers • Visit and watch them perform activities that your product/service offerings support (or will support) • Collect market research and customer information • Conduct focus groups • Involve customers in product design or improvement	• What are the pressing problems ("pains") that customers face? What must our customers (or potential customers) do to succeed and what can we do help them? • How well are customer needs being met today and how much are they willing to pay? • What is the current (and future) size of the customer base? • Are customer markets large and growing? Which segments are growing (or could grow) most rapidly? (Measure growth in terms of revenues, units sold, customer visits, number of customers/users, pricing, etc.) • Which of our current product/service offerings do our customers use today and how much revenue do we generate from each customer (or customer segment)? • What product/service offerings would our customers like us to offer? • What market share/"share of wallet" do we have today? What can we do to grow?

(*Continued*)

Business Model Strategy Audit: Suggested Approach and Sample Questions (*Continued*)

Competitor Analysis	Sample Questions
• Identify traditional rivals, potential new entrants, and substitute offerings • Benchmark current or potential new offerings • Ask potential customers why they use alternatives, what needs are not being met, and what would cause them to switch • Collect competitor data • Talk to experts	• Who are our competitors (including substitute products and services) and how do they differentiate their offerings by feature and price? • What prices do competitors charge and what margins do they get? • How sustainable are competitor positions? Can customers easily switch to other offerings? Who would lose share most quickly in a pricing or feature "war"? • What is the market share and share of wallet of key competitors/substitutes? What potential approaches could competitors take to increase their share? What approaches could we take to preserve or enhance our differentiated position? • How powerful are competitors? How might they respond to changes we might make?
Business Network Analysis	**Sample Questions**
• Identify the core activities, resources, and capabilities needed to achieve your goals (e.g., design, build, market, sell, and deliver products and services, innovate for the future, develop/manage talent) • Identify the support activities (e.g., payroll, recruiting, finance, and accounting) and infrastructure (property, equipment, data centers, networks) • Assess your capabilities and potential supplier and partner capabilities in performing these activities • Compare the cost and risk of performing activities inside versus sourcing from outside • Determine what you will do and what you will source • Develop governance structures and systems for end-to-end processes	• What activities, capabilities, and resources are required to execute strategy? • Which will my company perform and which will we source from the outside? • For the activities we outsource, how will we coordinate and control activities with key suppliers and partners? • How does the quality and cost of outsourced resources and capabilities compare to what we could provide inside? • How powerful are the individuals and organizations that control key activities, capabilities, and resources required to execute our strategy? • What is the source of power of different players in our business network? For example, does demand outpace supply or vice versa? Have suppliers or partners erected barriers to entry or exit or created high switching costs? • What relationships do we have with powerful individuals and organizations needed to execute strategy?

Business Model CapabilityAudit: Suggested Approach and Sample Questions

Process/Infrastructure Analysis	Sample Questions
• Build on your business network analysis to identify key activities needed to execute strategy • Group activities into roles that will be performed by people inside or outside your organization • Identify coordinating mechanisms that will enable the flow of goods and information through end-to-end processes • Identify infrastructure requirements	• What are the key activities needed to execute strategy? • How should those activities be grouped together to enable us to focus attention and resources while also developing the expertise needed in the future? • Which of the roles should we perform and which should we source from the outside? • What coordinating mechanisms (e.g., reporting relationships, liaison roles, steering committees) should we use to link activities and roles into efficient end-to-end processes? • What infrastructure (e.g., facilities, equipment, technology) is needed to support end-to-end processes?
People/Partner Analysis	**Sample Questions**
• Identify expertise and skills needed to perform activities and roles within end-to-end processes • Develop job descriptions for key roles • Analyze labor markets and determine which expertise and skills should be available inside the organization and which should be sourced from the outside • Analyze compensation patterns within labor markets and determine the cost of attracting, developing, and retaining talent • Develop and implement recruiting, hiring, development, and performance appraisal systems	• What skills and expertise do we need to perform the activities and roles as specified within our end-to-end processes? • Where do we find the talent we need and what do we need to pay for that talent? • How do we attract, develop, retain, and motivate the talent we need? • Do employees and partners understand what is expected of them, do they have the resources and authority needed to meet those expectations, and do we have performance measurement systems in place that provide them with timely feedback on their progress? • Do current development, compensation, and reward systems motivate employees and partners to work together to achieve shared goals, even as they fulfill personal goals?
Organization/Culture Analysis	**Sample Questions**
• Group employees and partners into work units that make it easy for them to accomplish individual and business goals while also focusing attention and effort and developing expertise • Clarify authority and accountability by role and unit • Develop formal reporting relationships to ensure a free flow of information on expectations and performance • Formalize authority and accountability and ensure people at all levels have the information needed to make decisions and take actions	• Are we organized to focus attention, develop necessary expertise, and reduce the friction that comes when people must work together to achieve shared goals? • Have we organized people into units and developed the reporting relationships needed to ensure authority and accountability for key decisions and actions? • Do we have the formal and informal coordination and collaboration systems required to get work done effectively and efficiently?

(*Continued*)

Business Model CapabilityAudit: Suggested Approach and Sample Questions (*Continued*)

Organization/Culture Analysis	Sample Questions
• Develop formal and informal coordination and collaboration mechanisms • Clarify values and behaviors and ensure consistency between incentives, performance measurement, and culture	• Do employees and partners at all levels have the information and resources needed to make timely decisions and perform core activities at highest standards of efficiency and quality? • Do they know how to use information to make informed decisions as individuals and teams? • Is information timely, relevant, and easily accessible? • Do we have the information and communication systems in place that make it easy for employees, partners, suppliers, customers, and other stakeholders to do business with us? Are our systems flexible enough to meet future needs?

Leadership/Governance Analysis	Sample Questions
• Identify key positions in your company and evaluate the strengths and weaknesses of people who fill those positions • Evaluate succession plans for key positions and the leaders who are being prepared to take on these positions • Evaluate leadership development and succession planning processes and systems, correct problems, and benchmark against world-class companies • Develop governance systems and structures to ensure strong operating and strategic controls and effective risk/culture management.	• Have the leaders in our company communicated a compelling and clear vision for the future that unites people and partners around shared goals? • Do we have leaders at all levels who can balance creativity and innovation with disciplined execution? Can they set goals, prioritize among competing projects, assemble resources, and deliver results? • Are our leaders well connected inside and outside and do they have a demonstrable track record of success? • Have we identified key positions throughout our company and our partner organizations? Do we have the right people in those positions and do we have an effective succession plan (and planning process) to ensure continuity? • Do we have a high-performing board of directors and executive team and strong governance systems?

Example of Amazon.com Strengths, Weaknesses, Opportunities and Threat (SWOT) in Early 2001

	Opportunities	**Threats**
Strategy Audit	• Established retailers desire quick entry into online markets but lack online retail capabilities • Toys"R"Us partnership demonstrates revenue and gross profit potential of established company markets • Online retail sales growing at 66% and forecasted to reach $2.7 trillion; key growth segments include digital products, consumer electronics, toys, and home & garden • 30 million loyal customers and strong brand; repeat customers ↑ to 79%	• Online retailers exit the market, dramatically decreasing revenues • Increased competition from traditional retailers • Investors exert significant pressure for capital efficient profitable growth • Increased complexity and speed of the business strain resources
Capability Audit	• Visionary, yet pragmatic, management • Demonstrated proprietary, best-in-class capabilities in online retailing, customer service, fulfillment, and distribution • Excess capacity and demonstrated capability for scaling operating capabilities • Inventory turns exceed traditional and Internet retailers • Advertising, marketing, and customer acquisition costs per customer while slightly higher than traditional retailers are trending down	• Need to leverage existing capabilities to enter new markets and launch new products more quickly and effectively • Fulfillment and customer acquisition costs exceed traditional retailers • While continuing to decrease, operating and gross margins continue to exceed traditional retailers • Gross profit margin lags online aggregators (e.g., Yahoo!) and auction businesses (e.g., eBay) that do not take ownership of inventory
	Strengths	**Weaknesses**

Appendix 1B

Analyzing Business Networks[19]

At the most basic level, organizations and the industries and markets within which they operate can be defined as networks of specialized *roles* that perform specific activities required to achieve a common purpose. These roles are united through *relationships* that manage the interdependencies as individuals, teams, and companies work together.[20] As companies consider how to organize and manage these networks, they are confronted with two fundamental questions:

- Which activities should we keep *inside* the boundaries of our firm and which should we source from the *outside*? The answer to this question determines how roles are defined and how the business network is structured.
- How should we *interact* with our customers, suppliers, distributors, and others? The answer to this question determines the relationships among different players within the network.

Defining Business Network Structure

There are three key choices that executives can consider when choosing how to structure business network activities.[21] (See Table 1B.1.) First, activities can be incorporated within a single *company*. Second, *selective sourcing partnerships* can be formed to enable two parties to work together to perform activities or to source activities to or from one another. Finally, a "*community*" can be created within which a firm retains only those activities that: (1) are considered a "core competency" or (2) are required to manage, coordinate, and control value chain activities within and across organizational boundaries.

Traditionally, executives chose to locate an activity within the corporation when a significant cost (or risk) was involved in coordinating and managing it on the outside. Costs and risks increased when: (1) a firm was required to make a *significant investment in physical facilities, people, or management systems* to coordinate and control activities with outside suppliers, distributors, or other parties; (2) the *services or activities were critical* to the effective and efficient delivery of the firm's products and services; or (3) a *high degree of uncertainty* surrounded the ongoing nature of the activities and relationship, which, in turn, made it difficult to develop a comprehensive contract to govern and control them.

Eastman Kodak, for example, was a highly integrated corporation even into the 1980s. Founded in the late 1800s on the principle of "commitment to quality," the firm established its own laundry to ensure that cloth for wiping film was of the highest quality; it bought its own blacksmith and built its own foundry to make its machines; and it managed its own credit union to finance its products. Having defined their strategy around quality, Kodak managers believed that the costs and risks associated with managing these activities on the outside were greater than the benefits that would

[19] This appendix is adapted from L. M. Applegate, "Electronic Commerce," in *The Technology Management Handbook*, ed. Richard Dorf, CRC Press, 1999; and L. M. Applegate, "Building Inter-Firm Collaborative Community," *The Firm as Collaborative Community: Reconstructing Trust in the Knowledge Economy*, ed. C. Heckscher and P. Adler, Oxford University Press, 2006.

[20] W. Baker, "Network Organizations in Theory and Practice," in *Networks and Organizations*, ed. Nohria, N. and Eccles, R., Boston: Harvard Business School Press, 1992.

[21] O. Williamson, "Comparative Economic Organization: The Analysis of Discrete Structural Alternatives," *Administrative Sciences Quarterly*, 36:269–296, 1991.

TABLE 1B.1 **Business Network Structure**

Options	Description
Corporation	Locate all but the most routine activities inside a vertically integrated firm.
Selective Sourcing Partnership	Source selected core activities from trusted partners.
Community	Develop a densely connected network of specialized, independent firms that work together to perform, coordinate, and control value chain activities—often across a shared platform.

be achieved through sourcing. General Motors followed a similar strategy in the early and mid-1900s; many recall its familiar slogan—"Genuine GM Parts."

Defining Business Network Relationships

Executives must also make choices about the nature of the relationships that they develop with customers, suppliers, and other external industry participants. These choices fall along a continuum from transactions to contracts to partnerships.[22] (See Table 1B.2.)

[22] J. Bradach and R. Eccles, "Price, Authority and Trust" *Annual Review of Sociology*, 15:97–118, 1989; M. Granovetter, "Economic Action and Social Structure: The Problem of Embeddedness," *American Journal of Sociology*, No. 91:481–510, 1985.

TABLE 1B.2 **Business Network Relationships**

	Transaction	Contract	Partnership
Basis of Interaction	Discrete exchange of goods, services, and payments (simple buyer/seller exchange)	Prior agreement governs exchange (e.g., service contract, lease, purchase agreement)	Shared goals and processes for achieving them (e.g., collaborative product development)
Duration of Interaction	Immediate	Usually short term; defined by contract	Usually long term; defined by relationship
Level of Business Integration	Low	Low to moderate	High
Coordination and Control	Supply and demand (market)	Terms of contract define procedures, monitoring, and reporting	Interorganizational structures, processes, and systems; mutual adjustment
Information Flow	Primarily one way; limited in scope and amount; low level of customization	One or two way; scope and amount are usually defined in the contract	Two-way (interactive); extensive exchange of rich, detailed information; dynamically changing; customizable

FIGURE 1B.1
Impact of IT on Industry Structure and Relationships

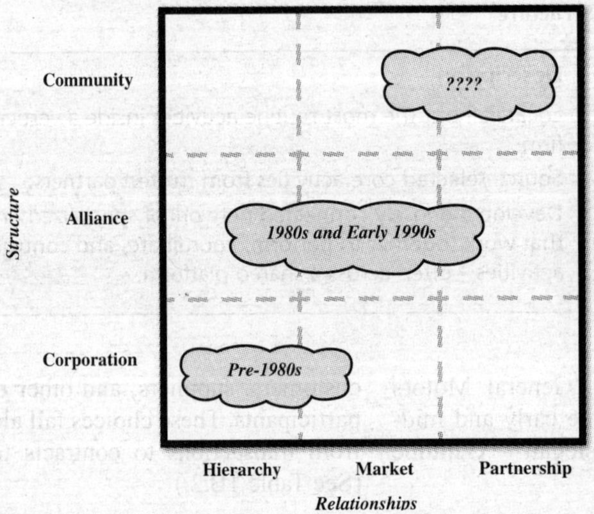

Transactions involve the simple exchange of goods, services, and payments, usually during a specific time period and with limited interaction or information sharing between the parties involved. In *contractual relationships* the products or services to be provided by each party and the length of the relationship are well defined at the start of the relationship and are clearly documented. The formal "terms of the contract" become the basis for coordinating and controlling the exchange of goods, services, payments, and information throughout the length of the contract. *Partnerships* are required when the activities to be jointly managed are complex, uncertain, and critical to the success of the firms involved. Partnerships require shared goals, complementary expertise and skills, and integration of activities across organizational boundaries. The exchange of goods and services is ongoing, and the interactions and relationships must adapt to the changing priorities of the parties involved. Partnerships often require significant investments in systems and people for carrying out, coordinating, and controlling shared activities.

Figure B1.1 summarizes these two perspectives and shows the evolution of business networks during the latter half of the twentieth century. As you will see in later chapters, IT played an important role in this evolution.

Chapter 2

IT Impact on Business Models[1]

Today's Chief Information Officers (CIOs) must enable the organization to meet its strategic goals and to envision goals that were never before possible.

Farber et al., 2008[2]

Long considered a tool to automate back-office activities—for example, payroll and accounts receivable—only recently has IT become an important tool for defining new strategic opportunities and building the capabilities needed to execute them. However, a huge proportion of IT investments fail to deliver their intended return each year; in the United States alone, this number is estimated at 40 percent. This phenomenon becomes even more significant when we consider that, on average, companies spend nearly 5 percent of revenues on IT.[3] On a worldwide basis in 2007, CIOs invested about $435 billion in computer equipment, $352 billion in communications equipment, and $336 billion in software, of which about two-thirds was for packaged software. In addition, CIOs across the globe spent $488 billion on IT services and outsourcing, plus nearly $660 billion on IT staff costs. Although IT investment growth is projected to slow in 2008, spending on IT services continues to grow and, in certain regions of the world, double-digit growth is the norm across all IT spending categories.[4]

This chapter presents a framework for analyzing IT impact on a company's business model. We begin by presenting a general framework that can be used to analyze the impact of an IT-enabled business initiative on business strategy and capabilities. The chapter provides numerous examples of companies that are using IT to transform their industry and company and ends with questions executives can use to assess the business model impacts of IT.

[1] Portions of this chapter are based on material developed by Professor Lynda M. Applegate for executive programs offered at Harvard Business School. Permission to reprint must be obtained from author.

[2] M. Farber, "The Visionary CIO, Strategy and Business," Booz-Allen Research Report (downloaded from www.strategy-business.com), p. 2.

[3] Forrester's Business Technographics®, November 2004, United States. SMB Benchmark Study found that enterprises spend an average of 4.9% of revenues on IT. Averages for specific industries range between 1% and 8%.

[4] A. Bartels, E. Daley, and H. Lo, "Global IT 2008 Market Outlook" Forrester Research, February 11, 2008.

Analyzing IT Impact

As you recall, the business model of a firm defines the alignment of a company's strategy with its environment and with the capabilities required to execute strategy and deliver value to all stakeholders.[5] Increasingly, IT has become central to designing and evolving a company's business model and value proposition. Given that a company's business model links decisions executives make to business performance, it also serves as a useful tool for analyzing the impact of IT on business performance and for framing IT investment decisions. The IT Impact Map describes the impact of IT along the two key dimensions of business model performance: strategy and capabilities.

- *IT impact on strategy* defines the role that IT plays in determining product, market, business network, and boundary positioning. It seeks to explain the mechanisms through which IT drives differentiation, sustainable advantage, and the development of proprietary assets. It also identifies the impact of IT on defining the growth path of the company over time.
- *IT impact on capabilities* defines the role that IT plays in building the capabilities needed to execute strategy. These capabilities include processes and infrastructure, people and partners, organization and culture, and leadership and governance. It is important to note that these capabilities may be located inside an organization or may be dispersed over a network of business partners. As such, it is important to analyze business network capabilities (for example, end-to-end processes and governance systems) and not just those located within the walls of an organization.

The IT Impact Map can be used to analyze the impact of a single project or it can be used to analyze a series of projects through which a company evolves its strategy over time. See Figure 2.1 for examples of how two companies have used IT to transform their business models.

Between 1994 and 2001, IBM spent significant effort reengineering and then centralizing its internal processes—starting with back-office processes (e.g., payroll, purchasing, and benefits management) and then proceeding to core operating processes such as supply chain management and new product development. These reengineered processes and internal shared services capabilities served as the foundation for launching IBM's Business Process Outsourcing (BPO) practice within its Global Services business unit. Thus, in addition to significant cost savings achieved through its reengineering efforts during the 1990s, IBM was also able to drive significant revenue growth from new service offerings that built on its internal IT-enabled business processes. Indeed, by 2002, IBM's Global Services business accounted for nearly 45 percent of the company's revenues and, by 2005, the percentage had grown to 52 percent. Today, IBM's Global Services business unit is one of three core businesses through which the company executes its strategy.[6] Its BPO practice is now

[5] L. M. Applegate, "Crafting Business Models Online Tutorial," Available from HBS Publishing, 2008.

[6] See the IBM 2007 Annual Report and the company Web site www.ibm.com//technologyservices for more information on IBM Global Services. Also see, Applegate, et al., "IBM's Decade of Transformation: Turnaround to Growth," Harvard Business School Publishing (No. 805-130), revised April 2008. This case is reprinted at the end of Module 1 of this book.

FIGURE 2.1
IT Impact Map

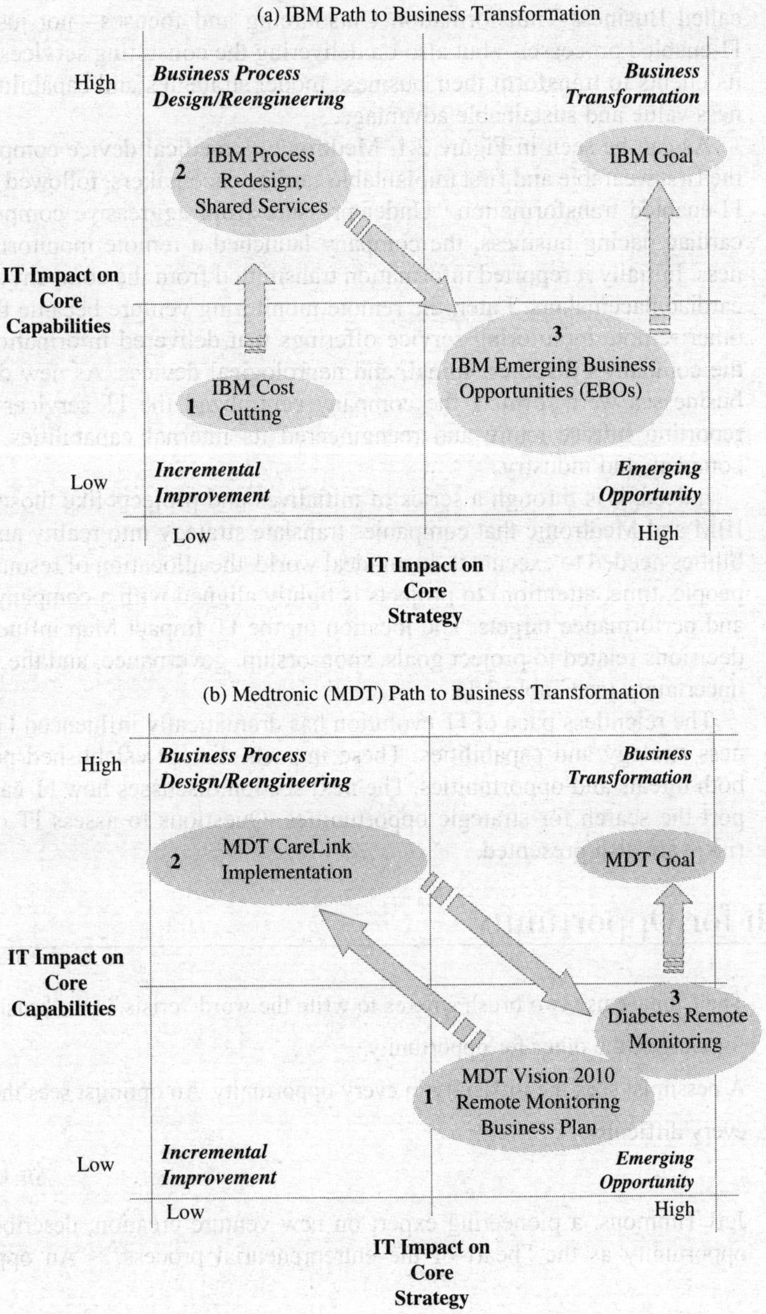

called Business Transformation Outsourcing and focuses—not just on outsourcing IT-enabled processes—but also on delivering the consulting services needed to enable its clients to transform their business model strategies and capabilities to drive business value and sustainable advantage.

As can be seen in Figure 2.1, Medtronic, a medical device company that invented the first wearable and first implantable cardiac pacemakers, followed a different path to IT-enabled transformation.[7] Under pressure from aggressive competitors in its core cardiac pacing business, the company launched a remote monitoring services business. Initially it reported information transmitted from the company's installed base of cardiac pacemakers. Later, the remote monitoring venture became the foundation for other remote monitoring service offerings that delivered information collected from the company's diabetes, spinal, and neurological devices. As new device monitoring businesses were formed, the company centralized the IT services and information reporting infrastructure and reengineered its internal capabilities to transform the company and industry.

Indeed, it is through a series of initiatives and projects like those implemented by IBM and Medtronic that companies translate strategy into reality and build the capabilities needed to execute it. In an ideal world, the allocation of resources (e.g., money, people, time, attention) to projects is tightly aligned with a company's strategic goals and performance targets. The location on the IT Impact Map influences IT resource decisions related to project goals, sponsorship, governance, and the levels of risk and uncertainty (see Table 2.1).

The relentless pace of IT evolution has dramatically influenced IT impact on business strategy and capabilities. These impacts disrupt established positions, creating both threats and opportunities. The next section discusses how IT can be used to support the search for strategic opportunities. Questions to assess IT opportunity—and risk—are also presented.

The Search for Opportunity

The Chinese use two brush strokes to write the word "crisis." One brush stroke stands for danger; the other for opportunity.

A pessimist sees the difficulty in every opportunity. An optimist sees the opportunity in every difficulty.

Sir Winston Churchill[8]

Jeff Timmons, a pioneering expert on new venture creation, described the search for opportunity as the "heart of the entrepreneurial process."[9] "An opportunity has the

[7] See L. M. Applegate, "Medtronic Vision 2010," Harvard Business School Publishing (No. 807-052), revised April 2008. Also see the Medtronic 2007 Annual Report and the company Web site www.medtronic.com for more information on Medtronic.

[8] Quotations are from Famous Quotations (www.famous-quotations.com; downloaded July 2004).

[9] J. Timmons, *New Venture Creation: Entrepreneurship for the 21st Century* (New York: McGraw Hill, 1995), pp. 3–11.

TABLE 2.1 Categories of IT Impact

IT Impact Category	Description
Local Improvements Sample projects: Automate functional support processes (e.g., payroll, budgeting); IT support for team project or business intelligence for a local decision	***Goal***: Use IT to improve local operating performance ***Business Sponsors***: Local managers, teams, and individuals ***Business Value***: Reduce costs and improve local operating performance ***Risk and Uncertainty***: Low to moderate; loss of focus on strategic goals; scope creep ***Project Investment and Management***: Local budgeting and management (may be ad hoc)
Business Process Design/ Reengineering Sample Projects: Business process reengineering; launch of shared services offering; ERP or sales force automation implementation	***Goal***: Use IT to improve end-to-end operating processes ***Business Sponsors***: Business unit and shared services leaders (may include suppliers, customers, or partners) ***Business Value***: Reduce costs, decrease cycle time, improve organizational or extended enterprise operating performance, and improve total cost of IT ownership ***Risk and Uncertainty***: Moderate to high; business and technology complexity and volatility; organizational change; often require integration of new capabilities with existing capabilities ***Project Investment and Management***: Corporate budgeting; steering committee with formal milestone reviews; change control processes and systems
Emerging Opportunities Sample Projects: Remote monitoring service offering; information-based product offerings	***Goal***: Pursue business opportunities that enable launch of new products or businesses or entry into new markets ***Business Sponsors***: Executive committee or business unit leadership, new venture/emerging technology or business ***Business Value***: Grow revenues and launch new businesses; enter high growth industries and markets ***Risk and Uncertainty***: High; new business models often require new capabilities and may involve new technologies ***Project Investment and Management***: Staged commitments and investments based on milestones; fund "experiments" and business plans; new venture risk management
Business Transformation Sample Projects: Global services business supports core product business; interactive online business sells or supports physical service offerings or products	***Goal***: Transform your organization and industry, differentiate strategy, and develop proprietary assets ***Business Sponsors***: Board, executive committee; strong project leadership ***Business Value***: Enable sustained capital efficient profitable growth, improve market share, and deliver sustainable competitive advantage ***Risk and Uncertainty***: High; new business models often require new capabilities and may involve new technologies; organizational change; often require integration of new business models with existing business ***Project Investment and Management***: Integrated with corporate strategy; board oversight with formal milestone reviews by executive committee; change control processes and systems

qualities of being attractive, durable, and timely," he continued, "and it must be anchored in a product or service that creates or adds value for the buyer or the end user." Paul Maeder, founder and managing general partner of the Boston-based venture capital firm, Highland Capital Partners, explained the criteria he uses to evaluate opportunities.[10]

> When we invest in [early-stage start-up] businesses, [we always ask]: Is this a unique value proposition? Do we have a real shot at being first in the market? . . . Is this a compelling enough business that people are going to be drawn to it, [initially employees and] managers and ultimately customers? Are there barriers to entry that we can erect so that when other people see our good ideas they don't pile in? Finally, can we build it with a reasonable amount of capital in a reasonable period of time? If the answers to those questions are satisfactory, we'll typically fund it.

As can be seen from the above quotes, while the search for opportunities often begins with a creative idea-generation process, opportunity identification requires a more analytically driven evaluation of the viability of the business model. Questions that executives can use as they search for ways to leverage IT to drive business model strategy are presented below. Chapter 3 discusses the role of IT in transforming business model capabilities.

- Can IT change the basis of competition?
- Can IT change the nature of relationships and the balance of power in buyer-seller relationships?
- Can IT build barriers to entry?
- Can IT raise switching costs?
- Can IT add value to existing products or services or create new ones?

Can IT Change the Basis of Competition?

At its core, IT is used to *automate* activities—whether they take place inside an organization or across its boundaries. But, as it automates, IT can also be used to both *inform* and to *transform*.

In the 1950s and 1960s, when IT was first introduced for commercial use, the primary target of IT applications was to automate routine, information-intensive back-office transactions (e.g., payroll processing, accounting, and general ledger postings). The primary goal was to increase efficiency and productivity. Businesses quickly learned to apply these same benefits to front-office activities that involved transactions with suppliers, distributors, customers, and other value chain participants. But the impact of IT increased dramatically when businesses learned to use it, not just to automate, but also to inform and transform—especially across business boundaries. A streamlined and integrated value chain helped eliminate redundancies, reduce cycle time, and achieve even greater efficiency and productivity. Information, a by-product of automation, also enabled executives, employees, partners, and other stakeholders to better understand fast-cycled operations. Moreover, timely—even real-time—information could be used to drive new benefits, including improved coordination and control; personalized products and services; enhanced strategic positioning and differentiation

[10] Interview with Paul Maeder by Professor Lynda Applegate, March 14, 2000.

of existing products and services; and, finally, the creation of IT-enabled products and services that attracted new market participants and generated new revenue streams.

American Hospital Supply Corporation (AHSC) and American Airlines (AA) were two early examples of how IT could be used to reengineer core operating processes and transform the basis of competition.[11] The story began during the late 1960s when an entrepreneurial sales manager at AHSC created a system that enabled hospital purchasing clerks to order supplies across telephone lines using punch cards and primitive card-reading computers. At about the same time, enterprising sales managers at AA were also paving new ground by giving large travel agencies computer terminals that allowed them to check airline schedules posted within American's internal reservation systems. Indeed, from these entrepreneurial actions grew two legendary strategic IT applications that changed the basis of competition in their respective industries.

Both AHSC and AA built their strategic systems upon internal systems that were originally designed to automate back-office transaction processing. AHSC, for example, first installed computers to manage internal inventory and order processing activities, and AA used computers to manage their internal reservation process. In both cases, the value of these early systems came from the ability to structure, simplify, standardize, and coordinate internal operations, thus reducing cost and cycle time while also ensuring consistency. But, once they had streamlined and structured activities inside the firm, both AHSC and AA recognized that they could allow customers to self-serve without fear of reducing quality. Because each firm had built its systems using proprietary technology, AHSC and AA owned the platforms upon which business was conducted—and they also owned the information flowing from the automated transaction systems. This information enabled executives and frontline workers to coordinate and control activities whether they took place inside the firm or outside. And, by harnessing the power of the information, both firms were able to differentiate existing services and to offer new information-based services to customers.

The benefits of conducting business online were so great that AHSC gave hospitals the card readers required to do business electronically and taught hospital supply clerks how to use them. AHSC even helped hospital personnel redesign their internal purchasing processes to fit with the new online process. AA did the same thing when it gave travel agents computer reservation terminals. Neither AHSC nor AA charged their customers for the computer equipment or the training. Why? The benefits to AHSC and AA from online purchasing, whether it was hospital supplies or seats on an airplane, more than offset the cost of giving away the terminals. For example, by 1985, AHSC saved over $11 million per year through online ordering and generated $4 to $5 million per year in additional revenue.

The AHSC and AA examples demonstrate how two firms used IT to fundamentally alter the basis of competition in their respective industries. This occurred when executives implemented strategies that radically changed both the cost structure for the industry and, at the same time, differentiated product/service offering and strategic positions, causing massive shifts in market share and demand.

[11] See J. L. McKenney, and D. G. Copeland, *Waves of Change* (Boston: HBS Press, 1995); and L. M. Applegate, "Electronic Commerce," in *The Technology Management Handbook*, ed. Richard C. Dorf (Englewood Cliffs, NJ: CRC Press, 1999), for an in-depth discussion of the evolution of early strategic systems.

Charles Schwab provides a more recent example of how a firm built upon existing capabilities and technology infrastructure to radically transform its industry—in this case financial services. Founded in 1975, Schwab accomplished this feat, not once, but twice. Initially, Schwab executives placed a bet that a growing number of individual investors would prefer to save money and time by using low-cost local branch office brokerage services rather than high-priced full-service brokers. Committed to delivering the levels of trust and responsiveness of a full-service broker but at a dramatically reduced cost, Schwab turned to IT. For example, by the late 1970s, the company had launched an IT-enabled 24×7 call center and customer relationship management system that quickly became the channel of choice for Schwab customers. In the mid-1980s and early 1990s, Schwab pioneered online trading capabilities—well before the Internet simplified adoption. Indeed, by 1997, revenues for Schwab's discount brokerage business—a new market segment that Schwab had started, built, and dominated for over 20 years—had reached US$2.3 billion.

When the commercial Internet appeared in the mid-1990s, Schwab was poised again to segment the market. Already, routine customer service requests (quotes, balances, positions) had migrated from Schwab branches to the call center and, to a lesser extent, to its proprietary online service. Indeed, at the time it launched its Internet online brokerage in January of 1998, only 5 percent of routine customer service was handled at a brokerage office—with the majority handled by phone. The Web-based service provided access to online and offline brokerage services for a single fee of $29.95 per trade (compared to an average $80 per trade for full-service brokerage commissions). Within less than one year, sales were up 19 percent. And, since the online self-service business dramatically lowered costs, profits were also up 29 percent.

Today, new "born digital" firms like Google and Amazon.com and established players like Boeing and IBM are pushing the boundaries of how IT can be used to transform business strategy and capabilities. In so doing, they are redefining the basis of competition in a wide range of industries.[12]

Can IT Change the Nature of Relationships and the Balance of Power in Buyer-Seller Relationships?

As mentioned above, AHSC rose to power within the hospital supply industry by streamlining channels, dramatically decreasing cost, improving order accuracy, and streamlining the supply chain between suppliers (e.g., Johnson & Johnson, Baxter, and Abbott) and hospital buyers. Initially, AHSC used traditional offline processes to buy supplies from manufacturers and to store them in AHSC-owned warehouses. But, once it succeeded in getting a large number of customers to buy online, AHSC sought to further streamline the supply chain. Sensing they were at risk of being excluded from the market and lacking the money, expertise, and time to respond, suppliers succumbed to the pressure to put their catalogs online and join the electronic market. Once electronic links to suppliers had been established, AHSC customers could order directly from supplier inventory, which enabled further reductions in cost and cycle time for all members of the online market.

[12] Both Amazon.com & Boeing are discussed in cases located at the end of this module. Readers can learn more about how Google is using IT to transform its industry in the Harvard Business School case (No. 806-105).

Customers encouraged this channel consolidation. While they recognized the value of a multivendor marketplace, they were unwilling to put up with the problems of using multiple different supplier systems to conduct business. Within a short time, AHSC became a powerful supply chain services provider within the hospital supply industry, controlling both the physical and information channels for conducting business. In fact, this neutral, third-party distributor created such a significant shift in the balance of power toward the channel that, in 1985, it was bought by Baxter Healthcare Corporation, a hospital supplier in the industry. A few years later, responding to pressure from market participants, Baxter was forced to spin out the supply chain exchange to ensure neutrality.

Initially, many believed that the Internet might similarly shift power from suppliers (e.g., manufacturers and service providers) to channel players (e.g., wholesalers, distributors, and retailers) and buyers. Indeed, during the late 1990s, Internet-based channel players flooded the market in an attempt to gain the position of power in this new online channel.

By 2004, however, many of the independent Internet marketplaces were struggling or had closed. As neutral, independent channel players faltered, established players rushed in—initially to defend their turf and later to drive efficiencies as the economy worsened. Once again, the health care industry provided an excellent view into the continued impact of IT on the changing nature of relationships and shifting power dynamics.

In March 2000, five of the largest health care suppliers—Abbott, Baxter, GE Medical, Johnson & Johnson, and Medtronic—launched the Global Healthcare Exchange, LLC (GHX).[13] GHX promised to eliminate inefficiencies in every step in the health care supply chain, from placing orders to tracking delivery. These inefficiencies accounted for an estimated $11 billion in unnecessary purchasing costs.[14] The five founding companies supplied over 70 percent of all products and services purchased by hospitals and did business with over 90 percent of potential buyers. Within months of the announcement of GHX's formation, more than half of the emerging independent health care Internet marketplaces disappeared as venture capital investors pulled back their funding and support in recognition that chances for success were slim given plummeting stock markets and the eroding economy.

Consolidation of the industry continued as the majority of the health care marketplaces joined forces with GHX. By mid-2003, GHX's board of directors and investors included representation by the largest buyers, distributors, and suppliers in the health care industry. As one of only two remaining large online supply chain marketplaces, GHX enabled over 1,400 health care buyers and distributors to transact over $2 billion in business with over 100 suppliers. In 2006, GHX purchased Neoforma, its last remaining health care supply chain competitor, and the industry moved to a neutral shared services platform.

[13] For a thorough discussion of GHX, see L. M. Applegate, "Global Healthcare Exchange," Harvard Business School Publishing (No. 804-002). Also see M. L. Applegate, "Building Inter-Firm Collaborative Community: Uniting Theory and Practice," in *The Firm as Collaborative Community: Reconstructing Trust in the Knowledge Economy,* ed. C. Heckscher, and P. Adler, 2006.

[14] R. Winslow, "Baxter International, Others Plan Net Concern for Hospital Purchases," *The Wall Street Journal Interactive,* March 30, 2000.

The GHX case provides a rare glimpse into the evolution of relationships and power dynamics within an industry as key participants in a business network worked together to drive efficiencies for all. When the Internet burst on the scene, it was initially believed that power would shift to independent channel players as they disintermediated traditional buyer-supplier relationships and fragmented industries. By 2000, the view had shifted as established players regained power and sought ways to consolidate it even more. Today, the evolution has come full circle as independent shared services providers—owned by the industry (e.g., GHX or Nasdaq) or by an independent provider (e.g., Google, Amazon.com, or eBay)—provide the online platform and services used by all players in an industry. While the evolution of GHX and Nasdaq as trusted, neutral collaborative marketplaces is facilitated by shared industry ownership, many voice concerns about the increasing power and ambitions of independent online platform and shared service providers such as Google.

Can IT Build Barriers to Entry?

Companies erect entry barriers by offering attractive products and services at a price and level of quality that competitors cannot match. Entry barriers can also be erected when companies possess assets and specialized expertise that would be costly, time consuming, and difficult to duplicate. Before the rise of the commercial Internet, first movers like AHSC and AA spent hundreds of millions of dollars over decades to establish a dominant position within electronic markets. The sheer magnitude of the investment and expertise required to build and operate proprietary networks, transaction systems, and databases created significant barriers to entry. For example, American Airlines and archrival United Airlines each spent hundreds of millions of dollars during the late 1970s and early 1980s to build the proprietary networks and computer systems required to launch and run online customer reservation systems. By the time other airlines recognized the opportunity—and threat—they were forced to tie into these two dominant online channels or risk being cut off from customers.

Over time, however, these technology-based advantages decreased. The more sustainable advantage came from second-order barriers to entry created when companies exploited the value of information generated by the technology and leveraged proprietary capabilities and assets to continuously innovate and evolve business strategy. Second-order barriers to entry were also erected by leveraging a loyal and engaged community of suppliers, customers, and partners that did business using a company's proprietary digital infrastructure and assets.

Initially, many believed that the overall impact of Internet technologies would be to lower entry barriers for all players in online markets.[15] This belief arose from the fact that Internet technologies dramatically lowered the cost of creating and participating in electronic markets. In addition, the shared, nonproprietary nature of the Internet made it easy for market participants to link to a shared, nonproprietary platform for conducting business online and, more importantly, to sever ties with one firm and link to another.

[15] M. Porter, "Strategy and the Internet," *Harvard Business Review*, March 2001.

After more than a decade of use, we have seen that the Internet's low cost and ease of penetration decrease the benefits to any one participant unless people within an organization are able to:

- Learn, respond, and innovate more quickly and more effectively than others.
- Build proprietary capabilities that are not easily replicable.
- Create a large, loyal community that remains committed and engaged despite the availability of seemingly comparable alternatives.

As we saw in the past, these capability and community barriers provide a sustainable entry barrier—even within open standard electronic markets. In most cases, we see that incumbent firms with large investments in proprietary infrastructure and channels to market are at a particular disadvantage relative to new entrants when attempting to create and quickly deploy second-order barriers to entry.

Amazon.com, one of the most celebrated new entrants of the dot-com era, provides an example of how new technology can lower entry barriers in an established industry. But, as we will see, while entry barriers were initially low, Amazon's initial online retail business model required the company to take ownership of physical inventory. This, in turn, required significant investments in building an online/offline retail infrastructure. While building and deploying the infrastructure delayed profitability, the company eventually found ways to capitalize on the infrastructure it had built, the community it had connected, and what it had learned, turning a profit during fourth quarter 2001—and building significant barriers to subsequent entry.

In July 1995, Jeff Bezos, Amazon's CEO and founder, launched his online bookstore from a 400-square-foot warehouse (about the size of a one-car garage) with only a few personal computers and a high-speed connection to the Internet. The company quickly became the number one online bookstore. Just two years after launch, sales had reached $148 million and the number of customers exceeded 2 million.

During its third year, Amazon executives demonstrated that the initial success in quickly dominating the online book market could be repeated. During the summer and fall of 1998, Amazon opened new online music and video "stores" and achieved the number one position in online music sales within four months and the number one position in online video sales within a record 45 days.

At this point, Amazon's success was due to the fact that the Internet had lowered entry barriers to the detriment of established players. But there was a deeper lesson here. Established competitors, such as Barnes & Noble, Borders, and Bertelsmann (in Europe), were not blind to Amazon's early success; they invested heavily but were unable to catch up. Why? Many erroneously believed that Amazon's dominance came from its first-mover advantage. While this was important, in other instances first movers were quickly crushed. CDNow, for example, was overtaken by Amazon.com in short order.

The secret to Amazon's success in entering and dominating multiple industries was the capabilities that it built behind its Web site to execute strategy. During 1999 and 2000, Amazon executives spent over US$400 million building a sophisticated, Web-based order fulfillment capability that enabled the company to fulfill orders for over 31 million units during the six-week 2000 holiday period from mid-November to the end of December. Over 99 percent of orders arrived on time.

Like the success stories from the 1980s, the automated transaction infrastructure generated valuable information that, in Amazon.com's case, was fed into a sophisticated business intelligence infrastructure that allowed executives and employees at all levels to develop a real-time understanding of the dynamics of the marketplace and of the needs of individual consumers and business customers. Amazon employees used the insights gained to coordinate and control operations—not only inside the firm but also across organizational boundaries. More importantly, it used its growing understanding of customer preferences to personalize its online services in a way that could not be matched by competitors and to feed valuable information to suppliers. The number of loyal customers increased quickly and, by late 2000, over 25 million people shopped on Amazon. These proprietary capabilities (which united people and technology) enabled Amazon to develop powerful barriers to entry that, to date, competitors have been unable to match. In Bezos' words:

> Amazon.com's platform includes its brand, customers, technology, distribution capability, deep e-commerce expertise, and a great team with a passion for innovation and serving customers well . . . We believe that we have reached a "tipping point," where this platform allows us to launch new e-commerce businesses faster, with a higher quality of customer experience, a lower incremental cost, a higher chance of success, and a clearer path to scale and profitability than perhaps any other company.[16]

By mid-2001, however, many wondered whether these proprietary assets would be enough. After the rapid decline in the price of Internet stocks during 2000 and the loss of investor confidence in online business models, the company found that sources of financing had dried up. Amazon executives altered the company's strategy and business model away from a dependence on retail product sales and toward a services model in an effort to attain profitability more quickly. This new strategy paralleled the approach used by AHSC and AA during the 1980s to shift from selling products to selling capabilities and expertise. The Amazon.com case, at the end of this module, tells this fascinating story and highlights the role of proprietary IT-enabled capabilities and assets in transforming organizations and industries.

Can IT Raise Switching Costs?

To provide a sustainable source of revenues, an IT system should ideally be easy to start using but difficult to stop using. Customers drawn into the system through a series of increasingly valuable enhancements should willingly become dependent on the system's functionality. Once use of the system becomes ingrained within day-today activities, switching to another system becomes difficult and costly.

In the past, when proprietary technologies were the norm, switching costs were high because switching usually required buying into different proprietary networks and systems owned and operated by another online service provider. As a result, first movers such as American Airlines in the travel industry, American Hospital Supply in the hospital supply industry, or Wal-Mart in the retail industry were able to hold customers and suppliers hostage. On the public Internet, however, the cost of a simple connection is relatively low and the technologies required to participate are not

[16] Amazon.com Annual Report, 1999.

proprietary. As a result, switching costs are often substantially reduced. For example, the cost to a customer of switching from shopping at Amazon.com to shopping at Barnes & Noble's online store is merely a few keystrokes' effort. Easy switching also makes for easy price comparisons, which led many to believe that it would be difficult to achieve strong customer loyalty.

While there appears to be a certain inevitability to this logic, savvy executives (for example, Scott Cook at Intuit) have identified ways to exploit the power of the Internet to increase, rather than decrease, switching costs. Launched in 1983, Intuit provided low-cost financial services software (Quicken, TurboTax, and QuickBooks) that were designed to be easy to use by individuals with little to no background in finance or technology. Initially, the products "hooked" the user by providing a much simpler and easier way to complete time-consuming and repetitive tasks. By also providing a simple way to store personal information, which would have to be re-entered if a customer switched to a different product, the company kept users hooked over time. This strategy enabled Intuit to quickly become the market leader for individual and small business financial software with over 80 percent market share across its product line and over 90 percent retention rates. Throughout the 1990s, the company continued to maintain this position despite aggressive competition by software giant Microsoft.

A decade after launching its first software product, the company launched an online financial services portal, Quicken.com, to complement and extend its packaged software offerings. By linking its Internet business to the company's traditional desktop software, Intuit was able to transition users from its desktop product line to a less costly Internet product line while also offering an even easier to use and more useful set of services. By 2001, consumers and small business owners could pay bills and bank online, calculate and pay taxes, and manage a portfolio of investments. Small business owners could also manage payroll, inventory, and customer accounts, and could purchase supplies. As these features were added to the service, and as customers benefited from their ease of use and convenience, switching became more difficult. Changing an online bill paying service, for example, involved setting up relationships between the new service and each company to be paid.

Intuit used the lessons learned from its successful software business to guide the launch and evolution of its Internet business. Careful attention was paid to creating a service offering that provided a unique value proposition for customers and that hooked users to its offering by providing a simple and easy-to-use way to complete time-consuming and repetitive tasks. And, once users invested the effort to store personal information and to set up online transaction relationships, it became much harder to switch. Using these principles, within less than one year of launch, Intuit's online version of its TurboTax software gained over 80 percent market share in the highly competitive market for online tax preparation and filing.

Can IT Add Value to Existing Products or Services or Create New Ones?

In addition to lowering cost, improving quality, and changing power dynamics, IT can also add value to existing products or services and create new ones. Indeed, over the past few decades, the information content of existing products has increased markedly. For example, by 2000, there were more computer chips in a late-model car than were in the entire U.S. Department of Defense in 1960. Today, computer chips control everything from a car's internal air temperature to the braking system, and they also provide valuable information to service mechanics and auto manufacturers to guide after-sales service and future product design. Most importantly, consumers can now tap into on-board computers, like General Motors' OnStar service, to get driving directions, make dinner reservations, contact police and rescue personnel, and even open the car door to retrieve keys inadvertently left inside. In fact, Nick Tredennick, technology analyst for Gilder Publishing, predicted that, by 2028, 99 percent of processors will be dedicated to embedded applications.[17]

Information-enabled products and services possess some very interesting properties. First, information is reusable. Unlike physical products, information can be "sold" without transferring ownership and "used" without being consumed. As one Internet business executive observed: "I sell information to you, and now you own it. Yet I still own it, and we both can use it." Second, information is easily customized. The same information can be presented in different forms (e.g., text, graphics, video, audio) and in varying levels of detail. It can be combined with information from other sources to communicate different messages and to create new products and services. Third, information-based products and services possess an inherent "time value." As the speed of business accelerates, the time value of information increases.

Boeing's launch of its 787 Dreamliner demonstrates the power of embedded IT to create what the company termed its "e-Enabled Advantage.[18] Planes in the Dreamliner fleet are equipped with networks and on-board computers that make it possible for them to serve as "flying Internet hubs." Specialized hardware, middleware, and applications connect the cockpit and cabin flight crews with all on-ground communication and data networks and systems. This "brain on the plane" manages and routes enormous quantities of real-time data input and output within the airplane and between the airplane and the outside world. Leveraging this core infrastructure, a suite of IT applications has been developed that integrates each aspect of flight operations and forms the foundation for new services offerings that generate new revenue streams and create value for Boeing and its customers, suppliers, and partners. Examples of the systems and services included as part of Boeing's e-Enabled advantage are:

- The Airplane Health Management in-flight monitoring system provides real-time information on airplane operations, diagnostics, and maintenance to pilots, airport ground personnel, airline management, and Boeing engineers and executives.
- The Boeing Electronic Flight Bag provides pilots and flight crews with integrated solutions for managing information and communicating with maintenance, scheduling, and a wide range of other service providers in the air and on the ground.

[17] Nick Tredennick presentation at the Embedded Systems Conference, April 2008.

[18] L. Applegate, J. Valacich, M. Vatz, and C. Schneider, "Boeing's e-Enabled Advantage," Harvard Business School Publishing (No. 806-106), 2006. Also see, Nolan et al., "Boeing 787: The Dreamliner," Harvard Business School Publishing (No. 305-101).

- The Portable Maintenance Aid provides mechanics and engineers with real-time information and diagnostic and monitoring systems to resolve technical issues at the work site, in the hangar, in the office, or on the flight line, and to troubleshoot airplanes in minimum time.
- Integrated resource planning and supply chain software enables Boeing to provide hosted airline materials management for the industry. This has resulted in improved service level reliability, lower parts costs, lower inventory, and streamlined logistics, while also enabling Boeing to leverage its supplier partnerships for improved asset management and supply chain functionality throughout the airline industry.
- Hosted Operations Control enables Boeing to provide airline customers and partners with a full suite of flight planning, logistics, and real-time operations control services.
- Business intelligence information and tools are available to operations personnel and executives at Boeing, its airline customers, and the myriad suppliers and partners that make up the airline business network.
- MyBoeingFleet.com, a portal available to airplane owners, operators; Maintenance, Repair, and Overhaul operators (MROs); and other third parties, provides direct and personalized access to information essential to the operation of Boeing-delivered aircraft.
- In-flight entertainment and communication systems provide passengers with access to video, audio, and Internet services.

To leverage its e-Enabled Advantage and deliver its new service offerings, Boeing needed new capabilities—so too did its customers, suppliers, and other members of the airline business network. Boeing built these capabilities by acquiring several high-growth airline industry software companies (e.g., Jeppesen) and by launching a Solutions Consulting business staffed with consultants, decision scientists, and information specialists with deep airline industry, technology, and business expertise. Teams of consultants worked with airline operation teams to identify opportunities to use Boeing's e-Enabled Advantage to create value for Boeing and its customers, suppliers, and partners. Sophisticated analytical models of end-to-end airline operations were built and those models, which simulated "as is" and "to be" operating processes and performance, enabled Boeing consultants and its airline partners to identify opportunities to reduce costs and improve performance that would translate to bottom-line financial performance improvements. For example, Boeing demonstrated to one airline customer how e-Enabling could help reduce fleet delays and create $225 million value over 10 years. "The process helps Boeing establish a jointly owned value proposition with our customers. This makes us a partner rather than a supplier," said a Boeing project director for its Aviation Services Value Analysis Consulting practice. Scott Carson, who in 2008 was president and CEO of Boeing Commercial Airlines, commented: "Whatever we do in e-Enabling will never be the sole reason that people buy Boeing airplanes. But it will certainly help create a preference for Boeing airplanes in the marketplace."[19]

[19] These quotes are from L. M. Applegate, et al., "Boeing's e-Enabled Advantage," Harvard Business School Publishing (No. 806-106), p. 11.

Sources of IT Risk

There are two key categories of risk that must always be considered when launching new business initiatives designed to evolve or transform a company's business model.

Strategic risk:

The following questions can be used to assess the impact of IT on strategic risk.

1. Can emerging technologies disrupt our current business model by enabling new business models with decidedly superior economics?
2. Can IT lower entry barriers, change industry power dynamics, or increase competitive intensity?
3. Can IT trigger regulatory action?

Project risk:

The following questions can be used to assess the impact of IT on project risk.

1. Is the project larger than our typical project?
2. How much uncertainty is there in the project? Do we know the requirements for key deliverables at the start of the project or are these requirements still evolving? (Note: Strategic uncertainties concerning market adoption, product design, or the availability of resources may influence both project and strategic risk.)
3. Do we have experience with the technology (or technologies)? If new technologies are involved, are they new to the world or just new to us?
4. Do we have the resources (time, money, talent, information) needed to implement the project?
5. Do we have the sponsorship and buy-in from key stakeholders?
6. Is the organization (including the extended enterprise and industry) ready to implement and use what we deliver?

While the Boeing case describes opportunities for creating business value by embedding IT in physical products and services, it is also possible to alter or even completely transform some products from analog to digital. For example, by 2008, books, magazines, music, videos, and games were often created, delivered, and used in a purely digital form. As mentioned earlier, these digital assets possess unique economic properties. Indeed, once information, interactions, and transactions are in digital form, they can be leveraged to increase business insight, to create new products and services, and to add value to existing ones.

The Management of Risk

While the above examples highlight the role of IT in pursuing new business opportunities, the importance of risk cannot be overlooked. Interestingly, the more successful a company is, the easier it is to forget about risk. "It's in good times that managers need to be most watchful for signs of impending danger," warns Bob Simons.[20] "[Success] has an uncanny way of setting a company up for trouble, if not impending attack. And, not just from outside sources such as competitors and regulators, but, just as important, from within the organization itself." While the earlier sections of this chapter focused on the impact of IT and the search for opportunities, this final section discusses IT impact on strategic risk. The text box entitled "Sources of IT Risk" provides an overview of the key categories of risk that must be addressed. Module 2 discusses approaches to managing project risk.

[20] R. Simons, "How Risky Is Your Company?" *Harvard Business Review*, May–June 1999, p. 85.

Summary

Exploiting IT opportunities requires vision, sound execution, and the ability to respond quickly. It also requires imagination—and a lot of creativity. This chapter presents frameworks and approaches for analyzing the strategic impact of IT projects and the role that IT plays in a company. The following questions can be used to assess IT impact, opportunities, and risks.

1. What is the business impact of IT projects currently under way in your organization? Do you have the right project sponsorship and implementation approach based on the level of impact and degree of uncertainty and risk? Identify the impact profile of the portfolio of projects in your organization. Are you focusing your resources (money, people, and time) on the right types of projects based on the strategic goals of your organization?
2. What are the opportunities for using IT to improve business model performance? Can IT:

    a. Change the basis of competition?
    b. Change the nature of relationships and the balance of power among buyers and suppliers?
    c. Build or reduce barriers to entry?
    d. Increase or decrease switching costs?
    e. Add value to existing products and services, create new ones, or enter new markets?

3. Are you identifying and managing IT risk?

Chapter 3

IT Impact on Organizations[1]

If the old model of organization was the large, hierarchical organization, the new model that is considered characteristic of the new competition is a network of lateral and horizontal interlinkages within and among firms.

Nohria and Eccles, 1992[2]

Today's executives are both fascinated by—and often skeptical of—the new business models that they read about in the business press. Some academics and business futurists argue that we are in the midst of an economic transition from the industrial economy to a global network economy that promises to be just as profound as the transition from the agrarian economy to the industrial economy during the latter half of the nineteenth century.[3] Others prefer to avoid such far-reaching predictions. But, no matter what their position, most agree that traditional organizational designs are inadequate for coping with today's turbulent and increasingly networked world. Executives in large, established firms increasingly find that their organizations must become much more agile, innovative, and entrepreneurial while not losing the efficiency, power, and reach that come with size and scale. And entrepreneurs and executives in small firms find that they must tap into an extended network of partners to achieve the scale and power needed to succeed in industries dominated by large, global players.

As they attempt to build lean yet agile businesses, these executives are finding that they can no longer rely on gut instinct alone. Neither can they simply copy organizational models that worked in the past. Instead, they must understand how organizational and design choices influence operational efficiency and flexibility and,

[1] This chapter is based on material developed by Professor Lynda M. Applegate for courses offered at HBS. Permission to reprint must be obtained from the author.

[2] N. Nohria and R. Eccles, *Networks and Organizations: Structure, Form and Action* (Boston: Harvard Business School Press, 1993), p. 2.

[3] During the late 1980s and early 1990s, academics and business futurists predicted the demise of the hierarchy and the rise of a more networked, intelligent, and agile organizational model. For examples, see Drucker, "The Coming of the New Organization," *Harvard Business Review*, January–February 1988; W. Powell, "Neither Market nor Hierarchy: New Forms of Organization," *Research on Organizational Behavior* 12 (1990), pp. 295–336; F. Ostroff and D. Smith, "The Horizontal Organization," *McKinsey Quarterly* 1 (1992), pp. 148–168.

even more important, they must determine how to best align the organization with the environment and the chosen strategy to quickly and effectively "sense and respond" to opportunities and threats.[4]

This chapter examines the capabilities required to build businesses that can survive and prosper in today's fast-paced and uncertain environment. The challenges of preserving the advantages of a big company while responding as quickly and innovatively as a small company are not new. Indeed, the insights presented in this chapter have emerged from over 20 years of work with hundreds of executives and entrepreneurs as they struggled to build businesses that could cope with the demands of a rapidly changing, increasingly networked global economy.[5] The insights from this research suggest that IT is an important enabler for developing the best-in-class capabilities required for success.

The Need for New Capabilities

Executives spent much of the twentieth century building and perfecting hierarchies—and the last few decades attempting to tear them down. During the 1980s and 1990s, downsizing, delayering, and reengineering swept through large companies. Rigid intra- and interfirm boundaries were shattered to enable companies to focus on core competencies while also delivering customized solutions in global markets. Strategic partnerships and alliances were formed to ensure access to capabilities and expertise that could not be efficiently and effectively built and managed inside organizations.

The vision of eliminating hierarchy was compelling, and the change initiatives—many of them enabled by emerging information technologies—shook business markets and the organizations within them to their foundations. But take a walk around most large, established firms, or talk with executives from established industries, and it soon becomes clear that the "hierarchy" is far from dead. Yet, when asked what their companies or industries should look like, most executives call immediately for new capabilities that enable them to work more effectively and efficiently within more diffuse and fluid business networks that are popularly called "ecosystems."[6] The problem confronting these executives, they report, is that they do not wish to sacrifice efficiency for speed; neither can they abandon authority and control as they empower others—be they employees, partners, or other loosely connected network

[4] S. Bradley and R. Nolan, *Sense and Respond: Capturing Value in a Networked Era* (Boston: Harvard Business School Press, 1998).

[5] L. M. Applegate, "In Search of a New Organization," in *Shaping Organizational Form: Communication, Connection and Community*, eds. G. DeSanctis and J. Fulk (Newbury Park, CA: Sage, 1999); L. M. Applegate, "Time for the Big-Small Company," *Financial Times Mastering Information Management*, April 1999.

[6] Applegate (1999) describes the features of early attempts at building intrafirm collaborative community. Also see Applegate (1994) for results of a survey of business executives who were asked to describe changing governance models during the early 1990s and expectations for future changes. L. M. Applegate, "Business Transformation Self-Assessment—1992–1993," Harvard Business School Publishing, 1994 (No. 194-013). L. M. Applegate, "Time for the Big Small Company," *Financial Times Mastering Information Management Series*, March 1, 1999.

members—to make decisions that directly influence real-time customer needs and business performance.

In the mid-1990s, Jack Welch, CEO of General Electric (GE) at the time, summarized the dilemma his company faced. "Our dream and our plan well over a decade ago were simple," he said. "We set out to shape a global enterprise that preserved the classic big company advantages while eliminating the big company drawbacks. What we wanted to build was a hybrid enterprise with the . . . power, resources, and reach of a large firm and the hunger, spirit, and fire of a small one."[7] This was not just a U.S. point of view: Percy Barnevik, CEO of Switzerland-based Asea Brown Boveri (ABB), was one of many in other countries who echoed Welch's comments. "ABB is an organization with three internal contradictions," he explained. "We want to be global and local, big and small, and radically decentralized with centralized reporting and control. If we resolve those contradictions, we create real competitive advantage."[8]

And it's not just large firms that face the dilemma of how to be big and small simultaneously. Small companies also struggle with the problems that come from doing business on an increasingly complex and global scale. Take, for example, LeapFrog, the educational toy company.[9] When LeapFrog was founded in 1995, executives outsourced manufacturing to seven Chinese factories and shipping and distribution to global logistics firms that, by 2002, were shipping LeapFrog products to Toys "R" Us and Wal-Mart retailers located in over 28 countries. Operating as the creative design and marketing hub of its global network of partners, LeapFrog rose from its position as the number 15 toy company in 2000, to the number 4 position in 2001, and the number 3 position in 2002—behind only Mattel and Hasbro, the giants in an industry that had been called a duopoly.[10]

But this rapid growth dramatically increased the complexity LeapFrog faced. In 2003, the company had launched five product platforms—hardware and software that could run a wide variety of content—with over 100 different content titles. In addition, the company had launched over 35 stand-alone toy products and had entered the educational software industry with the launch of its SchoolHouse division. Finally, its content had been translated into English, Spanish, French, Italian, and Japanese, and its products were sold in countries around the world.

With growth and increased complexity also came problems of control and talent management. Faced with the need to install systems and structure, founder and CEO Mike Wood worried that the company would lose its creative talent. IT was seen as a key enabler of controlling operations while also providing real-time information and analytical tools that allowed employees, executives, and even the company's retail customers to continue the steady stream of product innovation required for success in the fad-driven toy industry. Figure 3.1 summarizes the dilemma that drives executives of large and small firms alike to search for new organizational solutions.

[7] J. Welch, "Managing in the 90s," GE Report to Shareholders, 1988.

[8] R. Simons and C. Bartlett, "Asea Brown Boveri" Harvard Business School Publishing (No. 192-139).

[9] L. M. Applegate, et al., "Leapfrog Enterprises," Harvard Business School Publishing (No. 808-109), March 2008.

[10] A duopoly is an industry controlled by two large competitors. In the United States, the Sherman Antitrust Act prevents one player from gaining monopoly control.

FIGURE 3.1 The Organization Design Challenge

Source: © 2005 Lynda M. Applegate.

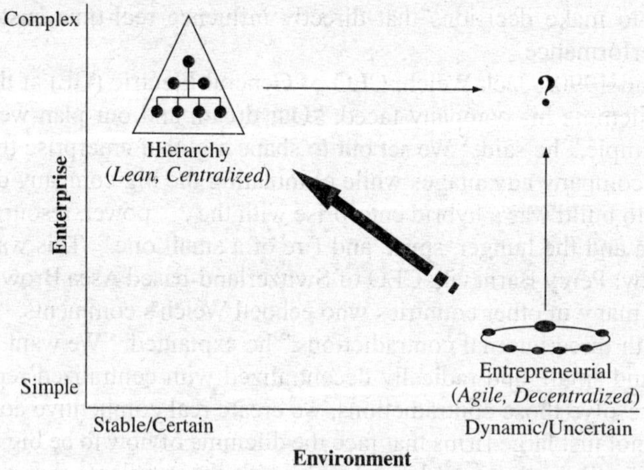

As timely as it seems, the management dilemma of designing a "big-small company" is not new. In fact, descriptions of "hybrid" organizations designed to enable companies to be lean and agile simultaneously were common in the 1950s and 1960s.[11] (Interestingly, these organizational models were pioneered by rapidly growing technology start-ups in the aerospace and computer industries.) One of these hybrid designs—the matrix—was originally billed as the "obvious organizational solution" to the need for control and efficiency, while simultaneously enabling flexibility and speed of response.[12] Decades ago, proponents of the matrix argued for an "adaptive, information-intensive, team-based, collaborative, and empowered" organization—all characteristics of today's twenty-first century organizations.

But companies that adopted the hybrid designs of the 1960s through 1980s soon learned that the new structures and systems bred conflict, confusion, information overload, and costly duplication of resources. Bartlett and Ghoshal discuss why many firms adopted the matrix only to abandon it several years later: "Top-level managers are losing control of their companies. The problem is not that they have misjudged the demands created by an increasingly complex environment and an accelerating rate of environmental change, nor that they have failed to develop strategies appropriate to the new challenges. The problem is that their companies are organizationally incapable of carrying out the sophisticated strategies they have developed. Over the past 20 years, strategic thinking has outdistanced organizational capabilities."[13]

[11] T. Burns and G. M. Stalker, *The Management of Innovation* (London: Tavistock, 1961); J. Woodward, *Industrial Organization, Theory and Practice* (London: Oxford University Press, 1965); J. D. Thompson, *Organizations in Action* (New York: McGraw-Hill, 1967); P. Lawrence, and J. Lorsch, *Organization and Environment* (Boston: Harvard Business School Press, 1967, 1986); L. Greiner, "Evolution and Revolution as Organizations Grow," *Harvard Business Review* 50, no. 4 (1972), pp. 37–46; J. Galbraith, *Designing Complex Organization* (Reading, MA: Addison Wesley, 1973).

[12] C. Bartlett and S. Ghoshal, *Managing across Borders: The Transnational Solution* (Boston: Harvard Business School Press, 1991).

[13] Ibid.

Is History Repeating Itself?

Given such problems, we might legitimately ask: "If these hybrid organizations failed in the past, why are we trying them again?" Interestingly, one of the major sources of difficulty with the matrix was the dramatic increase in the need for timely information to manage it successfully.[14] While the hierarchy managed complexity by minimizing it, the matrix demanded that managers deal with complexity directly. Product managers had to coordinate their plans and operations with functional managers. Country managers had to coordinate activities with headquarters. And senior managers, attempting to reconcile overall organizational performance and plan corporate strategy, were faced with a dizzying array of conflicting information.

In the large industrial economy hierarchies, paper-based and word-of-mouth information moved slowly and channels of communication were limited. While the mainframe computer systems of the day helped process some of this information, they were designed, like the hierarchy itself, to support centralized decision making and hierarchical communication. The microcomputer revolution of the 1980s provided tools to decentralize information processing—which helped improve local decision making—but the technology to support both local and enterprisewide information sharing and communication was inadequate.

Only recently has information technology (IT) become capable of meeting the information challenge inherent in the organization design challenge discussed above (see Figure 3.2). The "networked IT revolution," which began in the 1980s and picked up speed with the commercialization of the Internet and its associated technological innovations, has made possible new approaches to communicating and sharing information that redefine organizational possibilities. IBM CEO Sam Palmisano termed this new approach "Business On Demand" and has focused IBM's over 300,000 employee workforce and its global network of partners on making it a reality for IBM and its customers. He describes an On Demand enterprise as one that "unites information, processes, and people to create an enterprise in which end-to-end processes are integrated across a company, an industry, and globally to enable it to respond with speed and flexibility to any customer demand, market opportunity, or external threat."[15]

How can executives exploit the power of emerging IT infrastructures to enable organizations to act big and small simultaneously? Technology is not enough. New approaches to organizing and managing are required. But before we describe these design elements, it is helpful to review lessons from some classic organizational failures.

Learning from Mistakes

There is much to be learned from careful examination of a failure. Consider the disaster that befell Barings Bank.[16] A February 28, 1995, article in *The Wall Street Journal*,

[14] Research in the mid-1960s suggested that firms that are successful operating in uncertain and complex environments developed systems to improve vertical and lateral information processing in the firm. See J. Galbraith, *Designing Complex Organizations* (Reading, MA: Addison Wesley, 1973); and P. Lawrence and J. Lorsch, *Organization and Environment* (Boston: Harvard Business School Press, 1986).

[15] L. M. Applegate, et al., "IBM's Decade of Transformation: Turnaround to Growth," Harvard Business School Publishing (No. 805-130).

[16] R. Stevenson "Markets Shaken as a British Bank Takes a Big Loss," *The New York Times*, February 27, 1995; G. Millman, "Barings Collapses: Financial System Bears Up Well," *The Wall Street Journal*, February 28, 1995.

FIGURE 3.2
Building Lean, yet Agile, Enterprises

Source: © 2005 Lynda M. Applegate.

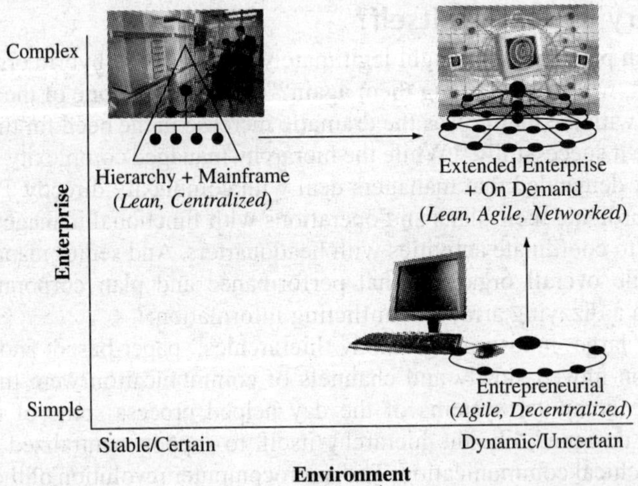

proclaimed: "The warning lights should have been blinking. The collapse of 233-year-old Barings PLC due to a staggering $1.2 billion loss from unauthorized derivatives trading raises an important question: How many other Barings are out there?"[17]

The huge losses were traced to the actions of a 27-year-old trader in Singapore who had been given authority to trade financial derivatives on behalf of the firm. While most securities firms grant similar authority to traders, the potential for abuse of power appeared to be greater at Barings because, according to the newspaper accounts, the 27-year-old trader also had control over the back-office transaction systems that reported on trades. Over a few months' time, the capital reserves of the bank were wiped out. The bank's risk management systems and executive oversight either did not detect or did not respond in time to prevent disaster.

More recently (January 2008) a 31-year-old trader at French bank, Société Générale, circumvented control systems resulting in a €4.9 billion ($7 billion) loss.[18] As in the case of Barings Bank, the problems arose in a unit that was growing quickly and generating significant profits, and there was evidence that a combination of faulty supervision and inadequate information reporting was among the underlying problems that led to the huge losses.

While no firm can totally insulate itself against such disasters, the hierarchy specifies a number of structures and systems that help to safeguard a large firm.[19] Authority systems limit decision making and actions by strict segregation of responsibility and duties, standardization of jobs, direct supervision, and restricted access to information and assets everywhere but at the very top of the firm. In theory, the hierarchy is designed so that, short of sabotage, no single employee or work unit can make a decision or take an action that can immediately threaten the entire organization. Even at

[17] S. Lypin and G. B. Krecht, "How Many Other Barings Are There?" *The Wall Street Journal*, February 28, 1995.

[18] "Soc Gen Post Mortem," *FT.com*, January 25, 2008 (downloaded June 14, 2008).

[19] In small, privately held firms, authority for most decisions is retained by the CEO/founder, and controls are based on direct oversight and supervision.

the top of a firm, the CEO is responsible to a board of directors that includes external members representing stakeholder interests.

Similarly, hierarchical control systems are designed to ensure tight control of operating processes through multiple intersecting checks and balances. At lower levels, control systems are based on action controls—employees are told exactly what they are supposed to do and supervisors watch to see that they do it.[20] As one moves up in the hierarchy, managers are evaluated and compensated based on their ability to meet predefined performance criteria; these results controls help focus managerial attention and actions on organizational priorities and ensure coordination of actions and decisions across functional boundaries. Personnel controls ensure that the right people with the right skills are recruited, hired, developed, motivated, and retained. Finally, transaction controls—accurate and complete documentation of financial and legal transactions with regular review by senior executives, the board of directors, and external auditors—ensure risk and asset management.

Current "new-age organization" buzzwords exhort executives to empower their people and expand their areas of responsibility; to wipe out middle management ranks and create self-managing teams. But they do not specify how control and authority are to be maintained once the traditional systems have been disrupted. Executives often learn important lessons about the complexity of organizational control and authority systems as they embark upon these change initiatives. Unfortunately some—like the executives at Barings Bank—learn their lesson too late.

Analysis of both failure and success has clarified several important lessons for designing organizations that can develop the "sense and respond" capabilities required of today's fast-paced, complex, and volatile business environment.

- ***Speed Counts, but Not at the Expense of Control***. When the business environment is highly competitive and turbulent, speed counts. New products must be introduced ever more quickly, order fulfillment cycles must be cut dramatically, and executives are exhorted to create organizations that can turn on a dime. But we know that taking one's time has its advantages. A driver racing along the freeway at 55 miles per hour is much more vulnerable to serious injury if something unexpected happens. Decisions must be made quickly; there is no margin for error. Skill and expertise—especially in dealing with unforeseen circumstances—are critical. Constant vigilance is necessary. In short, the faster we go, the more important it is—and the harder it is—to keep control of our car. Executives of fast-cycled organizations face the same dilemma. The faster the pace, the greater the need to monitor business operations and clearly define and enforce the rules of the road.
- ***Empowerment Is Not Anarchy***. When asked to define the term *empowerment*, some executives describe vague efforts to "push decision making down the line." Others equate empowerment with "getting rid of (or bypassing) middle management." Most have a hard time describing exactly who will make what decisions and fail to recognize that decisions concerning who is accountable and has authority to make a decision, take action, or commit resources on behalf of the firm is tightly linked to a more complex set of organization design features. These features include structure

[20] K. Merchant, *Rewarding Results* (Boston: Harvard Business School Press, 1989); R. N. Anthony *The Management Control Function* (Boston: Harvard Business School Press, 1988).

(how people are grouped into units and how those units coordinate activities to develop and deliver products and services to customers); reporting relationships and power (both formal and informal); and incentives and performance management (compensation, evaluation, and measurement systems). Many learn the hard way that isolated efforts to empower employees can lead to disaster when not accompanied by a more comprehensive redefinition of authority and control throughout the organization. For example, in an empowered organization, senior executives must be more involved, not less; and organizational boundaries and value systems must be more clearly communicated, closely monitored, and consistently enforced.

- ***Transforming an Organization Requires More Than Just Changing the Structure***. It is not enough to simply take out layers or redraw boxes on an organization chart. The resulting organizational confusion from structure changes can help to shake up an entrenched organization and create the "conditions" for change, but structural changes alone cannot harness the energy of the workforce to recreate an organization with a common purpose and direction. Nor can simple changes in structure promote the alignment of people, processes, and information.

These three key lessons from the field suggest that building the capabilities required to execute strategy in a fast-paced, uncertain business environment requires that managers adopt a comprehensive approach to organization design that includes analysis and realignment of capabilities within four key areas of business model design: processes and infrastructure, people and partners, organization and culture, and leadership and governance. Improved access to information and high-capacity networked communication systems are core elements of redesign in all four areas.

IT Impact on Capabilities

> Organizations are information systems. They are communication systems. And they are decision-making systems . . . If one thinks about it, every aspect of organizational functioning depends on information processing of one form or another.
>
> *Morgan, 1997*[21]

We have long known that organizations are information processing systems.[22] As such, limitations in vertical and horizontal information processing capacity directly influence the range of organizational choices available to managers as they attempt to execute strategy. We also know that the ability to align and adapt an organization's strategy and capabilities to the demands of a turbulent business environment is essential for building a high-performance organization.[23]

[21] G. Morgan, *Images of Organizations* (Thousand Oaks, CA: Sage Publications, 1997), p. 78.

[22] P. Lawrence and J. Lorsch, *Organization and Environment* (Boston: Harvard Business School Press, 1966); J. Galbraith, *Organization Design* (Reading, MA: Addison-Wesley, 1977).

[23] R. Miles and C. Snow, "Organizations: New Concepts for New Forms," *California Management Review* 28 (1986), pp. 62–73; M. Hammer, and J. Champy, *Reengineering the Corporation* (New York: Harper Business, 1993); J. Collins, and J. Porras, *Built to Last* (New York: Harper Business, 1994).

Earlier in this chapter, we described how executives spent the past two decades searching for a new organizational model that would enable their organization to survive and prosper in an increasingly volatile, complex, networked environment. Executives faced two key organizational design challenges as they attempted to design organizations and build capabilities. IT is a key enabler for addressing both challenges.

Can IT Enable Agility and Control?

As executives struggle to build a lean, yet agile, organization, we see them making a common mistake. They make changes to portions of their operations without considering the impact on other parts of the organization or on partners, suppliers, or even customer organizations, and then they are surprised when the results fall short of their goals. For example, Frito-Lay, Inc., a consumer products firm famous for its salty snacks, learned how to build a lean, yet agile, company the hard way.[24] In the mid-1980s, the senior executives attempted to accelerate the rate of new product development without ensuring that the supply chain, manufacturing, and order fulfillment processes could handle the increased complexity. In doing so, they failed to view their organization as a set of integrated, horizontal operating processes that must be redesigned in concert. Not surprisingly, chaos resulted.[25] Suppliers could not handle the demand, manufacturing defects rose, and inventory piled up in the warehouses.

Having failed in their first process redesign attempts, executives at Frito-Lay launched a second project—this time to integrate their new products development process with their supply chain, manufacturing, and order fulfillment processes. They eliminated bottlenecks and squeezed excess time and cost out of end-to-end operations but failed to redesign the organization and management systems needed to control these accelerated, real-time processes.

This example highlights two mistakes executive often make when attempting to balance agility with control: (1) failure to redesign end-to-end processes; and (2) failure to realign faster-cycled operations with organization structure, control, authority systems, incentives, and culture. Both problems can cause failures of execution.

Frito-Lay executives ran headlong into the first problem when they attempted to accelerate new product development without consideration for the end-to-end process. They increased the number of products and product variations, the rate of new product development, and the number of marketing campaigns and promotions. These actions dramatically increased operating complexity. Plans created by product managers and approved months in advance were being revised by field sales employees attempting to respond to local customer needs and competitive response. At the same time, marketing managers began offering promotions within targeted customer accounts. But neither manufacturing nor logistics were in on the decision nor were they informed in a timely enough manner to adjust supply and production schedules. Not surprisingly, within a short time, the company was out of control.

[24] L. M. Applegate, "In Search of a New Organizational Model: Lessons from the Field," in *Shaping Organization Form,* ed. G. DeSanctis and J Fulke, Sage Publishing, 1999, p. 33–70.

[25] It is important to note that the consumer products firm did make changes to isolated functional activities, but no attempt was made at end-to-end process redesign.

The problems during the second project were traced to the fact that the executives had failed to change the way the newly streamlined and integrated processes were aligned with control, authority systems, and incentives. As a result, the real-time business intelligence and early warning systems needed to make decisions and take actions in these faster time frames were not in place. Opportunities were missed and problems went undiscovered.

Frito-Lay executives learned important lessons from the series of problems they encountered. "I don't think any of us fully appreciated how highly leveraged and integrated our business truly was until the abortive attempt at accelerating new product development," the CEO explained. "The problems were so abrupt and severe that it made a lasting impression on all of us. Two major lessons came from this situation. First, it became very clear that we needed to recast our vision for change as an enterprisewide initiative rather than just a change within a specific function. Despite our functional organization, our operations were highly integrated. We couldn't make a change in one area without causing problems somewhere else. Second, we became aware that, as we sped up our processes, we needed to provide much more timely information to the people on the line who were being asked to respond more quickly within a much more complicated and less structured role. Finally, we needed to create a new management structure that would bring functional managers together as teams, which we called area operating teams, and provide them with the authority and accountability to coordinate and control these end-to-end processes."

FIGURE 3.3 Streamlining Operating and Management Process

Source: © 2005 Lynda M. Applegate.

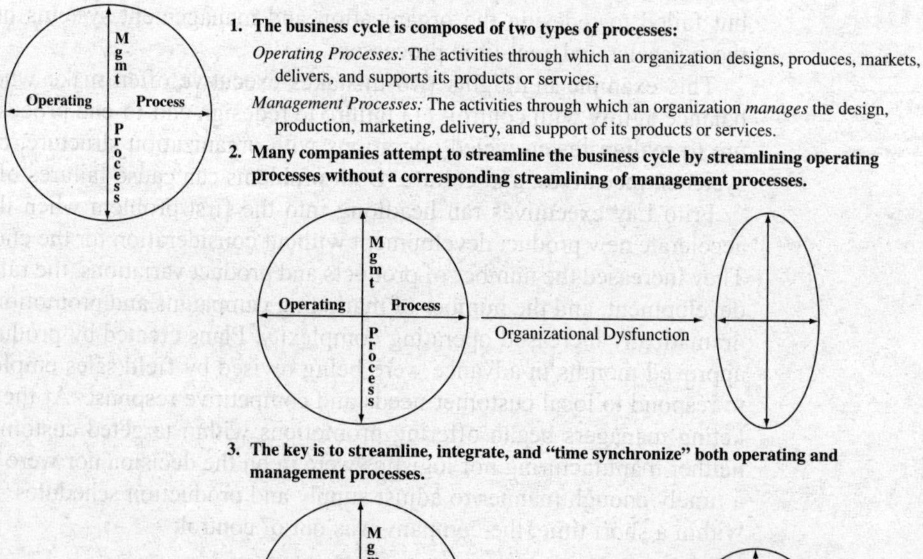

FIGURE 3.4 Redefining Control Systems

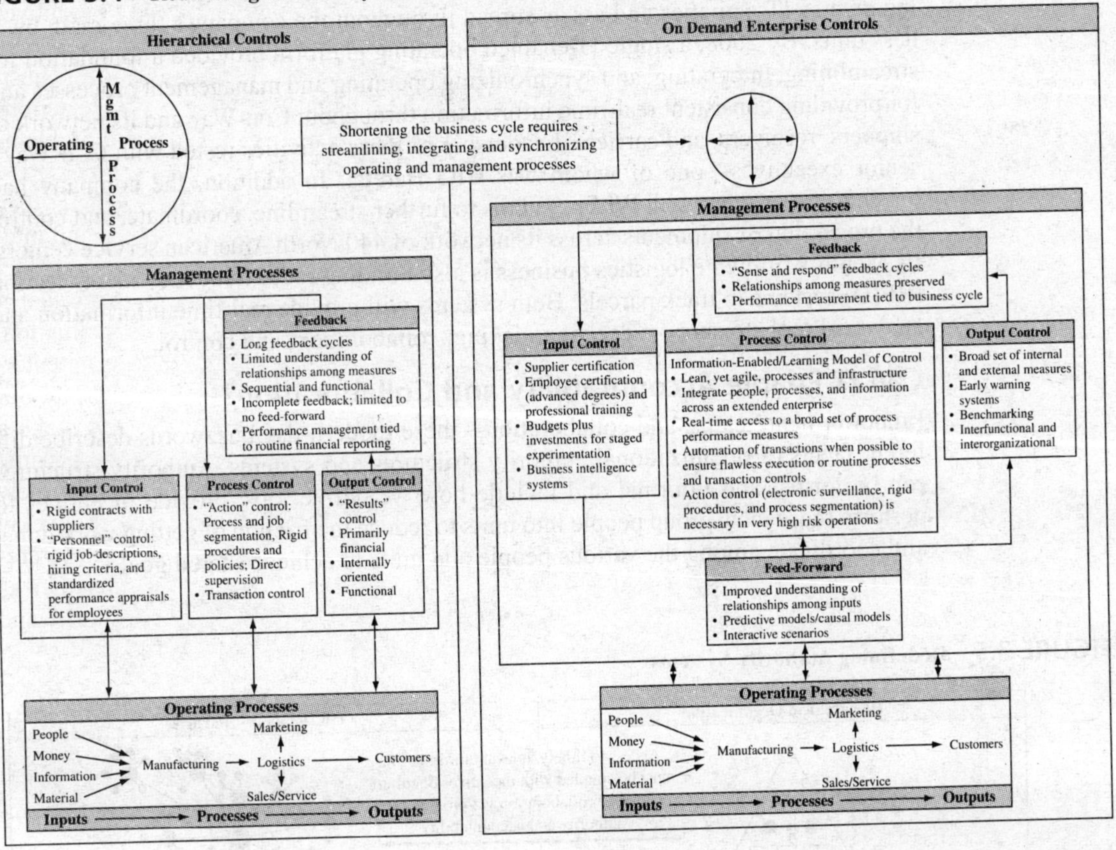

When attempting to build the capabilities to sense and respond quickly and effectively, executives like those at Frito-Lay are finding that it is important to recognize that organizational control is determined by two tightly integrated sets of processes. Operating processes are the series of activities that define how a firm designs, produces, distributes, markets, sells, and supports its products and services. Management processes are activities that define strategic direction and coordinate and control operations. As executives attempt to respond to a much faster business cycle, both operating and management processes must be—not only streamlined—but also integrated and synchronized to the cycle time of the business (see Figure 3.3).

As the Frito-Lay CEO learned, the ability to share information and perspective, while also providing much faster-cycled control systems, is critical for synchronizing operating and management processes (see Figure 3.4). More recently, Con-Way, Inc. has turned to IT to enable the real-time sense and respond organization and control systems needed to ensure it can respond quickly while maintaining control of its global network.[26] In February 2005, when Jacquelyn Baretta was appointed CIO of this $4.2

[26] Learn more about Con-Way's award winning IT systems on the 2008 CIO 100 Web site at http://www.cio.com/cio100/detail/1817 and on the company Web site's June 2, 2008 Press Release.

billion freight logistics company, she was faced with the daunting task of consolidating diverse IT activities and assets spread throughout the company's three main business units. By 2008, a single IT-enabled operating platform provided a foundation for streamlining, integrating, and synchronizing operating and management processes and for providing consistent real-time information throughout Con-Way and its network of shippers, receivers, and carriers. Leadership of these activities rested with Con-Way's senior executives—one of whom was CIO Baretta. In addition, the company had begun to experiment with Wi-Fi systems to further streamline, coordinate, and control the processing of shipments across its network of 440 North American service centers. Its Menlo Worldwide logistics business is also building radio frequency identification (RFID) systems to track parcels. Both systems will provide real-time information and analytical tools to support decision making, collaboration, and control.

Can IT Enable Accountability and Collaboration?

Empowerment, teams, and collaboration—these modern-day buzzwords describe different facets of organizational authority structures and systems. Authority structures can be formal and informal and include how we define jobs, provide incentives to perform those jobs, group people into units to reduce the friction of getting work done, and coordinate among the various people and units to achieve shared goals.

FIGURE 3.5 Redefining Authority Systems

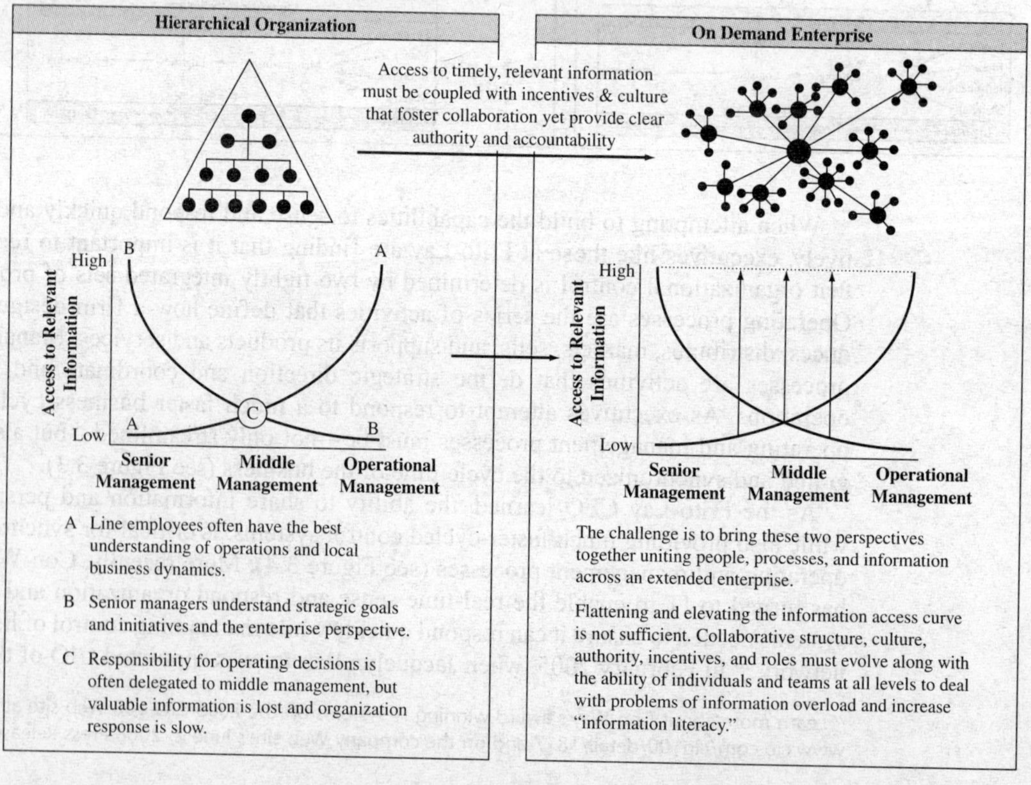

Traditionally, the formal distribution of authority within an organization has been viewed as a trade-off between centralization and decentralization (see Figure 3.5). Organizations were considered networks of relationships among principals (owners and senior executives) and self-interested "agents."[27] In hierarchical organizations, the cost and risk of coordinating local operations and aligning individual interests was minimized by centralizing decision making, structuring operations, and developing a deep hierarchy so that operations were executed efficiently and according to clearly defined procedures. This approach assumed that these centrally located executives and decision makers had access to the information they needed to understand local business dynamics. It also assumed that they had the time and expertise to analyze the information, make decisions, and ensure that the decisions were executed by operating employees.

As the complexity, uncertainty, and volatility in the business environment intensified, it became increasingly difficult to satisfy the assumptions required for centralized decision making. During the 1980s and 1990s, the solution adopted by many executives was to decentralize decision making to increasingly more focused and autonomous profit centers or "self-managing teams." In so doing, decisions could be made more quickly, but the cost of coordination and control increased and decisions made by local employees and teams often failed to consider the overall goals of the company.

The president of Phillips Petroleum recalled the "tyranny of control" that characterized his attempts to maintain control over decentralized decision making.[28] "When we attempted to decentralize decision making in our organization," he recalled, "we added controllers in all of the newly formed business units to ensure the senior management oversight we felt was required. Over time, the number of controllers in corporate headquarters also increased. We ended up having checkers checking the checkers!" As competition and price erosion increased, these slow-to-respond and costly authority structures and systems became a drag on innovation and a drag on earnings.

Executives at Phillips Petroleum initially responded by creating a matrix organization with centralized centers of excellence that provided shared services. Dramatic cuts in the number of middle management and staff were also made. Before long, employees in the field found that they no longer had the relevant information needed to make decisions and performance suffered. Eventually a business intelligence system was implemented and teams of operating managers were given authority for decision making. These actions enabled teams to make decisions in the field while also ensuring that senior executives could provide the required oversight.

[27] M. Jensen and W. Meckling, "Theory of the Firm: Managerial Behavior, Agency Costs, and Ownership Structure," *Journal of Financial Economics* (1973), pp. 305–360; E. Fama, "Agency Problems and the Theory of the Firm," *Journal of Political Economics* (1980), pp. 288–307.

[28] L. M. Applegate, "In Search of a New Organizational Model: Lessons from the Field," in *Shaping Organization Form*, ed. G. DeSanctis and J. Fulke, Sage Publishing, 1999, pp. 33–70.

Summary

Executives made significant efforts during the past decade in reorganizing to meet the challenges of operating in a more dynamic, hyper-competitive world. But as we entered the twenty-first century, it became clear that even more radical change was required. As IT transforms markets, industries, and the organizations that compete within them, executives are forced to respond even more quickly, deliver higher quality and more customized products and services, and cut costs even more deeply. In large companies, layers of management were cut and spans of authority increased to the point where many executives worried that their organizations were spinning out of control. Entrepreneurial start-ups and small firms were also being required to grow and expand their products and markets without losing their agility, speed, and responsiveness to local needs. In short, the assumptions behind traditional organizational models such as the hierarchy and the entrepreneurial model were pushed to the limit and found lacking. (The table in Appendix 3A compares the design features of traditional hierarchical and entrepreneurial organizations with the emerging IT-enabled networked organizations.)

Today, forward-thinking executives are using IT to streamline and synchronize operating and management processes. They are providing real-time information and business-intelligence tools to decision makers on the line while also providing teams of operating managers and senior executives with the information needed to ensure the right decisions are made.

The following questions can be used to guide organizational design decisions as executives attempt to leverage emerging networked IT to expand information processing capacity and build the lean, agile organizations required to compete and succeed in today's turbulent business environment.

1. Have we identified the key activities and decisions needed to execute strategy and achieve our goals?
2. Do we have, or can we acquire, the resources (people and expertise, information, technology, equipment and supplies, capital) we need to be successful?
3. Have we correctly identified the activities and decisions that should be performed inside our organization and those that should be sourced from the outside?
4. Have we integrated and streamlined end-to-end processes to ensure efficiency and quality? Are these processes synchronized with both cycle times in the business environment and with the management cycle times needed to coordinate and control operations?
5. Do individuals and teams at all levels within our organization and in customer, supplier, and partner organizations have the information and analytical tools needed to sense and respond to internal and external opportunities and threats?
6. Have we correctly grouped people and partners into teams and units to enable them to coordinate and control streamlined and integrated end-to-end processes?
7. Have we provided these teams with the tools and incentives needed to collaborate (both face-to-face and online) in making decisions and taking actions to ensure execution of today's strategy and a steady stream of innovations for success in the future?

8. Have we effectively developed, organized, and leveraged the creativity and full potential of our people and partners?
9. Have we created a culture of shared values and behaviors that unites the organization and its partners around a common shared purpose and the achievement of both personal and shared goals?

Appendix 3A

Characteristics of the Hierarchy, Entrepreneurial, and Networked Organization

Characteristic	Hierarchy	Entrepreneurial	Networked
Process integration & synchronization	• Process activities segregated into distinct tasks managed by functions. • Activities are synchronized during yearly planning sessions.	• Process activities defined on an ongoing basis by the people doing the work. • Activities synchronized through ad hoc discussion (face-to-face, e-mail, phone).	• Process activities integrated and synchronized through the flow of information in IT systems. • Changes discussed and planned through frequent interactions among those doing the work (face-to-face, e-mail, phone). • In the case of unstructured and uncertain activities, teams may meet daily or weekly to plan activities.
Process cycle time	• Operating cycle time based on organization's management cycle time. • For highly structured, routine, automated processes (e.g., factory operations), cycle time can be shortened. • In unstructured situations, time and inventory buffers used to manage uncertainty.	• The operating cycle time based on the cycle time of changes in the business environment. • Operating activities not structured; as a result, all activities managed in the same, unstructured way.	• Information on the market, industry, and operations available and acted on in real time. • The cycle time of operating activities approaches the cycle time of changes in the business environment.
Process complexity	• The inherent complexity of the business environment minimized through structure and slow response to change. • Standard products and services mass produced for mass markets to reduce business complexity. • Processes structured to reduce operating complexity.	• Start-up firms offer a limited product set to a limited market. • Within this simple business environment, significant customization provided to ensure that products meet the requirements of individual customers.	• Despite significant business complexity, real-time information and sophisticated analytical tools enable products and services to be customized for increasingly smaller customer segments. • At the limit, a company can personalize for a "market of one." • Real-time information and sophisticated analytics enable a large firm to manage complexity directly rather than managing through complexity reduction.

Management cycle time	• Defined around yearly planning and budgeting systems. • Yearly and quarterly performance monitoring and reporting dictated by country-level regulations for public and private firms.	• Management processes defined by the founder, often ad hoc. • Direct involvement of the founder in most decisions and activities cause the management cycle time to be timed directly to the business cycle.	• Real-time information and reporting enables the management cycle time to be tied directly to the operating cycle, which, in turn, has been timed to the inherent cycle time of the business environment.
Scope and granularity of business understanding	• Understanding of business limited to specific job an employee is hired to do. At operating levels, scope is limited to a specific task. Only top management team understands business dynamics across scope of enterprise but depth of understanding of any one portion of the business limited. • Employees at all levels unable to link specific decisions and actions to the firm's overall performance. • Planning targets and goals set on a yearly basis and monitored and adjusted quarterly. This results in quarterly cycles of feedback/feedforward. • Understanding business dynamics predicated on the organization operating as originally structured.	• Because of their direct involvement in all activities and decisions, founders and employees have an in-depth understanding of the business. • Business performance monitored and communicated in real time, enabling founders and employees to link actions to performance in a real-time cycle of feedback/feedforward. • Operations continually adjusted and refined in an ad hoc manner.	• Detailed information on the market, industry and business performance, and operations enables operating teams (which may include customers, suppliers, and business partners) to refine and adjust goals and activities *within the scope of their authority,* based on changes in the business environment. • Operating teams, rather than individuals, have authority over a broader set of business activities (processes), and senior management, like the founders in an entrepreneurial venture, take a more active role in monitoring business operations and participating in high-risk decisions.
Information and business literacy	• Employee understanding of business dynamics and information limited to specific assigned tasks.	• Employees and founders have access to all information required to run the company and are expected to use that information to solve problems, make decisions, and take actions to accomplish firm's goals.	• Employees at all levels have access to information on business goals and operations across a wide range of activities, and, working in teams within the scope of their collective authority, are expected to use that information to make decisions and take actions to accomplish firm's goals.

Characteristics of the Hierarchy, Entrepreneurial, and Networked Organization (*continued*)

Characteristic	Hierarchy	Entrepreneurial	Networked
Boundaries and values	• Activities and authority segmented so that no one individual has the power or authority (short of sabotage) to cause irreparable harm to company. (Even the CEO reports to a board of directors.) • In areas of high risk, special security precautions (e.g., restricted access, direct supervision) prevent sabotage. • Since broad decision-making authority limited to upper levels of management, companywide value systems not as crucial.	• Boundaries and values created in real time and transmitted directly by founders. • Founders directly involved in most decisions and actions. • The size of the company limits risk to the founders and a small number of investors.	• As decision authority pushed down, shared values become an important component of strategic control.
Units of work and chain of command	• Work highly segregated by function with duplication of resources within each operating unit. • Deep chain of command who report through business unit heads to corporate headquarters.	• Simple, functional chain of command. • Flat chain of command (3 or less) with functional managers reporting directly to the founder.	• Flat, team-based chains of command. • Market-focused operating teams composed of functional managers report to business unit managers, which report to corporate headquarters. • Broad chains of authority with work teams reporting to operating management teams.
Span of management	• Each manager supervises 5–7 direct reports.	• Varies with the size and stage of development. Spans of more than 10 are common.	• Spans of 30 or more are common.

Corporate headquarters	• Large corporate headquarters staff assume major responsibility for planning, budgeting, and performance management. • Large staff of analysts required to plan, monitor, and coordinate work.	• Single site for headquarters and operations. • Little formal planning, budgeting, and performance monitoring. • Operations planned, coordinated, and managed by those who do the work.	• Small corporate headquarters with minimal responsibility for planning, performance monitoring, and organizationwide resource management. • While formal planning, budgeting, and performance monitoring still take place, planning, coordinating, and managing operating activities takes place in operating units.
Coordinating mechanisms	• Work is primarily coordinated through direct supervision and the chain of command.	• Work is coordinated through ad hoc adjustments by those directly involved in the work.	• Work coordinated through the integrated flow of information. • Routine work coordinated through real-time feedback and adjustment. • Important decisions and actions coordinated through meetings of operating managers and employees who analyze real-time operating information to continually adjust and refine goals and their execution.
Roles	• Except at top levels of firm, roles and accountability defined in formal job descriptions. • Roles based on functional expertise and skills.	• Minimal to no formal specification of roles. • Emphasis on hiring innovators ("pioneers").	• All organizations, regardless of size, require innovators ("pioneers") and operators ("settlers"). • Senior executives must be skilled at leading and engaging. • Self-managing work teams define work and how it gets done.
Career progression	• Employees advance through functional hierarchical progression. • Seniority is as important as (and in some organizations is more important than) expertise and performance as a criteria for advancement.	• Career progression is often lateral. • In a rapidly growing firm, employees may move down in rank as senior managers are hired to ensure the leadership required by the more complex organization. Original employees may leave at this point.	• Minimal opportunities for advancement within flat hierarchical chains for command. • Innovators may have an opportunity to launch and grow new businesses. • Expanded jobs, increased lateral movement, and ownership incentives make work environment more challenging and rewarding.

Chapter 4

Making the Case for IT[1]

We continue pumping trillions of dollars annually into information technology to pursue competitive advantage and spur productivity. But extracting strategic value and productivity from IT has become increasingly challenging.

Harvard Business Review, 2003[2]

In spring 2003, Nicholas Carr published a controversial article entitled "IT Doesn't Matter."[3] Following on the heels of the dot-com meltdown and subsequent global economic recession, the article quickly became a best seller as business executives challenged chief information officers (CIOs) to explain—and sometimes defend—their IT budgets and requests for support of new IT investments. Carr's argument was built upon the premise that, in the past, legendary strategic IT applications—for example, American Airlines' Sabre reservation system and Wal-Mart's IT-enabled supply chains—were developed in-house using proprietary capabilities, with each application representing millions of dollars worth of investment and years of effort. These IT systems enabled each firm to differentiate its strategy, lock in key suppliers and customers, and build proprietary capabilities that others could not match. As such, IT became the foundation for strategic advantage. In doing so, American Airlines and Wal-Mart gained power within their respective industries and forced other players to adopt new business models to survive.

While these approaches worked in the 1980s, Carr argued that, by the late 1990s, many of the IT applications in use within firms were widely available from vendors and service providers. Others were being built internally but used development tools that dramatically decreased development cost and effort. Given that these tools were widely available, the systems could be quickly copied. More recently, IT systems have been built using common standards to enable them to be rapidly disseminated through "open" broadband networks. Since strategic positioning defines what makes

[1] This chapter is based on material developed by Professor Lynda M. Applegate for an executive tutorial entitled "Making the Case for IT," available from the author. Permission to reprint must be obtained from author.

[2] "Wringing the Real Value from IT," *Harvard Business Review OnPoint* (No. 5135), October 2003.

[3] N. Carr, "IT Doesn't Matter," *Harvard Business Review*, May 2003.

a company unique and that uniqueness must be sustained over time, Carr believed that IT could no longer enable sustainable proprietary advantage. Instead, he argued, IT should be considered a commodity—part of the infrastructure upon which a firm does business.

When Carr's article hit the streets, letters to the editor began pouring in. While some criticized Carr's entire article, thoughtful readers recognized that—while the title was designed to be provocative—the basic premises could not be totally dismissed. Many executives had been spending too much on IT believing that the technology itself could convey proprietary advantage. Many firms had been investing to build new infrastructure that duplicated what could have been bought much more cheaply. And the increased pace of innovation and the speed with which commoditization occurs had caused the window of opportunity, within which a new technological innovation must be exploited, to shrink. John Seely Brown, former chief scientist at Xerox Parc, and John Hagel, a management consultant, captured the mood of many letters.[4]

> Businesses have overestimated the strategic value of technology. They have significantly overspent on technology in the quest for business value. They need to manage large portions of their infrastructure more rigorously to reduce capital investment and operating expenses. As companies become more dependent on IT for their day-to-day operations, they must focus on potential vulnerabilities and more aggressively manage for reliability and security.

But Seely Brown and Hagel go on to argue that, despite the need for more disciplined management of IT infrastructure, "IT remains a profound catalyst for the creation of strategic differentiation."

> IT may be ubiquitous but the insight required to harness its potential [is not] . . . The gap between IT potential and business realization of that potential has not narrowed. Instead it has steadily widened over the past several decades. This gap creates enormous instability in the business world. Wherever there is so much potential for instability, there is also fertile ground for new strategies.

Vijay Gurbaxani, professor and director of the Center for Research on IT and Organization at the University of California at Irvine, agrees: "The scarce resource never was technology; it was always the set of managerial capabilities needed to create value with that technology."[5] Paul Strassman, executive advisor at NASA, goes further:[6]

> Easy availability of information technology is what makes IT increasingly valuable . . . I spent 40 years of my career implementing information technologies; for the first 30 years, that was a great pain. The technology was expensive, faulty, insecure, hard to manage, and unstable. I finally see the advent of an era in which low-cost ownership of information technologies is possible . . . Carr's logic is defective because his examples deal exclusively with capital intensive goods. Capital investments in machinery do indeed exhibit diminishing returns as markets saturate and the difference between marginal costs and marginal revenues disappears, but information goods are not subject to such effects.

[4] See "Does IT Matter? An HBR Debate," *Harvard Business Review*, June 2003, p. 2.

[5] Ibid., p. 14.

[6] Ibid., p. 7.

Indeed, Carr's arguments seem to be based on a view that new networked technologies will continue to be guided by the same economic principles that framed IT investment decision making in the stand-alone mainframe, PC, or early client-server eras. These approaches led to IT infrastructures that were costly to build, costly to maintain, and provided limited opportunity for leverage. Today's flexible, open standard and ubiquitous IT infrastructures are designed to be shared and actually become more valuable when shared. Rather than stifle innovation and value creation, this new breed of open standard, networked IT infrastructure has dramatically increased the range of business building opportunities that can be pursued, while also dramatically decreasing the cost and time required to launch them. IBM executives call this new era of IT-enabled business advantage "Innovation On Demand." An executive familiar with the emerging On Demand IT architecture model explained their impact:[7]

> I would argue that the commoditization of technology is the very thing that enables innovation in what many industry leaders now call an "On Demand" world. An On Demand enterprise is one that leverages standards-based, componentized technology to support integrated and flexible business processes. In a world where customer needs and global market forces are more dynamic than ever, it is these component-based technologies and flexible business processes that enable organizations to sense and respond to new opportunities and threats and to turn on a dime to meet new challenges. While technological innovation continually provides us with more powerful and efficient tools that do become commoditized and ubiquitous, strategic innovation using the technology—how we put the hardware and software together to solve pressing business problems and transform business models—is very much alive and well.

As discussed in earlier chapters, a company's business model frames the underlying mechanisms through which an organization creates value for all stakeholders.[8] These mechanisms are identified by examining how a business interacts with its environment to define a unique strategy, attracts the resources and builds the capabilities needed to execute strategy, and delivers value. As such, the business model audit framework, discussed in Chapter 1, can also provide an excellent foundation for understanding the mechanisms through which IT creates business value. These mechanisms, in turn, can be used to frame the business case for IT.

This chapter presents frameworks, approaches, and examples that executives can use to create a compelling business case for exploiting the power of IT to create value, both inside the firm and for customers, suppliers, and partners.

"Legacy" Mindset Limitations

It is little wonder that there is confusion over how to exploit IT to create business value. Most executives continue to view technology as a budgeted expense to be managed on a project-by-project basis within traditional budgeting cycles. This

[7] Author interview with IBM executives, July 2004.

[8] L. M. Applegate, "Crafting Business Models," Harvard Business School Publishing (No. 808705), 2008. (http://harvardbusinessonline.hbsp.harvard.edu/b02/en/common/item_detail.jhtml?id=808705&referral=2340).

Making the Case for IT at Progressive Insurance

Did you know that Glenn Renwick, the CEO and chairman of Progressive Insurance in 2008, was the company's CIO from 1998–2000 and, prior to that, he was the president of program operations within the consumer marketing division? It's no wonder that Progressive is well-known as a leader in using IT to drive strategy and build capabilities. While the company started on its path of IT-enabled innovation prior to the 1990s, Renwick continued the growth-through-innovation approach by trying to find creative solutions to solve compelling problems in the car insurance business. To help the company understand the value of these IT-enabled innovations, Renwick (CIO at the time) created an online business intelligence system that tracked the impact of IT on business profitability, focusing on cost savings, revenue generation, asset efficiency, and competitive advantage. In addition, long before it became fashionable, Progressive used technology to provide real-time information to insurance agents to enable them to make decisions on insurance coverage for high-risk customers that other companies would not insure. In 1997, Progressive took its world-renowned claims insurance systems online and began enabling customers to obtain quotes. As CIO and then CEO, Renwick extended Progressive's online services by providing increasingly sophisticated agent and customer intelligence systems. Named "Personal Progressive," Renwick considers these customer-focused systems to be key to the company's commitment to providing differentiated services at industry-leading prices.[9]

"legacy mindset"[10] is rooted in the early mainframe era of computing when IT infrastructure was composed of large stand-alone computers housed within a single data center, and tightly managed and controlled by a centralized group of IT professionals who were dedicated to keeping the technology running. Under the mainframe model, decisions on IT infrastructure investments—for example, in computers, networks, and facilities—were made along with other capital budgeting requests, and ongoing maintenance and operations were managed through the annual budgeting process.

Value-creating IT applications that were built to run on traditional mainframe infrastructures were funded as stand-alone projects. Each application performed a specific task and delivered well-specified benefits—usually involving cost savings that would come from increasing the efficiency of a structured, paper-intensive back-office process. Once deployed, the application became part of the operating environment, and routine operating and maintenance costs were factored into the annual operating budget. Since most applications could only be used for a single purpose and were tightly coupled with a highly structured task, the ability to reuse (or share) applications was limited. See textbox "The IT Legacy Challenge."

Exceptions to this norm were widely publicized, which increased executive awareness of strategic IT systems that could transform an organization and an industry,

[9] Learn more by visiting the Progressive Insurance Web site (www.progressive.com) and Answers.com (http://www.answers.com/topic/glenn-m-renwick?cat=biz-fin).

[10] Wikipedia (www.wikipedia.org/wiki/Legacy_system) defines a "legacy" IT system or application program as one that was developed using outdated development approaches. Here we categorize "legacy" approaches to IT system development and management within three eras: Mainframe (1960s through 1980s), Microcomputer (1980s through 1990s), and Client-Server (1990s and early twenty-first century). Today's open standard, networked IT systems may incorporate legacy systems but require a different approach to development, investment, and ongoing operations that is discussed in more detail in Module 2.

The IT Legacy Challenge

Large, established firms often have a long way to go to achieve best-in-class status of internal IT operations. Inefficiencies are often due to the fact that many companies assembled IT assets in a piecemeal fashion over the past 30 to 40 years. New technologies were adopted as they became available, with little consideration for how the different technologies might need to work together in the future. By the mid-1990s, this "legacy" IT infrastructure had become a hodgepodge of incompatible and inefficient technologies that were costly and difficult to manage and maintain. Given the state of IT infrastructure in most established firms, it is not surprising that massive investments have been required to simply keep critical systems up and running. In fact, most executives are shocked to learn that, despite an economic recession, global IT spending was projected to top $2 trillion in 2008, up 8 percent from 2007.[11] Even more shocking was the fact that the cost of maintaining and managing IT infrastructure often represented 80 percent or more of the yearly IT budget, leaving few resources to be directed towards creating proprietary business value.

generating significant proprietary advantage. For example, American Airlines' legendary Sabre computer reservation system was built on the company's internal reservation system that was running in company data centers. While the internal system had been built in the 1960s to lower the cost and improve the efficiency of the internal reservation process, insightful marketing executives soon recognized that a new front-end could be added to enable travel agents to book reservations directly. Given that the Sabre IT system was a fundamental component of American Airlines' business strategy to lock in travel agents, the IT system and strategy were tightly intertwined and evolved in tandem, creating proprietary advantage. In addition, the IT system development was funded as part of a larger strategic initiative and its success was measured based on the success of the strategy. As will be seen later in this chapter, this ability to leverage an existing IT system as a platform to implement a new IT-enabled strategic initiative is at the heart of the value proposition for today's open-standard, networked IT infrastructures.

As we saw with Sabre, since the 1960s, IT has become ever more tightly intertwined with business operations and strategy. During the 1990s, forward-thinking executives had begun to search for new approaches to making the business case for IT. But the proliferation of incompatible computers, operating systems, and applications within and across organization boundaries slowed the adoption of investment models that recognized the dual role of IT to create operating efficiencies while also driving business insight, innovation, and proprietary advantage.

The commercialization and rapid adoption of the Internet proved to be the "tipping point."[12] Rapid penetration and adoption of Internet standards for packaging, storing, accessing, and sharing information in all of its forms—voice, video, data, and graphics—catalyzed convergence of multiple technology platforms and a commitment to develop and adopt common standards. As we entered the twenty-first century, the stage was set for providing a shared infrastructure that would enable a dramatic decrease in the total cost of

[11] See A. Bartels, "Global IT Market Outlook 2008," Forrester Research Services, March 6, 2008.

[12] C. Kim and R. Mauborgne, "Tipping Point Leadership," *Harvard Business Review*, April 2003 (HBR #3353).

ownership and increase in the speed with which new value-creating IT applications could be developed and deployed across an organization, an industry, and the world.

More importantly, building on these industry standards, new approaches to system design and development enabled large, complex applications to be built from reusable modules linked together through shared "middleware" services and common interfaces. This approach dramatically increased the ability to reuse data, information, and applications and to share a common infrastructure, which further increased the flexibility and speed with which new value-creating IT-enabled business initiatives could be launched and globally deployed. Thus while infrastructure alone can't convey sustainable proprietary advantage, businesses that remain chained to a legacy of incompatible and inflexible proprietary infrastructures also find themselves at a significant strategic disadvantage as they attempt to keep pace with increasingly shorter cycles of innovation, productivity, and returns.

The "IT Business Value" Mindset: Framing Opportunities

A shared services approach to building and deploying IT infrastructure and applications demands a very different approach to investment decision making. Given that large portions of an IT investment involve shared infrastructure that serves as a platform upon which multiple business-building, value-creating applications can be deployed, IT development can no longer be considered as simply an investment that is managed on a project-by-project basis. Instead, we must think of business-building IT opportunities as a string of investments that must deliver value today and in the future. The value of these future uses can be thought of as the "options value" of IT, which will be discussed in more detail below.

As discussed earlier in this module, a business model frames how executives make decisions about strategies to pursue, capabilities to build, and the investments required to achieve business goals. As such, the business model also frames decisions concerning IT investments required to achieve business goals. Figure 4.1 shows how business models can be used to frame the evaluation of IT opportunities and the development of a business case for IT investments.[13]

The business model audit, discussed in Chapter 1, identifies key components of a company's strategy and capabilities that drive financial performance and proprietary advantage. Table 4.1 summarizes key questions and provides sample IT projects and metrics. Appendix 4A provides worksheets for completing a business model audit and identifying key IT drivers.

Can IT Be Used to Drive Cost Savings?

For years, many business executives have viewed IT as a black box—money, resources, and time go in and, hopefully, business value comes out. Traditionally, except for true infrastructure investments (e.g., investments in mainframe computers, operating systems, and networks), most IT investments are funded as an outgrowth of a business user's request. Given the recent emphasis on cost savings, many of these

[13] This approach was first described in L. M. Applegate, "Making the Case for IT," *Financial Times Mastering Information Management Series*, March 29, 1999.

FIGURE 4.1
Using Business Models to Frame the Business Case for IT

Source: L. M. Applegate, *Crafting Business Models*, Harvard Business School Publishing #808705, 2005.

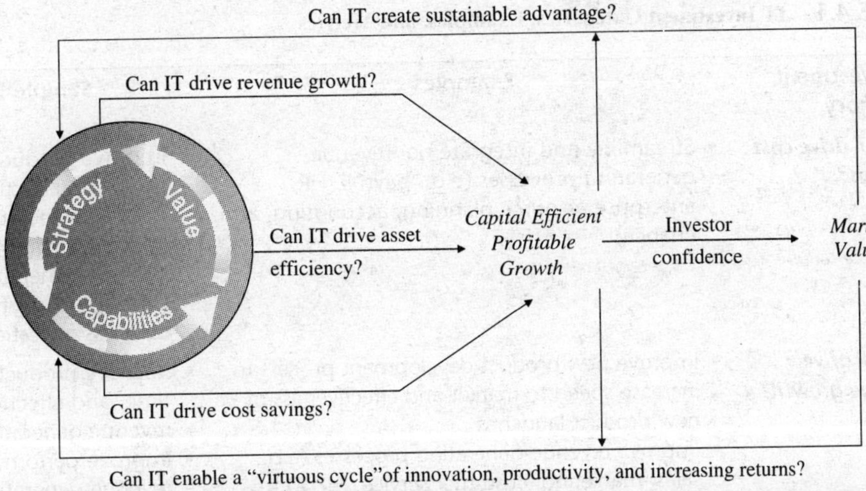

requests have required that IT demonstrate tangible cost savings. It is little wonder that many IT project portfolios emphasize incremental cost savings. Savvy IT and business executives, however, recognize that the benefits don't have to stop there. The IBM case study, available in the introduction of this book, provides an excellent example of how a project that started as a cost-saving effort ended up becoming the platform for driving revenue growth and proprietary advantage.

IBM was the most profitable company in the world during the 1980s and the second most profitable in 1990. But, beginning in the first quarter of 1991, IBM began posting substantial losses and, between 1991 and 1993, the company lost a staggering $16 billion. When Lou Gerstner took over as CEO in April 1993, he acted quickly to reverse IBM's plunging profits and stock price. He hired Jerry York, a former Chrysler CFO, and charged him with getting costs under control. Upon taking charge, York launched a study to benchmark IBM's costs in each of its businesses against its competitors. The results were daunting. Expenses needed to be cut by at least $7 billion, and the IT function was targeted as a major contributor to the company's runaway costs.

In fact, despite the leadership role that IBM had played in the IT industry, the company's internal IT infrastructure was out of date, inflexible, and costly to maintain. As a result, this poorly performing asset became a lightning rod for the first phase of the turnaround. When the dust cleared, IBM's internal IT operating budget had been cut in half. These cost savings contributed over $2 billion per year to the $7 billion per year cost reduction required. Key savings came from reducing the number of data centers from 155 to 3 regional "megacenters" fed by 11 "server farms," and a 60 percent reduction in headcount. IT leadership was centralized; 128 CIOs were reduced to 1. IBM's 31 incompatible networks were converted to one common Internet-standard network.[14]

The IT application portfolio was also rationalized. Prior to the IT restructuring, each of IBM's business units developed its own IT operating and development environment. Not surprisingly, these IT silos were built with incompatible technologies and methodologies. The result was a proliferation of duplicate applications, many of which were

[14] TCP/IP (Transport Control Protocol/Internet Protocol) is the standard used to communicate and share information on the Internet.

TABLE 4.1 **IT Investment Categories, Examples, and Metrics**

IT Investment Category	Examples	Sample Metrics
Can IT drive cost savings?	• Streamline and integrate nonrevenue-generating processes (e.g., payroll, HR, enterprise resource planning, accounting, and finance)	• Improve productivity, cycle time, and effectiveness of non-revenue-generating processes • Improve performance of non-revenue-generating employees • Decrease cost of current business operations
Can IT drive revenue growth?	• Improve new product development process to increase speed to market and effectiveness of new product launches • Improve revenue-generating processes (e.g., sales, marketing, customer service, M&A) to increase customer satisfaction, loyalty, lifetime value, and demand • Provide relevant, actionable information and analytical tools to business decision makers • Improve market segmentation and personalization to expand market penetration • Enter new markets or increase market spending from existing customers • Launch new information-based products, services, and solutions	• Improve productivity, cycle time, and effectiveness of revenue-generating processes • Improve performance of revenue-generating employees • Quantify value of improved decision making • Increase IT contribution to revenues while holding constant or decreasing expenses • Add new revenue streams from current customers • Launch new IT-enabled products, services, and solutions • Increase IT contribution to net income
Can IT drive asset efficiency?	• Create shared services, self-service portals, and centers of excellence • Outsource and offshore to take advantage of low-cost labor markets and scarce expertise • Build a modular, flexible, open source IT architecture • Attract, develop, and retain top IT talent • Create IT development, deployment, and operating processes that decrease the cost, time, and effort needed to launch new value-creating IT applications • Develop best-in-class security and risk management systems	• Decrease total cost of ownership of current infrastructure and operations • Improve asset efficiency (dollars of sales generated by each dollar of IT asset) • Decrease IT infrastructure and operations costs as a percentage of revenues • Decrease IT headcount costs as a percentage of sales
Can IT create sustainable advantage?	• Differentiate products (e.g., information value-added, improve ability to compete on price) • Launch new IT-enabled products or businesses in high-growth markets and industries • Increase barriers to entry or switching costs • Decrease the time, cost, and success of pursuing incremental and radical innovations	• Increase market share • Increase brand reputation and awareness • Increase market value • Increase success of innovation process (e.g., overall level of innovation activity, success in moving from idea to opportunity to launch to value creation)

Source: Author

designed to perform similar activities. As part of the restructuring, the application development process was reengineered to enable modularization and reusable code, and the number of internal applications that needed to be operated and maintained within the company's newly centralized data centers decreased from 16,000 to 5,200, further reducing the cost and complexity of delivering IT services.

As IT infrastructure costs were reduced and operations were centralized, Gerstner also focused on reengineering back-office business processes: for example, finance, enterprise resource planning (ERP), and payroll. In late 1993, each member of the corporate executive committee was assigned responsibility for one of these reengineering projects. He set two priorities: (1) get cost out as quickly as possible and (2) "clean sheet" the process and redesign it for global use. By 1996, these process reengineering efforts had reduced annual costs within newly centralized corporate procurement, HR, and finance units by another 50 percent, representing an additional $1 billion in direct savings per year.

Within a few short years of Gerstner's arrival, he had completed Phase 1 of the turnaround. The company was back on solid financial footing. After losing $5 billion on revenues of US$64 billion in 1992, IBM generated $3 billion in net profits on a slightly smaller revenue base in 1994. Further, the shift of IT infrastructure services and corporate back-office functions (e.g., finance, ERP, and HR) from decentralized silos to a centralized shared-services model was the first step in the executive team's strategic vision to return the company to a position of industry leadership by bringing the power of IBM's products and services together to solve its large global customers' most pressing business problems. As such, the centralized, streamlined IT infrastructure and corporate services functioned as a platform and a testing ground as the company tackled more complex business process reengineering projects aimed at streamlining core operating processes (e.g., supply chain, new product development, and customer-facing sales, marketing, and service) and driving revenue growth.

Can IT Be Used to Drive Revenue Growth?

With a lean, flexible IT infrastructure in place, companies like IBM are poised to pursue opportunities to drive revenue growth. While cost-control efforts can increase profits, companies (and the investors who finance them) cannot afford to see revenues stagnate for long periods of time. There are two key categories of IT-enabled, revenue-generating opportunities that can be pursued.

1. IT can be used to enhance revenue-generating capabilities. Opportunities in this category include:
    - ***Use IT to streamline and improve revenue-generating processes.*** Examples include IBM's redesign of its new product development process that enabled it to get new revenue-generating products to market faster and more successfully, Boston Coach's fleet optimization solutions that enabled it to centralize fleet logistics while expanding into new markets, and Charles Schwab's development of online and self-serve customer service centers that increased loyalty of existing customers while decreasing cost to serve and improving strategic differentiation.[15]

[15] Learn more about Charles Schwab's use of IT to drive strategy in L. Applegate, "Charles Schwab in 2002," Harvard Business School Pubishing No. 803-070, May 2004.

- ***Use IT to improve business intelligence.*** Provide real-time, relevant, and actionable information to revenue-generating employees to enable them to make better decisions or do their work in a more effective and productive way. For example, Canyon Ranch used IT to provide real-time, actionable information to sales, customer service, and marketing professionals whose performance evaluation was based on driving revenue growth. (To learn more, see the Canyon Ranch case at the end of Module 1.) Another example is Aflac's customer relationship management (CRM) systems that increased the productivity of its insurance agents, enabling them to spend more time selling and less time in nonvalue-added work, while also providing real-time actionable information. (See Aflac Field Agents Go Mobile Text Box.)

2. IT can also be used to launch new products, services, or solutions, or to add significant value to an existing product or service. Opportunities in this category include:
    - ***Embed IT*** into existing physical products. Examples of this include Boeing's decision to embed open-standard Internet systems and networks in its "e-Enabled" fleet of Dreamliner airplanes and Medtronic's decision to embed data-monitoring, collection, and storage capabilities within its pacemakers.[16] While embedded IT can improve functionality, grow revenues, differentiate products, and increase market share, the more compelling benefits often come when a company uses embedded IT to drive new revenue streams by launching new IT-enabled offerings or increasing revenues and market share of existing offerings.
    - ***Launch new IT product and service offerings*** that drive new revenue streams. Examples include Apple's decision to launch its iTunes service offering and Boeing's launch of its MyBoeingFleet.com, which enabled airlines to manage fleet operations and dramatically reduce time spent on maintenance and overall operating cost.
    - ***Add significant value to existing product and service offerings*** that enable a company to charge a price differential or to prevent price erosion. For example, Nike's ID online service that enables customers to design their own athletic shoes to meet specific training and fashion requirements.

Returning to the story of IBM's transformation, Phase 2 (during the late 1990s) was focused on driving profitable growth. Given that the entire industry was entering a period of rapid growth associated with the build out of Internet-based businesses and infrastructure upgrades associated with Y2K, IBM focused initially on building capabilities to meet high demand, customize solutions, and go to market as "One IBM." This required that the company reengineer and centralize its core operating processes (e.g., supply chain; new product development; customer acquisition, retention, and service).

The new product development process was among the first revenue-generating processes targeted for improvement. Benchmark studies had shown that, in over 85 percent of new product launches, IBM's time to market was at least 1.5 times slower than best-in-class competitors, and IBM's development expense to revenue-generation

[16] Learn more: L. Applegate, "Medtronic Vision 2010," Harvard Business School Publishing (No. 807-051), April 2007.

Aflac Field Agents Go Mobile

With 40 million customers around the globe, Aflac Insurance needed to be sure its over 100,000 field agents in Japan and over 70,000 agents in the United States had access to real-time, actionable information. That's why CIO Gerald Shields worked with business partners to launch AflacAnywhere and Mobile.Aflac. Today's field agents, many of whom are independent sales representatives, can access the information they need to close an account or deal with a claim in seconds. One agent remarked: "I saved an account because of it." Rather than having to call the company to answer the customer's question, the agent was able to get the information the customer needed immediately on his mobile phone. "Our goal is to empower the field force, to make them more successful," said CIO Shields. He stated that the business case was based on key revenue drivers—to make agents more effective and efficient, which enables the company to draw agents to Aflac. "We want to make our jobs attractive to agents, because we help them more than any other insurance company," Shields explained.[17]

ratio was over 2 times higher than best in class. By 1995, IBM executives had streamlined and integrated the new product development process to reduce time to market and lower development costs: abandoned project expenses were decreased by over 90 percent, the warranty expense to revenue ratio decreased by 25 percent, and time to market for new products improved by 67 percent. Overall, product development expenses were decreased by 50 percent, generating over $1.6 billion per year in cost savings and, more importantly, yielding increased revenues from the accelerated rate of successful new products that entered the market.

Having learned from earlier back-office reengineering efforts, in 1995, IBM also began to reengineer and centralize its global supply chain processes. The goal was to standardize and streamline core operating processes to enable IBM to go to market as "One IBM." An executive explained:[18]

> In 1995, each of our key brands handled its own procurement, logistics, and fulfillment activities. As a result, we had silos of these activities all over the company. During 1994 and 1995, we began to reengineer and standardize these activities. If there was someone on the outside that could perform the activity better, faster, and cheaper than us, we outsourced the physical activity and kept the strategy, planning, and management. For example, in logistics, we now handle all of the planning and management centrally, but we outsource all of the warehousing and distribution to a third-party partner. In addition, we decided to exit many of our software products that competed with enterprise application software vendors that our customers used and, instead, we partnered with former competitors, like SAP, PeopleSoft, and Siebel, so that we could run the same software internally as our customers used.

Within one year, procurement costs were down 20 percent and the time needed to complete and confirm supply orders had decreased from an average of 48 hours to 2.5 hours. By 2000, 94 percent of goods and services, representing $4.3 billion, were procured online from 24,000 worldwide suppliers at a cost savings of over $370 million annually. And, even as year-over-year growth in procurement volume increased by 60 percent between

[17] A. Sacco, "How Insurance Giant Aflac Made Mobile Applications Its Policy," CIO 100 2008 Web site (http://www.cio.com/cio100/2008/1).

[18] Author interview, 2004.

1999 and 2000, no new staff were added. More importantly, the ability to control supply chain operations enabled IBM to deliver the complex, customized solutions customers had begun to demand. Finally, real-time information was available to manufacturing, sales and marketing, customer service, and consultants who used the information to make more timely, customer-focused decisions—decisions that drove revenue.

As information became available from streamlined, standardized, real-time IT-enabled operating processes, IBM provided tools and IT support to help teams of employees create their own portals that would provide access to actionable information to support decision making and the collaboration tools needed to coordinate work. IBM Global Services consultants were among the first to develop a business intelligence portal to keep track of dynamically changing technology and customer requirements. At a cost of only $25,000 invested over several weeks, the consultants launched the portal and within one year had used the improved information and collaboration tools to decrease consultant engagement times by 40–80 percent, increase revenues per consultant by 20 percent, and improve contribution margin per consultant by 400 percent. In addition, the portal was also used to shift a significant portion of IBM's eLearning training programs online, saving $350 million in training costs per year.

While the initial return to profitability and a positive return on equity were driven by cost savings, during the late 1990s, IBM turned the corner and began to grow revenues. At only 5.7 percent average growth per year, however, IBM's revenue growth lagged the double-digit growth experienced by others in the industry. It was at this point that IBM began to look for ways to leverage its assets to continue to drive efficiency while also achieving sustainable proprietary advantage.

Can IT Be Used to Drive Asset Efficiency?

As we saw in earlier chapters, asset efficiency defines how many dollars of revenue are generated for every dollar of assets. Most firms measure asset value by counting up the dollars of financial and tangible assets "on their books." Financial assets often include cash, marketable securities, and accounts receivable, while tangible assets include physical inventory and physical facilities, equipment, and software that have not yet been depreciated. A firm's balance sheet has a category called "Goodwill," which is supposed to capture the value of intangible assets. But, while it often accounts for the value of acquisitions (the price paid over and above the book value of a business) or the value of intellectual property and patents, it rarely captures the full value of intangible assets within a company—especially if that company has significant investment in knowledge assets (e.g., the expertise and experience of people, proprietary information on customers or products that is stored in databases). Nor does it accurately reflect the value of strong relationships with customers, suppliers, and partners, or a strong brand that draws people to your firm and keeps them loyal.[19]

As we turn our attention to measuring IT asset efficiency, it is important to consider financial, tangible, and intangible IT assets. In addition, the impact of IT on the asset

[19] Learn more about how to value intangible assets in a more rigorous way in "Tangible Power of Intangible Assets," *Harvard Business Review On Point Collection* (No. 7706), 2004.

efficiency of the company and its customers, suppliers, and partners must be accounted for when defining the business case for IT. Key IT asset categories include:

1. ***IT operating infrastructure*** includes physical data centers, network centers, and call centers; middleware; and the people and operating systems that develop, run, and maintain these systems and solutions.
2. ***Enterprise solutions*** include ERP systems; CRM systems; payroll and HR systems; database management systems; e-mail systems and collaboration tools; and the people and partners that develop, run, and maintain these systems and solutions
3. ***Specialized business solutions*** include IT systems that support a specific business activity or team within a business and the people, partners, and software that develop, run, and maintain these specialized solutions.
4. ***Executive leadership and governance*** systems.

With the exception of the people involved, categories 1 and 2 are often considered to be tangible assets that can be valued on a firm's balance sheet. Categories 3 and 4 are often considered intangible assets and must be valued separately by the business executives. Measuring the efficiency of IT assets begins by calculating the total value of IT assets (tangible and intangible) within a company or business unit. Tangible asset value can be found on the firm's balance sheet or from the CFO. Intangible asset value can be calculated by estimating the market value of the asset. For example, the market value of IT professionals can be assumed to include the compensation and benefits that your firm pays to hire, retain, and incent these professionals. If your firm is not paying "market rates," the true market value may be higher.

IT asset efficiency increases when a company does something to drive more revenues from the same asset base or takes an underperforming asset off its books (usually by shutting it down, writing it off, or outsourcing it). Outsourcing legacy IT infrastructure has been a classic action that companies take to improve IT asset efficiency. Most view the action as simply removing unproductive or underperforming assets from the balance sheet (which improves asset efficiency ratios), while also lowering the expenses of operating and maintaining those assets (which improves profit margins). But this only works if outsourcing does not increase costs (including fees paid to outsourcing partners and the cost of coordinating and controlling the relationship) or reduce revenues secondary to poor performance by the company's outsourcing partner. In fact, a 2005 study of 25 "world-class" companies conducted by Deloitte Consulting (and reported in *California Management Review*) found that 25 percent brought outsourced IT activities back in-house after finding that the very act of outsourcing had enabled them to identify ways to lower the cost and improve the performance by doing the activity in-house. Another 44 percent found that outsourcing did not result in any cost savings, and over half found hidden costs that were not accounted for in the initial contract.[20]

[20] "Calling a Change in the Outsourcing Market," Deloitte Consulting, 2005, as referenced in S. Tadelis, "The Innovative Organization: Creating Value through Outsourcing," *California Management Review* 50, No. 1:261–277, November 2007. Also see S. Moore, "Offshore Outsourcing: Internal Preparation, Not Labor Rate, Is Key to Savings and Success," *Forrester Research Report*, December 2007.

But not all IT outsourcing contracts go bad. Some, like the IT outsourcing experience of a small title company, Tri*Source Title, show that benefits can be achieved that were not even envisioned at the time of the initial contract.[21] Tri*Source founder, Richard Blair, explained the benefits his company achieved after outsourcing IT operations to an IT services provider. "We've nearly eliminated faxes. We no longer have to do data entry of each title received and don't have titles lost in the shuffle. Now everything is in digital format." Network crashes, which had been frequent on the company's legacy system, were eliminated, and staff became more productive. "Now my staff can do their jobs, providing escrow service, disbursement, and ensuring titles, which increase revenues." In addition to improving the productivity of revenue-generating employees, costs per transaction decreased by 20 percent, even as the company doubled the number of transactions it processed each month. While Blair reports that he's paying approximately 25 percent per year more for the company's outsourced IT services, the improved productivity and flexibility have more than offset the added costs.

The experience of Tri*Source Title highlights the dual nature of IT asset value. While the assets have intrinsic value of their own, the more complex value measurements involve how IT assets drive financial and business value. The ability to deliver best-in-class IT asset value is based on choices made in developing and operating the assets. When IT assets are designed to be "lean and highly scaleable," they deliver best-in-class performance by lowering costs, achieving high levels of efficiency, and providing a reliable and scaleable platform for growing the current business. When IT assets are *also* designed to be "agile and leverageable," they can be quickly customized or changed to provide personalized customer solutions or to respond to new organizational or industry requirements. Indeed, it is the inability of IT assets to be both lean and agile that often doomed outsourcing partnerships. A 2006 survey of 420 IT professionals by *InformationWeek* identified service bottlenecks and lack of flexibility as key reasons for IT outsourcing failures.[22]

When assets are designed to be "lean and scaleable" and "agile and leverageable" *at the same time*, a company can scale its current business while it also pursues new business innovations and opportunities. These opportunities to leverage an IT platform to increase scale and scope are called "the options value of IT." (See the text box "Comparing Securities Options with IT Options.") Given that IT assets in most established companies are far from "best in class" in terms of being lean, yet flexible, significant value can be created through investments to modernize infrastructure.

Recall that IBM was able to save over 50 percent of its yearly IT operating costs by centralizing and reducing the number of data centers, networks, and IT professionals. The company then outsourced these centralized IT assets and their operation to IBM Global Services, which, in turn, then leveraged those assets by selling outsourced services to customers. For example, in September 2003, Procter & Gamble (P&G) signed a 10-year $400 million agreement with IBM to outsource payroll processing,

[21] G. Stern, "Inside a Small Title Company's IT Outsourcing Success," downloaded from www.sourcingmag.com, July 13, 2008.

[22] See P. McDougall, "In Depth: When Outsourcing Goes Bad," *InformationWeek*, June 19, 2006.

Comparing Securities Options with IT Options

In financial terms, a *securities option* gives the owner the right (as distinct from the obligation) to buy a security at a fixed, predetermined price (the exercise price) on or before some fixed date (the maturity date). Important features of securities options that determine value include (1) the nature of future benefits (risky projects often generate the highest returns); and (2) the length of time you have to exercise the option (the longer the time frame the greater the value of the option).

Using this same logic, an *IT option* provide executives with the right (as distinct from the obligation) to pursue value-added IT-enabled business opportunities at a lower cost, more quickly, and with less inherent risk throughout the useful life of the technology. Features of an IT option that determine value include (1) the cumulative value from business opportunities that could potentially be pursued (the value of these benefits depends upon the number, type, and range of business opportunities); (2) the ability to pursue riskier opportunities where there is a higher potential return (as we will see below, the IT option "cut off the downside risk for future investments"); and (3) the length of time for capturing value (keeping in mind that IT options can be exercised over and over again throughout the useful life of the technology).

benefits administration, compensation planning, expatriate and relocation services, travel expense management, and human resources data management for over 98,000 P&G employees in over 80 countries around the world.[23] In doing so, P&G gained access to partnerships that IBM had established with Fidelity, ADP, and Ceridian to provide HR services to internal IBM employees. In fourth quarter 2003 alone, IBM signed over $3 billion in similar outsourcing agreements that would provide ongoing revenues for years to come. In 2007, revenue from IBM's Global Services business unit, which was built by leveraging IBM's internal IT-enabled business transformation, totaled over $54 billion. This represented over 55 percent of IBM's total revenues and over 37 percent of profits.[24]

Can IT Be Used to Create Sustainable Advantage?

The question of how firms create sustainable advantage has been debated for decades. While some firms achieve sustainability based on strategic positioning (e.g., Apple iPod's product positioning–market positioning), others build capabilities (e.g., Wal-Mart's legendary sourcing capabilities) that lock in industry participants.[25] But, in the end, sustainability must be based on the ability to—not just take the lead—but also continue to innovate over time. Clearly, we have seen many examples of firms, like IBM, that were industry leaders for decades then floundered.

In fact, sustainable advantage comes from the fit of a company's business model—its strategy and capabilities—with the opportunities and demands of the environment and, more importantly, the ability to evolve that business model strategy and capability

[23] IBM Press Release, September 9, 2003.

[24] IBM 2007 Annual Report.

[25] See J. Williams, "How Sustainable Is Your Competitive Advantage," *California Management Review*, 34, No. 3: 29–49, Spring, 1992 and P. Ghemawat, "Sustainable Advantage," *Harvard Business Review* (No. 86507), September–October 1986.

to define a unique position and develop unique resources that stakeholders value over time. Economists call this cycle of innovation, productivity, and increasing returns a "virtuous cycle."[26] Refer back to Chapter 1 and Figure 4.1.

As demonstrated by the numerous examples discussed in this chapter and in earlier chapters in this module, IT can serve as a powerful driver of business model alignment and evolutionary potential. Key to sustainability is the development of IT capabilities to control IT-related costs, deliver value-creating business solutions, and enable the attainment of long-term and short-term business goals.[27] Key IT capabilities that enable sustainable advantage over time include: highly competent IT leaders and staff; a lean, yet agile, IT infrastructure; a strong partnering relationship with business; and a strong governance system for managing current IT assets and resources and for managing the portfolio of IT projects and investments. Modules 2 and 3 of this book provide an in-depth discussion of the development and management of strategic IT assets.

Developing the Business Case for IT

As seen above, defining the goal of IT opportunities determines the types of financial goals that can be achieved—from cost savings, to revenue growth, to asset efficiency, to sustainable advantage. These financial goals depend on identifying the impact of IT on strategy and capability drivers. Appendix 4B summarizes business model drivers and sample metrics.

But a good business case is more than just a set of metrics. Just like a business plan, an IT business case must tell a compelling story that answers three questions.[28] The key components of a good business case are presented in the text box, "Components of a Business Case."

- **Why this?** Is the logic sound? Have I clearly communicated why this is a good opportunity to pursue? Does this opportunity enable the business to achieve important goals today and/or in the future? Is the business case defined using language and metrics consistent with business funding priorities?
- **Why now?** What is the timing for the project? How long will it take to implement and deliver value to investors? How does the project timing fit with business needs?
- **Why you?** Why are you well positioned to exploit this opportunity? Are you well connected with key stakeholders and do you have the political power, credibility, and sponsorship you need? Do you have the passion and commitment needed to make the decisions and hard choices needed to turn the project "vision into reality"?

[26] Learn more about "virtuous cycles" in H. Chesbrough and R. Rosenbloom, "The Role of Business Models in Capturing Value from Innovation: The Role of Xerox Corporation's Technology Spin-Off Companies," *Journal of Corporate and Industrial Change*, 11, No. 3: 529–555, 2002; C. Shapiro and H. Varian, *Information Rules: A Strategic Guide to the Networked Economy*, Harvard Business School Publishing, 1999; D. Farrell, "The Real New Economy," *Harvard Business Review* (No. 5127), October 2003.

[27] J. Ross, C. Beath, and D. Goodhue, "Develop Long-Term Competitiveness through IT Assets," *Sloan Management Review*, Fall 1996.

[28] L. M. Applegate, "Analyzing and Pitching Opportunities Tool," in *Crafting Business Models*, Harvard Business School Publishing (No. 808705), 2008.

Components of a Business Case Pitch

Slide 1—Executive Summary: Provide a high-level summary of the problem or opportunity you plan to exploit, why it is important and to whom, the business goals that will be achieved, the solution you propose, the team expertise, the benefits, when you will deliver them, and current progress. Gear this to your audience and the purpose of the meeting. Let listeners know what you hope to accomplish during the meeting.

Slide 2—Users and Problem Description: Describe users and the problem ("pain") or opportunity you are addressing in greater detail. Highlight potential future users and options.

Slide 3—Project Description: Explain the solution you will deliver and how it will address user problem or opportunity. Provide a high-level description of any new technologies or features that differentiate your solution. (Avoid technical lingo; refer readers to a technical appendix and/or to a white paper for a more detailed description of key technologies.)

Slide 4—Project Team: Describe the team, including project sponsors, partners, vendors, etc. Highlight project and business relevant expertise, experience, power, and connections.

Slide 5—Alternatives: Discuss alternatives considered and why they were not chosen.

Slide 6—Stakeholders and Benefits: Show the key stakeholders, what they expect, and the benefits they will receive. Discuss how you will ensure buy-in and attract required resources and support. Highlight any potential barriers to adoption and use, and describe approaches you will use to overcome them.

Slide 7—Operations: Identify the key capabilities and resources you will need for ongoing operation and maintenance of the business and IT systems.

Slide 8—Financials and Metrics: Provide high-level performance metrics and financial projections, and identify the key assumptions behind your forecasts. Show best-case/worst-case scenarios around important assumptions, and discuss the influence of changes in key assumptions on your benefit and cost projections. Discuss financing raised to date and future needs, being sure to identify when the money is needed, what it will be used for, and when investors can begin to see a return on their investment. Provide more detailed financials and business model drivers in your narrative or appendix.

Slide 9—Implementation, Status, and Traction: Discuss key milestones (e.g., development deadlines, beta test, launch, follow-on projects), when they will be reached, and timing of reviews. If presenting to investors, include financing rounds, targets for returns to investors, and the size of the returns expected on this slide. Discuss current status, the activities you plan to complete in the next phase of implementation, resources required (including financing), and your progress at securing those resources.

Slide 10—Risks: Discuss key areas of risk and how they will be managed. Demonstrate that you understand all categories of risk (including business/strategy, user adoption, technology, resource, implementation, and financial) and that you have approaches to managing each category.

Closing Slide: At this point, return to your opening slide (or a variation of it) and summarize the business case you have made. Then open the discussion to answer questions, discuss issues, and, ultimately, achieve the objectives of the meeting.

Sources and Bibliography: Add key sources of data used in preparing the business case including analyst reports, company reports, interview notes, and other documents.

Appendices: Provide more detail regarding business, technology, bios, financials, etc.

Closing the Loop

Strategy is executed through projects. Defining a compelling business case that attracts investment is critical to executing business and IT strategy. But receiving funding is only the first step. Implementing the project, delivering on milestones, and then conducting the post-implementation audit are critical to maintaining credibility and receiving future funding. In fact, defining business case metrics so that they can be verified and audited is one of the most subtle elements in the construction of a sound business case. Equally challenging for many IT executives is how to validate benefits that are being captured by the business.

A recent survey of over 400 IT executives by Forrester analysts found that, in 2007, only 37 percent of companies performed post-implementation audits on IT projects.[29] In addition, while most IT steering committees evaluated and approved project funding and monitored achievement of critical project milestones, few adequately accounted for the uncertainty of business case assumptions. As a result, risk management and project financing approaches often treated all projects as if the assumptions used to create the business case were known with certainty. Many executives also fail to stop or revise project financing when assumptions prove wrong and project scope or requirements must be altered midstream.

A well-constructed business case is a dynamic document that is used to secure funding, guide implementation, and verify business benefits achieved. It assumes that there is uncertainty around assumptions and clarifies key areas of uncertainty up front. Scenario planning is then used to identify best-case/worst-case business cases. Most importantly, the business case is updated throughout the project.

Summary

In an on demand environment, measuring takes a different role. Measures should trigger actions and decisions, rather than just provide a state-of-the-business snapshot. And different types of measures are required—those that show progress to a business goal.

George Bailey, 2004[30]

As we enter the twenty-first century, excitement concerning the potential of IT to transform business and drive improved business performance has never been higher. But the fascination with IT-enabled business innovation comes at a time of significant uncertainty and change as entrenched players and new entrants struggle to define a sustainable proprietary position for success in the turbulent twenty-first century. While most agree that Internet-based technologies have progressed at lightning speed since they were introduced to the business world in the early to mid-1990s, developing common standards and robust commercial technologies usually takes time. The challenge of integrating new technologies into the "legacy" of computers, networks, and systems already in place within companies adds to the problem. To achieve the grand vision of the "Network Economy," a new approach to building businesses and measuring performance is needed. This chapter explored the challenges that executives face as they attempt to develop the business case for IT in the context of increasing volatility and uncertainty. IBM's journey from the brink of bankruptcy to providing leadership in the industry helps define the path to business transformation. Executives should consider the following questions as they attempt to forecast the value of IT investments.

[29] C. Symons, "Making the Right IT Investment Decisions," Forrester Research Report, July 19, 2007.

[30] Author interview with George Bailey, head of IBM Electronics Industry Consulting Practice, 2004.

1. How well do you understand the linkages among the elements of your company's business model—its strategy, the capabilities, and infrastructure built to execute the strategy, and the value that can be created for all stakeholders (e.g., customers, suppliers, partners, employees, investors)?
2. How well do you understand the key factors that drive business performance in your organization and industry? What must be done well to reduce costs, grow revenues, improve asset efficiency, and achieve sustainable advantage? How can IT be used to improve business performance?
3. Do you have a process and template that can be used to define the business case for IT projects? Does your process ensure that the business case is a "living document" that provides a roadmap—not just for investment decision making—but also for project implementation and post-implementation audit?
4. Have you defined business benefits to make it easier to conduct post-implementation audits? For projects designed to achieve business goals, can you engage the business in partnering with you to identify and revise the business case as the project unfolds and in conducting a post-implementation audit?
5. Do you have the political support required to ensure that projects can be completed quickly and effectively? Do project leaders have the resources, authority, and accountability required to get the job done?
6. Have you considered ways to limit the scope of your projects? Keep in mind the "80/20 rule": You can often achieve 80 percent of the benefit with 20 percent of the effort. Don't push to include hard-to-implement features and functions that are not critical to overall project success and business value.
7. Has an effective IT project governance process been implemented? Can you ruthlessly manage "project creep" while not losing sight of the good ideas that emerge during implementation?
8. How much are you spending to run and maintain current IT operations? On average, how long does it take and how much does it cost to implement a new IT-enabled business product, service, or solution? What are key bottlenecks that slow down IT-enabled business innovations and the key activities that increase the cost?
9. How efficient are your IT assets? Have you taken the steps needed to ensure that you are developing proprietary IT assets that provide the lean, yet agile, infrastructure required for business innovation today and in the future?
10. Use the worksheets in Appendix 4A to audit your company business model and develop opportunities for using IT to drive business model performance.

Appendix 4A

Analyzing IT Impact on Business Model Performance

Step 1: *Use these worksheets to rate a case study or a company or business unit. Start by rating strategy best practices. List key business opportunities and threats; then identify the role IT plays in exploiting opportunities and managing threats.*

Rating Scale: 1 = Key weakness; 2 = Weakness; 3 = Neutral; 4 = Strength; 5 = Key strength

Best Practices: Context and Industry	**Business Rating**	**Comments**
The market size and growth rate are sufficient to satisfy the company's growth goals.		
Opportunities exist to leverage our current position to expand into new markets, product categories, and channels, or to launch new businesses.		
Favorable competitive dynamics; few direct competitors and those that exist are unable to threaten our position; no single competitor controls significant market share; ability to raise entry barriers and increase switching costs.		
Favorable regulatory, legal, political, macroeconomic, technological, and societal context; no barriers to competition and growth today or anticipated in the future.		
Resources required to grow the business and compete (e.g., capital, talent, materials, information) are readily available and affordable.		
We have access to suppliers, distributors, and other partners needed to do business successfully; we have sufficient power and favorable relationships.		
Best Practices: Product/Market Positioning		
Target customers have a significant need and are willing and able to pay for products and services that meet that need.		
Our product/service offerings solve a significant customer need and are clearly differentiated from competitor offerings and other alternatives; benefits and unique features of our offerings are easy to communicate to customers, partners, employees, and investors.		
There are no significant barriers to marketing, selling, and distributing our products to customers.		

Key Business Opportunities	Key Business Threats

Role of IT in Exploiting Opportunities	Role of IT in Managing Threats

Review the information above and provide an overall rating of your company or business unit strategy; then rate the overall impact of IT on your company or business unit strategy.

Rating Scale: 1 = Very Weak; 2 = Weak; 3 = Neutral; 4 = Strong; 5 = Very Strong

Company or Business Unit Strategy Rating		Impact of IT on Strategy Rating	

Step 2: *Rate capability best practices. List key capability strengths and weaknesses; then identify the rold IT plays in developing strengths and reducing weaknesses.*

Rating Scale: 1 = Key weakness; 2 = Weakness; 3 = Neutral; 4 = Strength; 5 = Key strength

Best Practices: Processes and Infrastructure	**Business Rating**	**Comments**
Streamlined, integrated, best-in-class processes and infrastructure that: a. Generate and meet demand (marketing and sales). b. Manage your supply chain. c. Develop and produce products. d. Deliver services. e. Ensure continuous innovation. NOTE: Processes don't stop at the boundaries of your organization.	a. ______ b. ______ c. ______ d. ______ e. ______	
Recognized by customers and other industry participants as a quality leader; able to charge a price differential for the quality of your products and services.		
Best Practices: People and Partners		
Recognized leader in attracting and retaining top talent (include employees and partners).		
Recognized leader in rewarding employees and partners, in motivating commitment and loyalty, and in providing high-quality career development.		
Best Practices: Organization and Culture		
The organization is structured to support processes, develop talent, and reduce barriers to coordinating work and sharing information.		
Authority and accountability for key decisions and actions is clearly defined and consistent with business strategy and goals.		
Information needed to make decisions and take action is readily available and easily accessible; culture fosters information sharing and knowledge building.		
Best Practices: Leadership and Governance		
Visionary, yet pragmatic, leadership; experienced and committed leaders with a demonstrated track record of success; leaders are well connected within the industry and community.		
Strong governance and risk management ensure growth while also protecting the rights of all stakeholders (investors, customers, employees, partners, and society); shared values and culture guide decisions and actions.		

Key Capability Strengths	Key Capability Weaknesses
Role of IT in Developing Strengths	**Role of IT in Reducing Weaknesses**

Review the information above and provide an overall rating of your company or business unit capabilities; then rate the overall impact of IT on your company or business unit capabilities.

Rating Scale: 1 = Very Weak; 2 = Weak; 3 = Neutral; 4 = Strong; 5 = Very Strong

Company or Business Unit Strategy Rating		Impact of IT on Strategy Rating	

Step 3: *Link strategy and capability drivers to economic value. Identify factors in your strategy and capability audit that drive revenue growth, reduce costs, improve asset efficiency, and enable sustainable competitive advantage. Place a "+" beside factors that are positive drivers that create value and a "–" beside factors that are negative drivers that destroy value. Then identify the role of IT in growing revenues, reducing costs and improving asset efficiency, and in enabling sustainable competitive advantage.*

Key Revenue Growth Drivers	Key Cost and Asset Efficiency Drivers	Key Drivers of Sustainable Competitive Advantage
IT Role in Growing Revenues	**IT Role in Reducing Cost and Improving Asset Efficiency**	**IT Role in Enabling Sustainable Competitive Advantage**

Review the information above and provide an overall rating of your company or business unit economics; then rate the overall impact of IT on your company or business unit economics.

Rating Scale: 1 = Very Weak; 2 = Weak; 3 = Neutral; 4 = Strong; 5 = Very Strong

Business Model Economics Rating		Impact of IT on Business Model Economics Rating	

Appendix 4B

Business Model Drivers and Performance Metrics

What Drives Revenue Growth?

Below are samples of drivers and metrics. Choose among these examples or identify others that are appropriate for your business model.

Strategy Drivers	**Metrics**
Attractiveness of the Business Context	Industry rate of growth or decline, competitive intensity, consolidation or fragmentation Societal, regulatory, macroeconomic, environmental strengths/weaknesses
Market Attractiveness	Market size (e.g., sales, number of customers, units sold) Market growth (e.g., forecasts and historical trends) Level of unmet need ("pain") in customers able and willing to pay Length of time to sell and adopt Frequency of interaction and use of products and services
Product Differentiation	Features of product/service offering and attractiveness to customers Ability to clearly differentiate offerings and pricing vis-à-vis competitors and substitutes
Effectiveness of Demand Channels	Description of sales and marketing channels (roles played, activities performed, power dynamics) Revenues and volume by channel
Capability Drivers	**Metrics**
Effectiveness of Revenue Generating Processes	Product quality (e.g., defect levels, returns, customer satisfaction) Supplier and partner quality metrics Operating process effectiveness (e.g., order fulfillment, sales, marketing, customer service) Innovation process effectiveness (e.g., R&D, business development)
Value Drivers	**Metrics**
Customer Lifetime Value	Total revenues and revenue trends Number of customers and revenues per customer and per transaction Percent of first time vs. repeat customers Share of market and "share of wallet" Customer satisfaction with products, services, and experience of doing business with you Cost to serve, acquire, and retain Cost to serve: (operating expenses + cost of sales)/number of customers Cost to acquire and retain: (sum of all expenses related to customer acquisition and retention) Customer value: (number of customers) × (average monetary value of each visit) – (costs to acquire, retain, and serve) Lifetime value: (current value of a customer) × (estimated length of relationship) × (expected percent change in value over time)

Value Drivers	Metrics
Employee Lifetime Value	Number of employees and revenues per employee Number of offers made and accepted Average length of time to fill key positions Employee satisfaction and retention vs. industry and best practice benchmarks Cost to acquire, develop, and retain Employee value = (number of employees) × (revenues generated) – (costs to acquire, retain, and "serve") Lifetime value = (current value of an employee) × (estimated length of relationship) × (expected percent change in value over time)

What Drives Cost Savings?

Below are samples of drivers and metrics. Choose among these examples or identify others that are appropriate for your business model.

Strategy Drivers	Metrics
Industry Attractiveness	Number, size, and power of competitors Competitive intensity and price pressure No single competitor, supplier, or partner controls key resources
Product Differentiation	Price and perceived value vis-à-vis competitors and substitutes Features of product/service offering and attractiveness to customers Ability to clearly differentiate features of offering and benefits
Capability Drivers	**Metrics**
End-to-End Operating Process Efficiency	Cycle time of key processes and activities Operating costs by process, activity, product, customer segment, etc. Costs of supplies, parts, materials, services, etc. Cost of inventory and frequency of inventory turns Historical and potential savings from operating improvements and cost management practices
Product Quality	Cost of poor quality (e.g., returns, rework, waste, compliance) and savings from quality improvements Administrative costs to maintain quality
Value Drivers	**Metrics**
Activity-Based Cost	Product costs Fixed and marginal costs
Profit Margins	Gross profit margin = Gross profit/Net sales Operating profit margin = Operating profit/Net sales Profit margin = Net income (or EBIT)/Net sales

What Drives Asset Efficiency?

Below are samples of drivers and metrics. Choose among these examples or identify others that are appropriate for your business model.

Asset Value	Metrics
Tangible Assets	Value of current assets (e.g., cash and marketable securities, inventory, accounts receivable less allowance for doubtful accounts, etc.) Value of noncurrent assets (e.g., noncurrent securities, property, plant, and equipment or PPE, etc.)
Intangible Assets	Goodwill Value of patents and proprietary expertise/capabilities Value of loyal, engaged customers and employees Value of brand, image (e.g., Market Value to Book Value)

Productivity	Metrics
Tangible Assets	Fixed asset turnover Inventory turnover Capital turnover
Intangible Assets	Revenues per employee Percent of revenues from new products

What Drives Investor Confidence?

Below are samples of drivers and metrics. Choose among these examples or identify others that are appropriate for your business model.

Investor Returns	Metrics
Investor Returns	Return on Equity (ROE) = Net Income/Shareholder's Equity Return on Invested Capital (ROIC) = Profit/(Invested Capital + Capital Expenses) Earnings per Share (EPS) = Earnings/Number of Shares Outstanding
Investor Perceptions and Expectations	Brand value, image, and ethics Management capacity, leadership, and track record of success Strategy and performance guidance Proprietary assets (patents, knowledge, customers, etc.) and differentiation Historical earnings and returns Comparables and sector performance over time

Business Value	Metrics
Book Value	Working Capital = Current Assets – Current Liabilities Shareholders' Equity
Market Value	Market Value = Stock price × Number of Shares outstanding Price to Earnings ratio (PE) = Stock price/EPS (usually last 4 quarters) Market Value/Book Value Growth forecasts (especially Capital Efficient Profitable Growth)

The Five Competitive Forces That Shape Strategy

THE IDEA IN BRIEF

You know that to sustain long-term profitability you must respond strategically to competition. And you naturally keep tabs on your established rivals. But as you scan the competitive arena, are you also looking *beyond* your direct competitors? As Porter explains in this update of his revolutionary 1979 HBR article, four additional competitive forces can hurt your prospective profits:

- Savvy customers can force down prices by playing you and your rivals against one another.
- Powerful suppliers may constrain your profits if they charge higher prices.
- Aspiring entrants, armed with new capacity and hungry for market share, can ratchet up the investment required for you to stay in the game.
- Substitute offerings can lure customers away.

Consider commercial aviation: It's one of the least profitable industries because all five forces are strong. Established rivals compete intensely on price. Customers are fickle, searching for the best deal regardless of carrier. Suppliers—plane and engine manufacturers, along with unionized labor forces—bargain away the lion's share of airlines' profits. New players enter the industry in a constant stream. And substitutes are readily available—such as train or car travel.

By analyzing all five competitive forces, you gain a complete picture of what's influencing profitability in your industry. You identify game-changing trends early, so you can swiftly exploit them. And you spot ways to work around constraints on profitability—or even reshape the forces in your favor.

THE IDEA IN PRACTICE

By understanding how the five competitive forces influence profitability in your industry, you can develop a strategy for enhancing your company's long-term profits. Porter suggests the following:

Position Your Company Where the Forces Are Weakest

In the heavy-truck industry, many buyers operate large fleets and are highly motivated to drive down truck prices. Trucks are built to regulated standards and offer similar features, so price competition is stiff; unions exercise considerable supplier power; and buyers can use substitutes such as cargo delivery by rail.

To create and sustain long-term profitability within this industry, heavy-truck maker Paccar chose to focus on one customer group where competitive forces are weakest: individual drivers who own their trucks and contract directly with suppliers. These operators have limited clout as buyers and are less price sensitive because of their emotional ties to and economic dependence on their own trucks.

For these customers, Paccar has developed such features as luxurious sleeper cabins, plush leather seats, and sleek exterior styling. Buyers can select from thousands of options to put their personal signature on these built-to-order trucks.

Customers pay Paccar a 10 percent premium, and the company has been profitable for 68 straight years and earned a long-run return on equity above 20 percent.

Exploit Changes in the Forces

With the advent of the Internet and digital distribution of music, unauthorized downloading created an illegal but potent substitute for record companies' services. The record companies tried to develop technical platforms for digital distribution themselves, but major labels didn't want to sell their music through a platform owned by a rival.

Into this vacuum stepped Apple, with its iTunes music store supporting its iPod music player. The birth of this powerful new gatekeeper has whittled down the number of major labels from six in 1997 to four today.

Reshape the Forces in Your Favor

Use tactics designed specifically to reduce the share of profits leaking to other players. For example:

- To neutralize supplier power, standardize specifications for parts so your company can switch more easily among vendors.
- To counter customer power, expand your services so it's harder for customers to leave you for a rival.
- To temper price wars initiated by established rivals, invest more heavily in products that differ significantly from competitors' offerings.
- To scare off new entrants, elevate the fixed costs of competing: for instance, by escalating your R&D expenditures.
- To limit the threat of substitutes, offer better value through wider product accessibility. Soft-drink producers did this by introducing vending machines and convenience store channels, which dramatically improved the availability of soft drinks relative to other beverages.

Reading 1-1

The Five Competitive Forces That Shape Strategy

Awareness of the five forces can help a company understand the structure of its industry and stake out a position that is more profitable and less vulnerable to attack.

Michael E. Porter

In essence, the job of the strategist is to understand and cope with competition. Often, however, managers define competition too narrowly, as if it occurred only among today's direct competitors. Yet competition for profits goes beyond established industry rivals to include four other competitive forces as well: customers, suppliers, potential entrants, and substitute products. The extended rivalry that results from all five forces defines an industry's structure and shapes the nature of competitive interaction within an industry.

As different from one another as industries might appear on the surface, the underlying drivers of profitability are the same. The global auto industry, for instance, appears to have nothing in common with the worldwide market for art masterpieces or the heavily regulated health care delivery industry in Europe. But to understand industry competition and profitability in each of those three cases, one must analyze the industry's underlying structure in terms of the five forces. (See Exhibit 1, "The Five Forces That Shape Industry Competition.")

If the forces are intense, as they are in such industries as airlines, textiles, and hotels, almost no company earns attractive returns on investment. If the forces are benign, as they are in industries such as software, soft drinks, and toiletries, many companies are profitable. Industry structure drives competition and profitability, not whether an industry produces a product or service, is emerging or mature, high tech or low tech, regulated or unregulated. While a myriad of factors can affect industry profitability in the short run—including the weather and the business cycle—industry structure, manifested in the competitive forces, sets industry profitability in the medium and long run. (See Exhibit 2, "Differences in Industry Profitability.")

Understanding the competitive forces, and their underlying causes, reveals the roots of an industry's current profitability while providing a framework for anticipating and influencing competition (and profitability) over time. A healthy industry structure should be as much a competitive concern to strategists as their company's own position. Understanding industry structure is also essential to effective strategic positioning. As we will see, defending against the competitive forces and shaping them in a company's favor are crucial to strategy.

Forces That Shape Competition

The configuration of the five forces differs by industry. In the market for commercial aircraft, fierce rivalry between dominant producers Airbus and Boeing and the bargaining power of the airlines that place huge orders for aircraft are strong, while the threat of entry, the threat of substitutes, and the

Editor's Note: In 1979, *Harvard Business Review* published "How Competitive Forces Shape Strategy" by a young economist and associate professor, Michael E. Porter. It was his first HBR article, and it started a revolution in the strategy field. In subsequent decades, Porter has brought his signature economic rigor to the study of competitive strategy for corporations, regions, nations, and, more recently, health care and philanthropy. "Porter"s five forces" have shaped a generation of academic research and business practice. With prodding and assistance from Harvard Business School Professor Jan Rivkin and longtime colleague Joan Magretta, Porter here reaffirms, updates, and extends the classic work. He also addresses common misunderstandings, provides practical guidance for users of the framework, and offers a deeper view of its implications for strategy today.

Michael E. Porter is the Bishop William Lawrence University Professor at Harvard University, based at Harvard Business School in Boston. He is a six-time McKinsey Award winner, including for his most recent HBR article, "Strategy and Society," coauthored with Mark R. Kramer (December 2006).

power of suppliers are more benign. In the movie theater industry, the proliferation of substitute forms of entertainment and the power of the movie producers and distributors who supply movies, the critical input, are important.

The strongest competitive force or forces determine the profitability of an industry and become the most important to strategy formulation. The most salient force, however, is not always obvious.

For example, even though rivalry is often fierce in commodity industries, it may not be the factor limiting profitability. Low returns in the photographic film industry, for instance, are the result of a superior substitute product—as Kodak and Fuji, the world's leading producers of photographic film, learned with the advent of digital photography. In such a situation, coping with the substitute product becomes the number one strategic priority.

Industry structure grows out of a set of economic and technical characteristics that determine the strength of each competitive force. We will examine these drivers in the pages that follow, taking the perspective of an incumbent, or a company already present in the industry. The analysis can be readily extended to understand the challenges facing a potential entrant.

Threat of Entry

New entrants to an industry bring new capacity and a desire to gain market share that puts pressure on prices, costs, and the rate of investment necessary to compete. Particularly when new entrants are diversifying from other markets, they can leverage existing capabilities and cash flows to shake up competition, as Pepsi did when it entered the bottled water industry, Microsoft did when it began to offer Internet browsers, and Apple did when it entered the music distribution business.

The threat of entry, therefore, puts a cap on the profit potential of an industry. When the threat is high, incumbents must hold down their prices or boost investment to deter new competitors. In specialty coffee retailing, for example, relatively low entry barriers mean that Starbucks must invest aggressively in modernizing stores and menus.

The threat of entry in an industry depends on the height of entry barriers that are present and on the reaction entrants can expect from incumbents. If entry barriers are low and newcomers expect little retaliation from the entrenched competitors, the threat of entry is high and industry profitability is moderated. It is the *threat* of entry, not whether entry actually occurs, that holds down profitability.

Barriers to Entry

Entry barriers are advantages that incumbents have relative to new entrants. There are seven major sources:

1. *Supply-side economies of scale.* These economies arise when firms that produce at larger volumes enjoy lower costs per unit because they can spread fixed costs over more units, employ more efficient technology, or command better terms from suppliers. Supply-side scale economies deter entry by forcing the aspiring entrant either to come into the industry on a large scale, which requires dislodging entrenched competitors, or to accept a cost disadvantage.

   Scale economies can be found in virtually every activity in the value chain; which ones are most important varies by industry.[1] In microprocessors, incumbents such as Intel are protected by scale economies in research, chip fabrication, and consumer marketing. For lawn care companies like Scotts Miracle-Gro, the most important scale economies are found in the supply chain and media advertising. In small-package delivery, economies of scale arise in national logistical systems and information technology.

2. *Demand-side benefits of scale.* These benefits, also known as network effects, arise in industries where a buyer's willingness to pay for a company's product increases with the number of other buyers who also patronize the company. Buyers may trust larger companies more for a

[1] For a discussion of the value chain framework, see Michael E. Porter, *Competitive Advantage: Creating and Sustaining Superior Performance* (The Free Press,1998).

crucial product: Recall the old adage that no one ever got fired for buying from IBM (when it was the dominant computer maker). Buyers may also value being in a "network" with a larger number of fellow customers. For instance, online auction participants are attracted to eBay because it offers the most potential trading partners. Demand-side benefits of scale discourage entry by limiting the willingness of customers to buy from a newcomer and by reducing the price the newcomer can command until it builds up a large base of customers.

3. *Customer switching costs.* Switching costs are fixed costs that buyers face when they change suppliers. Such costs may arise because a buyer who switches vendors must, for example, alter product specifications, retrain employees to use a new product, or modify processes or information systems. The larger the switching costs, the harder it will be for an entrant to gain customers. Enterprise resource planning (ERP) software is an example of a product with very high switching costs. Once a company has installed SAP's ERP system, for example, the costs of moving to a new vendor are astronomical because of embedded data, the fact that internal processes have been adapted to SAP, major retraining needs, and the mission-critical nature of the applications.
4. *Capital requirements.* The need to invest large financial resources in order to compete can deter new entrants. Capital may be necessary not only for fixed facilities but also to extend customer credit, build inventories, and fund start-up losses. The barrier is particularly great if the capital is required for unrecoverable and therefore harder-to-finance expenditures, such as up-front advertising or research and development. While major corporations have the financial resources to invade almost any industry, the huge capital requirements in certain fields limit the pool of likely entrants. Conversely, in such fields as tax preparation services or short-haul trucking, capital requirements are minimal and potential entrants plentiful.

It is important not to overstate the degree to which capital requirements alone deter entry. If industry returns are attractive and are expected to remain so, and if capital markets are efficient, investors will provide entrants with the funds they need. For aspiring air carriers, for instance, financing is available to purchase expensive aircraft because of their high resale value, one reason why there have

EXHIBIT 1

The Five Forces That Shape Industry Competition

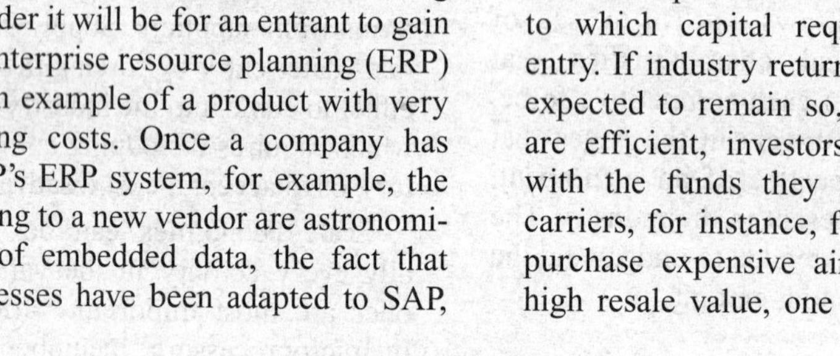

been numerous new airlines in almost every region.

5. *Incumbency advantages independent of size.* No matter what their size, incumbents may have cost or quality advantages not available to potential rivals. These advantages can stem from such sources as proprietary technology, preferential access to the best raw material sources, preemption of the most favorable geographic locations, established brand identities, or cumulative experience that has allowed incumbents to learn how to produce more efficiently. Entrants try to bypass such advantages. Upstart discounters such as Target and Wal-Mart, for example, have located stores in freestanding sites rather than regional shopping centers where established department stores were well entrenched.

6. *Unequal access to distribution channels.* The new entrant must, of course, secure distribution of its product or service. A new food item, for example, must displace others from the supermarket shelf via price breaks, promotions, intense selling efforts, or some other means. The more limited the wholesale or retail channels are and the more that existing competitors have tied them up, the tougher entry into an industry will be. Sometimes access to distribution is so high a barrier that new entrants must bypass distribution channels altogether or

EXHIBIT 2 Differences in Industry Profitability

The average return on invested capital varies markedly from industry to industry. Between 1992 and 2006, for example, average return on invested capital in U.S. industries ranged as low as zero or even negative to more than 50 percent. At the high end are industries like soft drinks and prepackaged software, which have been almost six times more profitable than the airline industry over the period.

Average Return on Invested Capital in U.S. Industries, 1992–2006

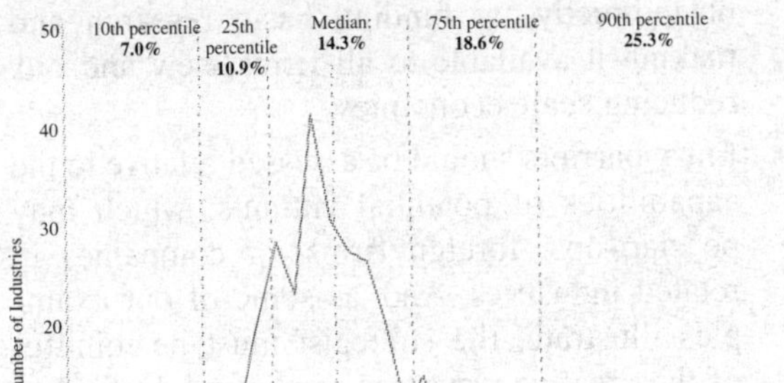

Return on invested capital (ROIC) is the appropriate measure of profitability for strategy formulation, not to mention for equity investors. Return on sales or the growth rate of profits fails to account for the capital required to compete in the industry. Here, we utilize earnings before interest and taxes divided by average invested capital less excess cash as the measure of ROIC. This measure controls for idiosyncratic differences in capital structure and tax rates across companies and industries.

Source: Standard & Poor's, Compustat, and author's calculations.

Profitability of Selected U.S. Industries
Average ROIC, 1992–2006

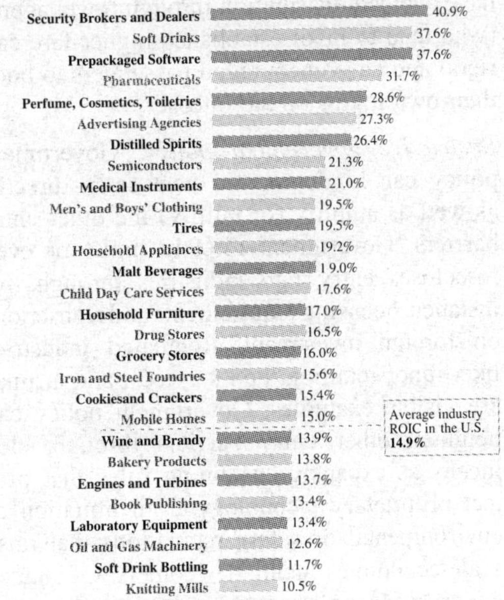

Industry Analysis in Practice

Good industry analysis looks rigorously at the structural underpinnings of profitability. A first step is to understand the appropriate time horizon. One of the essential tasks in industry analysis is to distinguish temporary or cyclical changes from structural changes. A good guideline for the appropriate time horizon is the full business cycle for the particular industry. For most industries, a three-to-five-year horizon is appropriate, although in some industries with long lead times, such as mining, the appropriate horizon might be a decade or more. It is average profitability over this period, not profitability in any particular year, that should be the focus of analysis.

The point of industry analysis is not to declare the industry attractive or unattractive but to understand the underpinnings of competition and the root causes of profitability. As much as possible, analysts should look at industry structure quantitatively, rather than be satisfied with lists of qualitative factors. Many elements of the five forces can be quantified: the percentage of the buyer's total cost accounted for by the industry's product (to understand buyer price sensitivity); the percentage of industry sales required to fill a plant or operate a logistical network of efficient scale (to help assess barriers to entry); the buyer's switching cost (determining the inducement an entrant or rival must offer customers).

The strength of the competitive forces affects prices, costs, and the investment required to compete; thus the forces are directly tied to the income statements and balance sheets of industry participants. Industry structure defines the gap between revenues and costs. For example, intense rivalry drives down prices or elevates the costs of marketing, R&D, or customer service, reducing margins. How much? Strong suppliers drive up input costs. How much? Buyer power lowers prices or elevates the costs of meeting buyers' demands, such as the requirement to hold more inventory or provide financing. How much? Low barriers to entry or close substitutes limit the level of sustainable prices. How much? It is these economic relationships that sharpen the strategist's understanding of industry competition.

Finally, good industry analysis does not just list pluses and minuses but sees an industry in overall, systemic terms. Which forces are underpinning (or constraining) today's profitability? How might shifts in one competitive force trigger reactions in others? Answering such questions is often the source of true strategic insights.

create their own. Thus, upstart low-cost airlines have avoided distribution through travel agents (who tend to favor established higher-fare carriers) and have encouraged passengers to book their own flights on the Internet.

7. *Restrictive government policy.* Government policy can hinder or aid new entry directly, as well as amplify (or nullify) the other entry barriers. Government directly limits or even forecloses entry into industries through, for instance, licensing requirements and restrictions on foreign investment. Regulated industries like liquor retailing, taxi services, and airlines are visible examples. Government policy can heighten other entry barriers through such means as expansive patenting rules that protect proprietary technology from imitation or environmental or safety regulations that raise scale economies facing newcomers. Of course, government policies may also make entry easier—directly through subsidies, for instance, or indirectly by funding basic research and making it available to all firms, new and old, reducing scale economies.

Entry barriers should be assessed relative to the capabilities of potential entrants, which may be start-ups, foreign firms, or companies in related industries. And, as some of our examples illustrate, the strategist must be mindful of the creative ways newcomers might find to circumvent apparent barriers.

Expected Retaliation

How potential entrants believe incumbents may react will also influence their decision to enter or stay out of an industry. If reaction is vigorous and protracted enough, the profit potential of participating in the industry can fall below the cost of capital. Incumbents often use public statements and responses to one entrant to send a message to other prospective entrants about their commitment to defending market share.

Newcomers are likely to fear expected retaliation if:

- Incumbents have previously responded vigorously to new entrants.
- Incumbents possess substantial resources to fight back, including excess cash and unused borrowing power, available productive capacity, or clout with distribution channels and customers.
- Incumbents seem likely to cut prices because they are committed to retaining market share at all costs or because the industry has high fixed costs, which create a strong motivation to drop prices to fill excess capacity.
- Industry growth is slow so newcomers can gain volume only by taking it from incumbents.

An analysis of barriers to entry and expected retaliation is obviously crucial for any company contemplating entry into a new industry. The challenge is to find ways to surmount the entry barriers without nullifying, through heavy investment, the profitability of participating in the industry.

The Power of Suppliers

Powerful suppliers capture more of the value for themselves by charging higher prices, limiting quality or services, or shifting costs to industry participants. Powerful suppliers, including suppliers of labor, can squeeze profitability out of an industry that is unable to pass on cost increases in its own prices. Microsoft, for instance, has contributed to the erosion of profitability among personal computer makers by raising prices on operating systems. PC makers, competing fiercely for customers who can easily switch among them, have limited freedom to raise their prices accordingly.

Companies depend on a wide range of different supplier groups for inputs. A supplier group is powerful if:

- It is more concentrated than the industry it sells to. Microsoft's near monopoly in operating systems, coupled with the fragmentation of PC assemblers, exemplifies this situation.
- The supplier group does not depend heavily on the industry for its revenues. Suppliers serving many industries will not hesitate to extract maximum profits from each one. If a particular industry accounts for a large portion of a supplier group's volume or profit, however, suppliers will want to protect the industry through reasonable pricing and assist in activities such as R&D and lobbying.
- Industry participants face switching costs in changing suppliers. For example, shifting suppliers is difficult if companies have invested heavily in specialized ancillary equipment or in learning how to operate a supplier's equipment (as with Bloomberg terminals used by financial professionals). Or firms may have located their production lines adjacent to a supplier's manufacturing facilities (as in the case of some beverage companies and container manufacturers). When switching costs are high, industry participants find it hard to play suppliers off against one another. (Note that suppliers may have switching costs as well. This limits their power.)
- Suppliers offer products that are differentiated. Pharmaceutical companies that offer patented drugs with distinctive medical benefits have more power over hospitals, health maintenance organizations, and other drug buyers, for example, than drug companies offering me-too or generic products.
- There is no substitute for what the supplier group provides. Pilots' unions, for example, exercise considerable supplier power over airlines partly because there is no good alternative to a well-trained pilot in the cockpit.
- The supplier group can credibly threaten to integrate forward into the industry. In that case, if industry participants make too much money relative to suppliers, they will induce suppliers to enter the market.

The Power of Buyers

Powerful customers—the flip side of powerful suppliers—can capture more value by forcing down prices, demanding better quality or more service (thereby driving up costs), and generally playing industry participants off against one another, all at the expense of industry profitability. Buyers are powerful if they have negotiating leverage relative to industry participants, especially if they are price sensitive, using their clout primarily to pressure price reductions.

As with suppliers, there may be distinct groups of customers who differ in bargaining power. A customer group has negotiating leverage if:

- There are few buyers, or each one purchases in volumes that are large relative to the size of a single vendor. Large-volume buyers are particularly powerful in industries with high fixed costs, such as telecommunications equipment, offshore drilling, and bulk chemicals. High fixed costs and low marginal costs amplify the pressure on rivals to keep capacity filled through discounting.
- The industry's products are standardized or undifferentiated. If buyers believe they can always find an equivalent product, they tend to play one vendor against another.
- Buyers face few switching costs in changing vendors.
- Buyers can credibly threaten to integrate backward and produce the industry's product themselves if vendors are too profitable. Producers of soft drinks and beer have long controlled the power of packaging manufacturers by threatening to make, and at times actually making, packaging materials themselves.

A buyer group is price sensitive if:

- The product it purchases from the industry represents a significant fraction of its cost structure or procurement budget. Here buyers are likely to shop around and bargain hard, as consumers do for home mortgages. Where the product sold by an industry is a small fraction of buyers' costs or expenditures, buyers are usually less price sensitive.
- The buyer group earns low profits, is strapped for cash, or is otherwise under pressure to trim its purchasing costs. Highly profitable or cash-rich customers, in contrast, are generally less price sensitive (that is, of course, if the item does not represent a large fraction of their costs).
- The quality of buyers' products or services is little affected by the industry's product. Where quality is very much affected by the industry's product, buyers are generally less price sensitive. When purchasing or renting production quality cameras, for instance, makers of major motion pictures opt for highly reliable equipment with the latest features. They pay limited attention to price.
- The industry's product has little effect on the buyer's other costs. Here, buyers focus on price. Conversely, where an industry's product or service can pay for itself many times over by improving performance or reducing labor, material, or other costs, buyers are usually more interested in quality than in price. Examples include products and services like tax accounting or well logging (which measures belowground conditions of oil wells) that can save or even make the buyer money. Similarly, buyers tend not to be price sensitive in services such as investment banking, where poor performance can be costly and embarrassing.

Most sources of buyer power apply equally to consumers and to business-to-business customers. Like industrial customers, consumers tend to be more price sensitive if they are purchasing products that are undifferentiated, expensive relative to their incomes, and of a sort where product performance has limited consequences. The major difference with consumers is that their needs can be more intangible and harder to quantify.

Intermediate customers, or customers who purchase the product but are not the end user (such as assemblers or distribution channels), can be analyzed the same way as other buyers, with one important addition. Intermediate customers gain significant bargaining power when they can influence the purchasing decisions of customers downstream. Consumer electronics retailers, jewelry retailers, and agricultural-equipment distributors are examples of distribution channels that exert a strong influence on end customers.

Producers often attempt to diminish channel clout through exclusive arrangements with particular distributors or retailers or by marketing directly to end users. Component manufacturers seek to develop power over assemblers by creating preferences for their components with downstream customers. Such is the case with bicycle parts and with sweeteners. DuPont has created enormous clout by advertising its Stainmaster brand of carpet fibers not only to the carpet manufacturers that actually buy them but also to downstream consumers. Many consumers request Stainmaster carpet even though DuPont is not a carpet manufacturer.

The Threat of Substitutes

A substitute performs the same or a similar function as an industry's product by a different means. Videoconferencing is a substitute for travel. Plastic is a substitute for aluminum. E-mail is a substitute for express mail. Sometimes, the threat of substitution is downstream or indirect, when a substitute replaces a buyer industry's product. For example, lawn-care products and services are threatened when multifamily homes in urban areas substitute for single-family homes in the suburbs. Software sold to agents is threatened when airline and travel Web sites substitute for travel agents.

Substitutes are always present, but they are easy to overlook because they may appear to be very different from the industry's product: To someone searching for a Father's Day gift, neckties and power tools may be substitutes. It is a substitute to do without, to purchase a used product rather than a new one, or to do it yourself (bring the service or product in-house).

When the threat of substitutes is high, industry profitability suffers. Substitute products or services limit an industry's profit potential by placing a ceiling on prices. If an industry does not distance itself from substitutes through product performance, marketing, or other means, it will suffer in terms of profitability—and often growth potential.

Substitutes not only limit profits in normal times, they also reduce the bonanza an industry can reap in good times. In emerging economies, for example, the surge in demand for wired telephone lines has been capped as many consumers opt to make a mobile telephone their first and only phone line.

The threat of a substitute is high if:

- It offers an attractive price-performance trade-off to the industry's product. The better the relative value of the substitute, the tighter is the lid on an industry's profit potential. For example, conventional providers of long-distance telephone service have suffered from the advent of inexpensive Internet-based phone services such as Vonage and Skype. Similarly, video rental outlets are struggling with the emergence of cable and satellite video-on-demand services, online video rental services such as Netflix, and the rise of Internet video sites like Google's YouTube.
- The buyer's cost of switching to the substitute is low. Switching from a proprietary, branded drug to a generic drug usually involves minimal costs, for example, which is why the shift to generics (and the fall in prices) is so substantial and rapid.

Strategists should be particularly alert to changes in other industries that may make them attractive substitutes when they were not before. Improvements in plastic materials, for example, allowed them to substitute for steel in many automobile components. In this way, technological changes or competitive discontinuities in seemingly unrelated businesses can have major impacts on industry profitability. Of course the substitution threat can also shift in favor of an industry, which bodes well for its future profitability and growth potential.

Rivalry among Existing Competitors

Rivalry among existing competitors takes many familiar forms, including price discounting, new product introductions, advertising campaigns, and service improvements. High rivalry limits the profitability of an industry. The degree to which rivalry drives down an industry's profit potential depends, first, on the *intensity* with which companies compete and, second, on the *basis* on which they compete.

The intensity of rivalry is greatest if:

- Competitors are numerous or are roughly equal in size and power. In such situations, rivals find it hard to avoid poaching business. Without an industry leader, practices desirable for the industry as a whole go unenforced.
- Industry growth is slow. Slow growth precipitates fights for market share.
- Exit barriers are high. Exit barriers, the flip side of entry barriers, arise because of such things as highly specialized assets or management's devotion to a particular business. These barriers keep companies in the market even though they may be earning low or negative returns. Excess capacity remains in use, and the profitability of healthy competitors suffers as the sick ones hang on.
- Rivals are highly committed to the business and have aspirations for leadership, especially if they have goals that go beyond economic performance in the particular industry. High commitment to a business arises for a variety of reasons. For example, state-owned competitors may have goals that include employment or prestige. Units of larger companies may participate in an industry for image reasons or to offer a full line. Clashes of personality and ego have sometimes exaggerated rivalry to the detriment of profitability in fields such as the media and high technology.
- Firms cannot read each other's signals well because of lack of familiarity with one another, diverse approaches to competing, or differing goals.

The strength of rivalry reflects not just the intensity of competition but also the basis of competition. The *dimensions* on which competition takes place, and whether rivals converge to compete on the *same dimensions*, have a major influence on profitability.

Rivalry is especially destructive to profitability if it gravitates solely to price because price competition transfers profits directly from an industry to its customers. Price cuts are usually easy for competitors to see and match, making successive rounds of retaliation likely. Sustained price competition also trains customers to pay less attention to product features and service.

Price competition is most liable to occur if:

- Products or services of rivals are nearly identical and there are few switching costs for buyers. This encourages competitors to cut prices to win new customers. Years of airline price wars reflect these circumstances in that industry.
- Fixed costs are high and marginal costs are low. This creates intense pressure for competitors to cut prices below their average costs, even close to their marginal costs, to steal incremental customers while still making some contribution to covering fixed costs. Many basic-materials businesses, such as paper and aluminum, suffer from this problem, especially if demand is not growing. So do delivery companies with fixed networks of routes that must be served regardless of volume.
- Capacity must be expanded in large increments to be efficient. The need for large capacity expansions, as in the polyvinyl chloride business, disrupts the industry's supply-demand balance and often leads to long and recurring periods of overcapacity and price cutting.
- The product is perishable. Perishability creates a strong temptation to cut prices and sell a product while it still has value. More products and services are perishable than is commonly thought. Just as tomatoes are perishable because they rot, models of computers are perishable because they soon become obsolete, and information may be perishable if it diffuses rapidly or becomes outdated, thereby losing its value. Services such as hotel accommodations are perishable in the sense that unused capacity can never be recovered.

Competition on dimensions other than price—on product features, support services, delivery time, or brand image, for instance—is less likely to erode profitability because it improves customer value and can support higher prices. Also, rivalry focused on such dimensions can improve value relative to substitutes or raise the barriers facing new entrants. While nonprice rivalry sometimes escalates to levels that undermine industry profitability, this is less likely to occur than it is with price rivalry.

As important as the dimensions of rivalry is whether rivals compete on the *same* dimensions. When all or many competitors aim to meet the same needs or compete on the same attributes, the result is zero-sum competition. Here, one firm's gain is often another's loss, driving down profitability. While price competition runs a stronger risk than nonprice competition of becoming zero sum, this may not happen if companies take care to segment their markets, targeting their low-price offerings to different customers.

Rivalry can be positive sum, or actually increase the average profitability of an industry, when each competitor aims to serve the needs of different customer segments, with different mixes of price, products, services, features, or brand identities. Such competition can not only support higher average profitability but also expand the industry, as the needs of more customer groups are better met. The opportunity for positive-sum competition will be greater in industries serving diverse customer groups. With a clear understanding of the structural underpinnings of rivalry, strategists can sometimes take steps to shift the nature of competition in a more positive direction.

Factors, Not Forces

Industry structure, as manifested in the strength of the five competitive forces, determines the industry's long-run profit potential because it determines how the economic value created by the industry is divided—how much is retained by companies in the industry versus bargained away by customers and suppliers, limited by substitutes, or constrained by potential new entrants. By considering all five forces, a strategist keeps overall structure in mind instead of gravitating to any one element. In addition, the strategist's attention remains focused on structural conditions rather than on fleeting factors.

It is especially important to avoid the common pitfall of mistaking certain visible attributes of an industry for its underlying structure. Consider the following:

Industry Growth Rate

A common mistake is to assume that fast-growing industries are always attractive. Growth does tend to mute rivalry, because an expanding pie offers opportunities for all competitors. But fast growth can put suppliers in a powerful position, and high growth with low entry barriers will draw in entrants. Even without new entrants, a high growth rate will not guarantee profitability if customers are powerful or substitutes are attractive. Indeed, some fast-growth businesses, such as personal computers, have been among the least profitable industries in recent years. A narrow focus on growth is one of the major causes of bad strategy decisions.

Technology and Innovation

Advanced technology or innovations are not by themselves enough to make an industry structurally attractive (or unattractive). Mundane, low-technology industries with price-insensitive buyers, high switching costs, or high entry barriers arising from scale economies are often far more profitable than sexy industries, such as software and Internet technologies, that attract competitors.[2]

Government

Government is not best understood as a sixth force because government involvement is neither inherently good nor bad for industry profitability. The best way to understand the influence of government on competition is to analyze how specific government policies affect the five competitive forces. For instance, patents raise barriers to entry, boosting industry profit potential. Conversely, government policies favoring unions

[2] For a discussion of how Internet technology improves the attractiveness of some industries while eroding the profitability of others, see Michael E. Porter, "Strategy and the Internet" (HBR, March 2001).

may raise supplier power and diminish profit potential. Bankruptcy rules that allow failing companies to reorganize rather than exit can lead to excess capacity and intense rivalry. Government operates at multiple levels and through many different policies, each of which will affect structure in different ways.

Complementary Products and Services

Complements are products or services used together with an industry's product. Complements arise when the customer benefit of two products combined is greater than the sum of each product's value in isolation. Computer hardware and software, for instance, are valuable together and worthless when separated.

In recent years, strategy researchers have highlighted the role of complements, especially in high-technology industries where they are most obvious.[3] By no means, however, do complements appear only there. The value of a car, for example, is greater when the driver also has access to gasoline stations, roadside assistance, and auto insurance.

Complements can be important when they affect the overall demand for an industry's product. However, like government policy, complements are not a sixth force determining industry profitability since the presence of strong complements is not necessarily bad (or good) for industry profitability. Complements affect profitability through the way they influence the five forces.

The strategist must trace the positive or negative influence of complements on all five forces to ascertain their impact on profitability. The presence of complements can raise or lower barriers to entry. In application software, for example, barriers to entry were lowered when producers of complementary operating system software, notably Microsoft, provided tool sets making it easier to write applications. Conversely, the need to attract producers of complements can raise barriers to entry, as it does in video game hardware.

The presence of complements can also affect the threat of substitutes. For instance, the need for appropriate fueling stations makes it difficult for cars using alternative fuels to substitute for conventional vehicles. But complements can also make substitution easier. For example, Apple's iTunes hastened the substitution from CDs to digital music.

Complements can factor into industry rivalry either positively (as when they raise switching costs) or negatively (as when they neutralize product differentiation). Similar analyses can be done for buyer and supplier power. Sometimes companies compete by altering conditions in complementary industries in their favor, such as when videocassette-recorder producer JVC persuaded movie studios to favor its standard in issuing prerecorded tapes even though rival Sony's standard was probably superior from a technical standpoint.

Identifying complements is part of the analyst's work. As with government policies or important technologies, the strategic significance of complements will be best understood through the lens of the five forces.

Changes in Industry Structure

So far, we have discussed the competitive forces at a single point in time. Industry structure proves to be relatively stable, and industry profitability differences are remarkably persistent over time in practice. However, industry structure is constantly undergoing modest adjustment—and occasionally it can change abruptly.

Shifts in structure may emanate from outside an industry or from within. They can boost the industry's profit potential or reduce it. They may be caused by changes in technology, changes in customer needs, or other events. The five competitive forces provide a framework for identifying the most important industry developments and for anticipating their impact on industry attractiveness.

[3] See, for instance, Adam M. Brandenburger and Barry J. Nalebuff, *Co-opetition* (Currency Doubleday, 1996).

Shifting Threat of New Entry

Changes to any of the seven barriers described above can raise or lower the threat of new entry. The expiration of a patent, for instance, may unleash new entrants. On the day that Merck's patents for the cholesterol reducer Zocor expired, three pharmaceutical makers entered the market for the drug. Conversely, the proliferation of products in the ice cream industry has gradually filled up the limited freezer space in grocery stores, making it harder for new ice cream makers to gain access to distribution in North America and Europe.

Strategic decisions of leading competitors often have a major impact on the threat of entry. Starting in the 1970s, for example, retailers such as Wal-Mart, Kmart, and Toys "R" Us began to adopt new procurement, distribution, and inventory control technologies with large fixed costs, including automated distribution centers, bar coding, and point-of-sale terminals. These investments increased the economies of scale and made it more difficult for small retailers to enter the business (and for existing small players to survive).

Changing Supplier or Buyer Power

As the factors underlying the power of suppliers and buyers change with time, their clout rises or declines. In the global appliance industry, for instance, competitors including Electrolux, General Electric, and Whirlpool have been squeezed by the consolidation of retail channels (the decline of appliance specialty stores, for instance, and the rise of big-box retailers like Best Buy and Home Depot in the United States). Another example is travel agents, who depend on airlines as a key supplier. When the Internet allowed airlines to sell tickets directly to customers, this significantly increased their power to bargain down agents' commissions.

Shifting Threat of Substitution

The most common reason substitutes become more or less threatening over time is that advances in technology create new substitutes or shift price performance comparisons in one direction or the other. The earliest microwave ovens, for example, were large and priced above $2,000, making them poor substitutes for conventional ovens. With technological advances, they became serious substitutes. Flash computer memory has improved enough recently to become a meaningful substitute for low-capacity hard-disk drives. Trends in the availability or performance of complementary producers also shift the threat of substitutes.

New Bases of Rivalry

Rivalry often intensifies naturally over time. As an industry matures, growth slows. Competitors become more alike as industry conventions emerge, technology diffuses, and consumer tastes converge. Industry profitability falls, and weaker competitors are driven from the business. This story has played out in industry after industry; televisions, snowmobiles, and telecommunications equipment are just a few examples.

A trend toward intensifying price competition and other forms of rivalry, however, is by no means inevitable. For example, there has been enormous competitive activity in the U.S. casino industry in recent decades, but most of it has been positive-sum competition directed toward new niches and geographic segments (such as riverboats, trophy properties, Native American reservations, international expansion, and novel customer groups like families). Head-to-head rivalry that lowers prices or boosts the payouts to winners has been limited.

The nature of rivalry in an industry is altered by mergers and acquisitions that introduce new capabilities and ways of competing. Or technological innovation can reshape rivalry. In the retail brokerage industry, the advent of the Internet lowered marginal costs and reduced differentiation, triggering far more intense competition on commissions and fees than in the past.

In some industries, companies turn to mergers and consolidation not to improve cost and quality but to attempt to stop intense competition. Eliminating rivals is a risky strategy, however. The five competitive forces tell us that a profit windfall from removing today's competitors often attracts new competitors and backlash from customers and suppliers. In New York banking, for example, the 1980s and 1990s saw escalating consolidations of commercial and savings banks, including Manufacturers Hanover, Chemical, Chase, and Dime Savings. But today the retail-banking landscape of Manhattan is as diverse as ever, as new entrants such as Wachovia, Bank of America, and Washington Mutual have entered the market.

Implications for Strategy

Understanding the forces that shape industry competition is the starting point for developing strategy. Every company should already know what the average profitability of its industry is and how that has been changing over time. The five forces reveal *why* industry profitability is what it is. Only then can a company incorporate industry conditions into strategy.

The forces reveal the most significant aspects of the competitive environment. They also provide a baseline for sizing up a company's strengths and weaknesses: Where does the company stand versus buyers, suppliers, entrants, rivals, and substitutes? Most importantly, an understanding of industry structure guides managers toward fruitful possibilities for strategic action, which may include any or all of the following: positioning the company to better cope with the current competitive forces; anticipating and exploiting shifts in the forces; and shaping the balance of forces to create a new industry structure that is more favorable to the company. The best strategies exploit more than one of these possibilities.

Positioning the Company

Strategy can be viewed as building defenses against the competitive forces or finding a position in the industry where the forces are weakest. Consider, for instance, the position of Paccar in the market for heavy trucks. The heavy-truck industry is structurally challenging. Many buyers operate large fleets or are large leasing companies, with both the leverage and the motivation to drive down the price of one of their largest purchases. Most trucks are built to regulated standards and offer similar features, so price competition is rampant. Capital intensity causes rivalry to be fierce, especially during the recurring cyclical downturns. Unions exercise considerable supplier power. Though there are few direct substitutes for an 18-wheeler, truck buyers face important substitutes for their services, such as cargo delivery by rail.

In this setting, Paccar, a Bellevue, Washington–based company with about 20 percent of the North American heavy-truck market, has chosen to focus on one group of customers: owner-operators—drivers who own their trucks and contract directly with shippers or serve as subcontractors to larger trucking companies. Such small operators have limited clout as truck buyers. They are also less price sensitive because of their strong emotional ties to and economic dependence on the product. They take great pride in their trucks, in which they spend most of their time.

Paccar has invested heavily to develop an array of features with owner-operators in mind: luxurious sleeper cabins, plush leather seats, noise-insulated cabins, sleek exterior styling, and so on. At the company's extensive network of dealers, prospective buyers use software to select among thousands of options to put their personal signature on their trucks. These customized trucks are built to order, not to stock, and delivered in six to eight weeks. Paccar's trucks also have aerodynamic designs that reduce fuel consumption, and they maintain their resale value better than other trucks. Paccar's roadside assistance program and IT-supported system for distributing spare parts reduce the time a truck is out of service. All these are crucial considerations for an owner-operator. Customers pay Paccar a 10 percent premium, and its Kenworth and Peterbilt brands are considered status symbols at truck stops.

Paccar illustrates the principles of positioning a company within a given industry structure. The firm has found a portion of its industry where the competitive forces are weaker—where it can

Defining the Relevant Industry

Defining the industry in which competition actually takes place is important for good industry analysis, not to mention for developing strategy and setting business unit boundaries. Many strategy errors emanate from mistaking the relevant industry, defining it too broadly or too narrowly. Defining the industry too broadly obscures differences among products, customers, or geographic regions that are important to competition, strategic positioning, and profitability. Defining the industry too narrowly overlooks commonalities and linkages across related products or geographic markets that are crucial to competitive advantage. Also, strategists must be sensitive to the possibility that industry boundaries can shift.

The boundaries of an industry consist of two primary dimensions. First is the *scope of products or services*. For example, is motor oil used in cars part of the same industry as motor oil used in heavy trucks and stationary engines, or are these different industries? The second dimension is *geographic scope*. Most industries are present in many parts of the world. However, is competition contained within each state, or is it national? Does competition take place within regions such as Europe or North America, or is there a single global industry?

The five forces are the basic tool to resolve these questions. If industry structure for two products is the same or very similar (that is, if they have the same buyers, suppliers, barriers to entry, and so forth), then the products are best treated as being part of the same industry. If industry structure differs markedly, however, the two products may be best understood as separate industries.

In lubricants, the oil used in cars is similar or even identical to the oil used in trucks, but the similarity largely ends there. Automotive motor oil is sold to fragmented, generally unsophisticated customers through numerous and often powerful channels, using extensive advertising. Products are packaged in small containers and logistical costs are high, necessitating local production. Truck and power generation lubricants are sold to entirely different buyers in entirely different ways using a separate supply chain. Industry structure (buyer power, barriers to entry, and so forth) is substantially different. Automotive oil is thus a distinct industry from oil for truck and stationary engine uses. Industry profitability will differ in these two cases, and a lubricant company will need a separate strategy for competing in each area.

Differences in the five competitive forces also reveal the geographic scope of competition. If an industry has a similar structure in every country (rivals, buyers, and so on), the presumption is that competition is global, and the five forces analyzed from a global perspective will set average profitability. A single global strategy is needed. If an industry has quite different structures in different geographic regions, however, each region may well be a distinct industry. Otherwise, competition would have leveled the differences. The five forces analyzed for each region will set profitability there.

The extent of differences in the five forces for related products or across geographic areas is a matter of degree, making industry definition often a matter ofjudgment. A rule of thumb is that where the differences in any one force are large, and where the differences involve more than one force, distinct industries may well be present.

Fortunately, however, even if industry boundaries are drawn incorrectly, careful five forces analysis should reveal important competitive threats. A closely related product omitted from the industry definition will show up as a substitute, for example, or competitors overlooked as rivals will be recognized as potential entrants. At the same time, the five forces analysis should reveal major differences within overly broad industries that will indicate the need to adjust industry boundaries or strategies.

avoid buyer power and price-based rivalry. And it has tailored every single part of the value chain to cope well with the forces in its segment. As a result, Paccar has been profitable for 68 years straight and has earned a long-run return on equity above 20 percent.

In addition to revealing positioning opportunities within an existing industry, the five forces framework allows companies to rigorously analyze entry and exit. Both depend on answering the difficult question: "What is the potential of this business?" Exit is indicated when industry structure is poor or declining and the company has no prospect of a superior positioning. In considering entry into a new industry, creative strategists can use the framework to spot an

Typical Steps in Industry Analysis

Define the relevant industry:

- What products are in it? Which ones are part of another distinct industry?
- What is the geographic scope of competition?

Identify the participants and segment them into groups, if appropriate:
Who are the

- Buyers and buyer groups?
- Suppliers and supplier groups?
- Competitors?
- Substitutes?
- Potential entrants?

Assess the underlying drivers of each competitive force to determine which forces are strong and which are weak and why.

Determine overall industry structure, and test the analysis for consistency:

- *Why* is the level of profitability what it is?
- Which are the *controlling* forces for profitability?
- Is the industry analysis consistent with actual long-run profitability?
- Are more-profitable players better positioned in relation to the five forces?

Analyze recent and likely future changes in each force, both positive and negative.

Identify aspects of industry structure that might be influenced by competitors, by new entrants, or by your company.

industry with a good future before this good future is reflected in the prices of acquisition candidates. Five forces analysis may also reveal industries that are not necessarily attractive for the average entrant but in which a company has good reason to believe it can surmount entry barriers at lower cost than most firms or has a unique ability to cope with the industry's competitive forces.

Exploiting Industry Change

Industry changes bring the opportunity to spot and claim promising new strategic positions if the strategist has a sophisticated understanding of the competitive forces and their underpinnings. Consider, for instance, the evolution of the music industry during the past decade. With the advent of the Internet and the digital distribution of music, some analysts predicted the birth of thousands of music labels (that is, record companies that develop artists and bring their music to market). This, the analysts argued, would break a pattern that had held since Edison invented the phonograph: Between three and six major record companies had always dominated the industry. The Internet would, they predicted, remove distribution as a barrier to entry, unleashing a flood of new players into the music industry.

A careful analysis, however, would have revealed that physical distribution was not the crucial barrier to entry. Rather, entry was barred by other benefits that large music labels enjoyed. Large labels could pool the risks of developing new artists over many bets, cushioning the impact of inevitable failures. Even more important, they had advantages in breaking through the clutter and getting their new artists heard. To do so, they could promise radio stations and record stores access to well-known artists in exchange for promotion of new artists. New labels would find this nearly impossible to match. The major labels stayed the course, and new music labels have been rare.

This is not to say that the music industry is structurally unchanged by digital distribution. Unauthorized downloading created an illegal but potent substitute. The labels tried for years to develop technical platforms for digital distribution

Common Pitfalls

In conducting the analysis avoid the following common mistakes:

- Defining the industry too broadly or too narrowly.
- Making lists instead of engaging in rigorous analysis.
- Paying equal attention to all of the forces rather than digging deeply into the most important ones.
- Confusing effect (price sensitivity) with cause (buyer economics).
- Using static analysis that ignores industry trends.
- Confusing cyclical or transient changes with true structural changes.
- Using the framework to declare an industry attractive or unattractive rather than using it to guide strategic choices.

themselves, but major companies hesitated to sell their music through a platform owned by a rival. Into this vacuum stepped Apple with its iTunes music store, launched in 2003 to support its iPod music player. By permitting the creation of a powerful new gatekeeper, the major labels allowed industry structure to shift against them. The number of major record companies has actually declined—from six in 1997 to four today—as companies struggled to cope with the digital phenomenon.

When industry structure is in flux, new and promising competitive positions may appear. Structural changes open up new needs and new ways to serve existing needs. Established leaders may overlook these or be constrained by past strategies from pursuing them. Smaller competitors in the industry can capitalize on such changes, or the void may well be filled by new entrants.

Shaping Industry Structure

When a company exploits structural change, it is recognizing, and reacting to, the inevitable. However, companies also have the ability to shape industry structure. A firm can lead its industry toward new ways of competing that alter the five forces for the better. In reshaping structure, a company wants its competitors to follow so that the entire industry will be transformed. While many industry participants may benefit in the process, the innovator can benefit most if it can shift competition in directions where it can excel.

An industry's structure can be reshaped in two ways: by redividing profitability in favor of incumbents or by expanding the overall profit pool. Redividing the industry pie aims to increase the share of profits to industry competitors instead of to suppliers, buyers, substitutes, and keeping out potential entrants. Expanding the profit pool involves increasing the overall pool of economic value generated by the industry in which rivals, buyers, and suppliers can all share.

Redividing Profitability

To capture more profits for industry rivals, the starting point is to determine which force or forces are currently constraining industry profitability and address them. A company can potentially influence all of the competitive forces. The strategist's goal here is to reduce the share of profits that leak to suppliers, buyers, and substitutes or are sacrificed to deter entrants.

To neutralize supplier power, for example, a firm can standardize specifications for parts to make it easier to switch among suppliers. It can cultivate additional vendors, or alter technology to avoid a powerful supplier group altogether. To counter customer power, companies may expand services that raise buyers' switching costs or find alternative means of reaching customers to neutralize powerful channels. To temper profit-eroding price rivalry, companies can invest more heavily in unique products, as pharmaceutical firms have done, or expand support services to customers. To scare off entrants, incumbents can elevate the fixed cost of competing—for instance, by escalating their R&D or marketing expenditures. To limit the threat of substitutes, companies can offer better value through new features or wider product accessibility. When soft-drink producers introduced vending machines and convenience store channels, for example, they dramatically improved the availability of soft drinks relative to other beverages.

Sysco, the largest food-service distributor in North America, offers a revealing example of how an industry leader can change the structure of an industry for the better. Food-service distributors purchase food and related items from farmers and food processors. They then warehouse and deliver these items to restaurants, hospitals, employer cafeterias, schools, and other food-service institutions. Given low barriers to entry, the food-service distribution industry has historically been highly fragmented, with numerous local competitors. While rivals try to cultivate customer relationships, buyers are price sensitive because food represents a large share of their costs. Buyers can also choose the substitute approaches of purchasing directly from manufacturers or using retail sources, avoiding distributors altogether. Suppliers wield bargaining power: They are often large companies with strong brand names that food preparers and consumers recognize. Average profitability in the industry has been modest.

Sysco recognized that, given its size and national reach, it might change this state of affairs. It led the move to introduce private-label distributor brands with specifications tailored to the food-service market, moderating supplier power. Sysco emphasized value-added services to buyers such as credit, menu planning, and inventory management to shift the basis of competition away from just price. These moves, together with stepped-up investments in information technology and regional distribution centers, substantially raised the bar for new entrants while making the substitutes less attractive. Not surprisingly, the industry has been consolidating, and industry profitability appears to be rising.

Industry leaders have a special responsibility for improving industry structure. Doing so often requires resources that only large players possess. Moreover, an improved industry structure is a public good because it benefits every firm in the industry, not just the company that initiated the improvement. Often, it is more in the interests of an industry leader than any other participant to invest for the common good because leaders will usually benefit the most. Indeed, improving the industry may be a leader's most profitable strategic opportunity, in part because attempts to gain further market share can trigger strong reactions from rivals, customers, and even suppliers.

There is a dark side to shaping industry structure that is equally important to understand. Ill-advised changes in competitive positioning and operating practices can undermine industry structure. Faced with pressures to gain market share or enamored with innovation for its own sake, managers may trigger new kinds of competition that no incumbent can win. When taking actions to improve their own company's competitive advantage, then, strategists should ask whether they are setting in motion dynamics that will undermine industry structure in the long run. In the early days of the personal computer industry, for instance, IBM tried to make up for its late entry by offering an open architecture that would set industry standards and attract complementary makers of application software and peripherals. In the process, it ceded ownership of the critical components of the PC—the operating system and the microprocessor—to Microsoft and Intel. By standardizing PCs, it encouraged price-based rivalry and shifted power to suppliers. Consequently, IBM became the temporarily dominant firm in an industry with an enduringly unattractive structure.

Expanding the Profit Pool

When overall demand grows, the industry's quality level rises, intrinsic costs are reduced, or waste is eliminated, the pie expands. The total pool of value available to competitors, suppliers, and buyers grows. The total profit pool expands, for example, when channels become more competitive or when an industry discovers latent buyers for its product that are not currently being served. When soft-drink producers rationalized their independent bottler networks to make them more efficient and effective, both the soft-drink companies and the bottlers benefited. Overall value can also expand when firms work collaboratively with suppliers to improve coordination and limit unnecessary costs incurred in the supply chain. This lowers the inherent cost structure of the industry, allowing higher profit, greater demand through lower prices, or both. Or agreeing on quality standards can bring up industrywide quality and service levels, and hence prices, benefiting rivals, suppliers, and customers.

Expanding the overall profit pool creates win-win opportunities for multiple industry participants. It can also reduce the risk of destructive rivalry that arises when incumbents attempt to shift bargaining power or capture more market share. However, expanding the pie does not reduce the importance of industry structure. How the expanded pie is divided will ultimately be determined by the five forces. The most successful companies are those that expand the industry profit pool in ways that allow them to share disproportionately in the benefits.

Defining the Industry

The five competitive forces also hold the key to defining the relevant industry (or industries) in which a company competes. Drawing industry boundaries correctly, around the arena in which competition actually takes place, will clarify the causes of profitability and the appropriate unit for setting strategy. A company needs a separate strategy for each distinct industry. Mistakes in industry definition made by competitors present opportunities for staking out superior strategic positions. (See "Defining the Relevant Industry.")

Competition and Value

The competitive forces reveal the drivers of industry competition. A company strategist who understands that competition extends well beyond existing rivals will detect wider competitive threats and be better equipped to address them. At the same time, thinking comprehensively about an industry's structure can uncover opportunities: differences in customers, suppliers, substitutes, potential entrants, and rivals that can become the basis for distinct strategies yielding superior performance. In a world of more open competition and relentless change, it is more important than ever to think structurally about competition.

Understanding industry structure is equally important for investors as for managers. The five competitive forces reveal whether an industry is truly attractive, and they help investors anticipate positive or negative shifts in industry structure before they are obvious. The five forces distinguish short-term blips from structural changes and allow investors to take advantage of undue pessimism or optimism. Those companies whose strategies have industry-transforming potential become far clearer. This deeper thinking about competition is a more powerful way to achieve genuine investment success than the financial projections and trend extrapolation that dominate today's investment analysis.

If both executives and investors looked at competition this way, capital markets would be a far more effective force for company success and economic prosperity. Executives and investors would both be focused on the same fundamentals that drive sustained profitability. The conversation between investors and executives would focus on the structural, not the transient. Imagine the improvement in company performance—and in the economy as a whole—if all the energy expended in "pleasing the Street" were redirected toward the factors that create true economic value.

Amazon.com: The Brink of Bankruptcy

The Amazon.com case traces the evolution of Amazon.com's business model from its founding in 1994 to early 2001. The case ends as the company stands poised on the "brink of bankruptcy." Jeff Bezos, founder and CEO, is convinced that the company will be able to leverage its strategic position, within a network of customers, suppliers, and partners, and the capabilities it built, to achieve profitability by year-end 2001. Do you agree? And, if so, how will he achieve this seemingly insurmountable goal? While all are familiar with the outcome of this case, the story of how Bezos achieved his goals provides powerful insights on the impact of IT on business model performance. As you read the case, consider the following questions: How did the Amazon.com business model evolve from the company's launch in 1995 to early 2001? What role did IT play in the company's strategy and the capabilities it built to execute strategy? As a member of the company's board of directors, what advice would you give to Jeff Bezos in early 2001?

Case 1-2

Amazon.com: The Brink of Bankruptcy

> We seek to offer the Earth's Biggest Selection and to be the Earth's Most Customer-Centric Company, where customers can find and discover anything they may want to buy online.
>
> *Jeff Bezos, CEO, Amazon.com, 2001*[1]

In early 2001, Amazon.com senior management faced tremendous pressures from Wall Street and the company's shareholders to achieve profitability. Incorporated in 1994 as the "Earth's Biggest Bookstore," Amazon.com enjoyed several years of tremendous growth fueled by the "irrational exuberance" that characterized the launch of Internet commerce.[2] The company's successful initial public offering (IPO) on May 15, 1997, netted approximately \$50 million, and the company quickly used that money and the capital associated with its soaring stock price to expand from an online retail bookstore into an online superstore offering books, music, videos, toys, videogames, consumer electronics, software, and a full line of kitchen/home improvement products. As a retailer, Amazon.com took ownership of the inventory it sold and, as its product line expanded, so too did the complexity of its warehousing, inventory management, distribution, and fulfillment. In addition, the company also began to explore new business models, initially adding auctions and an online marketplace where individuals and small businesses could leverage the company's proprietary online retail infrastructure to gain access to millions of loyal customers. Finally, in 2000, Amazon.com expanded its marketplace business model through a series of equity partnerships with leading online retailers (e.g., Drugstore.com, living.com, and pets.com). (Exhibit 1 provides a timeline of key events.)

Even as it expanded its retail strategy and explored new business models, during the late 1990s the company also invested heavily to quickly develop the best-in-class retailing, fulfillment, and customer service capabilities required to support its

Professor Lynda M. Applegate prepared this case from published sources as the basis for class discussion rather than to illustrate effective or ineffective management.

[1] Amazon.com Annual Report, 2001, p. 1.

[2] R. J. Schiller, *Irrational Exuberance* (Princeton, N.J.: Princeton University Press, 2000).

EXHIBIT 1 **Amazon.com Timeline of Key Events**

Source: Author. Based on company press releases and analyst reports.

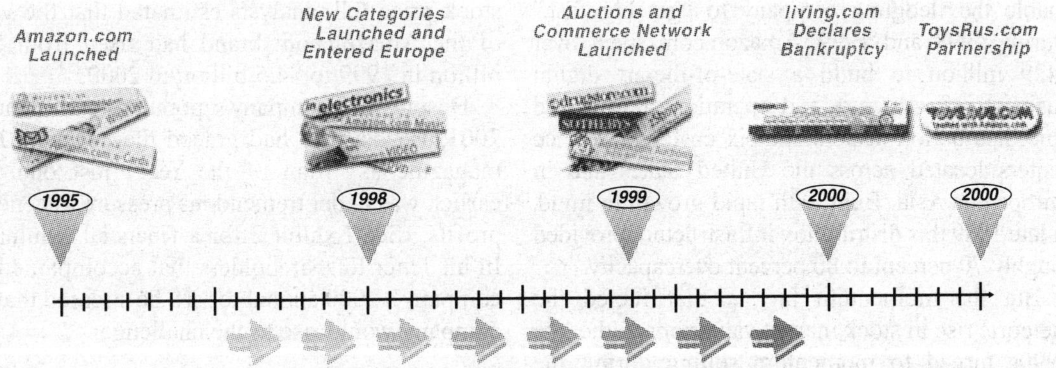

1994: Bezos, a N.Y. investment banker with no book publishing or retail experience, identifies book retailing as an industry segment that could exploit the power of emerging Internet technologies. Chooses Seattle as a location to be close to one of the largest book distributors. Writes the business plan and chooses the company name while driving cross-country with his wife.

1995: Between July 1994, when the company was incorporated, and July 1995 when the Amazon.com online bookstore was officially launched, Bezos and a few employees built the software that powered the Web site. By September 1995, the company was selling over $20,000 per week out of the founder's garage.

1996: Amazon.com focused on *enhancing* its product and service offerings and capabilities with increasingly sophisticated browsing and focused search capabilities, personalized store layout and recommendations, shopping carts, 1-Click shopping (which was later patented), wish lists, and greeting cards. Efforts to redefine and enhance the online shopping experience continued and, in 1999, Amazon.com was one of the first online retailers to enable shopping through wireless devices.

1997: By the first quarter of 1997, Amazon.com revenues had increased to $16 million (which was equivalent to the company's yearly revenues in 1996). Amazon.com went public on May 15, 1997.

1998: Beginning in 1998, Amazon.com began aggressively *expanding* into new product categories and into international markets. By early 2001, the company was not just an online bookstore; it was an online superstore selling a wide variety of products in over 160 different countries.

1999: During 1999, Amazon.com began *exploring* new business models including, auctions (low-end and high-end) and marketplaces (zShops). For these businesses, Amazon.com provided software and services but did not assume control of inventory. As such, it acted as an agent—not a retailer.

2000: During early 2000, Amazon.com *expanded* its marketplace business model through a series of equity partnerships with leading online retailers (Drugstore.com, living.com, pets.com). By late 2000, living.com and Pets.com had succumbed to the dot-com crash and had declared bankruptcy. This caused Amazon.com executives to reevaluate the company's business model. Rather than partner with dot-com retailers, attention shifted to traditional retailers that wished to develop online retailing capabilities and to upgrade their traditional distribution and fulfillment capabilities to enable the end-to-end visibility and speed required when doing business online. In August 2000, Amazon.com's partnership with Toys "R" Us enabled the company to *explore* a new business model as a logistics services provider as it simultaneously expanded into a new market (traditional retailers) with its existing online retail product.

rapidly growing and increasingly complex business. Talent was hired from leading retailers (e.g., Wal-Mart) and distributors (e.g., Federal Express) to enable the fledgling company to "get big fast." During 1998 and 1999, Amazon.com spent over $429 million to build a state-of-the-art digital business infrastructure and operations that linked nine distribution centers and six customer service centers located across the United States and in Europe and Asia. Built with rapid growth in mind, in late 1999 this distribution infrastructure provided roughly 70 percent to 80 percent overcapacity.[3]

But the momentum buying that fueled the meteoric rise in stock market valuations in the late 1990s turned to momentum selling during the latter half of 2000. Like most Internet businesses that had yet to achieve profitability, Amazon's stock price fell precipitously from its high of $113 on December 9, 1999, to around $15 by year-end 2000, and its market value declined from over $35 billion to less than $5 billion.[4] Despite the declining stock prices, however, the number of customers continued to rise, increasing from 14 million in 1999 to over 20 million in 2000. More importantly, these customers were not just shopping; they were also buying, and revenues increased from roughly $610 million in 1998 to $1.6 billion in 1999 then to $2.8 billion in 2000.[5] By 2000, over 75 percent of U.S. consumers recognized the Amazon.com brand, and Interbrand ranked the company as the 48th most valuable brand worldwide, immediately above Motorola (#49) and Colgate (#50) and well above Hilton (#68) and Pampers (#71). Indeed, even as the stock price fell, analysts estimated that the value of the Amazon.com brand had risen from $1.4 billion in 1999 to $4.5 billion in 2000.[6]

Despite the company's popularity, in January 2001, Bezos, who had graced the cover of *Time* magazine as "Man of the Year" just one year earlier, was under tremendous pressure to generate profits. (See Exhibit 2 for a financial summary.) In his letter to shareholders that accompanied the company's 2000 annual report, he stressed that the company would rise to the challenge:

> While there are no foregone conclusions, and we still have much to prove, Amazon.com today is a unique asset. We have the brand, the customer relationships, the technology, the fulfillment infrastructure, the financial strength, the people, and the determination to extend our leadership in this infant industry and to build an important, and lasting, company.[7]

Bezos believed that the key challenge to the company in late 2000 was to achieve profitability by year-end 2001. He advised investors that the company had a "tremendous amount of work to do and there could be no guarantees," yet also found time for humor:

> We've been called a lot of very funny things: Amazon dot toast, Amazon dot con, Amazon dot bomb and my personal favorite, Amazon dot org, because clearly we're a not-for-profit company.[8]

By summer 2000, some analysts had begun to question whether Amazon.com executives would be able to achieve profitability before the money ran out. Ravi Suria and Stan Oh, analysts at Lehman Brothers, published a report on Amazon.com's credit rating that raised the concerns of investors and hastened the stock price slide.

[3] M. Rowen, "Amazon.com," *Prudential Securities Research*, September 23, 1999, p. 3.

[4] Friday, April 14, 2000, ended a week of major downslides for both technology and blue-chip stocks. This downturn marked the end of what had become known as the "Internet Bubble." The NASDAQ tumbled 355.46 points (9.7%), which was the worst one-day price drop since the Nasdaq opened in 1971. The Dow Jones Industrial Average slipped 616.23 points (5.6%, its worst ever one-day point loss). A. Task, "Ruthless Selloff Hits All Sectors: This Was One for the Record Books," www.TheStreet.com (April 14, 2000).

[5] In 2000, Jupiter Research analysts estimated that U.S. retail sales had exceeded $2.7 trillion, while U.S. online retail sales were over $12 billion (up 66% from 1999). "Jupiter Consumer Survey Report," *Jupiter Media Metrix*, vol. 2, 2001.

[6] Founded in 1974, Interbrand was a leading global brand management consultancy. Its yearly ranking of the world's most valuable brands was published in *BusinessWeek* and was also available on the Interbrand Web site (www.interbrand.com).

[7] Amazon.com 2000 Annual Report.

[8] J. Bezos, Keynote Speech at Harvard Business School Cyberposium, February 26, 2000.

EXHIBIT 2 Amazon.com Historical Income Statements (in US$ thousands)

Source: Author. Based on data from Amazon.com annual reports and Web site.

	Year Ended December 31			
	2000	1999	1998	1997
Net sales	$ 2,761,983	$ 1,639,839	$ 609,819	$147,787
Cost of sales	2,106,206	1,349,194	476,155	118,969
Gross profit	655,777	290,645	133,664	28,818
Gross margin	*23.7%*	*17.7%*	*21.9%*	*19.5%*
Operating expenses:				
Fulfillment	414,509	237,312	65,227	15,944
Marketing	179,980	175,838	67,427	24,133
Technology and content	269,326	159,722	46,424	13,384
General and administrative	108,962	70,144	15,618	6,741
Stock-based compensation	24,797	30,618	1,889	1,211
Amortization of goodwill and other intangibles	321,772	214,694	42,599	—
Restructuring-related and other	200,311	8,072	3,535	—
Total operating expenses	1,519,657	896,400	242,719	61,413
Pro forma income (loss) from operations[(1)]	**(317,000)**	**(352,371)**	**(61,032)**	**(31,384)**
As a % of Sales	*−11%*	*−21%*	*−10%*	*−21%*
Income (loss) from operations	(863,880)	(605,755)	(109,055)	(32,595)
Interest income	40,821	45,451	14,053	1,901
Interest expense	(130,921)	(84,566)	(26,639)	(326)
Other income (expense), net	(10,058)	1,671	—	—
Other gains (losses), net	(142,639)	—	—	—
Total nonoperating expenses, net	(242,797)	(37,444)	(12,586)	1,575
Income (loss) before equity-related items	(1,106,677)	(643,199)	(121,641)	(31,020)
Other equity-related	(304,596)	(76,769)	(2,905)	—
Net income (loss)—GAAP	$(1,411,273)	$(719,968)	$(124,546)	$(31,020)
Basic income (loss) per share—GAAP	$(4.02)	$(2.20)	$(0.42)	$(0.12)
Diluted income (loss) per share—GAAP	$(4.02)	$(2.20)	$(0.42)	$(0.12)

(1) Pro forma income excludes the following items: stock-based compensation, amortization of goodwill and other intangibles, and restructuring and "related items"

EXHIBIT 2 **Amazon.com Historical Balance Sheet (in US$ thousands, except per share data) (*Continued*)**

	Year Ended December 31	
	2000	**1999**
Assets		
Current assets:		
Cash and cash equivalents	$ 822,435	$ 133,309
Marketable securities	278,087	572,879
Inventories	174,563	220,646
Prepaid expenses and other current assets	86,044	79,643
Total current assets	1,361,129	1,006,477
Fixed assets, net	366,416	317,613
Goodwill, net	158,990	534,699
Other intangibles, net	96,335	195,445
Investments in equity-method investees	52,073	226,727
Other equity investments	40,177	144,735
Other assets	60,049	40,154
Total assets	$ 2,135,169	$ 2,465,850
Liabilities and Stockholders' Equity (Deficit)		
Current liabilities:		
Accounts payable	$ 485,383	$ 463,026
Accrued expenses and other current liabilities	272,683	176,208
Unearned revenue	131,117	54,790
Interest payable	69,196	24,888
Current portion of long-term debt and other	16,577	14,322
Total current liabilities	974,956	733,234
Long-term debt	2,127,464	1,466,338
Commitments and contingencies		
Stockholders' equity (deficit):		
Preferred stock, US$ 0.01 par value:		
Authorized shares—500,000		
Issued and outstanding shares—none	—	—
Common stock, US$ 0.01 par value		
Authorized shares—5,000,000		
Issued and outstanding shares—357,140 and		
345,155 shares at Dec. 31, 2000 and 1999, respectively	3,571	3,452
Additional paid-in capital	1,338,303	1,194,369
Deferred stock-based compensation	(13,448)	(47,806)
Accumulated other comprehensive loss	(2,376)	(1,709)
Accumulated deficit	(2,293,301)	(882,028)
Total stockholders' equity (deficit)	(967,251)	266,278
Total liabilities and stockholders' equity (deficit)	$ 2,135,169	$ 2,465,850

EXHIBIT 2 Amazon.com, Inc. 2000 Historical Statements of Cash Flow (in US$ thousands) (*Continued*)

	Year Ended December 31		
	2000	**1999**	**1998**
Cash and Cash Equivalents, Beginning of Period			
Operating Activities:	$ 133,309	$ 71,583	$ 110,119
Net income (loss)	$ (1,411,273)	$ (719,968)	$ (124,546)
Adjustments to reconcile net income (loss) to net cash provided by (used in) operating activities:			
Depreciation of fixed assets and other amortization	84,460	36,806	9,421
Stock-based compensation	24,797	30,618	2,386
Equity in losses of equity method investees, net	304,596	76,769	2,905
Amortization of goodwill and other intangibles	321,772	214,694	42,599
Non-cash restructuring-related and other	200,311	8,072	1,561
Amortization of previously unearned revenue	(108,211)	(5,837)	—
Loss (gain) on sale of marketable securities, net	(280)	8,688	271
Other losses (gains), net	142,639	—	—
Non-cash interest expense and other	24,766	29,171	23,970
Changes in Operating Assets and Liabilities			
Inventories	46,083	(172,069)	(20,513)
Prepaid expenses and other current assets	(8,585)	(54,927)	(16,758)
Accounts payable	2,357	330,166	78,674
Accrued expenses and other current liabilities	93,967	95,839	31,232
Unearned revenue	97,818	6,225	—
Interest payable	34,341	24,878	(167)
Net cash provided by (used in) operating activities	$ (130,442)	$ (90,875)	$ 31,035
Investing Activities:			
Sales and maturities of marketable securities	$ 545,724	$ 2,064,101	$ 227,789
Purchases of marketable securities	(184,455)	(2,359,398)	(504,435)
Purchases of fixed assets, including internal-use software and web-site development	(134,758)	(287,055)	(28,333)
Investments in equity-method investees and other investments	(62,533)	(369,607)	(19,019)
Net cash provided by (used in) investing activities	$ 163,978	$ (951,959)	$ (323,998)
Financing Activities:			
Proceeds from exercise of stock options	$ 44,697	$ 64,469	$ 5,983
Proceeds from issuance of common stock, net of issuance costs	—	—	8,383
Proceeds from long-term debt and other	681,499	1,263,639	325,987
Repayment of long-term debt	—	(175,744)	(75,000)
Repayment of capital lease obligation and other	(16,927)	(13,142)	(3,108)
Financing costs	(1,122)	(35,151)	(7,783)
Net cash provided by (used in) financing activities	$ 693,147	$ 1,104,071	$ 254,462
Effect of exchange-rate on cash and cash equivalents	$ (37,557)	$ 489	$ (35)
Net increase (decrease) in cash and cash equivalents	$ 689,126	$ 61,726	$ (38,536)
Cash and Cash Equivalents, End of Period	$ 822,435	$ 133,309	$ 71,583
Supplemental Cash Flow Information			
Fixed assets acquired under capital leases	$ 4,459	$ 25,850	—
Fixed assets acquired under financing agreements	4,844	5,608	—
Equity securities received for commercial agreements	106,848	54,402	—
Stock issued in connection with business acquisitions	32,130	774,409	217,241
Cash paid for interest	67,252	30,526	26,629

EXHIBIT 2 Amazon.com Business Segment Analysis (in US$ thousands) (*Continued*)

	Revenues		Gross Profit		Operating Profit	
	1999	**2000**	**1999**	**2000**	**1999**	**2000**
US Books, Music & Video	1,308,292	1,698,266	262,871	417,452	(31,000)	62,836
Seq. Gwth	n/a	n/a	n/a	n/a	n/a	
Y-O-Y Gwth	122%	104%	59%	n/a	n/a	
% of Revenues	80%	20.1%	24.6%	(2.4)%	3.7%	
International	167,743	381,075	35,575	77,435	(79,223)	(139,215)
Seq. Gwth	n/a	n/a	n/a	n/a	n/a	
Y-O-Y Gwth	669%	618%	118%	n/a	n/a	
% of Revenues	10%	21.2%	20.3%	(47.2)%	(26.0)%	
Early-Stage Businesses & Other	163,804	535,442	(7,801)	50,790	(242,148)	(240,621)
Seq. Gwth	n/a	n/a	n/a	n/a	n/a	
Y-O-Y Gwth	n/a	n/a	n/a	n/a	n/a	
% of Revenues	10%	(4.8)%	9.5%	(147.8)%	(44.9)%	
Services (Toys "R" Us business)		147,200		110,100	(352,371)	(317,000)
Seq. Gwth	n/a	n/a	n/a	(21.5)%	(11.5)%	
% of Revenues		n/a	74.8%			
Consolidated Revenues	**1,639,839**	**2,761,983**	**290,645**	**655,777**		
Seq. Gwth	n/a	n/a	n/a			
Y-O-Y Gwth	169%	117%	126%			
Gross Margin		17.7%	23.7%			

Distribution & Shipping Services	**1999**	**2000**
Revenue	239,000	338,174
% of Revenues	14.6%	12.2%
Gross Profit	11,700	(1,341)
Gross Profit Margin	4.9%	(0.4)%
Customers	16,900	29,400
New Customers	10,700	12,200
Sales per Customer	$ 97.0	$ 93.9
Customer Acq. Cost	$ 16.3	$ 14.8

If Amazon.com had not generated $318 million in cash from options exercise [in 1999] and had paid its suppliers in the same quarter as it sold its goods,[9] its cash balance would have been down to $115 million, which would have proceeded to put the company in the poorhouse. With the buttressed cash level of $706 million showing up on the balance sheet as of the end of [1999], the company borrowed another $680 million in February of this year [2000]. If the company had not been able to borrow the money, the Amazon.com story might already have been over . . .[10]

[9] In their July 2000 report, Suria and Oh stated that Amazon.com did not pay its suppliers for Q4 inventory until Q1 of the following year.

[10] R. Suria and S. Oh, "Amazon.com Credit Update," *Lehman Brothers Investment Research,* June 22, 2000; R. Suria and S. Oh, "Amazon.com Credit Update," *Lehman Brothers Investment Research,* July 27, 2000.

Bezos knew its rising fulfillment costs, which increased from 11 percent of sales in 1998 to 14 percent in 1999, needed to be addressed quickly. Simply growing revenues and retaining customers in attractive market segments would not be enough. While he was happy to see that the company had achieved profitability in its book, music, and video categories, Bezos knew that the company needed to generate profits sufficient to support the cash flow needs of all of its businesses while also delivering returns to investors. To complicate the picture, while online revenues were expected to continue growing, strong competitors were lining up to exploit each market. (See Exhibit 3 for market size and competitor comparisons.)

Amazon.com believed that its digital business infrastructure—which linked its customer-facing processes (shopping, buying, paying, and customer service) to its back-end processes (supply chain, inventory, and order fulfillment)—was a proprietary asset that would provide sustainable advantage. It claimed that even its "picking-and-packing"—notoriously labor-intensive activities for retailers—were supported by technology that Bezos believed would enable the company to reduce fulfillment costs as a percentage of sales to the single digits when the company was operating at scale. But Amazon.com executives soon learned that supply chain, inventory management, and order fulfillment processes were difficult to efficiently scale across a diverse range of products. While its book, music, and video stores were breaking even, its toy, home and garden, electronics, and international stores continued to burn cash. The dot-com stock market crash exacerbated the company's problems and, by mid-2000, many of its online retail partners had declared, or were heading toward, bankruptcy.[11]

Bezos and the senior team immediately began to explore ways to quickly leverage its capabilities, fill excess capacity, and deal with competitive threats from traditional retailers. In August 2000, Amazon.com announced that it would close down its online toy store and partner with Toys "R" Us, Inc. to open a Toys "R" Us–branded online store. Under the terms of this partnership, Amazon.com would utilize its retailing technology to build and host the Toys "R"

[11] On August 28, 2000, *The Industry Standard* reported that, after selling inventory, Living.com, eToys, boo.com, and Garden.com had, or were in the process of, selling assets in bankruptcy court.

EXHIBIT 3 Addressable Market (U.S. only)

Source: Author. Based on data from K. Cassar, et al., "Shopping: Online Projections, Volume 3." Jupiter Media Metrix, 2001. Salomon Smith Barney. "Amazon.com." December 9, 1999. M. Rowen, "Amazon.com," Prudential Securities, September 23, 1999; and S. Farley and N. Modi, "Amazon.com," PaineWebber, February 23, 2000.

Categories	2000 U.S. Market		2005 U.S. Market Estimate	
	Online Retail	% of Total Market	Online Retail	% of Total Market
Books	$2.2B	9%	$3.7B	15%
Music	$0.7B	5	4.4B	25
Video/DVD	$0.5B	4	1.6B	10
Total BMV	$4.4B	7	9.7B	17
Toys	N/A	2.9	N/A	4.8
Video Games	N/A	N/A	N/A	N/A
Computers	6.1B	25	11.7B	46
Software	1.4B	17	3.8B	43
Consumer Electronics	1.1B	2.4	3.6B	2.9
Home & Garden	1.0B	0.3	12B	2.9
Auctions (Consumer Only)	3.3B	N/A	28.5B	N/A

EXHIBIT 3 Addressable Market (U.S. only) (*Continued*)

Comparison of Performance Metrics for Online and Offline Retailers

Source: Author. Based on data from *Standard & Poors' Research Insight*; H. Becker, "Amazon.com," *Salomon Smith Barney Equity Research*, December 9, 1999 (based on data from Media Metrix).

	Traditional Retailers				Online Retailers		
Fiscal Year: 1999	**Wal-Mart**	**Toys "R" Us**	**Barnes & Noble**	**Sears**	**Amazon.com**	**Barnesand Noble.com**	**eBay.com**
Sales ($ M)	165,013	11,862.00	3,486.04	41,071.00	1,639.84	202.57	224.724
COGS ($ M)	127,289	8,321.00	2,483.73	27,212.00	1,312.39	146.09	38.083
Gross margin (%)	23	30	29	34	20	28	83
Advertising as % sales	0.003	N/A	N/A	0.04	0.09	0.21	0.20
SG&A (% of sales)	.16	.23	.19	.23	0.41	0.816	0.72
Operating margin (%)	5.04	4.38	6.25	9.06	(36.45)	(60.54)	1.42
Employees (thousands)	1,140	76	37.41	326	7.6	1.24	1.212
Sales/Employee (US$)	144,748	156,079	100,347	125,985	215,768	163,363	185,416
Inventory turnover	6.91	4.24	2.43	5.51	10.49	53.46	N/A
Working capital turnover	112.91	168.26	10.99	2.73	6.12	0.8	1.01
Reach (%) (Oct. 1999)					17.8	6.9%	N/A
Unique visitors (Oct. 1999)					11,283,000	4,381,000	N/A
Average minutes/day (Oct. 1999)					6.5	5.0	N/A

EXHIBIT 4 Projected Economics of the Amazon.com / Toys "R" Us Partnership (in US$ millions)

Source: Author. Based on data from J.J. Patel and N. McCluskey, "Amazon.com," *Deutsche Bank Alex Brown Equity Research*, April 23, 2001.

	4Q 2000	2001E
Toys "R" Us product revenues	$130	$280
Amazon revenues		
Shipping fees ($6/order)	14.4	
Credit card fees (2.5% of product & shipping)	3.6	
Transaction fees ($6/order)	14.4	
Total Revenues	$32.4	$75
Amazon.com cost of goods sold		
Shipping costs ($5/order)	12.0	
Credit card costs (2% of product & shipping)	2.9	
Fulfillment costs ($4/order)	9.6	
Total costs	$24.5	
Amazon.com gross profit	$7.9	$22
Amazon.com gross margin	24.4%	30%

Us online store, while also providing customer service, inventory management, fulfillment, and logistics services in its state-of-the-art customer service and distribution centers. Toys "R" Us would maintain control of product sourcing and marketing, and would "own" the inventory in the Amazon.com distribution centers. (See Exhibit 4 for estimates of the economics of the Toys "R" Us deal.) As such, this partnership represented a further expansion of Amazon.com's service offerings to include hosting both physical and online customer and logistics services (including call center, fulfillment, inventory management, and distribution) in its global distribution and customer service network. By adding this new "Infrastructure Services" business model to its retail, marketplace, and auction models,[12] Bezos believed that this new combination of business models would be the "tipping point," enabling exponential growth in returns.[13]

> The Amazon.com platform is comprised of brand, customers, technology, distribution capability, deep e-commerce expertise, and a great team with a passion for innovation and serving customers well . . . We believe that we have reached a "tipping point," where this platform allows us to launch new e-commerce businesses faster, with a higher quality of customer experience, a lower incremental cost, a higher chance of success, and a clearer path to scale and profitability than perhaps any other company.[14]

While the concept of adding this new services business model was compelling, by early 2001, it was not clear how much longer the company could wait to begin cashing in on the "new Internet economics." Some analysts, such as Thomas Weisel Partners (TWP) "questioned [Amazon.com's] ability to gain the scale and operating efficiencies necessary to compete in the long run,"[15] but other analysts were more optimistic.[16]

As Bezos pondered his next moves, he knew that the risks were high but so too were the potential returns. Would Amazon.com achieve its aggressive goal of becoming cash flow positive by the end of 2001? Was it poised for exponential growth in revenues, profits, and returns to investors? Finally, how much time did the company have and how much would it need to spend to prove that it could create and sustain value over time?

[12] See L. M. Applegate, *Understanding Internet Business Models*, available from Harvard Business School Publishing.

[13] Economists define a market's "tipping point" as the point at which a dominant technology or player defines the standard for an industry in "winner-take-all" economies of scale and scope. See C. Shapiro and H. Varian, *Information Rules: A Strategic Guide to the Network Economy*, Boston: HBS Press, 1999 (p. 176–177 and 187-188) for a more in-depth discussion.

[14] Amazon.com 1999 Annual Report (Seattle: Amazon.com, 2000).

[15] S. D'Eathe and D. Bernstein, "Amazon.com—Underperform," *Thomas Weisel Partners Equity Research*, March 2, 2001.

[16] H. Becker and M. Gross, "Amazon.com, Inc., *Lehman Brothers Equity Research*, March 2, 2001.

Canyon Ranch

Founded in 1979, Canyon Ranch had become a leader in the health resort and spa industry. At the time of the case in 2004, however, the company was facing increased competitive pressure and had turned to its 20-person IT department to provide the information needed to better understand its customers, create loyalty, and cross-sell its offerings. Less than eight years before, the company's IT function had consisted of a single programmer who maintained a single dominant IT system—the company's Property Management System. While IT capabilities had increased, integration and information access remained a challenge. The case enables discussion of opportunities to use IT to drive business strategy and specifically addresses the role of customer relationship information and business intelligence as proprietary assets that drive business value. As you read the Canyon Ranch case, consider the following questions: What is the value of customer information to Canyon Ranch? As CIO, how would you make the case for customer relationship management (CRM) and business intelligence systems at Canyon Ranch? What impact would you anticipate these systems to have on the Canyon Ranch strategy and capabilities? What advice do you have for Canyon Ranch executives?

Case 1-3

Canyon Ranch

> No matter what feeling better or feeling healthier means to you, Canyon Ranch is a place that helps you connect to a happier lifestyle. Everyone experiences a different Canyon Ranch; we'll meet you where you are.
>
> *Harley Mayersohn, Vice President of Marketing*

> The real challenge is how do we get valuable information from a system that does not let it go easily and then use it for decision making.
>
> *Ben Campsey, Assistant Director of Finance*

As the year 2004 began, Canyon Ranch remained the undisputed leader in the luxury segment of the spa industry. Its unparalleled breadth and depth of offerings, its integrated portfolio of treatments spanning traditional spa and fitness as well as health and healing services, and its incomparable attention to guest needs made Canyon Ranch the gold standard in the industry. (See Exhibit 1).

The spa industry in the United States was set to continue to grow. Competitors were also starting to attack Canyon Ranch more directly.

The challenge for Canyon Ranch was twofold: to attempt to grow the business while maintaining the fundamental characteristics of Canyon Ranch, and to ensure that Canyon Ranch maintained its competitive advantage in the face of increasing competition.

Canyon Ranch

Canyon Ranch Health Resorts was a brainchild of Enid and Mel Zuckerman who, in 1979, sought to create a place where people would be inspired and motivated to translate their healthiest thoughts into action. As the company entered the twenty-first century, it had grown into the leading health resort and spa, with two destination resorts and three SpaClubs. While the company grew larger, it remained true to its founders' original vision: "Canyon Ranch is more than just a fabulous

Professor Lynda M. Applegate and Professor Gabriele Piccoli of Cornell University prepared this case as the basis for class discussion rather than to illustrate effective or ineffective management.

EXHIBIT 1 Canyon Ranch Business Units

Source: Company documents.

Destination/Health Resorts: Canyon Ranch, Tucson, Arizona (opened: 1979)

Facilities

- 62,000-square-foot Spa Complex: Health & Fitness Assessment Center; exercise physiology; fitness; Men's Program Office; hiking and biking; six gyms, including an indoor cycling room; strength training and cardio-fitness equipment; yoga and meditation dome; wallyball, racquetball, squash, and basketball courts; locker rooms with steam and inhalation rooms, sauna, cold dip, sunbathing decks, and whirlpools; skin-care rooms; beauty salon; art gallery
- Life Enhancement Center: Designed for small group interaction, home of Life Enhancement Program weeklong experience
- Aquatic Center: 11,000-square-foot facility with underwater treadmills, bikes, and cross-country ski simulators
- Golf Performance Center: pitch, chip, and putting greens; computerized fitness evaluation and three-camera perspective; priority access to Arizona National Golf Club

Services—Spa

- Massage and Bodywork: Ayurvedic herbal massage, herbal wrap, shiatsu, hydromassage
- Skin Care and Beauty Services: aloe-algae mask, European facial, seaweed paraffin body treatment

Services—Health & Healing

- Nutrition Classes and Workshops: antioxidant evaluation, digestive wellness, hands-on cooking classes
- Medical Services: acupuncture, cardiac treadmill stress test, cholesterol and heart health consultation
- Behavioral Health Services: biofeedback, hypnotherapy, adventure learning
- Exercise Physiology: basic fitness assessment, training for advanced and specialized needs
- Movement Therapy: aquatic therapy, Pilates

Services—Fitness

- Fitness Classes and Activities: aerobics, biking, personal training, private aqua lessons
- Outdoor sports: hiking, biking, aerobic walks
- Golf instruction for all levels
- Water exercise for sports conditioning, fitness, stress, and pain management

Destination/Health Resorts: Canyon Ranch in the Berkshires, Lenox, Massachusetts (opened: 1989)

Facilities

- 100,000-square-foot Spa Complex: Health & Fitness Assessment Center; six gyms; 75-foot indoor pool; exercise and weight-training rooms; indoor tennis, racquetball, squash, basketball, and wallyball; locker rooms with steam and inhalation rooms, sauna, cold dip, and whirlpools; indoor running track; therapeutic massage and bodywork rooms; beauty salon and skin-care services
- Inn: 126 guest rooms and suites

Services—Spa

- Massage and Bodywork: Austrian moor mud therapy, Ayurvedic herbal rejuvenation, reflexology
- Skin Care and Beauty Services: glycolic skin treatments, hair care, makeup consultation and application

Services—Health & Healing

- Nutrition Classes and Workshops: eating for weight loss, hands-on cooking classes, healing food
- Medical Services: acupuncture, cardiac treadmill stress test, cholesterol and heart health consultation

EXHIBIT 1 Canyon Ranch Business Units (*Continued*)

- Behavioral Health Services: biofeedback, changing eating habits, emotional healing, smoking cessation
- Exercise Physiology: comprehensive musculoskeletal evaluation, posture analysis
- Movement Therapy: aquatic therapy, Pilates, etc.

Services—Fitness

- Over 40 fitness classes and activities each day (e.g., aerobics, basketball, cross-training)
- Outdoor sports (e.g., biking, canoeing, cross-country skiing, hiking)
- One free round of golf at Cranwell Country Club

SpaClub: The Venetian, Las Vegas, Nevada (opened: 2000)

Facilities

- 65,000-square-foot Spa Complex: Health and Wellness Center; massage, skin-care, and body treatment rooms; therapeutic pools; three-story rock climbing wall
- 12,000-square-foot Living Essentials spa boutique: health-oriented store featuring in-store wellness education and demonstrations and environmentally sound merchandise

SpaClub: The Gaylord Palms, Kissimmee, Florida (opened: 2002)

Facilities

- 20,000-square-foot Spa Complex: 25 massage, body, and skin-care treatment rooms; fitness facility with cardiovascular and weight-training equipment; locker rooms with steam and sauna; salon with beauty services for men and women
- Living Essentials Spa Boutique: health-oriented store featuring in-store wellness education and demonstrations, and environmentally sound merchandise

SpaClub: The Queen Mary II—Cunard (opened: 2004)

Facilities

- 20,000-square-foot Spa Complex: located on two decks, 24 massage, body, and skin-care treatment rooms; coed relaxation lounge; Thermal Suite and Rasul room; thalassotherapy pool with airbed recliner lounges; neck fountains; deluge waterfall; air tub and body massage jet benches; whirlpool; thermal suite with herbal and Finnish saunas; reflexology basins; aromatic steam room

vacation. It's an experience that can influence the quality of your life, from the moment you arrive to long after you return home. Canyon Ranch is a place to relax, enjoy yourself, and explore your potential for a happier, healthier, more fulfilling life."[1]

Destination Resorts

The two destination resorts were the backbone of the company. While they differed in their physical layout, both resorts offered a similar portfolio of services and had the same organizational structure. Each was divided into three revenue-generating departments: Health and Healing, Hotel, and Spa, with a director overseeing each one.

As the company grew, so did its stunning array of services. The most recent guide to services for Canyon Ranch in the Berkshires, for example, detailed more than 230 different services in both the Spa and Health and Healing departments (see Exhibit 2). Guests also had access to numerous lectures and fitness classes as well as multiple opportunities for outdoor activities at no extra charge (see Exhibit 3). Central to the mission

[1] Canyon Ranch Web site, http://www.canyonranch.com/misc/whatis.asp.

EXHIBIT 2 **Canyon Ranch Services**

Source: Company documents.

Over 500 services, plus between 10 to 20 lectures a day, about 50 fitness classes, not including outdoor activities.

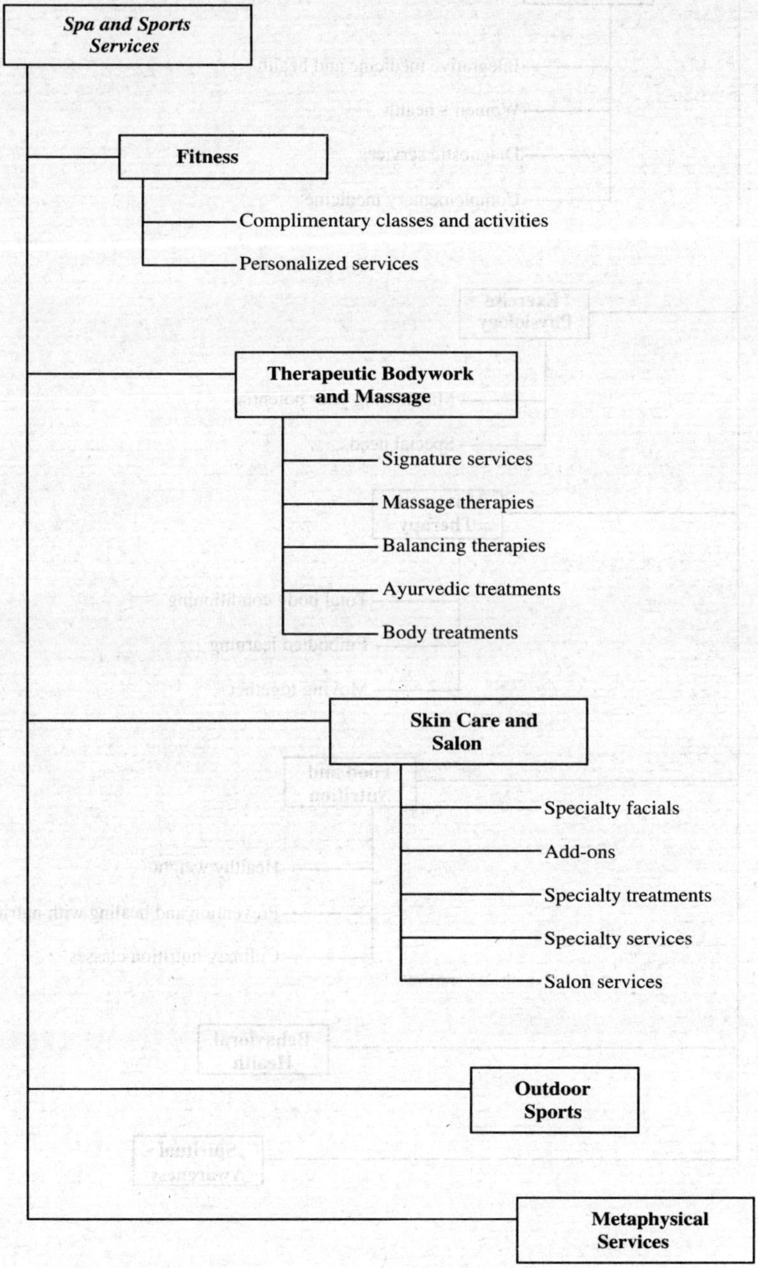

EXHIBIT 2 Canyon Ranch Services (*Continued*)

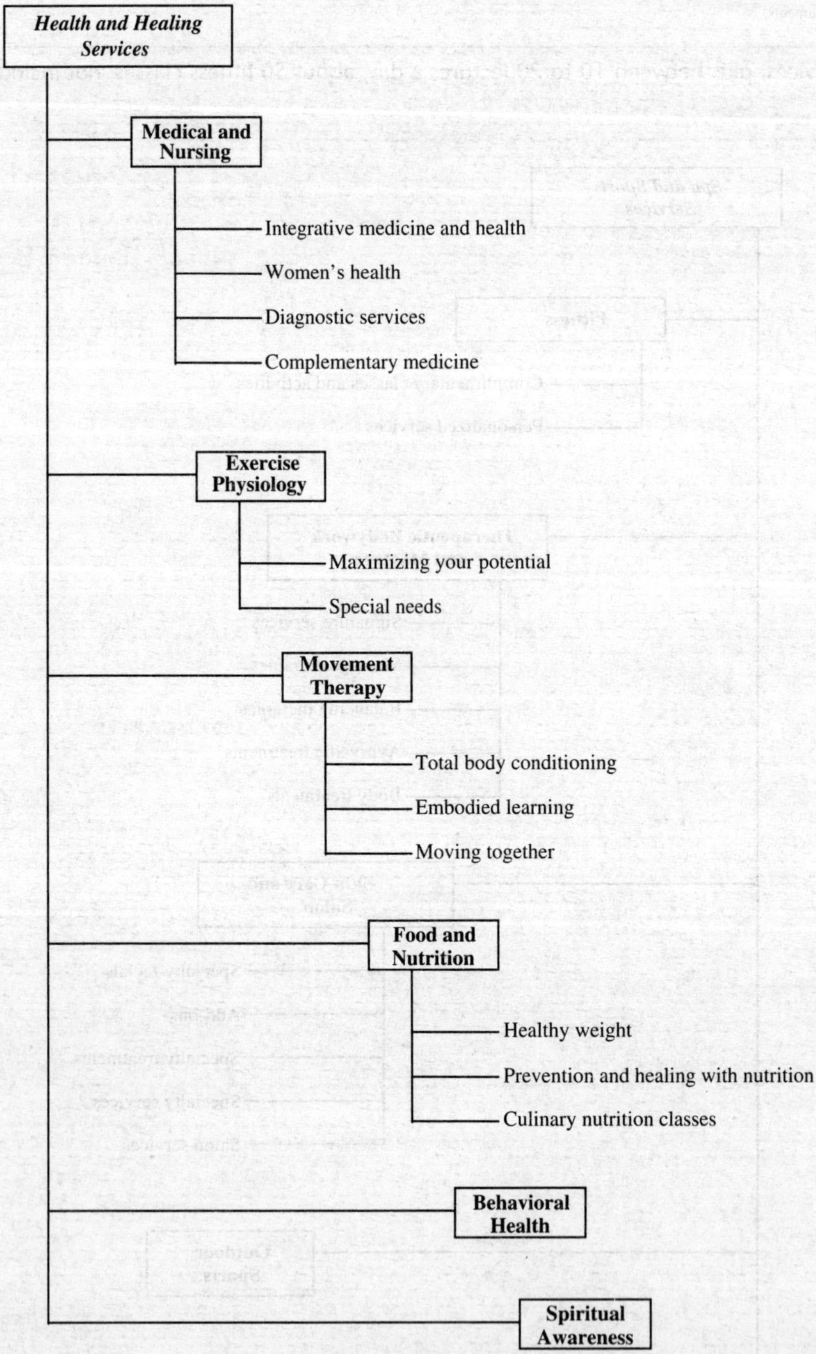

EXHIBIT 3 New Services and Sample Packages and Services

Source: Company documents.

new services

special health packages
- Ayurvedic Health
- Brain Wellness: Preventive Medicine for the Mind
- Pregnancy Health

medical
- Breast Cancer Prevention
- Natural Medicine for the Home
- Pregnancy & Childbirth Counseling

movement therapy
- Align & Lengthen
- Energize Your Relationships
- Movement Principles for Yoga
- Real Bodies Moving

food & nutrition
- All About Carbohydrates, Insulin Resistance & Blood Sugar
- Beauty of Nutrition
- CustomVite™
- Digestive Wellness
- Eating for Energy
- Fastest Meals Imaginable
- Maximize Metabolism for Weight Loss
- Menopause Matters
- Neuronutrition, Stress & Brain Health

spiritual awareness
- Embodying Yoga
- Total Yoga

fitness
- Express Workout
- Forever Fit
- Weight Loss Workout

therapeutic bodywork & massage
- Bindi Shiodhara
- Canyon Hydra-Stone
- Integrative Bodywork
- Lymphatic Massage

skin care & salon services
- Ayurvedic Facial
- Ayurvedic Pedicure
- Buff Nails
- Gentleman's Scalp Renewal
- Hey Mom!
- Infusia Treatment
- Sisley Anti-Aging Facial

package allowances

Your package stay includes allowances for services in two categories, Health & Healing and Spa & Sports (refer to your confirmation information for allowance details). Your Program Coordinator can help you choose the services that you'll enjoy and benefit from most.

Health & Healing Services
- Medical & Nursing
- Behavioral Health
- Acupuncture & Energy Medicine
- Exercise Physiology
- Spiritual Awareness
- Movement Therapy
- Food & Nutrition

Spa & Sports Services
- Fitness & Sports
- Outdoor Sports
- Therapeutic Bodywork & Massage
- Skin Care & Salon
- Metaphysical

Complimentary
Many experiences at Canyon Ranch are available without charge. Lunch & Learn, hikes, bike rides, cross-country skiing are all complimentary. Check the postings in the Spa and *This Week at Canyon Ranch* for information.

EXHIBIT 3 New Services and Sample Packages and Services (*Continued*)

SPECIAL HEALTH PACKAGES

Sign up: Ext. 5325 or 5439

○ OPTIMAL LIVING[SM] *4 nights or longer* **Fee: $985**

Work with an integrated team of Canyon Ranch health professionals who will create a personalized plan to help broaden your awareness in health, fitness, nutrition, movement, stress management and creative expression.

Your package begins with an Optimal Health Consultation with a physician or psychotherapist and may include a combination of sessions with a physician, psychotherapist, movement therapist, Chinese medicine practitioner, exercise physiologist, nutritionist or demo chef. You'll work closely with our team to develop a plan to take home.

These services are in addition to those in a spa package:

- Pre-arrival interview
- 50-minute Optimal Health Consultation
- $630 allowance for Health & Healing Services
- Final wrap-up and phone follow-up

Note: *For people over 50 who have not had recent health evaluations, we recommend the Ultraprevention package.*

○ ARTHRITIS/PAIN MANAGEMENT *4 nights or longer* **Fee: $1,250**

If you have chronic pain from arthritis or any other condition, this package can help you live a fuller life. Our integrated approach uses nutritional and natural therapeutics, mind-body techniques, immune system modulation and musculoskeletal assessment.

We combine physical, behavioral, nutritional and spiritual approaches that lead to relief or better coping mechanisms. We can also provide follow-up communication with your primary care physician.

These services are in addition to those in a spa package:

- Pre-arrival interview
- 50-minute consultation with a physician
- Special Needs Assessment with a physical therapist
- Movement Therapy consultation
- Acupuncture or Chinese Herbal consultation
- Behavioral health consultation
- Healing Foods nutrition consultation
- 30-minute follow-up with a physician
- Healing Touch
- Final wrap-up and phone follow-up

○ ULTRAMETABOLISM: NEW APPROACHES TO WEIGHT LOSS *3 nights or longer* **Fee: $1,800**

Let an experienced team of Canyon Ranch specialists guide you through new approaches to diagnosis and treatment of obesity or weight problems. The latest clinical advances are available to help you balance the hormones, behavior, and brain chemistry that govern your eating pattern and weight loss or gain. Go beyond the frenzy of high-carb/low-carb, high-fat/low-fat and other confusing diets to unlock the gateway to healthy weight, increased energy and healthy aging.

These services are in addition to those in a spa package:

- Pre-arrival interview
- 50-minute Optimal Health Consultation
- Metabolic Exercise Assessment and Exercise Assessment follow-up
- DEXA Body Composition Test
- $500 allowance toward laboratory tests that may include:
  - Blood Glucose and insulin levels before and after glucose challenge
  - Thyroid function
  - Cholesterol & Heart Health Profile

(Other specialized testing may be recommended for an additional fee.)

- Maximize Metabolism for Weight Loss
- Two Food Habit Management Consultations
- Final wrap-up
- 30-minute phone follow-up with physician
- 30-minute phone follow-up with nutritionist

EXHIBIT 3 New Services and Sample Packages and Services (*Continued*)

SPA & SPORTS SERVICES • therapeutic bodywork & massage

Sign up: Ext. 5439

signature services

Canyon Ranch has created special treatments for you to enjoy at any of our properties.

MANGO SUGAR GLO

Fee: $120

The organic healing effects of the desert's aloe plant and the fragrant quality of the mango fruit combine in this truly luxurious Canyon Ranch original treatment. Derived from natural products – raw sugars, jojoba oil and aloe vera among others – this body scrub enhances your skin with rejuvenating and moisturizing effects. It begins with a light exfoliation to clear and balance skin. The vitamin-enhanced, hydrating qualities of the mango bodywash gently cleanse and condition. Ultimately, a vitamin-enriched mango moisturizer is applied to soften and smooth even the most sensitive skin. 50 minutes.

CANYON STONE MASSAGE

Fee: $165

Smooth, rounded basalt stones are heated in water then lubricated with essential oil and applied to the body as an extension of the therapist's hands. The heat within the stones penetrates your muscle tissue inducing deep relaxation without overheating. Only available from 10 a.m. to 5 p.m. 75 minutes.

EUPHORIA℠

Fee: $230

In the candlelit environment of our Spa Suite, music plays softly as you are draped in bath sheets, and your face is enveloped in towels dipped in sage oil. An aromatherapy scalp massage is followed by a warm botanical body mask. After the mask is gently buffed, you're immersed in a soaking tub for a revitalizing bath. Your experience concludes with a light, soothing massage using warm herb-infused oil. 100 minutes.

LULUR RITUAL

Fee: $230

This luxurious beauty ritual from Central Java begins with an effective combination of energetic massage techniques using jasmine frangipani oil followed by exfoliation with turmeric and a yogurt wash. Then enjoy a relaxing soak in a bath with floating rose petals. An application of jasmine frangipani aloe body lotion completes the ritual. Lulur leaves the skin with a radiant glow. 100 minutes.

massage therapies

Our therapists use a variety of subtle, stimulating and effective techniques to achieve overall relaxation and muscle rejuvenation.

CANYON RANCH MASSAGE

Fee: 50 minutes – $95; 100 minutes – $190

This classic full-body massage is a Canyon Ranch staple. Therapists adapt their eclectic massage techniques to your needs to increase circulation, relieve tense muscles and promote relaxation. Choose a 50- or 100-minute session.

SHIATSU

Fee: 50 minutes – $95; 100 minutes – $190

Shiatsu uses pressure and passive stretches throughout the body to shift the chi into better balance. This balances and improves the energetic system of the body, leaving you feeling centered and connected in mind, body and spirit. Please wear loose, comfortable clothing. Choose a 50- or 100-minute session.

SPORTS MASSAGE

Fee: $95

This personalized massage focuses on areas of need. The therapist applies specific techniques to reduce muscle tension, increase range of motion and provide a warm-up or cool-down for a particular activity. (Not a full-body massage.) 50 minutes.

of Canyon Ranch was the Health and Healing operation, a function staffed with medical doctors, nutritionists, behaviorists, and exercise physiologists. Canyon Ranch executives believed that, if properly integrated, the Health and Healing Department could offer important synergies with other departments. Michael Tompkins, assistant general manager at the Lenox, Massachusetts, resort, was in charge of all revenue-generating departments. In early 2004, he explained: "If Health and Healing recommends that you have shiatsu, that recommendation elevates the level of that service because a health professional recommended you do it. It raises the caliber of the spa services."

Of the three departments, Health and Healing showed the fastest growth but accounted for the lowest contribution to profitability. The leading department on the profitability front was the Hotel, followed by the Spa. Simon Marxer, Spa director, explained:

> When Health and Healing was started, it was accepted that we were going to lose money every year on it. This is no longer the case, but the flow-through remains much lower. A nutritionist makes around $60 out of the $105 you pay for the service, while a fitness instructor will make around $40 and a massage therapist around $30. As a result of the higher commissions paid to the Health and Healing professionals, the profit for Canyon Ranch is lower.

SpaClubs

The SpaClubs complemented the Canyon Ranch destination resorts and focused on spa, fitness, and salon services but lacked a strong health and healing component. In 2004, the two SpaClubs were housed in third-party properties—the Venetian resort in Las Vegas, Nevada, and the Gaylord Palms Resort & Convention Center in Kissimmee, Florida. The SpaClubs were designed to serve the needs of the guests of these properties—largely convention goers. A third SpaClub had recently been opened on the cruise ship Queen Mary 2. Mayersohn explained the role of the SpaClubs: "SpaClubs are 'a touch of Canyon Ranch.' They were designed to introduce customers to the brand. The synergy between the SpaClubs and resorts is still a little tenuous, but we expect the SpaClub on the Queen Mary 2 to be more of a feeder because the demographics are similar."

Canyon Ranch Talent Strategy

As a luxury destination, Canyon Ranch was extremely attentive to service with a 2.5:1 staff-to-guest ratio. For example, Canyon Ranch in the Berkshire Mountains of western Massachusetts had approximately 700 employees on property for an estimated "full-house" count of 212 guests. But executives were quick to point out that a visitor to Canyon Ranch would receive uniquely attentive service. Tompkins explained: "The service is not five-star stuffy; there are no bellmen in white gloves here. Our staff are real people acting in a genuine manner to help you achieve your goals."

During recruitment, Canyon Ranch focused on finding people who would provide excellence in the position and would complement the set of skills currently available at the site. The fit of a new recruit's personality with the firm's culture was also an important factor. Applicants in Health and Healing were given a topic and were asked to give a presentation to the area directors and other members of the recruiting team. Applicants in the Spa Department were asked to perform two or three services in their area of expertise.

Outstanding professional qualifications, though, had to be complemented by an outgoing personality, friendliness, and genuine excitement about the job. Selecting people with the right personality was considered one of the critical factors for new hires at Canyon Ranch. Marxer aptly captured this culture: "We just don't say no. We'll find a way to meet guests' requests."

The Canyon Ranch Customer

Canyon Ranch executives had developed substantial knowledge about customers over the years. This was particularly true of the approximately 17,000 customers (some returning multiple times) visiting each destination resort every year. Mayersohn explained: "Our prototypical guest is a 47-year-old woman, with grown kids, with a high household income, active, generally fit, and who does not compromise on wanting the best."

While women represented about 75 percent of Canyon Ranch's customer base, men represented a growing segment. This growth was imputed to the aging of the baby boomer generation and the increasing attention that men paid to their health and well-being. This trend appeared to be confirmed by the growing interest customers showed in the Health and Healing Department, with 6 percent of guests purchasing a package focusing on this area and generating about 16 percent of ancillary service revenue. Senior management was intent on fostering the trend. Tompkins explained:

> We have been in business for 25 years, and we have not been known for our wellness component. We have been known for being the best spa in the world. The majority of our clientele comes here looking for the spa vacation. We are attempting to create an awareness of our health and healing component without disrupting the spa vacationers. Ideally, after customers try it, a whole new world opens up for them.

The primary feeder markets for both health resorts were the New York metro and the eastern corridor areas. As a consequence, Tucson relied almost exclusively on fly-in customers, while Lenox served almost exclusively a drive-in market. Cross-property traffic was estimated to be just below 10 percent. Most customers bought packages. These included the hotel stay and meals, as well as some services or vouchers that could be used toward the purchase of services in specific areas (see Exhibit 4). Guests were required to stay for either three or four nights and spent $2,000 to $2,500 per stay, taking, on average, a little over two services a day (either included in their package or a la carte). Lectures, fitness classes, and outdoor activities were all complimentary except when one requested a one-on-one session with the instructor. Some guests also purchased ancillary products such as books or CDs. Particularly popular were beauty supplies, generally purchased after service at the salon. The success of these sales, estimated to exceed half a million dollars at the Lenox resort alone, had convinced Canyon Ranch executives to launch their own proprietary line of skin-care products.

At any given time, about 55 percent of the in-house guests had visited Canyon Ranch before. The firm calculated that 18 percent of the customers returned more than once to Canyon Ranch health resorts, with guests returning multiple times over their lifetime and some guests returning multiple times a year. Tompkins reasoned:

> People return over and over several times a year when they get what Canyon Ranch is all about and we become part of their lifestyle. We have a true integrative-care model. When was the last time that you spent an hour with your physician? When you go see a doctor and you say, "I feel OK, I just want to feel better," they look at you like you are crazy, whereas here this is what Canyon Ranch is all about.

Particularly loyal customers had the option of becoming centennial members. Membership offered significant discounts and perks. After paying a flat fee proportional to the number of free nights the guest wanted to purchase, members were entitled to stay at Canyon Ranch for 50 percent of the room rate and receive a 10 percent discount on services purchased a la carte for the seven-year duration of the membership. The 798 current centennial members were also allowed to visit for only two nights when current occupancy levels allowed. Returning customers received tokens of appreciation (branded merchandise such as T-shirts and bags), but Canyon Ranch did not have a formal recognition or reward program.

Canyon Ranch did not advertise heavily, instead focusing on direct communication and affiliations with similar suitable partners. Mayersohn commented:

> We are a word-of-mouth referral business with a long sales lead time, not an impulse buy. Our core strategy is creating word of mouth. We do customer events and give parties with partners—like Williams-Sonoma, for example. We invite customers, and they bring a guest who has never been to Canyon Ranch. Partners will become the most important part of our growth in the next two years. We get one or two calls a week from people who want to do something with us, but we have to be carefully selective.

While Canyon Ranch did receive about 20 percent of its business from travel agents (including group business), the firm had recently expanded the direct communication to the electronic space using e-mail and its Web site for direct marketing.

EXHIBIT 4 Canyon Ranch: Rates and Packages

Source: Company documents.

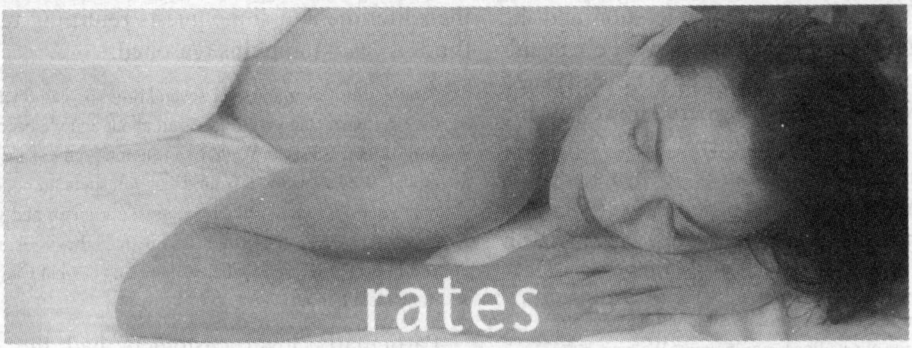

OCTOBER 19 THROUGH NOVEMBER 29, 2003

		Deluxe Room		Luxury Suite		
		Single	Double	Double	Triple	Quad
3 Nights	Arrive Sun. - Tues.	$2,030	$1,670	$2,030	$1,670	$1,480
	Arrive Wed. - Sat.	$2,490	$2,060	$2,490	$2,060	$1,760
4 Nights	Arrive Sun. - Tues.	$2,670	$2,230	$2,670	$2,230	$2,020
	Arrive Wed. - Sat.	$3,130	$2,670	$3,130	$2,670	$2,290
5 Nights	Arrive any day	$3,500	$2,930	$3,500	$2,930	$2,640
7 Nights	Arrive any day	$4,960	$4,140	$4,960	$4,140	$3,740

NOVEMBER 30, 2003 THROUGH MARCH 18, 2004

Excluding December 24 to 31 and February 13 to 15

		Deluxe Room		Luxury Suite		
		Single	Double	Double	Triple	Quad
3 Nights	Arrive Sun. - Tues.	$1,890	$1,520	$1,970	$1,460	$1,320
	Arrive Wed. - Sat.	$2,320	$1,900	$2,360	$1,860	$1,610
4 Nights	Arrive Sun. - Tues.	$2,420	$1,960	$2,420	$1,960	$1,710
	Arrive Wed. - Sat.	$3,100	$2,480	$3,100	$2,480	$2,150
5 Nights	Arrive any day	$3,270	$2,710	$3,270	$2,710	$2,390
7 Nights	Arrive any day	$4,850	$3,920	$4,850	$3,920	$3,520

MARCH 19 THROUGH JUNE 30, 2004

		Deluxe Room		Luxury Suite		
		Single	Double	Double	Triple	Quad
3 Nights	Arrive Sun. - Tues.	$2,030	$1,670	$2,030	$1,670	$1,480
	Arrive Wed. - Sat.	$2,490	$2,060	$2,490	$2,060	$1,760
4 Nights	Arrive Sun. - Tues.	$2,670	$2,230	$2,670	$2,230	$2,020
	Arrive Wed. - Sat.	$3,130	$2,670	$3,130	$2,670	$2,290
5 Nights	Arrive any day	$3,500	$2,930	$3,500	$2,930	$2,640
7 Nights	Arrive any day	$4,960	$4,140	$4,960	$4,140	$3,740

Rates are per person and include 18 percent service charge and applicable sales tax. Rates are subject to change without notice. Minimum 3-night stay.

EXHIBIT 4 Canyon Ranch: Rates and Packages (*Continued*)

Thousands of guests have discovered the vacation of a lifetime at Canyon Ranch, an environment entirely dedicated to relaxation, recreation, total health and well-being, and going further than you thought possible.

At Canyon Ranch in the Berkshires, anything is possible. Come out and play, or simply unwind – every moment belongs to you.

Discover an astounding, uncommonly valuable vacation. Find your happiest self at Canyon Ranch.

Your all-inclusive Canyon Ranch in the Berkshires getaway includes

- Gracious accommodations - all with Frette bed linens to satisfy, delight and surround you in comfort
- Three meals daily – fresh gourmet creations combining taste and nutrition, beautifully presented
- Use of all spa facilities, indoor and outdoor pools, and tennis & sports courts – no extra spa or court fees
- Fitness activities – more than 45 each day for all levels and interests
- Hiking – in dramatic mountain splendor
- Biking – seasonal daily tours through the charming New England countryside
- Seasonal skiing and snowshoeing
- Health & fitness assessment and brief consultation with a registered nurse
- Presentations by fitness, nutrition, stress management and medical experts
- Lunchtime cooking instruction in our fully equipped Demonstration Kitchen
- Self-service laundry and supplies
- Lending library of books, CDs and videos
- All gratuities – no additional tipping is required or expected
- Round-trip airport transfers for Hartford or Albany airports or Albany (Renssalaer) train station
- Unlimited local calls and incoming fax transmissions
- Access to long-distance carriers and toll-free numbers without surcharge

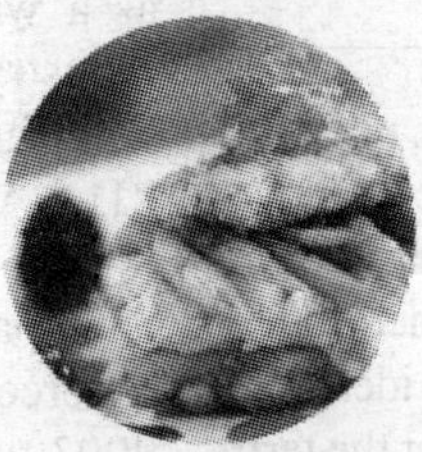

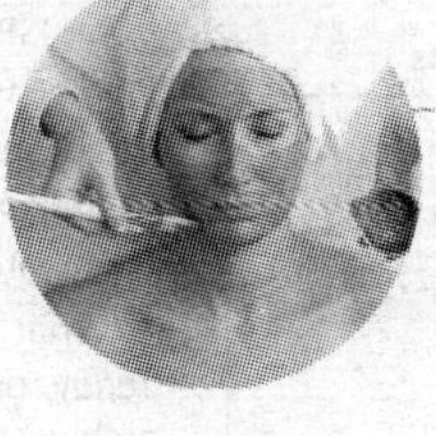

Each Canyon Ranch vacation includes allowances for Health & Healing and Spa & Sports Services.

You'll make your selection during an appointment with a Program Coordinator who will help you plan your stay.

Choose from the following:

Health & Healing Services

More than 75 consultations and workshops in:

- Preventive & integrative medicine
- Acupuncture & energy medicine
- Behavioral health
- Nutrition & food management
- Exercise physiology
- Movement therapy
- Spiritual awareness

Spa & Sports Services

- Fitness & racquet sports
- Seasonal outdoor sports including canoeing, kayaking, cross country skiing and snowshoeing
- Therapeutic massage & bodywork
- Skin care
- Beauty salon
- Metaphysical

Over 2 million unique visitors viewed the Canyon Ranch Web site in 2003. Executives were entertaining proposals to improve the Web site from its current static design to an interactive one. Mayersohn discussed the philosophy behind it: "Because your Canyon Ranch experience is customized to your needs, we want your Web site experience to be customized to your interests and needs as well."

The Spa Industry

Since the times of ancient Greece and Rome, mankind had enjoyed a variety of thermal and aquatic therapies for healing and relaxation purposes. The term "spa" originated from a town in Belgium renowned for its baths and mineral springs and had come to identify a place to receive a wide range of services. Yet the term had lost some of its meaning due to its broad use to include a wide range of services, traditional or modern, and sizes. In fact, in the United States, the spa industry was dominated by many small operations and a few large companies. According to the International Spa Association (ISPA), in June 2002 there were 9,632 spas in the United States—up from 1,374 in 1990.[2] The census included such diverse outfits as day spas (outfits without a lodging element), spas housed in resorts and hotels, destination spas (outfits where the spa is the principal draw for the customer), and so on—operated by approximately 7,400 different organizations (see Exhibit 5).[3]

EXHIBIT 5 Composition of the Spa Industry

Source: The ISPA's 2002 SPA Industry Study, PricewaterhouseCoopers, p. 3.

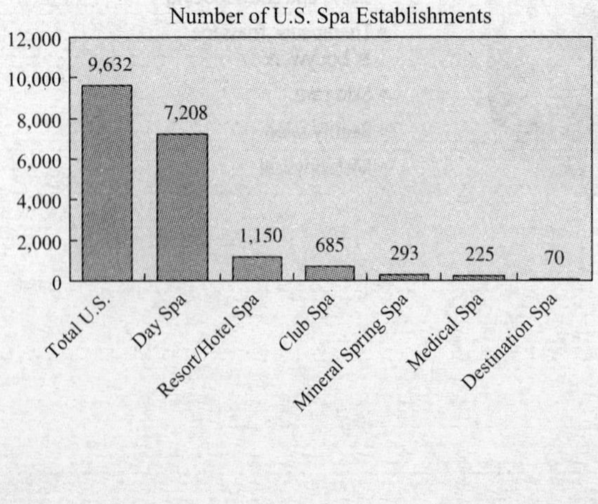

This growth in offerings was fueled by the growth in spa visits—from an estimated 57 million in 1997 to 155.8 million in 2001.[4] All this growth, attributed in large part to the aging baby boomer population seeking longevity, propelled a $10.7 billion industry by 2001,[5] up significantly from two years earlier (see Exhibit 6). This trend was confirmed by many customers no longer simply seeking a spa experience to be pampered but as a way to a healthier life.[6] But while the spa industry was growing, the spa experience was still far from being mainstream. According to "The American Spa-Goer Survey," 11 percent of the U.S. population (over 16 years old) visited a day spa, 7 percent visited a resort/hotel spa, and 1 percent visited a destination spa in the 2002 to 2003 time frame (see Exhibit 6).

Despite industry growth, operations remained generally low tech, and relatively little attention was paid to the potential offered by information technology. Because of its very nature as a service business characterized by personal attention and coproduction,[7] the spa industry had traditionally been a high-touch, people-intensive business. Computerization was often seen as a threat, rather than an opportunity, due to its perceived potential to depersonalize and dehumanize the experience. Moreover, since many spa goers were seeking an escape from their increasingly stressful office lives, the industry was very careful to avoid any technology that might damage the carefully choreographed atmosphere of the setting.

[2] The ISPA's 2000 SPA Industry Study, PricewaterhouseCoopers, 2001, p. 26.

[3] Ibid., p. 3.

[4] The ISPA's 2000 SPA Industry Study, PricewaterhouseCoopers, 2001, p. 29.

[5] "What Really Drives the Spa Industry?" *Massage Today*, online at http://www.massagetoday.com/archives/2003/01/21.html, accessed January 14, 2004.

[6] The ISPA's 2002 SPA Industry Study—Executive Summary, http://spas.about.com/library/weekly/aa090602f.htm, accessed January 14, 2004.

[7] The term *coproduction* characterizes industries where the customer has to be actively present in the creation of the product or service.

EXHIBIT 6 Industry Growth

Source: *The ISPA's 2002 SPA Industry Survey*, PricewaterhouseCoopers, 2001.
Source: *The American Spa-goer Survey*, 1999 and 2003, ISPA.

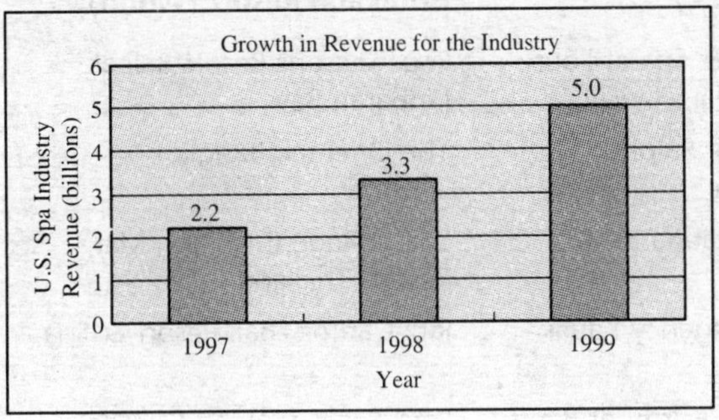

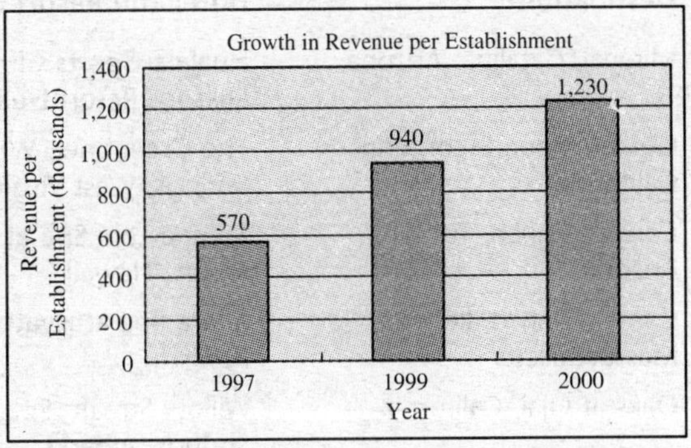

Percentage of Spa Visitors

Visited Once or More in the Last 12 Months	1999[a]	2003[a]
Day Spa	7%	11%
Resort/Hotel Spa	5	7
Destination Spa	1	1

[a] People ages 16 or above.

Frequency of Visiting a Spa during the Last 12 Months (1999)

	Day Spa Visitor		Other Type of Spa Visitor	
	One or More[a]	Mean[b]	One or More[a]	Mean[b]
Day Spa	100%[c]	5.0[c]	44%	2.1
Resort/ Hotel Spa	31	1.8	84[c]	2.5
Destination Spa	16	2.1	41[c]	1.9
Cruise Spa	8	2.1	15[c]	1.7

[a] Does not equal 100% due to multiple response.
[b] Among those who took one or more trips.
[c] Denotes a statistically significant difference from the comparison group at 95% confidence.

The Competition

Canyon Ranch was widely recognized as the gold standard in the industry. It commanded rates 25 percent to 30 percent higher than other destination spas—with the possible exception of Golden Door. Moreover, its astonishing array of services and its Health and Healing Department set it apart from most competitors. Mayersohn discussed the competition:

> We do compete with the destination resorts that have spas. Two things differentiate us: the health and healing component that is unmatched in any similar setting, and the totality of all that is available under one roof. If a massage is all you want, there are many places to go. If you want to be open to the possibility of a life-enhancing experience, Canyon Ranch provides more options than anywhere else.

Customers who simply sought standard spa services such as massages, fitness, and salon services often included location as an important driver of the purchase decision and had a number of options to choose from (see Exhibit 7). Many of these guests also traveled to different destinations

EXHIBIT 7 Top Spas according to *Travel and Leisure Magazine*

Source: *Travel and Leisure Magazine*, online at http://www.travelandleisure.com/worldsbest/pressrelease-spas.cfm, accessed January 14, 2004.

Destination	Hotel and Resort (U.S.)	Hotel and Resort (World)
Miraval, Catalina, Arizona	Hualalai Sports Club & Spa at Four Seasons Resort Hualalai, Hawaii	Four Seasons Resort Bali at Jimbaran Bay
Golden Door, Escondido, California	The Greenbrier, White Sulphur Springs, West Virginia	The Oriental, Bangkok
Canyon Ranch, Tucson, Arizona	Mauna Lani Spa at Mauna Lani Resort, Hawaii	Spa at Regent Chiang Mai Resort, Thailand
Canyon Ranch, Lenox, Massachusetts	Anara Spa at Hyatt Regency Kauai Resort	Ritz-Carlton, Bali Resort & Spa
Oaks at Ojai, California	Willow Stream Spa at Fairmont Banff Springs, Alberta	Four Seasons Hotel George V, Paris
Mii Amo, Sedona, Arizona	Spa Bellagio, Las Vegas	Banyan Tree Spa Phuket, Thailand
Rancho La Puerta, Tecate, Mexico	Golden Door Spa at the Boulders, Carefree, Arizona	Brenner's Park-Hotel & Spa, Baden-Baden, Germany
Ten Thousand Waves, Santa Fe, New Mexico	Plaza Spa, New York City	Le Sirenuse, Positano, Italy
BodyHoliday at LeSport, St. Lucia	Four Seasons Resort Maui at Wailea	The Ritz, Paris
Palms at Palm Springs, California	Spa Grande at Grand Wailea Resort Hotel, Maui	Las Ventanas al Paraíso, Los Cabos, Mexico

seeking variety of setting between purchases. Yet Canyon Ranch, because of its history and reputation, was able to attract a substantial number of spa goers, as Marxer explained: "Over 50 percent of our customers visit Health and Healing because it is part of their package. But there is a big chunk of our guests that are here to get nothing but spa services and be pampered."

While senior management believed that no other spa resorts could currently compete head on with Canyon Ranch, there were signs of increasing competition. Tompkins explained: "Most of our competitors have either a very high spa component or a very high health and healing component. Because of our longevity, we have a huge menu of services that most spas don't have as well as fitness classes and lectures. Our differentiator the whole time has been Health and Healing. It has become part of the spa, integrated under one roof."

But there were signs that some competitors were beginning to encroach on Canyon Ranch's unique value proposition. Industry observers were seeing some convergence between medicine and spa services. This trend was manifested in day spas aligning themselves with medical professionals, not only plastic surgeons and dermatologists, but also those practicing many other branches of medicine, such as nutritionists, homeopathic doctors, physical therapists, and general practitioners. At the same time, some medical professionals were beginning to include spa treatments in their practice, and some hospitals were including alternative treatments in their portfolio. While precisely estimating the extent of this trend remained difficult, management was watching it closely, as Mayersohn indicated: "These are potential threats to our uniqueness. Many of the large luxury destination resorts with sizable spas now are building a medical or wellness component. On the other side, hospitals are adding spas and wellness centers with nutritionists."

Substantially more difficult was the analysis of competition from substitute luxury purchases. A destination spa was a big-ticket item that often competed with other vacation opportunities. But, as Mayersohn explained, the potential pool of substitutes was virtually unlimited: "We debate constantly what substitutes to our product are. We compete with trips to Europe, cruises. . . . really, we compete with anything that may cost five grand of discretionary income. . . . We could compete with a plasma-screen TV, for example."

Information Technology at Canyon Ranch

The corporate IT function at Canyon Ranch numbered 20 professionals headed by Mike Randle, corporate IT director, who reported to the COO and CFO. The function was responsible for internal software development and maintenance, as well as evaluating software packages and performing help-desk and support tasks. Randle recounted this evolution: "In 1996, the IT director position was created. At the time, Canyon Ranch had one programmer, one or two tech-support people, and one manager who had worked her way up from the accounting department. The focus was on maintaining the only computer system—the property management system."

The growth had come following the evolution of the role that IT played at Canyon Ranch. While the IT function had historically been regarded as a support function with the main goal of supporting the many operational systems—property management system, reservations, spa and wellness service scheduling, accounting, purchasing, payroll—IT was now being viewed as increasingly strategic. This change was a result of the need for business intelligence, decision-support functionalities, and expected growth, as well as some turnover in senior management. The business expectation of what IT could deliver was growing rapidly. The pressure came from the top and from operational personnel who saw the potential value of information to enable better decision making. But, as Marxer explained, some difficulties remained:

> It can be a big transition to make decisions based on numbers rather than anecdotal information. In beauty services, for example, we found out that the utilization of therapists after 4:00 PM was high, but utilization of facilities was low. This indicates few people on staff who are booked all the time. But traditionally, beauticians believe that nobody wants a pedicure after four—it's late, their nails are wet before going to dinner. Using the utilization report, I was able to convince them.

Canyon Ranch relied on a decentralized IT infrastructure with both the destination resorts and the SpaClubs working relatively independently. The heart of the infrastructure at the destination resorts was the property management system—Computerized Lodging Systems (CLS)—a UNIX-based legacy application written in BASIC that the company had been using since 1986 through multiple versions. Canyon Ranch owned the source code to CLS, which made it easy to customize, and had worked in partnership with Computerized Lodging Systems Inc. to develop its complex and robust scheduling component for Spa and Health and Healing services. Other activities were not tracked by CLS. Like most operational computer systems, CLS focused on efficiently processing transactions rather than collecting decision-support data. This data was used to generate utilization reports for Spa and Health and Healing services. For popular services and activities, paper-based waiting lists were maintained. Campsey explained: "To sign up for activities included in the rate such as fitness classes, outdoor sports, and lectures, the guests use a paper-based system. For reporting purposes, the instructors input the number of people who took the service in a database I have recently created."

CLS also represented the primary source of guest data. Traditionally, the company had been able to collect stay information (e.g., type of room, number of guests in the party, room rate and charges, address). Randle explained: "We have guest-history data dating back 10 years, even though beyond 1999 it gets questionable. We know when they were here, and we know more or less what they spent, but we don't necessarily know what they spent it on."

The depth of this information had increased significantly with the 1999 upgrade of CLS to version 16. The firm could now track what paid services a customer scheduled, when, with whom they took the service, and similar transactional data. Like many luxury operations, the company had also been compiling significant amounts of data about guest stays (e.g., when guests asked for specific accommodations or visited on anniversaries or other important dates). This information was recorded in free-form text and could not be easily parsed by automated software.

To complement the functionality of CLS, Canyon Ranch in the Berkshires had recently implemented Guestware, a software application designed to collect preferences and support incident tracking, rapid response, and guest surveying. While Guestware had the potential to improve relationships with customers, it was currently a stand-alone application used primarily to record guest preferences. Campsey expanded on the current use of Guestware: "We mainly use Guestware for preferences and incident tracking, but it does not integrate well with CLS yet. The manager on duty should be able to go in and look at what happened during the day and take action immediately. But this does not happen."

The firm did not have point-of-sale (POS) software either in the restaurant or the salon, where customers could purchase beauty products. A guest would schedule an appointment with the salon, and the appropriate charge was posted to CLS. If a guest purchased beauty products, the value of the purchase would be added to the salon services, but it could not be tracked independently. As the profile of the IT function continued to rise, Randle explained his role: "One of the most important things I focus on is to enable management to use technology to answer operational questions without us being the bottleneck."

Delivering the Canyon Ranch Experience: Canyon Ranch in the Berkshires

Typically a guest booked a Canyon Ranch vacation by calling the property they were interested in visiting. Three weeks prior to their scheduled arrival, the guest called a 1-800 number and spoke to prebooking personnel (part of the reservation department). This call was designed to obtain some background information about the prospective guest's goals for their stay (e.g., relieve stress and relax, quit smoking, relieve back pain, lose weight) and some relevant background information (e.g., current exercise level, preferences for treatments, such as time of day, preferred pressure level, therapist's gender). If possible, specific services were also booked at this time. Prospective guests were sent a health questionnaire that they were asked to return prior to their arrival.

Upon arrival, guests checked in at the security gate and were announced and greeted by name once they drove up to the inn. After checking in and getting settled in their room, new guests received a brief orientation and a tour of the facilities. Then guests met with a program coordinator who could look up services prebooked by the reservations department and counsel guests. This "handoff" between reservations and program coordination was sometimes problematic, as Marxer, formerly a program coordinator, explained: "Ideally, program coordinators will know what you want upon arrival; you don't have to repeat what your goals are, what your history is. If you suffered from bulimia as a youth, you don't want to have to repeat yourself. The program coordinator should say: 'I know that eating has been an issue for you before, and here is how I think we should proceed.'"

Canyon Ranch in the Berkshires employed 15 full-time coordinators, seven part time, and a few on call who could fill in during high-demand periods. As Marxer explained, the program coordinators served both as counselor, trying to connect with guests to understand their needs and make appropriate recommendations, and as concierge, helping the guest navigate the staggering array of services and options available:

> Program coordinators need a unique blend of skills; they need to make the guest's entry into the environment as easy as possible. Sometimes they need to probe and connect with the guest, but they also need to be very practical and efficient in booking services. Tenure in the job helps a lot. When you are new and trying to remember what the heck the code was for that one service, you are not really tuned in to what the guest is telling you. You can't really connect with the guest.

Staffing the position was challenging, with a lead time of six weeks of training before the program coordinators could begin to interact with guests and an estimated six months on the job for them to become proficient in the position. Turnover in the position was high, with the department turning over an estimated 50 percent every year and 20 percent of trainees not completing the preliminary six weeks. Reflecting on the causes of this high turnover, Marxer reasoned: "Right now the program coordinator is not a highly paid position. Paying them more would challenge our entire compensation scheme. Moreover, how many people want to make program coordinator their career? It can be stressful; some guests don't want to hear that 4:00 PM is prime time for a massage and their preference is not available."

Program coordinators needed to be very flexible and be able to think on their feet, as every scheduling request could pose conflicts that needed to be quickly and efficiently resolved. When conflicts arose, coordinators tried to satisfy the guest request, working in tandem with therapists on their schedules and using waiting lists, or they provided alternative options for the customer to evaluate. With their schedule worked out, guests were free to enjoy the many services that Canyon Ranch had to offer and returned to the program coordinators when they had changes in their plans.

Guests were provided with a daily schedule of services they had signed up for—printed from CLS. The service providers had individual vouchers, also printed daily from CLS, for each guest who would visit that day. The vouchers indicated the name of the guest, the service they had booked, and whether they were new or a returning guest. At the scheduled time the guest would either go to the Health and Healing Department or to the Spa and Fitness locker room, depending on the service. If they needed health and healing services, they completed a short questionnaire and then were greeted by the service provider, who would introduce himself or herself, welcome or welcome back the guest, and discuss any issues, concerns, or preferences regarding the service. Upon completion of the service, there was a brief wrap-up session during which the service provider would provide any suggestions and referrals for other services before walking the guest back to the reception area.

The experience in the spa was similar, with the guest being walked to the therapist by a locker room attendant. Any medical alerts or other noteworthy issues (e.g., three months pregnant, recent surgery) that had been noted by medical staff or program coordinators appeared in the form of a code, directly on the voucher. Before beginning, the treatment therapist also introduced himself or herself and discussed any issues or preferences with the guest. Upon completion of the session, he or she walked the guest back to the locker room.

The Future

In early 2004, Canyon Ranch remained the undisputed leader in the destination segment of the spa industry. Yet, in the face of increasing competition from within the industry as well as from substitutes, Canyon Ranch executives were constantly seeking ways to leverage this preeminent position to extend the Canyon Ranch brand and to maintain future dominance in the destination spa segment. The challenge, as Mayersohn framed it, was to grow the company by extending the brand and by improving the performance of the existing business units: "We must integrate our growing array of products under one brand, making sure that we continue to raise the level of consistency among all our business units."

Each business unit was intent on improving the level of customer service and personalization of the Canyon Ranch experience. Canyon Ranch in the Berkshires was at the forefront of this trend, and its management was strongly committed to providing an unparalleled standard of customer service. Yet there existed no readily available blueprint for how to improve on the "best-in-the-business" spa experience. Canyon Ranch management was keenly aware of the potential that customer data offered, as well as the risks of not using it appropriately and with care. A number of questions remained unanswered: Should Canyon Ranch in the Berkshires develop a clear customer relationship management strategy and make it a cornerstone of its positioning as a preeminent destination spa? If so, what should this initiative look like? What was the value of the substantial amounts of data generated during the customer experience? Were there any opportunities to use this data during prospecting? Or during the customer stay? Or even after the stay?

Boeing's e-Enabled Advantage

In 2004, Boeing was the world's largest aerospace company and, for decades, it had dominated the world's commercial aviation market. But the airline industry was reeling from simultaneous blows, including terrorist attacks, rising fuel prices, consolidation, cost pressure, and increasing competitive intensity. Every player in the industry was struggling to survive. Boeing's main rival, European-based Airbus, responded to these pressures through massive investments from its European government owners that enabled it to build planes to compete head-on with Boeing and then to sell them at lower prices. In 1999, Airbus outsold Boeing for the first time in history and Standard & Poor's analysts stated that there was no clear differentiation between Airbus and Boeing planes. While airplanes had long depended on embedded IT for flight controls and operations, it was not until United Airlines flew the first Boeing 777 in 1995, that a Boeing plane had an installed local area network inside the aircraft that could provide real-time information to flight crews, ground personnel, airline executives, and passengers. By 2004, Boeing executives believed that its "e-Enabled Advantage" would be the source of differentiation and leadership for decades to come. As you read the Boeing story, consider the following questions: What steps did Boeing take in its journey to build its e-Enabled Advantage? Is this a sustainable advantage and, if so, for how long? What recommendations do you have for Scott Carson, leader of the company's e-Enabled Advantage initiatives and newly named CEO of Boeing Commercial Airplane Company?

Case 1-4

Boeing's e-Enabled Advantage

> We're asking people at Boeing and in the industry to do things differently. The biggest risks aren't technical; they're cultural.
>
> *Scott Carson, Vice President of Sales, 2005*[1]

In 2004, Boeing was one of the United States' largest manufacturers, with nearly 160,000 employees and a net income of $1.87 billion. It was the world's largest aerospace company, and, for decades, had dominated the world's commercial aviation market. But as the industry reached maturity, Boeing's position in the market began to change. In 1999, its main rival, European-based Airbus, outsold Boeing for the first time, and in 2003, it delivered more airplanes. Pressures intensified after the terrorist attacks of September 11, 2001, which translated into rescheduled airplane orders. Furthermore, airlines in the United States—which made up a large part of Boeing's customer base—were undergoing fundamental changes as they focused on cost structure and consolidation, and increasing operating efficiency became a means for survival. The combination of the industry downturn—catalyzed by the terrorist attacks—and the underlying cost position shortcomings of the industry caused several airlines to either go bankrupt or be on the verge of bankruptcy. Finally, confronted by a highly successful competitor, Boeing faced yet another challenge: differentiating its product. Industry

Professors Lynda M. Applegate and Joseph S. Valacich (Washington State University) and Research Associates Mara E. Vatz and Christoph Schneider prepared this case as the basis for class discussion rather than to illustrate effective or ineffective management.

[1] Author interview, May 24, 2005.

analysts, noting that the market had matured, offered as evidence the "increasing difficulty in differentiating between Airbus and Boeing planes."[2]

It was clear that Boeing needed to adapt to the changing climate. In June 2003, Boeing unveiled a new strategy that executives believed would help its airline customers improve efficiency and profitability and also differentiate its products in the marketplace. The idea was to take advantage of an "e-Enabled" operating environment in which every aspect of an airline's and its suppliers' and partners' operations would be integrated through information technology. By providing airplane information systems that could be better networked with airline ground systems as well as new products, services, and solutions within the networked environment, Boeing could help airlines operate more efficiently while also creating preference for Boeing products and services. While Boeing had long sold services associated with its products, the company was now formulating plans to become a broader services provider by growing the services business around its core products.

In 2004, the leadership of Boeing's commercial airplanes division assembled a team to begin analyzing how the new strategy would affect the airlines, how it would affect Boeing internally, and how it might reposition Boeing in the marketplace. The team presented its findings, and although the new strategy would require great coordination among different business units within Boeing, and the transition into services wouldn't be easy, the idea caught on quickly.

After about two meetings, there was general concurrence that the new strategy was a key part of Boeing's future success. At that point, Lou Mancini, vice president of commercial aviation services, appointed Chris Kettering to serve as the program director. In February 2004, the key players were assembled: Mancini, Kettering, and Scott Carson, who was vice president of the Connexion by Boeing™ business unit at the time. The team had broad support among leaders in Boeing Commercial Airplanes (BCA) as they embarked on this new strategy, but the biggest challenges still lay ahead.

"It's one thing to come up with the answers, and another to actually implement them," Kettering explained. "Getting e-Enabled operations to work in an organization involves personalities, it involves careers and culture."

The group met often to address the challenge of translating ideas into processes. Carson's main concern was breaking down the silos of communication among the different business units. How could they effectively communicate the important points of the strategy, and then open the forums for dialogue? Mancini's objective was to integrate the strategy into each business unit while continuing to run a profitable business. Kettering was tasked with coordinating the entire effort. How would the new strategy fit into each business unit? How could the broad, general ideas be translated into a blueprint, or a process and technical architecture that each business unit would follow? How could they create an integrated message that would help get everyone—both inside and outside Boeing—on board, and would the initiative help transform the company and the industry?

Company Background

In 1916, William Boeing founded an aircraft manufacturing company in the Puget Sound region of Washington State. Boeing, who had made his fortune in the timber industry of the Northeast, had moved to the West Coast in 1903—the same year the Wright Brothers made their famous first flight—and became fascinated with flying after he attended the 1910 Air Meet in Los Angeles. Soon after, he began building planes as a hobby with Navy engineer Conrad Westervelt. Their first plane, the B&W, named for their initials, was a 27.5-foot seaplane that had a top speed of 75 mph. Westervelt was relocated to the East Coast before the plane was

[2] S&P, 2005, p. 24.

completed, but Boeing stayed in Washington, launching the Pacific Aero Products Company (which he renamed, one year later, "the Boeing Airplane Company"). His first customer was the government of New Zealand, which used the B&W for airmail and pilot training. Boeing's new company really took flight, however, when the Navy ordered 53 training sea planes as the United States prepared to enter World War I.[3]

Between World War I and World War II, Boeing grew to be one of the largest aircraft manufacturers in the United States by supplying the military with training and fighting planes, pioneering airmail planes and routes, and developing early passenger planes.[4] During World War II, Boeing was "one of the country's leading defense and space contractors."[5] The B-17 "Flying Fortress" and B-29 "Super Fortress" bombers were an essential military force,[6] and the B-52, an eight-engine bomber that made its debut in 1952, was later used in the Vietnam War, the Persian Gulf War in 1991, and in Afghanistan in 2001.[7] The research and development that took place during the war years set the stage for the coming age of commercial jetliners, which Boeing would dominate for the remainder of the twentieth century.

In 1954, Boeing made its entry into commercial aviation with the Boeing 707—a four-engine jetliner based largely on the C-97 "Stratofreighter," a military-tanker transport—which competed directly with the Douglas DC-8. While Boeing's foray into commercial aviation was risky at first (one major airline president wondered at the time whether Boeing was "in the commercial business to stay"[8]), the success of the 707 eventually helped establish Boeing as a leader in commercial aviation, which until then had been dominated by the Douglas Aircraft Company.[9] The 707 was followed by the 727 in 1962 and the 737 in 1967, and in 1968, Boeing rolled out the 747—its flagship aircraft and the largest civilian aircraft at the time.[10]

In 1968, Thornton "T" Wilson became president of the company and was immediately faced with "impending disaster:"[11] the Apollo project of the 1960s was drawing to a close; Congress had pulled the plug on funding for development of the Super Sonic Transport, which would have been the country's first supersonic commercial jetliner; the cyclical aviation industry was in a downturn; and the 747 had unexpectedly high start-up costs.[12] Wilson was forced to cut Boeing's workforce from 105,000 to 38,000—a move that had a "profound effect on the local economy," raising unemployment in Seattle to 14 percent[13] and inspiring the now famous billboard that read, "Will the last person leaving Seattle turn out the lights."[14]

Ultimately, the layoffs were enough to save the company, and, in the 1970s, Boeing entered a period of prosperity. With its brush with disaster in mind, the company attempted to diversify. Boeing employees embarked on a wide range of projects—from irrigating an eastern Oregon desert, to managing projects for the Federal Department of Housing and Urban Development, to building voice scramblers for police departments?[15] By the 1980s, however, Boeing had returned to its core of building airplanes, adding the 757 and 767 to the 7-series and releasing upgraded versions of the 737.

Throughout the 1980s, Boeing was virtually unrivaled in commercial aviation. Its two main competitors, McDonnell Douglas in the United

[3] *International directory of company histories*, St. James Press: Chicago.

[4] Boeing Annual Report, 1990.

[5] Eugene Rodgers, *Flying High: The Story of Boeing and the Rise of the Jetliner Industry* (New York: The Atlantic Monthly Press, 1996), p. 6.

[6] *International directory of company histories.*

[7] www.boeing.com, accessed March 2006.

[8] Robert J. Serling, *Legend and Legacy: The Story of Boeing and Its People* (New York: St. Martin's Press, 1992), p. 137.

[9] *International directory of company histories.*

[10] http://www.boeing.com/history/boeing, accessed December 2005.

[11] *International directory of company histories.*

[12] http://www.boeing.com/history/boeing, accessed December 2005.

[13] *International directory of company histories*, St. James Press: Chicago.

[14] http://boeing.com/history/boeing/markets.html, accessed December 2005.

[15] Ibid.

States and Airbus in Europe, held less than half of the market share combined, and neither had a family of airplanes that could compete with Boeing's versatile 7-series (see Exhibit 1A).

The second half of the 1980s and the early 1990s witnessed nearly unmitigated growth for Boeing. Although the defense and space sectors struggled as the U.S. government cut funding, the commercial aviation division prospered. Air travel had been growing steadily since 1970,[16] and Boeing broke its own sales records for six years in a row, starting in 1985.[17] In the 1980s alone, Boeing received orders for more than 3,500 jetliners, which represented half of all jetliners sold by Boeing since the first 707 order was placed in 1956;[18] and in 1987, the 737 surpassed the 727 as the world's best-selling jetliner.[19] In 1989, Boeing announced plans to develop the next airplane in the 7-series, the 777, to be released in 1995.

By 1992, Boeing employed nearly 150,000 people and posted net earnings of $1.55 billion[20] (see Exhibit 2A). It was the country's leading exporter and was considered one of the nation's most admired companies. The company that started as a mere hobby had become "the king of the jet makers."[21]

Mature Market

> Boeing, with its towering 60 percent share of the world's commercial airliner market, appears to have reached the pinnacle of its corporate might. Decay often follows, bred by resistance to change and complacency. Could it be that Boeing is fated to wither like so many other once-world-class U.S. manufacturers?
>
> *Barron's National Business and Financial Weekly, 1993*[22]

In 1990, Frank Shrontz, Boeing's president and CEO, wrote in the annual report that, despite the steady production increases over the last three years, "contingency plans [were] in place to respond if market demand declines significantly."[23] Shrontz's anticipation of a downturn in the market was well timed. Boeing faced new challenges in the 1990s. The Gulf War and an economic slowdown had put an end to the decades-long growth in air travel.[24] Orders plunged, and Boeing's production model, which dated back to WWII, when the company turned out 20 B-17s a day, was increasingly seen as a model of inefficiency, earning the company the unflattering nickname "The Lazy B."[25] *Fortune* declared 1994 to be Boeing's "annus horribilis": "Earnings shrank by nearly half, to $856 million, and Boeing slashed 9,300 employees from its payroll of 126,000."[26] But simply shrinking the company would not save Boeing. The company needed a new strategy to revitalize its mature market. The pace of new airplane technology was slowing down and its competitors were catching up (see Exhibits 1B and 1C).

Airbus, which entered the market in 1970 as a consortium of European manufacturers, made its first profit in 1991 (see Exhibit 2B). Just three years earlier, the *Economist* wrote that Airbus was "losing as much as $8 million on each airliner it sells."[27] But Airbus stayed afloat with the help of significant government subsidies toward the development of new aircraft—subsidies that Boeing and McDonnell

[16] "Will Boeing's Tails Turn White?" *The Economist*, April 13, 1991, p. 61.

[17] Boeing Annual Report, 1990.

[18] Boeing Annual Report, 1989.

[19] Boeing Annual Report, 1987.

[20] Boeing Annual Report, 1993.

[21] Eugene Rodgers, p. 4.

[22] Jonathan R. Laing, "Restless in Seattle: Plane Builder Boeing Prepares for Takeoff," *Barron's National Business and Financial Weekly*, July 26, 1993, p. 8.

[23] Boeing Annual Report, 1990.

[24] Jonathan R. Laing, p. 8.

[25] Shawn Tully, "Boeing: Is 'the Lazy B' a Bad Rap?" *Fortune*, January 25, 1993, p. 10.

[26] Alex Taylor III, "Boeing: Sleepy in Seattle," *Fortune*, August 7, 1995, p. 92.

[27] *Economist*, January 30, 1988, p. 50.

EXHIBIT 1A Boeing Aircraft

Source: www.boeing.com

Model	Versions	Range	Capacity	First in Service	Details
707	120, 320	5,681km–9,913km	141–189	October 1958	First successful commercial jet; replaced propeller planes.
727	100/C, 200/F	2,750km–4,020km	141–189	February 1964	First Boeing jet with completely automated flight controls.
737	100, 200/C/Adv, 300-800, 900/ER	5,645km–6,235km	110–177	February 1968	Best-selling commercial aircraft in history.
747	100-300, 400/ER/F	13,570km–14,038km	416	January 1970	World's first jumbo jet, largest commercial aircraft for over 30 years. Boeing's most profitable plane.
757	200/F/M, 300	6,287km	243–280	January 1983	Pioneered digital and electronic display systems on flight deck. High fuel efficiency, low noise levels, able to do both short- and long-haul trips.
767	200/ER, 300/ER/F, 400/ER	12,220km	181–245	September 1982	First twin-engine airplane to achieve 180-minute Extended Twin-Engine Operations (ETOPS) approval, allowing trans-Atlantic and trans-Pacific flights.
777	200/ER/LR, 300/ER/F	9,640km–16,890km	301–368	June 1995	Most technologically advanced plane and first to be designed completely using CAD programs.
717	200	2,645km–3,815km	106	October 1999	Most efficient plane for short-haul flights.
787		14,800km–15,741km	200–300	Expected 2008	Majority of the primary structure will use composite materials, and will be up to 20% more efficient than existing planes. May incorporate airplane health monitoring systems and other e-Enabled services.

EXHIBIT 1B Airbus Aircraft

Source: Adapted from www.airbus.com

Model	Versions	Range	Capacity	First in Service	Details
A300	B2, B4	7,500km	266	May 1974	Introduced weight-saving composite materials.
A310		9,600km	220	May 1983	Uses composite materials in primary structures, including fin. First commercial aircraft to have drag reducing wing tips.
A320	A318, A319, A320, A321	5,600km	185	March 1988	Full digital, computer-driven controls and sidestick controller. Establishes common systems across its fleet.
A330	200, 300	10,500km	335	December 1993	Entry into service of the A330 and A340 in the same year established "Mixed Flying Fleet," whereby pilots certified to fly one fly-by-wire Airbus aircraft could easily switch to another, due to the airplanes' commonality.
A340	200, 300, 500, 600	13,900km	380	January 1993	First four-engine Airbus.
A380	A380F	15,000km	555	April 2005	World's largest commercial jet. Twenty-five percent composite materials.

EXHIBIT 1C Airbus and Boeing Orders and Deliveries

Source: Adapted from www.boeing.com and www.airbus.com.

Airplane Orders

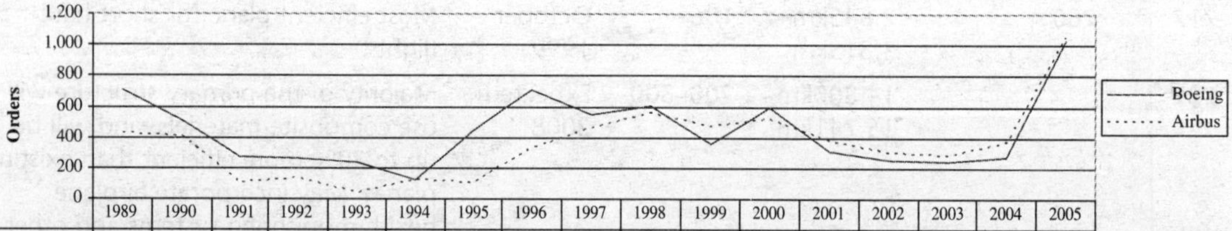

	1989	1990	1991	1992	1993	1994	1995	1996	1997	1998	1999	2000	2001	2002	2003	2004	2005
Boeing	713	513	275	267	236	125	441	712	544	606	355	598	314	251	249	277	1,031
Airbus	421	404	101	136	38	125	106	326	460	556	476	520	375	300	284	370	1,055

Airplane Deliveries

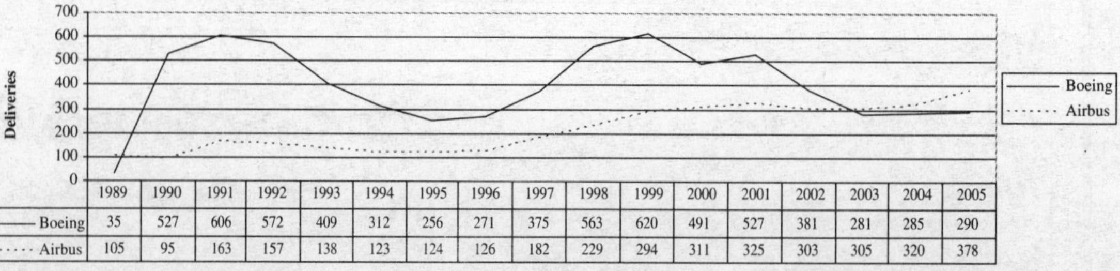

	1989	1990	1991	1992	1993	1994	1995	1996	1997	1998	1999	2000	2001	2002	2003	2004	2005
Boeing	35	527	606	572	409	312	256	271	375	563	620	491	527	381	281	285	290
Airbus	105	95	163	157	138	123	124	126	182	229	294	311	325	303	305	320	378

EXHIBIT 2A **Boeing Income Statement ($ millions)**

Source: Thomson Financial, Global Vantage, accessed January 2006.

	Dec86	Dec90	Dec91	Dec92	Dec93	Dec94	Dec95	Dec96	Dec97	Dec98	Dec99	Dec00	Dec01	Dec02	Dec03	Dec04	Dec05
Sales	16,341.0	27,595.0	29,314.0	30,184.0	25,438.0	21,924.0	19,515.0	22,681.0	45,800.0	56,154.0	57,993.0	51,321.0	58,198.0	54,069.0	50,485.0	52,457.0	54,845.0
Cost of Goods Sold	13,885.0	23,355.0	23,826.0	24,105.0	19,959.0	16,801.0	15,293.0	18,062.0	39,186.0	49,077.0	49,884.0	42,453.0	47,406.0	44,303.0	42,693.0	43,550.0	44,346.0
Gross Profit	2,456.0	4,240.0	5,488.0	6,079.0	5,479.0	5,123.0	4,222.0	4,619.0	6,614.0	7,077.0	8,109.0	8,868.0	10,792.0	9,467.0	7,617.0	8,907.0	10,499.0
Selling, General & Administrative Expense	1,363.0	2,032.0	2,708.0	3,078.0	2,763.0	2,830.0	2,287.0	2,274.0	4,111.0	3,888.0	3,385.0	3,776.0	4,325.0	4,173.0	4,419.0	5,536.0	6,433.0
EBITDA	1,093.0	2,208.0	2,780.0	3,001.0	2,716.0	2,293.0	1,935.0	2,345.0	2,503.0	3,189.0	4,724.0	5,092.0	6,467.0	5,294.0	3,198.0	3,371.0	4,066.0
Depreciation & Amortization	463.0	678.0	826.0	961.0	1,025.0	1,142.0	1,033.0	991.0	1,458.0	1,622.0	1,645.0	1,479.0	1,750.0	1,182.0	1,099.0	1,125.0	1,503.0
Operating Profit	630.0	1,530.0	1,954.0	2,040.0	1,691.0	1,151.0	902.0	1,354.0	1,045.0	1,567.0	3,079.0	3,613.0	4,717.0	3,950.0	1,748.0	2,246.0	2,563.0
Interest Expense	27.0	28.0	57.0	133.0	189.0	217.0	216.0	203.0	573.0	518.0	512.0	527.0	730.0	801.0	873.0	790.0	653.0
Non-Operating Adj.	425.0	470.0	307.0	349.0	319.0	209.0	274.0	212.0	587.0	348.0	307.0	451.0	302.0	-15.0	560.0	507.0	909.0
Special Items	0.0	0.0	0.0	0.0	0.0	0.0	-600.0	0.0	-1,400.0	NA	450.0	-538.0	-725.0	46.0	-885.0	-3.0	NA
Pretax Income	1,028.0	1,972.0	2,204.0	2,256.0	1,821.0	1,143.0	360.0	1,363.0	-341.0	1,397.0	3,324.0	2,999.0	3,564.0	3,180.0	550.0	1,960.0	2,819.0
Total Income Taxes	363.0	587.0	637.0	702.0	577.0	287.0	-33.0	268.0	-163.0	277.0	1,015.0	871.0	738.0	847.0	-185.0	140.0	257.0
Discontinued Operations	665.0	1,385.0	1,567.0	552.0	1,244.0	856.0	393.0	1,095.0	-178.0	1,120.0	2,309.0	2128.0	2827.0	492.0	718.0	4872.0	2,572.0
Net Income	665.0	1,385.0	1,567.0	552.0	1,244.0	856.0	393.0	1,095.0	-178.0	1,120.0	2,309.0	2,128.0	2,827.0	492.0	718.0	1,872.0	2,572.0
Available for Common	665.0	1,385.0	1,567.0	1,554.0	1,244.0	856.0	393.0	1,095.0	-178.0	1,120.0	2,309.0	2,128.0	2,826.0	2,319.0	718.0	1,820.0	2,562.0
EPS (Primary)—Excl. Extra Items & Disc Op.	1.0	2.0	2.3	2.3	1.8	1.3	0.6	1.6	-0.2	1.2	2.5	2.4	3.5	2.9	0.9	2.3	3.26
EPS (Fully Diluted)—Incl. Extra Items & Disc Op.	1.0	2.0	2.3	0.8	1.8	1.3	0.6	1.6	-0.2	1.1	2.5	2.4	3.4	0.6	0.9	2.3	3.2
Dividends per Share	0.3	0.5	0.5	0.5	0.5	0.5	0.5	0.5	0.6	0.6	0.6	0.6	0.7	0.7	0.7	0.8	1
ROA (%)	6.0	9.5	9.9	8.6	6.1	4.0	1.8	4.0	-0.5	3.1	6.4	5.1	5.8	4.4	1.4	3.4	4.3
ROE (%)	13.8	19.9	19.4	19.3	13.8	8.8	4.0	10.0	-1.4	9.1	20.1	19.3	26.1	30.1	8.8	16.1	23.2
Market Value (US$ Mil.)	7,929.2	15,589.7	16,296.5	13,619.2	14,711.0	16,021.3	26,957.3	36,994.2	47,639.2	32,596.7	38,725.0	58,637.6	30,945.4	26,370.3	33,721.1	43,465.9	56,702.3
Book Value (US$ Mil.)	4,826.0	6,973.0	8,093.0	8,056.0	8,983.0	9,700.0	9,898.0	10,941.0	12,953.0	12,316.0	11,462.0	11,020.0	10,825.0	7,696.0	8,139.0	11,286.0	11,059.0
Market to Book Ratio	1.6	2.2	2.0	1.7	1.6	1.7	2.7	3.4	3.7	2.6	3.4	5.3	2.9	3.4	4.1	3.9	5.1

(continued)

EXHIBIT 2A **Boeing Balance Sheets ($ millions) (*Continued*)**

	Dec86	Dec90	Dec91	Dec92	Dec93	Dec94	Dec95	Dec96	Dec97	Dec98	Dec99	Dec00	Dec01	Dec02	Dec03	Dec04	Dec05
Assets																	
Cash and Equivalents	4,172	3,326	3,453	3,614	3,108	2,643	3,730	5,258	5,149	2,462	3,454	1,010	633	2,333	4,633	3,523	5,966
Net Receivables	1,201	2,057	2,099	1,657	1,833	1,914	1,675	2,138	3,382	4,069	4,252	5,923	6,209	6,296	5,571	5,269	5,613
Inventories	3,105	3,332	3,277	2,701	3,434	4,979	6,933	6,939	8,967	8,349	6,539	6,794	6,920	6,184	5,338	4,247	7,940
Current Assets—Other	0	55	0	115	800	878	840	745	1,765	1,495	1,467	2,137	2,444	2,042	1,716	2,061	2,449
Current Assets—Total	8,478	8,770	8,829	8,087	9,175	10,414	13,178	15,080	19,263	16,375	15,712	15,864	16,206	16,855	17,258	15,100	21,968
Gross PPE	5,247	9,711	11,342	13,181	14,347	14,604	14,758	14,986	21,435	23,276	23,280	25,178	25,812	27,326	27,694	21,405	NA
Accumulated Depreciation	2,931	4,633	5,196	5,737	6,364	7,055	7,614	7,915	11,253	11,976	12,270	12,556	12,791	13,371	13,718	12,962	NA
Net PPE	2,316	5,078	6,146	7,444	7,983	7,549	7,144	7,071	10,182	11,300	11,010	12,622	13,021	13,955	13,976	8,443	8,420
Intangibles	0	NA	NA	0	0	0	0	2,478	2,395	2,312	2,233	5,214	6,443	3,888	2,948	2,903	2,799
Other Assets	274	743	809	2,616	3,292	3,500	1,776	2,625	6,184	6,685	7,192	8,328	12,673	17,644	18,853	27,517	26,871
Total Assets	11,068	14,591	15,784	18,147	20,450	21,463	22,098	27,254	38,024	36,672	36,147	43,504	48,978	52,342	52,986	53,963	60,058
Liabilities																	
Debt Due in 1 Year	14	4	4	21	17	6	271	13	608	650	480	538	1,321	1,814	1,144	1,321	1,189
Notes Payable	0	0	0	0	0	0	0	0	123	219	272	694	78	0	0	0	0
Accounts Payable	1,716	2,586	2,335	2,869	2,731	3,207	3,017	3,554	5,609	5,263	4,909	5,040	4,793	4,431	3,822	4,563	16,513
Other Current Liabilities	5,504	5,947	5,491	4,247	4,788	4,676	5,501	6,672	9,966	9,616	10,416	14,961	18,184	18,516	18,375	20,502	10,486
Total Current Liabilities	5,659	7,132	6,276	6,140	6,531	6,827	7,415	8,642	14,152	13,422	13,656	18,289	20,486	19,810	18,448	20,835	28,188
Long-Term Debt	263	311	1,313	1,772	2,613	2,603	2,344	3,980	6,123	6,103	5,980	7,567	10,866	12,589	13,299	10,879	9,538
Deferred Taxes	219	161	102	0	0	51	0	0	0	0	172	0	177	0	0	1,090	2,067
Investment Tax Credit	101	14	NA	0	0	0	0	0	0	0	0	0	0	0	0	0	0
Other Liabilities	0	0	0	2,004	2,148	2,282	2,441	3,691	4,796	4,831	4,877	5,152	5,989	12,247	13,149	9,873	9,206
Equity																	
Preferred Stock	0	0	0	175	175	0	0	0	0	0	0	0	0	0	0	0	0
Common Stock	776	1,746	1,746	1,746	1,746	1,746	1,746	1,802	5,000	5,059	5,059	5,059	5,059	5,059	5,059	5,059	5,061
Capital Surplus	562	581	583	418	413	586	615	1,951	1,090	1,147	1,684	2,693	1,972	2,141	2,880	3,420	4,371
Retained Earnings	3,497	4,840	6,064	6,276	7,180	7,696	7,746	8,447	8,127	8,666	10,481	12,081	13,855	10,217	10,262	13,640	15,498
Less: Treasury Stock	9	194	300	384	356	328	209	1,259	1,264	2,556	5,762	8,813	10,061	9,721	10,062	10,833	13,871
Common Equity	4,826	6,973	8,093	8,056	8,983	9,700	9,898	10,941	12,953	12,316	11,462	11,020	10,825	7,696	8,139	11,286	11,059
Total Equity	4,826	6,973	8,093	8,231	9,158	9,700	9,898	10,941	12,953	12,316	11,462	11,020	10,825	7,696	8,139	11,286	11,059
Total Liab. and Equity	11,068	14,591	15,784	18,147	20,450	21,463	22,098	27,254	38,024	36,672	36,147	42,028	48,343	52,342	53,035	53,963	60,058

EXHIBIT 2A **Boeing Cash Flow Statement (*Continued*)**

	Dec86	Dec90	Dec91	Dec92	Dec93	Dec94	Dec95	Dec96	Dec97	Dec98	Dec99	Dec00	Dec01	Dec02	Dec03	Dec04
Indirect Operating Activities																
Income before Extraordinary Items	665	1,385	1,567	1,554	1,244	856	393	1,095	-178	1,120	2,309	2,128	2,826	2,319	718	1,820
Depreciation and Amortization	463	678	826	961	1,025	1,142	1,033	991	1,458	1,622	1,645	1,479	1,750	1,497	1,468	1,509
Extraordinary Items and Disc. Operations	0	0	0	0	0	0	0	0	0	0	0	0	0	0	0	1
Deferred Taxes	297	-118	95	-26	-536	NA	NA	NA	0	0	0	0	0	0	0	NA
Equity in Net Loss (Earnings)	-17	-5	1	-13	-1	3	NA	0	0	NA	NA	NA	NA	NA	NA	NA
Sale of Property, Plant and Equip. and Sale of Investments—Loss (Gain)	NA	-74	0	0	0	0	0	0	0	0	-87	-34	-21	-44	-7	-23
Funds from Operations	0	0	0	0	0	0	600	133	1,301	153	281	886	420	492	1,674	1,635
Receivables—Decrease (Increase)	NA	-534	-141	635	-187	-49	194	243	-251	-167	-225	-768	342	-155	357	-241
Inventory—Decrease (Increase)	NA	1,585	55	NA	-733	-1,545	-1,954	250	-1,008	618	2,030	1,097	-19	1,510	351	611
Income Taxes—Accrued—Increase (Dec.)	NA	227	-453	206	202	-117	37	-94	-451	145	462	421	-762	905	NA	NA
Other Assets and Liabilities—Net Change	NA	192	-516	45	203	787	763	-395	1,229	-1,124	-191	733	-722	-2,149	-680	-1,854
Operating Activities—Net Cash Flow	NA	3,336	1,434	3,362	1,217	1,077	1,066	2,223	2,100	2,367	6,224	5,942	3,814	4,375	3,881	3,458
Investing Activities																
Investments—Increase	0	NA	NA	1,140	1,560	975	1,239	420	1,889	2,660	2,398	2,571	5,073	3,595	2,291	4,142
Sale of Investments	NA	0	0	50	626	770	2,638	1,482	1,030	1,418	1,842	1,433	1,297	1,040	1,497	1,400
Short-Term Investments—Change	NA	0	623	-388	137	NA	NA	NA	NA	NA	NA	NA	NA	NA	NA	NA
Capital Expenditures	795	1,586	1,850	2,160	1,317	795	629	762	1,391	1,584	1,236	965	1,189	1,001	741	978
Sale of Property, Plant and Equipment	0	NA	NA	NA	NA	NA	NA	NA	NA	NA	NA	NA	NA	NA	NA	NA
Acquisitions	57	16	0	0	0	0	0	NA	NA	0	0	5,727	22	22	-289	34
Investing Activities—Other	NA	171	-3	-19	8	0	0	0	0	0	359	169	152	157	186	2,385
Investing Activities—Net Cash Flow	NA	-1,431	-1,230	-3,657	-2,106	-1,000	770	300	-2,250	-2,826	-1,433	-7,628	-4,714	-3,421	-1,060	-1,369
Financing Activities																
Sale of Common and Preferred Stock	13	27	23	35	23	26	146	214	NA	NA	NA	NA	NA	NA	NA	NA
Purchase of Common and Preferred Stock	30	156	127	109	0	0	0	891	141	1,397	2,937	2,357	2,417	0	0	752
Cash Dividends	186	328	343	340	340	340	342	379	557	564	537	504	582	571	572	648
Long-Term Debt—Issuance	247	15	993	482	837	0	6	NA	232	811	437	2,687	4,567	2,814	2,042	0
Long-Term Debt—Reduction	12	0	0	0	0	21	0	822	867	693	676	620	1,124	1,564	2,024	2,208
Current Debt—Changes	NA	NA	NA	NA	NA	NA	NA	NA	NA	NA	NA	NA	NA	NA	NA	NA
Financing Activities—Other	NA	0	0	0	0	0	0	0	434	65	93	136	79	67	33	90
Financing Activities—Net Cash Flow	NA	-442	546	68	520	-335	-190	-1,878	-899	-1,778	-3,620	-658	523	746	-521	-3,518

EXHIBIT 2B **Airbus Income Statement ($ millions)**

Source: Thomson Financial, Global Vantage, Accessed January 2006.

	Dec94	Dec95	Dec96	Dec97	Dec98	Dec99	Dec00	Dec01	Dec02	Dec03	Dec04	Dec05
Sales/Turnover (Net) + Operating Revenues—Other	8,771.0	9,875.9	9,951.1	9,660.6	9,316.4	13,757.7	17,951.5	27,573.6	28,268.3	34,100.6	39,502.4	40,352.82
Operating Expense	8,249.6	9,343.3	9,435.6	9,170.3	8,974.8	12,861.9	16,497.0	22,135.5	25,885.0	30,967.0	34,812.3	
Depreciation and Amortization—Total	490.9	404.5	371.6	307.4	272.2	384.1	1,291.8	3,187.3	2,232.1	2,080.0	2,016.1	
Operating Income	30.5	128.2	143.9	182.9	69.4	511.7	162.6	2,250.8	151.3	1,053.6	2,674.0	
Interest and Related Expense	343.3	360.3	257.9	163.5	153.7	176.9	38.8	209.5	573.9	745.8	779.8	
Amortization	490.9	404.5	371.6	307.4	272.2	384.1	1,291.8	3,187.3	2,232.1	2,080.0	2,016.1	
Operating Income	30.5	128.2	143.9	182.9	69.4	511.7	162.6	2,250.8	151.3	1,053.6	2,674.0	
Interest and Related Expense	343.3	360.3	257.9	163.5	153.7	176.9	38.8	209.5	573.9	745.8	779.8	
Non-Operating Income/Expense	209.7	-105.7	221.4	191.2	239.9	-193.2	-1,180.9	-249.8	599.4	475.3	465.2	
Pretax Income	-103.1	-337.9	107.4	210.6	155.7	141.6	-1,057.1	1,791.5	176.8	783.1	2,359.4	2,990.54
Appropriations to Untaxed Reserves	0.0	0.0	0.0	0.0	0.0	0.0	0.0	0.0	0.0	0.0	0.0	
Income Taxes—Total	-0.2	-29.9	3.3	-3.1	-25.8	66.3	-243.9	578.4	428.3	536.4	825.8	
Minority Interest	-9.4	-92.5	-38.9	0.9	19.2	25.5	21.3	-15.2	31.2	74.7	252.5	
Net Items—Total	6.3	18.7	15.8	30.5	13.8	-17.2	0.0	0.0	0.0	0.0	0.0	
Income Before Extraordinary Items	-87.2	-196.8	158.8	243.3	176.1	32.5	-834.4	1,228.4	-282.7	172.0	1,281.1	2,017.287
Extraordinary Items	0.0	0.0	0.0	0.0	0.0	0.0	0.0	0.0	0.0	0.0	0.0	
Dividends—Total	0.0	0.0	0.0	0.0	0.0	32.8	0.0	0.0	0.0	0.0	0.0	
Ratios												
ROA (%)	NA	-1.4	1.2	2.0	1.3	0.2	-3.0	3.0	-0.6	0.3	1.7	
ROE (%)	-11.9	-32.8	21.8	27.8	15.7	2.0	-8.7	14.0	-2.1	0.8	5.6	
Return on Average Equity (%)	NA	-29.6	23.9	30.3	17.6	2.4	-14.8	13.3	-2.5	1.0	5.9	
Capitalization Ratio (%)	NA	4.8	5.1	6.5	7.3	8.2	17.0	22.5	23.6	28.3	29.4	

EXHIBIT 2B Airbus Balance Sheet ($ millions) (*Continued*)

	Dec94	Dec95	Dec96	Dec97	Dec98	Dec99	Dec00	Dec01	Dec02	Dec03	Dec04	Dec05
Assets												
Cash and Short-Term Investments	1,863.1	1,942.4	1,564.0	1,797.7	1,943.6	2,852.4	7,437.5	7,152.3	6,507.6	9,926.8	12,478.7	
Accounts Receivable/Debtors—Total	4,093.5	4,388.4	3,902.5	3,634.9	4,431.2	5,161.2	5,605.9	6,959.1	9,834.9	6,262.2	8,917.4	
Inventories/Stocks—Total	4,422.1	4,114.2	4,097.0	3,665.8	5,305.9	5,717.4	1,953.7	2,198.3	2,834.0	4,134.9	4,178.1	
Current Assets—Other	938.8	952.3	912.0	892.3	1,137.5	1,153.7	4,296.2	4,481.2	4,153.3	16,380.7	16,905.4	
Current Assets—Total	11,317.5	11,397.3	10,475.4	9,990.8	12,818.3	14,884.8	19,293.3	20,791.0	23,329.7	36,704.6	42,479.6	
Fixed Assets (Net)—Total	4,678.7	5,289.0	4,845.6	4,379.4	5,148.2	5,485.6	11,773.1	14,619.0	18,435.4	24,636.6	29,532.2	19,415.5
Investments—Permanent Subsidiaries	302.8	368.5	387.8	389.8	305.4	127.0	0.0	1,114.7	1,399.1	2,068.1	2,361.5	
Investments and Advances—Other	186.6	140.7	127.9	154.1	532.0	407.5	4,327.1	3,093.1	3,717.7	3,138.7	3,195.8	
Intangible Assets	113.9	82.4	78.3	89.4	105.1	435.8	7,665.7	9,427.2	10,274.7	12,224.4	13,598.3	
Assets—Other	26.4	14.5	9.8	4.5	0.0	0.0	0.0	0.0	0.0	0.0	0.0	
Assets—Total	13,674.0	13,806.3	12,648.6	12,018.6	15,386.3	17,625.8	38,909.6	43,374.4	49,751.6	68,571.9	79,169.7	83,033.18
Liabilities												
Short-Term Borrowings—Total	781.2	985.0	286.0	438.7	363.9	532.1	861.9	1,301.7	1,243.8	1,233.3	978.3	
Accounts Payable/Creditors—Trade	3,289.2	3,407.1	3,347.7	3,043.0	3,614.6	4,220.8	4,007.0	4,866.8	5,321.5	6,452.7	7,962.2	
Current Liabilities—Other	4,663.7	4,537.1	4,751.0	4,692.4	6,408.7	7,516.4	10,434.3	12,099.2	13,609.3	17,371.8	20,695.0	
Current Liabilities—Total	8,734.1	8,929.2	8,384.7	8,174.1	10,387.2	12,269.3	15,303.2	18,267.7	20,174.6	0.0	29,635.5	
Provision—Deferred Taxes	20.6	0.4	0.0	0.2	12.7	14.5	1,059.0	717.6	2,113.9	4,620.4	5,617.0	
Long-Term Debt	2,511.4	2,287.8	1,841.8	1,515.2	1,571.8	1,646.2	4,563.7	4,485.7	3,979.1	4,778.0	5,986.6	
Minority Interest	319.3	253.8	212.4	185.5	204.8	200.2	207.5	497.7	1,428.5	2,747.8	3,220.2	
Reserves—Untaxed	0.0	0.0	0.0	0.0	0.0	0.0	0.0	0.0	0.0	0.0	0.0	
Liabilities—Other	1,356.6	1,735.0	1,480.7	1,267.5	2,086.6	1,879.1	8,153.0	10,611.4	8,657.2	11,003.7	11,648.5	
Liabilities—Total	12,942.1	13,206.1	11,919.6	11,142.4	14,263.1	16,009.3	29,286.4	34,580.2	36,353.3	48,207.6	56,107.8	
Shareholders' Equity	731.9	600.2	729.0	876.2	1,123.2	1,616.5	9,623.2	8,794.2	13,398.3	20,364.3	23,061.9	16,400.19

(*continued*)

EXHIBIT 2B **Airbus Cash Flow Statement ($ millions) (*Continued*)**

	Dec94	Dec95	Dec96	Dec97	Dec98	Dec99	Dec00	Dec01	Dec02	Dec03	Dec04
Indirect Operating Activities											
Income before Extraordinary Items	-96.6	-289.3	119.9	244.2	195.3	58.1	-834.4	1,228.4	-282.7	172.0	1,281.1
Depreciation and Amortization	408.7	638.0	125.5	219.5	429.4	613.3	1,035.9	3,187.3	2,616.9	2,687.7	2,016.1
Extraordinary Items	0.0	0.0	0.0	0.0	0.0	0.0	0.0	0.0	0.0	0.0	0.0
Deferred Taxes	0.0	0.0	0.0	0.0	0.0	0.0	-641.3	97.6	241.1	-156.2	667.9
Sale of Fixed Assets and Sale of Investments-Disposables-(Gain)-Loss	-26.2	16.9	-11.1	-39.6	-189.3	-302.3	44.4	NA	NA	-310.1	-119.4
Provisions	0.0	0.0	0.0	0.0	0.0	0.0	1,387.9	42.1	-798.9	278.4	-294.8
Reserves	0.0	0.0	0.0	0.0	0.0	0.0	0.0	0.0	0.0	0.0	0.0
Funds from Operations—Other	757.3	798.9	829.0	746.7	839.6	0.0	0.0	-2,144.3	-47.3	297.6	-248.7
Accounts Receivable/ Debtors–Dec. (Inc.)	277.6	31.9	321.3	-118.2	-670.3	-224.4	NA	-800.4	846.1	190.1	-501.2
Inventories/Stocks—Dec. (Inc.)	342.3	444.6	-16.6	64.2	-251.8	-411.9	NA	-586.4	259.0	181.1	350.7
Assets and Liabilities-Other (Net Change)	16.4	-57.2	-121.6	-56.8	33.3	4.2	NA	702.8	-213.7	1,782.4	1,890.5
Operating Activities—Net Cash Flow	1,703.0	1,225.2	1,685.5	1,412.0	715.3	905.1	2,385.0	2,377.9	2,520.4	5,329.0	6,234.9
Investing Activities											
Investments—Increase	132.6	58.2	57.9	166.5	368.8	159.2	NA	1,330.4	1,072.1	0.0	599.5
Investments—Decrease	0.0	0.0	0.0	0.0	0.0	0.0	NA	761.0	802.6	470.8	611.9
Short-Term Investments	NA	NA	NA	NA	NA	NA	NA	0.0	-249.6	380.2	12.4
Capital Expenditures	208.4	296.9	357.5	399.7	371.2	554.6	1,428.6	1,966.1	2,187.6	3,339.6	4,568.3
Sale of Fixed Assets—Tangible	NA	NA	NA	NA	NA	NA	NA	NA	NA	NA	NA
Acquisitions	0.0	0.0	0.0	0.0	0.0	0.0	-2,468.1	NA	NA	NA	124.4
Investing Activities	-701.9	-707.6	-678.4	-593.3	-653.5	0.5	0.0	141.5	-561.6	-1,506.3	-176.6
Investing Activities—Net Cash Flow	-982.2	-969.4	-896.4	-914.7	-874.3	-139.5	1,489.6	-2,034.1	-3,041.3	-3,932.6	-4,662.8
Financing Activities											
Purchase of Common & Preferred Stock	0.0	0.0	0.0	0.0	0.0	0.0	0.0	0.0	0.0	0.0	0.0
Equity Stock—Addition	367.4	2.0	13.7	0.0	0.0	0.0	1,423.0	18.8	15.1	23.8	53.5
Cash Dividends	0.7	2.2	0.0	0.0	0.0	0.0	28.6	361.7	381.0	271.6	477.6
Taxation	0.0	0.0	0.0	0.0	0.0	0.0	0.0	0.0	0.0	0.0	0.0
Current Debt—Change	-50.2	-16.5	-544.0	177.8	-87.1	0.0	0.0	NA	NA	NA	NA
Financing Activities—Other	-0.7	2.2	-11.7	-12.4	-217.3	0.0	-14.8	199.7	-2.8	9.1	0.0
Financing Activities—Net Cash Flow	-76.6	-363.5	-1,091.0	-29.5	-429.1	160.5	1,284.4	-606.1	-1,368.0	964.2	64.7
Exchange Rate Effect	0.0	0.0	0.0	0.0	0.0	0.0	5.5	12.5	-77.5	-93.9	-2.5
Cash and Cash Equivalents—Inc. (Dec.)	661.4	-89.1	-267.5	460.6	7.1	926.0	5,164.5	-249.8	-1,966.4	2,266.7	1,634.3
Direct Operating Activities											
Income Taxes Paid	NA	NA	NA	NA	NA	NA	NA	465.6	300.6	433.4	375.6
Interest Paid (Net)	NA	NA	NA	NA	NA	NA	NA	299.9	384.8	351.9	456.5

Douglas long contended gave Airbus an unfair advantage.[28]

Most analysts believed that the airplane manufacturer segment of the industry was about to enter an era of unprecedented price competition, "one that would lead Boeing to disaster unless it drastically cut costs."[29] The fate of the country's other once-great manufacturers, such as IBM and GM, loomed large: "It could happen to us if we don't do things differently," said Shrontz.[30] IBM's leaders saved the company from the brink of disaster. Could Boeing's leaders save the company before disaster struck?

New Leadership, New Vision

> In a year filled with big events and changes, one of the biggest was this: We stopped thinking of ourselves as just an aerospace manufacturer and began to think of ourselves in a much broader way as a provider of integrated products and services to all of our customers.
>
> *Phil Condit, President and CEO, 1999*[31]

In 1996, Shrontz retired as CEO and was succeeded by Phil Condit, a 30-year Boeing veteran who had been the company's president since 1992. Condit recognized that in the face of stiff competition and the cyclical nature of the industry, Boeing could not survive on selling airplanes alone. He acknowledged early in his term that he may be "Boeing's first CEO not to roll out a new aircraft during his tenure."[32] Instead, Condit launched the company's transformation into "a more agile, geographically diverse, more broadly based company less dependent on the highly cyclical commercial jetliner market."[33] Condit wrote in the 1996 annual report that Vision 2016 called for Boeing to become "an integrated aerospace company and a global enterprise, designing, producing, and supporting commercial airplanes, defense systems, and defense and civil space systems" by its 100th anniversary in 2016 (see Exhibit 3).[34] Boeing's Vision 2016 was centered on three strategic initiatives: Run a healthy core business, leverage strengths into new products and new services, and open new frontiers.

Run a Healthy Core

> Just a decade ago, our profile looked very different, and we were a company that was dependent on a very cyclical commercial airplane market. We were 80 percent commercial airplanes and only 20 percent defense and other business . . . Fortunately, we look very different, and today your company is a billion-dollar-a-week company with a better-balanced portfolio mix.
>
> *Phil Condit, 2003*[35]

In the 1990s, Boeing's core—which had always been a mix of commercial and defense work—was heavily weighted towards commercial aviation, leaving the company vulnerable to the industry's cycles. In his self-described "momentous" first year, Condit attempted to restore the balance: in

[28] In 1992, the U.S. government and the European community reached a bilateral agreement that capped direct government support to Airbus for the development of new aircraft—or "launch aid"—at 33% of nonrecurring costs. (Previous Airbus projects had received up to 100% of the financing in the form of favorable government loans.) The agreement also stipulated that neither Airbus nor Boeing could receive annual "indirect" support (benefits to commercial activities stemming from government contracts) in excess of 4% of its annual civil turnover. But Airbus continued to pressure Boeing and, in the early 1990s, expanded its family of aircraft with the release of the A330 and the A340 in 1993. Demand for Airbus planes increased. In 1999, Airbus surpassed Boeing in orders and, in 2003, it surpassed Boeing in deliveries. In 2004, the U.S. government reignited the subsidies dispute. Robert Zoellick, the U.S. trade representative, argued that Airbus's success should disqualify it from further government subsidies, and said that: "If there were ever justification in 1992 or earlier for [financing] a start-up, that has long been overcome." (Source: Boeing press conference, July 8, 2004.) Upon learning that Airbus planned to use launch aid to develop a midsize aircraft that would compete with Boeing's planned 787, the United States withdrew from the 1992 agreement and both sides filed complaints with the World Trade Organization. (Source: Author interview, February 22, 2006.)

[29] Shawn Tulley, "Can Boeing Reinvent Itself?" *Fortune*, March 8, 1993, p. 66.

[30] Ibid., p. 66.

[31] Boeing Annual Report, 1999.

[32] Eugene Rodgers, p. 464.

[33] Paul C. Proctor, "Boeing Ascendant," *Frontiers*, May 2002.

[34] Boeing Annual Report, 1996.

[35] Address to Shareholders, Chicago, April 28, 2003.

EXHIBIT 3 Vision 2016

Source: Company documents.

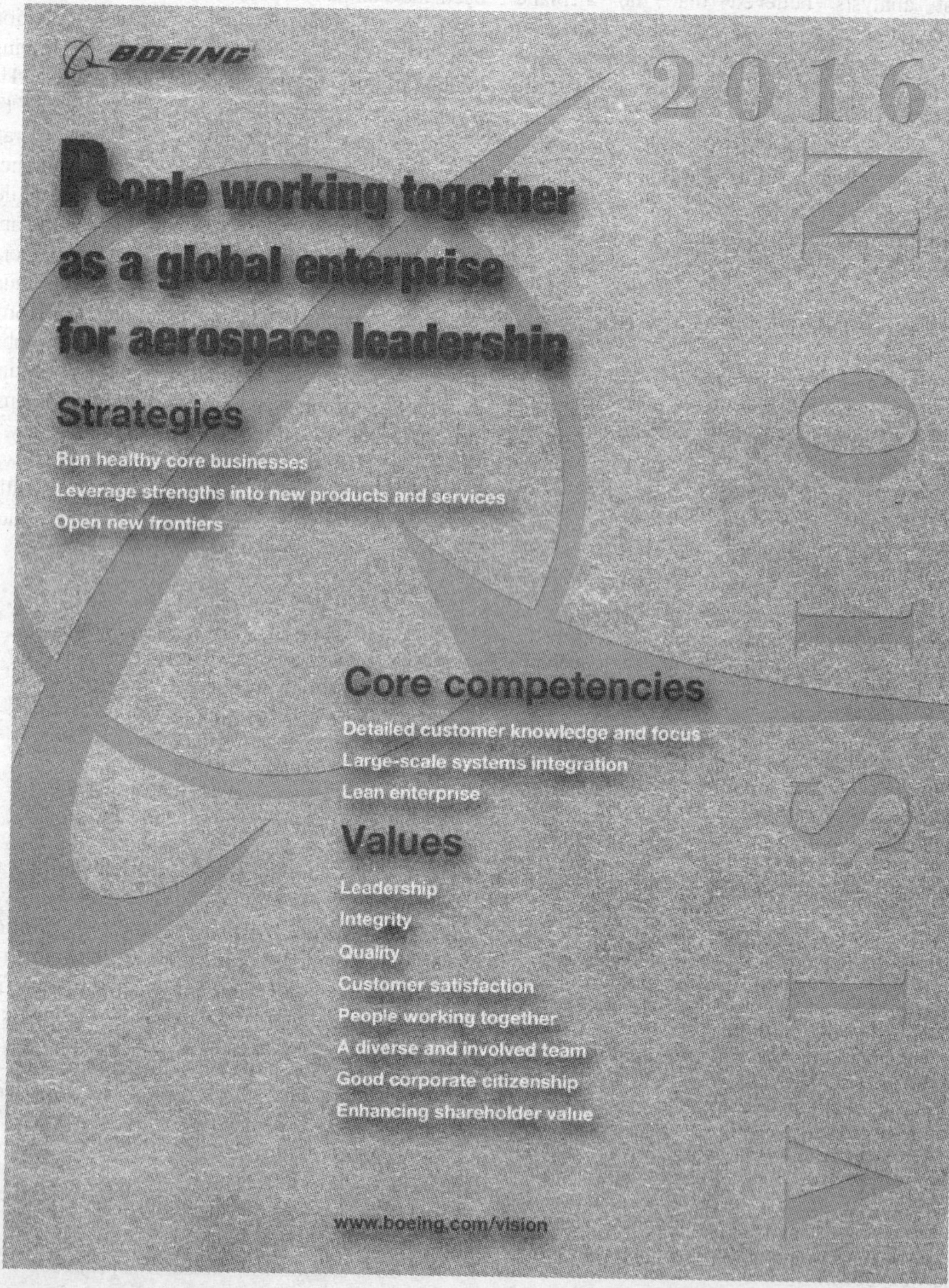

EXHIBIT 3 Vision 2016 (*Continued*)

Vision 2016

People working together as a global enterprise for aerospace leadership

Strategies

Run healthy core businesses
Leverage strengths into new products and services
Open new frontiers

Core competencies

Detailed customer knowledge and focus
We will seek to understand, anticipate and be responsive to our customers' needs.

Large-scale systems integration
We will continuously develop, advance and protect the technical excellence that allows us to integrate effectively the systems we design and produce.

Lean enterprise
Our entire enterprise will be a lean operation, characterized by the efficient use of assets, high inventory turns, excellent supplier management, short cycle times, high quality and low transaction costs.

Values

Leadership
We will be a world-class leader in every aspect of our business – in developing our team leadership skills at every level; in our management performance; in the way we design, build and support our products; and in our financial results.

Integrity
We will always take the high road by practicing the highest ethical standards and by honoring our commitments. We will take personal responsibility for our actions and treat everyone fairly and with trust and respect.

Quality
We will strive for continuous quality improvement in all that we do, so that we will rank among the world's premier industrial firms in customer, employee and community satisfaction.

Customer satisfaction
Satisfied customers are essential to our success. We will achieve total customer satisfaction by understanding what the customer wants and delivering it flawlessly.

People working together
We recognize that our strength and our competitive advantage is – and always will be – people. We will continually learn, and share ideas and knowledge. We will encourage cooperative efforts at every level and across all activities in our company.

A diverse and involved team
We value the skills, strengths and perspectives of our diverse team. We will foster a participatory workplace that enables people to get involved in making decisions about their work that advance our common business objectives.

Good corporate citizenship
We will provide a safe workplace and protect the environment. We will promote the health and well-being of Boeing people and their families. We will work with our communities by volunteering and financially supporting education and other worthy causes.

Enhancing shareholder value
Our business must produce a profit, and we must generate superior returns on the assets entrusted to us by our shareholders. We will ensure our success by satisfying our customers and increasing shareholder value.

BOEING®

DO 6000 5880 REV (20MAR2001)

www.boeing.com/vision

(*continued*)

EXHIBIT 3 Vision 2016 (*Continued*)

1996	• August: Boeing acquires Rockwell International Corporation aerospace and defense businesses
	• December: Boeing announces merger with long-time rival McDonnell Douglas
1997	• Hurt by production delays, Boeing continues to improve production process; adopts "lean manufacturing"
1998	• Alan Mulally replaces Ron Woodard as president of Boeing Commercial Airplanes; Scott Carson named chief financial officer
	• Commercial Aviation Services business unit formed within Boeing Commericial Airplanes
1999	• Acquires Preston Aviation Solutions
2000	• Acquires Hughes Electronics Corporation's space and communications businesses, Jeppesen Sanderson, Inc., and Continental Data Graphics
	• Creates two new services business units: Air Traffic Management and Connexion by Boeing™; Scott Carson named president of Connexion by Boeing™
2001	• Acquires SBS international
	• Launches MyBoeingFleet.com
	• Moves corporate headquarters to Chicago
	• Reorganizes into six business units
2003	• e-Enabled Advantage unveiled at 2003 Paris Air Show
	• ValSim Launched
2004	• e-Enabled Advantage program launched, led by Chris Kettering
	• Carson named senior vice president of marketing and sales for Boeing Commerical Airplane Company

August 1996, the company acquired Rockwell International Corporation's aerospace and defense businesses, making Boeing "one of the world's strongest aerospace companies";[36] and in December, in what *Fortune* magazine called "the sale of the century," Boeing announced plans to merge with McDonnell Douglas Corporation.[37] The Boeing-McDonnell merger further tipped the balance of commercial to defense work from 75:25 to 60:40.[38]

Condit was also faced with rehabilitating the commercial sector. If 1994 was Boeing's "annus horribilis,"[39] 1997 was worse, and this time, the problem came from within. In response to the "largest surge of new orders in the history of the jet age," Boeing faltered with "an embarrassing failure to meet delivery schedules." Production delays caused Boeing to take "a $178 million loss in 1997—its first red ink in 50 years—and to report a 90 percent drop in profits for the first quarter of 1998."[40]

The problem stemmed from cost-cutting measures that Shrontz had implemented at the beginning of the decade. On the brink of a price war, Shrontz had set a goal of cutting production costs by 25 percent.[41] The company set to work modernizing its inventory system and streamlining the manufacturing process. It slowed production rates of the 737 and 757, laid off 12,000 employees, and put plans to build a new superjumbo plane on hold.[42] But these efforts, meant to strengthen the commercial sector by making it lean and agile, backfired; when the industry rebounded from the downturn of the early 1990s, "Boeing suddenly faced the task of transforming the way it built planes while furiously ramping up production of new jets."[43] Condit likened it to "trying to change the tire on my car while going 60 miles an hour."[44] Boeing was plagued by production delays because it "simply lacked the parts and labor to more than double its production as planned."[45]

Nevertheless, Boeing forged ahead with its production reforms. It adopted simpler procedures for configuring aircraft to customer specifications, scheduling and ordering parts, and managing inventory; it also implemented the "principles and practices of 'lean' manufacturing to eliminate waste and promote greater efficiency."[46] By 1998, Boeing Commercial Airplanes was on the road to recovery under the new leadership of Alan Mulally, who replaced Ron Woodard as president, and Scott Carson, who was named chief financial officer (see Exhibit 4 and Exhibit 5). By the end of the year, Boeing Commercial Airplanes was "largely back on track," with 563 jetliner deliveries (up from 256 in 1995) and "greatly reduced out-of-sequence work and parts shortages."[47]

Leverage Strengths

> We can increase Boeing value to our customers by offering services in addition to airplanes. We need to get involved with our customers and know where they're going, where they are in their business models, and how we can help them be successful.
>
> *Lou Mancini, Vice President, Commercial Aviation Services, 2005*

With Boeing Commercial Airplanes' core business of making, selling, and supporting airplanes back on solid ground, Condit began to expand the company into adjacent markets with a series of acquisitions (see Exhibit 6). In 2000, Boeing purchased Jeppesen Sanderson Inc., a leading provider of print and electronic flight information services. Also in 2000, the company

36 Paul C. Proctor.

37 David Whitford. "Sale of the Century," *Fortune*, February 17, 1997, p. 92.

38 Boeing Annual Reports 1996, 1997.

39 Alex Taylor III, p.2.

40 John Greenwald, "Is Boeing Out of Its Spin?" *Time*, July 13, 1998, p. 67.

41 Shawn Tulley.

42 Alex Taylor III, p. 2.

43 John Greenwald.

44 Ibid.

45 Ibid.

46 Boeing Annual Report, 1997.

47 Boeing Annual Report, 1998.

EXHIBIT 4A Boeing Organization, 2006

Source: Company documents.

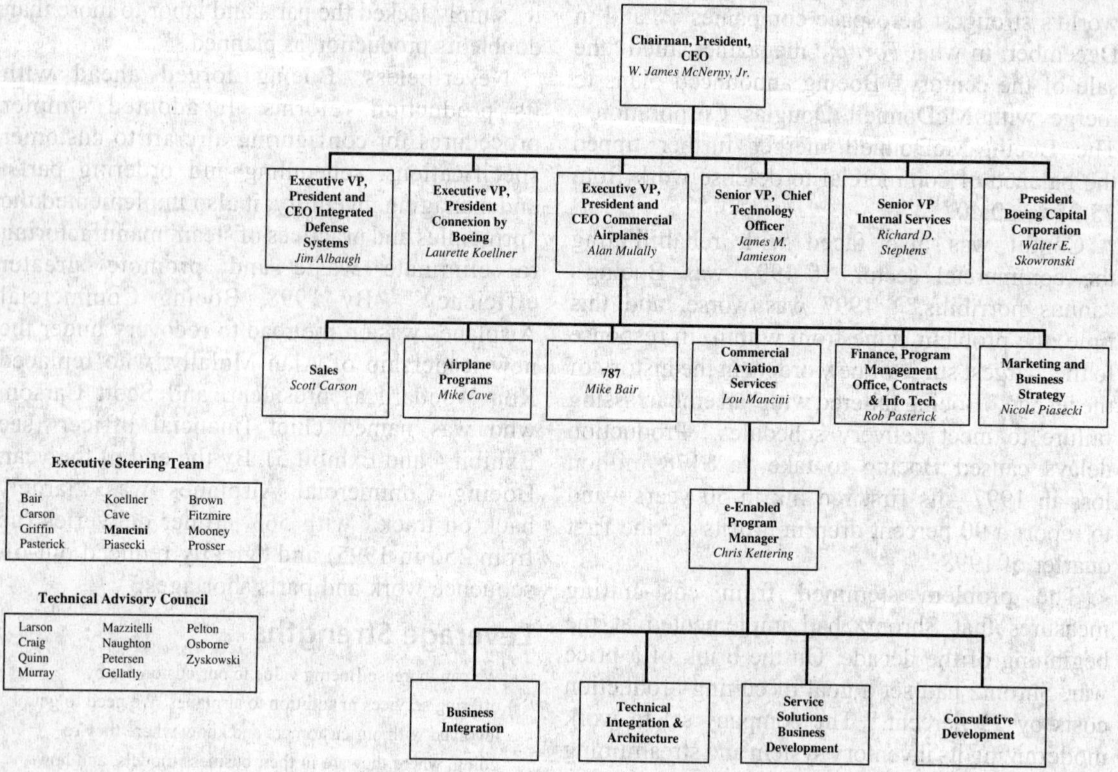

EXHIBIT 4B **An Alternate View of the Boeing Organization in 2004**

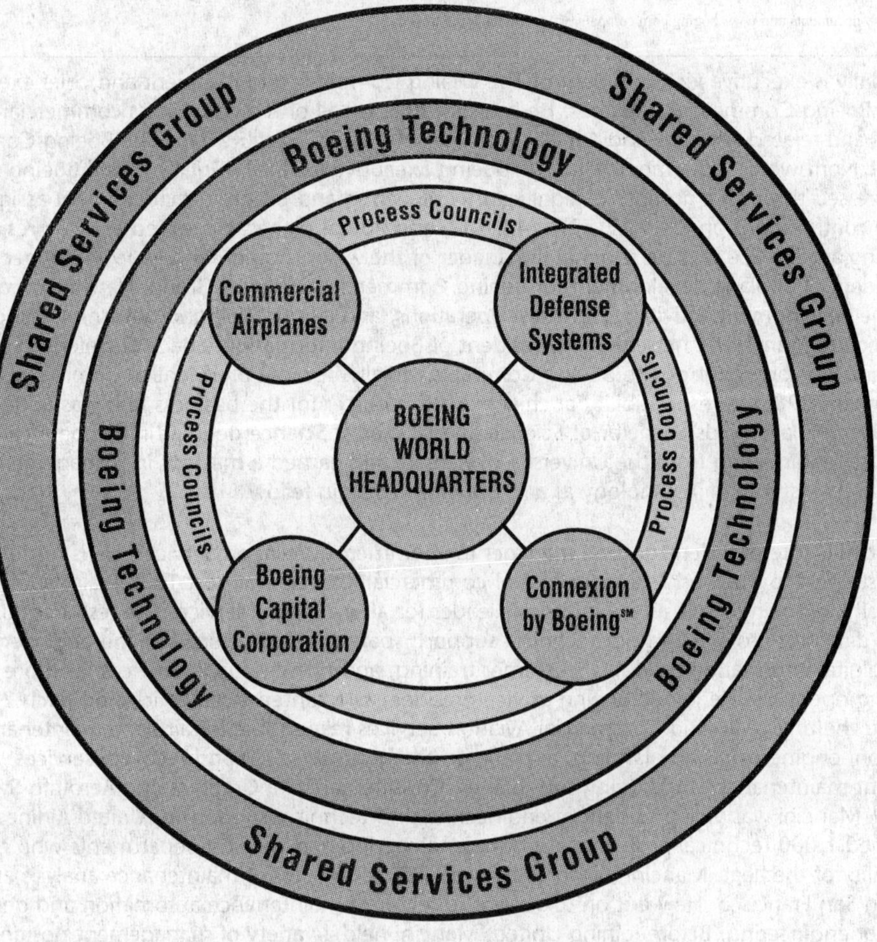

acquired Hughes Electronics Corporation's space and communications businesses and "became the world's premier space-based communications company."[48] "Simply put, we intend to run Boeing as a business that has the flexibility to move capital and talent to the opportunities that maximize shareholder value," Condit said.[49]

As Boeing moved towards offering more products and services and introducing new technologies, Condit and Mulally restructured the business units within Boeing Commercial Airplanes. They combined the existing customer services and logistics support units to form a new business unit called Commercial Aviation Services (CAS), which would contain all the existing support-related offerings: Both those provided free of charge to customers in conjunction with their ownership of a Boeing airplane and those offered as independent businesses. Over the next few years, CAS would leverage Boeing Commercial Airplanes' vast repository of airplane data and its detailed customer knowledge to create new business opportunities around its healthy core of selling and supporting airplanes in service.

[48] Boeing Annual Report, 2000.

[49] Paul C. Proctor.

EXHIBIT 5 Biographies in December 2005: Alan Mulally, Lou Mancini, Scott Carson, and Chris Kettering

Source: Company documents and www.boeing.com/companyoffices/abouts/execprofiles.

Alan Mulally is executive vice president of The Boeing Company, and president and chief executive officer of Boeing Commercial Airplanes. He is responsible for all of the company's commercial airplane programs and related services. Additionally, Mulally is the senior executive for The Boeing Company in the Pacific Northwest, and a member of the Boeing Executive Council. Mulally joined Boeing in 1969 and progressed through a number of significant engineering and program-management assignments, including contributions on the 727, 737, 747, 757, and 767 airplanes. He served as vice president of engineering and as vice president–general manager of the 777 program, and in 1994, he became senior vice president of airplane development for Boeing Commercial Airplanes Group. He was responsible for all airplane development activities, flight test operations, and certification and government technical liaison. Beginning in 1997, he served as president of Boeing Information, Space & Defense Systems and a senior vice president of The Boeing Company. Mulally became president of Commercial Airplanes in September 1998; the responsibility of chief executive officer for the business unit was added in March 2001. Mulally holds Bachelor of Science and Master of Science degrees in aeronautical and astronautical engineering from the University of Kansas, and earned a master's in management from the Massachusetts Institute of Technology as a 1982 Alfred P. Sloan fellow.

Lou Mancini is vice president/general manager for Commercial Aviation Services. He is responsible for ensuring support to the world's largest fleet of commercial jetliners—almost 12,000 airplanes—and for maintaining Boeing's role as the industry's leader for after-delivery service. The resources under Mancini's direction provide 24-hour technical support, spare parts, modification and engineering services, digital information products, customer training, and other valuable services for more than 800 Boeing operators. He joined Boeing as vice president of Maintenance Services in March 2002, overseeing the unit of Boeing Commercial Aviation Services responsible for airplane maintenance information, engineering and planning; airplane-on-the-ground (AOG) and recovery services; component maintenance; and Boeing subsidiaries, Continental Data Graphics and AeroInfo Systems. Previously, Mancini was vice president of engineering and technical support for United Airlines, where he managed 1,000 technical professionals in the engineering and training departments who ensured the reliability of the fleet. Mancini joined United in 1985 as director of maintenance analysis and research in San Francisco. He went on to serve as director of maintenance automation and general manager of engineering. Before joining United, Mancini held a variety of management positions at Shell Development Co. in Houston and Chevron in San Francisco. He has also held positions as vice president of technical operations and as vice president of engineering, inspection, and quality assurance at Northwest Airlines. Mancini earned a doctorate and master's degree in operations research from Stanford University. He also holds a bachelor's degree in general engineering from the University of Illinois at Champaign-Urbana.

EXHIBIT 5 Biographies in December 2005: Alan Mulally, Lou Mancini, Scott Carson, and Chris Kettering (*Continued*)

Scott Carson is senior vice president of sales and marketing for Boeing Commercial Airplanes and has responsibility for the sales of commercial airplanes and related services to airline customers and leasing companies around the world. Prior to this assignment, he led Connexion by Boeing™, bringing the high-speed in-flight Internet service to market with airlines in Europe and Asia. Prior to this, Carson had served as executive vice president and chief financial officer of Boeing Commercial Airplanes. Carson joined Boeing in 1973 as a financial analyst on the B-1 bomber avionics program. He held a series of management positions in the Boeing Defense & Space Group, and in 1985 he moved to Boeing Company offices where he served as operations assistant corporate controller, controller for Aerospace & Electronics, and director of planning and computing, before returning to the Defense and Space Group in 1992. In 1993, he was named Space Station transition program director and went on to serve as Space Station business operations deputy program manager. In 1997, Carson was named executive vice president of business resources for the former Boeing Information, Space & Defense Systems (ISDS). Carson graduated from Washington State University with a bachelor's degree in business administration and he received an MBA from University of Washington.

Chris Kettering is director of the e-Enabled program in Boeing Commercial Airplanes. His primary responsibilities include leading the enterprisewide effort to develop and deploy an integrated architecture for product hardware, software, content, and connectivity and to bring new e-Enabled commercial products and services to market. Kettering joined Boeing in 1986 and has held a series of engineering, marketing, and management positions in Commercial Airplanes. Prior to rejoining Commercial Airplanes, he was the director, enterprise integration for air traffic management. As an early member of the 777 team, Kettering was involved in the 777 aerodynamic wing design and wind-tunnel testing. He also supported design-build teams, sales campaigns, flight-testing, and certification. During 1998, Kettering held a three-month guest management position at BMW AG in Munich, Germany. In 1993 he worked for five months at British Airways flight operations and engineering in London studying all facets of the day-to-day operation of the airline. Previously, Kettering was a configuration engineer for Douglas Aircraft Company in Long Beach, California, and an engineering consultant for United Technologies in Mountain View, California. Kettering holds a Bachelor of Science degree in aeronautical engineering from California Polytechnic State University in San Luis Obispo, California.

In September 2001, Condit relocated Boeing's corporate headquarters from its long-time home in Seattle to Chicago. The move was part of a greater corporate reorganization. Condit restructured the company into business units that would align with the new strategic footprint. The presidents of Boeing's two largest business units—Integrated Defense Systems and Commercial Airplanes—were promoted to chief executive officers.

Condit advocated a low-risk approach to expanding into new markets: Either apply new technology to existing markets, or test new markets with familiar technology.[50] However, in the mid-1990s, Boeing had run into several dead-ends with the new technology proposed for the 777. The 777's Electronic Library System featured an onboard Local Area Network (OLAN) and an onboard server that could gather and store significant maintenance, flight, and cabin information. Even after several years of marketing, the airlines didn't adopt the new systems. The technology was ahead of its time.

[50] Paul C. Proctor.

EXHIBIT 6 Boeing Subsidiaries and MyBoeingFleet.com (December 2005)

Source: Company documents and Dick Schleh, "Info at Your Fingertips," *Frontiers*, September 2000.

Preston Aviation Solutions provides a comprehensive suite of IT solutions to meet the needs of aviation customers. Its mandate is to increase market share and aggressively expand offerings to further meet the simulation and scheduling needs of the aviation industry. Boeing acquired Preston in 1999.

Continental Data Graphics Corp. provides customized information and documentation to airlines, including illustrated parts catalogs, provisioning/procurement data, customized fleet and owner/operator catalogs, and component maintenance manuals. Using 9,700 proprietary software programs, Continental has developed an unsurpassed expertise in parts-related information management services. Boeing acquired Continental Data Graphics in 2000.

Hughes Electronics Corporation is recognized as the technological world leader in space-based communications, reconnaissance, surveillance, and imaging systems. Hughes Space and Communications is also the world's leading manufacturer of commercial communications satellites, with a backlog of more than 36 satellites valued at more than $5 billion in 2000. Boeing acquired Hughes Electronics Corporation's space and communications business and related operations in October 2000. The acquisition made Boeing the world's largest space company, boosted its space-related revenues, and provided for significant future growth in information and communications products and services, which had been identified as a major growth area for Boeing in the coming decade.

Jeppesen Sanderson Inc. provides a full range of print and electronic flight information services, including navigation data, computerized flight planning, aviation software products, aviation weather services, maintenance information, and pilot training systems and supplies. Jeppesen's customer base includes the majority of airlines around the world and all U.S. airlines. It also serves the large general aviation and business aviation markets. Boeing acquired Jeppesen Sanderson, Inc. in October 2000.

SBS International provides powerful and flexible tools to manage crew scheduling in both regulated and deregulated environments. It enables airlines to deal with rapidly changing flight schedules, growing crew forces, and increasingly complex logistic requirements. SBS International's planning suite includes four key product areas: crew planning, crew management, operations control, and groundstar. Boeing acquired SBS International in July 2001.

MyBoeingFleet.com is a password-protected portal that provides a single point of customer entry into Boeing information for maintenance, engineering, and flight operations data. Millions of engineering drawings, a full range of maintenance manuals, service bulletins, fleet statistics, flight manuals, and other documents are accessed quickly via the portal. Updated daily, its contents assure users access to the latest and most accurate information for safe, efficient fleet operations. "MyBoeingFleet.com is more than simply a repository of data," said Barb Claitman, director of e-commerce for Commercial Aviation Services. "It offers interactive and collaborative features as well. For example, it provides direct access to the Boeing PART page, where airlines order and track their spare parts shipments. Another feature, known as the FLEET TEAM Digest and Resolution Process, provides a forum for airlines and Boeing to identify, prioritize, and resolve technical issues." As of 2006, the site had grown to 10 million hits per month.

However, with the creation of CAS and with four additional acquisitions—Preston Aviation Solutions, an airport and air traffic solutions provider; Continental Data Graphics, a provider of information and documentation to airlines; SBS International, a crew scheduling systems provider; and AeroInfo Systems Inc., a provider of advanced maintenance software applications for the airline industry—Boeing was in a better position to introduce new IT-enabled products and services (see Exhibit 7 for the evolution of e-Enabling). Building on elements of the 777's advanced network technology and leveraging the strengths of its new subsidiaries, CAS announced new service offerings. These businesses focused primarily on airplane maintenance, flight operation solutions, and cabin/passenger services. Most notable of these was MyBoeingFleet.com, which was a Web portal to airplane data and applications hosted on Boeing servers.

In addition to businesses within CAS, two other important businesses were started in CAS and then "spun out" into independent divisions of the company: The first, Connexion by Boeing™, which began in 2000, provided in-flight broadband Internet service to passengers. The business unit, then led by Scott Carson, found early success with four airlines signing up for the service on 1,500 planes in the first year. But Connexion by Boeing™ was greatly affected by the market changes after September 11, 2001, and several airlines pulled out of their contracts.

Carson recast the value of Connexion by Boeing™, showing airlines that it was more than an in-flight perk, and showing Boeing that it was a service that could be leveraged companywide. He took great effort to learn exactly what Boeing's customers (the airlines) as well as the airlines' customers (the passengers) needed from technology. He initiated a thorough three-month trial period for Connexion by Boeing™, during which Lufthansa Airlines and British Airways dedicated an Airbus 340 and a Boeing 747 full time to conducting passenger tests twice a day.[51] Carson described the benefits of thorough testing:

> At Connexion by Boeing™, it cost a lot of capital to acquire a commercial jetliner and convert it to a full-time flying laboratory so that we could develop and validate the technology. It was inconvenient to codesign our service with 15 of the world's leading airlines. It was not cheap to run two overlapping passenger-service demonstrations across the Atlantic for three months earlier this year. But our best minds couldn't think of a better way of understanding what our airline customers needed—and just as importantly—what their customers needed.[52]

In the spring of 2004, Connexion by Boeing™ began commercial service on Lufthansa Airlines, and it was on 11 airlines by the spring of 2005.[53] Later that year, Carson moved from Connexion by Boeing™ and was named senior vice president of sales for Boeing Commercial Airplanes, where he would have an opportunity to drive the marketing and selling of the vision of the e-Enabled environment to airplane customers. Laurette Koellner replaced him as president of Connexion by Boeing™. In addition, in 2004, Connexion by Boeing™ branched out to offer its services beyond the aviation industry; Laurette Koellner said that Connexion by Boeing™ "offers the potential to improve efficiency and customer service, and it appears to have potential to bring significant value to the maritime industry."[54]

The second business that was "spun out" from CAS was Boeing's Air Traffic Management service, launched in 2000 as well. This business would take advantage of the many Boeing capabilities around the e-Enabled environment, and, in partnership with the U.S. Government Federal Aviation Administration (FAA), international air traffic control organizations, and

[51] http://www.boeing.com/news/speeches/2003/carson_030923.html, accessed December 2005.

[52] Ibid.

[53] Company documents.

[54] Laurette Koellner, "An Amazing Year for In-Flight Connectivity," *Connexion by Boeing eUpdate*, November–December 2004.

EXHIBIT 7 The Evolution of e-Enabling

Source: Company documents.

Year	What	Comment
1960s and 1970s	Airline Computer Reservations Systems	Sabre (Semi Automated Business Research Environment) launched in the early 60s and United Airline's Apollo in travel agencies by 1976.
1970s and 1980s	ACARS	Aircraft Communication Addressing and Reporting System (or ACARS) is a digital datalink system for transmission of small messages between aircraft and ground stations via radio or satellite.
1980s	Mileage programs	American AAdvantage, May 1981.
1989	Boeing 747-400	Fly-by-wire system, glass cockpit.
1995	Boeing 777	First computer designed airplane, fly-by-wire, glass cockpit, fully software configurable avionics, digital data download capability.
1990s	Online reservation and revenue management systems changed ticketing	Created ease for customers and integrated information for airline route and fare optimization.
1990s	e-Tickets	Goal of 100% tickets issued globally by end of 2007.
1990s	Check-in kiosks streamlined the airport experience	Las Vegas McCarran Airport becomes first to use kiosks for multiple airlines in 2003.
2001	My Boeing Fleet (MBF)	Commercial Airplanes external customer portal. 1.4 million hits per month in 2001, 4.6 million hits per month in 2002, 10 million hits per month in 2006.
2008	Boeing 787	Fully e-Enabled airplane with onboard router/server, wireless cabin communications, digital software and data loading, electronic flight deck with cockpit/cabin interface.

other companies, developed future solutions to meet global air traffic control needs. By 2005, a Boeing-led industry team had launched an Internet-like system that linked the air traffic control systems of the U.S. FAA, Department of Defense, and Homeland Security, providing shared situational awareness, real-time information, and integrated network operations. Future plans involved expanding the network internationally and adding new customers, including passenger and cargo airlines, business jet operators, and corporations.[55]

While the acquisition of several airline services companies paved the way for building the Commercial Aviation Services Company within Boeing, it soon became clear that the "biggest challenges and risks we face are cultural and organizational—not technical."[56]

Open New Frontiers

> We saw some pockets of need and how to fill those pockets. But there was no systemic, holistic view of how to add them together. [Our task] is to take these building blocks and allow them to work together to further increase efficiency.
>
> *Chris Kettering, 2005*[57]

If the transition into the new frontier of services was risky, it was also inevitable. "You can't imagine a future where airplanes aren't networked to the airlines' information systems," said Larry Coughlin, director of strategic projects for Boeing Commercial Airplanes. "It's going to happen, and the mindset was, if Boeing doesn't do it first, someone else will."[58]

And if the transition was inevitable, the September 11, 2001, terrorist attacks made it urgent as they catalyzed the transformation of the airlines' business models. "In the first half of 2002, the top 10 U.S. airlines . . . posted staggering operating losses of $12.3 billion. These losses came on top of $7.3 billion of red ink for full year 2001, which was the biggest deficit in the history of the airline industry."[59] The airlines were focused on short-term survival, not long-term investments. They faced immense pressure to cut costs as revenues declined, and several filed for bankruptcy. Boeing was in a unique position to help: Its new array of products and services could be used to greatly improve efficiency and to help the airlines cut operating costs on a day-to-day basis.

In June 2003, at the Paris Air Show, Boeing unveiled its new strategy, which it called e-Enabled Advantage. The term reflected a concept whereby all data and information systems relating to airplane maintenance, flight operations, and passenger needs would be seamlessly interconnected to effectively bring the airplane into the airline's network during flight.[60] The e-Enabled Advantage would "help airlines cut costs, improve dispatch reliability, reduce delays and cancellations, improve passenger service, enhance aviation security, and provide real-time situational awareness for both flight crew and airline operations centers."[61]

At the time of the announcement, e-Enabled Advantage was little more than a bright idea based on a scattered selection of products and services. "The e-Enabled Advantage is a way of doing things; it's not one tangible product or service," said Tim Mooney, senior strategist, marketing business strategy.[62] But introducing the term to the public helped set Boeing in motion to develop a clearly defined strategy. "The concept became bigger and more extended than we realized as we talked to the airlines," Mooney said, "and we realized that we had to figure out what kind of partnerships, what kind of standards, and the other technologies we needed to make the vision a reality." At the time, various segments of

[55] http://www.boeing.com/atm/organization/index.html, accessed December 2005.

[56] Author interview, May 2005.

[57] Debby Arkell, "Subsidiaries: On the Same Team," *Frontiers*, May 2005.

[58] Author interview, January 18, 2006.

[59] Standard & Poor's Industry Survey: Aerospace and Defense, April 2003.

[60] Author interview, January 6, 2006.

[61] "Boeing Revamps Aviation Strategy," *Satellite News*, June 23, 2003.

[62] Author interview, May 24, 2005.

EXHIBIT 8 e-Enabled Advantage Components

Source: Company documents.

Component	Capability
Solutions Consulting	Consulting engagements with airline operating personnel to address areas of operational improvements; involves modeling of airline's operations, simulations of "as is" and "to be" operational processes and supporting technologies, and sophisticated analytics to identify opportunities to reduce cost and improve business performance.
Portable Maintenance Aid	Interactive maintenance software that enables mechanics and engineers to resolve technical issues at the work site, in the hangar, in the office, or on the flight line, and to troubleshoot airplanes in minimum time.
Airplane Health Management	Software and Web-based capability which e-Enables maintenance by letting airlines monitor engine and airframe systems information in real time. Allows both diagnostic and predictive analysis. Reduces aircraft delays, cancelations, air turn-backs, and diversions.
Integrated Materials Management	Maintenance supply chain software that transitions airline materials management responsibility to Boeing. Provides service level reliability, lower parts costs, lower inventory, better logistics, while leveraging supplier partnerships for improved asset management and supply chain functionality. Allows global planning and collaboration as well as improved quality assurance.
SBS Products	Provides resource planning, scheduling, and management solutions to the worldwide aviation industry. These services are offered by Boeing Commercial Aviation Services to enhance the safety, security, and efficiency of the global air transportation system.
Enterprise One	Suite of integrated software applications optimized for efficient management of configuration, logistics, maintenance planning and scheduling, engineering, and document management.
Electronic Flight Bag (EFB)	Electronic charts, performance calculations, electronic documents, checklists, real-time weather and notice-to-airman, fault finder, and electronic log book to reduce or eliminate paper, improve data accuracy, aircraft utilization, safety, and performance. Performance tools provide real-time exact data, which facilitates more sophisticated and accurate aircraft performance.
Jeppesen Data	Jeppesen Electronic Flight Bag data supporting electronic log books, e-documents, charts, performance calculators, and other EFB features.
e-Link	Jeppesen e-Link is an Internet delivery service. This allows airlines to access and print their full library of tailored electronic charts and data via a secure Internet connection.
Hosted Ops Control	OPS Control is Jeppesen's flight operations management solution. It incorporates a suite of flight planning products and operations control, offering dynamic system interfaces that facilitate quick and easy access to all types of flight information.
Core Network	The hardware, middleware, and applications connecting the cockpit and cabin flight crews with all on-ground communication and data capabilities and providing passengers with both communications and entertainment connections. The "brain on the plane," managing and routing enormous quantities of data input and output within the airplane and between the airplane and the outside world. Consists of both computer and network hardware and software, which facilitate functions in cockpit/cabin for crew and in the cabin for passengers. Based on IEEE 80.11 and IEEE 802.11B wireless standards.
Connexion by Boeing™	High-speed Internet service. Provides data and entertainment to passengers and forms the foundation of the high-speed network needed for delivering the full range of e-Enabled Advantage services. In use on both the Boeing and non-Boeing aircraft fleet of 11 airlines, as of April 2005.
My Boeing Fleet	Web portal to the world's largest repository of aviation information and services. Includes flight operations support, maintenance and engineering services, fleet enhancement and modification data, and spares and logistics support.
VPN Access	Boeing application service provider enables an airline customer and/or aircraft in its fleet to connect through a hosted Boeing network. Boeing also sells VPN services and tools to companies so that they can host their own networks and solutions.

the e-Enabled environment, the fundamental precursor to the e-Enabled Advantage, existed in different areas of the company with little coordination. "We realized we were spending a heck of a lot of money on research and development and on new programs and products, all valid by their own right, and we didn't understand how they all fit into a comprehensive strategy," said Coughlin.

In early 2004, Boeing launched a concerted effort to develop a strategy for how it should support and generate value from the e-Enabled environment—to take a step back and evaluate the existing products and services, "and to say, do these all fit together, do they work together, do they cannibalize existing products or services or are they synergistic?" said Coughlin. Just two months into the strategy effort, Boeing decided there was enough demand and that it had sufficient resources to form a program to coordinate the myriad service efforts into one cohesive effort (see Exhibit 8).

In February 2004, Kettering was brought on to lead the e-Enabled Program, which was sponsored by the leaders of Boeing Commercial Airplanes and housed within the CAS unit. For Boeing, which had always been based on a product model, "the shift into services and solutions [was] a big mindset change,"[63] according to Kettering. But consolidating the fragmented efforts to offer new products and services in one program would help the transition. "Many companies wanted to have a single point of contact with Boeing," said Carson. "We needed to break down these silos to better integrate our message and solutions for our customers."[64]

e-Enabled Environment

> Our vision of the future of flight is fundamentally linked with technology, services, and keeping customers flying. We believe Boeing and its subsidiaries will take a network-centric approach to flight operations and aircraft maintenance, to enhance airlines' productivity.
>
> *Lou Mancini, 2005*[65]

Boeing saw the e-Enabled environment as the next "lever" that the airlines could pull to dramatically reduce costs and to shift from short-term management to long-term value planning.[66] Airlines had used IT in the past to cut costs and streamline operations but had traditionally invested in commercial operations such as computer reservation systems, self-service check-in, revenue management systems, and customer data warehouses.[67] "While commercial IT systems were effective in cutting costs and increasing revenues and customer switching costs, they did this within one silo of the airline, stopping short of improving end-to-end operating processes across all members of an airline's business network. In order to survive, airline executives knew they would need to invest in broader and more holistic IT solutions,"[68] said Kettering.

And that's exactly what e-Enabled environment was designed to do. Boeing thought of the airplane as the "factory" of an airline, where the service was provided. "Unfortunately, it's a factory that is 'unplugged' from the airline while flying—which can be up to 15 hours—depriving airlines of valuable information and data that could be used to improve efficiency and safety," said Coughlin.[69] With the e-Enabled environment, the airplane was "plugged in" to every aspect of airline operations—from flight operations managers to maintenance managers to crew members and regulatory agencies—creating one seamless network that could deliver crucial information to the people who needed it most, when they needed it most.

An early implementation of the e-Enabled environment for some airplanes was an onboard server called the Core Network, a component of Connexion by Boeing™, the high-speed data communications service.[70] The Core Network was

[63] Ibid.

[64] Ibid.

[65] Debby Arkell.

[66] Company documents.

[67] Ibid.

[68] Author interview, May 24, 2005.

[69] Ibid.

[70] http://www.boeing.com/news/releases/2003/q2/nr_030617j.html, accessed December 2005.

"the brain of the plane," said Carson. "It manages and routes data within the airplane and between the airplane and the outside world."[71] Connexion by Boeing™ delivered high-speed Internet service to the airlines, the crew, and the passengers. With this infrastructure in place, Boeing and its industry partners could launch any number of cost-cutting or time-saving applications based on other internal and external capabilities, and airlines could pick and choose the specific applications to meet their needs. For example, in case of delays, crew members could alter their schedules from the airplane using scheduling software (provided by SBS International) hosted on ground systems but accessible from the airplane through Connexion by Boeing™ service. The software avoided rule violations and penalties, amended hotel and ground transportation arrangements, and allowed crew to view their schedules online. It "[streamlined] the planning process facilitating faster, more effective, real-time crew management decisions and [safeguarded] against inadvertent contractual or regulatory oversights. All of which [led] to a direct reduction in an airline's operating costs."[72]

Indeed, Boeing executives and their airline customers believed that the e-Enabled environment was most effective in improving the efficiency of maintenance operations. According to Peter Smith, project director of solutions valuations for the Boeing's services businesses, "this [the e-Enabled environment] can improve reliability by 0.5 percent and, more importantly, it can decrease cost by $100 per hour out of $400 per hour total maintenance costs."

To address a portion of this opportunity, in 2002, CAS began developing Airplane Health Management (AHM), an in-flight airplane monitoring system that would help airlines reduce flight-schedule interruptions.[73] With AHM, airlines could use MyBoeingFleet.com to "monitor an entire fleet in real time." That information could then be sent to the ground crew in real time, during a flight, using Connexion by Boeing™ or other communications methods, so the necessary technicians, spare parts, and specialized tools could be ready and waiting by the time the plane arrived at the gate.[74] The real benefit of AHM was not just knowing what needed to be fixed by the time the plane landed, but that it converted nonroutine maintenance problems into scheduled, or scheduleable, tasks. Anytime maintenance surprises could be eliminated, maintenance productivity naturally improved.[75] This kind of decision support tool has computers doing what they do best: analyzing data and presenting it as information and knowledge; and people doing what they do best: making the decision on the proper course of action.

Boeing estimated that, in 2002, the total airline operating expenses that the e-Enabled environment could affect reached nearly $250 billion, and the potential impact of the e-Enabled Advantage for Boeing's airline customers could range from $23 billion to $44 billion in savings per year (see Exhibit 9).[76] "Given this much benefit," said Coughlin, "there should be a huge market pull for e-Enabled sometime in the future."[77]

A New Customer Engagement Model

> To be effective, we have to take a consultative approach. We have to ask, what are an airline's areas of pain or need, and what can we do to help solve that? It can't be, "I come bearing a gift of technology," but "I'm helping you examine what you need to become more efficient."
>
> *Tim Mooney, 2005*[78]

[71] Author interview, December 2004.

[72] http://www.sbsint.com/solutions/products2.html, accessed December 2005.

[73] http://www.boeing.com/news/releases/2004/q1/nr_040223h.html, accessed December 2005.

[74] "Technology Drives." *Aviation Today*, October 1, 2005.

[75] Ibid.

[76] Company documents.

[77] Author interview, May 2005.

[78] Jim Proulx, "Tomorrow Takes Shape," *Frontiers*, April 2005.

EXHIBIT 9 **Airline Costs and Potential Benefits of e-Enabled Advantage**

Source: Company documents.

Cost Areas[a]	Overall Spend ($ million)	e-Enabled Benefit Low (%)	e-Enabled Benefit High (%)	e-Enabled Benefit Low ($ million)	e-Enabled Benefit High ($ million)
Flight Operations	$80,349	2%	4%	$1,991	$3,398
Maintenance Operations	27,231	10	30	2,662	8,038
Passenger Services	26,437	1	1	132	264
Own/Lease	28,023	16	27	4,371	7,433
Ground Operations	38,098	0	6	144	2,455
Ticket Sales and Promotion	26,437	16	26	4,230	6,874
Other	18,767	0	5	0	938
G&A	19,027	4	7	731	1,310
Scheduled Services[b]	237,472	4	6	9,171	14,259
Totals	273,588[c]			23,433	44,970

[a] Based on world top 80 airlines.
[b] Total revenue.
[c] Includes revenue from nonscheduled flights and incidental revenue.

Aggregate Benefit Categories: $23–$44B

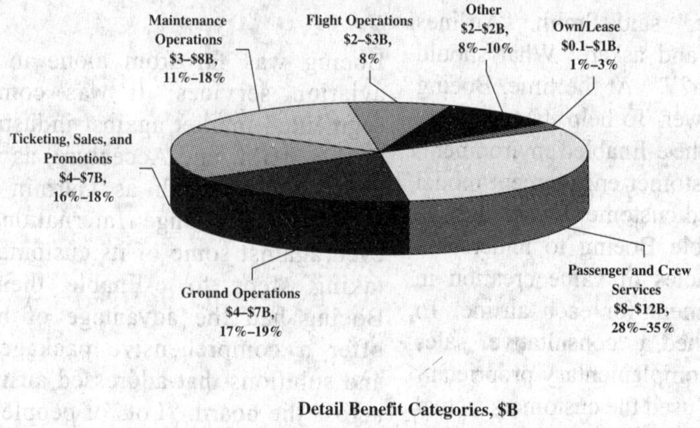

Detail Benefit Categories, $B

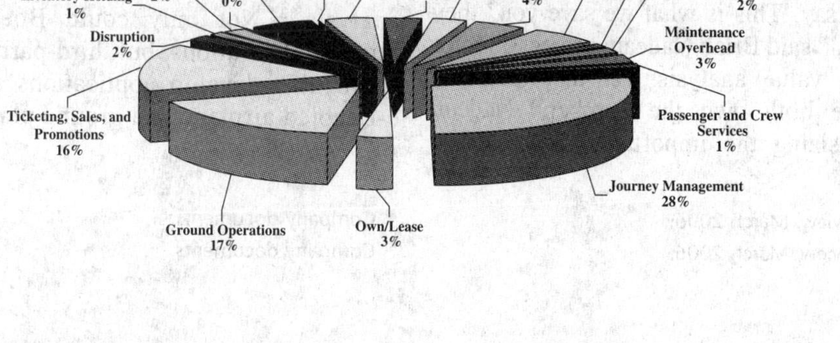

As Boeing shifted into services with the launch of its maintenance and flight operations services and Connexion by Boeing™, its executives and employees had to learn how to best apply emerging information technology to serve its customers. But even more challenging were other factors. First, Boeing had to get its customers to start thinking of it as a service provider. Second, Boeing had to convince a very skeptical customer base that the e-Enabled environment would yield value to their businesses. And third, Boeing had to separate the value created by its airline services from the value created by the airplanes themselves. For example, it was not uncommon for an airline customer to comment: *"How dare you, Boeing, charge me so your airplanes perform the way they were supposed to."*[79] But the value of the e-Enabled environment is not about the airplane; rather it is about improving the performance of the people in the airline.

When the first elements of the e-Enabled environment were launched in the 1990s—such as the 777's on-board LAN and server—the major customers "didn't bite," said Smith. "Airlines came back to Boeing and asked, 'What should we do with all this data?'"[80] At the time, Boeing didn't have a great answer. To help its customers understand the value of the e-Enabled environment, it needed to adopt a customer engagement model that emphasized detailed customer knowledge—a model that would enable Boeing to understand and convey the intricacies of value creation in the e-Enabled environment for each airline. To that end, Boeing launched a "consultative" sales approach and created complementary proprietary software. The approach used the customers' actual airplane fleet information and operations models to understand an airline's *As Is* and *What If* processes. "I've been on lot of sales calls. If you walk in and say 'This is what we save you,' they say 'Prove it,'" said Brian Nadeau, project director for aviation value analysis. "If they discover with us, we both own the number," Nadeau said, emphasizing the importance of a shared perspective.

Boeing's consultative selling approach showed airlines in a quantifiable way how various products and services within the e-Enabled suite could improve their day-to-day operations. For example, Boeing demonstrated to one airline customer how the e-Enabled environment could create $225 million value over 10 years; these cost savings were primarily from decreasing delays for their 747 fleet. "The process helps Boeing establish a jointly owned value proposition with our customers. This makes us a partner rather than a supplier,"[81] said Heide Tacheron, project director, aviation services value analysis.

Competition

> Whatever we do in e-Enabling will never be the sole reason that people buy Boeing airplanes. But it will certainly help create a preference for Boeing airplanes in the marketplace.
>
> *Scott Carson, 2005*

Boeing was far from alone in the field of aviation services: It was competing in a segmented market against industry giants like Oracle, IBM, and Accenture, as well as many niche players such as Garmin International and Aero Exchange International, Inc., and even against some of its customers, who were taking steps to e-Enable themselves. But Boeing had the advantage of being able to offer a comprehensive package of services and solutions that addressed airline operations across the board. "Lots of people [were] doing individual systems, but not a lot were doing integrated solutions that add real value," said Jeff Deckrow, senior manager, CAS market analysis.[82] Not only could Boeing provide integrated solutions, but third-party developers could also develop applications for Boeing's e-Enabled airplane and ground platforms.

[79] Author interview, March 2006.

[80] Author interview, March 2006.

[81] Company documents.

[82] Company documents.

Boeing also had to develop a plan to retrofit existing Boeing planes with e-Enabling capabilities. The worldwide fleet was expected to grow by nearly 20,000 in 20 years, but almost 10,000 planes that were flying in 2003 were expected to still be in service in 2023. "If you want to impact e-Enabled, it can't just be on new aircraft; it needs to be on the retained fleet as well,"[83] Mooney explained. And in a break from traditional practice, Boeing's e-Enabled Advantage was designed to be independent of airplane manufacturer—meaning it worked on both Boeing and Airbus planes. Indeed, the first installation of Connexion by Boeing™ was on an Airbus 340 for Lufthansa Airlines. "It wasn't easy for Connexion by Boeing™ or for Lufthansa," said a Boeing manager. "Lufthansa really had to leverage Airbus to put the system on the airplanes. That was a big deal for us, and at the end of the day, that's something we're going to have to think about. Are we branded correctly and are we structured correctly [inside Boeing] or are we selling ourselves short?"

Sure enough, Boeing's e-Enabled Advantage strategy faced fierce competition from Airbus. "Airbus matched us with everything we did,"[84] said Peter Niklaus, director maintenance information and engineering services for CAS. For example, Airbus offered an in-flight Internet service, OnAir, which competed with Connexion by Boeing™; it offered an aircraft fault management tool, AIRMAN, to compete with Boeing's AHM; and it had its own technical data Web viewer, AirN@v, to match Boeing's Portable Maintenance Aid. Although "everyone agrees our technology is better," said Bob Manelski, director of Boeing Commercial Airplanes Operations Center, referring specifically to Boeing's Airplane Health Management and MyBoeingFleet.com versus Airbus' AIRMAN, "they are overtaking us in signing on new customers because they are selling the product at a significant discount."

The Commercial Aviation Services group had ongoing debates on whether and how much to discount some of the e-Enabling services to seed the market for Boeing's solutions and to define the standards going forward. Products like MyBoeingFleet were provided free of charge and experienced high adoption rates. "But at the end of the day, there's a clarity to your products when they have to earn their way into customers through creating value on their own merit, and we still have to run a business based on profit and loss for products and services," said Mooney.[85]

The e-Enabled Program knew that Boeing had reason to be concerned about Airbus: "Quite frankly, they're a very good competitor," they said. Nevertheless, and in spite of the aforementioned executive's claims, neither Boeing nor Airbus was a clear leader in e-Enabling. "I think we're both eyeballing each other, looking across the no-man's land, saying, 'O.K., they did this, so what are we going to do?'" Coughlin said. "Right now, it's sort of like a very pre-emptive chess game. The e-Enabled environment is going to happen, and the question is, are we going to be following or leading?"

The Silver Bullet?

In mid-2005, Boeing Commercial Airplanes faced a mixed outlook. Although both independent industry analysts as well as Boeing's analysts forecasted an average annual growth in passenger volume of around 5 percent over the next two decades,[86] there remained some elements of uncertainty. The 2004 annual report warned that: "We can make no assurance that any customer will purchase additional products or services from us after our contract with the customer has ended."[87] Although many of the legacy carriers were struggling, low-cost carriers had demonstrated that, given the right operating structure, sustained

[83] Company documents.

[84] Company documents.

[85] Author interview, January 18, 2006.

[86] AVITAS GOAT 2005.

[87] Boeing Annual Report, 2004.

profitability could be achieved. Thus, increasing operational efficiencies was seen as key for the major airlines' survival. Boeing's executives saw these pressures for reducing costs as a factor that could have a strong impact on Boeing's own market position and profitability. The 2004 annual report stated that:

> The commercial jet aircraft market and the airline industry remain extremely competitive. We expect the existing long-term downward trend in passenger revenue yields worldwide (measured in real terms) to continue into the foreseeable future. Market liberalization in Europe and Asia has continued to enable low-cost airlines to gain market share. These airlines have increased the downward pressure on airfares. This results in continued cost pressures for all airlines and price pressure on our products. Major productivity gains are essential to ensure a favorable market position at acceptable profit margins.[88]

Many within Boeing believed that the e-Enabled Advantage could prove to be the "silver bullet" to deal with the situation. The efficiency gains in the airlines' day-to-day operations—made possible by the products and services of the e-Enabled environment—could help them survive in difficult times. At the same time, offering an integrated suite of e-Enabled solutions could help to develop the airlines' preference for Boeing's jetliners.

As the e-Enabled Program and CAS navigated through the transformation into services, they understood the importance of defining a compelling and consistent message that would communicate the value that e-Enabling could offer—not only to Boeing's customers, but to the individual business units within Boeing as well. But questions remained. Could e-Enabling create the kind of sustainable advantage that the airplanes used to provide? And would the advantage be able to withstand the competition so close at hand? Would Boeing's transition into services prove to be the silver bullet—the solution to the airlines' financial woes and to Boeing's aggressive competition with Airbus?

[88] Ibid.

Royal DSM N.V.: Transforming for the Twenty-First Century

The Royal DSM N.V. case provides an excellent summary for Module 1 and a transition to Module 2. It enables examination of the impact of IT on the rapidly changing business model of the company while also enabling a thorough exploration of how to build IT capabilities to execute strategy. As you read the DSM case, consider the following questions: What challenges and opportunities do senior executives at DSM N.V. face in 2000? What challenges and opportunities does newly hired CIO Jo van den Hanenberg face when he assumes his position in 2000? How should van den Hanenberg position IT as a strategic asset and organize and govern the IT function?

Case 1-5

Royal DSM N.V.: Information Technology Enabling Business Transformation

In 2000, Royal DSM N.V., a Netherlands-based company that had its origins in coal mining but had expanded into industrial chemicals, performance materials, and life sciences products, was poised for change. In an effort to move away from the cyclical petrochemicals business and into the more stable and growing life sciences and performance materials businesses, DSM planned to radically alter its portfolio through divestitures and acquisitions. The corporate strategy, termed "Vision 2005: Focus and Value," called for the company to divest a significant part of its core petrochemicals business and to make acquisitions in areas in which the company had relatively little experience.

DSM executives anticipated that the transition would be complex yet wanted to move quickly. One of the biggest challenges would be upgrading the company's Information and Communication Technology (ICT) to meet the demands of the new diversified company and to enable execution of the company's new business strategy, which called for aggressive growth through mergers and acquisitions. Specifically, to gain operational efficiency, the company needed to standardize its ICT infrastructure and enterprise applications and transform the way it built and managed ICT. To support its new strategy, DSM also needed to improve its ability to rapidly disentangle an acquired business from a parent company and simultaneously integrate it into DSM. In 2000, Jo van den Hanenberg was hired as corporate CIO and was charged with building these capabilities, and building them fast. (See Exhibit 1 for a summary of the background of van den Hanenberg and other key players.)

Professors Lynda M. Applegate and Edward Watson of Louisiana State University and Research Associate Mara Vatz prepared this case as the basis of discussion rather than to illustrate effective or ineffective management.

Company and Industry Background

> Some 40 years ago, DSM took the last step in the transition from mining to chemicals. Since then, the company has gradually evolved from a national to a European organization. Our strategies of the past ten years accelerated the company's internationalization towards a global player. Important drivers in this development were significant portfolio changes, technological progress, new cooperative patterns, and increasing efforts to exploit the opportunities of emerging economies.
>
> *DSM 2005 Annual Report*

EXHIBIT 1 DSM Executive Biographies

Source: DSM Internal documents.

Peter Elverding (CEO and Chairman of the Managing Board of Directors) joined DSM in 1985 and held various managerial posts at subsidiaries such as DSM Resins and DSM Research. In 1995, he was appointed to the managing board as Vice President, Personnel and Organization. In July 1999, he succeeded Simon de Bree as chairman of the DSM Managing Board. Elverding studied Dutch law at the University of Amsterdam, with specialization in labor law and organizational theory, and began his career in 1973 in the health care industry.

Jo van den Hanenberg (CIO) joined DSM in March 2000 and serves on the Group Management Committee, the ICT Governance Board, and the DSM Nutritional Products Executive Committee. Prior to joining DSM, he was senior vice president and a member of the board at Philips Business Electronics NV. Prior to that, van den Hanenberg served in various managerial capacities at Philips, including research, IT, technology, and purchasing. He currently sits on the advisory councils of Dell Europe, EDS Europe, Getronics, and Microsoft Netherlands. Furthermore, he is, a member of the research board. Van den Hanenberg graduated with honors, receiving a bachelor's and master's degree in electrical engineering, as well as an MBA in informatics.

Ruud Neeskens (Vice President, DSM ICT Services and Competences) joined DSM in 2005. Prior to joining DSM, he was Industry Director at Atos Origin, where he managed large international ICT programs for companies like DSM, Shell, and SAP. In September 2003, he started working with DSM to manage the ICT disentanglement of Roche Vitamins and ICT integration into DSM. After completion of the vitamins unbundling program, he joined DSM, in 2005, to lead the DSM Global Applications department. Neeskens holds a BSc in electrical engineering and started his career in 1980 as a software and hardware developer.

Theo de Haas (Senior Director, Global Client Services) joined DSM in 2001 and drove the development of the e-business platform. With the acquisition of Roche Vitamins, he assumed the responsibility for the integration of this acquisition within DSM. Before joining DSM, he was IT director EMEA for Ashland Inc., before that, responsible for service delivery for a ERP vendor for the Benelux market. After his chemistry study, he chose information technology and now has 25 years of experience in that field.

Titus Looman (Director, Apollo at DSM Business Support) studied chemical engineering at the University of Eindhoven, the Netherlands, with specialization in polymer chemistry. He joined DSM in 1989 and held several positions ranging from product development to business management. In 2005 he was appointed as Director, Apollo, the DSM global initiative to develop standardized business processes and implement these in all of the DSM business groups, with the aim of achieving more efficient and effective organizations.

Hans Vossen (Director of Strategy) joined DSM in 1991 and held various finance positions at subsidiaries such as DSM Polyethylene and DSM Resins. In 2000, he joined the corporate strategy department of DSM. He was involved in the sales of the petrochemical business to SABIC and the vitamins acquisition from Roche. Vossen studied Economics and Business Administration at the University of Tilburg, with specialization in Information Management, and began his career in 1986 at KPMG.

EXHIBIT 1 DSM Executive Biographies (*Continued*)

Gerard van der Zanden (Manager, Communications) joined DSM in 2000 and held various posts at DSM Corporate Communications (Heerlen, NL), DSM Nutritional Products (Basel, CH) and DSM Netherlands (Geleen, NL). He was involved in the "carve-out" of DSM Petrochemicals and sale to SABIC Europe, the acquisition of Roche Vitamins, and many other important projects. Van der Zanden studied at the Educational Academy, Veghel (NL), and specialized, later on, in the communications business. He started his career in 1978 and worked at the Royal Netherlands Airforce, the Royal Netherlands Army, and the Province of Limburg. Furthermore, he is examiner at the Fontys College (communications), a member of the communication board of VNCI (NL Association of Chemical Industries), and chairman of the communication board of NIABA (Biotech Industry Association of the Netherlands).

Jim Richard (Program Manager, DSM Nutritional Products) joined DSM in 2000 as ICT Manager for DSM Elastomers Americas and, in 2003, went on to manage the DSM Corporate ICT affiliate in the USA. He joined the eVita program in DSM Nutritional Products, in March 2004, in Switzerland. He studied finance at LSU and received his Master of Accountancy from Weatherhead School of Management, Case Western Reserve University, in 1991.

In its first 100 years, the "De Nederlandse Staatmijnen" company, or Dutch State Mines (DSM), evolved from producing coal and fertilizer, to petrochemicals and performance materials, and finally to life science products and biomaterials. In 1989, the company was privatized and went public on the Amsterdam Stock Exchange (AEX), which, in 2005, was part of Euronext Amsterdam. During the 1990s, DSM focused on creating a balance between commerce and research and on developing specialty chemical products for the pharmaceutical and food industries as well as high-performance materials for the automotive, transport, and electronics industries.

Evolving DSM

In the early 1900s, coal was the only indigenous source of energy in the Netherlands, and, as a result, it was considered a commodity of strategic importance. Starting with only six workers in 1902, DSM first mined coal in 1906, and by 1921 was producing coke-oven gas—a by-product of the coal processing operation and an important energy source. But by 1929, the market for coke-oven gas began to shrink and DSM began leveraging its position and capabilities to produce chemicals such as nitrogenous fertilizer and ammonia.

After World War II, the chemicals industry began expanding into plastics and DSM opened its first research lab. During the 1950s, DSM began to produce caprolactam—a compound used in the production of nylon—and by the 1960s had opened both polyethylene and melamine plants. By the early 1970s, the company exited coal mining altogether, closing its last mine in 1973. DSM restructured during the 1980s and expanded its products, through acquisitions, to include a wider variety of specialty chemicals. (See Exhibit 2 for a timeline of DSM's 100 years of evolution and an example of its value chain.)

Simon de Bree was appointed CEO in 1993. Under his leadership, DSM continued to refocus its portfolio by repositioning its business into markets with higher growth and earnings potentials. By the end of the decade, DSM had moved forward on a series of joint ventures with Asian manufacturers. In 1998, DSM acquired Gist Brocades, which specialized in food ingredients and penicillin and, in 2001, Catalytica, a pharmaceutical intermediates, sterile formulation, and packaging company.

When de Bree stepped down mid-1999, he was praised for his efforts to reduce the company's cyclical exposure and to shift its product portfolio towards a larger share of value-added products. Peter Elverding was appointed as CEO and chairman of the managing board of directors and was charged with overseeing the completion of DSM's strategic transformation into a specialty chemicals company.

EXHIBIT 2 Company Timeline and Value Chain

Source: DSM internal documents.

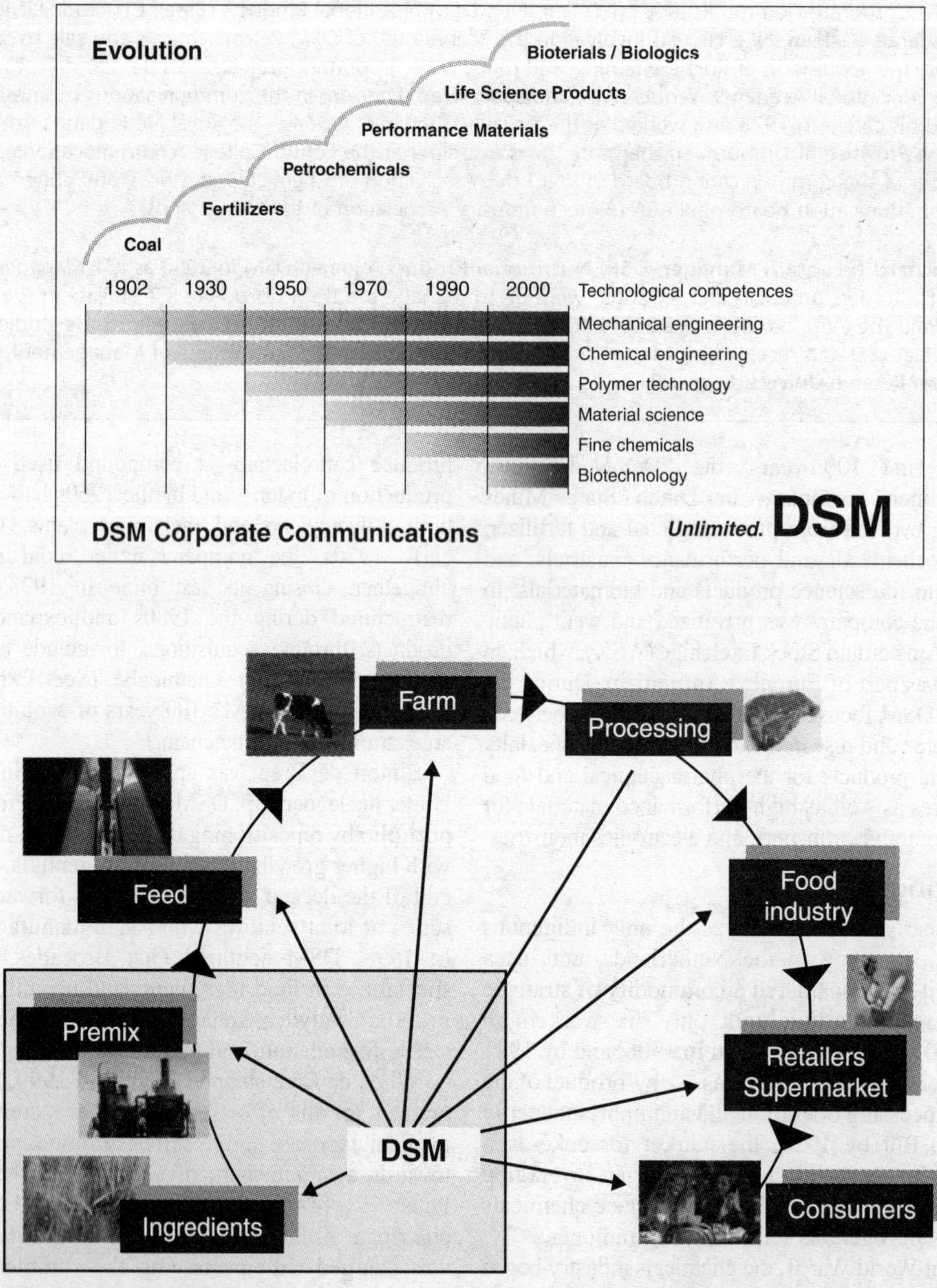

Disruption in the Late 1990s

The pressure to restructure DSM was strongly influenced by changes in the petroleum and chemicals industries. During the 1990s, DSM identified a number of global trends that executives believed could threaten current positions while also providing opportunities for growth in the twenty-first century. Certain technological advances—especially in ICT, biotechnology, materials, and alternative energy sources—promised to accelerate innovation and revolutionize the way business was conducted across a wide variety of industries, including those in which DSM competed. Five key trends that focused DSM executive attention included global industry consolidation; increasing market transparency and price pressure; increased capital market pressure for specialization in value-added growth businesses; and new business models that dramatically reduced costs and improved asset efficiency by outsourcing manufacturing, logistics, and even research to lower-cost labor markets.

During the 1990s, DSM had witnessed rapid consolidation of the oil and gas industry. While many expected smaller players to be gobbled up by large players, the December 1, 1998, announcement of a merger between Exxon and Mobil—the largest corporate merger in history—shook the industry.[1] On December 31, 1998, British Petroleum responded by announcing the acquisition of Amoco to form BP Amoco. The dust had barely settled, however, when, in April 1999, BP Amoco announced its intention to acquire Atlantic Richfield (ARCO). In early 1999, French giant TOTAL acquired the Belgian oil firm PetroFina to form TotalFina and then led a hostile bid to acquire Elf Acquitane. Two weeks later, Elf responded by launching a hostile bid for TotalFina with the intent of separating the combined company into two integrated entities—petroleum and chemicals. Other petroleum and chemical players responded by spinning out their petrochemical businesses into independent entities, such as Borealis and Basell.

Meanwhile, the fragmented pharmaceutical and food sectors were also undergoing consolidation. But unlike the oil industry consolidation—which led to global giants—the pharmaceutical and food sector consolidation led to spin-offs in the form of life sciences products (LSP) and performance materials (PM) companies. These newly formed companies offered potential acquisition opportunities for DSM. Most performance materials/specialty chemicals businesses were global, growing at 5 percent to 10 percent per year, and were financially attractive due to their promise of stable earnings. (See Exhibit 3 for changes in DSM's business environment.)

DSM believed that ongoing industry restructuring in the performance materials and specialty chemicals fields would lead to opportunities for further growth through acquisition, and that it was well positioned to take advantage of those opportunities. (see Exhibit 4 for more on the European chemical market.)

Making the Transition

> We had to choose. Did we want to be a Petrochemicals company or a life sciences and performance materials company? Those were the choices we had . . . but we could only spend the money once.
>
> *Hans Vossen, Director Corporate Strategy and Planning, 2005*

By 2000, DSM essentially stood on four pillars: roughly half of its €8 billion sales came from petrochemicals and industrial chemicals, and the other half came from life sciences products and performance materials. As DSM executives formed the company's strategy for the twenty-first century, management was confronted with a dilemma: either build on the past—the core petrochemicals business—or invest in the future by exploiting the growing life sciences and performance materials businesses.

Based on DSM's competitive processes in its plants, the company had a very strong position in the European petrochemicals business. However, in the wake of consolidation among the industry's global players, additional growth in petrochemicals would require massive capital expenditures. Although DSM management felt that the timing was right to be a part of the petrochemicals consolidation, they anticipated significant antitrust problems,

[1] Standard and Poors' Industry Research, *Oil and Gas*, October 7, 1999.

EXHIBIT 3 Changes in DSM's Business Environment

Source: DSM internal documents.

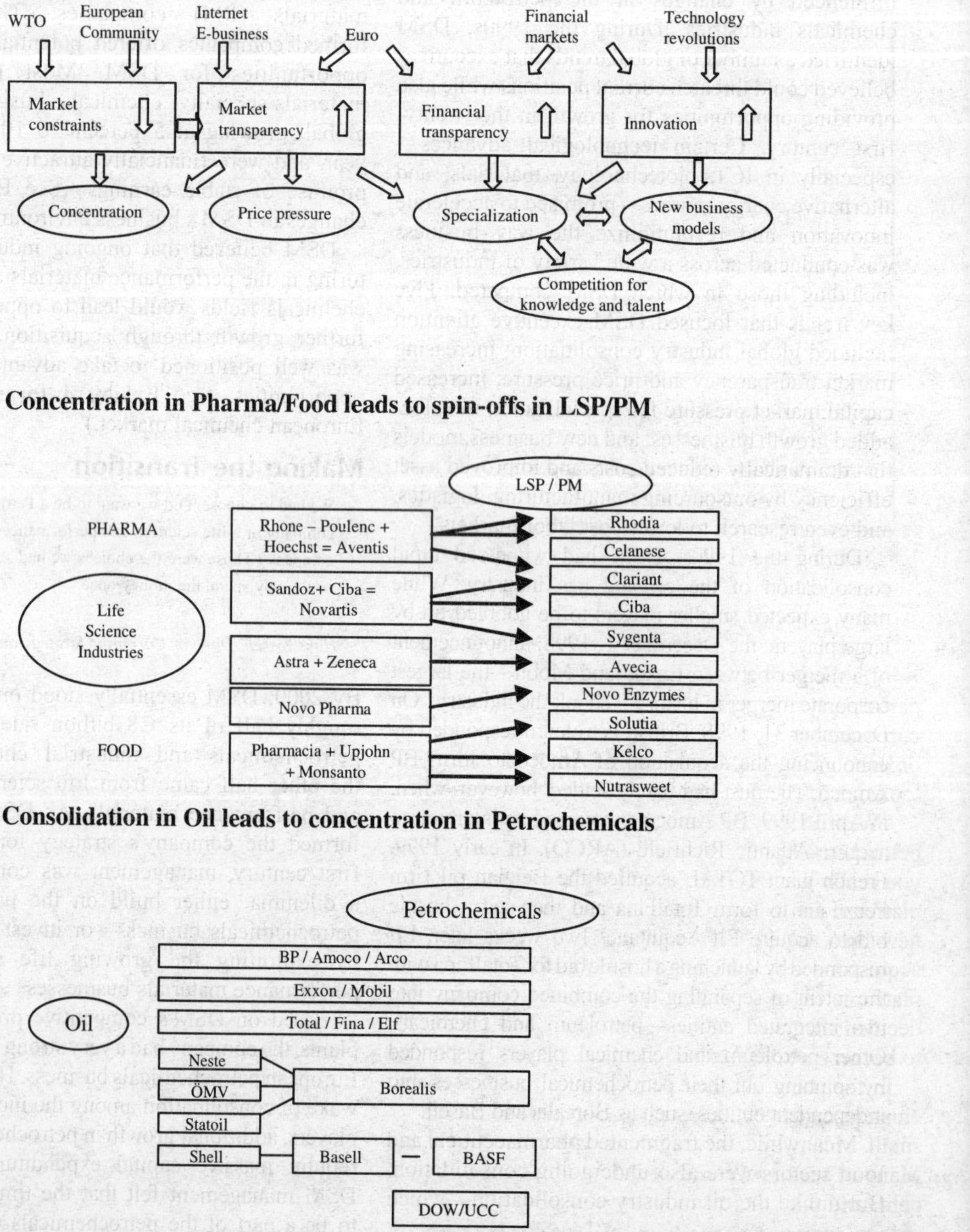

EXHIBIT 4 **Sales by Subsector, European Chemicals: 1989–2006e**

Source: Company data CSFB estimates.

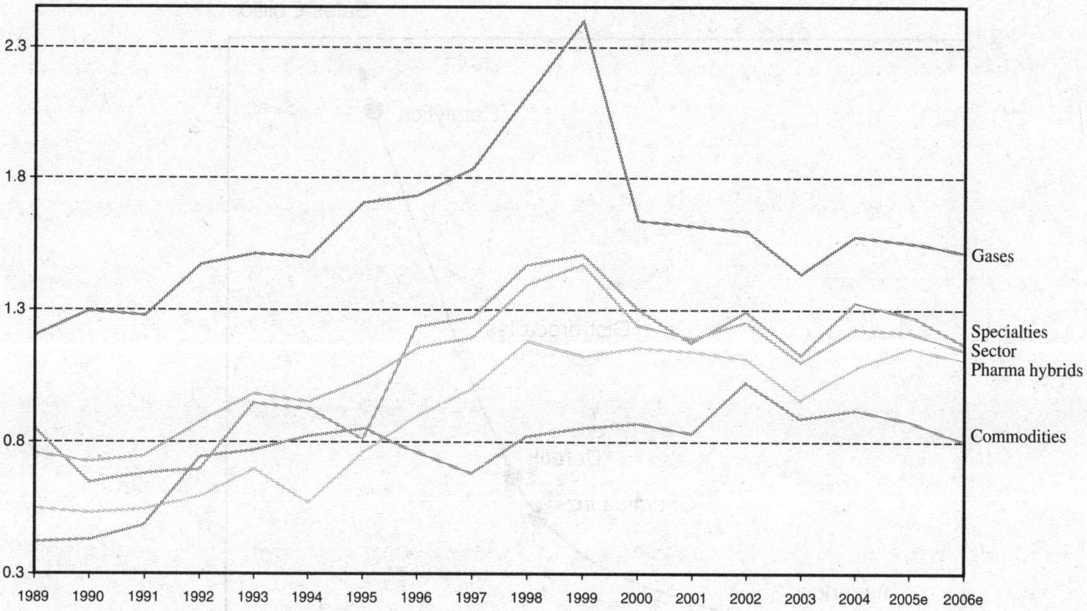

particularly in Europe. Hans Vossen, director of corporate strategy and planning, explained that in order to grow in that industry, DSM would have to look outside of Europe.

"We could easily survive in European petrochemicals for some time," he said, "but if you really want to grow, it means you need a new platform for the future. If [we were to] go to a new area, we would first need to make a huge acquisition; then we would have to build on the platform to grow in the region. In the end, we decided that, without partners, we were too small to become a global petrochemicals company."

In the performance materials and life sciences clusters, on the other hand, the players were mostly small spin-offs—not consolidations—of giants. Many of these spin-offs were heavily loaded with debt, and were thus vulnerable to takeover. DSM saw an opportunity to expand through acquisition in sectors where it already had a strong position.

Vision 2005: Focus and Value

In 2000, DSM launched its major new corporate strategy, called "Vision 2005: Focus and Value." Its primary objective was to focus the company on growth opportunities, but when first launched, DSM was unsure of the steps it would take to meet Vision 2005's goals. Initially, DSM intended to keep its petrochemicals business and to participate in the global industry consolidation. After additional analysis, however, the company instead chose to totally divest its petrochemicals business. At the same time, DSM intended to build on its earlier acquisition of Gist Brocades, Deretil, and Chemie Linz, in the food ingredients and pharmaceuticals industries, and further expand its position in the life sciences and performance materials markets. (See Exhibit 5 for growth in life science products)

EXHIBIT 5 Growth of Life Science Products

Source: DSM internal documents.

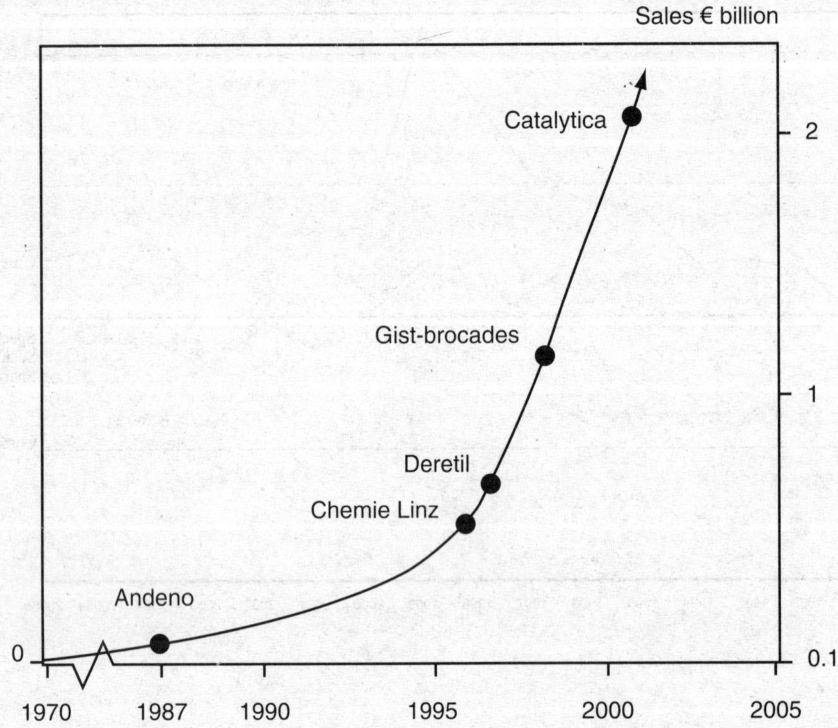

Vision 2005 called for the company to reach sales of €10 billion, 80 percent of which would come from specialties markets, such as life sciences, performance materials, and specialty chemicals, and the remaining 20 percent from the company's well-integrated global positions in the petrochemicals caprolactam and melamine. Execution of Vision 2005, therefore, would require DSM to successfully divest a large portion of its current business while acquiring new business comparable in size to what was being divested. In preparation for this, DSM created a separate petrochemical entity within the company, consisting of the Hydrocarbons, Polyethylene, and Polypropylene business groups. The relationship between this petrochemical entity and other DSM units was at arm's length until its divestiture, which the company hoped to achieve between 2001 and 2004.

Over that same four-year time frame, DSM planned to achieve accelerated growth in their Life Science Products and Performance Materials divisions and build on their global leadership positions in caprolactam and melamine. DSM expected that this coordinated implementation would allow it to maintain sufficient corporate size and financial critical mass while radically changing its profile.

Information Communication Technology

In 2000, DSM's Information and Communications Technology (ICT) organization was completely decentralized. Each business group had its own systems and infrastructure (desktops, e-mail, networks, data centers, applications, vendors, and employees), and organizational control of technology resided with each business site. As a result, there was no standardized technology infrastructure across departments and business groups. The acquisition of Royal Gist-Brocades N.V. in 1998—though it was considered a successful part of DSM's strategy to increase its participation in attractive sectors—only complicated matters by adding yet more complexity to DSM's diverse array of ICT infrastructures.

It was clear to DSM's CEO Peter Elverding that, in the future, acquisitions would require a different kind of ICT organization—one that could deal with tremendous complexity and change in a short period of time; one that was not only on top of the latest technology developments but also had an ear to the ground and engaged in projects that made business sense. Finally, ICT needed to be sensitive to user needs and responsive to the business.

In 2000, Elverding hired Jo van den Hanenberg to the new corporate CIO position and charged him with bringing consistency to the decentralized ICT organization. A clear vision and a common agenda would be required to create an organization that could serve the needs of an €8 billion company going through rapid transformation. To van den Hanenberg, it was clear that a complete transformation of the ICT organization and philosophy was necessary.

A New ICT Strategy

> There is a lot of euphoria over mergers—but often the euphoria stops with the acquisition and, in the end, nothing happens because there is not sufficient direction and no real "merging" to achieve the expected synergies. What I experienced here in ICT is that if you have a vastly diversified set of systems and infrastructures it's hard to effectively merge two organizations.
>
> *Jo van den Hanenberg, Executive Vice President and Chief Information Officer, 2005*

Upon his arrival at DSM in 2000, van den Hanenberg knew what needed to be done in order to support the corporate strategy, *Vision 2005: Focus and Value*. Twenty-four years as an executive at Philips Electronics in research, technology, procurement, and business management areas gave him significant experience in an environment with heavy acquisition and divestiture activity. He was aware of the challenges of such an environment, and he knew what his ICT organization had to do in order to overcome them.

> When DSM acquired Gist-Brocades, there were still numerous email systems, numerous wide-area networks, numerous desktops [in place], so what do you implement in that new company? Where do you want that new company to roll in? So we started in 2000 to reach to a standardized ICT infrastructure—the networks, the desktops, and the larger applications, like SAP.

To create an ICT environment conducive to a dynamic, uncertain, and highly competitive business environment, van den Hanenberg developed an ICT strategy focused on three important concepts: global standardization of ICT infrastructure and enterprise models, a service delivery-oriented ICT organization, and an ICT organization that was not only business-oriented but was itself governed by the business.

The first element, global standardization of ICT, involved organizationwide acceptance of a standardized ICT infrastructure (e.g., desktops, servers, networks, Internet, business application software, service providers, etc.) and common enterprise models of DSM business processes. Shortly after his arrival, one of van den Hanenberg's first moves was to restructure his supply base so that he only had to deal with a handful of reliable suppliers for hardware, software, and services. He advised, "If you really want to steer your ICT, then you can't do that with more than 107 suppliers. We used to have a lot of local suppliers and now we have a handful of key suppliers."

The second part of his strategy was the transformation of the ICT organization itself from a purely technical organization—built around highly skilled people solving technical problems—into a business-oriented management organization with service delivery skills. ICT was focused on understanding business problems and determining the best solution using technology, as indicated, to achieve value. To achieve this, ICT staffers would need new consultant-like skill sets, chief among them being project management.

In the new environment, instead of focusing on developing single solutions for a technology problem, ICT employees would likely find themselves managing projects consisting of diverse groups of technologies and business unit professionals from both DSM and vendor organizations. The technical work was to be done by whatever entity—inside or outside—was best equipped to do it. Outsourcing partners that had been developed over the years would continued to be utilized: EDS for e-mail and distributed computing, Getronics for end-user support, KPN/Infonet for networking, Deloitte and Accenture for business process development and reengineering, and Atos Origin for data center and application hosting. This ICT standardization and business process simplification would effectively facilitate the acquisition process and enable faster and smoother integration into the DSM organization. Van den Hanenberg realized that this new ICT model would result in "a completely different organization than that which we had prior to 2000."

The third component of his ICT strategy revolved around how ICT initiatives were identified, justified, and paid for (i.e., ICT governance). Again building on the notion of service delivery rather than technical problem solving, under the new model, all major ICT investment projects had to be approved by DSM's ICT governance board, heavily weighted towards business oversight, which consisted of two managing board members, the CIO, and four business group directors who rotated periodically.

Implementing Vision 2005: Focus and Value

Divesting Petrochemicals

Under van den Hanenberg's direction, the new ICT strategy got its first workout during the planned divestiture of DSM's petrochemical business. In order to facilitate the divestiture and to enable a more accurate valuation, his organization initiated what came to be called a "carve-out," a disentangling of the ICT infrastructures and business systems of the petrochemicals business from its DSM parent. Van den Hanenberg described how the carve-out supported the divestiture process:

> We went through a detailed analysis of what needed to be done to decouple our ICT systems, the DSM systems, and the petrochemical systems. It took us half a year to really define that. By specifying it very exactly, we knew what part of the business we could separate immediately and what required some support from the mother company. Then we could use this information in the negotiations processes.

A key consequence of the carve-out strategy was the realization by the business units that standardization on the SAP enterprise system platform (e.g., work processes, data standards, reporting templates) was a critical step towards operational simplification and efficiency. As a result, management saw the importance of involving ICT from the first day in the due diligence process of an acquisition. Hans Vossen recalled: "The experience I got out of the divestiture was directly used in the acquisition process." When DSM divested petrochemicals, they first sorted out the parts of the business that had previously been managed by DSM, but for which the buyer would now have responsibility. Vossen elaborated, "You put the problem to the buyer, so the seller does not have the problem of solving it."

In June 2002, DSM sold its petrochemicals business to Saudi Arabian Basic Industry Corp (SABIC) for €2.25 billion, a move that signaled a major milestone in DSM's transition from a bulk commodity to a specialty player.

Acquiring Roche Vitamins

That same month, DSM began negotiations for the acquisition of the Vitamins & Fine Chemicals Division from Roche, the Swiss-based health care group, for €1.75 billion. (See Exhibit 6 for an organizational chart of the newly configured DSM.) The division would be called DSM Nutritional Products, or DNP. At the time, Roche's Vitamins & Fine Chemicals business was the world's leading maker of vitamins and carotenoids. Vossen, in his strategy

EXHIBIT 6 DSM Organization

Source: DSM internal documents.

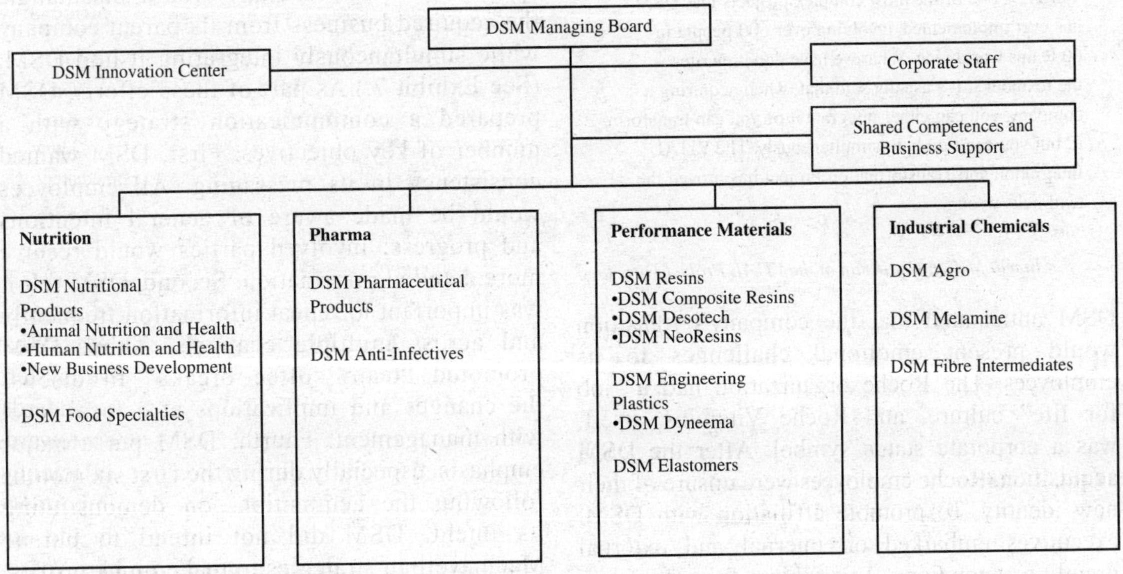

role, recalled the challenge: "Adding a €1.5 billion business . . . made it from our side very risky . . . We did a lot of internal preparation and market studies, and Roche allowed us to have a lot of discussions with their internal and external experts to understand the business really well."

Because of DSM's recent experience in divesting its petrochemicals business, the company had a thorough understanding of what would be required to separate the Vitamins & Fine Chemicals Division from the parent Roche organization. This knowledge helped DSM navigate that part of the negotiations process, as van den Hanenberg recalled:

> When we started with the acquisition of Roche vitamins, DSM [executives] realized that they had to involve ICT from day one in the due diligence. And I think, thanks to that decision, it saved us a very large amount of money because initially they had underestimated the cost of disentanglement and integration by a factor of 20. The more realistic costs were taken into account in the price negotiations, and later on we could clearly budget those costs into the restructuring budget.

This acquisition alone doubled the size of DSM's life sciences business. DSM acquired Roche's Vitamins business when its prospects were declining. A price fixing scandal and the entrance of new low-cost Asian producers in the late 1990s/early 2000s had resulted in margins falling to just 5 percent in 2003, according to a Citigroup report. Ruud Neeskens, DSM's senior manager for ICT applications, spoke about the role ICT played in turning around the newly acquired vitamin business:

> Roche had been run much more like a pharmaceutical company, looking at growth in the top line but not paying much attention to operational excellence and growth in the bottom line. That's okay if you are in high-growth phase, but that phase was over for vitamins. So DSM acquired this company clearly with the intention of bringing in its operational excellence knowledge. We would be able to improve significantly on profitability . . . and still make it a very interesting business for many years to come.

Integrating Roche Vitamins: The VITAL Program

> VITAL is one of the most complex projects that DSM has ever implemented, involving over 600 people in 60 teams worldwide. What we have done rewrites the textbooks. It's usually said that, when acquiring a company, you can either integrate it or you can transform it, but you can't do both simultaneously. The VITAL Integration and Transformation Project has proved the textbooks wrong.
>
> *Emmo Meijer, Chairman of the VITAL Project Directors*[2]

DSM anticipated that the company's transition would present emotional challenges to its employees. The Roche organization had a "job for life" culture, and Roche Vitamins, itself, was a corporate status symbol. After the DSM acquisition, Roche employees were unsure of their new identity. To promote affiliation with DSM, executives embarked on internal and external branding campaigns. Everything from business cards to property signage, e-mails, product labeling (e.g., packaging and product info. sheets), had to be changed. A Web site was used to communicate the new branding and to encourage employees to be consistent in their representation of the "new" DSM.

DSM was also sensitive to the need to ensure the integrity and sustainability of the Roche Vitamins brand. The external branding campaign, termed "DNP Unlimited," promoted DSM's desire to act with an unlimited spirit in many different markets by delivering their brand attributes: innovation, ambition, the ability to change, and responsibility. A guerilla advertising campaign "DSM Loves Roche Vitamins" was launched in the leading business press of the Netherlands, Switzerland, Germany, and the USA, as well as the Asia edition of *The Wall Street Journal*.

To coordinate its myriad integration initiatives, DSM created the Vital program to specify how the company would disentangle the acquired business from its parent company while simultaneously integrating it into DSM. (See Exhibit 7.) As part of these efforts, DSM prepared a communication strategy with a number of key objectives. First, DSM wanted consistency in its messaging. All employees would be made aware of general intentions and progress; involved parties would receive more detailed information. Second, DSM felt it was important to repeat information frequently and across multiple channels. Third, DSM promoted "team coffee breaks" to discuss the changes and implications at a local level with management. Fourth, DSM put a major emphasis, especially during the first six months following the acquisition, on demonstrating its intent. DSM did not intend to pursue Machiavellian strategies to make quick profits. Instead, the company wanted to signal that its future growth was critically dependent on the success of its newly acquired nutritional products division.

Various media strategies were designed to get these messages across: Nine issues of a magazine called *Vital* provided news on the integration; the company intranet featured more technical information; e-mail was used to communicate daily and weekly project updates.

In October 2003, DSM launched a series of management communication sessions which took representatives of DSM's managing board of directors and of DSM Nutritional Products' senior management to most European and U.S. sites of the former Roche V&FC division. Management team members felt it was important to explain in their own words why DSM had made this acquisition. They also wanted to communicate the urgent need for restructuring. But, most importantly, they wanted to meet their new colleagues in their place of work, to welcome them to DSM, to discuss with them their concerns, and also to learn from them about their products, markets, and ways of working.

[2] Source: "Reflections from the VITAL Project Directors" in *VITAL: The Internal Magazine of DSM Nutritional Products*, Issue 9, June 2005.

EXHIBIT 7 Vital Program

Source: DSM internal documents.

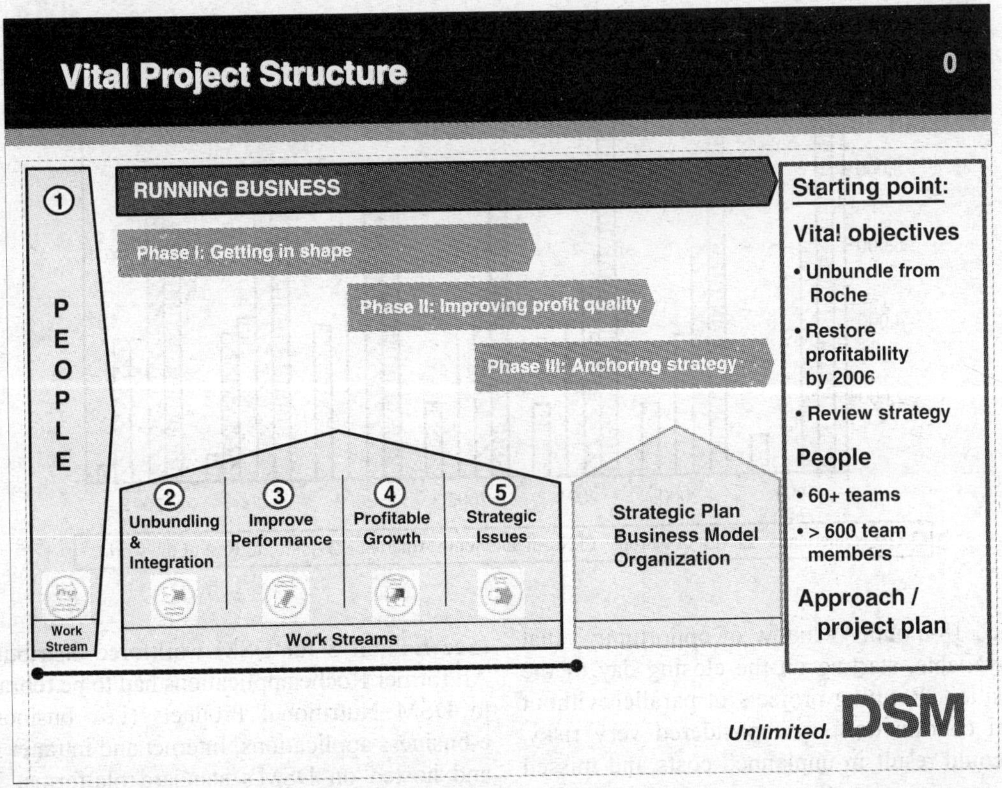

ICT's One-Jump Transition Strategy

> So this was a paradox . . . DSM had to keep things the same . . . but they had to change everything.
>
> *Gerard van den Zanden, Manager, Communications*

In ICT, the goal was to have the vitamin business up and running 100 percent in the DSM environment by the end of the transition period, with no business disruption. This aggressive approach could only be accomplished with a "one-jump" strategy to disentangle Roche Vitamins & Fine Chemical's ICT infrastructure from Roche and, at the same time, to integrate Roche V&FC, immediately, into the DSM-branded ICT infrastructure. The one-step strategy was not typical, but it was necessary in order to maintain the momentum of the acquisition, secure sufficient funding, and ensure the cooperation from both organizations. According to Ruud Neeskens:

> Normally what you see a company do when they acquire another company, from an ICT perspective, is separate it from the mother company and leave it, more or less on its own for a while, then slowly start integrating. This was not the approach DSM took here . . . it was a very fundamental decision that in one jump we would do both the uncoupling from Roche and at the same time immediately integrating into the DSM standard ICT infrastructure. This was quite a jump to take immediately after closing, but I think it was a very fundamental one because . . . it created a window of opportunity . . . If you miss that moment of opportunity immediately after the acquisition, you are struggling for years to get [the system] up.

The strategy required significant projects related to networks, system hosting, desktop, applications, and external, internal, and e-business (Internet). All of these projects ran in parallel during a

EXHIBIT 8 DSM Workforce Distribution

Source: DSM Web site.

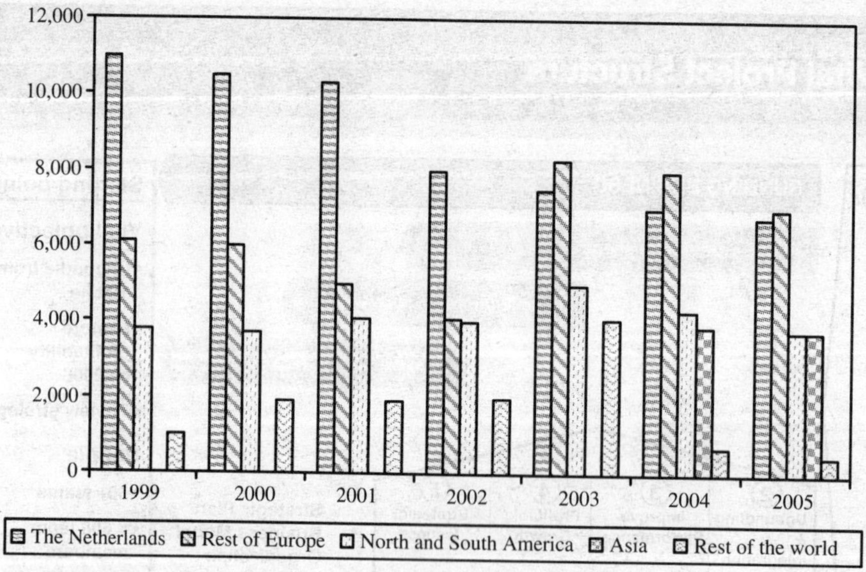

planned 18-month "window of opportunity" that was available, starting on the closing day of the acquisition. Running projects in parallel without central coordination was considered very risky, as it could result in unplanned costs and missed deadlines.

The EVITA Initiative

> We had more than 360 projects running in parallel during the peak period, with a lot of dependencies between them. So if you get sand in the wheels of that complex machine then you can have the whole machine stop; then we would have had a disaster on our hands.
>
> *Ruud Neeskens, Senior Manager ICT Applications, April 12, 2006*

Prior to the acquisition, nearly 6,400 Roche employees accessed over 100 business applications, from 5,700 desktops at 89 global sites, to conduct their business on a daily basis. Customers, suppliers, and employees utilized 37 Internet sites to access content or e-business applications. The acquisition accelerated the growth of DSM's global workforce. (See Exhibit 8 for DSM workforce distribution.) All former Roche applications had to be rebranded to DSM Nutritional Products (i.e., business & e-business applications, Internet and intranet sites) and hosted on DSM's standard platforms. Their local and wide area networks had to be fully separated from Roche, and e-mail, desktops, and printers had to be consistent with DSM standards. All systems and servers had to be hosted in DSM datacenters, independent of Roche.

As Jim Richard, a DSM eVita program manager for business applications, recalled, "We wanted everything to be based on DSM ICT standards. From an ICT perspective, this was a best practice—to implement a pure DSM ICT foundation. We felt this was achievable in the 18 months defined for the disentanglement." Since the integration of business processes would take longer, this step was postponed until after the initial 18-month transition was complete.

DSM developed a program that would be responsible for separating all of DNP/Roche shared applications—either through cloning, installing replacement systems, discontinuing

EXHIBIT 9 Evita Program

Source: DSM internal documents.

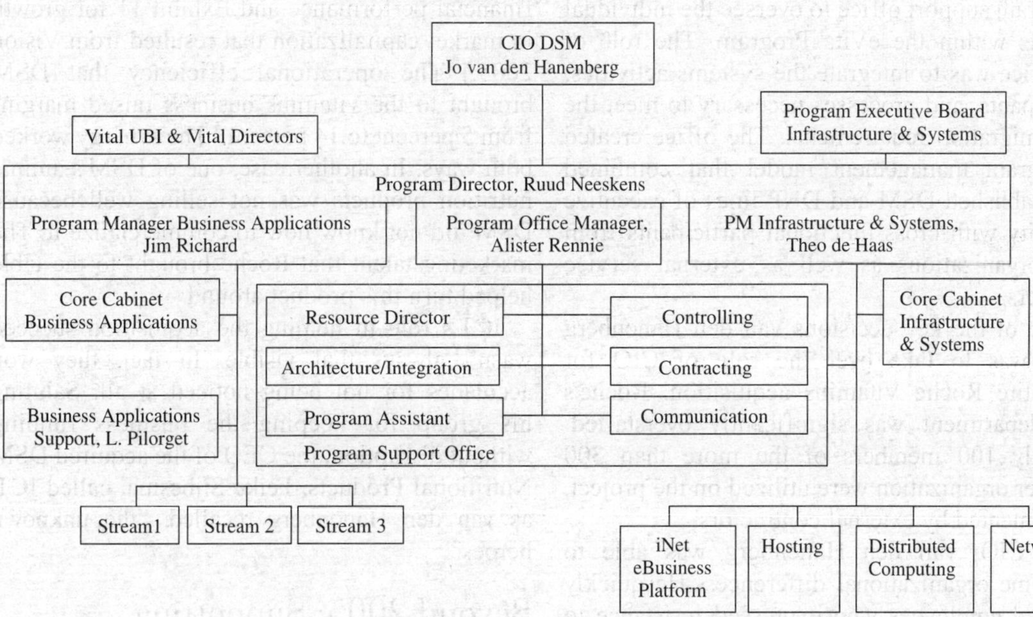

their use, or, under exceptional circumstances, leasing the application through a supplier-buyer relationship. The program, named EVITA, which stood for Experience Vitamins IT Anywhere, was critical to the success of VITAL, and therefore to DSM's Vision 2005 (see Exhibit 9).

At the peak, over 360 projects were running simultaneously, each being managed by a project manager. Progress was tracked and problems were flagged for immediate attention and swift resolution. In order to organize and manage this activity, the EVITA initiative was divided into five distinct, but interdependent, work streams: Business Applications, Internet & e-business, Hosting, Distributed Computing, and Network. Each stream was then assigned a specific stream manager who had a strong history of achievements. (See Appendix A for a description of the work streams.)

DSM also implemented a 23-week project cycle for each site, regardless of its size. This approach took careful coordination with multiple partners, because DSM outsourced most of its infrastructure. Networking was coordinated by KPN, mail servers were handled by EDS, Getronics was involved with desktop and File & Print server roll-out and organizing end-user support, and Roche delivered the data and information. Theo de Haas, manager, Global ICT Client Services, explained the process:

> We made cookbooks and said, from day to day . . . what should be done on day 1, day 2, day 3, day 4 . . . until 23 weeks were up. If you look at the success that we had, it was really based on the cookbooks—going through day-to-day what kind of activities you should do, what kind of problems could occur, and how you should tackle them.

Vision 2005: Success Factors

> All of this went on and on with multiple systems every weekend for over a year . . . and all of this had to happen without the slightest business disruption . . . A lot of people had doubts that we would ever succeed, but we managed to do it in 15 months.
>
> *Ruud Neeskens, DSM Senior Manager ICT Applications*

To reduce risks, increase efficiency, and manage the inevitable resistance to change, DSM installed a program support office to oversee the individual projects within the eVita Program. The role of the office was to integrate the systems activities, participants, and processes necessary to meet the DNP migration requirements. The office created a program management model that combined the established DSM and DNP lines of executive authority with cross-functional participants from both organizations as well as external service suppliers.

One of the key decisions van den Hanenberg made was to take over the role of CIO for the entire Roche Vitamins acquisition. Roche's ICT department was significantly overstaffed: Roughly 100 members of the more than 300 member organization were utilized on the project, supplemented by external contractors.

As CIO, van den Hanenberg was able to overcome organizational differences. He quickly replaced employees who expressed resistance to the transition plan. Neeskens explained that in any major transformation, there are three main camps: a big group which quickly accepts the new program, another big group that may be in doubt but goes along with the plan, and a smaller group made up of those who are resistant to change. "The only way to move forward," he said, "was to get [the reluctant employees] either into another position in the organization that's outside of ICT, or to remove them from the company completely. We had 15 to 18 months to execute the transition . . . It was a tough approach, but it was the only way to make this work."

To ensure a standardized infrastructure, ICT imposed conditions: Business groups had no influence on what type of network was installed, nor could they specify what type of desktop they got. These decisions were standardized globally across DSM businesses. All this was done within 15 months, bringing the DNP ICT environment very quickly in close alignment with the DSM ICT standards and policies.

Soon after the acquisition, there were signs that the Roche Vitamins integration would pay off and that the Vision 2005's goals would be achieved. (See Exhibit 10 for the portfolio changes and financial performance and Exhibit 11 for growth in market capitalization that resulted from Vision 2005.) The operational efficiency that DSM brought to the vitamins business raised margins from 5 percent to 14 percent.[3] The synergy worked both ways. In another case, one of DSM's animal nutrition products was not selling well because DSM did not know how to commercialize it. The marketing talent that Roche brought to the table helped turn this product around.

ICT's role in helping the acquisition succeed wasn't always that visible. In fact, they won accolades for not being noticed at all. Saluting his group for keeping the business running without disruption, the CEO of the acquired DSM Nutritional Products, Feike Sijbesma, called ICT, as van den Hanenberg recalled, "the unknown heroes."

Beyond 2005: Supporting *Vision 2010*

> All in all, I would qualify 2005 as a very good year for DSM . . . DSM is financially sound, technology rich, and has embarked on a new strategic course with new opportunities and challenges. The successful completion of Vision 2005 has paved the way for the next logical step, Vision 2010—Building on Strengths. In fact, we have already started. And more will follow as we further leverage the capabilities and performance of our company in order to successfully execute this strategy.
>
> *Peter Elverding, Chairman of the Managing Board, as cited in DSM 2005 Annual Report*

The success of its *Vision 2005* strategic plan encouraged the company to set yet another aggressive transformation target. As with Vision 2005, DSM pursued a careful and comprehensive strategic planning process, (see Exhibit 12). In October 2005, Peter Elverding, the chairman of

[3] Source: M. Heslop, et al. "DSM," Citigroup Analyst Report, December 2005, p.6.

EXHIBIT 10 Portfolio Changes Resulting from Vision 2005 M&A Activity, Sales, and EBIT

Source: DSM internal documents.

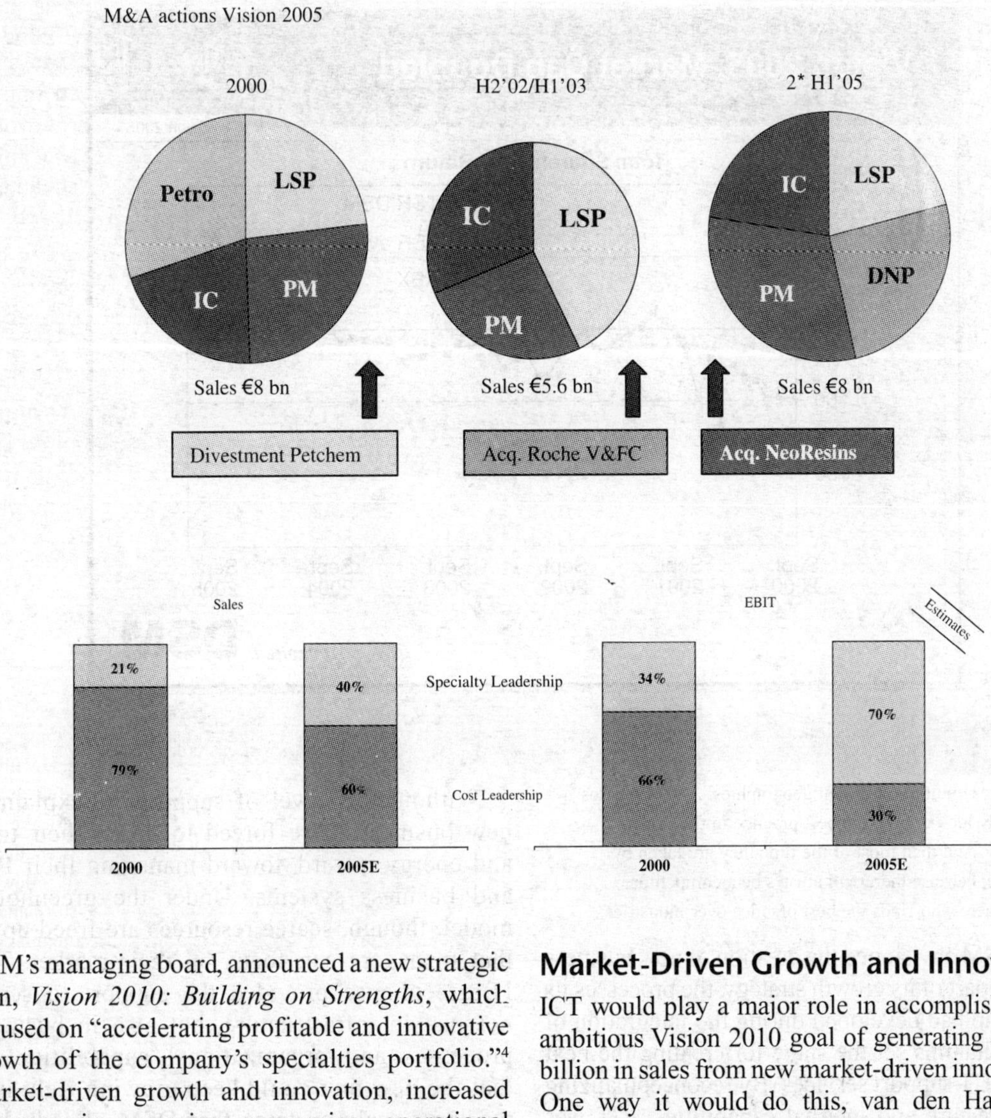

DSM's managing board, announced a new strategic plan, *Vision 2010: Building on Strengths*, which focused on "accelerating profitable and innovative growth of the company's specialties portfolio."[4] Market-driven growth and innovation, increased presence in emerging economies, operational excellence, and value creation were the plan's key components. And once again, ICT would be critical to the realization of these goals.

Market-Driven Growth and Innovation

ICT would play a major role in accomplishing the ambitious Vision 2010 goal of generating over €1 billion in sales from new market-driven innovations. One way it would do this, van den Hanenberg explained, was through modeling best practice in sourcing innovative ideas. ICT's cross-industry outlook gave it an advantage over other functional groups, which tended to look only within their own industry for innovation, as he explained:

> When you are in the IT industry, you have to look across very broadly, because . . . the pockets of innovation, and the trends, are happening across multiple different

[4] See the DSM Web site (http://www.dsm.com/en_US/html/about/vision_2010.htm) for a summary of Vision 2010, viewed on January 31, 2007.

EXHIBIT 11 Market Capitalization and Accelerated Growth Performance: Results from Vision 2005

Source: DSM internal documents.

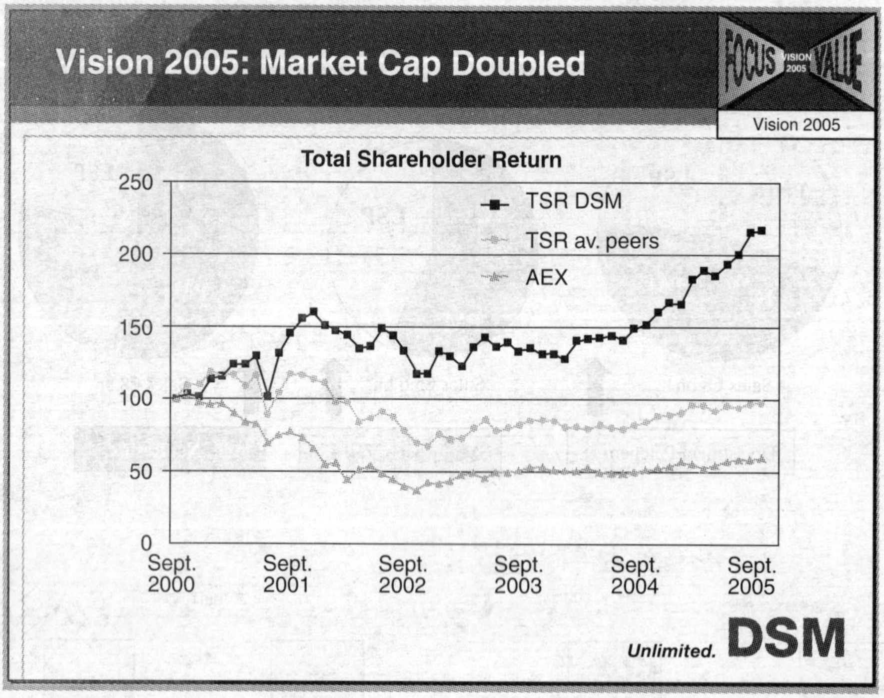

> industries, multiple different geographies. . . . Businesses normally look only to the best practice in their own industry. And then most of the time they are taken by surprise, because there will always be a competitor somewhere who finds the best practice over industries.

As DSM envisioned the creation of new business as a core part of its growth strategy, the processes its ICT group had developed during the integration of Roche Vitamins set the stage for creating the next level of ICT support services. By reconceptualizing its architecture and internal capabilities, ICT was able to support innovation processes and give new ventures a leg up. Van den Hanenberg described what he called "the IT greenhouse for innovation": "In a greenhouse, we set up an IT system backbone, on which you can place new start-ups. And then they automatically, in a very natural way, learn the business processes for that new start-up company. And you can easily scale up and scale down."

Without this level of support, he explained, new businesses are forced to divert their time and energy inward, toward managing their ICT and business systems. Under the greenhouse model, though, scarce resources are freed up so that managers can focus on their market. The IT greenhouse provided the support to scale, not just in infrastructure, but also in business processes and organizational capabilities, so that the new unit could keep growing right into the large-scale systems that DSM already had in place.

Increased Presence in Emerging Markets

To support the company's plans for a greater presence in emerging markets, van den Hanenberg built a virtual global ICT organization. He elaborated on this concept: "Instead of steering

EXHIBIT 12 Corporate Strategy Process

Source: DSM internal documents.

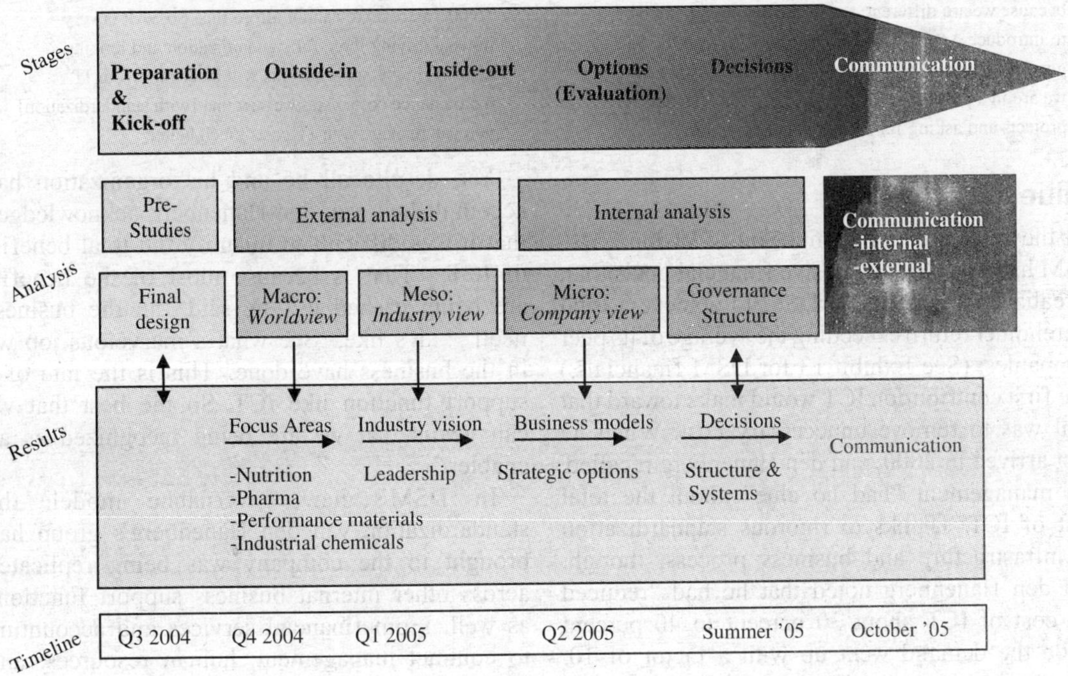

and delivering services from one location here in the Netherlands, I have now six affiliate locations in Parsippany [New Jersey], Sao Paolo, Switzerland, Singapore, Shanghai . . . With those footholds, I can support the growth of DSM in the emerging markets."

These globally distributed sites provided another important benefit as well. By accessing his Brazil, Singapore, or Shanghai affiliates, van den Hanenberg could take advantage of low-cost labor markets while maintaining more control over the process than was possible with typical outsourcing and offshoring arrangements.

Operational Excellence

The standardization around SAP led a program of business processes standardization, dubbed Project Apollo. This enhanced clarity around business operations led to some surprises, as previously uncovered aspects of their operations were made visible when processes were documented and data was delivered. Van den Hanenberg remarked:

> The business units have discovered . . . how much more transparent their business is becoming because of ICT. For instance, one business discovered that they had 85 different pricing structures, and, nowadays, they have only three. You can imagine if you have 85 different pricing structures, you have no control over your pricing policy. Another unit had over 40,000 different product codes in one area. You can't manage your product portfolio if you have 40,000 product codes . . . and it only is discovered at the moment that IT provides them the right systems and the data.

While they may have been initially reluctant, DSM managers quickly saw what ICT could contribute to their business success, as van den Hanenberg recalled,

> Way back in 2000, every business group director came to me and said it is impossible that we have a shared IT organization, standard IT infrastructure, and systems, because we are different. . . . In the beginning, we had to introduce Apollo by pushing from ICT with the ICT governance board and the managing board. Nowadays, we are in a pull mode, as the business is . . . asking for projects and asking for further standardization."

Value Creation

For the value creation component of Vision 2010, DSM had set itself aggressive financial goals that, if realized, would enable DSM to achieve a total shareholder return exceeding the average of its peer companies. (See Exhibit 13 for DSM financials.) The first contribution ICT would make toward that goal was to remove unnecessary cost. When he first arrived in 2000, van den Hanenberg recalled, top management "had no clue" about the total cost of ICT. Thanks to rigorous standardization of infrastructure and business process, though, van den Hanenberg noted that he had "reduced the cost of ICT about 30 percent to 40 percent while the demand went up with a factor of 10. So, if we had not standardized all of these, then we would have had outrageous IT cost. And lousy performance."

Titus Looman, DSM manager, Apollo Program, provided an example of how standardization created value for the company:

> In DNP we had 15,000 pieces of customized programs completely modeled for DNP. Suppose that SAP comes with a new upgrade. You have to redo every bit of these 15,000 pieces. We cannot afford this. So SAP is very much a driving force for standardization and looking at cost. How you handle this will determine your IT maintenance costs. And we saw that [with standardization] you can manage your IT costs much better.

Yet, despite all he and his organization had accomplished, van den Hanenberg acknowledged that it was difficult to quantify the total benefits of ICT: "That is because most of the benefits are being cashed in," he said, "in the business itself . . . it's like, 'See what a marvelous job we in the business have done.' This is the fate of a support function like ICT. So the best that we can get is that we are being recognized as an enabler."

In DSM's new governance model, the standardization van den Hanenberg's group had brought to the company was being replicated across other internal business support functions as well. From financial services and accounting to contract management; human resources; and safety, health, and sustainability systems, ICT was the reference point for how to create internal value through service delivery. If van den Hanenberg continued to lead his team to the same high level of achievement, perhaps by 2010 his ICT staff would still be heroes, but unknown no more.

EXHIBIT 13 DSM Financials

Source: DSM internal documents.

DSM Full P&L	1992	1993	1994	1995	1996	1997	1998	1999	2000	2001	2002	2003	2004	2005	2006E	2007E	2008E
DSM Nutritional Products												496	1,899	1,914	1,969	1,992	2,018
Performance Materials	1,616	1,588	1,809	2,133	2,032	1,846	1,924	1,835	2,188	1,855	1,767	1,774	2,007	2,447	2,529	2,426	2,408
Life Science Products	1,314	1,040	1,238	1,388	1,672	687	1,681	1,666	1,853	2,237	2,168	1,963	1,484	1,479	1,470	1,477	1,490
Industrial Chemicals	1,207	1,093	1,096	1,071	1,020	2,752	2,679	2,704	3,877	1,302	1,268	1,416	1,570	1,687	1,784	1,632	1,572
Other activities	92	80	146	125	168	400	135	128	172	357	433	401	474	485	485	485	485
Intragroup Sales	(188)	(152)	(216)	(261)	(235)												
Associates & discontinued										2,219	1,029		398	183	0	0	0
Total Sales	4,041	3,648	4,074	4,457	4,657	5,629	6,361	6,333	8,090	5,751	5,636	6,050	7,832	8,195	8,237	8,013	7,974
Sales Growth	(4.7%)	(9.7%)	11.7%	9.4%	4.5%	20.9%	13.0%	(0.4%)	27.7%	(28.9%)	(2.0%)	7.3%	29.5%	4.6%	0.5%	(2.7%)	(0.5%)
Volume growth	(4.7%)	(9.7%)	11.7%	9.4%	2.7%	9.0%	3.0%	7.0%	8.0%	(2.0%)	6.0%	2.0%	8.0%	0.0%			
Other operating income	133	33	99	174	148	154	143	163	274	(31)	(141)	131	197	223	223	223	223
Raw material cost	(1,944)	(1,737)	(1,855)	(1,990)	(2,163)	(2,733)	(2,955)	(3,021)	(4,449)	(2,723)	(2,414)	(2,895)	(3,574)	(4,338)	(4,530)	(4,407)	(4,389)
Personnel cost	(878)	(818)	(779)	(761)	(824)	(883)	(873)	(887)	(927)	(924)	(915)	(958)	(1,342)	(1,352)	(1,366)	(1,379)	(1,393)
Gross profit, predepreciation	1,352	1,125	1,539	1,879	1,819	2,168	2,676	1,588	1,988	2,073	2,166	2,328	3,113	2,728	2,564	2,450	2,418
Other operating cost	(904)	(829)	(895)	(869)	(1,025)	(1,220)	(1,620)	(1,540)	(1,734)	(1,332)	(1,399)	(1,605)	(2,046)	(1,417)	(1,298)	(1,298)	(1,294)
EBITDA	448	296	643	1,010	794	948	1,056	1,012	1,254	741	767	723	1,067	1,311	1,267	1,152	1,124
Depreciation & gw amortisation	(320)	(338)	(363)	(319)	(341)	(403)	(470)	(458)	(503)	(405)	(384)	(429)	(504)	(503)	(518)	(508)	(507)
EBIT from continuing	128	(41)	280	691	453	545	586	554	751	336	383	294	546	799	748	644	617
		-132.3%	-778.0%	146.7%	-34.4%	20.4%	7.5%	-5.5%	35.5%	-55.3%	14.0%	-23.2%	85.6%	46.3%	-6.4%	-14.0%	-4.1%
Net interest	(55)	(61)	(66)	(26)	(27)	(33)	(71)	(69)	(57)	(97)	(14)	(31)	(56)	(70)	(67)	(57)	(30)
Pre-tax Profit	73	(102)	214	664	426	512	515	485	694	424	436	263	490	729	682	586	587
Tax	22	57	(10)	(213)	(119)	(149)	(108)	(118)	(171)	(69)	(84)	(49)	(95)	(173)	(161)	(150)	(150)
Non-consolidated	22	20	35	36	24	34	19	15	48	14	(3)	5	9	(2)	(5)	0	5
Net profit on ord. activities	117	(25)	239	487	331	397	426	382	571	369	349	219	404	554	496	436	442
Preference dividend	0	0	0	0	(13)	(16)	(15)	(19)	(22)	(22)	(22)	(22)	(22)	(16)	(16)	(16)	(16)
Minorities	(5)	(2)	0	0	(2)	0	(2)	2	(1)	1	(1)	14	11	7	7	7	7
Net before extraord	112	(27)	239	487	316	381	408	365	548	348	326	211	393	545	487	428	433
Net extraordinaries	(10)	(26)	3	(1)	(2)	(2)	(9)	(13)	10	1,045	840	(94)	(122)	(34)	0		
	102	(54)	241	486	314	379	399	352	558	1,393	1,166	117	271	511	487	428	433
Ordinary Dividend	65	25	(98)	(111)	(131)	(148)	(165)	(153)	(168)	(168)	(170)	(168)	(168)	(191)	(190)	(190)	(190)
Retained	37	(79)	339	597	445	527	564	199	390	1,225	996	(51)	103	320	297	237	243

(Continued)

EXHIBIT 13 DSM Financials (*Continued*)

DSM Full P&L	1992	1993	1994	1995	1996	1997	1998	1999	2000	2001	2002	2003	2004	2005	2006E	2007E	2008E
Total sales growth	-4.7%	-9.7%	11.7%	9.4%	4.5%	20.9%	13.0%	-0.4%	27.7%	-28.9%	-2.0%	7.3%	29.5%	4.6%	0.5%	-2.7%	-0.5%
Gross Margin predepreciation	33.5%	30.8%	37.8%	42.2%	39.1%	38.5%	42.1%	40.9%	36.9%	36.0%	38.4%	38.5%	39.7%	33.3%	31.1%	30.6%	30.3%
Change in raw material costs	-1.6%	-10.6%	6.8%	7.3%	8.7%	26.3%	8.1%	2.2%	47.3%	-38.8%	-11.3%	19.9%	23.5%	21.4%	4.4%	-2.7%	-0.5%
Raw material/sales	48.1%	47.6%	45.5%	44.7%	46.4%	48.5%	46.5%	47.7%	55.0%	47.3%	42.8%	47.9%	45.6%	52.9%	55.0%	55.0%	55.0%
Change in personnel costs				-1.0%	3.7%	3.3%	-1.1%	1.6%	4.5%	-0.3%	-1.0%	4.7%	40.1%	0.7%	1.0%	1.0%	1.0%
Personnel costs/sales	21.7%	22.4%	19.1%	17.1%	17.7%	15.7%	13.7%	14.0%	11.5%	16.1%	16.2%	15.8%	17.1%	16.5%	16.6%	17.2%	17.5%
Change in other operating costs	4.0%	-8.3%	8.0%	-2.9%	17.9%	19.0%	32.8%	-4.9%	12.6%	-23.2%	5.0%	14.7%	27.5%	-30.7%	-8.4%	0.0%	-0.3%
Other operating costs/sales	22.4%	22.7%	22.0%	19.5%	22.0%	21.7%	25.5%	24.3%	21.4%	23.2%	24.8%	26.5%	26.1%	17.3%	15.8%	16.2%	16.2%
EBITDA margin	11.1%	8.1%	15.8%	22.7%	17.1%	16.8%	16.6%	16.0%	15.5%	12.9%	13.6%	12.0%	13.6%	16.0%	15.4%	14.4%	14.1%
Deprcn as % of sales	7.9%	9.3%	8.9%	7.2%	7.3%	7.2%	7.4%	7.2%	6.2%	6.5%	6.3%	6.7%	6.4%	6.1%	6.3%	6.3%	6.4%
No of employees (year end)	9,982	9,528	8,672	7,709	8,361	7,953		22,000	22,000	19,150	18,375	26,111	24,204	21,820	21,820	21,820	21,820
No of employees (average)						8,228			19,505	19,505	19,505	20,516	24,503	22,839	21,820	21,820	21,820
wages & salaries								(1,145)	(1,191)	(1,251)	(1,217)	(1,215)	(1,382)	(1,337)	(1,303)	(1,329)	(1,356)
Cost per employee	39.9	39.0	40.7	44.8	44.7	50.4			(61,061)	(64,137)	(62,394)	(59,222)	(56,401)	(58,540)	(59,711)	(60,905)	(62,123)
Pension service cost													(89)	(112)	(112)	(112)	(112)
Pension interest													(215)	(210)	(210)	(210)	(210)
Expected return on assets													283	305	305	305	305
Operating lease rentals											(1)	(2)	(1)	(2)	(2)	(2)	(2)
No of shares (m) year end							193.1	194.4	192.0	192.2	194.0	191.6	192.0	190.9	190.4	190.4	190.4
No of shares (m) average	212.6	216.2	216.6	217.0	182.6	174.4	199.5	194.0	192.4	192.2	193.1	189.4	191.6	190.8	190.4	190.4	190.4
EPS before extraordinaries & gw	0.5	(0.1)	1.1	2.24	1.73	2.18	2.05	1.88	2.85	1.96	1.83	1.25	2.05	2.86	2.56	2.25	2.27
EPS after extraord	0.5	(0.2)	1.1	2.24	1.72	2.17	2.00	1.82	2.90	7.25	6.04	0.62	1.41	2.68	2.56	2.25	2.27
EPS growth					-22.8%	26.2%	-6.4%	-8.0%	51.4%	-31.1%	-6.8%	-31.8%	64.5%	39.3%	-10.4%	-12.2%	1.3%
Dividend	0.3	0.1	0.5	0.6	0.7	0.8	0.8	0.8	0.9	0.9	0.9	0.9	0.9	1.0	1.0	1.0	1.0
Pay-out ratio	26.2%	-40.9%	18.7%	12.2%	17.7%	15.7%	36.9%	40.4%	30.7%	44.6%	47.8%	70.2%	42.7%	35.0%	39.1%	44.5%	44.0%
Tax rate	30.6%	-56.0%	-4.9%	-32.0%	-28.0%	-29.2%	-21.0%	-24.3%	-24.6%	-16.3%	-19.3%	-18.6%	-19.4%	-23.7%	-26.5%	-25.6%	-25.6%

EXHIBIT 13 DSM Financials (*Continued*)

DSM Cash Flow Schedule	1992	1993	1994	1995	1996	1997	1998	1999	2000	2001	2002	2003	2004	2005	2006E	2007E	2008E
EBIT	128	(41)	280	691	453	545	586	554	751	336	383	294	562	808	748	644	617
D&A of tangible assets & gw	320	338	363	319	341	402	470	458	503	521	442	429	504	503	518	508	507
Dec. (inc.) in net working capital	(91)	97	51	25	(176)	114	(111)	(137)	(60)	(58)	10	111	209	(201)	2	39	7
Provision related cash items	20	22	(44)	54	20	16	36	16	(63)	(37)	(139)	(173)	(153)	(202)	(120)		
Other adjustments	(5)	(26)	(20)	(16)	(10)	(10)	4	86	(60)	138	109	3	(81)	(11)			
Minority int. of adjusted net profit	(5)	(2)	0	0	(2)	0	(2)	2				(1)			7	7	7
Operating cash flow	443	286	542	844	684	806	985	977	1,071	900	805	663	1,041	897	1,156	1,198	1,138
Interest	(55)	(61)	(66)	(26)	(27)	(33)	(71)	(69)	(57)	(97)	(20)	(31)	(66)	(71)	(67)	(65)	(44)
Tax	22	57	(10)	(10)	(213)	(119)	(149)	(108)	(118)	(171)	(69)	(49)	(77)	(133)	(181)	(148)	(148)
Dividends	(89)	(22)	(33)	(123)	(118)	(102)	(78)	(91)	(87)	(190)	(191)	(187)	(194)	(183)	(207)	(206)	(206)
Capital Expenditure of tangible fixed assets	(477)	(312)	(168)	(345)	(484)	(458)	(585)	(647)	(598)	(652)	(457)	(433)	(349)	(393)	(512)	(563)	(551)
Trading cash flow	(157)	(52)	265	339	(158)	93	102	62	211	(210)	68	(37)	355	117	189	216	189
Acquisitions	(18)	(38)	(49)	(22)	(214)	(120)	(1,292)	(31)	(883)		(1)	(1,469)		(564)	(30)		
Disposals	53	93	77	90	51	91	28	49	32	1,244	1,998	12	28	222	120		
Increase in Share Capital/ Repurchases	0	0	9	0	(273)	0			(119)			(109)	(108)	(68)	(100)		
Other adjustments	69	(12)	(90)	45	(36)	(12)	(92)	(148)	(71)			(15)	57	33	0		
Change in Net Cash (Debt)	(53)	(10)	211	452	(630)	52	1,254	(68)	(830)	1,034	2,066	(1,618)	332	(260)	179	215	189
Net cash (debt) year end	(944)	(853)	(515)	(1)	(567)	(248)	(1,456)	(1,373)	(2,148)	(867)	1,038	(671)	(572)	(832)	(653)	(438)	(249)
Net cash (debt) average	(889)	(898)	(684)	(258)	(284)	(408)	(852)	(1,415)	(1,761)	(1,508)	86	184	(622)	(702)	(742)	(545)	(343)
Acquisitions/sales	0.4%	0.9%	1.3%	0.5%	4.8%	2.6%	23.0%	0.5%	13.9%								
Interest										6.4%	(23.4%)	4.6%	11.5%	8.5%	10.0%	10.0%	10.0%
FCF to equity	(68)	(30)	297	462	(40)	195	180	153	298	(20)	259	150	549	300	396	421	395

Appendix A

EVITA Work Streams

To manage the volume of activity, DSM established a series of ICT work streams, each with its own function and staffing.

The Business Applications stream was responsible for separating over 100 business applications that, immediately following the acquisition, were shared both by Roche and DNP. DSM followed a very strict ICT principle: ICT would provide the business with the tools and instructions it needed, but the business itself was responsible for using the tools to change the management and implementation within the organization. This principle demanded a complete split of governance between the application side and the infrastructure side. On the infrastructure side, there was strong governance driven directly from the board to the global ICT organization, and this drove all the infrastructure-related streams, like network and distributed computing. On the application side, ICT had business responsibility to support the business. As Neeskens explained:

> We went to the business with a long list of 104 applications and we said, for each of these applications, what are you going to do in the future? E.g.: You are now sharing your HR system with Roche. In 18 months from now you have to be on your own. What will your action be? Do you want to have your own HR system or do you want to outsource it to a payroll service provider? The business had to make the decision on how they wanted to move forward with each application.

The iNet and eBusiness stream focused on separating DNP from the Internet and intranet structure of Roche. It was important to immediately show all employees and customers of DNP that they had become a part of a new organization. Thousands of Web pages were migrated out of the Roche environment and integrated into the DSM environment. In total, 37 Internet sites, 3 major business applications, 11 intranets, 34 Web applications (such as registering for a company parking space), and 59 Web services (e.g., making restaurant reservations) were moved. All e-business applications that were involved in selling over the Internet and had been previously dispersed over many different small systems were moved off the Roche infrastructure and integrated into the DSM environment.

While not all of the applications were mission-critical, the internal Web applications were important as they had a big impact on employee morale. As Theo de Haas explained, "There are all kind of things that, while nitty-gritty, can be very annoying to people [if they don't work]. Maybe I can't park my car; I can't eat anymore because I can't pay in the canteen . . . all those kind of things you have to take into account."

During the migration of Web content, ICT managers were careful to involve Corporate Communications to ensure the integrity of the DSM brand. After porting content into the new DSM layout, the business units verified the accuracy of the content and revised it to meet the new corporate policies and standards. Getting business unit staff to do this work required some effort on the part of ICT project managers. De Haas recalled his conversations with new employees, some of whom were concerned with whether they would still have a job next year: "Then I come in and say, 'Your information on the Internet is not correct. Can you please change it?' It's not a top priority for the business, that's for sure," said Haas. "But if you don't correct it, things won't work anymore, and you'd have a totally dead Internet."

The Hosting stream took charge of relocating over 350 systems (i.e., servers) from Roche data centers to DSM hosted data centers located in Eindhoven, Netherlands, and Arlington, Texas. Each system move required three to four months of preparation with meticulous planning down to the hour. The typical routine involved stopping a system on a Friday night, dumping all the information onto tapes, sending via courier to Eindhoven, loading onto the systems, and finally bringing the systems up on Sunday morning. The responsible business unit then checked their system integrity and accuracy, problems were fixed, and, on Monday morning, the systems were available for business again. Functionality was not changed, only the physical location of the system. This required a weekend routine of shutting down the old system, copying information, relocating it, reloading, and testing. De Haas commented on challenges of effecting these transitions in a live work environment:

> The whole aim was that all the business functions must be available without any interruption so people can keep on working from 8 to 5. And if you make any changes, the changes must come at night or in the weekend. When people came back the day after or on Monday, the system should work again as it did before . . . And I'm proud to say that there was no business outage whatsoever.

The Distributed Computing stream was tasked with redeploying or replacing over 5,700 desktops and laptops at 89 former Roche locations across the globe. This involved adopting the DSM desktop standards and installing the standard file and print servers and email infrastructure. All of the data had to be migrated out of the Roche environment and into the DSM environment while maintaining the integrity of the user's e-mail and shared files.

"I think the main success of the whole project was what we call a dry-run. . . . We urged people in that dry run to come up with problems so that we could test. Then we'd select one site as a pilot site to see if it really did run in practice," said de Haas.

The Network stream managed the removal of all of the global network sites from the Roche Global Network while simultaneously integrating them into the DSM global network (DGN). This required a period of double connectivity. A solution was designed to enable DNP employees to access systems from both Roche and DSM during the transition period, requiring close cooperation between both ICT groups who were distributed across the globe.

Secure tunnels were built between the Roche network and the DSM environment so users, still in the Roche environment, could access systems that had already been moved to the DSM environment. This required coordination around the connections between the Roche and DSM networks during that transition period, with teams at both Roche and DSM guarding the double fire walls. Approval from both teams was necessary in order to get the traffic from one environment into the other while maintaining network integrity and security.

Module 2

The Business of IT

Robert D. Austin

More than ever, companies depend on IT capabilities to execute their business models. Without sound management, frameworks to deliver operational results, strategies, investments, plans, and innovations—however visionary, shrewd, careful, or original—cannot create business value. In recent years, advances in computing technology have led to fundamental shifts in how firms use IT to execute their intentions. New technologies bring new opportunities but also new risks. Realizing opportunities and managing risks require innovations in IT delivery service models and management approach. Today's manager of the business of IT needs a modern arsenal of methods and techniques for contending with many new challenges while also continuing to meet past commitments.

The chapters in this module focus on frontline operational issues. They examine how changing technology infrastructure affects business, how management frameworks and priorities must shift, and how opportunities can be exploited and risks minimized. The module is organized within four chapters. Chapter 5 introduces the basic elements of modern IT infrastructure and surfaces the management issues to be pursued in depth later in the module. Chapter 6 addresses the robustness of IT capabilities, with emphasis on issues of system availability and security. Chapter 7 explores new service models made possible by advances in computing technologies and discusses frameworks for managing these services, including those provided by external partners (via outsourcing). Chapter 8 addresses issues of project management, an activity that remains very critical to the delivery and enhancement of IT capabilities. The article and five cases at the end of the module provide a basis for further discussion on how to tackle value creation's all-important last step: Execution.

Chapter 5

Understanding IT Infrastructure

"Seventy-five percent of all IT dollars go to infrastructure. Isn't it time you learned what it is?"[1]

Information technology (IT) infrastructure[2] lies at the heart of most companies' operating capabilities. Changes in IT lead therefore to fundamental changes in how businesses operate. Because many companies depend on these technologies, adept management of this infrastructure has become vital.

Recent advances have led to major changes in how IT services are delivered. For some time, low-cost computing power has propelled a shift toward more distributed processing. *Internetworking technologies*, which provide a low-cost way to connect everyone on the same network, present new possibilities for addressing business computing needs. The operational mechanisms at the heart of many businesses continue to evolve. New technologies add to, improve, and interconnect older systems to yield infrastructures with complex operational characteristics.

Infrastructure evolution brings with it many benefits. IT services few envisioned several years ago have become commonplace. Older services can be delivered in new, more customer-responsive ways, and the cost structures underlying new service delivery methods are superior to those of older methods. New business models enabled by the new service possibilities have emerged. Industries restructure to realize greater efficiencies and capabilities as part of a long-term trend that will continue and accelerate regardless of occasional technology market slumps.

Along with benefits, however, come challenges. In this chapter and the next three, we address the challenges associated with changing infrastructure. Our focus is on frontline issues of execution. Grand visions are of little use unless they can be translated into reality. New business models and systems cannot succeed unless they

This chapter is adapted from Professor Robert D. Austin's *Managing Information Technology Infrastructure* course module, Harvard Business School Publishing No. 603-104.

[1] From an IBM advertisement that ran in major newspapers in the fall of 2001.

[2] In this and the following chapters, we use the word *infrastructure* to refer to the entire layered fabric of hardware, software, systems, and media that collectively deliver IT services.

can be relied on to operate at key moments. New technologies provide less value if they cannot inter-operate effectively with the older technologies still present in most companies. Most seriously, IT infrastructure greatly determines a company's differentiating capabilities; effective infrastructure enhances capabilities, while ineffective infrastructure destroys them. In today's environment, a seemingly minor IT decision made two or three years ago by a low-level technical employee can turn out to be the decisive factor in defining a winning strategy, closing a sale or deal, or surviving a competitive challenge.

The constraints of past IT infrastructure decisions can be severe, for example, when a company deploys a technology that proves to be a loser in the marketplace; such a company can be left with poor (or no) vendor support, inferior business capabilities, and costly-to-maintain infrastructure that cannot easily be shut down or replaced. Infrastructure decisions are difficult because they arise in a dimly illuminated realm halfway between business and technology. In this realm, technology issues are tightly interwoven with business issues, and it is unclear who should be making the decisions. Often general managers are tempted to "leave it to the techies," but this is often a mistake. Technological aspects of decisions may seem alien to nontechnical managers, but technologists may see business issues in similar terms. The deepest challenges of infrastructure management, then, are in understanding and assigning responsibility for making these not just technical, not just business decisions, in bridging the gap between the business and technology domains. Only when we are successful in this will we see clearly how evolving technologies affect business, how management priorities should evolve, and how we can reduce the risks that affect day-to-day operations.

The Drivers of Change: Better Chips, Bigger Pipes

In 1965, Gordon Moore, who would later cofound Intel, noted that the performance of memory chips doubled every 18 to 24 months, whereas their size and cost remained roughly constant. He predicted that the trend would continue and that its impact on the world would be profound. Nearly four decades later, most people are familiar with consequences of Moore's "Law." The computing power in a twenty-first-century desktop, laptop, or even handheld computing device far exceeds that of machines the size of large rooms at the time of Moore's observation (see Figure 5.1). Equally significant is the low cost of modern devices. Once scarce, expensive, and therefore centrally controlled computing power is now abundant, inexpensive, and widely distributed in everything from general-purpose computers to toaster ovens.

Centralized computing architecture prevailed during the 1960s and 1970s (see Figure 5.2). Specialized data processing staffs presided over large mainframe computers accessed via awkward punch card, Teletype, and terminal machines. Dealings between humans and computers were not very interactive; programs ran infrequently, in batches, often only once each day. Access devices were "dumb"; they had little inherent capability but served merely as murky windows into complex mainframes. Mainframes provided all computational and storage capabilities. The occasional need to share information between mainframes led to the development of networks. These early networks were simple because they only had to handle traffic between a few large mainframe computers.

FIGURE 5.1
A Graphical Representation of Moore's Law

Source: Adapted by Mark Seager from *Microprocessor Report,* 9 no. 6, May 1995, and Aad Offernan, "ChipLisi 9.9.5." July 1998, http://einstein.et.tudelft.nl/~offerman/chiplist.html. See http://www.physics.udel.edu/wwwusers/watson/scen103/intel.html, April 20, 2000, George Watson, University of Delaware, 1998.

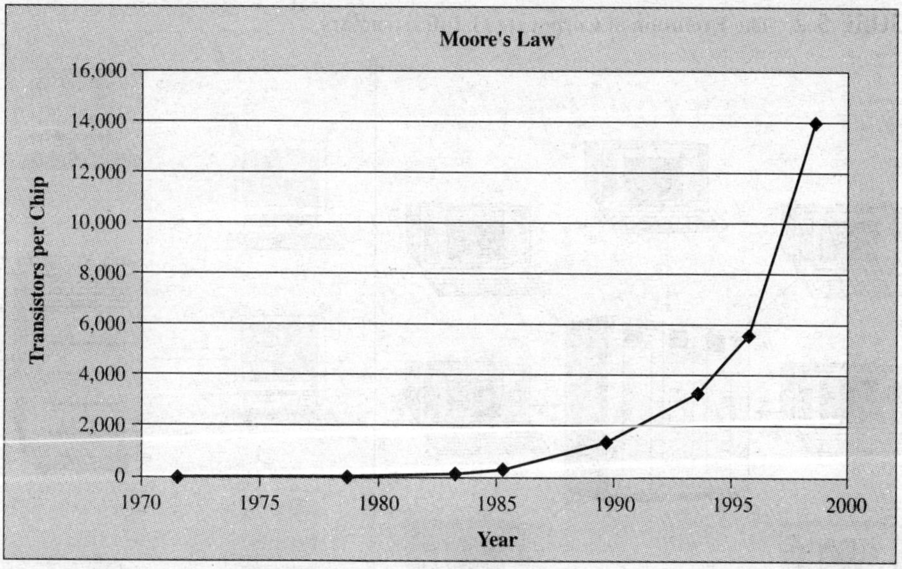

The impacts of Moore's Law disrupted the mainframe paradigm. An advertisement for the Intel 4004 in the Fall 1971 issue of *Electronic News* exaggerated when it announced "a new era in integrated electronics," a "computer on a chip."[3] But the new era was not long in coming. The immediate successors of the programmable 4004 were the basis for the first general-purpose desktop computing machines capable of real business functionality: personal computers (PCs). When the IBM PC appeared in late 1981, few realized how radically it would change business computing.

With the emergence of PCs, computing that had resided in centralized data processing enclaves spread throughout the organization and into the eager hands of business users. Financial analysts embraced spreadsheets. Marketers designed and analyzed their own databases. Engineers adopted computerized drawing packages and programmed their own PCs for more specialized purposes. For a growing number of computing tasks, reliance on the data processing staff became a distant memory.

As newly empowered computer users sought to share work, new communications infrastructures emerged. Local area networks (LANs) allowed businesspeople to share spreadsheets, word processing, and other documents, and to use common printers to obtain hard copies of their work. PCs and LANs became more sophisticated as users' computing needs expanded and as underlying technologies that were fundamentally different from earlier mainframe technologies advanced. The client-server movement was the culmination of this model: Higher-powered but still distributed computers (servers) combined with more elaborate networks and desktop PCs (clients) to provide IT services (i.e., payroll, order management, sales support, and beyond) formerly delivered by mainframe.

In the early 1990s, the rise to prominence of the commercial Internet, the Web, and underlying protocols (rules for how data would be moved across networks) led to new

[3] Paul Frieberger and Michael Swaine, *Fire in the Valley: The Making of the Personal Computer* (New York: McGraw-Hill, 2000), p. 20.

FIGURE 5.2 **The Evolution of Corporate IT Infrastructure**

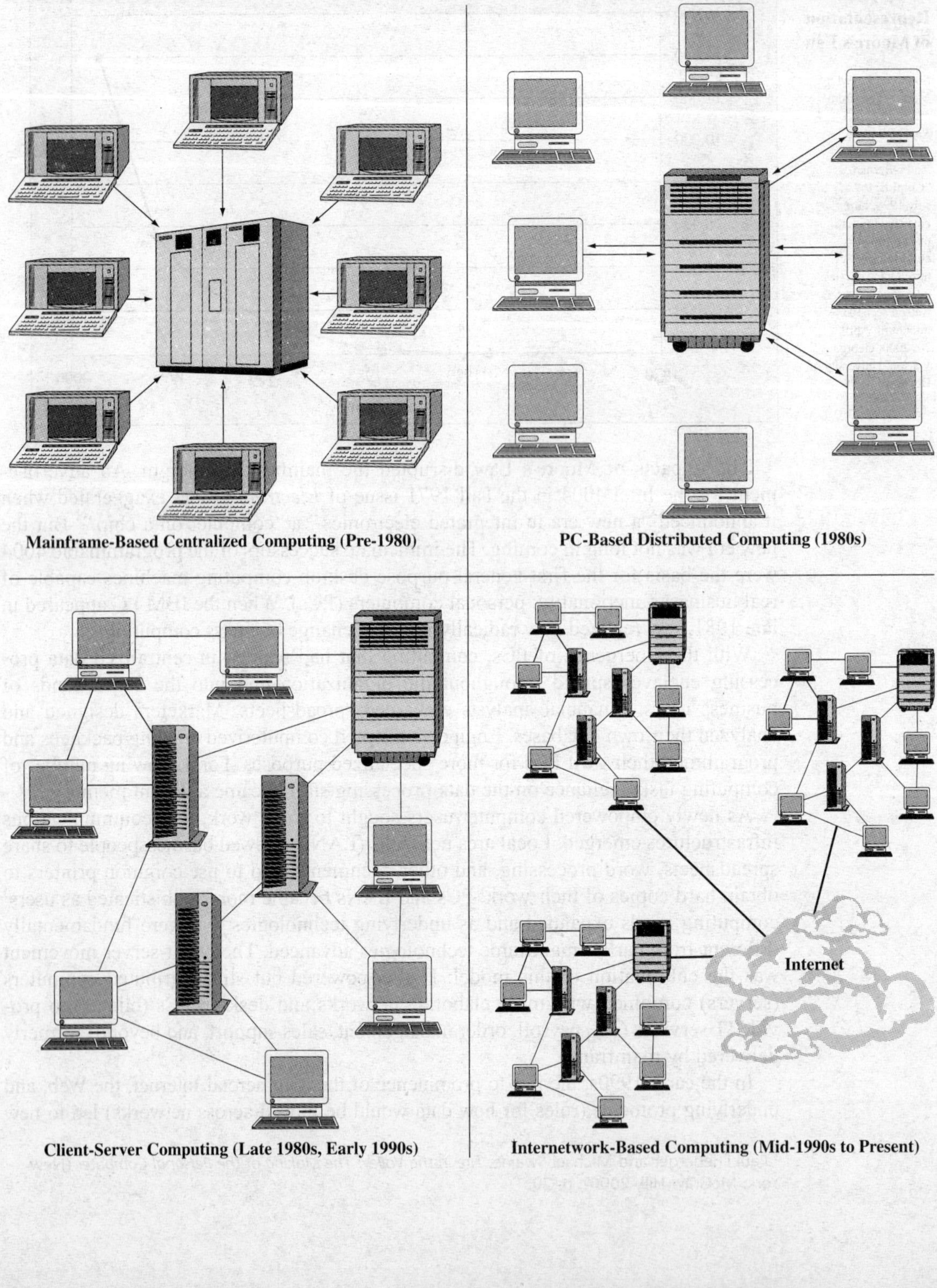

FIGURE 5.3
A Graphical Illustration of Metcalfe's Law

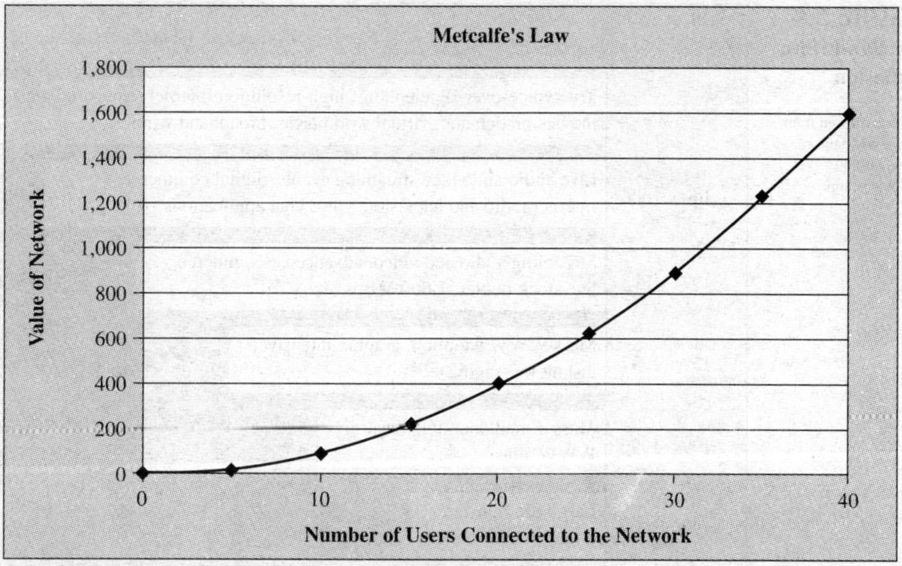

stages of evolution.[4] Transmission control protocol and Internet protocol, together known as TCP/IP, provided a robust standard for routing messages between LANs and created the potential to connect all computers on an ever-larger wide area network (WAN). Internetworking technologies were the legacy of U.S. Department of Defense (DOD) research (conducted in the 1960s against the backdrop of the Cold War) to develop communication networks without critical communication lines or nodes that could be targeted by an enemy. Because of their publicly funded origins, TCP/IP and other Internet protocols and technologies were *open* standards, not owned by any person or company. Computers could be connected at low cost and with minimal central orchestration. Self-service hookup facilitated rapid growth in the worldwide Internet.

At first, the Internet was useful primarily for exchanging e-mail and large data files, but the Web, with its graphical user interfaces, made Internet communication valuable to those who were not computer specialists. Just as PCs had made computing accessible to a wide variety of nontechnical users, the Web made network resources (such as distant databases) and capabilities (such as over-the-Net collaboration) accessible. The number of connected computers shot skyward, and the value of the network increased according to Metcalfe's Law: "The usefulness of a network increases with the square of the number of users connected to the network" (see Figure 5.3).[5]

As the number of users grew, commercial potential mounted and network capacity expanded. Network capacity followed a curve steeper than the one that applied to chips (see Figure 5.4). The combination of powerful chips and large communication "pipes," both at low cost, fueled a process that would lead to qualitatively different computing infrastructures.

[4] The Internet was not new in the 1990s. It had been in use by the military and by researchers since the 1960s. But commercial uses of these technologies accelerated dramatically in the 1990s.

[5] Metcalfe's Law is commonly attributed to Robert Metcalfe, one of the inventors of the Ethernet standard and the founder of 3Com Corporation.

FIGURE 5.4
The Bandwidth Explosion

Source: Adapted from http://www.stanford.edu/~yzarolia/Challenges.htm.

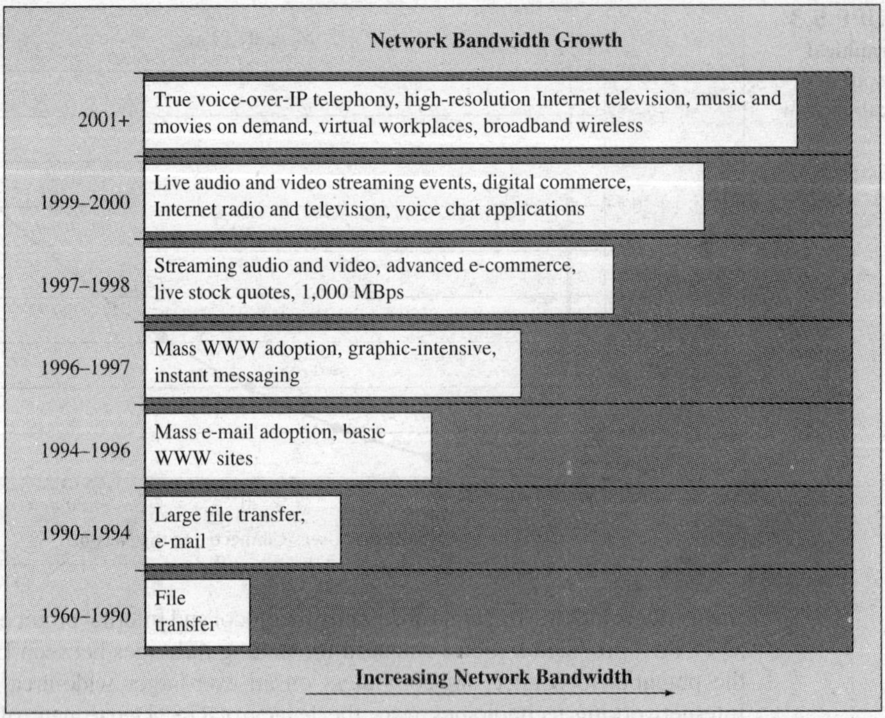

These related exponential trends—reduction in the cost of computing power and reduction in the cost of exchanging information between computers—have been fundamental drivers of changes in the business landscape that we continue to experience and try to understand. Because changes have been rapid, many businesses own a mix of technologies from different computing eras. Some companies still rely heavily on mainframes. At the same time, companies have moved boldly to seize the benefits of newer technologies. Mainframes have been redefined and reborn as enterprise servers. The constant intermingling of old and new technologies adds to the complexity of infrastructure management problems. Understanding how shifting technology might combine with "legacy" systems to change business capabilities is a prerequisite for understanding how to manage IT infrastructures.

The Basic Components of Internetworking Infrastructures

For our purposes, IT infrastructures can be divided into three categories: network, processing systems, and facilities. *Network* refers to the technologies (hardware and software) that permit exchange of information between organizations. As network capacity increases, the network takes on greater importance as a component of IT infrastructure. *Processing systems* encompass the hardware and software that together provide an organization's ability to handle business transactions. They are newly interesting in the age of internetworking because they are being redesigned to better capitalize on the advantages offered by internetworking technologies. Facilities,

TABLE 5.1
Fundamental Components of Internet-working Infrastructure

	Core Technologies	Key Management Issues
Network	Fiber optics, cable systems, DSL, satellite, wireless, internetworking hardware (routers, switches, firewalls), content delivery software, identity and policy management, monitoring	• How to select technologies and standards • How to select partners • How to manage partner relationships • How to assure reliability • How to maintain security
Processing Systems	Transaction software (enterprise systems offered by companies such as SAP and Oracle or more targeted solutions, sometimes homegrown), servers, server appliances, client devices (PCs, handhelds), mobile phones	• What to keep internal and what to outsource • How to deploy, grow, and modify • Enterprise system or best-of-breed hybrid • Relationships with legacies • How to manage incidents • How to recover after a "disaster"
Facilities	Corporate data centers, collocation data centers, managed services data centers, data closets	• Internal or external management • Choosing a facilities model suited to one's company • How to assure reliability • How to maintain security • How to maximize energy efficiency and reduce environmental impact

the physical systems that house and protect computing and network devices, are the least glamorous infrastructure components. But they too are growing in importance as demand increases for high levels of availability, reliability, and security and as greater network capacity makes new facilities models possible.

Each of these infrastructure components generates opportunities and issues managers must understand and be able to address. Table 5.1 lists some of the supporting core technologies and identifies some of the key management issues that arise for each component. A major theme underlying the evolution of these components is that *internetworking creates many more degrees of freedom in how components can be arranged and managed.* Having more degrees of freedom creates possibilities for cost reduction, new capabilities, and new business models but also poses challenges in understanding the implications of possible infrastructure designs and management actions.

FIGURE 5.5
A Simple LAN

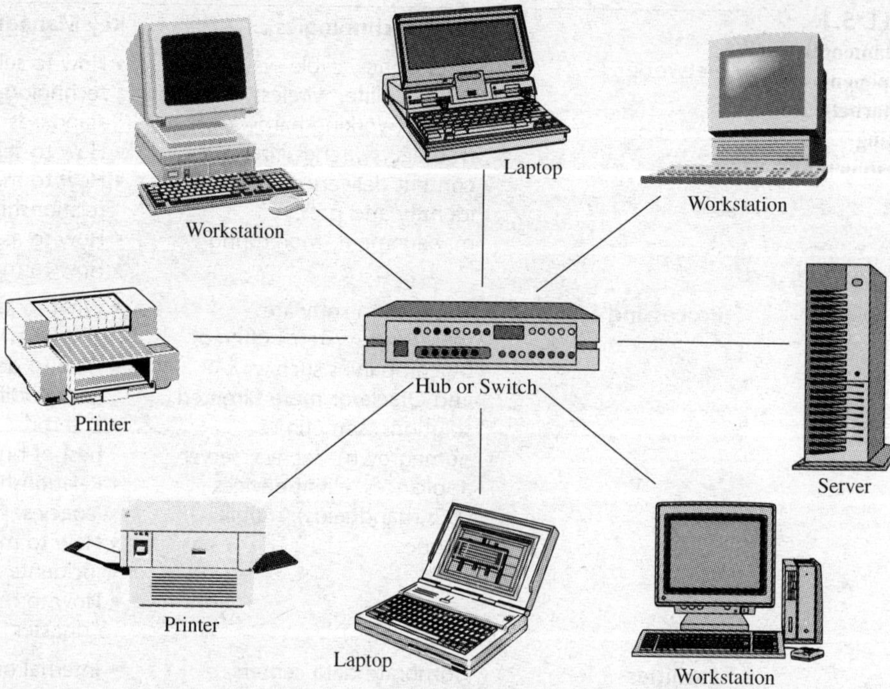

The Technological Elements of Networks

Networks can be decomposed into technological elements; these are the key components that managers must understand, arrange, and maintain. Although the underlying technologies that constitute these elements vary, anyone involved in managing networks will need to make decisions about the design, management, and improvement of the following.

Local Area Networks

Local area networks (LANs), as the name implies, provide a way for computers that are physically close together to communicate (see Figure 5.5). LAN technologies define the physical features of solutions to local communication problems and also the protocols—the rules—for "conversations" among devices.

Hubs, Switches, Wireless Access Points, and Network Adapters

Hubs, switches, "WAPs," and network adapters allow computers to be connected in LANs. Hubs and switches serve as central junctions into which cables from the computers on a LAN are connected. Wireless access points connect wireless devices into hubs and switches. Hubs are simple connection devices, but switches vary in complexity and capability from very simple to very large and sophisticated. Sophisticated switches connect LANs and larger networks to each other. Network adapters that are physically fitted into the computers on a LAN translate the computer's communications into a language that can be broadcast over the LAN and understood by listening computers. Network adapters also listen for communications from other computers and translate them into terms that can be understood by the connected computers (see the accompanying feature on p. 243).

How LAN Protocols Work

The problem of computers "conversing" on a LAN is much like the problem of students conversing in a classroom. In a classroom, the air in the room (the "ether") readily supports students in speaking to each other. But if two people speak at the same time, they cannot be sure of communication. To avoid such problems in the classroom we employ protocols—rules—that govern our interactions. One possible set of rules might require that students speak in turn, To keep track of whose turn it is, we might pass a small object (a "token") in a pattern (maybe a "ring") around the room. Whoever has the token at the moment has speaking rights; everyone else must listen. These rules are very much like those used by computers as they speak onto the captive ether of LAN network cables, or into the actual ether of a wireless LAN, by using the Token Ring protocol. The popular Ethernet protocol is a little different. With Ethernet, computers speak out whenever they (1) have something to say, and (2) hear silence on the network for a moment. If two or more computers speak at the same time, the computers notice this—they detect the "collision"—and stop talking. Each waits a random amount of time and tries again. The Ethernet protocol works well as long as the amount of time it takes a computer to say something is small compared to the time available.

Wide Area Networks

Wide area networks (WANs), as the name implies, provide a way for computers physically distant from each other to communicate (see Figure 5.6). WANs are networks of networks, and enable LANs to connect and communicate. WAN technologies define the physical features of solutions and the standards for conducting conversations between computers and communication devices over long distances. A WAN inside the boundaries of a company's physical premises is sometimes called an *intranet*. A WAN that extends outward from a company's physical premises to business partners

FIGURE 5.6
An Example of a WAN

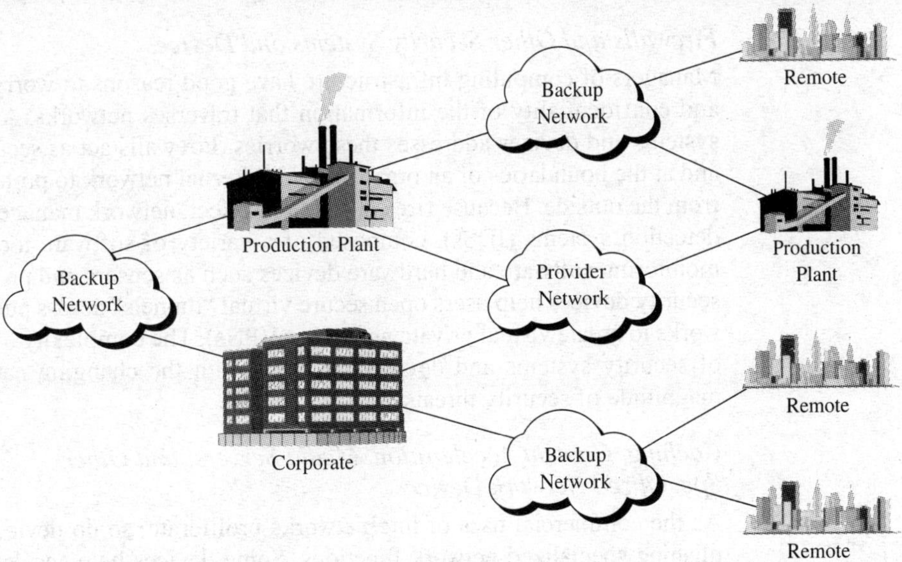

An Internetworking Analogy

Imagine a complex highway system on which millions of cars are always moving. There are groups of cars that belong to the same travel party and are heading to the same place. But individual drivers know only the address where they are heading. They have no maps and no sense of direction. Members of groups make no attempt to stay together. At junctures along the highway network there are routing stations where cars stop, show their destination addresses, and are told, "Try going that way." A single routing station may send cars heading for the same destination in different directions. Eventually, though, a car arrives at its destination. It waits for other members of the travel party to arrive, and then they all do something useful together. This is an overly simple but fairly accurate analogy for how messages traverse internetworks.

is sometimes called an *extranet*. Choices between different technologies and standards in building internetworks, whether they are intranets or extranets, involve trade-offs of cost versus data capacity, reliability, and security.

Routers

Routers are the devices that enable internetworking, the means by which messages are relayed across large distances. A router listens in on LAN conversations and recognizes messages intended for computers that are not on that LAN. The listening router relays those messages to other routers. Each router has some notion of the approximate direction of the message's destination across the larger network. As a message makes its way through a series of between-router "hops," it gradually arrives at routers that know more details about the location of the destination computer. Eventually a message finds a router that knows the destination machine's LAN and can complete the delivery of a message. Like switches, routers come in simple and sophisticated varieties. They are the glue with which networks are connected to each other and provide many degrees of freedom in network design (see the accompanying feature).

Firewalls and Other Security Systems and Devices

Managers of computing infrastructure have good reasons to worry about the security and confidentiality of the information that traverses networks. A variety of network systems and devices addresses these worries. Firewalls act as security sentries within and at the boundaries of an organization's internal network to protect it from intrusion from the outside. Because firewalls are imperfect, network managers employ intrusion detection systems (IDSs), composed of a variety of software tools such as network monitoring software and hardware devices such as sensors and probes. Other network security devices help users open secure virtual "tunnels" across public and private networks to create virtual private networks (VPNs). The complexity of the configurations of security systems and devices increases with the changing nature and escalating magnitude of security threats.

Caching, Content Acceleration, Media Servers, and Other Specialized Network Devices

As the commercial uses of internetworks proliferate, so do devices aimed at accomplishing specialized network functions. Some devices help accelerate the delivery of information across the network, sometimes by "caching" (e.g., storing) information in a location close to the destination machine. Other specialized devices help assure the efficient transmission of time-dependent information such as the sound and image data that accompany internetwork-based video delivery or video teleconferencing. As infrastructure evolves, there will be continuing growth in specialized network systems and devices for metering and management of messages and transactions to assure timely and error-free quality of services (QoS), facilitate information-based transactions, and accomplish a variety of other functions.

The Technological Elements of Processing Systems

Processing systems are also composed of technological elements managers must understand, arrange, and maintain. Although there is tremendous variety in the underlying hardware and software that constitute these elements, anyone involved in managing a company's processing systems will need to make decisions about the design, management, and improvement of the following.

Client Devices and Systems

Until recently, it was safe to think of client devices as PCs; in the last few years, however, variety in client devices has exploded to include handheld devices, cell phones, and even automotive components. Client systems are the software that runs on these devices to perform business functions, manage interactions with other computers, and handle certain low-level client machine operations (such as storing saved information). As the name implies, clients are often on the receiving end of IT services delivered from elsewhere in the network. Business users experience internetworking infrastructure primarily through client devices and systems. Unlike the terminals of the mainframe era, modern clients are not dumb; often they are capable of performing significant business functions even when separated from a network. Mobile users often use clients in both network-connected and unconnected modes; client software must manage intermittently connected devices and systems in a way that provides business advantage to users.

Server Devices and Systems

Servers occupy a role in internetworking infrastructure roughly equivalent to that of mainframe computers in an earlier era. Although based on microcomputer technology, servers handle the heavy processing required for high-volume business transactions and permit sharing of information across a large number of computer users. Servers are the source of many of the IT services that clients receive from across the network. Server systems consist of software to carry out mainline business functions (such as order or inventory management), manage transactions from other computers (such as those that update inventory information), and handle low-level machine operations (such as storing saved information). In essence, clients perform front-end processing (interaction with users) while servers perform back-end processing (heavy computation or interaction with other back-end computers). Servers are often physically located in data centers and managed by central staffs, as their mainframe ancestors were. Both they and their systems are increasingly designed as specialized appliances

FIGURE 5.7
Servers in a Possible E-Commerce Configuration

Source: Robert D. Austin, Larry Leibrock, and Alan Murray, "The iPremier Company; Denial of Service Attack (A)," Hardvard Business School Case No. 9-601-114.

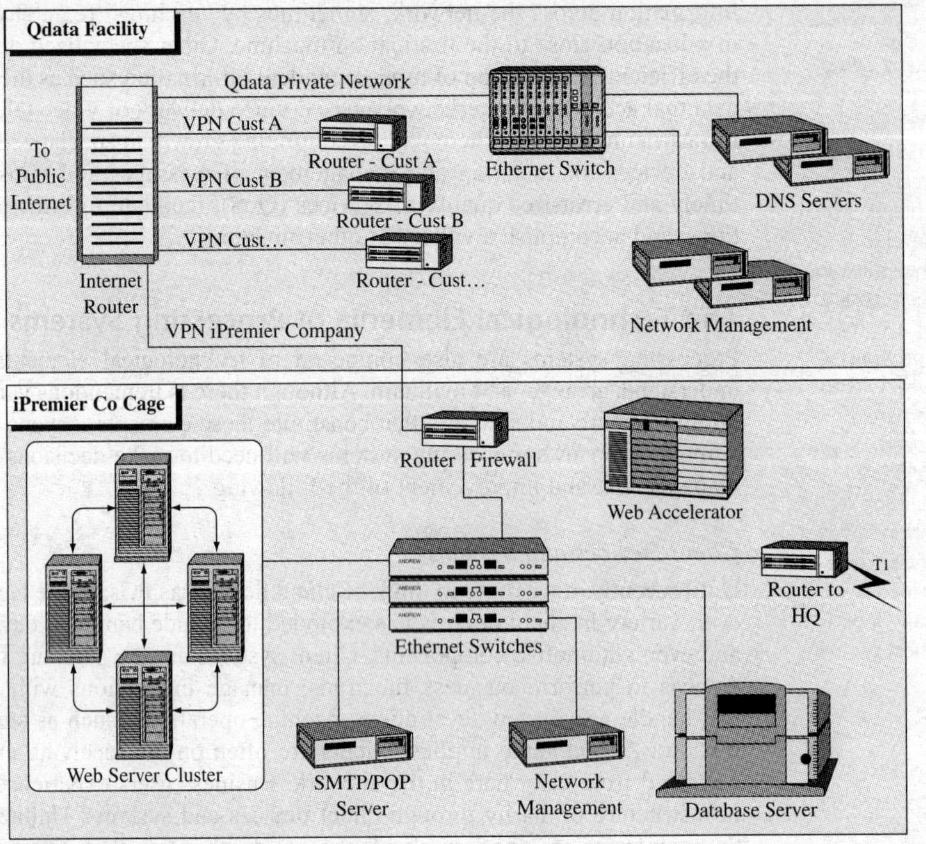

targeted at specific functions: database servers, Web servers, and application servers, for example (see Figure 5.7). Software systems that run on distributed, specialized architectures must be designed very differently from those of mainframe systems in which all processing happens on the same machine.

Mainframe Devices and Systems

Mainframe computers remain very much a part of modern IT infrastructure. In many companies, mainframes still do the majority of business-critical transaction processing. Some mainframes are modern, high-performance machines, the equivalent of very powerful servers that interoperate well with internetworks. Others are relics of an earlier era that are still performing vital business functions. As computing infrastructures become more interconnected, legacy mainframe systems pose complications. The open protocols of the internetworking world are not the native language of older mainframe computers. Mainframe manufacturers have developed systems that enable interaction between legacy mainframes and internetworks. These advanced systems allow users to access information on mainframes via new technologies, such as Web browsers. But interfaces between legacy mainframes and internetworks cannot always overcome the problems associated with the interaction of such different

Open Source Software

Many companies use "open source software" (OSS) systems, such as the Linux operating system or the Apache Web Server, as vital components of their IT infrastructure. OSS is neither purchased nor homegrown; rather, it is freely available from a worldwide community of volunteers who have worked together via the Internet to develop a product of common interest. You might think that software developed by informally organized volunteers could not perform well enough to become parts of a corporate IT infrastructure. But OSS (notably Linux and Apache, but there are other examples) performs *very* well. Often it outperforms commercially developed counterparts on important measures (e.g., reliability, security, speed). Experts attribute the excellent performance of OSS to the extreme transparency of the methods used to develop it; whereas commercial firms usually keep secret the inner workings of their software, OSS developers make their "code" available for anyone to see. When so many experts—potentially thousands of software developers—can "look under the hood" to see how a system works, most problems get noticed and fixed quickly.

When companies use open source, they pay no license fees. Although significant monetary savings may result from this fact, operating OSS does incur costs. Some commercial software vendors have argued that OSS is *more* expensive to operate than commercial software (e.g., support workers may need to be retrained). Critics of OSS also point to concerns about who "stands behind" software developed by an amorphous community of volunteers (when something goes wrong, who do you call?), and to the difficulty in assuring that no components within an OSS system are owned by a commercial firm (if proprietary software has found its way, perhaps inadvertently, into OSS, this could generate legal difficulties for companies using the software). OSS enthusiasts counter these complaints by noting that many large, reputable firms, such as IBM and Novell, will now provide support for OSS (thus, "standing behind it"), and that OSS development practices are transparent enough to assure that proprietary software will not appear in OSS to any consequential degree.

technologies. For example, some mainframe systems still process jobs in batches. Native internetworking systems and more modern mainframe systems, in contrast, usually are designed to operate in real time, to process new orders at the time they occur. Overcoming fundamental operational incompatibilities often eventually necessitates the replacement of a legacy system, but this takes time and money. Where mainframes remain in more modern renditions, their mission has changed so that they function effectively as real-time transaction processors.

Middleware

Middleware is the hodgepodge of enabling utilities, message handling and queuing systems, protocols, standards, software tool kits, and other systems that help clients, servers, mainframes, and their systems coordinate activities in time and across networks. Middleware, which often runs on servers, could be considered a category of server system, but it is important enough in orchestrating the activities of internetworking infrastructure to deserve separate mention. Many managers know little and understand less about middleware; it is a classic example of difficult-to-manage infrastructure. Few people know enough about both the technology and the business needs to make intelligent decisions in this area. And yet increasingly sophisticated middleware is the key to many new approaches to IT service delivery, such as those sometimes called *software as a service, utility* or *on demand* or *grid* computing. The middleware domain is where important "Web services" technologies usually operate. Middleware plays an increasing role in improving the flexibility, capacity utilization, efficiency, and effectiveness of modern IT infrastructure.

Infrastructure Management Systems

A company must have systems for managing its computing infrastructure. These systems monitor the performance of processing systems, devices, and networks. They include systems that support the help desks when users are having trouble with computers or networks, and the systems that deliver new software to computers throughout an organization. The quality of infrastructure management systems influences how efficiently a company obtains value from its computing assets. Without strong systems management, expensive internetworks may become tied in knots; for example, too many transactions may flow to one computer while another is underused.

Business Applications

Computer users interact with the business applications layer of infrastructure constantly and directly. Most companies house an immense variety of installed business applications. Many applications are custom built by the IT staffs in the companies that use them. Others are off-the-shelf packages ranging from small client applications, such as a spreadsheet program, up to huge packages that cost tens of millions of dollars and take years to install, such as enterprise resource planning (ERP) systems. As the name suggests, business applications deliver actual business functionality. In a real sense, it is the job of the rest of an internetworking infrastructure to make possible the delivery of business functionality by this top layer.

The Technological Elements of Facilities

Facilities also can be decomposed into technological elements. Once a non-technical backwater left to real estate managers, facilities management has become an important aspect of infrastructure management, primarily due to the demands for always on, 24-hour, 7-days-a-week (24×7) operations. At the same time, there is increasing recognition that providing this level of operational functionality imposes significant environmental costs: Computers and other IT infrastructure consume phenomenal and increasing amounts of electrical energy, placing a heavy burden on electric supply and contributing to greenhouse gas emissions. In addition, both the manufacture and disposal of computing equipment have an environmental impact. Consequently, anyone involved in managing a company's processing systems eventually will face decisions about the operationally effective and environmentally sound design, management, and improvement of the following.

Buildings and Physical Spaces

The physical characteristics of the buildings and rooms that house computing infrastructure strongly influence how well devices and systems function and how efficiently and effectively they can be managed (see Figure 5.8). The size of a facility, its physical features, how readily it lends itself to reconfiguration, and how well it protects its contents from external disruptions are important factors to consider in managing physical structures. Design decisions such as minimizing the footprint of the building; using

FIGURE 5.8
A Modern Data Center

Source: Allegiance Telecom.

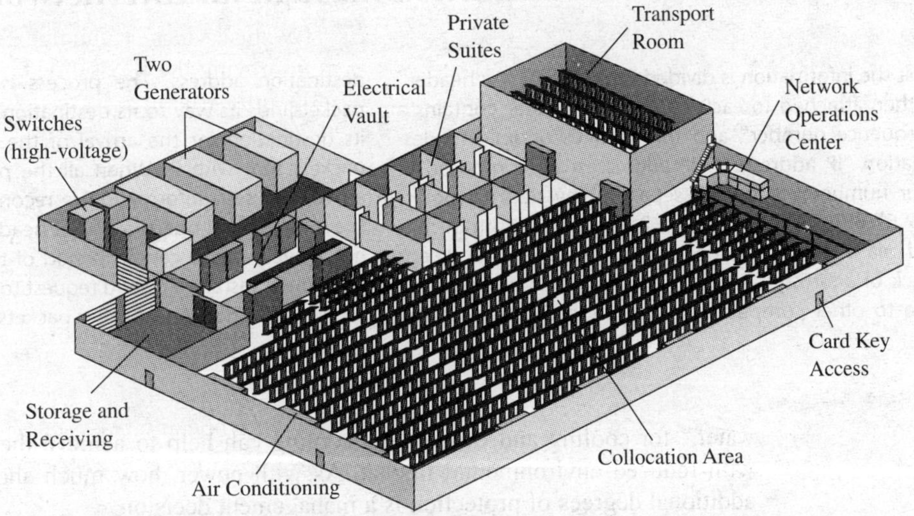

low-emission building materials, carpets and paints; recycling waste, and sustainable landscaping can minimize the environmental impact of a data center.

Network Conduits and Connections

The way in which systems within a facility are connected to wider networks also influences IT infrastructure performance. Among the factors managers must consider are the amount of redundancy in physical network connections, the number and selection of partners who will provide "backbone" connectivity to external networks, and the capacity of the data lines leased from service providers. All these factors involve trade-offs in terms of cost, performance, availability, and security. At stake in trade-off decisions are relationships with customers, suppliers, and other business partners.

Power

Computers do not run without power, and many businesses do not run without computers. Assuring that firms will have power when they need it is, then, a major concern for infrastructure managers. Indeed, access to sufficient and affordable power can be a critical factor in choosing a data center location. Decisions in this area involve trade-offs between cost and redundancy. Systems can obtain power from multiple power grids, uninterruptible power supplies (UPSs), backup generators, and even privately owned power plants. Access to clean, renewable, or alternative sources of energy is an increasing concern. Choices to use more energy-efficient equipment can also reduce a facility's power needs. Determining which measures are worth their cost and impact is a management decision.

Temperature and Humidity Controls

Computers are delicate devices (although less so than in the past). They do not tolerate wide variations in temperature or combine well with moisture. Shielding computers from environmental hazards is another effort that can be pursued more or less thoroughly and at varying cost. Approaches such as the use of recycled water, or "gray

How Information Is Transmitted through an Internetwork

First the information is divided into packets. A "header" is then attached to each packet; the header contains a "sequence number" and the packet's origin and destination "IP addresses." IP addresses are composed of four numbers, 0 to 255, separated by decimal points (19.67.89.134, for example). Packets are then transmitted via a router—a specialized computer that keeps track of addresses—across an available communication line to other computers in the rough direction of the destination address. The process is repeated until a packet finds its way to its destination. A packet waits at its destination for the arrival of the other information packets sent with it. When all the packets in a group arrive, the sent information is reconstructed by using the sequence numbers in packet headers. If a packet has not arrived after a certain period of time, the receiving machine transmits a resend request to the origin address found in the headers of other packets in the group.

water," for cooling and evaporative cooling can help to achieve the desired control with reduced environmental impact. As with power, how much should be paid for additional degrees of protection is a management decision.

Security

Computer devices and systems also must be protected from malicious attacks, both physical and network-based. Physical security requires facilities and methods that control access to machines, such as security guards, cages, and locks. Network security—a field of growing complexity—has numerous facilities implications. The threat from hacker attacks and intrusions is a growing problem. As with other facilities elements, security involves trade-offs, in this case between cost and level of protection.

Operational Characteristics of Internetworks

Taken together, internetworking technologies have operational characteristics that distinguish them from other information technologies. In many ways, these characteristics determine the challenges of managing infrastructures based on internetworking technologies. Important operational characteristics of internetworking technologies that make them different from the technologies of previous eras, in terms of how they perform and should be managed, include the following (see the accompanying feature).

Internetworking Technologies Are Based on Open Standards

TCP/IP is the primary common language of internetworking technologies. TCP/IP standards define how computers send and receive data packets. Because the standards were developed using public funds, they are public and not owned by anyone; they are open, not proprietary. The fact that TCP/IP can be freely used by anyone makes internetworks less dependent on solutions developed and marketed by private companies. Decreased reliance on proprietary technologies has generated huge economic benefits for purchasers of new technology by making systems from different vendors more interoperable and thus increasing competition. Prices are lower and performance better than they might have been if these technologies had remained proprietary. Insistence on open standards and solutions has become part of the ethos of the internetworking community of administrators and developers. This ethos has led to development of other important open standards, such as hypertext transport protocol (HTTP), used to deliver Web content.

Internetworking Technologies Operate Asynchronously

Information sent over an internetwork does not employ dedicated, bidirectional connections between sender and receiver, as for example, a telephone call. Instead, packets of information with accompanying address information are sent toward a destination, sometimes without any prior coordination between the sender and the receiver. Network services that exchange information quickly, such as the Web, require the sender and the receiver to be connected to the internetwork at the same time. But such communication is still asynchronous in that no dedicated link is established. For other services, such as e-mail, the receiver's computer need not even be switched on at the time the message is sent. As with postal mail, an e-mail recipient has a mailbox where mail can accumulate until it is accessed. Unlike regular mail, though, e-mail messages can be sent around the globe almost instantaneously.

Internetwork Communications Have Inherent Latency

The computers that make up internetworks are connected by links of varying capacity. As packets carry information along different paths toward a common destination, some packets flow quickly through wide links while others move more slowly through narrow links. Packets that together constitute a single message do not arrive at the destination in the same moment. Thus, there is variable wait time between the sending of a message and the arrival at the destination of the last packet in a message.

Because traffic volume is somewhat unpredictable, wait time—often called *latency*—can be difficult to predict. Managers can take actions to make it likely that latency will be within certain tolerances. At the very least, they can assure that network capacity between two points is great enough to avoid unacceptable wait times. New routing technologies provide more options; some make it possible to move high-priority packets to the top of the queues that form at narrow network links. But some degree of latency, and hence unpredictability, is inherent in internetworking technologies and must be taken into account in the design and management of internetworking systems.

Internetworking Technologies Are Decentralized

Largely due to their Defense Department heritage, which dictated that computer networks contain no single points of failure, internetworks have no central traffic control point. Computers connected to the network do not need to be defined to a central control authority, as is the case with some networking technologies. There is, in fact, no central authority that oversees or governs the development or administration of the public Internet except the ones that assign TCP/IP addresses. As a result, individuals and organizations are responsible for managing and maintaining their own facilities in a way that does not hinder the operation of the network as a whole.

Internetworking Technologies Are Scalable

Because communication is intelligently routed along multiple paths, adding to an internetwork is as simple as connecting to another machine. An internetwork as a whole is not affected significantly when a path is removed (packets simply get routed a different way). Additional paths can be added in parallel with overworked paths. Furthermore, internetworking technologies allow relatively easy reorganization of subnetworks; if a network segment has become overloaded, the network can be split up into more manageable subnetworks. In general, these new technologies allow more flexible expansion than do most other network technologies.

The Rise of Internetworking: Business Implications

Dr. Eric Schmidt, Google's chief executive officer (CEO), has observed that high-capacity networks enable a computer to interact just as well with another physically distant computer as with one that is only inches away. Given enough bandwidth, the physical location of computers ceases to matter much. Operationally, the communication pathways inside a computer become indistinguishable from the pathways that connect computers. The network itself becomes part of a larger processor composed of the network and all of its connected computers. To paraphrase a Sun Microsystems slogan: The network *becomes* a computer.

The idea of an increasingly connected network, both inside and beyond the boundaries of organizations, in which the physical location of processors matters less and less, is of great practical importance. Improved connections between machines, departments, companies, and customers mean *quicker realization of economic value* when parties interact; internetworking infrastructure is the means by which value is created and captured in real time. Transactions are initiated and consummated quickly. Activities that once were sequential occur almost simultaneously. Because the physical location of processing is less important, new possibilities for outsourcing, partnerships, and industry restructuring emerge. Along with these beneficial outcomes come drawbacks: Rising complexity, unpredictable interactions, and new types of threats to businesses and consumers. As a result, executives must understand the business implications of these powerful and pervasive networks.

The Emergence of Real-Time Infrastructures

In the mainframe era, scarcity of processing capacity required that business transactions be accumulated and processed in batches. A credit card account might, for example, be updated by a batch run once each day. A stranded traveler who needed to reactivate a mistakenly deactivated card might have to wait for the once-a-day batch run for the card to be reactivated. As processing and communication capacity became more abundant, however, batch processing became less necessary. Delays between initiating a transaction and completing its processing have been greatly reduced. With real-time internetworking infrastructures, customers are serviced and economic value is realized immediately rather than over hours, days, or weeks. The potential benefits of real-time infrastructures are discussed below.

Better Data, Better Decisions

In most large organizations, people in different locations need access to the same data. Until recently, organizations had to keep copies of the same data in many places. But keeping the data synchronized was difficult and frequently did not happen.

Discrepancies between copies of data led to errors, inefficiencies, and poor decision making. Abundant communication capacity has not eliminated the need for multiple copies, but it has reduced it. In addition, it has made it much easier to keep copies synchronized. For the first time, it is becoming possible to run a large business based on a set of financial and operational numbers that are consistent throughout an enterprise.

Improved Process Visibility

Older IT systems based on proprietary technologies often communicated poorly with each other. Consequently, viewing the progress of orders or other transactions across system boundaries was difficult. People in a company's sales organization could not access data in manufacturing, for example, to obtain information about the status of an order. New technologies based on open standards and compatible back-office transaction systems let users instantaneously view transactions with each step in procurement and fulfillment processes, beyond specific system boundaries, and even beyond the boundaries of a company into partners' systems.

Improved Process Efficiency

Many efficiency improvements result directly from enhanced process visibility. In manufacturing, workers who can see what supplies and orders are coming their way tend to hold less buffer stock ("just-in-case" inventory) to guard against uncertainty. Holding less buffer stock reduces working capital, shortens cycle times, and improves return on investment (ROI). A manager in charge of supplying plastic cases for portable radios, for example, can notice that orange radios are not selling well and quickly reduce orange in the color mix.

From Make-and-Sell to Sense-and-Respond[6]

Real-time infrastructures are a prerequisite for achieving highly responsive operations, those based on "sense-and-respond" principles rather than make-to-sell principles. The fundamental insight here is that if operating infrastructures can come close enough to real time, value-adding activities can be performed in response to *actual* customer demand rather than *forecasted* customer demand. Sense-and-respond organizations avoid losses caused by demand-forecasting errors. The most celebrated example is Dell Computer Corporation's make-to-order manufacturing process, which makes computers only in response to actual customer orders. But many other companies in both manufacturing and service industries are seeking ways to move to sense-and-respond models, including some with very complex products, such as automobiles.

In many companies, especially older ones, moving to real-time systems involves reengineering transaction systems to take advantage of greater processing and network capacities. Some companies have renewed transaction infrastructures by implementing large enterprise systems made, for example, by SAP or Oracle. Others have designed best-of-breed transaction infrastructures by connecting what they consider the best products from a variety of vendors. Whichever approach a company takes, the objective is to remove elements from the transaction infrastructure that do not operate in real time, thereby realizing almost immediate economic value from transactions.

[6] See Richard L. Nolan and Steven P. Bradley, *Sense and Respond: Capturing Value in the Network Era* (Boston: Harvard Business School Press, 1998).

A company that succeeds in reengineering transaction and communication systems to operate more or less in real time has ascended to a new and important stage of evolution. When a company achieves real-time IT operations, it not only creates value more quickly; it also creates options for fully leveraging a shared public infrastructure, the Internet, for that company's private gain.

But there are drawbacks in how real-time infrastructures operate. The same characteristics that allow immediate value creation also allow crisis acceleration. The connections to public networks that create leverage also increase exposure to external threats. While the drawbacks do not outweigh the benefits, they must be understood and managed.

Broader Exposure to Operational Threats

On October 19, 1987, the Dow Jones Industrial Average plummeted more than 500 points in the twentieth century's single largest percentage decrease. The 22.6 percent plunge was almost double the 12.9 percent drop in 1929 that foreshadowed the Great Depression. Unlike 1929, the market in 1987 quickly recovered, posting major gains in the two days after the crash and regaining its precrash level by September 1989. Nevertheless, the suddenness of these events prompted a search for explanations.

Many singled out the role of computerized program trading by large institutional investors as a primary cause of the 1987 crash. In program trading, computers initiate transactions automatically, without human intervention, when certain triggering conditions appear in the markets. No one anticipated that automatic trades could lead to a chain reaction of more automatic trades. Automatic trades themselves created market conditions that set off more automatic trades, which created conditions that set off more automatic trades, and so on, in a rapid-fire progression that was both unexpected and difficult to understand while it was in progress.

This example reveals a dark side of real-time computing that extends to internetworking infrastructures. As batch-processing delays are eliminated and more transactions move from initiation to completion without intervention by human operators, the potential grows for computerized chain reactions that produce unanticipated effects. Favorable effects such as value creation happen more immediately, but so do unfavorable effects. Malfunctions and errors propagate faster and have potentially broader impacts. Diagnosis and remediation of problems that result from fast-moving, complex interactions present major challenges to organizational and, indeed, human cognitive capabilities. Just figuring out what is going on during or in the immediate aftermath of an incident is often difficult.

IT infrastructures of the twenty-first century therefore must be less prone to malfunctions and errors that might trigger a chain reaction and more tolerant of them when they occur. Real-time operations demand 24×7 availability.[7] Because some unintended effects will occur despite the best intentions and plans, responsible managers need to think in advance and in detail about how they will respond to incidents. Effective "disaster recovery" requires anticipating that incidents will occur despite the fact that one cannot anticipate their exact nature and practicing organizational responses. The range of incidents that require detailed response plans also includes those of a more sinister sort: malicious attacks. Infrastructure managers

[7] That is, operations that run 24 hours per day, 7 days per week.

must anticipate and protect systems from the many dangers creative yet malevolent individuals—hackers—introduce.

Technologies of the past were designed to deny access to systems unless someone intervened to authorize access. Internetworking systems are different. Because they evolved in an arena not oriented toward commerce but intended to support communities of researchers, internetworking technologies allow access unless someone intervenes to disallow it. Security measures to support commercial relationships, therefore, must be retrofitted onto the base technologies. Moreover, the universality of Internet connections—the fact that every computer is connected to every other computer—makes every computer a potential attack target and a potential base from which to launch attacks.

The average computer is connected to the Internet for only a few minutes before it is probed for vulnerability to intrusion or attack. Many attempted incursions are the electronic equivalent of kids playing a prank. But recent evidence shows that more serious criminals have begun to explore the possibilities presented by the Internet. The threat is real, even from pranksters. Damaging attacks are alarmingly simple to initiate. As the Internet and the Web have risen to commercial prominence, computer security problems have progressed from being tactical nuisances that could be left to technicians into strategic infrastructure problems that require the involvement of business executives at the highest levels.

New Models of Service Delivery

In the early days of electric power generation, companies owned and managed their own power plants. Later, as standardization and technological advances made it possible to deliver power reliably via a more centralized model, companies began to purchase electric power from external providers. A similar shift is under way in the IT industry.

In today's companies, as increasingly reliable networks make the physical location of computers less important, services traditionally provided by internal IT departments can be acquired externally, across internetworks, from service providers. Fundamental economic forces such as scarcity of IT specialists and desire to reduce costs are driving this shift. The shift, which parallels the maturation of other industries, reveals a common pattern: Standardization and technology advances permit specialization by individual firms in value chains, resulting in economies of scale and higher service levels.

The transition under way is analogous to the move from telephone answering machines to voice mail. Telephone answering machines were purchased by companies and attached to individual telephones. When they broke,. it was the company's job to fix or replace the machines. Messages were stored inside the machine. In contrast, companies acquire voice mail from service providers for a monthly fee. The hardware that supports the service is owned by the provider and physically resides in a central location unknown to most voice mail users. When voice mail breaks, the service provider is responsible for fixing it. Fixing it is easier and less expensive because the infrastructure that delivers the service is centralized and easily accessible. The potentially sensitive contents of voice mail messages no longer reside on the end user's desk; instead, the service provider is entrusted with their care and security.

The move to over-the-Net service delivery has been gradual and is far from complete. As supporting infrastructure matures, however, the economic advantages become more compelling. Even if actual software functionality is not acquired externally, external infrastructure management may still make sense. For example, a company may rent space in a vendor-owned IT hosting facility rather than incur the capital expenses required to build a data center, even as it retains internal management of the software.

As IT service models proliferate, service delivery depends on a growing number of service providers and other partners. One implication is that the reliability of vital services is only as good as the weakest link in the service provider chain. Selecting strong partners and managing relationships are vital to reliable service delivery.

New service models that offer new capabilities and cost reduction cannot realize their full potential without being integrated into the rest of a company's IT infrastructure. Ideally, over-the-Net services would exchange data seamlessly, in real time, with a company's installed base of systems. Unfortunately, this is not easily accomplished. The questions involved in deciding how new services should interact with existing IT and organizational systems lead to the subject of managing legacies.

Managing Legacies

Few companies are so new that they have no artifacts left over from earlier eras that must coexist with new technologies. Legacy *systems* present one set of challenges. They are often based on outdated, obsolete, and proprietary technologies. Yet they are vital to the business as it operates from day to day. Fitting new infrastructure into complex legacy infrastructure, or vice versa, presents formidable challenges and uncertain outcomes.

But systems are not the only legacies companies must manage. Even more significant are legacy *processes, organizations*, and *cultures*. Changing the IT infrastructure has unavoidable effects on nontechnical elements of a company's operations. New technologies change how people work and interact. Managers must decide how much they want the company's culture to drive the design of its infrastructure or vice versa. In some companies, managers go to great lengths to make sure the IT infrastructure does not constrain culture or process. In others, managers use IT systems as "sledgehammers" to bring about organizational change. Both approaches can work, but the issues and decisions involved are complex.

The Future of Internetworking Infrastructure

The basic technology that supports moving data packets around an Internetwork has existed in something like its present form since the late 1960s. The technologies we use to access internetworks—PCs, e-mail packages, and Web browsers, for example—have been appearing and maturing over the last 30 or so years. Although internetworking infrastructure continues to evolve significantly in both of these areas, there is a third area in which internetworking technologies are evolving even more rapidly.

The smooth functioning of markets and other kinds of business interactions presumes prerequisites that internetworking infrastructure still does not perfectly fulfill. We have mentioned some of these already. Markets do not tolerate the uncertainties of unreliable or unavailable infrastructure. Customers of a financial services firm, for example, will not tolerate loss of access to stock market trading. Similarly, business transactions cannot flourish when infrastructure is not highly secure. As we have seen, internetworks already are reasonably good at reliability, availability, and security, and they are getting better. But there are other, more subtle aspects of business support for which these technologies are not yet mature.

Ultimately, internetworking technologies must support all or nearly all the elements of business transactions that can occur in face-to-face transactions. If you are videoconferencing, for example, you need to be able to purchase guaranteed network bandwidth sufficient to make the conference approximate a productive face-to-face work experience; this is not yet possible everywhere. Consider another example: In business, you need to be sure the party you are interacting with is who he says he is, so he cannot later say, "That was not me you contracted with." This "nonrepudiation" requirement still presents difficulties in some internetworks. In general, the elements of infrastructure that support financial transactions are works in process; they constitute the above-mentioned third area in which infrastructure is evolving most rapidly.

How we transport information within internetworks and how we access network resources are well defined, if continually changing, at this point in history. How companies will in the long run engage each other in real-time transactions, negotiate the terms of transactions, establish business linkages, and settle accounts depends on standards and technologies not yet fully developed.

Summary

Internetworking infrastructures include the totality of existing client and server systems, new externally provided services, and older legacy systems. They interact with living organizations and have distinctive characteristics that are coming into clear view in the twenty-first century. They offer many more degrees of freedom in designing organizations and contain larger numbers of smaller components that interact in complex ways. Some of the components exist outside a firm's boundaries and thus are not fully under the control of company managers. The overall effect on a company's business is that there is *more inherent uncertainty in the operational environment*. This is at least partially offset by *more incremental options for managing that uncertainty*. Our ability to predict how a planned system will perform is limited, but options for experimenting to improve our understanding of emerging infrastructures are becoming more numerous and less expensive. Not surprisingly, our management frameworks are evolving in a way that reflects the uncertain and incremental nature of emerging infrastructure.

In this chapter we have described the technologies, functions, and components of internetworking infrastructure and how they are changing. We have explained how the changes generate new benefits, challenges, and threats. Approximately 75 percent of most companies' IT dollars go to infrastructure investments. In many companies, that 75 percent approaches half of all capital expenditures. Executives can use the following questions to assess the implications of the emergence of new technologies and infrastructures for their companies' operational capabilities:

1. What does the public infrastructure of the Internet mean to our business operations? Are we leveraging this infrastructure to maximum advantage? How dependent are we still on proprietary technologies?

2. How close do our company operations come to running in real time? What value creation opportunities can still be obtained by moving more in the direction of real-time value capture?
3. Has our company taken appropriate advantage of the many degrees of architectural and operational freedom offered by internetworking technologies? Have we thought through the inherent complexities and risks in those additional degrees of freedom?
4. Are we exploring new service delivery models aggressively enough?
5. Have we reexamined our management frameworks in light of the new and more adaptive capabilities that internetworking technologies offer? Most important, do senior business managers play an active and informed role in infrastructure design and planning decisions?

Chapter 6

Assuring Reliable and Secure IT Services

The emergence of Web-based commerce has accelerated the expansion of a worldwide network capable of transmitting information reliably and securely across vast distances. The inherent reliability of modern internetworks is a legacy of U.S. Department of Defense research in the 1960s that led to technologies robust enough to withstand a military attack. The key to this inherent reliability is *redundancy*: the exceptionally large number of potential paths a message can take between any two points in a network. Because internetworking technologies automatically route messages around network problems, transmissions are highly likely to be successful.

Unfortunately, some components of a *firm's* infrastructure are *not* inherently reliable. The reliability of processing systems, for example, depends on how they are designed and managed. As with internetworks, the key to reliable systems is redundancy; however, reliability through redundancy comes at a price. It means buying extra equipment (computers, switches, software, electric generators, etc.) to guard against failures. Every increment of additional redundancy makes outages less likely, but every increment increases expenses as well.

How much reliability to buy is a management decision highly contingent on numerous, mostly business, factors. How costly is a 15-minute failure of the order management system? How costly is a 3-hour failure or a 12-hour failure? How likely are these failures? How about the e-mail system and the human resources system? Answers to these questions differ across businesses. Some costs of failures are intangible and hard to quantify. It may be possible to estimate the direct revenues your company will lose if your Web-based retail site goes down for two hours, but it is much harder to gauge how many customers, frustrated by the outage, will never return.

Redundant systems are more complex than nonredundant systems, and this complexity must be managed. Businesses need policies that determine how to integrate redundant elements into a company's overall infrastructure: how backup systems and equipment will be brought online, how problems will be diagnosed and triaged, and who will be responsible for responding to incidents. Since the efficacy and efficiency of incident response improve with practice, the frequency and form of rehearsals are also management decisions. Charles Perrow suggests in *Normal Accidents: Living with High Risk Technologies* that failures are inevitable in "tightly coupled" complex systems. Typical precautions, Perrow writes, such as adding redundancy, help create new categories of accidents by adding complexity.[1] Thus, our efforts to make infrastructure designs more robust also make operational management more difficult.

Managers also must guard against malicious threats to computing infrastructure. Malicious threats, which are similar to accidental failures in their potential cost and unintended ripple effect, are designed specifically to damage a company's business. Attacks, intrusions, viruses, and worms have no legitimate uses when perpetrated against others' systems. Their designers, often extremely creative, are motivated by a desire to cause mayhem.

Instigators of malicious threats, called *hackers*,[2] range from pranksters to organized criminals and even international terrorists. Securing systems against malicious threats is an arms race, a high-stakes contest requiring constantly improving defenses against increasingly sophisticated weaponry. Some businesses have particular reason to fear being targeted. But even the most unobtrusive firms cannot count on low profiles ("security through obscurity") as a defense. Increasingly, attacks are automated and systematic, carried out by wrecking routines turned loose on the Internet to probe for vulnerabilities and inflict damage randomly.

In an age of real-time systems, global operations, and customers who expect always-on performance, the reliability and security of systems takes on new importance. Technologies to assure 24×7 operations[3] get better all the time, but every increment of capability comes with additional infrastructure complexity and management challenges. Add new malicious threats to the mix and we see that twenty-first century infrastructure managers have their hands full. Making the wrong decision in designing or maintaining infrastructure or in responding to incidents can severely harm a business.

Availability Math

The reliability of computing infrastructure is often discussed in terms of the *availability* of a specific information technology (IT) service or system. A system that is 98 percent available is, on average, running and ready to be used 98 percent of the time. It is down, or not available for use, 2 percent of the time. In a day, 98 percent availability translates into just under one-half hour of downtime, which might be fine for some systems and businesses.

This chapter is adapted from Professor Robert D. Austin's *Managing Information Technology Infrastructure* course module, Harvard Business School Publishing No. 603-104.

[1] Charles Perrow, *Normal Accidents: Living with High Risk Technologies* (Princeton, NJ: Princeton University Press, 1999).

[2] The term *hacker* is controversial. Although the word is now used to describe a computer expert with malicious intent, it originally had no negative connotations. UNIX programming enthusiasts, beginning in the 1960s, called particularly excellent programmers hackers. Some have tried to preserve the positive interpretation by proposing the word *cracker* to describe malicious hackers. To most people, *hacker* implies malicious intent, so that is how we use it in this book. We extend our apologies to purists on this point.

[3] That is, operations that run 24 hours per day, 7 days per week.

A business's tolerance for outages varies by system and situation. Downtime that occurs in large chunks, say, a two-hour outage every four days, might be more of a problem than the same total amount of downtime occurring in increments that never exceed three minutes in a single outage. Whether outages occur at predictable times matters too. A half-hour outage that always happens at 3:00 AM may not be a problem. Some systems require planned outages; a system might need to be shut down each night to have all its data files copied to a backup tape. But planned outages are increasingly rare in the world of real-time infrastructures; and unplanned outages are not usually well behaved.

In modern contexts, a 98 percent availability rating for a system usually means that its probability of being up and running at any given time is 98 percent—period. A strong underlying presumption is that planned outages will be minimized, if not eliminated. Moreover, for real-time infrastructure, 98 percent is not nearly good enough. In fact, the availability of today's IT infrastructure is often expressed in terms of a number of "nines." "Five nines" means 99.999 percent availability, which equates to less than a second of downtime in a 24-hour day, or no more than a minute in three months, on average. Not surprisingly, keeping systems available at such a high level requires much redundancy and highly sophisticated operations management.

We can better appreciate how difficult it is to achieve very high levels of reliability if we consider how rates of availability for components combine into overall system or service availability. Most IT services are not delivered by a single component but by a number of components working together. For example, a service that sends transactions from one server to another via a corporate internetwork might require two or more routers, one or more switches, and both servers—all up and running at the same time. Each of these devices has its own individual availability. Thus, overall *service* availability is generally lower than the availability of individual components. Many managers do not appreciate how rapidly service availability decreases as components are added in series. Let's consider how this works.

The Availability of Components in Series

Suppose you have five components connected in series that together deliver an IT service (see Figure 6.1). Assume that each component has an availability of 98 percent, which means, as we have noted, a half hour per day of downtime for each component on average. Computation of service availability is straightforward.

For the service to be up and running, all five components must be up and running. At any given time, the probability that a component is up and running is .98 (that's what 98 percent availability means), and so the probability that Component 1 *and* Component 2 *and* Component 3 *and* Component 4 *and* Component 5 are all up and running is

$$.98 \times .98 \times .98 \times .98 \times .98 = .9$$

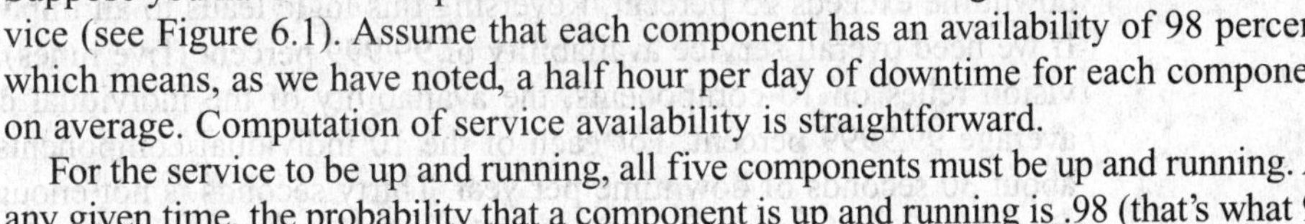

FIGURE 6.1 Five Components in Series (Each 98 percent Available)

FIGURE 6.2
Combining Components in Series Decreases Overall Availability

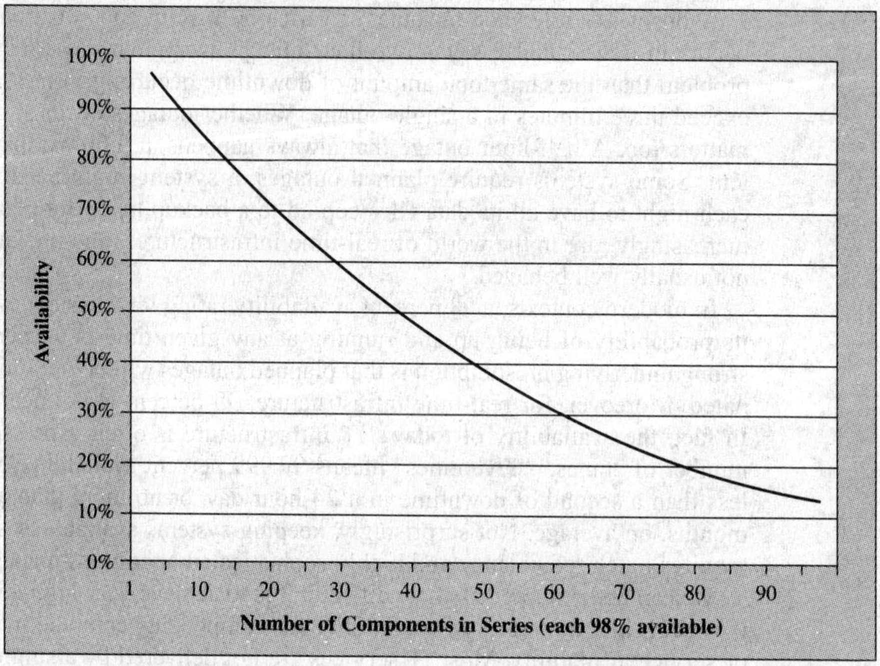

The overall service availability is 90 percent, which means the service is unavailable 10 percent of the time, or almost two and a half hours a day. If we take into account the fact that most services rely on many more than five devices operating in series, we can see that service availability degrades quite severely as we add components in a chain.

Figure 6.2 shows how service availability falls as we add components, assuming that individual components are 98 percent available. Notice that by the time we get to 15 devices in series—which is not hard to imagine in a modern IT infrastructure—downtime exceeds 25 percent. Reversing this logic leads to an important conclusion: If we need overall service availability of 99.999 percent (five nines) and service provision relies on 10 components, the availability of the individual components must average 99.9999 percent. For each of the 10 individual components, that equates to about 30 seconds of downtime per year. Thirty seconds is not enough time to restart most servers. If only one server needs rebooting in a year, that blows a five nines availability rating. How, then, can we achieve five nines of availability? The answer to this question: redundancy.

The Effect of Redundancy on Availability

Suppose you have five components connected in *parallel* involved in the provision of an IT service (see Figure 6.3). The components are identical, and any one of them can perform the functions needed to support the service. As in the earlier example, each individual component has an availability of 98 percent, and each component experiences outages randomly. The computation for the overall availability of these parallel components is also straightforward.

FIGURE 6.3
Five Components in Parallel (Each 98 percent Available)

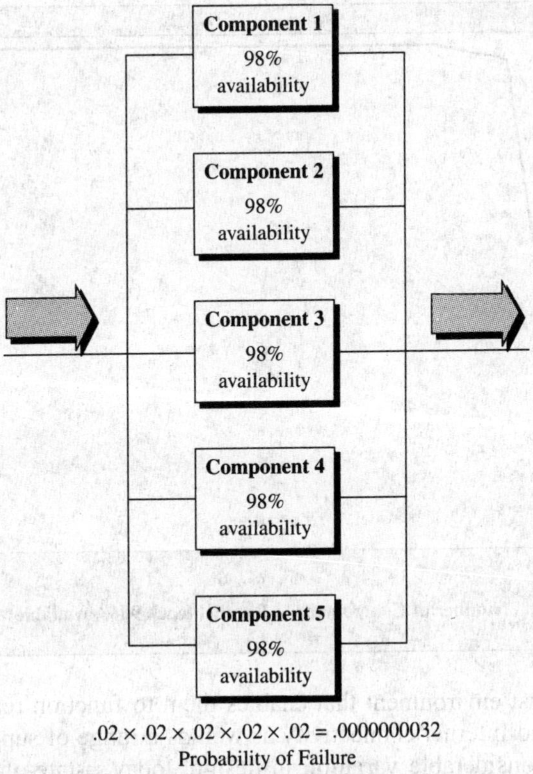

Because any of the individual components can support the service, all five must fail at the same time to render this combination of components a failure. At any given time, the probability that a component is down is .02 (98 percent availability means 2 percent downtime), and so the probability that Component 1 *and* Component 2 *and* Component 3 *and* Component 4 *and* Component 5 will all fail at the same time is

$$.02 \times .02 \times .02 \times .02 \times .02 = .0000000032$$

The overall availability of these components combined in parallel is therefore 99.99999968, which is eight nines of availability. Figure 6.4 shows how availability increases when components that are 98 percent available are combined in parallel. Of course, to deliver a service, we must place the parallel combination in series with other components. From this example and the previous one, however, we can see that even if a component does not satisfy our five nines availability requirement, several connected in parallel may.

High-Availability Facilities

A close look at modern data centers provides a concrete sense of the availability decisions faced by infrastructure managers. Data centers physically house Web, application, database, and other servers; storage devices; mainframes; and networking

FIGURE 6.4
Redundancy Increases Overall Availability

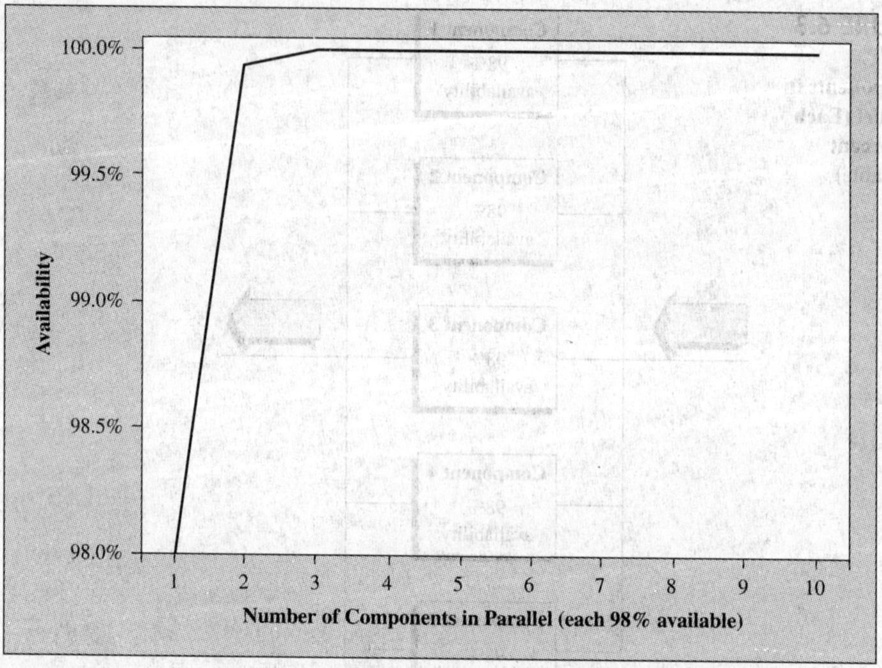

equipment in a robust environment that enables them to function reliably. They supply space, power, and Internet connectivity as well as a range of supporting services. Although there is considerable variation in design, today's state-of-the-art facilities tend to offer the following features.

Uninterruptible Electric Power Delivery

High-availability facilities provide redundant power to each piece of computing equipment housed in them, literally two or more power cables for each computer (high-availability computing equipment accepts two or more power inputs). Power distribution inside the facility is fully redundant and includes uninterruptible power supplies (UPSs) to maintain power even if power delivery to the facility is interrupted. Connections to outside sources of power are also redundant; usually, facilities access two or more utility power grids. Diesel generators stand by for backup power generation; on-site fuel tanks contain fuel for a day or more of operation. Facilities managers have a plan for high-priority access to additional fuel in case of a long-lasting primary power outage (e.g., delivery by helicopter). High-end data centers may obtain primary power from on-site power plants, with first-level backup from local utility power grids and second-level backup from diesel generators; UPSs may employ batteryless, flywheel-based technologies.

Physical Security

Security guards, posted in bulletproof enclaves, protect points of entry and patrol the facility regularly. Closed-circuit television monitors critical infrastructure and provides immediate visibility into any area of the facility from a constantly attended security desk. Access to internal areas requires photo ID and presence on a prearranged list.

Entry is through a buffer zone that can be locked down. Guards open and inspect the items (e.g., boxes, equipment) people bring into the facility. The building that houses the data center is dedicated to that use, not shared with other businesses. In some high-end facilities, the building is "hardened" against external explosions, earthquakes, and other disasters. Advanced entry systems force everyone through multiple, single-person (hostageproof) buffers with integrated metal and explosive detection. Visitors may be automatically weighed on arrival and departure to detect when they are removing something they didn't arrive with or leaving something behind. Biometric scanning technologies such as retinal scanners, palm readers, and voice recognition systems control access to zones within data centers. Motion sensors supplement video monitoring, and perimeter fencing surrounds the facility.

Climate Control and Fire Suppression

Facilities contain redundant heating, ventilating, and air-conditioning (HVAC) equipment capable of maintaining temperatures in ranges suitable for computing and network equipment. Mobile cooling units alleviate hot spots. Integrated fire suppression systems include smoke detection, alarming, and gas-based (i.e., no equipment-damaging water) fire suppression.

Network Connectivity

External connections to Internet backbone providers[4] are redundant, involve at least two backbone providers, and enter the building through separate points. The company that owns the data center has agreements with backbone providers that permit significant percentages, say, 50 percent, of network traffic to travel from origin to destination across the backbone company's private network, avoiding often-congested public Internet junctions. A 24×7 network operations center (NOC) is staffed with network engineers who monitor the connectivity infrastructure of the facility; a redundant NOC on another site is capable of delivering services of equal quality as those provided by the primary NOC. High-end facilities have agreements with three or more backbone providers that allow even more traffic, up to 90 percent, to stay on private networks.

Help Desk and Incident Response Procedures

Customers can contact facility staff for assistance at any time during the day or night. The facility has procedures for responding to unplanned incidents. Automated problem-tracking systems are integrated with similar systems at service delivery partner sites, so complex problems involving interactions between services can be tracked down and quickly solved.

N + 1 and N + N Redundancy

Most modern data centers try to maintain at least an "N + 1" level of redundancy of mission-critical components. N + 1 means that for each type of critical component there should be at least one unit standing by. For example, if a facility needs four

[4] Backbone providers own the very large data transmission lines through which large quantities of data are moved long distances.

TABLE 6.1 Data Center Uptime Levels

Uptime Level	Availability
Level 1	99 to 99.9 percent
Level 2	99.9 to 99.99 percent
Level 3	99.99 to 99.999 percent
Level 4	99.999 to 99.9999 percent

diesel generators to meet power demands in a primary power outage, N + 1 redundancy requires five such generators, four to operate and one to stand by. N + 1 redundancy provides a higher level of availability if the underlying number of components, the N in the N + 1, is small (you can verify this for yourself by using probability calculations such as those that we demonstrated earlier).

Some companies aspire to higher levels of infrastructure redundancy. "N + N" redundancy requires twice as many mission-critical components as are necessary to run a facility at any one time. For example, a facility that needs four diesel generators to meet its power demands needs eight generators to achieve N + N redundancy. Where N + 1 facilities are able to commit to service levels in the 99.9 percent availability range, N + N facilities can ensure availability levels at the 99.999 percent (five nines) level. Facilities are sometimes categorized according to the "level" of uptime they support (see Table 6.1). Level 1 data centers, which employ N + 1 redundancy, are available 99 to 99.9 percent of the time. Level 2 and Level 3 centers feature more redundancy. Level 4 data centers, the highest level of availability in current common usage, have N + N or better redundancy and achieve uptime in the range of 99.999 to 99.9999 percent. Downtime at a Level 4 facility, literally seconds per year, is unnoticeable by most users.

Not surprisingly, high levels of availability are costly. Increasing the availability of *a single* Web site from 99 percent to 99.999 percent might require additional spending of millions of dollars. A 99.999 percent availability data center costs many times more than one capable of 99 to 99.9 percent availability.

Management decisions about the design of IT infrastructures always involve trade-offs between availability and the expense of additional components. Figure 6.5 depicts an e-commerce infrastructure used by a real company for delivering a basic Web-based IT service. Notice that many infrastructure elements are redundant: the firewall devices, the Web servers, the application servers, and the policy servers. Notice, though, that the switch and the database server are not redundant. Why?

Although you cannot tell from the diagram, both the switch and the database servers have built-in redundancy. Both have redundant power supplies. In addition, the switch has redundant modules. The database server is shown connected to an array of disks set up to write data to at least two separate disks at the same time.[5] Nevertheless, there are single points of failure in these two components. Thus, the question remains:

[5] Notice that there are usually many options for adding redundancy, some more expensive than others. For most high-availability equipment, redundancy is a matter of degree and can be purchased incrementally. Note also that redundancy does not necessarily mean purchasing another instance of exactly the same technology platform; cheaper platforms are sometimes used as temporary backups for expensive system components.

FIGURE 6.5
A Representative E-Commerce Infrastructure

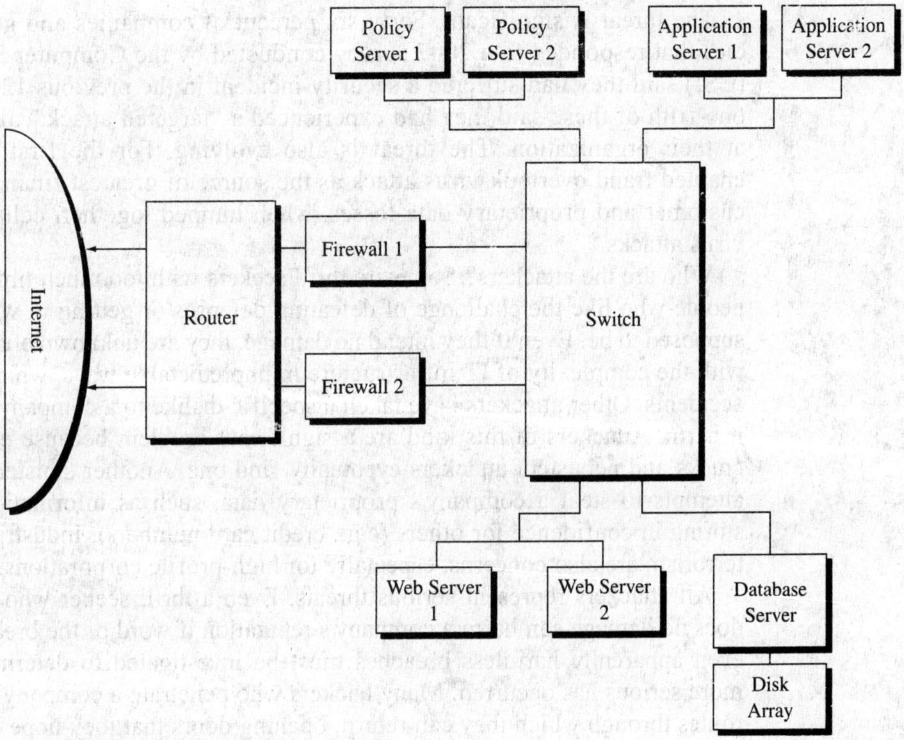

Why would managers leave these two obviously central components without redundancy when they have made all the other components redundant?

The reason boils down to one word: money. The two nonredundant components represent approximately half the cost of this setup. Making the switch and database server redundant would add about 50 percent to the overall cost. Managers of this infrastructure have made a deliberate decision to rely on the redundancy built into these two devices. Depending on the company's business, this decision might make sense or it might not. Such choices are not unusual, however.

Securing Infrastructure against Malicious Threats

Richard Clarke, the former U.S. national coordinator for security, infrastructure protection, and counterterrorism, often chided companies for spending less on information security than on coffee. "If you spend as much on information security as you do on coffee," he argued, "you will be hacked, and you'll deserve to be hacked."[6]

Business leaders are becoming more interested in security. The September 11, 2001, terrorist attacks against the United States seem to have prompted new visibility for information security. But even before that, a series of high-profile attacks, viruses, and worms had been drawing attention to security concerns.

[6] *InformationWeek Daily*, February 20, 2002, http://update.informationweek.com.

The threat is significant. Forty-six percent of companies and government agencies that responded to a 2007 survey conducted by the Computer Security Institute (CSI) said they had suffered a security incident in the previous 12 months. Almost one-fifth of these said they had experienced a "targeted attack," aimed specifically at their organization. The threat is also evolving. For the first time, computer-enabled fraud overtook virus attack as the source of greatest financial loss; theft of customer and proprietary data losses, when lumped together, eclipsed losses from virus attacks.[7]

Who are the attackers? Some are thrill seekers with too much time on their hands, people who like the challenge of defeating defenses or getting in where they are not supposed to be. Even if they intend no damage, they are unknown elements interacting with the complexity of IT infrastructure in unpredictable ways, which can precipitate accidents. Other attackers have taken a specific dislike to a company and intend to do it harm. Attackers of this kind are a significant problem because every defense has cracks and persistent attackers eventually find one. Another sinister type of attacker attempts to steal a company's proprietary data, such as information a company is storing in confidence for others (e.g., credit card numbers). Industrial espionage and terrorism are also concerns, especially for high-profile corporations.

All attackers represent serious threats. Even a thrill seeker who gains access but does no damage can harm a company's reputation if word of the breach gets out. And even apparently harmless breaches must be investigated to determine that nothing more serious has occurred. Many hackers who penetrate a company's defenses set up routes through which they can return, opening doors that they hope company managers will not notice. Many also share information with each other about how to break in to certain companies or open doors they left ajar after their own break-ins. A thrill seeker who intends no real harm may pass information to people with malevolent aims.

Responsible managers must build defenses to secure a company's information-related assets—its data, infrastructure components, and reputation—against this escalating threat. When it comes to securing IT infrastructure, one size does not fit all, and so defenses must be customized to a company's situation, business, infrastructure technologies, and objectives. Sound approaches to securing IT infrastructure begin with a detailed understanding of the threats.

Classification of Threats

Hackers are always inventing new ways to make mayhem. There are many kinds of attacks, and there are subtle variations on each kind. Some threats are common, only too real in actual experience, while others are hypothetical, theoretically possible but not yet observed. Despite the variety, threats can be divided (very roughly) into categories: external attacks, intrusions, and viruses and worms.

External Attacks

External attacks are actions against computing infrastructure that harm it or degrade its services without actually gaining access to it. The most common external attacks

[7] "2007 CSI Computer Crime and Security Survey," www.gocsi.com.

are "denial of service" (DoS) attacks, which disable infrastructure devices (usually Web servers) by flooding them with an overwhelming number of messages. Attackers send data packets far more rapidly than the target machine can handle them, and each packet begins what appears to be an authentic "conversation" with the victim computer. The victim responds as it usually does to the beginning of a conversation, but the attacker abruptly terminates the conversation. The resources of the Web site are consumed by beginning a very large number of bogus conversations. Figure 6.6 compares how normal and DoS conversations proceed between network-connected computers.

If attacks always came from a single location on the Internet, defeating them would be easy. Network monitoring software can automatically read the origin IP address from incoming packets, recognize that the flood is coming from a single address, and filter out flood traffic before it reaches its target. Attackers counter this defense, however, by sending packets that originate from multiple locations on the Internet or that appear to originate from multiple locations (see Figure 6.7). *Distributed* denial of service (DDoS) attacks are carried out by automated routines secretly deposited on Internet-connected computers ("zombies" organized into "botnets") whose owners have not secured them against intrusion (a large percentage of DSL and cable modem–connected home PCs fall into this unsecured category). Once implanted on the computers of unsuspecting users, these routines launch packets at targeted Web sites for a predefined duration or during a predetermined interval. Because the flood comes from many different addresses, network-monitoring software cannot easily recognize the flood as an attack. Clever attackers can simulate a distributed attack by inserting false origin information into packets to mislead filtering software at a target site (providing packets with false origin addresses is called "spoofing"; see Figure 6.8).

FIGURE 6.6
Normal and DoS Handshakes

Source: Robert D. Austin, "The iPremier Company, (A), (B), and (C): Denial of Service Attack," Harvard Business School Teaching Note No. 602-033

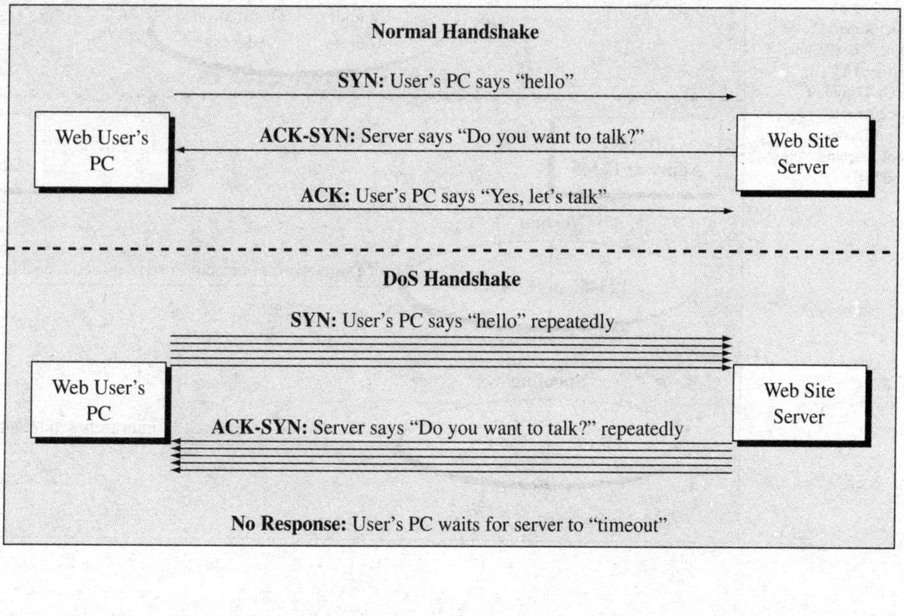

FIGURE 6.7
A Distributed Denial of Service Attack

Source: Robert D. Austin, "The iPremier Company, (A), (B), and (C): Denial of Service Attack." Harvard Business School Teaching Note No. 602-033.

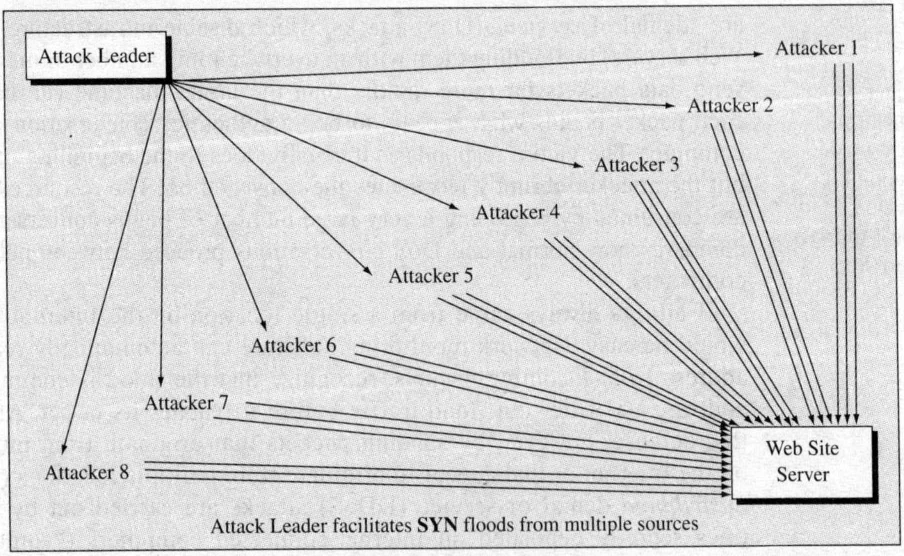

Unfortunately, DoS attacks are extremely easy to execute. Attack routines are available for download from sources on the Internet. Using the routines is almost as easy as sending e-mail. Attackers need not be programming experts; many, in fact, are "script kiddies," relatively unsophisticated computer users who run routines that others have written. Although DDoS and spoofing attacks are more difficult, they require no great technical skill. Computer users who do not secure their computers against mischievous use provide unintended assistance to attackers.

FIGURE 6.8
"Spoofing"

Source: Robert D. Austin, "The iPremier Company, (A), (B), and (C): Denial of Service Attack." Harvard Business School Teaching Note No. 602-033.

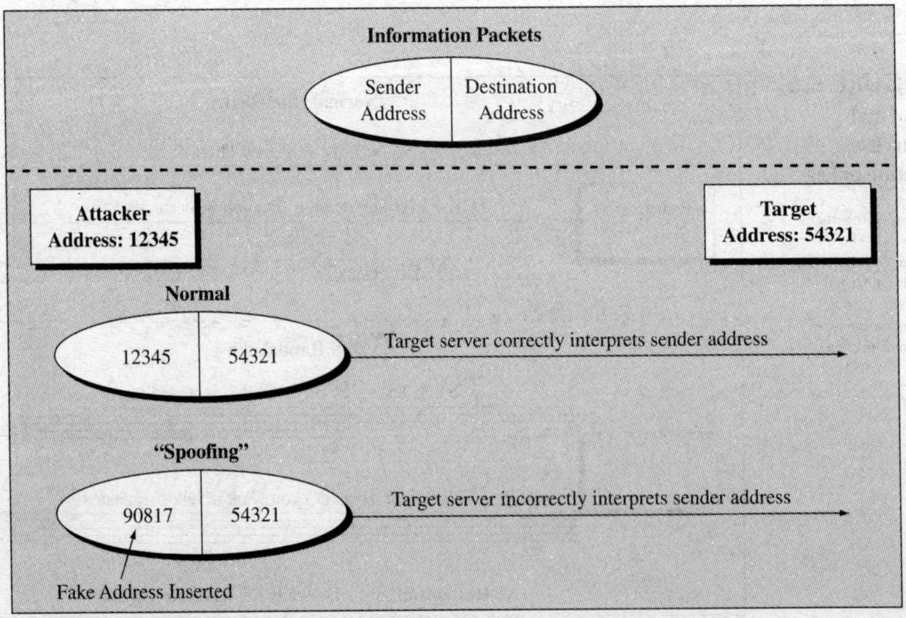

Like a Tour Bus at a Fast Food Restaurant: A DoS Attack Analogy

Have you ever stopped for fast food while driving on a major highway only to discover that a full tour bus has just unloaded its passengers at the restaurant? The restaurant is overwhelmed by the sudden burst of business. A DoS attack is like this, only worse. In a DoS attack, it is as if tour bus customers were standing in line, interacting with the cashier at the front of the line, and then deciding not to buy anything. Customers who really intend to buy food are stuck at the back of the line. The restaurant wastes resources on fake customers who are indistinguishable from real customers.*

* We first heard this analogy from Dr. Larry Liebrock, a freelance computer forensics expert.

DoS attacks are very difficult to defend against. Most defensive methods rely on monitoring that can detect recognizable attack patterns, but it is relatively simple for attackers to vary their patterns of attack. Patterns of attack can be very similar to legitimate e-commerce traffic. A slow-motion DoS attack—attacks of this kind have been called "degradation of service" attacks—looks almost exactly like real e-commerce traffic. Although these attacks do not cause outages, they do affect infrastructure performance, waste company resources, and reduce customer satisfaction (see the accompanying feature).

There are now active markets in which established platforms for attack (usually unsuspecting network-connected PCs infected with unknown-to-the-user "malware") can be bought and sold. Frivolous DoS attacks have declined, partly, some have suggested, because hackers have become less willing to squander "assets" that now have monetary value (infected PCs that will become useless as attack platforms after they are used).

Intrusion

Unlike external attackers, intruders actually gain access to a company's internal IT infrastructure by a variety of methods. Some methods involve obtaining user names and passwords. Most people's user names and passwords are not hard to guess; user names usually are constructed by using a consistent convention (e.g., John Smith's user name might be jsmith). Many people use birthdays or children's names for passwords; many more use the same password for numerous applications, which means an intruder can gain access to many systems with the same password. Few people change passwords frequently, and it is not uncommon to find passwords taped to computer monitors or sent out in the trash to dumpsters behind office buildings. The term *social engineering* describes low-tech but highly effective techniques for getting people to freely divulge privileged information. Many people will reveal a password to an official-sounding telephone caller who pretends to be a company network engineer.

There are also high-tech ways to get inside a company's defenses. Hackers who gain physical access to a network can acquire passwords by eavesdropping on network conversations by using "sniffer" software; because network traffic often traverses many local area networks (LANs), a sniffer need not be attached to the LAN where traffic originates to get a password. Or intruders can exploit vulnerabilities left in software when it was developed to gain access to systems *without* first obtaining passwords. In some cases, software development mistakes allow hackers to trick a company's computer into executing their own code or to cause a failure that leaves them in control of the computer. Such vulnerabilities in software are common. New vulnerabilities in widely deployed software systems are discovered daily, sometimes by good guys, who notify vendors so that they can fix the problem, and sometimes by bad guys, who take advantage of the opening. Computers are "port scanned"—probed for vulnerability to intrusion—within a few minutes of connecting to the Internet. Hackers use automated routines that systematically scan IP addresses and then report back to their masters which addresses contain exploitable vulnerabilities.

Once inside, intruders have the same rights of access and control over systems and resources as legitimate users. Thus empowered, they can steal information, erase or alter data, or deface Web sites (internal and external). Or they can use a location inside a company to pose as a representative of the company. Such an imposter could, for example, send a message canceling an important meeting or send scandalous information that appeared to originate from official sources inside the company. Intruders can leave behind routines that use the company's computers as a base for attacks against other companies. Or they can deposit "time bombs," seemingly innocuous bits of code scheduled to explode unexpectedly into catastrophic action at a future date.

One of the most difficult problems arising from intrusion is figuring out what exactly intruders might have done while they were inside company defenses. It can take companies a long time to discover trespassing on their systems or networks (see the accompanying feature on p. 273). Hackers generally try to cover their tracks. They may make subtle changes in a system, opening obscure doors, adding a small file to a disk drive, or slightly altering some data. Finding out what intruders have done, or whether they have done anything, can be very costly for victim companies, yet it must be done. A company that does not know exactly how its systems have been compromised may have difficulty deciding what to tell customers, business partners, and others about the security of data entrusted to the company. There is a very high public relations penalty for not knowing something consequential about your infrastructure that you should have known or, perhaps worse, for issuing assurances about the security of your systems that turn out to be spectacularly inaccurate.

Viruses and Worms

Viruses and worms are malicious software programs that replicate, spreading themselves to other computers. The damage they do may be minor, such as defacing a Web site, or severe, such as erasing the contents of a computer's disk drive. Although people disagree about the exact definitions of viruses and worms, they often are distinguished by their degree of automation and ability to replicate across networks. Simply put, viruses require assistance (often inadvertent) from users to replicate and propagate (e.g., opening a file attached to an e-mail message or even opening a Web page), whereas worms replicate and move across networks automatically.

What is perhaps most alarming about viruses and worms is that they increasingly incorporate and automate other kinds of attacks. The Code Red Worm, for example, moved across networks, automatically invaded systems with certain vulnerabilities, deposited a program to launch a DoS attack against another computer, and replicated itself across the Internet at an exponential rate. Although Code Red did little damage

Unauthorized Intrusion at the TJX Companies Places Millions of Credit and Identity Records at Risk

On January 17, 2007, the TJX Companies admitted they had experienced an "unauthorized intrusion" into their computer systems that process and store customer transactions including credit card, debit card, check, and merchandise return transactions for most of their stores. Although the intrusion was discovered mid-December 2006, it was not announced until January 2007, drawing negative public reactions and suggestions that they knew they had a security problem but did not want to interrupt the busiest shopping time of the year. Florida law enforcement officials later reported that information stolen from TJX's systems was already being used fraudulently in November 2006 in an $8 million gift card scheme.

Initially, TJX reported that the intrusion had been in operation for seven months prior to its detection and that transaction data from mid-May through December 2006 had been accessed. A month later, the company admitted that the hackers might have already breached their systems in July 2005 and on subsequent occasions that year, gaining access to records dating back to early 2003. It estimated that 45.7 million credit and debit card numbers were accessed, as well as 455,000 merchandise return records containing customers' driver's license numbers, Military ID numbers, or Social Security numbers.

TJX acknowledged that it could not verify the full scope of the breach, in part because the hackers accessed its encryption software and might have known how to unscramble customer information. In addition, in the normal course of business, TJX had deleted much of the transaction data between the time of the breach and the time that TJX detected it, making it impossible to know how many total cards were affected. In May 2007, it emerged that TJX had an outdated wireless security encryption system, had failed to install firewalls and data encryption on computers using the wireless network, and had not properly installed another layer of security software it had bought. As a result, thieves were able to access data streaming between handheld price-checking devices, cash registers, and the store's computers.

The impact on TJX and its customers was substantial. The company soon faced multiple U.S. and Canadian lawsuits from banks seeking damages from the retailer for reissuing compromised cards. Court filings later in the year claimed that the number of accounts affected by the theft exceeded 94 million, while the total number of records affected increased to 215 million. During the summer of 2007, U.S. Secret Service agents found TJX customers' credit card numbers in the hands of Eastern European cyber thieves who created high-quality counterfeit credit cards. Shortly thereafter, they intercepted and charged an organized fraud ring in South Florida with aggravated identity theft, counterfeit credit-card trafficking, and conspiracy. About 200,000 stolen credit card numbers were recovered in this effort.

TJX was forced to set aside a $107 million reserve intended to settle lawsuits on behalf of Visa, Inc. and TJX customers affected by the data security breach. Proposals for customer compensation included credit monitoring for those who suffered identity theft, as well as reimbursement of document replacement costs, store vouchers, and discount opportunities. TJX's total expenses in dealing with the breach have been estimated between $500 million and $1 billion.

to infected systems (it defaced their Web sites), it is significant for the possibilities it suggests. Human hackers can attack companies at human speeds only, but self-propagating, automated attackers can potentially wreak havoc much faster and against arbitrary targets.

Defensive Measures

Defense against hackers is difficult. The threats are varied, sophisticated, and ever-evolving, and security is a matter of degree rather than absolutes. There is no master list against which a company can compare its defenses and, after checking off everything, declare its infrastructure secure. But there are defensive measures that are effective in combination, elements of fortification that companies can erect around vital networks, computers, and systems. Like the fortifications of ancient castles, they must be able to repel hostile forces while admitting friendly parties. Elements of information security often marshaled for this task include security policies, firewalls, authentication, encryption, patching and change management, and intrusion detection and network monitoring.

Security Policies

To defend computing resources against inappropriate use, a company must first specify what is meant by "inappropriate." Good security policies specify not only what people should avoid doing because it is dangerous but also what people should do to be safe. A good policy also explains company decisions not to offer certain services or features because the security risks more than outweigh the benefits.

Security policies address questions such as the following:

- What kinds of passwords are users allowed to create for use on company systems, and how often should users change passwords?
- Who is allowed to have accounts on company systems?
- What security features must be activated on a computer before it can connect to a company network?
- What services are allowed to operate inside a company's network?
- What are users allowed to download?
- How is the security policy enforced?

Because a security policy cannot anticipate everything users might want to do or any situations that might arise, it is a living document. It must be accessible to the people who are expected to comply with it and not be written in overly technical language. And it must be reasonable from the standpoint of a user; a policy people perceive as unreasonable usually is ignored or subverted.

Firewalls

A firewall is a collection of hardware and software designed to prevent unauthorized access to a company's internal computer resources. Computer users outside a company's physical premises often have a legitimate need to access the company's computers. An employee who is traveling, for example, may need to access a system he or she often uses at work. A primary function of a firewall, then, is to facilitate legitimate interactions between computers inside and outside the company while preventing illegitimate interactions.

Firewalls usually are located at points of maximum leverage within a network, especially at points of connection between a company's internal network and the external public network. Some work by filtering packets coming from outside the company before passing them along to computers inside the company's production facilities. They discard packets that do not comply with security policies, exhibit attack patterns, or appear harmful for other reasons. Others use a sentry computer that relays information between internal and external computers without allowing external packets direct entry.

Firewalls are also useful in other ways. They enforce aspects of a security policy by not allowing certain kinds of communication to traverse the internal network. They have a limited ability to filter out viruses as they enter company networks. Firewalls are located at excellent points at which to collect data about the traffic moving between inside and outside networks and across internal networks. Often they are used between segments of an internal network to divide it into regions so that an intruder who penetrates one part will not be able to access the rest. Firewalls also conceal internal network configurations from external prying and thus serve as a sort of electronic camouflage that makes breaking in harder.

Firewalls do not provide perfect protection. Every design has weaknesses, some of which are not known at any point in time. They provide no defense against malicious insiders or against activity that does not traverse the firewall (such as traffic that enters a network via an unauthorized dial-up modem behind the firewall). It is best to think of a firewall as part of an overall strategy of defense. Although it reduces risks, it does not eliminate them.[8]

Authentication

Authentication describes the variety of techniques and software used to control who accesses elements of computing infrastructure. Authentication can occur at many points. *Host* authentication controls access to specific computers (hosts); *network* authentication controls access to regions of a network; *data* authentication controls access to specific data items. Host authentication, network authentication, and data authentication are used in combination. When used with sophisticated and well-managed directory technologies, which keep track of identities and access rights, access can be very granular, allowing many layers of access control throughout the infrastructure.

Strong authentication implies that passwords expire regularly and that forms of passwords are restricted to make them harder to guess. For example, a company might require that passwords be changed weekly and be composed of a combination of at least eight alpha and numeric characters. What minimally constitutes strong authentication is a matter of debate, but simple user name and password authentication does not meet the test. Strong authentication requires user name/password plus one other factor, such as certificate authentication (see the accompanying feature on p. 276) or biometric verification of identity (e.g., iris scanning).

Encryption

Encryption renders the contents of electronic transmissions unreadable by anyone who might intercept them. Modern encryption technologies provide a high degree of protection against the vast majority of potential attackers. Legitimate recipients can decrypt transmission contents by using a piece of data called a "key" (see the accompanying feature on p. 277). The recipient typically possesses the key for decryption as a result of a previous interaction. Like passwords, keys must be kept secret and protected from social engineering, physical theft, insecure transmission, and a variety of other techniques hostile forces use to obtain them. Encryption does little good if the

[8] Elizabeth D. Zwicky, Simon Cooper, and D. Brent Chapman, *Building Internet Firewalls,* 2nd ed. (Sebastapol, CA: O' Reilly, 2000), is an excellent reference on firewalls and their capabilities.

Digital Certificates

Digital certificates are analogous to the official physical documents people use to establish their identity in face-to-face business interactions. When someone writes a check at a retail store, the store may ask for proof of identity. To provide proof, people often offer a driver's license. Businesses trust a driver's license because they trust the issuing authority (the state agency that regulates motor vehicle use) to verify identity by using a rigorous procedure and because driver's licenses are difficult to forge. A digital certificate is much like the driver's license, a signed document that a trusted third-party organization stands behind that provides evidence of identity. Digital certificates are in fact much harder to forge than physical documents, although it is possible to trick people into issuing real certificates in error. Also, digital certificates are "bearer instruments," rather like driver's licenses with no photo on them; it is possible that the person presenting a certificate is not the person the certificate represents her or him to be.

key that decrypts is available to attackers. Nevertheless, modern encryption techniques provide excellent concealment of the contents of messages if the key is secret regardless of what else hackers might know about the encryption algorithm itself. By setting up encryption at both ends of a connection across public networks, a company can in effect extend its secure private network (such network extensions are called virtual private networks; see the accompanying feature on p. 278).

Encryption does not conceal everything about a network transmission. Hackers still can gain useful information from the pattern of transmission, the lengths of messages, or their origin or destination addresses. Encryption does not prevent attackers from intercepting and changing the data in a transmission. The attackers may not know what they are changing, but subtle changes can still wreak havoc, especially if the intended recipient is a computer that expects data to arrive in a particular format.[9]

Patching and Change Management

A surprising number of attacks exploit weaknesses in systems for which "patches" (fixes) already exist at the time of the attack. Successful attacks of this kind sometimes represent administrative failures, but there are also a large number of contributing factors, such as shortage of IT staff to apply fixes to existing systems, or legitimate concerns about the unintended negative consequences of a system patch. Keeping track of the variety of systems in a company's infrastructure, their security weaknesses, the available patches, and whether patches have been applied is nontrivial. Consequently, attacks against known and presumably patched weaknesses often are successful.

Knowing exactly what software is running and whether it is patched is important for another reason: After an attack, this knowledge is essential to discerning whether attackers have changed anything within a company's infrastructure. Detecting a change in a file size or finding a file that should not be there would be an obvious sign of intruder activity. Best practice calls for keeping detailed records of all files that are *supposed* to be on production computers, including file sizes or even file

[9] Jalal Feghi, Jalil Feghi, and Peter Williams, Digital Certificates: Applied Internet Security (Reading, MA: Addison-Wesley, 1999), is an excellent reference on the subject of encryption and digital certificates.

Public-Private Key Encryption and Digital Signatures

Public-private key encryption uses a mathematical algorithm with an interesting characteristic: If one unique key is used to transform a plain text message into encrypted form, a different unique key must be used to decrypt the message back into plain text at its destination. Typically, one key is made public and the other is kept private. A message can be sent confidentially if it is encrypted using the public key; then only a person possessing the private key can decrypt the message. A message can be "signed" by using the same process in reverse; if the public key can successfully decrypt the message, only the person in possession of the private key could have encrypted it; hence, it must have come from the person known to possess the private key.

"fingerprints."[10] Sadly, many companies fall short of this practice, sometimes for what seem like good business reasons. For example, managers hurrying to fix a customer-impacting problem may be tempted to shortcut formal change management procedures. The result is a gap in formal knowledge about what files and programs ought to be present on company systems.

Intrusion Detection and Network Monitoring

Intrusion detection and network monitoring together help network administrators recognize when their infrastructure is or has been under attack. Network monitoring automatically filters out external attack traffic at the boundary of company networks. Sophisticated intrusion detection systems include combinations of hardware probes and software diagnostic systems. They log activity throughout company networks and highlight patterns of suspicious activity for further investigation. Along with formal change management, which provides a baseline description of company system configurations, the information logged by intrusion detection systems can help companies reconstruct exactly what an intruder did.

A Security Management Framework

Securing a company's infrastructure involves design decisions, operating policy and procedure development, and steely execution. Information security is an evolving field with an evolving state of the art. Nevertheless, the following principles of security management have ongoing relevance.

Make Deliberate Security Decisions

This may seem obvious, but too many companies rely on a combination of blissful ignorance and security through obscurity. These are not reasonable approaches for companies seeking to connect to and leverage the public Internet. Ignorance is neither a strategy nor an excuse. General managers must educate themselves on security-related subjects and take responsibility for decisions in this area.

Consider Security a Moving Target

The forces of digital darkness are constantly searching for new ways to attack. Companies must maintain a solid defense, attack their own systems (do a safety

[10] There are technologies available to capture images of disk drives that act as a sort of fingerprinting.

Virtual Private Networks

Virtual private networks (VPNs) use encryption to create a connection across public networks that extend a company's private network. Traffic between two points—for example, a remote user and a computer inside a company's network—is encrypted at one end of the transmission, encapsulated inside new packets, and sent on to a destination where the packets are unencapsulated and decrypted. VPNs allow a secure private network to be extended securely across a public network to arbitrary points. There is a dark side to this, however. If an attacker can gain access to a remote VPN node, a company's network can be attacked as if from the inside. Thus, although VPNs extend security usefully, they also add to the complexity of the security management task.

check), and hire outside firms to audit their defenses for vulnerability to new threats on a regular basis. Indeed, companies must stay plugged in to sources of information about threats, such as the Computer Emergency Response Team (CERT) (www.cert.org). Information security is not something a company can do once and then forget about.

Practice Disciplined Change Management

The fix that needs to be rushed into production may be important, but if shortcutting formal procedures makes reconstructing the facts of a subsequent attack impossible, the costs of informality ultimately may be far greater. Companies need to know what they have running at all times and need a disciplined process for migrating infrastructure changes through testing and into production use. Not following such procedures represents reckless behavior for which general managers are ultimately responsible. Conversely, failure to promptly install available patches to counter known threats also risks unnecessary incidents. Best practice requires the prompt installation of patches, while remaining within change management procedures.

Educate Users

Make sure users understand the dangers inherent in certain activities, such as sharing passwords and connecting behind-the-firewall dial-up modems to their desktop computers. Help them understand the reasons for security measures that may inconvenience them in some situations. Enlist them as allies in maintaining security.

Deploy Multilevel Technical Measures, as Many as You Can Afford

Use security at the host and network levels. Acquire defensive technologies as they develop. No company can afford an infinite amount of security, but managers need to be sure they have thought through the consequences of a breach of security. Managers must prioritize security measures appropriately.

Risk Management of Availability and Security

Companies cannot afford to address every threat to the availability and security of IT infrastructure with equal aggressiveness. Even if they could, doing so would not make business sense. Instead, risks must be characterized and addressed in proportion to their likelihood and potential consequences. Management actions to mitigate risks must be prioritized with an eye to their costs and potential benefits.

Figure 6.9 suggests a way of thinking about potential failures in terms of their probabilities and consequences. Incidents in the upper right corner are both likely and costly; mitigating these risks is obviously important. Risks in the other quadrants must be prioritized. One method of prioritizing involves computing the *expected loss* associated with incidents in these quadrants by multiplying the probability of an incident and its cost if it occurs. Incidents with higher expected losses get higher priorities. Needless to say, incidents in the upper left and lower right quadrants receive higher priorities than do the low-probability, low-cost incidents in the lower left quadrant.

For most companies, however, the logic of risk management is more complicated. Managers' attitudes toward risk may be too complex to be summarized by simple probabilities and costs. For example, managers may dread high-cost incidents so much that they prefer to address high-cost incidents first, even if those incidents are very unlikely to occur and their associated expected loss (probability × cost) is small. Or

FIGURE 6.9
Managing Infrastructure Risks: Consequences and Probabilities

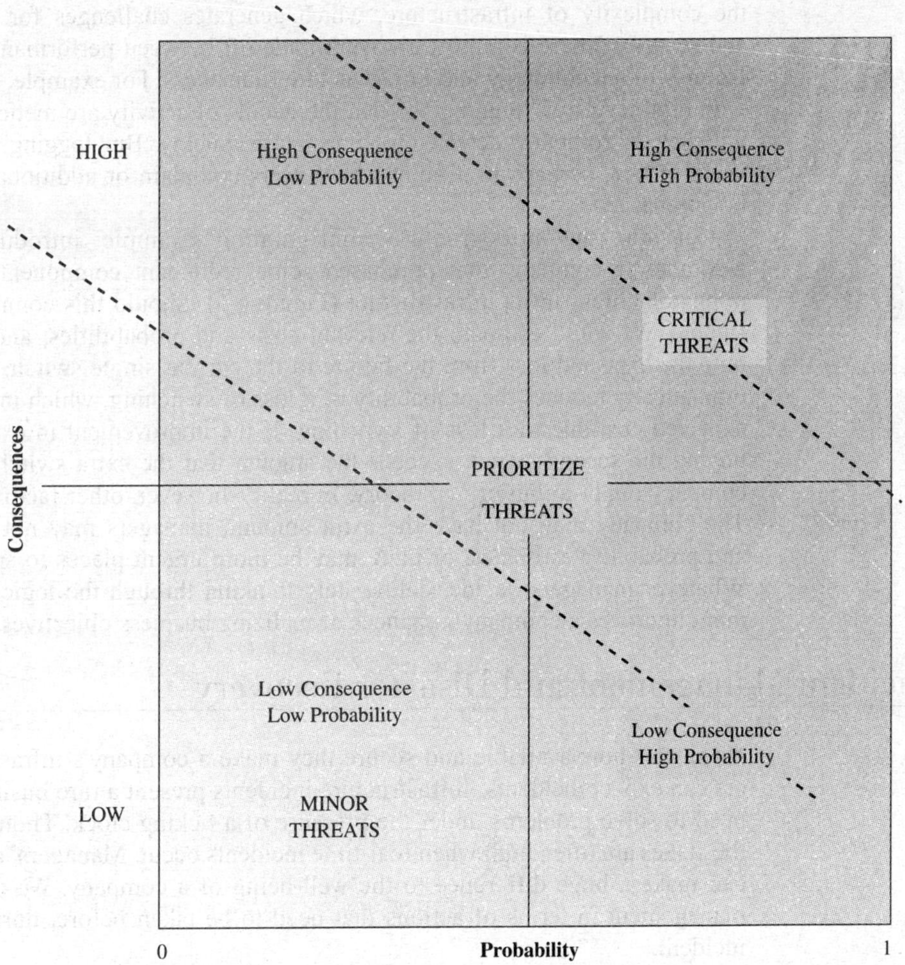

managers may fear specific events for reasons that go beyond cost. A further complication arises from the difficulty of estimating costs and probabilities in some situations. The intangible costs of some incidents are exceedingly difficult to predict, and estimating probabilities often is no easier.

In addition, not all risks can be countered with well-defined management actions. Most companies choose between courses of action that vary in cost and address risks to varying degrees. Sometimes none of the possible actions address some serious risks. Sometimes addressing a serious risk is prohibitively expensive. Thus, after assigning priorities to risks, most companies perform an additional assessment step to decide which actions to take. This step takes into account not only the expected losses from incidents but also the costs of actions to reduce or eliminate risks.

New capabilities that come with new technologies generate another wrinkle in risk management thinking. Although new capabilities provide benefits, they often require taking on new risks to availability or security. Thus, managers also engage in risk management as they decide which new services to offer. A new service to support the business—for example, a collaborative videoconferencing technology—increases the complexity of infrastructure, which generates challenges for both availability and security. There is almost always a trade-off between performance or richness of features of a technology and infrastructure robustness. For example, running software with high levels of "logging" so that the details of activity are meticulously recorded will help a company detect intrusions more quickly. But logging degrades system performance, perhaps to a point where users complain or additional hardware must be purchased.

Consider the infrastructure configuration example introduced earlier: an e-commerce company that purchased some redundant components but left single points of failure in its infrastructure (Figure 6.5). Should this company buy another switch? We could estimate the relevant costs and probabilities, and we could compute the expected loss from the failure of the current single switch. A second switch dramatically reduces the probability of a loss of switching, which in turn reduces the expected cost due to a loss of switching. If the improvement in expected loss from buying the second switch exceeds the amount that the extra switch would cost, the company ought to buy it—in theory. In reality, however, other factors may intervene. The company may not have the extra amount, managers may not believe the cost and probability estimates, or there may be more urgent places to spend that money. Whatever managers decide, deliberately thinking through the logic of risk management improves a company's chances of realizing business objectives.

Incident Management and Disaster Recovery

No matter how available and secure they make a company's infrastructure, managers can expect incidents. Infrastructure incidents present a rare business challenge: a need to solve problems under the pressure of a ticking clock. Though they are rare, the stakes are often high when real-time incidents occur. Managers' actions in a crisis can make a huge difference to the well-being of a company. We consider incident management in terms of actions that need to be taken before, during, and after an incident.

Managing Incidents before They Occur

The range of options available to managers in the middle of a crisis is largely determined by decisions made before the crisis. Precrisis practices that make incidents more manageable include the following:

Sound infrastructure design. If infrastructure has been designed with an eye to recoverability and tolerance for failures, the losses associated with an incident are more likely to be contained.

Disciplined execution of operating procedures. Change management procedures make the diagnosis of problems more effective by maintaining a baseline of knowledge about infrastructure configurations. Data backup procedures preserve data in case the data are lost. Scheduled infrastructure health audits uncover lurking problems or vulnerabilities.

Careful documentation. If procedures and configurations are carefully documented, crisis managers need not guess about crucial details. Reliable documentation saves time and increases certainty in dealing with a crisis.

Established crisis management procedures. Procedures for managing incidents guide the diagnosis of problems, help managers avoid decision-making traps, and specify who should be involved in problem-solving activities. Managing in a crisis is difficult enough without having to make up every response as you go. Crisis management always involves creativity, but familiar and useful procedures serve as bases from which managers can innovate under fire.

Rehearsing incident response. Rehearsing responses to incidents makes decision makers more confident and effective during real crises. Even if the way an incident unfolds is different from the way it was practiced, practice makes a crisis situation more familiar and better prepares managers to improvise solutions.

These preparations may seem basic, but a large number of companies do not make them. There is a tendency for other urgent business concerns, such as growing revenues, profits, product functionality, or the customer base, to take priority over hypothetical problems nobody wants to think about. In most companies, staff members who execute responses to incidents have no training in that area and are not necessarily trained in the nature of threats. Nevertheless, managers clearly bear responsibility when they do not foresee exposure to availability and security incidents. Good managers find the time to plan for high-cost events.

Managing during an Incident

When faced with a real-time crisis, human decision makers have numerous psychological obstacles to surmount in addition to the usually very serious technical difficulties inherent in the crisis. These obstacles include the following:

- Emotional responses, including confusion, denial, fear, and panic
- Wishful thinking and groupthink
- Political maneuvering, diving for cover, and ducking responsibility
- Leaping to conclusions and blindness to evidence that contradicts current beliefs

Awareness of psychological traps helps decision makers avoid them when situations turn dire.

Another difficulty managers face in crises is "public relations inhibition." Sometimes managers are reluctant to admit the seriousness of a problem because they do not want to take actions that communicate to others (customers, the public) that a serious incident has occurred. For example, the managers of an e-commerce company might not want to shut down their online retail site to confound a hacker until they have definitive proof of an intrusion. A shutdown would have to be explained to the press and might alarm customers. Obviously, the stakes of such a decision are high.

Managing after an Incident

After an incident, infrastructure managers often need to rebuild parts of the infrastructure. Sometimes erasing and rebuilding everything from scratch is the only way to be sure the infrastructure is restored to its preincident state. If configurations and procedures have been carefully documented in advance, recovery can happen swiftly. But if records of how systems should be put together are not exact, rebuilding can run into hiccups: problems that must be solved under the time pressure of getting the business back online. Rebuilding processes may have to be reinvented "on the fly." Furthermore, if there have been change management lapses—for example, if changes made to systems have not been documented—a rebuild can result in lost functionality (a problem solved earlier by an informal change in production may reappear).

To avoid future incidents of the same type, managers need to understand what happened. Figuring out exactly what caused an incident is sometimes difficult, but it must be done. Typically, a company owes business partners information about the nature of a failure so that those partners can determine the consequences that might flow to them as a result. There is no one best way to explain or disclose an incident to partners, customers, or the press and public. In formulating actions after an incident, however, it is essential to communicate the seriousness with which a company protects the information entrusted to it. A possible intrusion need not be a public relations disaster if subsequent steps to secure infrastructure are framed as "taking no chances."

Summary

The challenges of keeping real-time infrastructures always operational are formidable and evolving. Nevertheless, in this chapter we have outlined management actions and frameworks that will, if applied with discipline and effort, improve the chances of success. The economic consequences of ignoring or failing to take effective action in these areas may be dire indeed. We have demonstrated how the arithmetic of availability calls for increasing sophistication in infrastructure design and how redundancy, the primary means of increasing robustness, also adds operational complexity and management challenges. We have outlined a series of new and serious malicious threats to IT infrastructure, and proposed frameworks for reducing the threats and for managing incidents when they occur. Executives can use the following questions to assess their own preparedness for these twenty-first century challenges:

1. How available do our systems need to be? Are our infrastructure investments in availability aligned with requirements?
2. Are we taking security threats seriously enough? How secure is our current infrastructure? How do we assess information security on an ongoing basis? Have IT staff members received adequate training? How do we compare with information security best-in-class organizations?
3. Do we have a solid security policy in place? Were business managers as well as IT managers involved in creating it? Do users know about it and understand it? Do they accept it? How is the policy enforced?
4. Do we have plans for responding to infrastructure incidents? Do we practice them on a regular basis? Are staff members trained in incident response? What are our plans and policies for communicating information about incidents to external parties such as customers, partners, the press, and the public?
5. Do we practice risk management in availability and security decisions? Is our approach to dealing with hypothetical problems deliberate, structured, and well reasoned? Have the company's general managers embraced responsibility for availability and security?

Chapter 7

Managing IT Service Delivery

Before the emergence of the commercial Internet in the 1990s,[1] companies accomplished some of what they now achieve through public internetworks entirely on their own by using proprietary technologies installed and managed inside each firm. For several reasons, this approach was expensive and unsatisfactory:

- To reach business partners and customers, every company had to develop its own communication infrastructure, a process that led to massive duplication in infrastructure investment. Often the multiplicity of technologies confused and confounded the partners and customers businesses wanted to reach.
- The technologies did not interoperate well. Many companies maintained complex software programs that had no purpose except to serve as a bridge between otherwise incompatible systems.
- Reliance on proprietary technologies meant that companies were locked in to specific vendor technologies. Once locked in, firms had little bargaining power and were at the mercy of the margin-maximizing inclinations of their technology providers.

Companies that installed hardware and software from many vendors suffered performance and reliability difficulties. IT managers, seemingly trapped in a losing game, were perennially blamed by business managers for delivering expensive systems that performed poorly or, worse, never worked at all.

The emergence of an accessible public Internet based on open standards has changed the way companies build IT capabilities. Corporate systems now gain leverage from their connections to public infrastructure. The new approaches compare favorably with previous approaches in numerous ways. Today, for example,

- Companies can share a communication infrastructure common to all business partners and customers. Customers and business partners can interact via common interfaces (usually Web browsers). This seamless interaction dramatically reduces complexity and confusion.

This chapter is adapted from materials developed by Professor Robert D. Austin and Professor F. Warren McFarlan.

[1] The Internet itself arose much earlier, of course, but the commercial Internet really took off only with the introduction of Web browsers in the early 1990s. Some companies were using the Internet productively in the 1980s, but not very many.

- Because of the open Transmission Control Protocol/Internet Protocol (TCP/IP) standard, communication technologies interoperate well. Software that bridges systems is simple, standardized, and inexpensive. In some cases it can be acquired for free.
- Companies are much less locked in to specific vendor technologies, a fact that creates more competition among vendors. More competition leads to lower prices and better-performing technology.

Companies can combine technologies from numerous vendors and expect them to interconnect seamlessly. Although the job of the information technology (IT) manager remains formidable, it is not the losing game it once was.

Reliable and secure connections to public networks provide new options for delivering IT services. Services historically provided by IT departments now can be acquired from service providers. This is outsourcing, but of a kind different from large-scale outsourcing programs. As communication technologies improve and become more compatible and modular, firms can obtain smaller increments of service from outside vendors, with shorter lead times and contract durations. "Web services" take incremental service ideas to a logical conclusion, depicting a world in which functions as narrow as, say, currency conversion can be obtained externally for prices negotiated whenever a conversion is needed.

Although the standards and infrastructure necessary to bring this vision to reality are still works in progress, major IT vendors such as IBM and Microsoft profess a commitment to it. The underlying trend toward external acquisition of increasingly incremental services appears irresistible. Infrastructure that lends itself to incremental improvement enjoys favorable management attributes; for example, investment and implementation risks are easier to manage when improvements involve a series of many small steps rather than a few large "all-or-nothing" steps. Incremental improvement also facilitates experimentation and learning.[2]

Incremental service delivery also makes new business models possible, and those models act as catalysts for restructuring in service delivery industries. More and more, IT services are delivered by collections of service partners, each of which must perform well to deliver the service reliably and securely. Working with service providers means that IT managers must be especially careful in selecting and managing relationships with these business partners. Managing service provider relationships means sharing information—"virtually integrating," if you will—which requires surmounting technical communication challenges as well as challenges of incentive design.

Service-level contracts provide a foundation for aligning incentives between parties collaborating in service delivery, but successful relationship management goes beyond contract administration.

When evolving service models connect to corporate systems, diverse IT infrastructure is the result. In many companies, legacy systems still perform vital functions and must be supported. In most companies, there is an accelerating trend toward heterogeneity in supported client devices. Increasingly, cell phones and personal digital assistants (PDAs), not personal computers (PCs), are the tools people use to interact with

[2] David Upton has written extensively on the benefits of incremental improvement strategies, especially the need to design operational infrastructures so that they can be incrementally improved. See, for example, *Designing, Managing, and Improving Operations* (Upper Saddle River, NJ: Prentice-Hall, 1998).

IT systems to conduct business. The variety of service delivery models and technologies creates complexity and generates management challenges. Not surprisingly, new ways of thinking are needed to manage diverse, distributed, and complex information and technology assets.

New Service Models

Since the emergence of PCs and client-server computing, end-user software has been designed to execute on PCs or on servers housed locally. Saved documents and other forms of data usually remain on a PC's hard drive or on storage devices connected to a nearby server or mainframe. In this scenario, there is close physical correspondence between the places where people use software and the location of the machines that deliver services. One can point to a nearby computer and say, for example, "that server runs our e-mail system."

With the advent of reliable, high-capacity networks, however, local software execution and data storage is no longer the only alternative or the best alternative from a business standpoint. Increasingly, software is designed to operate in geographically distant facilities that belong to service providers who deliver similar services to many customers. Even when software execution remains inside a company, it may happen in faraway places. Servers and storage are shared among applications and users, so that it becomes much more difficult to associate a particular machine with particular IT services. Such service delivery scenarios offer efficiency and flexibility advantages. But they also pose management challenges.

In some scenarios, the end-user's company owns little of the infrastructure involved in service delivery and instead pays a monthly fee for a service bundle, which includes technical support services. When something goes wrong, business users call another company rather than their internal IT department to request resolution of the problem. Even when software applications are not managed externally, components of the infrastructure that delivers IT services may be outsourced. A company might, for example, rent space in a vendor-owned hosting facility rather than build its own data center. Or it might employ a specialized outside firm to monitor its intrusion detection systems and guard against sophisticated new security threats. The benefits of this kind of "incremental outsourcing" include the following:

Managing the shortage of specialized IT workers: Incremental outsourcing helps individual firms overcome the shortage of specialized skills by reducing the need for internal staff a firm must hire. This benefit is especially important to small and medium-size businesses that have difficulty attracting and retaining top IT talent.

Reducing time to market: Network-based service delivery models help companies develop new capabilities quickly. For example, existing companies can use externally hosted retailing packages to sell over the Web without having to purchase equipment or develop software.

The shift to 24×7 operations: Consumers expect company Web sites and supporting systems to be always available. Real-time operations require computers that are always on. But in many enterprises, facilities and equipment are not designed for high levels of availability. High availability requires large investments in redundant infrastructure. Because vendors are able to spread investments across many customers, they can achieve economies of scale that justify large investments. Vendors often can invest in levels of availability and security that individual firms cannot afford.

Favorable cash flow profiles: Traditionally, IT investments required large up-front cash outlays that only yielded deferred and often uncertain benefits (because of high project failure rates). Subscription-based IT services have a different cash flow profile. Firms pay a monthly fee to acquire services equivalent to those provided by internal systems in the past. With limited up-front purchases, payback flows in more quickly. This benefit is particularly important to small and medium-size companies that cannot afford the large up-front investments associated with some IT services. Figure 7.1 compares the cash flow profile of a traditional IT investment with that of a subscription-based service delivered through a prebuilt external infrastructure.

Cost reduction in IT service chains: Centralized service delivery can reduce support costs in many ways. With business functionality delivered from servers, upgrades to new versions of the software are done centrally, eliminating the need for support personnel to upgrade individual client computers. This service delivery approach also reduces the risk (and costs) of software piracy, because the software is never physically distributed. In addition, there is no inventory of physical media (e.g., CD-ROMs) for distributors and systems administrators to manage because services are distributed in real time to users. Vendors realize savings from economies of scale in using staff, which may be passed along to customers in the form of reduced prices.

Making applications globally accessible: When IT services are delivered over the Net, the geographic location of a computer is unimportant. Services are available at any computer with a Web browser for any user who has the authority to access the service. Traveling employees can access the same virtual workspace regardless of where they are in the world. Because the IT infrastructure is geography-neutral, much of the cost of moving a worker from one location to another is eliminated. This advantage combines with the continuing evolution in client devices (cell phones and PDAs, for example) to create new value opportunities.

Over-the-Net delivery models that permit realization of these advantages may take different forms. Many companies now manage certain corporate functions, such as human resource benefits administration, by procuring over-the-Net services from a vendor with benefits expertise; many employees manage investment of their retirement plan contributions using a Web browser to access a Web site owned and operated by a financial services company. Salesforce.com provides sales force automation to many companies via the "Software as a Service" (SaaS) model, which entails renting software functionality from a vendor for a monthly fee and accessing the functionality via a Web browser; data is stored securely in a central location managed by the service provider.

The "Web services" model allows for highly dynamic provision of IT services. Rather than establish a long-term relationship with specific service providers, firms using Web services negotiate and procure services in real time from an ever-changing market composed of companies offering those services. For example, a firm in need of

FIGURE 7.1
Purchase versus Subscribe Cash Flows

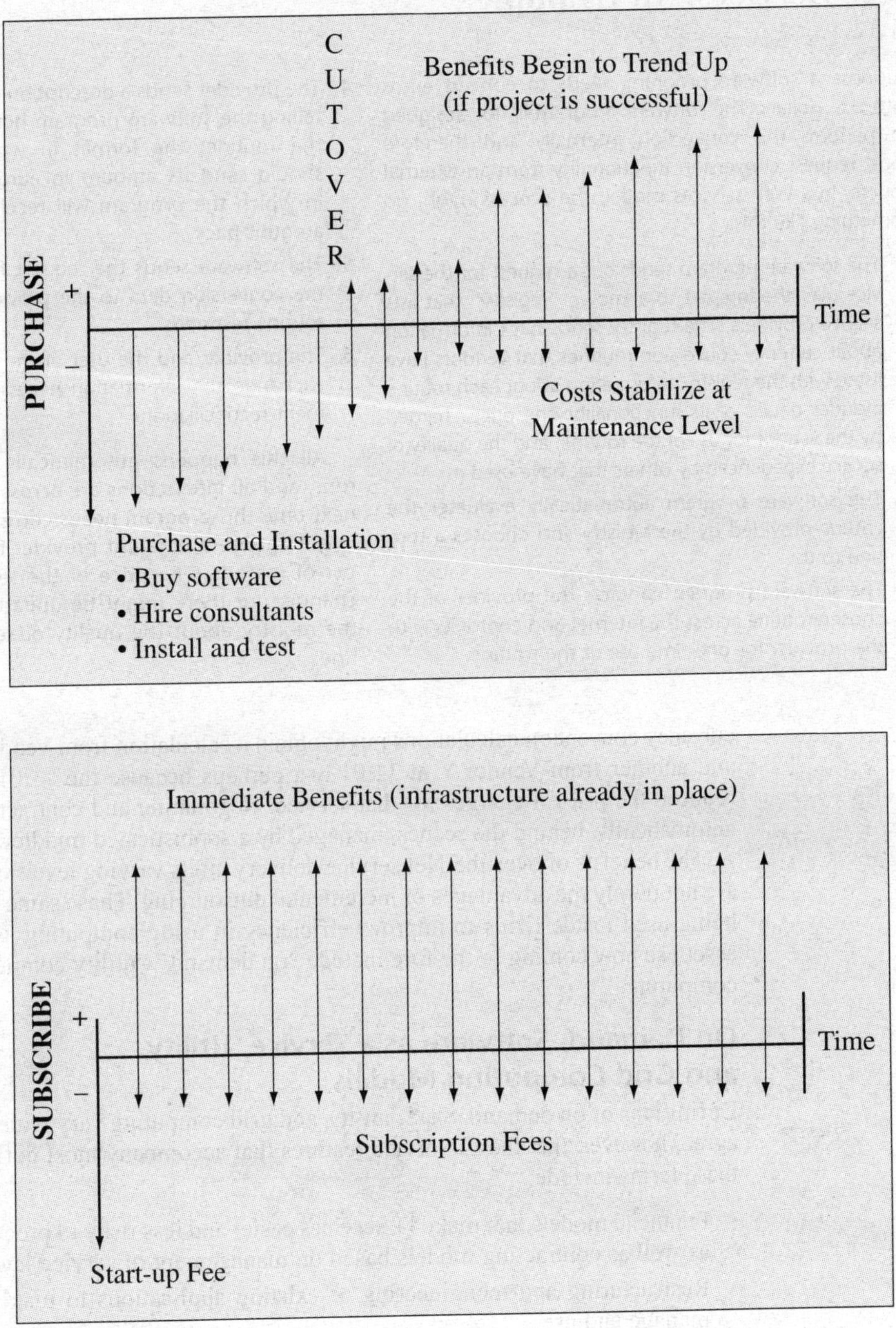

Web Services: An Example

Suppose a software program needs to convert euros into U.S. dollars. The software program is not designed to perform this conversion internally and therefore must request conversion functionality from an external source. In a Web services model, the process might go something like this:

1. The software program sends out a request for the service over the Internet to a known "registry" that lists service providers. The registry sends back information about currency conversion routines that vendors have listed with the registry. Information about each routine indudes details of its functionality, the price charged by the vendor for use of the routine, and the quality of service experienced by others that have used it.
2. The software program automatically evaluates the criteria provided by the registry and chooses a routine to use.
3. The software program contacts the provider of the chosen routine across the Internet and contracts with the provider for one-time use of the routine.
4. The provider sends a description across the Internet telling the software program how to interact with the routine: the format in which the program should send its amount in euros and the format in which the program will receive the U.S. dollar amount back.
5. The software sends the request for conversion and the conversion data to the provider; the provider's routine responds.
6. The provider and the user of the conversion service exchange the information necessary to assure payment reconciliation.

All this happens automatically as the program runs, and all interactions are across the Internet. The next time this program needs currency conversion, it might choose a different provider for any of a number of reasons. The price of the service might have changed, or there might be updated information in the registry about the quality of service of the routine.

currency conversion calculations might obtain a calculation from Vendor X at 11:00 AM and another from Vendor Y at 11:01 AM, perhaps because the 11:01 AM vendor had reduced the price it charges for that service. Negotiating and contracting would occur automatically, behind the scenes, managed by a sophisticated middleware layer.

The benefits of over-the-Net service delivery, in its varying levels of sophistication, are not purely the advantages of incremental outsourcing. These same technologies are being used inside firms to improve efficiency in using computing assets. Models of asset use now coming to the fore include "on demand," "utility computing," and "grid computing."

On Demand, Software as a Service, Utility, and Grid Computing Models

Definitions of on demand, SaaS, utility, and grid computing vary widely. Most experts agree, however, that the IT service features that accompany most definitions of all of these terms include:

- Financial models that make IT services easier and less risky to procure and manage, as well as contracting models based on management of service levels.
- Restructuring and reengineering of existing applications to make them easier to manage and use.
- Enhancements to infrastructure to improve interoperability and efficiency in use of computing assets.

There is tremendous diversity in the possible and actual configurations of IT infrastructure to support these models, which creates great potential for cost savings and new capabilities, but which also creates additional infrastructure complexity.

In simplest form, financial models that underlie such service models can seem mundane, as when an IT vendor makes equipment available to a customer via favorable leasing arrangements, rather than traditional purchases. Taken to a more sophisticated extreme, financial models may allow customers to contract for a variable amount of computer power or storage capacity (or both), to be provided by a vendor for a fee that varies in proportion to the amount of power or capacity used. Such contracts may also include pricing that allows handling of surges in the load systems must bear. A customer firm that has to pay for surge capacity only when it is required, instead of maintaining it all the time even though it is usually not needed, can realize substantial savings from this kind of financial arrangement. In general, such financial arrangements allow cost savings or reduction in financial risk by adjusting the cash flow profiles involved in procuring services (as was illustrated in Figure 7.1).

Financial arrangements do not always correspond to characteristics of physical implementation—a company might obtain equipment via a lease labeled "on demand," for example, even when the use of the equipment is quite conventional—but the advantages of the financial arrangements can often be magnified by rearrangement of existing applications. Sometimes this means centralizing and commonizing applications, so that they can be managed in a central data center and accessed from anywhere. Other times it means large-scale reengineering of business processes, and rewriting or replacing with off-the-shelf packages large chunks of a company's applications portfolio. Still other times, restructuring applications might mean replacing existing applications with Software as a Service applications. In all cases, the idea is to better align application functionality with more efficient modes of management and use.

At the infrastructure level, on demand, SaaS, utility, and grid computing refer to steps companies might take to make access to IT services more like access to traditional utilities, such as electricity and telephone. If, for example, server capacity or disk storage capacity can be managed as a fluid resource and easily reallocated to handle surges or to create efficiencies from sharing of equipment, then significant savings can be realized. The critical enablers of this approach to managing IT resources reside deep below the "floorboards" of IT infrastructure, in middleware layers that most business users never see. Middleware in support of these modes must address issues such as:

- *Provisioning,* providing access to new services or additional capacity in an automated and "on-the-fly" manner.
- *Resource virtualization,* which allows server or storage capacity to be accessed and referenced independent of its physical characteristics and location, which in turn allows power or capacity to be tapped in variable increments independent of how much capacity a particular server or disk array might have to offer.
- *Change management,* which permits centralized changes to infrastructure, to reduce the cost of making changes and to exert additional levels of control over processes critical to maintaining high availability.

- *Performance monitoring and analytics,* which allow constant evaluation of the performance of computing infrastructure, both in terms of functionality and financial return, and suggests ongoing adjustments to improve the performance or return on investment in computing assets.

Figure 7.2 depicts an on demand computing environment that includes applications residing on an enabling middleware layer that provides virtualized and performance-managed access to storage, server, and network resources.

Managing Risk through Incremental Outsourcing

As IT service chains proliferate and mature, companies often face the question of which services to outsource. Figure 7.3 outlines the steps many companies consider in making this decision. IT services that are unique to a company and provide it with significant advantages over competitors tend not to be outsourced, at least not to vendors that are trying to sell similar services to all of their customers. Such services are so core to a company's business that an internal capability to manage and extend them must be maintained. The exception to this rule arises when companies find themselves unable to develop a vital capability internally and must therefore rely on outsourcing to acquire the capability.

FIGURE 7.2(a)
An "On Demand" Computing Environment

Source: Adapted from work by Arjun Chopra and Meghna Rao, Harvard Business School MBAs from the class of 2004.

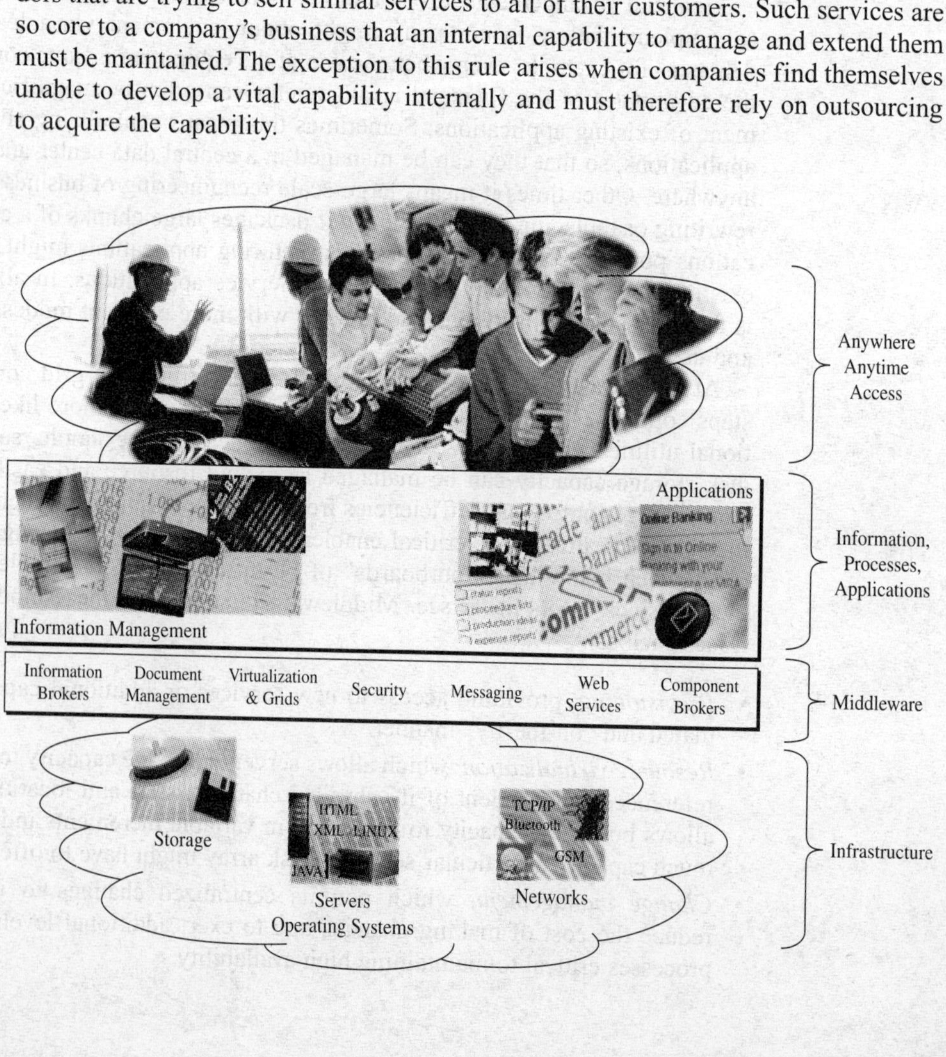

FIGURE 7.2(b)
An "On Demand" Computing Environment (*continued*)

	IBM—Computing Portfolio
Server Farms	BladeCenter on Intel (Win/Linux/Netware); xSeries on Intel (Linux/Win/Netware); Midrange iSeries (OS400/Linux); pSeries on IBM power4+ processors (AIX/Linux); zSeries MainFrames (z/OS/Linux); 32/64 bit Servers on AMD Opteron (Linux)
Storage Farms	IBM Total Storage Disks/Tapes/SAN/NAS H/W
Network Resources	Use of third-party products (e.g., Cisco, Juniper)
Server Virtualization/App Provisioning	Purchased ThinkDynamics (5/03=$undisclosed) Tivoli Configuration/Provisioning Mgr
Storage Mgmt	IBM Total Storage SAN F/S & SAN Vol Controller Tivoli Storage Manager
Network Mgmt	Tivoli NetView for network provisioning
Systems Mgmt	Tivoli Suite for Managing Multiple Platforms: Access Mgr, Systems Discovery, Provisioning, Monitoring, Reporting
Higher Level Web Services Apps	WebSphere e-business products. Rational (12/02 =$2bn) dev tools, Lotus collaboration products, DB2 database

Many IT services do not provide competitive advantage. These services are essential in running a modern business, but there may be no reason one company's service must be different from that of its competitors. A company probably needs, for example, e-mail and word processing software, but the success or failure of a company usually has little to do with the features of these products. For these commoditylike services, the priorities are reliability and low cost (or a more favorable cash flow profile).

The logic of incremental outsourcing decisions parallels the logic of outsourcing large segments of the IT function. But there are also differences. With incremental outsourcing, the economic stakes are not as high and the potential consequences of mismanagement are not as far-reaching. When a firm outsources only its travel expense reporting, for example, as opposed to its entire IT organization, risk is contained. Mistakes are more reversible and less painful. Also, because mistakes cost less, more experimentation is feasible. Trying something does not mean managers must suffer its effects for the duration of a long-term contract.

However, incremental outsourcing decisions cannot be taken lightly. A decision to outsource hosting or network management can have serious across-the-company implications if there are service problems. Furthermore, many individually correct incremental decisions can add up to a significant negative overall impact. Incremental decisions made in isolation must not add up to an incoherent or inconsistent business strategy.

Incremental outsourcing, however, offers new and attractive choices to managers seeking to improve IT infrastructure. In the past, managers often felt they faced two equally unpleasant choices: (1) do nothing and risk slipping behind competitors, or (2) wholesale replacement of major components of computing infrastructure, which risks huge cost overruns and potential business disruptions as consequences of an implementation failure. Decisions to replace legacy networks with TCP/IP-based networks have run this second risk, as have decisions about whether to implement

FIGURE 7.3
Internal versus External Service Delivery

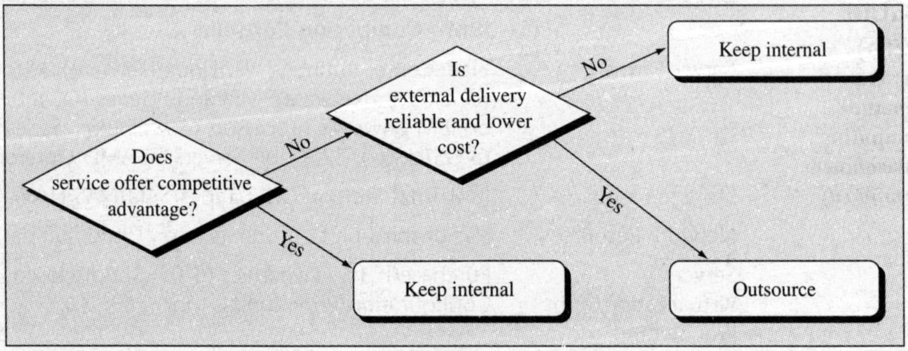

enterprise systems. With the TCP/IP networks installed today, however, managers have intermediate options that lie between all-or-nothing choices. The importance of these options cannot be overemphasized. For perhaps the first time in the history of IT, it is possible to imagine incremental improvement paths, ways of getting from A to B and then to C and capturing significant economic benefits without putting the entire future of the firm at stake each time.

An Incremental Outsourcing Example: Hosting

Outsource hosting of a company's systems involves deciding where they should be located physically. Although on the surface this may seem like an all-or-nothing choice, a company can, in fact, precisely determine which management functions it turns over to a vendor when moving computers to a vendor's site. Some basic support functions, such as electrical power, are necessarily ceded, but beyond those, managers can choose the size of the increment of outsourcing. By doing so, managers exercise control over the risks that executing the outsourcing initiative entails. In this section, we consider hosting as an illustration of the incremental nature of modern service delivery options even in cases when, at first glance, outsourcing seems to present all-or-nothing options.

The Hosting Service Provider Industry

Hosting companies own and manage the facilities that house computers that provide over-the-Net services. In online retailing, for example, back-office functions (e.g., shopping cart, checkout, and credit card processing) that enable Web-based consumer purchases often reside on computing platforms in hosting facilities rather than on the selling company's premises.

The benefits of outsourcing hosting are many. Outsourcing hosting can reduce downtime and costs, and provide access to new technologies without large investments in capital equipment.

Service Levels in Hosting[3]

Table 7.1 shows the layers of services a hosting provider can offer. The base service level—real estate services—is similar to the business of leasing office space.

[3] Some of the material in this section is adapted from Robert D. Austin, "Web and IT Hosting Facilities: Technology Note," Harvard Business School Publishing Note No. 601-134.

TABLE 7.1 Levels of Service from Hosting Providers

Level of Service	Description of Service
Business operating services	Administering and operating an application
Application support services	Support for software above the operating system level; application support; application performance monitoring and tuning; design of applications for scalability, reliability, security
Platform services	Support for hardware, operating system; reboot services; data backup and disaster recovery services; URL monitoring
Network services	Connectivity within the facility and externally to the public Internet and to private peering networks; monitoring of network traffic at the transport layer; service-level assurances at the packet loss and network availability layers; network security
Real estate services (lowest level)	Suitable floor space and physical facilities; maintenance of the space and facilities

Although this level of outsourcing provides robust facilities, it leaves the management and ownership of networks, computers, and software applications to the client firm. All that has changed is the physical location of the computers delivering IT services. The same development and maintenance staff members care for the computers, and the client firm continues to own all application computing equipment.

In addition to space and utilities, most hosting providers can manage networks, physical computing equipment, application performance, and even applications. As we move up the levels of service in Table 7.1, the outsourcing increment—the dollars the client firm spends and the percentage of effort outsourced—grows larger.

Hosting models can be roughly categorized along service level lines, as follows:

Colocation hosting: Colocation hosting companies provide no-frills access to a facility and its infrastructure. Customers rent floor space, connectivity, and power. Everything beyond these basics is provided à la carte and not necessarily by the hosting provider. Customer space is usually enclosed inside floor-to-ceiling cages, and the customer owns and retains responsibility for all the servers and equipment inside the cages. Often the hosting company knows little about the equipment or business operations inside customers' cages. This model requires customers to have (or acquire from a third party) the expertise to design, maintain, and operate the equipment inside the cages. This model, which supports a wide range of architectural possibilities, generally offers high availability.

Shared hosting: In shared hosting, servers are owned and operated by the hosting provider and customers purchase space on servers. Multiple client companies share a single physical server. Providers use sophisticated clustering technologies to achieve highly secure and reliable performance. Although some client companies are wary of the degree of sharing implicit in this model because of its perceived negative implications for security and reliability, this approach is becoming more prevalent as companies move to on demand, SaaS, utility, and grid computing.

Dedicated hosting: As with shared hosting, in dedicated hosting, servers are owned and operated by the hosting provider. Unlike a shared model, however, client firms do not share servers; the servers are "dedicated" to individual client firms. Other infrastructure components that provide network, storage, and some other services are shared across client companies. Usually, dedicated hosting providers offer a complete managed services package that includes everything needed to run the client company's systems at the required level of security and availability. Dedicated servers support high levels of security and availability, but forego some of the efficiencies promised by new service models.

Outsourcing data center infrastructure management is not an all-or-nothing choice. Connectivity service providers—to take another example—offer increasingly incremental service levels with much more attractive risk and expense management profiles for customers. How much speed do you need as your systems communicate to the Internet backbone? The options in service provision are multiplying, and infrastructure managers now often can purchase exactly the service increments they want.

Managing Relationships with Service Providers

When companies acquire IT services externally, they find themselves engaged in relationships with a growing number of service providers. As the operations of service providers and their clients become intertwined, the client firm comes to rely on the provider's capabilities as a basis for its own capabilities. Consequently, as with all outsourcing of important business functions, whether supplying just-in-time parts to a manufacturing assembly line or managing computing platforms, healthy relationships with vendors are critical to how well a company performs its primary business mission. Mistakes by vendors can be costly. Services are only as good as the weakest link in the service provider chain. Choosing reliable service providers and managing strong vendor relationships therefore are critical skills for an IT manager.

Selecting Service Partners

The most critical step in assembling an IT service chain is the selection of providers. Providers differ greatly in the service increments they offer, how they charge for services, the guarantees they *can* make, and the guarantees they are *willing* to make. No expertise in relationship management can overcome choosing an unreliable service provider. Infrastructure managers therefore must take tremendous care in selecting business partners that perform vital service chain functions.

The most common process for selecting service providers involves writing a "request for proposal" (RFP) and submitting it to a set of apparently qualified vendors. An RFP asks prospective providers for information relevant to their service capabilities across a spectrum that includes financial, technical, and operational information. Responses become a primary basis for deciding among vendors. Companies, however, rarely rely entirely on RFP responses but instead gather additional information from industry analysts, from other companies that have used providers' services, and from visits to service provider sites. Many companies employ elaborate scoring mechanisms for combining information gathered from all sources into comparable bases. But selection always comes down to the judgment of management.

There is no single format for RFPs, nor are there universally agreed on categories of information or sources that should be consulted in selecting providers. RFPs, however, typically request information in the following categories:

Descriptive information: How a service provider describes its business reveals much about its priorities and likely future direction. Descriptive information is equally relevant in evaluating the prospective provider's capacity to provide services (e.g., is the provider big enough to meet your demands?).

Financial information: A service provider's financial strength is a critical factor in evaluating the continuity of service and service quality a vendor is likely to provide. Providers that struggle financially may have trouble maintaining service quality or may require financial assistance that reduces or eliminates the economic benefits of acquiring a service externally. Worse, they may fail and shut down, leaving the customer firm to navigate the provider's bankruptcy.

Proposed plan for meeting service requirements: How the provider offers to meet the requirements laid out in the RFP indicates whether it truly understands the requirements. The plan for meeting the requirements can be evaluated on its merits and compared with proposed plans from other vendors. Partner firms that will be involved in the vendor's plan should be identified so that the customer firm can be assured of the qualifications of all the parties involved in service provision.

Mitigation of critical risks: A good RFP asks specific questions about potential service risks. Availability and security are two areas where it pays for customers to be sure they understand a service provider's approach.

Service guarantees: A service provider's guarantees (the levels of performance it is willing to back with penalty clauses in a contract) are important signals of the real level of confidence vendor managers have in their services. Often there is a substantial gap between what the performance service providers claim is their norm and what they are willing to guarantee. If the gap is too wide, services may not be as robust as advertised. Service guarantees are essential to aligning incentives between service providers so that, overall, the service chain performs well.

Pricing: Pricing usually includes one-time and variable components and may be structured in other ways as well. Although pricing is important for most companies, usually it is not the most important factor in deciding among vendors.

Table 7.2 shows a summary of information about three hosting providers that might be gathered from an RFP and other sources.[4] A close look at the information demonstrates that choices between vendors are often nontrivial. Providers that are strong in one area may be weak in another, and often no clear choice emerges.

For example, in Table 7.2 the fact that Provider 1 seems unwilling to supply financial information is probably a red flag that signals further investigation. Even if Provider 1's funding sources are gold-plated, customers need specific assurance that a service provider has a viable business model and will be a strong partner well into the future. Similarly, infrastructure managers might reasonably be worried about

[4] This example is taken from Robert D. Austin, "Selecting a Hosting Provider," Harvard Business School Exercise No. 601-171.

TABLE 7.2 Summary Grid for Comparing Hosting Providers

Source: Adapted from Robert D. Austin, "Selecting a Hosting Provider," Harvard Business School Exercise No. 601-171. Although based on real cases, these data arc fictitious and do not pertain to any real hosting provider.

Comparison Dimension	Provider 1	Provider 2	Provider 3
Company description	Regional hosting and broadband (backbone, DSL) service provider	National hosting services provider	Regional telco, backbone and broadband service provider
Employees	1,600	3,300	28,000
Financial profile	Declined to provide (private company)	After-tax loss $180 million on sales of $600 million; strong cash position; new facilities building offered as explanation for lack of profitability	After-tax profit of $1.1 billion on sales of $13 billion (most not from hosting business)
Number of data centers managed/ total square feet	3 data centers/160,000 sq. ft.	28 data centers/1.6 million sq. ft.	5 (2 operational) /220,000 sq. ft. (45,000 operational)
Space offered (RFP specified space for six racks of equipment)	3 8′ × 8′cages (192 sq. ft.), partitions removed to provide contiguous space	3 8′ × 7′ cages (168 sq. ft.), partitions removed to provide contiguous space	280 sq. ft. enclosed room
Physical security	Fully meets requirement	Fully meets requirement	Some concerns (see notes from site visit)
Power	Fully meets requirement	Fully meets requirement	Connected to only one power grid; two promised within 6 weeks
Connectivity	Fully meets requirement	Fully meets requirement	Not redundant to backbone; promised redundancy in 6 weeks
Service-level Guarantees	Fully meets requirement	Fully meets requirement	Partially meets requirement
One-time setup cost, space	$6,500	$7,800	$10,800
Monthly space rental	3 × $6,500	3 × $6,800	$9,800
One-time setup cost, connectivity	$1,200	$1,500	$1,600
Variable connectivity cost	$1,200 per month plus $525 per month for each mbps above 10	$1,500 per month plus $589 per month for each mbps above 10	$900 per month plus $412 per month for each mbps above 10

Provider 2's lack of profitability. Provider 2 relates the losses to its expansion plans, but prospective customers might wonder if the company can transition as easily to profit-making as its managers suggest. In this scenario, Provider 3 looks like the solid choice because it is large and profitable and its fees are lower.

Unfortunately, there are also reasons to worry about Provider 3. Most of the company's revenues come from business other than hosting services. This situation may translate into a lack of focus on the hosting business. Furthermore, Provider 3 seems to have some serious operational problems. Table 7.3 shows a discouraging report from a team that visited Provider 3's data center. In light of the report, one wonders whether Provider 3's lower prices are a miscalculation and perhaps evidence of the company's inexperience in hosting services. If so, the low prices eventually may become a problem for Provider 3's customers as well, especially if low profitability in the hosting business causes that provider's managers to further reduce their attention to hosting. Worse yet, if Provider 3 discovers it is losing money on hosting, it may seek to reduce costs in ways that affect service levels or even discontinue its hosting business.

We have stumbled here onto a general truth of outsourcing: *An outsourcing deal that is too one-sided, too favorable to one party at the expense of the other, usually ends up as a bad deal for both sides.* As they realize the deal is a loser, managers of a disadvantaged vendor almost always divert resources away from the relationship. This realization brings us to the next subject: managing relationships with providers once they are in place.

Relationship Management

Relationships with service provider partners require ongoing attention. Processes must be in place so that partners can share information and problems in the service chain can be solved quickly, even when they result from complex interactions of infrastructure components owned by different players. Problem-tracking and customer relationship systems, for example, must be able to exchange problem-tracking information as well as, sometimes, customer account information. Procedures and technical interfaces between partner systems must be properly designed and maintained.

More significant than problems with information-sharing systems, though, are the many incentive problems that attend service relationships. The most formidable obstacles are sometimes not technical but "political." When avoiding responsibility for a problem intrudes into the process of solving it, service collaboration becomes less effective. The key to effective relationships is aligned incentives among partners.

A service-level agreement (SLA) aligns incentives in relationships with service providers. SLAs describe the specific conditions by which the service provider is held liable for a service interruption and the penalties that the service provider will incur as a result. Table 7.4 illustrates the kinds of contractual terms one finds in an SLA. In keeping with our earlier examples, this SLA is for a hosting provider. Notice that failure is specifically defined, penalties apply only when the service provider is responsible for the service interruption, and penalties are prespecified and limited. Why a service provider insists on careful definitions is clear: To limit its liability for problems not under its control. But the specific nature of the agreement complicates service quality assurance. What matters to the client company is any failure, regardless of which service provider causes it.

TABLE 7.3 Sample Facility Visit Report for Hosting Provider

Source: Robert D. Austin, "Selecting a Hosting Provider," Harvard Business School Exercise No. 601-171. Information in this report is fictitious and not intended to pertain to a real hosting provider.

Initial walk around exterior: Renovated warehouse building (conventional brick, not hardened) shared with a delivery service. Urban setting amid a complex of warehouses. City workers doing roadwork near the facility, with heavy-duty digging (potentially fiber cable slicing) equipment. Data center on third floor: First floor and basement include a garage used by the delivery service. Panel trucks come and go on the lower levels on the north side. Second floor includes offices and appears to be empty. Never spoke to anyone who could tell us definitively how the second floor would be built out or if even that was the plan.

CCTV cameras visible around the perimeter of the facility. Diesel generators enclosed in 12-foot-high chain link, HVAC on roof. West side of building composed of a series of loading doors.

On day of visit, three loading doors were open. We succeeded in climbing up onto the loading dock and walking right into a power infrastructure room where many UPSs were housed. Waited there, expecting CCTV or alarm to summon security; no one ever showed up. (Staff later explained this lapse by saying that the door was open to facilitate construction and renovation and that the guard who was posted there had been reprimanded.)

Entering facility: First-level security is building security. Guard appeared not to realize that there was a data center in the building. Ushered us up to the third floor, where we encountered an unoccupied security desk behind a sliding glass partition. One CCTV console visible at desk. It would have been easy to climb through the opening to the security desk and let ourselves into the facility. Biometric palm reader visible but dust-covered at door. Security guard who had walked us up called someone on radio, and someone came to let us in. Person who let us in came from somewhere outside the data facility, then let us in by leaning through the opening and hitting the buzzer, which was in reach. We stood inside the door while he made out visitor badges for us. He did ask to see picture IDs, but security was kind of a farce by this point and everyone was a little embarrassed (including us for them), The room we were standing in while he prepared badges approximated a man trap in that there was another door about 20 feet away that opened into the data center proper. Unfortunately, that door was propped open.

Cages: No cages. Everyone gets an enclosed room with keypad access. No raised floor; power comes in from above, as do comms. Bolt-in racks and shelves provided. Walls of rooms do not extend to roof, so possible to climb over walls or to toss something into enclosed room.

Verification of redundancy, security, etc.: Redundant power and connectivity not yet in place, although promised within six weeks. Network hardware for facility was exposed in an open area anyone walking to his or her own enclosed space would need to pass. No on-site NOC, although they expressed willingness to provide specific network monitoring on site on a contract basis; noted too that network operations were monitored from a regional NOC. Guy giving tour kept apologizing for the construction.

Concerns: This facility is not fully built yet, although some customers are operational. Provider promises to have it in shape in time consistent with our project, but fact is that we cannot compare this facility on an equal basis with the others. Facility being under construction did not explain all the lapses we saw.

Overall assessment: These guys don't appear to have the hosting business figured out yet. Maybe it's just that they are in a construction phase. But there was little that we saw that offered warm feelings during our tour.

TABLE 7.4 An SLA Offered by a Hosting Provider

- Downtime—defined as sustained packet loss in excess of 50 percent for 15 consecutive minutes due to the failure of the hosting provider to provide services for that period (does not include scheduled maintenance time).
- Excess latency—defined as transmission latency in excess of 120 milliseconds round-trip time between any two points within the hosting provider's U.S. network.
- Excess packet loss—defined as packet loss in excess of 1 percent between any two points in the hosting provider's network.
- Each downtime period entitles customer to receive a credit equal to one day's recurring connectivity charge.
- Hosting provider guarantees two-hour response time in diagnosing problems within hosting provider and customer network.
- If problem is not within hosting provider and customer network, hosting provider will determine source within an additional two hours.
- Customer will be advised of reason for problem within one hour of hosting provider's discovery of the reason for the problem.
- If problem is within control of hosting provider, remedy for problem is guaranteed in two hours from diagnosis of the problem.
- Inability to deliver diagnosis or remedies within the times stated above entitles customer to an additional service credit for each two-hour period of delay.
- Customer can collect credits for no more than seven days' charges in a calendar month.
- Customer must request credits in writing within seven days of the event for which credits are compensation.
- Credits are granted at the sole discretion of the hosting provider.

Managers of customer firms must therefore manage SLAs with many service providers. SLAs must interlock so that penalty payments flow through the service chain in a way that provides appropriate incentives. Suppose, for example, a company offering over-the-Net software functionality agrees to an SLA that requires it to pay a penalty if the system is not available for a period longer than 10 minutes. Suppose also that the actual cause of a failure is a different vendor, say, an Internet service provider (ISP). In that case an SLA in place between the software company and an ISP should specify that the ISP will reimburse the software company for the penalty it owes to the client company. Although the SLA arrangement between the software company and the ISP might seem a matter best left to those two entities, it is to the customer company's advantage to ensure that incentives are aligned. Disputes between partners in a service chain can have dire implications for the users of a service.

The conventional wisdom in defining SLAs calls for designing them with "teeth," so that service providers feel pain when failures occur. In practice, however, it is difficult to determine appropriate penalty levels. SLAs provide service providers with both incentives and a way to credibly express their intention to deliver reliable service, and so it is important that they be in place. But setting penalties too low has little impact. Setting them too high is detrimental to a provider's willingness (and, if penalties are high enough, ability) to be a strong partner. Thus it is a mistake to consider SLAs the only means by which partners are managed. The most successful relationships emphasize shared objectives and helping all the partners earn a reasonable return.

Since many outsourced services involve entrusting data to service providers, contractual relationships need to contain provisions about a customer firm's rights to control its own data. The concern here is not that a vendor might try to claim ownership of customer data but that the vendor might try to lock the customer into a relationship by making it inconvenient to switch vendors. The interests of service providers and their customers are poorly aligned when it comes to the degree of entanglement in their relationship. Managers who take insufficient care in avoiding unnecessary entanglements will find themselves at the mercy of service providers, forfeiting a principal benefit of incremental outsourcing: the ability to alter and improve IT infrastructure in small steps in an ongoing manner.

Managing Large-Scale Outsourcing Arrangements[5]

Sometimes companies outsource not merely services but all or large parts of their IT function. Major outsourcing programs involve larger investments, longer durations, higher stakes, and greater overall risks than do incremental outsourcing deals. Usually they arise from strategic rather than operational motivations, and their impacts on IT end users are broader.

These special characteristics of big outsourcing agreements make them more complex to manage than incremental service contracts. A major outsourcing contract can extend over, say, 10 years while computer chip performance is improving by 20 to 30 percent per year; the strategic relevance of IT capabilities can change during such an interval, in a manner that suggests midcourse contract adjustments. The way benefits to the client and vendor unfold over time can also trigger the need for such adjustments. Early in a relationship, the client receives clear benefits, often including a one-time payment in exchange for assets being transferred to the vendor; but as time passes, the client begins to look for more value in exchange for the ongoing payments to the vendor. From the vendor's perspective, the situation is reversed; the early years of a new contract involve making a big payment while absorbing the punishing costs of taking on the client's IT function, in anticipation of profits from efficiencies to come later in the contract term. Too often, however, just as the vendor finally begins to experience those profits, the customer, looking for more value and feeling the need for new services, begins chafing under payment terms that look less lucrative than they did earlier. Profound tensions can develop. A healthy arrangement anticipates such difficulties by writing contract terms that facilitate communication about midcourse adjustments.

Large-scale outsourcing deals have become common across the corporate landscape. Like marriages, however, such outsourcing arrangements are easier to enter than to sustain or dissolve. Big outsourcing involves more than managing a relationship: In effect, it entails managing a strategic alliance.

[5] This section was originally adapted from F. Warren McFarlan and Richard L. Nolan, "How to Manage an IT Outsourcing Alliance," *Sloan Management Review* 36, no. 2 (Winter 1995).

Why Companies Enter into Large-Scale Outsourcing Relationships

The decision to place large components of your ability to execute your business model into the hands of another firm should not be taken lightly. The reasons companies make this choice vary widely, but we can identify some common themes.

Cost Savings: A large outsourcing vendor can potentially save money for a client. A vendor may be able to manage infrastructure shared among clients, especially the capacity of hardware and facilities, more efficiently, reducing overhead costs. A vendor with wider geographic reach may enable access to lower-cost labor for operations and new development. A vendor with many clients may be able to command more favorable purchasing terms with technology vendors than a client company could demand for itself.

Dissatisfaction with Existing IT Capabilities: In some companies, cumulative IT management neglect over a period of years can eventually culminate in an out-of-control situation; when this happens, general managers may see outsourcing as a way to enhance an inadequate capability. An additional driving factor toward outsourcing is the need for companies to rapidly retool IT back-office operations to remain competitive. Alternatively, the dynamics of an industry might change in a way that more broadly demands technological proficiency from firms to stay competitive; a firm's managers may doubt that the existing IT department is up to the challenge. In any such situations, outsourcing might seem like a good choice to the company's leaders.

Desire to Focus Firm Strategy in Other Areas: A firm under competitive pressures that does not consider IT a core competence may see outsourcing as a means to better strategic focus. With IT outsourced, such a firm then can concentrate its energy on other competitive differentiators.

Forcing Major Organizational Changes: Sometimes organizational rigidity and inertia make it hard for managers to make changes in operations. Outsourcing, driven by senior management, can provide a fulcrum to force movement past such impasses; changes that could never be accomplished internally can sometimes be accomplished by moving locus of the change to a vendor.

Access to Skills and Talent: Many firms, especially those in apparently nontechnological industries, have trouble attracting sufficiently skilled and talented IT staff. Such firms may perceive little choice other than outsourcing to meet their strategic and operational IT needs.

Other Factors: A major outsourcing deal provides an opportunity to liquidate the firm's intangible IT assets, strengthen the balance sheet, and avoid some future capital investments. A one-time cash payment to the client by the vendor in exchange for transfer of IT assets can be consequential; the $200 million General Dynamics received from CSC as part of an IT outsourcing deal arrived at an important time in the life of the former firm. Outsourcing can transform fixed-costs business into variable costs, as fees for vendor services replace large investments in IT equipment; such a change can be particularly important for clients that experience volatility in demand for their own products and services. A vendor relationship also brings new dynamics to a client firm's view of its own

IT expenditures, as soft dollar budget allocations for IT services are replaced by hard dollar expenditures; this can bring to IT decision making a discipline and tough-mindedness an internal IT department has trouble inspiring.

Designing Large-Scale Outsourcing Alliances

The potential for success of a big outsourcing deal lies with the structure of the arrangement between client and vendor. The right structure is not a guarantee of success, but the wrong structure will make the governance process almost impossible. Several factors are vital to a successful alliance.

Contract Flexibility: Evolving technology, changing economic conditions, and new service options make change inevitable during the life of an outsourcing relationship, for both client and vendor firms. Outsourcing contracts must therefore be written to allow evolution. Because contracts often need adjustments, noncontractual aspects of the relationship are also extremely important. If there is mutual interest in the relationship and if there are shared approaches to problem solving, the alliance is more likely to be successful. For these reasons, the process of drafting the contract, which often takes many months, is sometimes more important than the contract itself. During this time, each side gains insight into the other's values. When the process is successful, it forms a basis for personal relationships that go beyond the written contract.

Standards and Control: Reasonably enough, companies worry about handing control over a major part of a firm's operations to an outsourcing vendor, particularly if IT innovation is vital to the firm's success or if the firm is very dependent on IT for smooth operations. The outsourcing agreement must address these concerns. Control is, in part, a state of mind. Most organizations are accustomed to having other firms in control of parts of their businesses. For example, third parties normally provide electricity and telephone services, even though interruption of those services can cripple an organization. Explicit assurances a vendor can make about backup plans provide an important means of addressing concerns in such areas. As with incremental outsourcing, the key here is careful development of detailed performance standards for systems response time, availability of service, responsiveness to systems requests, and so on.

The Scope of Outsourcing: A company may choose to outsource large parts of its IT operations without outsourcing everything. In determining the scope of a major outsourcing arrangement, factors of connection and coordination enter into discussion. Can the portion of IT proposed for outsourcing be feasibly separated from the rest of the client firm's systems and infrastructure? Even if it can be, will coordination costs be manageable, or will the complexity of the arrangement offset potential gains?

Expected Cost Savings and Rate of Technology Renewal and Improvement: Though it might seem obvious, it is important that both parties to a major outsourcing deal agree on expected costs savings, the rate at which those will appear, and how they will be divided between the client and vendor. Similarly, expectations about rates of equipment replacement, new technology implementation, and systems renewal are best spelled out in the contract.

Putting together a decade-or-more long, flexible, evolving relationship requires more than just technical skill and contract wizardry. A shared approach to problem solving, similar values, and good personal chemistry among key staff people are the intangible determinants of long-term success. A wise client firm might give up something in price to engage an outsourcing partner that its managers believe will be a good fit over the long term. Personal chemistry among the dealmakers is an insufficient condition for success. Years after the people key to establishing the initial relationship have moved to other assignments, the outsourcing relationship will remain in place.

Managing the Alliance

The transition to a large-scale outsourcing relationship is a period of peak stress. Uncertainties about career paths and job security of staff contribute to the potential for problems. The sooner plans and processes for dealing with staff career issues, outplacement processes, and separation pay are addressed, the more effective the results will be. Fear of the unknown is almost invariably worse than any reality. Often, opportunities for IT staff will be greater at a vendor focused on IT than they were at the client company.

Once the relationship is in place, ongoing management of the alliance is the single most important factor in success. Three critical areas require close attention:

The CIO Function: The client firm must retain a strong, active CIO function. The heart of the CIO's job is planning—ensuring that IT resources are at the right level and are appropriately distributed. This role has always been distinctly separate from the active line management of networks, data centers, and systems management. Line activities can be outsourced, but sustained internal CIO responsibility for certain critical areas must be maintained even in a company that has fully outsourced its IT function. First and foremost, the CIO must manage the relationship with the vendor; monitoring performance against the contract and dealing with issues that arise helps an outsourcing alliance adapt to change. Second, the CIO and staff must retain certain planning responsibilities, for visualizing and coordinating the firm's long-term approach to networks, hardware and software standards, database architectures, and so on; the client can delegate execution in these areas but not its assessment of what it needs to support the firm in the long term. Third, the CIO and staff must maintain an ability to evaluate emerging technologies and their potential applications; assessing technology alternatives cannot be delegated to a third party because an outsourcing vendor has an incentive to suggest new ideas that lead to additional work and to downplay ideas that might lead to greater vendor costs.

Performance Measurement: Realistic measurement of outsourcing success is difficult, but companies must do their best to develop performance standards, measure results, and interpret them continuously. Many of the most important measures of success are intangible and play out over a long period of time. Early benefits—immediate reductions in capital expenditure or staff headcount reductions, for example—are easier to measure than eventual ones. This means that a firm should not stay satisfied too long with its current measures of outsourcing success, but should constantly look for more ways to probe for additional value from the relationship.

Relationship Interface: The importance of the sensitive interface between the client and the outsourcing vendor cannot be overestimated. First, outsourcing cannot imply delegation of final responsibility to the outsourcing vendor. The reality is that oversight cannot be entrusted to someone outside the firm, and as we have mentioned, a CIO and the supporting staff need to manage the agreement and relationships. Additionally, the interfaces between the customer and the outsourcing vendor are very complex and usually must occur at multiple levels. At the most senior levels there must be links to deal with major issues of policy and relationship restructuring, whereas at lower levels there must be mechanisms for identifying and handling more operational and tactical issues. For some firms, discussions with an outsourcing vendor happen at the CEO level and involve the board of directors.

Large-Scale Outsourcing: Here to Stay

During the last two decades, an entirely different way of managing overall IT capability has emerged, and it is likely here to stay. While outsourcing on such a scale is not for all companies, many successful organizations have made this leap. What primarily determines success or failure? Managing the relationship more as a strategic alliance and less as a contract.

Managing Legacies

Not too long ago, tax accountants at a major U.S. company discovered they were not taking full advantage of a benefit they could claim under the U.S. tax code. The tax law details of this story are unimportant, but the benefit was worth a substantial amount of money to the company, if the accountants could claim it. But to claim the tax benefit, the company needed to process receivables in a very specific way. The tax accounting managers, therefore, convened a large meeting of all the people in the company who might have something to say about a change in how receivables were processed.

The meeting was nearly two-thirds finished when a young junior employee, seated near the back of the room, interrupted the smooth flow of the meeting, to the mild irritation of the senior manager from tax accounting.

"Excuse me," the young man said. Everyone knew he was from the IT department. "Can you help me . . . do I understand . . . ?" the young man stuttered as the room's attention turned entirely to him. "What you are proposing? Is it . . . ?" He then summarized his understanding of the proposal.

"Yes," the senior tax accounting manager answered. "That is the proposal, although we are working it through in detail with everyone here to make sure no one sees any issues with the change."

The young man smiled. "I've got news for you," he said. All those in the room braced themselves, expecting an explanation in incomprehensible IT terms of why the change could never be made within the company's IT infrastructure, at least not at a reasonable cost. What he said instead surprised everyone:

"We've been processing our receivables that way for the last 20 years. That's the way the system does it. That's how the program logic works." The meeting was quickly adjourned as the tax accountants returned to their offices to see if they could figure out a way to apply for the benefit retroactively.

This story illustrates two very serious points. First and most obvious, company operations often are constrained by the way legacy systems process information. Old computer code often disturbingly manifests what have been called "core rigidities," the ossified remains of what were once capabilities.[6] Second, business managers often do not even know how their company performs certain vital business functions because the details are buried in how legacy systems operate. In this story, the managers' discovery about their company's operations was a happy one; more often, though, such discoveries are less welcome.

The difficulties that arise from legacy systems can be roughly categorized as follows:

Technology Problems: Sometimes the constraints embedded in legacy systems result from inherent incompatibilities in older technologies. As we have seen, proprietary technologies that predate the internetworking era were not designed to converse easily with technologies from other vendors. This kind of problem must be worked around in modern internetworking infrastructures.

Residual Process Complexity: Some difficulties with legacy systems arise because the systems address problems that no longer exist. One example is the substantial amount of batch processing some companies still perform. Legacy systems were designed to operate in batch mode because processing power needed to be rationed and because the bandwidth available at that time did not allow computers to operate in real time. Now computing power and bandwidth are relatively abundant, but many batch systems have not been redesigned or replaced because of other priorities.

Local Adaptation: Many legacy systems were developed for very focused business purposes within functional hierarchies. When such systems were designed, their architects had little inkling of the enterprise systems and real-time architectures of the then-distant future. Instead, systems were intended to solve a particularly narrow business problem. Not surprisingly, a system designed in the 1970s does not facilitate global uniform parts management in the twenty-first century, although it still may do its narrowly defined job very well.

Nonstandard Data Definitions: Throughout most companies, business units and divisions have used different conventions for important data elements. For example, the parts division might use a 15-character part number whereas the product development organization uses a 13-character part number. This may seem like a small difference (only two characters), but the legacy system implications are far-reaching. Differences in fundamental data definitions are built into a company's IT infrastructure in many specific places. They are difficult to change not only because they touch so many elements of the IT infrastructure but because making definitions common requires an expensive and difficult to achieve companywide consensus.

Because of the tremendous variety in legacy systems across companies, it is not possible to develop a prescriptive approach to dealing with legacy issues. Tactics for

[6] For a deeper discussion of core rigidities, see Dorothy A. Leonard, *Wellsprings of Knowledge: Building and Sustaining the Sources of Innovation* (Boston: Harvard Business School Press, 1998, paperback edition).

solving legacy problems must fit individual companies and their specific situations. However, there are questions managers should think through carefully before they contemplate growing infrastructure by adding new systems or services on top of existing systems.

Table 7.5 lists questions managers might ask about legacy systems that will have to interact with a new system or service. The first issue is whether legacy systems can, in any modified or enhanced form, perform consistently with real-time infrastructure objectives. If the answer is no, replacement may be the only option. Often, though, the answer is not definitively negative. Questions then focus on "work-arounds," contrivances needed to facilitate interaction between new and old infrastructure elements: whether they are sustainable and whether they represent reasonable cost/functionality trade-offs.

Many businesses have succeeded in adding interfaces to legacy systems that enable them to work with internetworking systems. This interfacing approach is sometimes called enterprise application integration (EAI). EAI practitioners recommend "noninvasive" interfaces that minimize changes to the internal operations of legacy systems. Even EAI enthusiasts, however, acknowledge limits to how well legacy systems can perform as components of real-time infrastructure. Sooner or later, getting work-arounds to operate satisfactorily becomes more difficult and more expensive than just replacing old systems. Infrastructure managers always must ask whether the complexity of workarounds is unreasonable.

When installing new infrastructure or acquiring new services, infrastructure managers also run up against organizational rather than technical legacies. Sometimes the rigidity of workers' attachment to how a legacy system works is more of an obstacle to change than the system itself or any technological factor. Moreover, changes in how systems work almost always force changes in how people work . Managers must decide the degree to which a new system implementation should force cultural and process changes. The second half of Table 7.5 suggests questions that managers should ask as they confront organizational legacies that interact with system legacies.

TABLE 7.5 Key Questions in Managing Legacies

Legacy systems	• How will new infrastructure exchange data with legacy systems? • Will new infrastructure obtain needed real-time interaction with legacy systems? • What work-arounds are necessary? Are they sustainable? • What is long-term strategy for renewing legacy systems?
Legacy organizations and cultures	• How will new infrastructure affect ways of working and communicating? Are anticipated changes acceptable? • Should technology drive organizational and cultural change? • Should organization and culture be protected from technology effects? • What are organizational expectations about common processes in different parts of the organization? • What are criteria for deciding whether systems or process will change when the two are not compatible?

Managing IT Infrastructure Assets

In the past, keeping track of the assets that made up a company's IT infrastructure was relatively easy. The majority consisted of a small number of large mainframe machines in the corporate data center. A company's investment in IT had a tangible presence. Senior business managers could point to it, even rap their knuckles against it if they wished. Because a company's infrastructure was centralized and because services were deployed from mainframe assets, companies found it relatively easy to track how systems were being used and estimate how much value they were providing.

Since the emergence of PCs, clients and servers, the Web, portable devices, and distributed network infrastructure, a company's investments in IT have become much more diffuse. Computing assets are increasingly scattered in a large number of small machines located in different buildings. Some (e.g., laptops) now move around with their users and leave the company's premises on a regular basis. Some new service delivery models cause assets (e.g., servers) to migrate back to the corporate data center, which might seem to herald a return to centralized management models. Other model variations, such as outsourced hosting, make it clear, though, that complex infrastructure and distributed IT assets are here to stay. As service delivery models proliferate and improve, the variety of IT asset configurations will increase.

The variety of asset configurations in modern IT infrastructures makes certain business questions hard to answer: How are IT investments deployed across business lines or units? How are IT assets being used? Are they being used efficiently? Are they deployed to maximum business advantage? How can we adjust their deployment to create more value? Although never easy to answer, these questions were at least reasonable when assets were centralized.

IT management frameworks over the past decade have focused on reclaiming management control over now largely decentralized IT assets. One approach to this problem has been called total cost of ownership (TCO) analysis. IT services are analyzed in terms of the costs and benefits associated with service delivery to each client device. For example, the total cost of delivering office productivity services to a PC desktop within an enterprise might be expressed as "$250 per desktop per month." Arriving at this number requires a detailed study to determine the total monthly costs associated with the delivery of each service available on that desktop, including costs shared with other desktops and costs not necessarily accounted for as line items in budgets or accounting systems. Once monthly costs are computed, they must be allocated on a per desktop basis. Totaling costs without missing any that are material is difficult, as is allocating costs to desktops in a way that preserves the management usefulness of the information.

Completing the analysis on the benefit side of the equation is also difficult but essential if IT assets are to be used efficiently. Many who attempt TCO analyses settle for usage information—what services are used and with what frequency—on the benefit side of the equation, rather than attempting to estimate the actual benefits to each user. Usage information on a per desktop, per month basis is more intuitively helpful compared with cost of service delivery on a per desktop, per month basis. Usage information also may be useful when computed on the basis of other platform types. For example, usage information on a per server basis might be useful in server-to-server comparisons, in planning for growth in server capacity, or in discovering opportunities for consolidating underused servers into a smaller number nearer their capacities.

Cost and benefit analysis for IT assets and platforms provides a basis for evaluating a company's current IT services against new service alternatives. Outsourcing vendors often are asked to bid on a per platform basis. These prices can be compared to study results to evaluate a company's options and identify incremental opportunities for service delivery improvement. Where a firm's costs of delivering an IT service are out of line with the price at which it can be acquired externally, outsourcing becomes comparatively appealing.

Summary

This chapter has explored the increasingly diverse nature of the infrastructure used to deliver IT services in twenty-first-century companies. We have described how more available and secure network connections are creating more service delivery options and how new options have led to the creation and restructuring of the service provider industry. Today, companies acquire services externally from chains of service providers and integrate those external services into their internal legacy infrastructures. The shift toward incremental outsourcing and multiple collaborating service delivery partners dictates a shift in management emphasis. The following questions should help a company assess the opportunities and the risks:

1. What services within our IT infrastructure are candidates for incremental outsourcing? Are there opportunities to convert large up-front IT investments into spread-over-time subscription services?
2. Are our service delivery partners technically and financially capable of supporting our evolving IT service needs? Do we have well-defined processes for partner selection to ensure that we will continue to have highly capable partners?
3. Do we have detailed service-level agreements in place with our service providers? Have we made sure that the SLAs in our service delivery chains interlock and that incentives are aligned up and down the chain? Do we have systems in place for virtually integrating with service delivery partners? Have we specified contract terms with service providers that preserve our options for incrementally improving our infrastructure?
4. If we are engaged in a large-scale outsourcing relationship, have we built the need to change the relationship over time into the contract? Do we have specific mechanisms in place to indicate when an adjustment to the contract might be called for?
5. Have we retained an internal CIO function to perform the IT planning and contract monitoring functions that cannot be delegated? Have we adequately funded and staffed this internal group?
6. What are our short-term and long-term strategies for dealing with legacy system issues? What systems should we replace, and when should we replace them?

Chapter 8

Managing IT Project Delivery

Many IT service delivery arrangements, whether they involve internally or externally provided services, begin with a project. But despite 40 years of accumulated experience in managing such projects, major disasters still occur. Consider the following examples:

A division of a major chemical company halts its SAP installation and takes a major write-off. Although the company had successfully implemented SAP before, this time an inexperienced project manager misjudges the amount of change that must be managed during the project. The company starts over with an experienced project manager and a change management consultant. Losses add up to millions of dollars.

A major credit card company underestimates processing requirements by a factor of ten as it moves its online credit card processing to a new service provider, and it discovers this mistake only as the system "goes live." One and one-half million accounts are at risk. Service levels plunge. The chief information officer (CIO) and one of his direct reports lose their jobs.

A manufacturing company consolidates activities from more than 50 plants, field offices, and order entry points into a national service center. Only after consolidation is well under way does the company realize that wait time to confirm orders averages 25 seconds. In the estimation of the firm's line managers, any wait longer than 2 seconds makes the system unusable.

Two major insurance companies attempt to install the same software package to solve an identical problem with their field sales forces. In one company, the new technology generates a 46 percent increase in sales from one year to the next. In the other, all the money is wasted; $600 million is written off with no benefit.

In this chapter we examine the sources of implementation risk and suggest strategies for managing IT project delivery.

This chapter is adapted from materials developed by Professor Robert D. Austin and Professor F. Warren McFarlan.

Managing Sources of Implementation Risk

Risk is an essential characteristic of projects that promise benefits. The idea of taking on higher risk for a higher return is basic to business thinking. All beneficial business activities undertake risk, and project management is no different. Sound project management requires minimizing risks that lead to benefits and avoiding unnecessary risks.

Project feasibility studies typically provide estimates of financial benefits, qualitative benefits, implementation costs, target milestone and completion dates, and staffing levels. Developers of estimates often provide voluminous supporting documentation. Only rarely, however, do they deal frankly with the risks of late delivery, cost overruns, or the possibility of outright failure to deliver a working system. This need not be the case. Discernible characteristics of projects can be translated into indicators of project risk that are every bit as tangible as project cost or duration.

Three important project dimensions influence *inherent* implementation risk:

1. **Project size**. The larger the project in terms of budget, staffing levels, duration, and number of departments affected, the greater the risk. Multimillion-dollar projects carry more risk than do $50,000 efforts and tend to affect the company more if the risk is realized. Project size across departments and companies is relative. A $1 million project in a department whose average undertaking costs $2 million to $3 million usually has lower implicit risk than does a $250,000 project in a department whose projects have never cost more than $50,000.
2. **Experience with the technology.** Project risk increases when the project team and organization are unfamiliar with the hardware, software, or other project technologies. New technology projects are intrinsically more risky than are projects that use familiar technologies. A project posing a slight risk for a large, leading-edge IT group may be highly risky for a smaller, less technically advanced group. By hiring consultants with expertise in those technologies, a company can potentially reduce the risk associated with unfamiliar technologies, but hiring experts is not a cure-all.
3. **Requirements volatility**. For some projects the nature of the task fully and clearly defines what is required of project outputs. From the project's beginning and throughout its duration, outputs remain fixed. Inherently stable requirements make these projects easier to manage. Other projects do not have such convenient characteristics; their requirements are difficult to determine and tend to evolve throughout the project.

Figure 8.1 shows how the project characteristics just identified influence project risk. If we consider large project size, high technology, and high requirements volatility to be risk factors, then each factor that we add increases the project risk. Moreover, as risk factors accumulate, the risk increases at an even greater pace. In other words, a project with two risk factors—say, large size and high requirements volatility—is more than twice as risky as a project with just one of those factors.

Of course, in reality, projects have degrees of size, technology, and requirements volatility, and they may not fit cleanly into categories defined as "high" or "low" (some may be "medium" or "medium high"). But even this simplistic view can be of great use for understanding relative implementation risk and for communicating that risk to senior executives. Having the ability to show senior executives that a project leans toward high technology or high requirements volatility, and that it is therefore more

FIGURE 8.1
Effect of Adding Risk Factors (Large Size, High Technology, High Requirements Volatility) on Project Risk

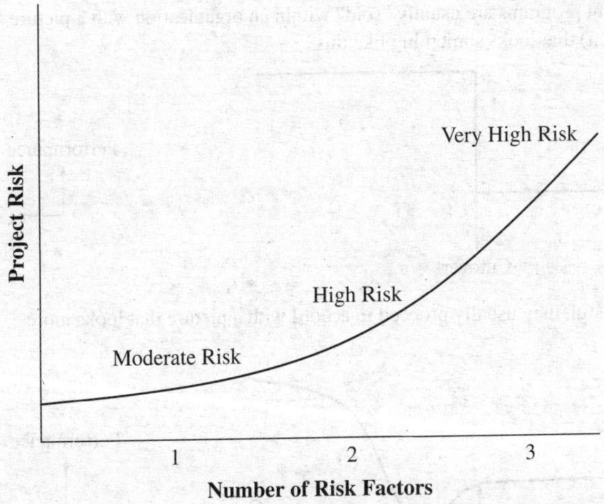

difficult to manage, is significant progress over the state of affairs in many companies. This kind of risk analysis helps ensure that all stakeholders have the same understanding of a project's inherent risks.

Managing the "Dip" during Project Implementation[1]

In most IT projects, there arrives a time when substantial difficulties materialize, even if managers and IT staff have planned and executed well. This most often happens at "cutover," when the new system goes live. Even some of the most successful implementations experience a feeling of everything going bad or everything suddenly being broken at cutover. When this occurs, business users and their managers can quickly lose confidence in the system and the IT staff. A crisis may ensue. How managers handle such a crisis is a major determinant of project success; thus, managing this "dip" in performance is an important part of managing project risk.

Figure 8.2 compares the expectations of business users about the performance impact of a new computer system with the way such impacts actually happen. Not surprisingly, business users and executives primarily think about new systems in terms of the improvement they will provide. Indeed, advocates of a new system may have engaged in a certain amount of "selling" of a project as they sought approval to go ahead with it. Frequently a project is sold on the basis of the pattern in Figure 8.2a, so people are surprised when it unfolds in a pattern more like that in Figure 8.2b.

Moreover, when a company arrives at that point in time corresponding to the downward slope of the dip, business managers see only the downward trend, which ends in disaster if it continues, not the eventual upturn. As we suggested with the examples at the beginning of this chapter, concerns that the dip might be deep or that it might end in disaster are far from misplaced. Many projects do go bad or become disasters, often at cutover. Business users may even feel betrayed. They were promised improvement but instead the new system

[1] Andrew McAfee has done important research on this phenomenon. See, for example, Andrew McAfee, "The Impact of Enterprise Technology Adoption on Operational Performance: An Empirical Investigation," *Production and Operations Management Journal* 11, no. 1 (Spring 2002).

FIGURE 8.2 What People Expect and What Often Happens at System Cutover

a. Major improvement programs are usually "sold" within an organization with a picture (sometimes implicit) that looks something like this:

b. Even when successful, they usually proceed in accord with a picture that looks more like this:

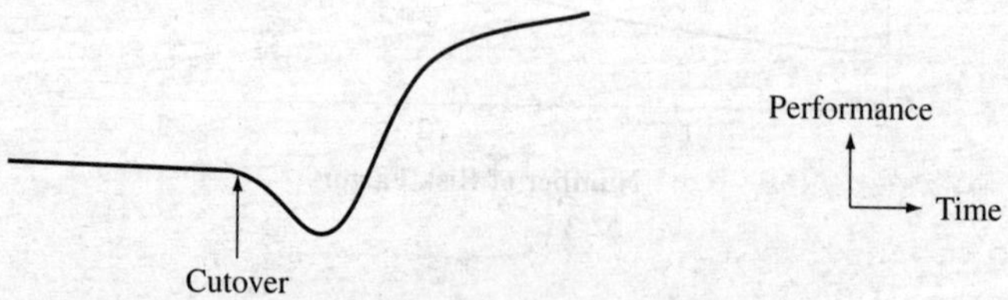

seems to have made their jobs harder. Nostalgia for the old system appears rapidly, and the new system gets compared to an ideal version of the old system, its shortcomings forgotten amid the trauma of cutover to a new system.

When faced with cutover difficulties, project managers must find a way to focus, despite a possibly overwhelming torrent of problems and complaints. Problems must be tackled one at a time, in order of importance. IT managers must work hard to educate senior business managers about the inevitability of the dip and the likelihood of upturn, and also to enlist business managers in helping to set priorities for solving problems. Everything may seem like an emergency in such situations, but it is crucial to differentiate between degrees of urgency, between bad problems and very bad problems, so the latter can be handled first. Business managers can also help during a cutover crisis if they are willing to intervene to protect the project team from unconstructive complaints, which are not uncommon when people are very frustrated. For example, if a business user sends an e-mail "rant" to everyone in a department or company, his or her manager might provide assistance by reminding the user to provide feedback in a professional manner.

Ideally, IT managers will work to communicate the likelihood of a performance dip before it occurs. If business managers expect a dip, they may be less prone to panic when it actually happens. But no amount of expectations management can fully prepare business users and their managers for the shock of sudden and severe difficulties that they may face at cutover. This point in a project often amounts to a moment of truth; managers can respond constructively or not. How well managers, both IT and business, perform during cutover crises is a factor that separates companies destined for successful major project implementations from those destined to descend into disaster.

Portfolio Risk

In addition to determining relative risk for single projects, a company should develop a profile of aggregate implementation risk for its portfolio of systems projects. Different portfolio risk profiles are appropriate to different companies and strategies.

For example, in an industry where IT is strategic, managers should be concerned if there are no high-risk projects in the project portfolio. Such a cautious stance may open a product or service gap through which the competition may seize advantage. A portfolio loaded with high-risk projects, however, suggests that the company may be vulnerable to operational disruptions if projects are not completed as planned. In companies where IT plays a critical support role, heavy investment in high-risk projects may not be appropriate; they should not be taking strategic gambles in the IT arena. Yet even these companies should have some technologically challenging ventures to ensure familiarity with leading-edge technology and maintain staff morale and interest.

These examples suggest that the aggregate implementation risk profiles of the portfolios of any two companies can legitimately differ. The risk profile should include projects executed by outside systems integrators as well as those of the internal systems development group. IT's aggregate impact on corporate strategy is an important determinant of the appropriate amount of implementation risk to undertake.

Figure 8.3 depicts a way of thinking about a portfolio of projects in terms of aggregate risk. Projects tend to cluster around the diagonal in this picture because, in business, high risk tends to be associated with the potential for high reward. But projects may be distributed differently along the diagonal; they could be spread out evenly, or they could be clumped at the upper left or lower right. How they should be distributed depends on the firm's business strategy. If a company includes "aggressive use of technology to maintain competitive advantage" in its strategy statements but has IT projects clumped at the bottom right in this picture, managers ought to contemplate whether this makes sense. If a company's managers do not expect new IT systems to contribute significantly to the firm's competitive strategy, projects clumped in the upper left corner should prompt a serious review.

In many companies, project portfolios drift out of alignment with business strategy. The most prominent reason: Projects are usually conceived and financially justified one at a time, not as a group. Formal financial criteria, such as return on investment, often favor derivative projects, which are similar to projects already completed and known to be valuable. Breakthrough projects do less well in formal project evaluation because their potential benefits are less certain and because they entail higher risk. In companies that rely heavily on formal approval processes, project portfolios may shift down and to the right over time. Periods of great technology enthusiasm, such as the late 1990s, produce the opposite problem: Project portfolios shift to the upper left, toward more risk than may be consistent with a company's business strategy. Obviously, it is important to avoid off-diagonal projects in the upper right in Figure 8.3, which provide little benefit but generate high risk. Poorly executed projects can all too easily take on this sort of profile.

Managing Project Execution

The trend in the last decade has been toward projects with more volatile requirements that challenge traditional tools for project management and entail high implementation risk. Business requirements for many enterprise systems are not well

FIGURE 8.3 Risk and Return Distribution for a Portfolio of Projects

Source: Adapted from Steven C. Wheelwright and Kim B. Clark, *Revolutionizing Product Development: Quantum Leaps in Speed, Efficiency and Quality* (New York: Free Press, 1992).

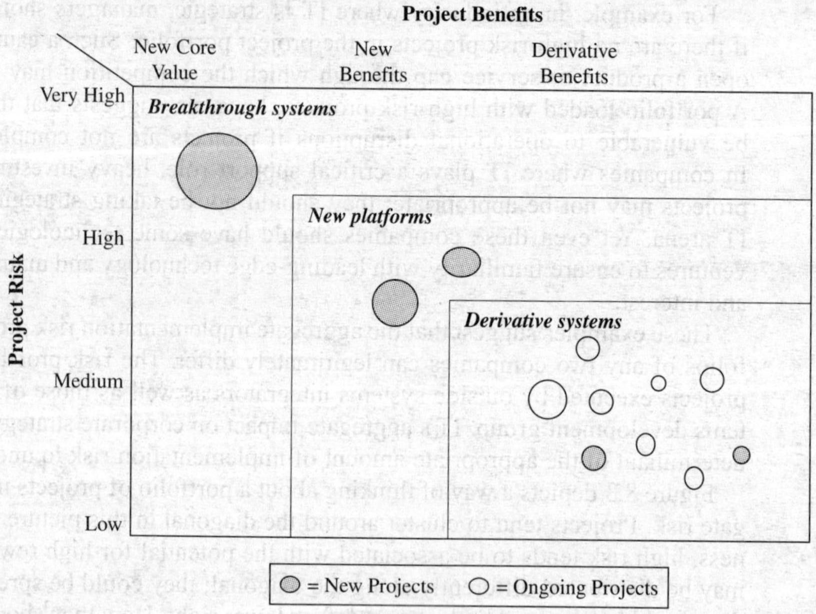

defined in advance and also involve new technologies. As investments, these systems have unattractive profiles. They require large investments, most of which must be spent up-front, to achieve uncertain (high implementation risk) benefits.

Traditional planning methodologies do not work well in the presence of so much outcome uncertainty. Project managers who are experts in project technologies and in communicating with the user can help mediate the risks. Increasingly, however, outcome uncertainty and difficulty in determining system requirements are leading to evolution in the project management process.

An emerging response to these conditions is adaptive methods approaches to design, deployment, implementation, and investment that assume a need to gather information and to learn as one goes. To be used successfully, adaptive methods require that project staff be able to experiment during a project without incurring prohibitively high costs. Although evolving prototyping technologies allow low-cost project experimentation, adaptive methods are not yet universally applicable. Let's consider these approaches to project execution in turn.

Development Methodologies

Traditionally, the activities necessary to design, implement, and operate information systems have been combined into "development methodologies."[2] A development

[2] It is worth noting that the list of responsibilities inherent in this methodology remains with the firm regardless of whether all or a portion of the system development process and IT operations/management is outsourced. The job of IT and business management is to ensure that those tasks are performed in the most effective and efficient manner regardless of where or by whom they are performed.

methodology represents IT projects in a sequence of phases. The names of the phases vary, but most are more or less consistent with the following:

Analysis and design. The traditional process begins with a comprehensive analysis of requirements, followed by documentation of the desired capabilities of the system in a form that can be used by system developers to code and implement the system. Either a user request or a joint IT department/user proposal, which includes a formal statement of costs and benefits, often initiates the process. IT professionals typically manage the design process. Today, business users and technology specialists—often supported by vendors and/or consultants—determine the requirements for developing a new system or adapting a software package or in-place system.

Construction. Once requirements, costs, and benefits are defined and specifications are developed, the system can be assembled. Traditionally, construction combined high levels of technological skill with a large dose of art and experience. Today, system construction more often involves selecting appropriate computer equipment and then creating, buying, and adapting the computer programs needed to meet system requirements. The final step is to test the system, both in the laboratory (often called alpha testing) and in the real-world user environment (often called beta testing). Intense coordination and control are required to ensure that the project remains on track, within budget, and focused on user requirements. Even the best designs require numerous interdependent decisions that must be made in real time as the system is being constructed. Large, often dispersed project teams must coordinate closely to ensure that the system components will work together. The decision to outsource portions of the project or the entire project markedly increases coordination and control costs; all technical decisions and tasks still must be managed, but now across firm boundaries.

Implementation. Implementing a new IT system involves extensive coordination between the user and the technologist as the transition is made from the predominantly technical, IT-driven task of construction to user-driven, ongoing management of the completed system. Whether the system is bought or made, the implementation phase is very much a joint effort. Extensive testing, which may disrupt normal business operations, must be performed; training is required; and work procedures and communication patterns may be disrupted. Often, achieving the benefits of the system is dependent on the ability of individuals and groups to learn to use information from the system to make better decisions and add value to the business. It is essential to shape the organization's operational and management structure, processes, and incentives to exploit the potential of an IT system. In this world of electronic commerce, the impact of the system often extends to groups and individuals outside the organization, which further complicates implementation.

Operation and maintenance. To avoid ongoing problems, system operation (after implementation) and maintenance (fixes and changes to the system after launch) are planned in advance, ideally during the early stages of requirements definition and design. Maintenance is complex, particularly for older systems. It requires highly competent professionals to perform the necessary changes safely and in a way that does not bring the system (and the firm) to a crashing halt.

Adaptive Methodologies[3]

Adaptive and prototyping-intensive methodologies call for quickly building a rough preliminary version of the system without going through a lengthy or formal requirement definition or design phase. Interacting with an early prototype makes the system easier to visualize for both users and developers. Thus, adaptive approaches quickly iterate through the traditional phases of design, construction, implementation, and operation, improving the performance of the product each time. Instead of moving slowly and deliberately through development phases, adaptive projects try to loop through each phase every week or even every day. Early prototypes are typically crude, but, throughout development, they are an excellent basis for discussions about system requirements between developers and users.

Companies that have implemented large enterprise systems successfully, such as Cisco and Tektronix, have tended to restructure projects to formally incorporate the ideas of in-progress learning and midcourse adjustment. Although adaptive projects are carried out in a variety of ways, they share five basic characteristics:

1. They are iterative. Design, construction, and implementation occur incrementally with each iteration so that more manageable tests can be carried out on outcomes and interactions as they appear.
2. They rely on fast cycles and require frequent delivery of value so that incremental implementation does not slow down a project. Long lead times and variable delivery timing are discouraged.
3. They emphasize early delivery to end users of functionality, however limited, so that feedback can be incorporated into learning and improvement cycles.
4. They require skilled project staff capable of learning and making midcourse adjustments in the middle of deployment.
5. They complicate the use of return on investment (ROI) and other similar tools for investment decision making that implicitly assume predictability of outcomes; instead they emphasize "buying of information" about outcomes as a legitimate expenditure.[4]

Although Cisco's managers did not explicitly identify their project management approach as "adaptive," they explicitly emphasized "rapid, iterative prototyping" as the basis for their approach. Tektronix divided its project into more than 20 "waves" that provided formal opportunities for deliberation, adjustment, and learning.

In recent years, adaptive methods have made significant inroads into the ways in which developers create systems and software. As more off-the-shelf system

[3] The materials on "adaptive methods" are based on work by Professor Austin. For a more thorough discussion of such approaches, see Robert D. Austin and Lee Devin, *Artful Making: What Managers Need to Know about How Artists Work* (Upper Saddle River, NJ: Financial Times, Prentice Hall, 2003).

[4] Robert D. Austin and Richard L. Nolan have suggested in the paper "Manage ERP Initiatives as New Ventures, Not IT Projects" (Harvard Business School Working Paper 99–024) that very large IT projects have risk profiles that resemble those of new ventures more than those of traditional IT projects. Venture investors cope with risky venture profiles by using a variety of adaptive techniques that legitimize the notion of buying information about the new venture. Large IT projects must adopt a similar approach that recognizes the impossibility of knowing everything in advance and the importance of in-progress learning.

components and more over-the-Net IT services become available, many firms are doing less and less software development internally. But even installing vendor software requires systems development. "Extreme programming" (or XP)[5] and "adaptive software development"[6] are examples of popular adaptive development approaches. Open-source software development, a technique that has produced widely used infrastructure components such as the Linux operating system and the Apache Web server, also has adaptive characteristics.[7]

Adaptive methods emphasize low-cost experimentation and rapid delivery of system prototypes. They deemphasize up-front planning intended to "get it right the first time." In essence, the adaptive approach is to create something that works roughly as quickly as possible, to begin to experience unexpected effects as soon as possible, and then, just as rapidly, to change and improve the system. Adaptive methods are designed to offset the inevitability of unexpected outcomes.

Adaptive Methods and Change Management

Adaptive methods do not aspire to finalize a design in a discrete early phase of a project; instead, they call for an acceptable design to emerge gradually during the development process. It would be a serious mistake, however, to conclude that change management is less important for adaptive projects.

Adaptive projects achieve change management in part by intensely involving users in evaluating the outcome of each development iteration and deciding on the next enhancement to be introduced into the system. Users are forced to confront, at every iteration, trade-offs between delay in obtaining useful results and implementation of their "great ideas." When the development process is an active collaboration between users and the IT staff, a natural discipline evolves to control unreasonable user requests.

But change management becomes important for adaptive projects in a different sense as well. Adaptive methods are an emerging response to outcome uncertainty in systems development. Rigorous change management is the corresponding response to the same kind of uncertainty when one changes existing systems vital to a company's operations. The approaches are two halves of a management system for balancing IT systems' agility with rigorous operational control.

The essence of sound change management is to strictly control the migration of system features from development, through testing, into production with a clear understanding of the benefits and the potential for unanticipated problems at each stage. Successful change managers introduce new system features into production infrastructure with high confidence in the changes. They know, at all times, exactly what is running in their production environment and are therefore better able to diagnose problems and respond to incidents quickly. Effective change management, in

[5] Kent Beck and Cynthia Andreas, *Extreme Programming Explained: Embrace Change* (2nd ed., Reading, MA: Addison-Wesley, 2004).

[6] James A. Highsmith III, *Adaptive Software Development: A Collaborative Approach to Managing Complex Systems* (New York: Dorset House, 1999).

[7] Eric S. Raymond, *Cathedral & the Bazaar: Musings on Linux & Open Source by an Accidental Revolutionary* (O'Reilly & Associates, 2001).

fact, makes adaptive development possible by insulating the production environment from the negative effects of adaptive experimentation. Adaptive methods make sense only when the experiments do not result in catastrophic consequences, and effective change management prevents such consequences.

Process Consistency and Agility in Project Management

In practice, project management always involves balancing a tension between process consistency and process agility. Project managers need to ensure a thorough and disciplined approach so that "no balls are dropped," all requirements are met adequately, and no important details go unnoticed. This usually is accomplished through formal specification of project steps, required documentation, and compliance mechanisms (such as reviews or progress reports). At the same time, however, companies need to retain an ability to change direction, in the middle of a project if necessary, when business conditions require it. The tension between process consistency and process agility arises from the fact that the tools used to improve consistency—specifications, documentation, compliance mechanisms—often are perceived as encumbrances that work against project responsiveness and agility. A firm that is well practiced and expert in its established routines may have trouble changing them. A firm that has grown accustomed to using certain tools may continue to try to use them in business conditions in which they are less appropriate.

In the last decade, many companies have struggled with this issue, including many technology companies for which responsiveness to market and time to market were overriding concerns. For the most part, these companies resisted full-fledged adoption of traditional project methodologies because they perceived that adoption as too damaging to project agility. In place of traditional project management methodologies, many companies have attempted to develop "light" methodologies that contain the essential elements of "heavy" methodologies but are not as cumbersome.

The companies that have been most successful in balancing discipline and agility have neither eschewed process formalization altogether nor let process formalization efforts overwhelm them. Rather, they have developed simple process management tools based on the idea that the best balance is one that includes the minimum formal specification critical to the success of a project. These simple tools fall into three categories:

Flow. People working on projects need to understand the relationships between their activities and those of others. That is, they need to understand the overall process "flow." Process tools in this category can be simple depictions of the process context that are intended to give decision makers, at specific points in the process, a sense of the overall business picture. Deep detail is not required or recommended. Simple schedules and flowcharts work well here.

Completeness. People working on projects need to be sure that everything is being done, that no ball is being dropped. This is where mastery of the essential details comes into the picture. Tools in this category can be simple lists to convey what needs to be done, when it needs to be done, by whom, and whether it is complete. Simple checklists work well here.

Visibility. People working on projects need to be able to review processes, while they are being executed, to get status information. Ideally anyone, whether from the engineering department, the marketing department, or elsewhere, can review the same "picture" and come away with the information he or she needs. Visibility is not easy to achieve. Computerized status-reporting systems can provide this kind of visibility, but some of the best solutions are simple wall charts that allow status to be tracked in a way that everyone (in one physical location, anyway) can see.

In some contexts, another category of tools must be added: tools to ensure that project activities are auditable. This may be true of projects that will result in government systems or safety-related systems.

Managing the tension between consistency and agility is, for most companies, a general process issue that extends well beyond project management. Process frameworks from earlier times, when systems were proprietary and the common Internet platform was not available for commerce, significantly encumber many firms. As these companies work to make the transition to new ways of doing business, they face the difficult task of distilling processes down to essential elements to reclaim lost project and organizational agility.

Summary

This chapter focused on key issues associated with IT project delivery. All IT projects entail both benefits and risks. Firms can better manage IT project implementation risk by assessing a project on three critical dimensions—project size; experience with the chosen technologies; and volatility of project requirements—and then adopting control processes suitable for the level of risk identified. Moreover, the use of new development techniques and management approaches can reduce the risks associated with those critical project dimensions. In addition, firms should recognize the risk that accrues from their overall project portfolio and choose a mix of projects that is aligned with the role of IT in their organizations.

Executives can use the following questions to assess whether they are managing the risks inherent in IT projects to maximize gain:

1. Have we established suitable criteria and procedures for evaluating the risk of IT projects? Are these criteria and procedures effective in communicating this risk to management?
2. Do we have project planning, tracking, and control processes that accommodate different degrees of project risk?
3. Are we using adaptive approaches appropriately for projects that entail high requirements volatility or other sources of uncertainty? Do we have processes in place that will allow us to learn and adjust during the duration of a project?
4. Is the overall risk of our project portfolio a good fit with our business objectives and strategies?

CareGroup

CareGroup examines the causes and consequences of a three-day network outage at Beth Israel Deaconess Medical Center, one of the world's top hospitals and an acclaimed leader in the use of IT in the health care industry. The company's experiences demonstrate how vital IT has become in modern organizations. Difficulties arose because of a series of incremental changes to the institution's computing infrastructure, none of them individually harmful, each a reasonable change to fix a pressing problem; the accumulated changes, however, led to a serious collapse. The case prompts discussion of the challenges that derive from infrastructure complexity and the importance of strong IT leadership in a crisis. As you read the case, consider these questions: What caused the outage at CareGroup? How well did the company handle the crisis? What should CareGroup's IT managers do differently in the future? Are the 10 lessons that CIO John Halamka learned from this situation the right ones?

Cases 2-1

CareGroup

"The good news," reported John Halamka, CareGroup CIO, as he opened his November 21, 2002, presentation to the board of directors, "is that health care did not suffer." Over the next 20 minutes, Halamka recounted a remarkable tale that explained why CareGroup information technology (IT) systems had completely collapsed for three-and-a-half days the previous week, the steps staff members and vendors had taken to recover, and how the hospital had reverted to paper-based systems, many of which had not been used for a decade or more. Though his story contained challenges and travails, in the end the paper-based systems and recovery efforts had worked well. Care to some patients had been delayed, but not a single adverse event related to the outage had been reported. Even so, there were numerous lessons learned and some line items to be added to the IT budget; Halamka now outlined these for the board.

Professors F. Warren McFarlan and Robert D. Austin prepared this case as the basis for class discussion rather than to illustrate effective or ineffective management.

CareGroup

CareGroup was a team of health care professionals dedicated to providing the best quality care to patients in a highly personalized manner. CareGroup and its members offered a broad spectrum of health services to residents of eastern Massachusetts in a variety of settings, ranging from world-renowned academic health centers and outstanding community hospitals to physician offices and community health centers. CareGroup hospital members included Beth Israel Deaconess Medical Center in Boston, Mount Auburn Hospital in Cambridge, New England Baptist Hospital (NEBH) in Boston, Deaconess-Glover Hospital in Needham, and Deaconess-Nashoba Hospital in Ayer. With more than 13,000 employees and 2,000 medical staff, CareGroup offered community-based primary care and a wide range of specialty services close to where individuals lived or worked.

CareGroup had been formed in a three-way merger on October 1, 1996. The Beth Israel Hospital, the Deaconess Hospital, and the Mount Auburn Hospital came together on that day. The Beth Israel and Deaconess Hospitals, which were physically adjacent, merged into a single hospital; every department was merged and headed by one individual (e.g., the two surgical units were merged and a head of surgery appointed). The Mount Auburn Hospital, located in Cambridge, reported to CareGroup management as a separate entity, as did four other hospitals that had formerly been a part of the Pathway Network, assembled over the previous decade by the Deaconess Hospital. (See Exhibit 1 for the organizational chart of CareGroup and Exhibit 2 for descriptions of the different hospitals.)

This merger produced a hospital group with \$1.6 billion in revenue, the second-largest group of hospitals in eastern Massachusetts. The merger was driven by the intense competitive environment in the mid-1990s. On December 13, 1994, the Massachusetts medical community was stunned to discover that the two largest and most prestigious hospitals in Boston, Massachusetts General Hospital and the Brigham and Women's Hospital, had agreed to merge in a holding-company structure called Partners. The perceived pressure that this large organization was going to be able to put on health maintenance organizations (HMOs, which stood between individual patients and employees and the hospitals and doctors) led many hospitals to conclude they had subcritical mass in terms of their number of "covered lives"; in this new world, you would need a critical mass to get survival prices from the HMOs (the more covered lives you had, the more the HMOs needed you). The hospitals felt they needed bulked-up negotiating power to push back against the HMOs, which themselves were under great financial pressure from companies in the region such as FleetBank and Raytheon that were trying to drive down their medical costs. Specifically, the factors that brought CareGroup together were:

1. The contracting power needed by the hospitals against the HMOs.
2. The possibility of developing integrated services across the hospitals that could improve quality of care and drive down costs.
3. The need for a strong balance sheet in a complex price war, in which there were more than 40 percent excess hospital beds in the region. Because of this excess supply, some hospitals were closing their doors.

EXHIBIT 1 CareGroup Organizational Chart, January 1, 2003

Source: CareGroup internal documents.

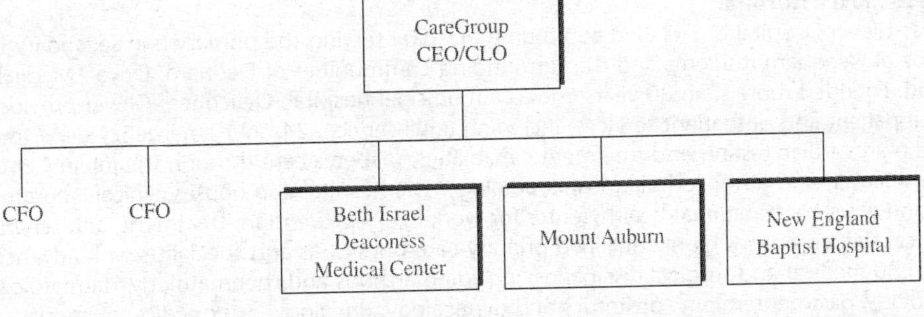

By December 31, 2002, Deaconess-Waltham Hospital and Deaconess-Nashoba Hospital were no longer part of CareGroup, and Nashoba-Glover Hospital reported to the Beth Israel Deaconess Medical Center.

EXHIBIT 2 Major CareGroup Medical Facilities

Source: CareGroup Internal documents.

Beth Israel Deaconess Medical Center

Beth Israel Deaconess Medical Center is a Harvard-affiliated, research-intensive teaching hospital located in Boston's Longwood Medical Area. Serving as the principal academic and clinical resource of CareGroup, Beth Israel Deaconess Medical Center is home to several nationally recognized clinical centers of specialized expertise, including solid-organ transplantation, diabetes/vascular surgery, obstetrics, cardiology and cardiac surgery, gastroenterology, trauma, cancer (with a particular interest in breast cancer), and AIDS. Complementary, state-of-the-art inpatient and outpatient facilities, in addition to two regional outpatient centers, primary-care offices in more than 30 communities, and transitional and palliative care units, enhance the broad array of clinical services available.

Mount Auburn Hospital

Mount Auburn Hospital in Cambridge is an acute-care, Harvard-affiliated community teaching hospital, serving the health-care needs of residents in Arlington, Belmont, Cambridge, Lexington, Medford, Somerville, Watertown, and Waltham. The hospital offers comprehensive inpatient and outpatient medical, surgical, obstetrical, and psychiatric services and is a leading provider of advanced, specialized care in cardiology, cardiac surgery, oncology, orthopedics, neurology, and vascular surgery. In addition, Mount Auburn Hospital offers an extensive network of satellite primary-care practices in seven communities, as well as a broad range of community-based programs including Mount Auburn Home Care, outpatient specialty services, and occupational health. The hospital's Prevention and Recovery Center is a provider of education, intervention, and support programs for public health issues such as substance abuse and violence. The Mount Auburn Center for Problem Gambling is the first such outpatient clinic in the state.

New England Baptist Hospital

Established in 1893, New England Baptist Hospital is a 150-bed adult medical/surgical hospital located in the Mission Hill neighborhood of Boston, with specialty services in musculoskeletal care, sports medicine, occupational medicine, and cardiology.

New England Baptist Hospital ranks among the nation's foremost providers of hip- and knee-replacement surgery. To solidify its commitment to musculoskeletal care, the hospital, in 1995, formed the New England Baptist Bone & Joint Institute. The institute is the region's leading resource for a full range of prevention and education, diagnostic, treatment, and rehabilitation services in orthopedics and rheumatology, joint replacement, spine care, foot and ankle care, hand surgery, occupational medicine, and sports medicine. The hospital has a 40-bed skilled nursing unit specializing in rehabilitative care for the orthopedic patient, in addition to post-surgical medical patients. NEBH is the sports medicine hospital of the Boston Celtics.

Deaconess-Glover Hospital

Deaconess-Glover Hospital is a 41-bed community hospital serving the primary and secondary health care needs of Needham residents and the surrounding communities of Dedham, Dover, Medfield, and Westwood. Founded more than 80 years ago as a municipal hospital, Deaconess-Glover provides a wide range of inpatient and outpatient services, including a full-service, 24-hour emergency department, state-of-the-art cardiac testing and treatment capabilities, diabetes care through the Joplin Center at Deaconess-Glover, and advanced diagnostic radiology. The hospital also houses clinical laboratory facilities and a new occupational health center for work-injury prevention, treatment, and rehabilitation. The medical staff comprises highly qualified primary-care physicians and specialists with advanced training in 30 medical and surgical disciplines, including arthritis and rheumatology, dermatology, endocrinology, gastroenterology, obstetrics and gynecology, oncology, orthopedics, pulmonary medicine, and urology, as well as plastic, thoracic, and vascular surgery.

EXHIBIT 2 Major CareGroup Medical Facilities (*Continued*)

Deaconess-Nashoba Hospital (spun off December 31, 2002)
Deaconess-Nashoba Hospital is a 41-bed community hospital serving 11 communities in north central Massachusetts. Located in Ayer, the hospital boasts a highly qualified medical staff with 122 active and associate member physicians offering community-based primary care and a wide range of specialty services. Founded in 1964, Deaconess-Nashoba has many clinical strengths, including emergency medicine, cardiology, gastroenterology, oncology, orthopedics, and surgery. The hospital also offers a diverse array of outpatient services in its ambulatory care center, including a Joslin Diabetes Center. Other hospital facilities include a 123-bed nursing and rehabilitation center and a medical office building. The hospital also offers an on-site occupational health center, which focuses on prevention of work-related injuries and illnesses, rehabilitation, and management of return-to-work issues.

Over the next seven years, under the leadership of two CEOs, CareGroup sought to deal with these issues. A brief summary of progress would include the following observations:

1. It was a time of extraordinary financial pressure for CareGroup. First the Mount Auburn Hospital, which had been profitable for over 15 years, suddenly produced a $10 million loss and had to reengineer its operations. Just as it recovered, Beth Israel Deaconess began losing significant amounts of money. Not until mid-2002, under the leadership of a new CEO, Paul Levy, did it begin to recover. At about that same time, the Baptist Hospital suddenly incurred a $20 million loss, which led to the appointment of new management there. By early 2003, these problems were largely behind CareGroup. Each hospital in the group was headed by a different CEO than at the time of the merger, and financial stability issues were fading into the past.
2. Operational coordination across the hospitals had turned out to be extremely difficult because of their history of independence. Financial synergy in terms of lower debt costs, however, had been a strong feature. Similarly, joint contracting with the HMOs had been very successful.
3. An unexpected glittering success was the development of an integrated technology system that linked the entire group together. The system was widely touted, nationally; it was considered not only the best in health care but also one of the very best in any industry.

In 2003 CareGroup senior management consisted of a CEO/chief legal officer, a CFO, and a CIO. In the past several years, one of the subsidiary hospitals, Waltham Hospital, had run into difficulty, and the CareGroup Board had begun the process of closing it down. This led to a real estate specialist stepping in and, in return for a third of the hospital's land, providing Waltham with additional funding that allowed it to emerge as a stand-alone organization with strong community support.

On December 31, 2002, Deaconess-Nashoba Hospital was spun off to Essent, a for-profit organization that committed significant funds to a massive renovation of the hospital over the next two years (which CareGroup's capital structure did not permit). Finally, Deaconess-Glover Hospital was reorganized as a part of the Beth Israel Deaconess Medical Center because of its strong referral pattern there. All three of these hospitals continued to get all their IT support through CareGroup's IT organization, which had become a *de facto* outsourcing vendor for the hospitals no longer part of CareGroup; they were in very capable hands.

On November 1, 1998, Halamka became CIO of CareGroup as it was systematically working through a $41 million project to deal with the Y2K problem. At the time, the IT organization had 380 staff members and annual expenditures in excess of $50 million. Halamka brought an extraordinary background to the task. As an undergraduate at Stanford University majoring in computers and economics, he had founded a software company in his dorm room at age 18. After Stanford, he enrolled simultaneously at UCSF Medical School and Berkeley Engineering School, where he completed a combined mechanical/electrical engineering and medical school program. At residency time, he sold his software company, which had by then grown to 35 people, and became an emergency medicine specialist in Los Angeles. In his spare time, he authored several books on computing subjects and wrote a hypertext system to coordinate all clinical information in the county hospital in Los Angeles. In 1996, he moved to Harvard to practice emergency medicine at the Beth Israel Deaconess Medical Center and undertook postdoctoral work at the Massachusetts Institute of Technology in medical informatics. He also headed a group of 50 data analysts and Web specialists developing Web applications for CareGroup.

Halamka, in 2000, assumed the additional role of CIO of the Harvard Medical School. (Mount Auburn and Beth Israel/Deaconess were both Harvard teaching hospitals.) In talking about his background, Halamka observed:

> The reason why I've been successful is because I know all the technologies, I program in 12 languages, and I've written books on Unix system administration. I'm a doctor, so I understand the clinical domain and the technical requirements. But as I tell people, my own blind spot—I've wired a telephone closet, I've built 100 servers, hundreds of desktops, but never built anything beyond a home network. It's just the reality. But, I have now.

CareGroup IT

The IT organization that Halamka took over in October of 1998 was a decentralized, nonstandardized operation. Each of the hospitals ran its own homegrown legacy systems that predated the merger. At the Beth Israel Deaconess Medical Center, computer operations were complicated by having to run a mishmash of the systems from each of the merged hospitals. In addition to internal IT staff, CareGroup employed 78 consultants. Deaconess-Nashoba had an antiquated lab system with hand-typed results (IBM Selectric), no e-mail, and few PCs. Deaconess-Glover had a pathology system hosted at Neponset Valley with no electronic outputs and financials hosted by a third-party vendor that would fail during each thunderstorm. Deaconess-Waltham had a 10-year-old homegrown system with nonintegrated lab and radiology systems. NEBH had $500,000 per year outside consultants, a problematic lab system, a self-developed payroll system, a failed operating room system installation, and a limited network incapable of remote access. Mount Auburn Hospital, the most sophisticated of the nonmedical center hospitals, was running on its own homegrown system built around the Meditech package.

By 2002, all of these hospitals had been brought together on a common system with the Meditech software at the center. All had state-of-the-art e-mail, networking, PCs, and clinical/financial information systems at costs similar or reduced from those at the time Halamka took over. For example, NEBH's IT budget dropped $135,000 in fiscal year 2002, and it was expected to drop another $400,000 in fiscal year 2003. By 2003, CareGroup believed it had the most advanced network in health care, the most advanced e-mail system in health care, the most advanced voice/wireless system in health care, the most advanced data center in health care, and the most advanced Web infrastructure in health care. It served 3,000 physicians, processed 40 terabytes of data per day, and handled 900,000 patient records dating back to 1977, all supported by a staff of 200.

All applications were Web-enabled. In late 2002, the case author, using Halamka's password, was able to access all of his own personal health records, X-rays, and records of office visits for the past decade on a PC five miles away from the hospital where he had received those services (and was delighted to find that they were accurate). The IT organization ran a complete "lights-out" data center with three backup generators and had not suffered a data center power outage in three years. In the first quarter of 2003, the final IBM mainframe was scheduled to be decommissioned, and the network would be exclusively built around clustered Unix/Linux servers. Storage was 100% EMC (with no local server-based storage). Paired central processing units (CPUs) for development, testing, and production assured that new software performed well by the time it was in use.

Hewlett-Packard was the primary supplier of the Unix boxes, and Compaq (now HP) was the primary supplier of Wintel boxes; Dell supplied machines for Linux clusters. Following a McKinsey study at Harvard, IBM came in with a bid that undercut Dell prices for PCs by 50 percent. As a result, over a five-year period, all desktops (including at CareGroup, because it included Harvard teaching hospitals) were being replaced by IBM PCs. The data center housed tape-backup systems that did incremental backups on the 40 terabytes of daily data, transferring them onto three-gigabyte tapes. Every night those tapes were taken to an Iron Mountain storage facility that had once been a missile silo. PeopleSoft software handled HR, payroll, accounts payable, and the general ledger. Physicians were provided free e-mail accounts, and they had begun experimenting with wireless messaging devices. As of the first quarter of 2003, all networks became IP based; Novell IPX would be replaced by year-end 2002, and AppleTalk would be gone by the end of the following quarter.

In 2002, there were two events that were not considered major when they happened but that took on significance in retrospect. First, at Halamka's request, Cisco conducted a study of the CareGroup overall network in the summer, delivering its final report, complete with detailed recommendations for modernizing the network, in October; the results of the study were being analyzed in November, but nothing in it suggested imminent peril. Second, CareGroup's networking guru, who had long provided the last word on anything to do with the overall network, left his position in CareGroup IT to pursue another opportunity; although a replacement was being sought, no immediate impact was apparent as a result of his departure.

CareGroup had cut capital budget expenditures by 90 percent in the three years prior to 2003 (see Exhibit 3). The Meditech installations in the various hospitals were done without consultants in half the usual time, at 20 percent of the cost. (Exhibit 4 shows CareGroup's operating expenses vis-à-vis Partners and Gartner standards. Exhibit 5 shows the IT operating costs for the various hospitals.) In September 2001, the CareGroup IT organization was ranked number one in America by *Information Week,* and it had been in the *Information Week* top 100 companies for the last three years. By November 2002, CareGroup's IT systems and services were widely viewed as critical to building clinical loyalty, and they were believed to provide the best knowledge management service in the United States. All of this was exhilarating and exciting, BUT . . .

November 13, 2002

In the days leading up to November 13, 2002, a researcher on the CareGroup network had begun experimenting with a knowledge management application based on file sharing, a sort of "Napster for health care." The software was

EXHIBIT 3 CareGroup IT Operating and Capital Expenses, FY1998–FY2001

Source: CareGroup internal documents.

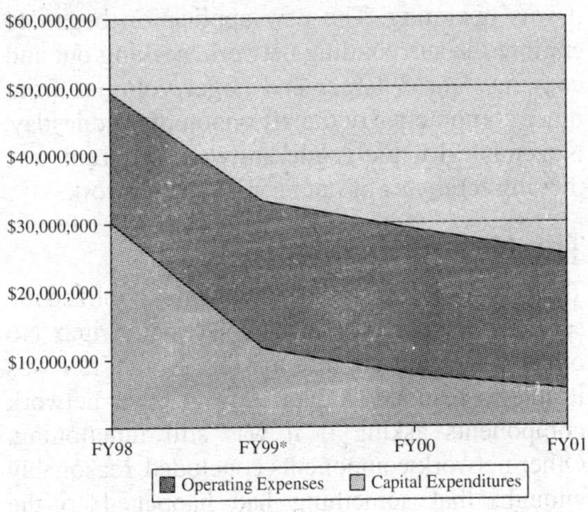

EXHIBIT 4 Benchmark Comparisons, FY2001

Source: CareGroup Internal documents.

IT Operating Expenses as a Percentage of Organization Revenues	
CareGroup	1.9%
Partners	2.3%
Gartner benchmarks for 1B IDNs[a]	2.7%
Range for 2nd/3rd quintiles—1.9%–2.9%	
IT as a Percentage of Total Hospital Capital Expenditures	
CareGroup	10.0%
Partners	25.0%
Gartner benchmarks for 1B IDNs	21.0%
Range for 2nd/3rd quintiles—10%–6%	

[a]IDN = Integrated Delivery Network.

EXHIBIT 5 Community Hospital IT Budgets (% of revenues)

Source: CareGroup internal documents.

	FY2001	FY2002
Mt. Auburn	0.7%	.8%
NEBH	1.6%	1.5%
Waltham	1.8%	1.9%
Nashoba	1.2%	1.3%
Glover	1.0%	1.1%
All CareGroup, including BIDMC/PSN	1.9%	1.9%[a]

[a]Adjusted for PSN and capital reallocations in FY2002.

designed to locate and copy information across the network automatically. No sooner had this researcher set up the software in its original configuration than he received a call from his wife telling him she was in labor. He departed hurriedly for a three-week paternity leave. The new software was left running in a basic mode, not yet tested or tuned for the environment in which it was operating. The new application began to explore the surrounding network, seeking out and copying data in larger and larger volumes from other computers. By the afternoon of Wednesday, November 13, the rogue software program was moving terabytes of data across the network.

The Network Collapse

These huge data transfers quickly monopolized the services of a centrally located network switch. No other data could get through this switch, nor was it able to respond to queries from other network components asking if it was still functioning. Other network components concluded, reasonably enough, that something had happened to the monopolized switch, that it had ceased to function as a reliable part of the network. Other network components then began to compute alternative paths for data flow through the network, paths that did not traverse the troubled switch.

Fortunately, the network was physically redundant throughout (see Exhibit 6); there *were* alternative paths along which data could flow. Network components had a built-in ability to recompute data paths in the event of failures. Theoretically, any computer on the CareGroup network could still communicate with any other computer, even though a major switch was no longer available.

Unfortunately, the evolved complexity of the overall network—the way individual smaller networks had been added one at a time, none of them resulting in issues when they were added—had created a hidden problem that kicked in with a vengeance now that the network had lost the services of a major switch. As network components tried to calculate new paths along which data would flow, as they decided which redundant network components would now act as primaries and which would act as backups, they became confused. Because the many smaller networks had been "glued" together over time, the network had gradually crept "out of spec"; algorithms for computing alternative data paths could no longer operate correctly.

EXHIBIT 6 The Existing Network at the Time of the Outage (loss of the east campus switch labeled ly030 triggered the event)

Source: "CareGroup Network Outage," presentation by John D. Halamka, M D, November 25, 2002.

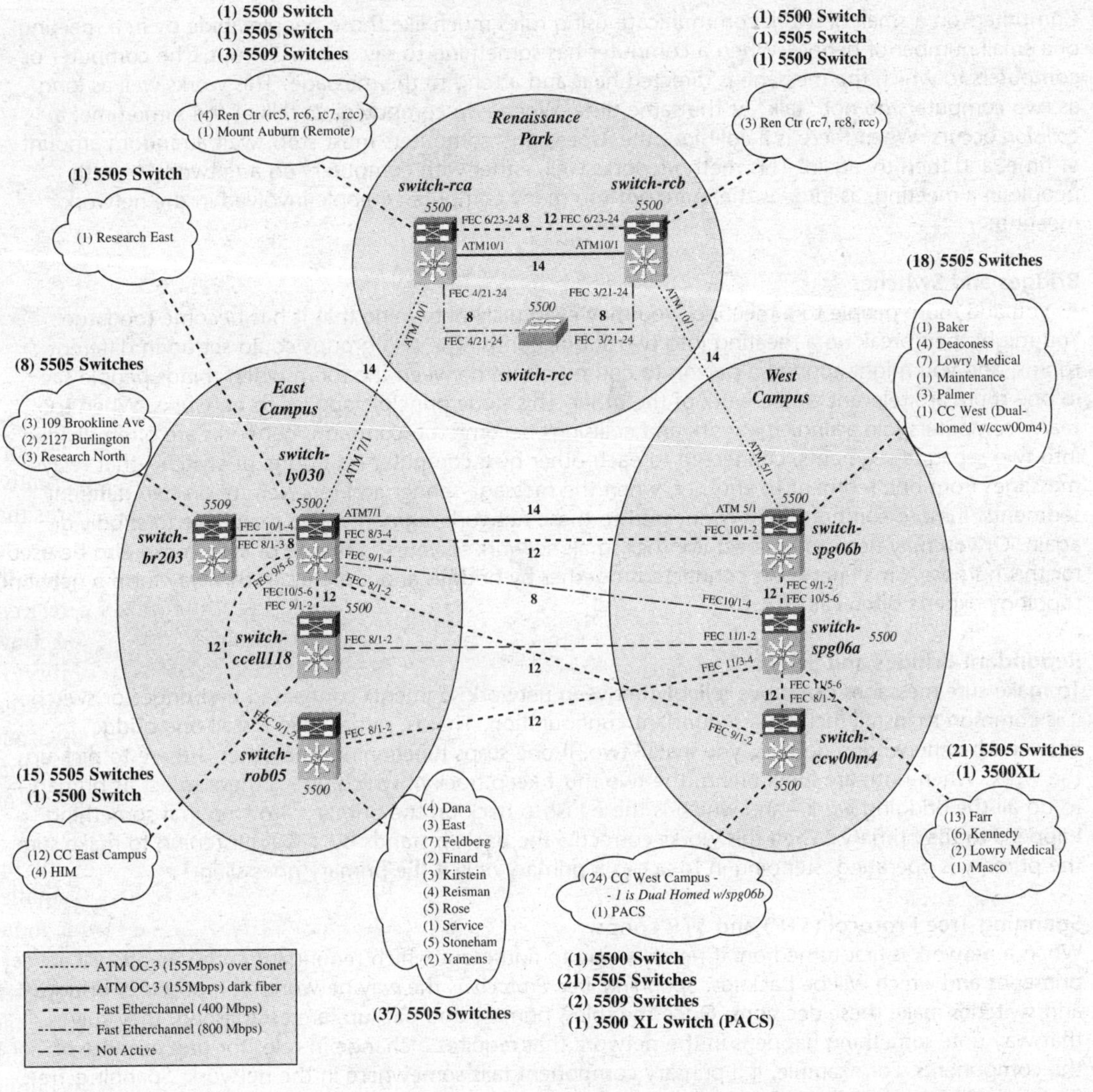

Redundant components intended to operate in tandem, one as primary and the other as backup, began to operate at cross purposes, both becoming primary. They began to duplicate each other's functionality. Each relayed the other's messages; one switch would relay a single message to the other; then that switch would relay the same message back to the first, which would then relay it to the second again. All messages on the network began repeating in this way, reproducing rapidly in an endless loop until the network was totally disabled. (See Exhibit 7 for a more detailed account of this problem and Exhibit 8 for a graphic of network traffic levels during the outage.)

EXHIBIT 7 **Simplified Description of the Problem That Caused the Network Outage**

Source: Based on interviews with John Halamka and CareGroup documents, including http://home.caregroup.org/templatesnew/departments/BID/network_outage/.

The Ethernet Protocol

Computers on a small network communicate using rules much like those people abide by in a meeting of a small number of people. When a computer has something to say, it blurts it out. The computer or computers to which the message is directed hear and attend to the message. This works well as long as two computers do not "talk" at the same time. When two computers *do* talk at the same time, a *collision* occurs. When there is a collision, the "speaking" computers must stop, wait a random amount of time, and then try again. This method works well, either with computers on a network, or with people in a meeting, as long as there are not too many computers/people involved in the network/meeting.

Bridges and Switches

As you add more people to a meeting, you may eventually determine that it has become too large. You might then break up a meeting into two submeetings. The two groups could set up in different rooms, and you might appoint a person to communicate between the room when things people say in one room are relevant to the work of the other. This same principle applies to networks. When too many computers join a single network and collisions become too common, networks are often divided into two separate segments, connected to each other by a computer—a bridge or switch—that relays messages from one segment to another, when the message sender and receiver are on two different segments. If more computers are connected to these network segments, you may have to subdivide again. Or you may need to connect another small network to yours; a bridge or switch can also be used for this purpose. Small networks connected together by bridges and switches in this way form a network topology experts often call "flat."

Redundant Bridges and Switches

To make sure messages can move reliably between network segments connected by bridges or switches, it is common to install them in a redundant configuration. That is, rather than install one bridge between two network segments, you install two. If one stops functioning, the other is there to pick up the work. When both are functioning, the two must keep track of which one is there to act as primary—to do all the bridging work—and which is there just to back up the primary—to step in if something happens to the primary. When this works correctly, the backup stands by, always listening to make sure the primary is operating, stepping in to act as a primary only if the primary goes silent.

Spanning Tree Protocol (STP) and STP Loops

When a network is first turned on, it needs a way to figure out which redundant components will act as primaries and which will be backups. *Spanning Tree Protocol* is the way networks composed of bridges and switches make these decisions. Once the roles, primary and backup, are established, they stay that way until something happens in the network that requires a change in roles for one or more of the components. For example, if a primary component fails somewhere in the network, Spanning Tree Protocol will once again kick in to decide roles for network components. Components communicate to decide their roles using special network messages. These messages have, within them, counters that keep track of how many "hops" they have made—how many network segments they have traversed. In Spanning Tree Protocol, if this counter exceeds seven (7), the special network message is dropped (ignored). What this means, in effect, is this: When the number of network segments connected together by bridges or switches exceeds seven (7), the network can have trouble resolving primary and backup roles properly. Rather than primary and backup pairs, you may end up with two redundant components operating as primary.

EXHIBIT 7 Simplified Description of the Problem That Caused the Network Outage (*Continued*)

What happens when redundant components both operate as primary? They relay every message they hear to each other. A single message gets relayed by both components, to both components; each one then faithfully relays the same message again, as if it were new. A single message multiplies into many, reproducing in an endless, exponential loop, until all network capacity is consumed. When the switch in the CareGroup network was overwhelmed by the software package left running by a researcher, this is exactly what happened to the CareGroup network.

Getting the Network "In Spec"

The CareGroup network was "out of spec" because it contained numerous instances of more than seven (7) network segments connected by bridges or switches. To fix this flat topology network, it needed to be made less flat. Rather than connecting segments with bridges and switches, *routers* were substituted in some cases. Routers permit more intelligent transfer of messages across networks. By using routers to break up the evolved complexity of the many bridge- and switch-connected network segments, the network topology was made less flat and became immune to Spanning Tree Protocol loops.

The intelligence in routers arises from their ability to use addressing information in the TCP/IP packets that encapsulate transmitted information in a modern Internetwork. Before routers will work, therefore, a network must be able to run TCP/IP. This is one reason the CareGroup network drifted out of spec. At the time that some smaller networks were added to the overall network, those smaller networks were based on proprietary technologies rather than TCP/IP. The messages that traversed those proprietary networks were therefore not "routable." Getting the network "in spec," so that routers could be used in place of bridges/switches, thus required getting rid of old proprietary networking technologies that were not routable.

None of these details of what was happening was apparent to users, operators, or managers of CareGroup's IT systems and network. All anyone could see on that November afternoon was that every software application that required network communication had stopped working, suddenly and without warning.

At Beth Israel Deaconess Medical Center, key areas and systems were affected: clinical units, e-mail, admitting-office functions, operating room functions, clinical laboratories, radiology, ambulatory services, pharmacy, medical records, fiscal/payroll systems, and Emergency Department functions. Physicians prescribing drugs for their patients had grown accustomed to computer assistance in identifying drug interactions; when a doctor placed a drug order for a patient, the system, which remembered perfectly which other drugs the patient was taking, flagged possible interactions and even popped up recent Food and Drug Administration (FDA) advisories. For years, X-rays had been digitized, and computer tools for viewing them provided many options for enhanced views that were widely used. The emergency room had come to rely on immediate access to often available patient medical history, extremely valuable if a patient was incapacitated.

But with the network down, none of this worked. Doctors had to check drug interactions for themselves; radiology residents who had never actually touched an X-ray in "primitive" photographic film form got a crash course in diagnosis, the old-fashioned way. Medical histories had to come entirely from patients. All across the community of caregivers, myriad problems appeared. Telephones replaced e-mail. Paper forms were hauled out of closets and dusted off; old-timers began to explain to younger staff how the paper systems worked. "We became a hospital of the 1970s in an instant," explained Halamka.

EXHIBIT 8 **Core Router CPU Use during the Outage (November 11, 2002 to November 15, 2002)**

Source: "CsreGroup Network Outage," presentation by John D. Halamka, M.D., November 25, 2002.

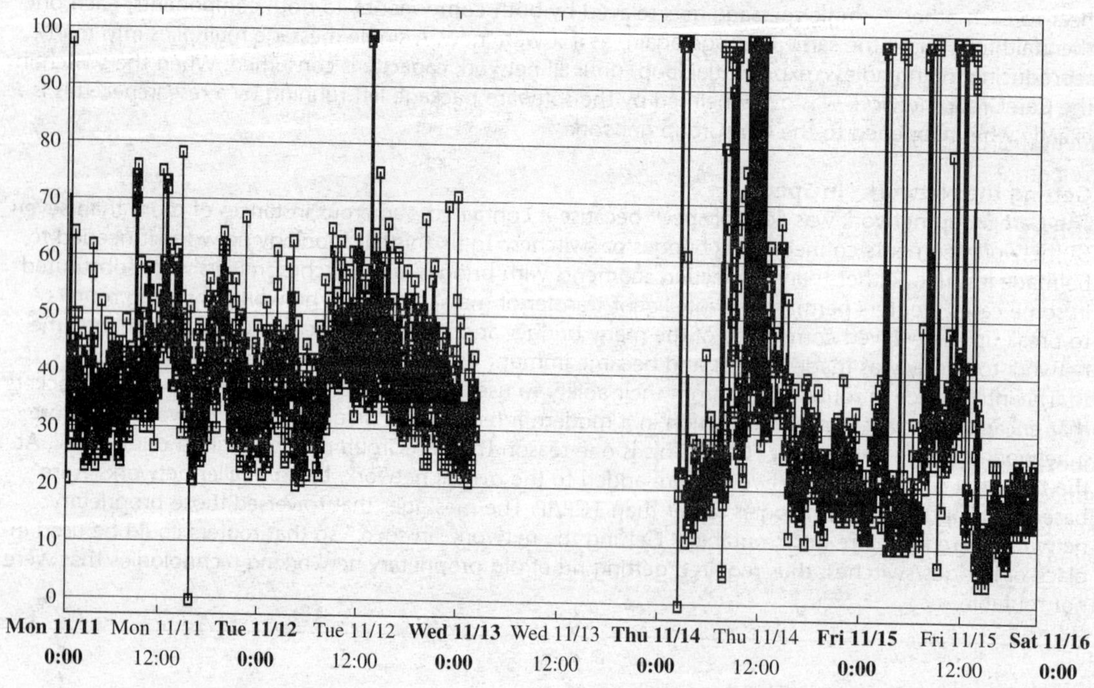

The community hospitals used the Meditech package for all clinical operations and did not depend on access to the central CareGroup data center or Beth Israel Deaconess networks to retrieve clinical information. Thus, these hospitals were largely unaffected by the outage, other than by e-mail across the system. (Meditech had an internal messaging system that kept communications going inside a hospital.)

The CareGroup IT staff set themselves, urgently, to diagnosing the problem at Beth Israel Deaconess and trying to restore functionality. It was a formidable challenge. The primary symptom of the problem was that "nothing worked"; though extremely impressive in its effects, this fact conveyed little detailed information about *why* that might be. The network seemed like a strong candidate as the problem source since it was a common element in all that was not working, but it was not the only possible problem source. Even assuming that the network was the problem, there were a vast number of possible reasons for that. People began frantically forming ideas about what was wrong and suggesting changes based on their ideas. Halamka, who had begun personally overseeing recovery efforts almost as soon as the incident had commenced, described what was happening:

> One person would say, "Oh, I know what the problem is. It's the wide-area network connection out to Mount Auburn—we should shut off Mount Auburn." And somebody else would say, "Well, I don't know; I'm worried about the configuration of this network component." Everyone wanted to go and make a change. And the problem is that as soon as you make one change, then diagnosis of the problem gets harder.

Using tactical measures such as restarting network equipment, the IT group was able to restore services by 4:00 AM on Thursday, November 14, about 12 hours after the incident had begun.

But as users began resuming business as usual, the network again misbehaved. Throughout the day on Thursday, systems bounced up and down. Sometimes they were usable; sometimes they were not. Thursday evening, the IT staff once again believed that systems were restored. But by early morning on Friday, November 15, it was evident that network instability remained; failures were continuing to occur.

Calling in Cisco

At 4:00 PM on Thursday, about 24 hours after the first difficulties with the network, Halamka called Cisco and asked for urgent assistance. With his Cisco networking equipment under maintenance contract and a riveting story to tell, he had no trouble getting the attention of Cisco's advanced support engineering group. Cisco support engineers took the story to John Chambers, the Cisco CEO, who approved escalating the incident to "CAP status"; this set the company's customer support SWAT team in motion.

Within hours, Cisco had dispatched from Santa Clara, California, a Boeing 747 loaded with network equipment and support engineers. At the same time, an expert team from North Carolina, consisting of staff from Cisco and Callisma (a Cisco consulting partner), boarded commercial airline flights headed for Boston. The team and equipment were adequate to build an entire redundant core network to get CareGroup systems up and running again, should that prove necessary. In the late hours of Thursday night, as Halamka drove to the airport to meet the Cisco engineers, he realized just how tired he was; by then he had been awake for 36 consecutive hours. He knew that other members of his team were also tired and badly needed the strong support he hoped he would get from Cisco.

When the Cisco team arrived at CareGroup, they took charge, immediately instituting their "CAP process." Halamka explained:

> Cisco has learned over the years that too many cooks in the kitchen do not ever heal a network. So the CAP process basically says, "We will freeze all changes." Cisco owns the problem and will put its entire business resources at your disposal until you become stable again. But you delegate *all* authority to solve this problem to Cisco. You don't do anything on your own.

Throughout the night, Cisco worked rapidly, carefully mapping the existing network. About 1:00 on Friday morning, they had zeroed in on at least part of the problem and decided to install a large, modern switch (a Cisco 6509) in place of an existing network component. They spent all night reconstructing a major part of the network. "In one night," recounted Halamka, "they did a month of work."

While implementing the CAP process, Cisco kept an average of about 10 people on-site at Beth Israel Deaconess. But that was only the tip of the support iceberg. On-site engineers worked continuously with teams throughout the world. Halamka explained:

> They follow the sun. North Carolina to Japan to Amsterdam. We literally had worldwide teams handing off to each other. They had about 10 folks here, at least three engineers 24 by 7, from Thursday at about 6:00 until Tuesday. And their network reconstruction isolated that part of the CareGroup network. And we said, "Oh great, this is wonderful; we've got it now." We went into Friday and Saturday thinking "things are looking really pretty good." Until we discovered that there were two other parts of the network that had the same kind of problems.

The Decision to Remain on Backup Procedures

With each of the network failures, the medical center had enacted established backup procedures. When systems were believed restored, the medical center would attempt to revert to standard procedures. But by the morning of November 15 it was obvious that the frequent switching between backup and standard processes carried more potential risk to patient care than remaining on backup processes for a more prolonged period. Halamka therefore recommended, and it was quickly agreed by CareGroup senior management, that the hospital remain on backup procedures until it was clear that the network was fully and definitively restored. Halamka described the rationale for this decision:

> The challenge for me, from a leadership standpoint, was that you want to believe you're one configuration change away from getting everybody back up to where they should be. So you've got the CEO, the COO saying, "OK, where are we?" "Oh, we're almost there," you think. My people tell me we're almost there. Cisco tells me we're almost there.
>
> And so you had the organization, which is entirely electronic, saying, "OK, we'll go to downtime; we'll do paper—oh, I hear the network is back up, let's go to electronic." Just as the network is oscillating, they're oscillating their workflows. What I ended up telling [CEO] Paul Levy and [COO] Michael Epstein is, "I will believe what Cisco says and I will tell you when the network will be back up. When we have 24-hour functionality at full load, the network itself will be telling us it's back up. So in the meantime, let's move the entire organization to paper and keep them on paper, so that the engineers have the opportunity to make changes, and the organization isn't suffering this error likelihood of going between two workflows."

On November 15, Beth Israel Deaconess Medical Center activated an internal command center to coordinate a prolonged period on backup procedures. Access to the network was blocked so that intermittent use of computer systems would not occur. The Massachusetts Department of Public Health was notified upon activation of the command center. The command center was manned at all times by senior administrators, and key contacts were established within each clinical and administrative department. Experience during the period of intermittent outages revealed that clinical laboratories faced the greatest disruption in workflow in relation to the outage, and so these areas received particular attention and support.

Specific processes that were followed, beginning on November 15 and throughout the outage, included:

- Establishment of the command center as the central point for all communication
- Establishment of morning and afternoon briefing sessions each day as part of a regular schedule. At each meeting, clinicians and staff were reminded that patient safety was of paramount importance, and special mechanisms for reporting patient safety concerns were established.
- Establishment of a system of "runners" available to retrieve specimens, tests, equipment, documentation, or supplies at any time
- Paper documentation of all activity that was previously recorded electronically, using systems established as part of backup procedures
- Call-back of all urgent lab results to the responsible clinician
- Establishment of staggered lab draws so as to even out the demand on the clinical laboratories
- Implementation of manual processes for orders and pharmacy dispensing
- Implementation of manual census lists by the admitting office, updated every few hours
- Establishment of a contingency plan for the outsourcing of all ambulatory laboratory volume (this never became necessary)
- Creation of hot lines for requesting/reporting lab results, patient care concerns, and the need for any other forms of support

The planning CareGroup had done to prepare for Y2K had made Halamka reasonably confident that the medical center could operate entirely paper based. But things had changed since Y2K. No one knew where paper forms were. Medical staff wandered the halls, saying, "I know we have those paper forms somewhere. Where are they?" In one instance, forms were retrieved from the recycling center, literally pulled out of recycling bins. Additional personnel were called in to move forms around. Data that would normally have been sent along a wire had to be sent over "sneakernet" instead. Halamka described the teamwork and resourcefulness that allowed the medical center to quickly adapt to paper operations:

> All day Friday we worked to optimize the backup processes. So we're on computerized order entry to the pharmacy entirely—how is it that we go back to handwritten orders and dose checking and drug-drug checking and drug-allergy checking? So you have [CEO] Paul Levy running Xerox copies of lab results that

runners would then pick up and take to the intensive care unit (ICU). The director of pharmacy manually reviewed every paper order for drug-drug interactions and drug-allergy interactions. It was amazing what people were able to do. The teamwork and problem-solving spirit was just awesome.

It turned out that we actually could run the entire hospital on paper just fine. You just can't go back and forth because you take all of your paper orders and then you key them into the computer, and then the computer takes over—oh, but now the network is down again; you have to rewrite them all on paper. So you at least duplicate, if not triplicate, your work by oscillating back and forth.

The decision to function predominantly on a paper-based information system also helped the IT group in their efforts to diagnose the problem. Network tests could be conducted and problems isolated without concern for disruption of routine clinical activity.

In the end, services to patients and the Boston community were minimally interrupted. For approximately four hours on November 14, when it was not yet clear that patient throughput could be maintained, the Emergency Department announced to Boston Emergency Medical Services that it was closed. Also, the medical center was on ambulance diversion for a total of 13.5 hours from November 13–15. This amount of time on diversion was not highly unusual for any hospital in the city of Boston. Otherwise ambulatory clinic activity, operating room activity, patient transfer, and patient walk-in activity continued according to standard policy and procedure during the outage.

After full restoration of computer systems, the directors of all clinical services were contacted to reinforce the importance of reporting any adverse clinical events related to the network outage. Twelve events were reported in response to this solicitation. The records relating to each of these were reviewed; they revealed that care had been delayed in some instances, but in no instance was there evidence of an adverse outcome relating to the network outage. Incident reports and patient complaints were also reviewed for unexpected outcomes related to the network outage; no other events were documented.

Solving the Problem(s)

Subsequent mapping by the Cisco support team eventually discovered other places where the network had "evolved" until it was out of spec—until the algorithms for recalculating data paths across the network could not function correctly. Across the CareGroup wide-area network, mapping revealed problems from changes to the network that had been casually made by users. Halamka offered an example:

> Some researchers ran out of ports on one of the switches. So what did they do? They daisy-chained a switch to a switch. Imagine that you have to run your barbecue to your hot tub to your Christmas lights, and you've got five extension cords without a breaker. You're going to blow! And so we discovered that was another source of the looping problem. Cardiology had also made some changes to the network that caused problems.

CareGroup IT and the Cisco SWAT team spent Saturday fixing all of the looping issues in the overall network. At the end of that task, they were disappointed to discover that there was still a problem somewhere in the network, which they tracked down to an old model router. The old router had a problem in its "firmware," the software that was permanently written into the microchips within the device. There was no way to upgrade the old router, so it was replaced.

The computer network was restored on November 18, but processes were transitioned back to computer-based formats gradually and in staggered fashion. Paper-based systems were retired only after information systems in each area had functioned continuously and without incident for at least 24 hours.

Following restoration of computer systems, all paper-based information was transferred to the appropriate electronic format within approximately 48 hours. The very large majority of documentation was easily located, but approximately 300 clinical test requests could not be reliably paired with a specimen or clinical result. For each of these cases, the ordering physician was contacted, and patients needing to be retested were informed that fees would be waived and parking/transportation costs reimbursed by the hospital.

Lessons Learned

For everyone who had been affected by the network outage, one lesson was deeply felt, as Halamka explained: "People realized, many for the first time, just how dependent they are on the technology. It had become so much a part of the culture. You didn't even think about it. We had begun to think about it like we think about the telephone. You pick up your phone and hear a dial tone. It's just there." Halamka also cited 10 more specific lessons that he, his staff, and the CareGroup management team had extracted from the experience:

Lesson #1: *Do not hesitate to bring in the experts to make sure your network is configured properly*. Since the network incident, Halamka had signed a $300,000 per year agreement for support from Cisco's advanced engineering services. As part of this deal, Cisco would make any changes to the CareGroup network that were considered significant. Cisco's ongoing review would assure that the network would stay "in spec." Two Cisco engineers would remain on-site at Beth Israel Deaconess permanently.

Lesson #2: *Do not let any one individual in your IT group become the sole point of failure*. In retrospect, Halamka realized that the CareGroup IT Department had relied too heavily on a single employee to maintain the network. Because the IT staff relied exclusively on one expert, there was no one to offer a second opinion about the network's configuration or to notice any precursors to the problem (if there had been any). "It's better to excise an excellent employee who may be brilliant and seems indispensable, if he or she is recalcitrant and not willing to open up, to work and share with others," suggested Halamka.

Lesson #3: *Keep your working knowledge current*. Not only had CareGroup depended too much on one networking expert; it had also allowed his knowledge to become out-of-date. After the fact, Cisco's support engineers summarized the problem at CareGroup this way: "The network at CareGroup was state of the art for the early 1990s. In the late 1990s it had evolved into a fragile state, and the group's networking staff, which hadn't kept up on networking technologies, didn't see problems coming."

Lesson #4: *Beware of users armed with just enough knowledge to be dangerous*. A user experimenting with a new software package had triggered the outage. Although users, and especially researchers, would always engage in some experimentation with local IT resources, it was important that the IT group remain vigilant, noting changes and supervising user experiments as appropriate.

Lesson #5: *Institute rigorous network change control*. After the network outage, CareGroup established a formal procedure for making changes to the network. A Network Change Control Board was created with multidisciplinary membership to review and approve all network infrastructure changes. The group classified changes into three categories: minimal, moderate, or substantial impact. Substantial changes required review by Cisco's advanced engineering team. Changes to the network were only made between 2 AM and 5 AM on weekends, and testing and incident-recovery plans had to be in evidence before changes were allowed to go forward.

Lesson #6: *Adapt to externalities*. The CareGroup network had evolved into its "out of spec" condition as a result of mergers, reorganizations, and other external activities and events. The November network outage led IT staff to examine more carefully all events in the outside environment for possible impacts on existing IT functionality.

Lesson #7: *There are limits to customer-centric responsiveness*. The CareGroup IT staff could not take an "anything the customer wants" approach, but rather needed to balance customer-centricity with the risks to the network and IT systems posed by requests to support new technologies. Halamka offered an example of the IT group's new perspective on customer responsiveness in the aftermath of the outage:

> The Department of Surgery has decided that minimally invasive surgery is a top priority. They've hired a guy to come help them with that who is planning to use video over IP. He's going to need gigabit-speed networks to show endoscopy to the world. He'll be here in February. Is that a problem? In the past, the idea was, "Of course we will support video over IP by February." Now it's a, "Nope, we'll bring in Cisco to look at the impact on the total environment." We'll place much more severe restrictions on what protocols and services anyone can run, what load you can put on the network, where you run it, and changes that we have to make.

A formal change-control process would achieve little if processes were short-circuited every time there was an "urgent" business need.

Lesson #8: *Have backup procedures in which you can have confidence*. CareGroup was able to run the hospital on paper systems because of Y2K preparedness. With Y2K past, however, there remained an ongoing need to make sure backup procedures worked. Backup procedures needed to be effective enough to operate for a prolonged period. In the event of a serious outage, it would not be productive to move back and forth between computer and paper processes, so the paper system would need to be robust.

Lesson #9: *Component redundancy is not enough; you need alternative access methods*. During the outage, some important systems could have continued to operate, albeit more slowly, if they could have been emergency connected to dial-up modems. Telephone lines could have become a rudimentary backup network that would have preserved a significant amount of system functionality. After the outage, CareGroup acquired additional analog telephone capacity and added low-tech dial-up modem capabilities to 50 PCs throughout the medical center.[1]

Lesson #10: *Life-cycle-manage your network components*. Routers, switches, and other network components needed to be replaced every four years. During the CareGroup outage, a component more than four years old had caused a serious problem because of a flaw in its firmware; it was unable to function properly in a modern network. Replacing network components needed to be budgeted. The upgrades required after the CareGroup outage amounted to a multimillion-dollar one-time expense and an ongoing requirement for upgrades every year.

There were many other lessons as well, important though perhaps not as deserving of headlines (Exhibit 9 lists actions taken in the aftermath of the outage). The entire incident had been a tremendous opportunity to learn, and Halamka was convinced that sharing information about what had happened, and talking about it with others, would ultimately strengthen CareGroup and its capabilities. The incident had also provided tutorials in both positive and negative aspects of human psychology. Halamka had been tremendously impressed by how the organization—doctors, nurses, researchers, IT staff, and many others—had pulled together to perform extremely well in the crisis. But he also had renewed respect for the damaging human tendency to respond to a problem by just "doing something," by making impulsive changes to the IT infrastructure; if Halamka and his colleagues had not overcome that urge, diagnosis and recovery from the problem would have been much more difficult.

The outage also reminded Halamka that computer operations in a large organization have tens of thousands of "moving parts" and that his job was to manage the process of getting all of those moving parts to work in harmony. "They call me the 'chief information officer,'" noted Halamka, "but I'm really the 'chief *integration* officer'; I make everything talk to everything else."

[1] For security reasons, these modems are only accessible from inside the CareGroup internal telephone network and only in the event of an emergency.

EXHIBIT 9 Changes Made or Planned in Response to Network Outage

Source: Summarized from "CareGroup Network Outage," presentation by John D. Halamka, MD, November 25, 2002.

Specific improvements already put in place include:

- Redesign and rebuilding of the radiology computer network, the research campus network, and the clinical campus network
- Placement of 50 dial-up computers in strategic areas of the hospital
- Addition of clinical system dial-up capability to 21 physician order entry desktops on patient care floors
- Implementation of a redundant core network that can be plugged in to replace the existing core network

The following improvements are either completed or will be completed within the next few weeks:

- Selective upgrade of noncore network hardware to increase the redundancy and stability of our network
- Scheduling of downtime on weekends 2:00 AM–5:00 AM to make network changes
- Implementation of a strict change-control process with all engineering changes overseen by Cisco

The following improvements will be completed within one year:

- Reconfiguration of the core network
- Introduction of redundancy in all hardware and links
- Implementation of the most modern hardware and topologies
- Implementation of network management software improvements
- Scheduling of appropriate downtimes with emphasis on network stability

The iPremier Company: Denial of Service Attack (A)

A security crisis is in progress. A luxury goods retailer with high-income customers is under attack by unknown hackers. As events unfold, company managers discover problems with their plans for responding to crises and struggle to understand and control the situation. First order problems, such as how to get the business back up and running, give way to second order, but no less serious, issues—such as what, if anything, to explain to customers, investors, or the public about the incident. As you read the case, consider these questions: How well did this company perform during the attack? What should they have done differently, before or during the event? What should they do in the aftermath of the event? What, if anything, should they say to customers, investors, and the public about what has happened?

Case 2-2

The iPremier Company (A): Denial of Service Attack

January 12, 2007, 4:31 AM

Somewhere a telephone was chirping. Bob Turley, CIO of the iPremier Company, turned beneath the bed sheets, wishing the sound would go away. Lifting his head, he tried to make sense of his surroundings. Where was he?

The Westin in Times Square. New York City. That's right. He was there to meet with Wall Street analysts. He'd gotten in late. By the time his head had hit the pillow it was nearly 1:30 AM. Now the digital display on the nearby clock made no sense. Who would be calling at this hour? Why would the hotel operator put a call through?

He reached for the phone at his bedside and held it to his ear. Dial tone. Huh? The chirping was coming from his cell phone. Hanging up the hotel phone, he staggered out of bed, located the cell phone, and flipped it open.

"This is Bob Turley."

"Mr. Turley?" There was panic in the voice at the other end of the line. "I'm sorry to wake you, Joanne told me to call you."

"Who is this?"

"It's Leon. Leon Ledbetter. I'm in Ops. We met last week. I'm new. I mean, I was new, last month."

"Why are you calling me at 4:30 in the morning, Leon?"

"I'm really sorry about that Mr. Turley, but Joanne said—"

"No, I mean what's wrong? Why are you calling?"

"It's our Web site, sir. It's locked up. I've tried accessing it from three different computers and

Professor Robert D. Austin, Dr. Larry Leibrock, Chief Technology Officer, McCombs School of Business, University of Texas at Austin, and Alan Murray, Chief Scientist, Novell Service Provider Network prepared this case as the basis for class discussion rather than to illustrate effective or ineffective management. The situation described in this case is based on real accounts of denial of service attacks directed against several companies during 2000 and 2001. Company names, product/service offerings, and the names of all individuals in the case are fictional, however. Any resemblance to actual companies, offerings, or individuals is accidental.

nothing's happening. Our customers can't access it either; the help desk is getting calls."

"What's causing it?"

"Joanne thinks—if we could only—well, someone might have hacked us. Someone else might be controlling our site. Support has been getting these e-mails—we thought it was just the Web server, but I can't access anything over there. Joanne is on her way to the colo.[1] She said to call you. These weird e-mails, they're coming in about one per second."

"What do the e-mails say?"

"They say 'ha.'"

"Ha?"

"Yes, sir. Each one of them has one word in the subject line, 'ha.' It's like 'ha, ha, ha, ha.' Coming from an anonymous source. That's why we're thinking—."

"When you say they might have hacked us—could they be stealing customer information? Credit cards?"

"Well, I guess no firewall is perfect but, well[2]—Joanne says—actually we're using a firewall service we purchased from the colo, so—."

"Can you call someone at the colo? We pay for monitoring 24×7, don't we?"

"Joanne is calling them. I'm pretty sure. Is there anything you want me to do?"

"Have we set our emergency procedures in motion?

"Joanne says we have a binder, but I can't find it. I don't think I've ever seen it. I'm new—"

"Yes, I got that. Does Joanne have her cell?"

"Yes sir, she's on her way to the colo. I just talked to her."

"Call me back if anything else happens."

"Yes sir."

Turley stood up, realizing only then that he had been sitting on the floor. His eyes were bleary but adrenaline was now rushing through his bloodstream. Steadying himself against a chair, he felt a wave of nausea. This was no way to wake up.

He made his way to the bathroom and splashed water on his face. This trip to New York was an important assignment for someone who had been with the company for such a short time. It demonstrated the confidence CEO Jack Samuelson had in him as the new CIO. For a moment, Turley savored the memory of the meeting in which Samuelson had told him he would be the one to go to New York. As that memory passed, another emerged, this one from an earlier session with the CEO. Samuelson was worried that the company might eventually suffer from "a deficit in operating procedures." "Make it one of your top priorities," he had said. "We need to run things professionally. I've hired you to take us to the next level."

Looking himself over in the mirror, seeing his hair tussled and face wet, Turley lodged a protest with no one in particular: "I've barely been here three months."

The iPremier Company

Founded in 1996 by two students at Swarthmore College, the iPremier Company had evolved into one of the few success stories of Web-based commerce. From its humble beginnings, it had risen to become one of the top two retail businesses selling luxury, rare, and vintage goods on the Web. Based in Seattle, Washington, the firm had grown and held off incursions into its space from a number of well-funded challengers. For the fiscal year 2006, profits were $2.1 million on sales of $32 million. Sales had grown at more than 20 percent annually for the last three years, and profits, though thin and somewhat variable, had an overall favorable trend.

Immediately following its initial public offering in late 1998, the company's stock price had nearly tripled. It had continued up from there amid the

[1] "Colo" is short for "colocation facility," where Internet companies often house their vital computing hardware. Colocation facilities are sometimes called "Internet Data Centers" or simply "hosting facilities." They provide floor space, redundant power supplies, high-speed connectivity to the Internet, and a variety of other services to their customers.

[2] A "firewall" is a combination hardware/software platform that is designed to protect a local network and the computers that reside on it against unauthorized access.

euphoria of the 1999 markets, eventually tripling again. A follow-on offering had left the company in a strong cash position. During the NASDAQ bloodbath of 2000, the stock had fallen dramatically but had eventually stabilized and even climbed again, although not to pre-2000 levels. Since then, the company had held its own, recovering from a difficult period by streamlining and focusing its business to achieve profitability when others couldn't. Eventually the company began to grow again, though more slowly than before. In the treacherous business-to-consumer (B2C) segment, iPremier was one of a very few survivors.

Most of the company's products were priced between fifty and a few hundred dollars, but there were a small number of items priced in the thousands of dollars. Customers paid for items online using their credit cards. The company had flexible return policies, which were intended to allow customers to thoroughly examine products before deciding whether to keep them. The iPremier customer base was high-end—so much so that credit limits on charge cards were rarely an issue, even for the highest-priced products.

Management and Culture

The management team at iPremier was a mix of talented young people who had been with the company for a long time and more experienced managers who had been gradually hired as the firm grew. Recruitment had focused on well-educated technical and business professionals with reputations for high performance. Getting hired into a senior management position required excelling in an intense series of three-on-one interviews. The CEO interviewed every prospective manager at the director level and above. The reward, for those who made the grade, was base compensation above the average of managers at similar firms, and variable compensation that could be a significant multiple of the base. All employees were subject to quarterly performance reviews that were tied directly to their compensation. Unsuccessful managers did not last long.

Most managers at iPremier described the environment as "intense." The company stated its governing values in terms of "discipline, professionalism, commitment to delivering results, and partnership for achieving profits." Unlike many Internet companies, iPremier had taken a balanced approach to growth and profitability, although growth had tended to rule the day. Throughout the company, there was a strong orientation toward doing "whatever it takes" to get projects done on schedule, especially when it came to system features that would benefit customers. The software development team was proud of its record of consistently launching new features and programs a few months ahead of a major competitor, MarketTop. Value statements aside, it was well understood by senior managers that their compensation and future prospects with the company depended on executing to plan. Managers pursued "the numbers" with zeal.

Technical Architecture

The company had historically tended to outsource management of its technical architecture and had a long-standing relationship with Qdata, a company that hosted most of iPremier's computer equipment and provided connectivity to the Internet. Qdata was an early entrant into the Internet hosting and "colocation" business, but it had been battered by the contraction of the Internet bubble and lost any prospect of market leadership. The facility was close to the corporate offices of iPremier; some felt there was little else to recommend it. Qdata was a steady provider of basic floor space, power, connectivity, environmental control, and physical security, and it offered some higher-level "management services," such as monitoring of Web sites for customers at its Network Operations Center (NOC) and some Internet security services (such as the firewall service used by iPremier). But Qdata had not been quick to invest in advanced technology and had experienced difficulty in retaining staff.

The iPremier Company had a long-standing initiative aimed at eventually moving its computing to another facility, but several factors had conspired to keep this from happening. First,

EXHIBIT 1 The iPremier Company's Technical Architecture

Source: Casewriter.

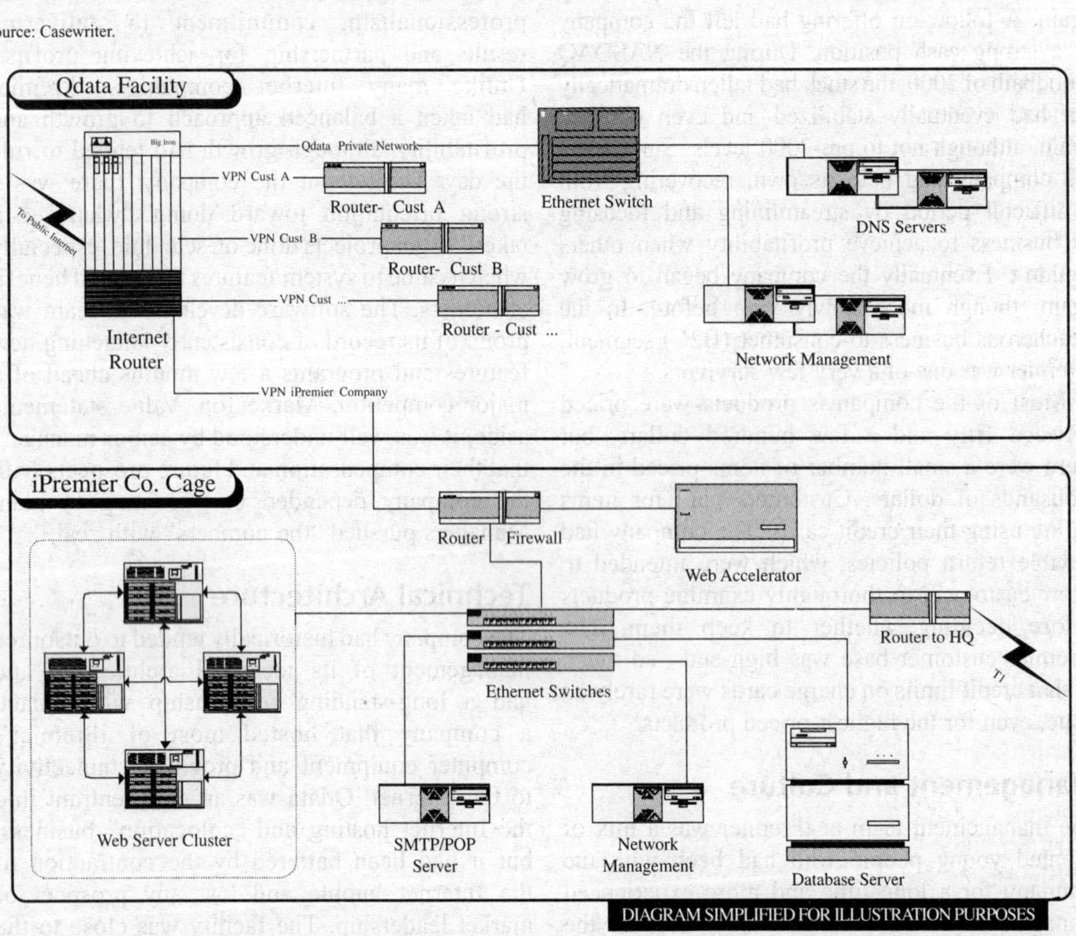

and most significant, iPremier had been very busy growing, protecting its profits, and delivering new features to benefit customers; hence the move to a better facility had never quite made it to the top of the priority list. Second, the cost of more modern facilities was considerably higher—two to three times as expensive on a per-square-foot basis. The computers at iPremier occupied a great deal of space, so a move to another facility would have increased costs enough to affect the slender but increasing profit trend the company was eager to maintain. Third, there was a perception—not necessarily supported by fact, according to the operations staff—that a move might risk service interruption to customers. The operations staff maintained that with appropriate modernization of the computing infrastructure, growth could be accomplished by adding installations in other facilities, rather than by expanding floor space in the existing facility. The work of planning how this might be carried out had never been done, however. Finally, one of the founders of iPremier felt a personal commitment to the owners of Qdata because the latter company had been willing to renegotiate their contract at a particularly difficult time in iPremier's early days.

Exhibit 1 provides a diagram of iPremier's technical architecture.

4:39 AM

Turley situated himself at the desk in his hotel room and began paging through the digital phonebook on his cell phone. Before he could find the number for Joanne Ripley—his technical operations team leader—the phone began to chirp. The incoming call was from Ripley.

"Hello, Joanne. How are you this morning?"

A cautious laugh came from the other end of the circuit. "About the same as you, I'm guessing. I assume Leon reached you."

"He did, but he doesn't know anything. What's going on?"

"I don't know much either, yet. I'm in the car, on my way to the colo."

"Can't you do something from home?"

"Well—no. Leon can't access any of the boxes behind the firewall via the line at the office,[3] so something is screwy with our connectivity to the colo. Sounds like a problem outside the perimeter of our architecture. I called Qdata, but they assured me there's no problem with connectivity into or out of the building. They're looking into it further, but their night shift is on duty. I don't know where they get those bozos. I haven't talked to anyone yet who knows what he's doing."

"How long till you get there?"

"I'm driving fast and running red lights. I ought to be there in five minutes."

"How long after that until we are back up and running?"

"That depends on what's wrong. I'll try restarting the Web server as soon as I get there, but if someone has hacked us, or if there's some kind of attack going on, that might not do it. Did Leon tell you about the e-mails?"

"The 'ha, ha' e-mails? Yeah. Makes it sound like something deliberate."

"I'd have to agree with that."

"No chance it's a simple DoS attack?"

"I doubt it's a *simple* DoS attack; we've got software that deals with those."

"Can we track the e-mails?"

"Not soon enough. They're coming through an anonymizer that's probably in Europe or Asia. If we're lucky we'll find out sometime in the next 18 months who sent them. Then we'll discover they're originating from some DSL-connected PC in Podunk, Idaho, and that the Joe Schmo who owns it has no idea that it's been compromised by hackers."

"Any chance they're stealing credit cards?"

"There's really no way of knowing without more info."

"Should we pull the plug? Physically disconnect the communications lines?"

"We could. But if we start pulling cables out of the wall it may take us a while to put things back together. Right now most of our customers are asleep."

"Joanne, don't we have emergency procedures for times like this, a binder or something at least? I don't think I've seen it but it comes up when people mention our business continuity plan. When I mentioned it to Leon, he seemed to have no idea what I was talking about."

"We've got a binder," said Ripley. "I've got a copy with me. Keep it in my car. There's one at the office too, even if Leon can't find it. But to be honest, well—it's out of date. Lots of people on the call lists don't work here anymore. I don't think we can trust the cell phone numbers and I *know* some of the technology has changed since it was written. We've talked about practicing incident response but we've never made time for it."

"Hmm. So what's the plan when you reach the colo?"

"Whoops." There was a pause while Ripley negotiated a traffic obstacle. "Sorry. Let me restart the Web server and see what happens. Maybe we can get out of this without too much customer impact."

Turley thought about it for a moment. "Okay. But if you see something that makes you think credit cards are being stolen, I want to know that immediately. We may have to take drastic action."

[3] The hosting facility where the production computer equipment was housed was connected to the iPremier Company's offices via a leased communication line. This line would ordinarily permit people at the office to connect to production computers without traversing the public Internet.

"Understood. I'll call you back as soon as I know anything."

"Good. One more thing: Who else knows this is going on?"

"I haven't called anyone else. Leon might have. I'll call him and call you right back."

"Thanks."

Turley flipped his cell closed then picked up the hotel phone. After a series of transfers, he found someone who would bring coffee to his room, despite the odd hour. Never before had he so desperately wanted coffee.

Just as he replaced the hotel phone his cell rang again.

"Damn." It was Warren Spangler, VP of business development. Turley remembered vaguely that Leon Ledbetter had come into the organization via a recommendation by Spangler. They were old high school buddies or something. Ledbetter had almost certainly called Spangler.

"Hi, Warren," said Turley, flipping the phone open.

"Hi, Bob. I hear we've got some kind of incident going on. What's the story?"

"Something's definitely going on, but we're not sure what yet. We're trying to minimize customer impact. Fortunately for us it's the middle of the night."

"Wow. So is it just a technical problem or is somebody actually doing it to us?"

Turley was eager to call the chief technology officer (CTO), so he didn't really have time for this discussion. But he didn't want to be abrupt. He was still getting to know his colleagues.

"We don't know. Look, I've got to—"

"Leon said something about e-mails—"

"Yes, there are suspicious e-mails coming in so it could be someone doing it."

"Oh, man. I bet the stock takes a hit tomorrow. Just when I was going to exercise some options. Shouldn't we call the police?"

"Sure, why don't you see what you can do there; that'd be a big help. Look, I've got to—"

"Seattle police? Do we know where the e-mails are coming from? Maybe we should call the FBI? No. Wait. If we call the police, the press might hear about this from them. Whoa. Then our stock would really take a hit."

"I've really got to go, Warren."

"Sure thing. I'll start thinking about PR. And I'll work with Leon on this end. We got you covered here, bro. Keep the faith."

"Will do, Warren. Thanks."

Turley ended that call and began searching through his cell phone's memory to find the number for Tim Mandel, the company's CTO. He and Mandel had already cemented a great working relationship. Turley wanted his opinion. Just as Turley was about to initiate the call, though, another call came in from Ripley.

Turley flipped the phone open and said: "Leon called Spangler, I know. Anything else?"

"Ah, no. That's it for now. Bye."

Turley dialed Mandel. At first the call switched over to voice mail, but he retried immediately. This time Mandel answered sleepily. It took five full minutes to wake Mandel and tell him what was happening.

"So what do you think, should we just pull the plug?" Turley asked.

"I wouldn't. You might lose some logging data that would help us figure out what happened. Whatever we do, we want to preserve evidence of what has happened or else we may never know exactly."

"I'm not sure that's the most important thing to me right now, knowing exactly what is happening."

"I suggest you change your mind about that. If you don't know what happened this time, it can happen again. Worse than that, if you don't know what happened, you won't know what, if anything, you need to disclose publicly."

Turley thought about that for a moment. What if they halted the attack but he could not be sure of the danger, if any, to customer information? What would the company need to say publicly? It was too much to sort out on the fly. Mandel was saying something else.

"Come to think of it, Bob, preserving the logs is irrelevant because I'm pretty sure detailed logging is not enabled. Detailed logging takes up a lot of disk space on the server. To run at higher logging levels we would have to add significantly to our storage arrays and I've never been able to convince the finance guys that the expenditure was necessary. Plus detailed logging adds a performance penalty of about 20 percent, which impacts the customer experience; nobody's been game for that."

"So we aren't going to have evidence of what happened anyway."

"There'll be some, but not as much as we'll want."

Another call was coming in.

"Hold on, Tim." Turley kicked the phone over to the waiting call. It was Peter Stewart, the company's legal counsel. What was *he* doing awake?

"This is Turley."

"Hey, Bob, it's Pete. Pull the plug, Bob. Shut off the power, pull the cords out of their sockets, everything. We can't risk having credit cards stolen."

"Spangler call you?"

"Huh? No, Jack. Samuelson. He called me three minutes ago, said hackers had control of our Web site. Told me in no uncertain terms to call you and 'provide a legal perspective.' That's just what he said: 'provide a legal perspective.'"

So the CEO was awake. The result, no doubt, of Spangler's "helping" from that end. Stewart continued to speak legalese at him for what seemed like an eternity. By this time, Turley was incapable of paying attention to him.

"Thanks for your thoughts, Pete. I've got to go, I've got Tim on the other line."

"Okay. For the record, though, I say pull the plug. I'll let Jack know you and I spoke."

"Thanks, Pete."

Turley switched back over to the call with Mandel.

"Spangler's got bloody everybody awake, including Jack. I recommend you get dressed and head into the office, my friend."

"Is Joanne on this?"

"Yes, she's at the colo by now." Turley's phone rang. "Got a call coming in from her now."

He switched the phone.

"What's up Joanne?"

"Well I'm at Qdata," she said in an angry voice, "and they won't let me into the NOC. There's no one here who knows anything about the network monitoring software and that's what I need to use to see the traffic coming into our site. The Qdata guy who can do it is vacationing in Aruba. I tried rebooting the Web server, but we've still got a problem. My current theory is an attack directed at our firewall, but to be sure I've got to see the packets coming in, and the firewall is their equipment. You got an escalation contact to get these dudes off their butts?"

"I'm in New York, Joanne. I've got no Qdata contact information with me. But let me see what I can do."

"Okay. I'll keep working it from this end. The security guard doesn't look too fierce. I think I could take him."

"Do what you can."

Turley hung up. He noticed that Mandel had disconnected also. For a moment Turley sat back in the chair, not sure what to do next. There was a knock at the door. Coffee. Good news, for a change.

5:27 AM

He had just taken his first sip of hot coffee when he got the call he'd been dreading. It was from Jack Samuelson, the CEO.

"Hi Jack."

"Bob. Exciting morning?"

"More than I like it."

"Are we working a plan?"

"Yes, sir. Not everything is going according to plan, but we are working a plan."

"Is there anything I can do?"

"Actually, Jack, there is. Call someone senior at Qdata and tell them we need their full and immediate support. They're giving Joanne the runaround about access to their NOC."

"I'll do that right now, Bob."

"Thanks, Jack."

"Bob, the stock is probably going to be impacted and we'll have to put a solid PR face on this, but that's not your concern right now. You focus on getting us back up and running. Understand?"

"I do."

The call ended. It had gone better than Turley had feared. He avoided the temptation to analyze Samuelson's every word for clues to his innermost thoughts. Instead, he dialed Joanne.

"Hi, Bob," she said, sounding mildly cheerful. "They let me in. I'm sitting in front of the console right now. It looks like a SYN flood[4] from multiple sites directed at the router[5] that runs our firewall service. So it *is* a DoS attack, just not a simple one. By the way, this is not a proper firewall, Bob; we need to work on something better."

"Fine, but what can we do right now?"

"Well, looks like the attack is coming from about 30 sites. If the guys here will let me, I'm going to start shutting down traffic from those IP addresses."[6]

"Samuelson is waking up the senior guys at Qdata. If the night shift gives you any trouble, tell them it's going to be raining executives really soon."

"Samuelson, huh? So everybody's up for our little party. Okay, I'm going to try shutting off traffic from the attacking IP addresses. I'll have to set the phone down for a minute."

There was a pause of a couple of minutes. Turley heard some muffled conversation in the background, then several exclamations. Ripley came back on the line.

"Damn it, Bob, they're spawning zombies. It's Dawn of the Dead out there."

"You're going to have to translate that one for me, Ripley."

"Every time we shut down traffic from an IP address, the zombie we've shut off automatically triggers attacks from two other sites. I'll try it a few more times, but right now it looks like that's just going to make things worse."

"If it's a denial of service attack, they haven't hacked us, right? It means it's not an intrusion. They haven't gained entry to our system. So credit cards and customer data are safe. Can we say that?"

"There's nothing that makes a DoS attack and an intrusion mutually exclusive. And targeting the firewall strikes me as a fairly sophisticated tactic. I'm not so sure these are script kiddies,[7] Bob."

It was not the comforting answer he had hoped for, but it would have to do for the time being. "I'll let you get back to it. Call me with an update when there is something to tell."

Turley hung up and thought about whether to call Samuelson and what to tell him. He could say that it was a DoS attack. He could say that the attack, by itself, was not evidence that customer information was at risk. But Turley wanted to think some more before he went on record. He'd talk to Tim, see what he thought.

For a moment, everything was quiet. He put the cell phone down and poured another cup of coffee. Pacing across the room, he picked up the TV remote and hit the "on" button. A movie appeared, an old Hitchcock film. An airplane was strafing Cary Grant. He muted the sound then walked to the window and pulled the curtain aside. There was a red glow in the sky to the east.

[4] Each "conversation" with a Web server begins with a sequence of "handshake" interactions. The initiating computer first sends a "SYNCHRONIZE" or "SYN." The contacted Web server responds with a "SYNCHRONIZE-ACKNOWLEDGE" or "SYN-ACK." The initiating computer then completes the handshake with an "ACKNOWLEDGE" or "ACK." A "SYN flood" is an attack on a Web server intended to make it think a very large number of "conversations" are being initiated in rapid succession. Because each interaction looks like real traffic to the Web site, the Web server expends resources dealing with each one. By flooding the site, an attacker can effectively paralyze the Web server by trying to start too many conversations with it.

[5] As the name suggests, a "router" is a hardware platform that routes traffic across internal networks and the Internet.

[6] An "IP address" corresponds to a particular machine located somewhere on the Internet.

[7] "Script kiddies" are relatively unsophisticated hackers who use automated routines—"scripts"—written by other more sophisticated hackers. These scripts are available to anyone willing to spend a little time searching for them on the Internet.

His cell phone rang. He went and picked it up. It was Ripley.

"It stopped," she said excitedly. "The attack is over."

"What did you do?"

"Nothing. It just stopped. The attack just stopped at 5:46 AM."

"So—what do we do now?"

"The Web site is running. A customer who visits our site now wouldn't know anything had ever been wrong. We can resume business as usual."

"Business as usual?"

"Actually, I'd recommend that we give everything a proper going-over after an attack like this. We really ought to do a thorough audit. I've been thinking about how they targeted the firewall, and I don't think it sounds like script kiddies."

"Sit down when you get a chance and write me an e-mail that summarizes what you think we should do. Tell me how whatever you recommend will impact on customers, if at all. I've got to figure out what to tell Samuelson."

Ford Motor Company: Supply Chain Strategy and the Power of Virtual Integration: An Interview with Dell Computer's Michael Dell

A century-old U.S. manufacturer considers whether it should model its operations on the celebrated and IT-enabled operations of a much younger company. Examining this question leads managers at the older firm to confront a series of complex questions about how IT should support business operations. The article and case together provide an introduction to Dell's computerized direct fulfillment system while exploring the many ways in which "legacies"—systems, organization, and relationships—constrain an established company's capabilities. As you read the article and case, consider these questions: What advantages does Dell derive from virtual integration? How important are these advantages in the auto business? What challenges must Ford overcome that Dell does not face? Is the Dell model really relevant to Ford? What should Teri Takai recommend to Ford's senior executives about how closely the company should emulate the Dell model? What might be the consequences for Ford if executives are too aggressive or too timid concerning these issues?

Case 2-3

Ford Motor Company: Supply Chain Strategy

Teri Takai, Director of Supply Chain Systems, had set aside this time on her calendar to contemplate recommendations to senior executives. The question they'd asked was widely agreed to be extremely important to Ford's future: How should the company use emerging information technologies (e.g., Internet technologies) and ideas from new high-tech industries to change the way it interacted with suppliers? Members of her team had different views on the subject.

Some argued that the new technology made it inevitable that entirely new business models would prevail and that Ford needed to radically redesign its supply chain and other activities or risk being left behind. This group favored "virtual integration," modeling the Ford supply chain on that of companies like Dell,[1] which had aggressively used technology to reduce working capital and exposure to inventory obsolescence. Proponents of this approach argued that although the auto business was very complex, both for historical reasons and because of the inherent complexity of the automotive product, there was no reason such business models could not provide a conceptual blueprint for what Ford should attempt.

Another group was more cautious. This group believed that the differences between the auto business and relatively newer businesses like computer manufacturing were important and substantive. Some noted, for example, that relative to Dell the Ford supplier network had many more layers and many more companies, and that Ford's purchasing organization had historically played a

Professor Robert D. Austin prepared this case as the basis for class discussion rather than to illustrate effective or ineffective management.

[1] Information on Dell included in this case was obtained by Ford from public sources, including the 1997 Dell Annual Report, the Dell Web site (www.dell.com), and from "The Power of Virtual Integration: An Interview with Dell Computer's Michael Dell" by Joan Magretta, *Harvard Business Review*, March–April 1998 (reprint 98208).

more prominent and independent role than Dell's. These differences and others posed complications when examined closely, and it was difficult to determine the appropriate and feasible scope for redesign of the process.

As Takai read through the documents provided by her team, she thought about CEO Jac Nasser's recent companywide emphasis on shareholder value and customer responsiveness. It was widely acknowledged that Dell had delivered on those dimensions, but would the same methods deliver results for Ford?

Company and Industry Background

Based in Dearborn, Michigan, the Ford Motor Company was the second-largest industrial corporation in the world, with revenues of more than $144 billion and about 370,000 employees. Operations spanned 200 countries. Although Ford obtained significant revenues and profits from its financial services subsidiaries, the company's core business had remained the design and manufacture of automobiles for sale on the consumer market. Since Henry Ford had incorporated in 1903, the company had produced in excess of 260 million vehicles.

The auto industry had grown much more competitive over the last two decades. Since the 1970s, the Big Three U.S. automakers—General Motors (GM), Ford, and Chrysler—had seen their home markets encroached upon by the expansion of foreign-based auto manufacturers, such as Toyota and Honda. The industry was also facing increasing overcapacity (estimated at 20 million vehicles) as developing and industrialized nations, recognizing the wealth and job-producing effects of automobile manufacturing, encouraged development and expansion of their own export-oriented auto industries.

Although manufacturers varied in their degree of market presence in different geographical regions, the battle for advantage in the industry was fast becoming global. Faced with the need to continue to improve quality and reduce cycle times while dramatically lowering the costs of developing and building cars, Ford and the other large automakers were looking for ways to take advantage of their size and global presence. One element of the effort to achieve advantage in size and scale was a movement toward industry consolidation. In the summer of 1998, Chrysler merged with Daimler-Benz to form a more global automaker. In early 1999, Ford announced that it would acquire Sweden's Volvo, and there were rumors of other deals in the works.

Previously, in 1995, Ford had embarked on an ambitious restructuring plan called Ford 2000, which included merging its North American, European, and International automotive operations into a single global organization. Ford 2000 called for dramatic cost reductions to be obtained by reengineering and globalizing corporate organizations and processes. Product development activities were consolidated into five Vehicle Centers (VCs), each responsible for development of vehicles in a particular consumer market segment (one VC was in Europe). By making processes and products globally common, Ford intended to eliminate organizational and process redundancies and realize huge economies of scale in manufacturing and purchasing. Major reengineering projects were initiated around important company processes, such as order to delivery (OTD) and Ford production system (FPS), with goals such as reducing OTD time from more than 60 days to less than 15.

Ford's new global approach required that technology be employed to overcome the constraints usually imposed by geography on information flow. Teams on different continents needed to be able to work together as if they were in the same building. Furthermore, in virtually every reengineering project, information technology (IT) had emerged as a critical enabler. The link between reengineering success and the company's IT groups was made explicit in the Ford 2000 restructuring—IT was placed within the process reengineering organization. In the supply chain area, there was general agreement that IT could also be deployed to dramatically enhance material flows and reduce inventories—substituting information for inventory, as the expression went.

As Ford 2000 unfolded, the Internet revolution unfolded in parallel, creating new possibilities for reengineering processes within and between enterprises. Ford launched a public Internet site in mid-1995; by mid-1997 the number of visits to the site had reached more than 1 million per day. A companywide *intra*net was launched in mid-1996, and by January of 1997, Ford had in place a business-to-business (B2B) capability through which the intranet could be extended in a secure manner beyond company boundaries into an *extra*net, potentially connecting Ford with its suppliers. Ford teamed with Chrysler and General Motors to work on the Automotive Network Exchange (ANX), which aimed to create consistency in technology standards and processes in the supplier network, so that suppliers, already pressed to lower costs, would not have to manage different means of interaction with each automaker.

On January 1, 1999, Jac Nasser took over the CEO job from Alex Trotman. Nasser had been Trotman's second-in-command throughout the Ford 2000 rollout, and had a long-standing reputation as a tough-minded cost-cutter and a capable leader. Even before taking the helm, he had begun to focus Ford senior management on shareholder value. In the period between 1995 and 1999, Ford had seen companies with fewer physical assets and much lower revenues and profits achieve market capitalization well in excess of Ford's. Corporate staff members began to study models such as Cisco and Dell to try to understand whether Ford could produce shareholder value in the ways that these newer companies had.

As the end of 1998 approached, Ford had amassed profits of $6.9 billion, employees enjoyed record profit sharing, and return on sales (3.9 percent in 1997) was trending solidly upward. The company was the world leader in trucks. It had taken over the U.S. industry lead in profit per vehicle ($1,770) from Chrysler, and it was the most improved automaker on the 1997 J. D. Power Initial Quality Study (in fourth place overall, behind Honda, Toyota, and Nissan).

Ford's Existing Supply Chain and Customer Responsiveness Initiatives

Ford had a number of initiatives under way that were aimed at favorably positioning the company for success in integrating with the extended enterprise that also included suppliers and customers. In addition, there were historical factors that would need to be taken into account in any virtual integration strategy.

Ford's Existing Supply Base

The existing supply base was, in many respects, a product of history. As the company had grown over the years, so had the supply base, to the point where, in the late 1980s, there were several thousand suppliers of production material in a complex network of business relationships. Suppliers were picked primarily based on cost, with little regard for overall supply chain costs, including the complexity of dealing with such a large network of suppliers.

Beginning in the early 1990s, Ford had begun to actively try to decrease the number of suppliers the company dealt with directly. Rather than fostering strong price competition among suppliers for individual components, there was a shift toward longer-term relationships with a subset of very capable suppliers who would provide entire vehicle subsystems. These "tier one" suppliers would manage relationships with a larger base of suppliers of components of subsystems—tier two and below suppliers. Ford made its expertise available to assist suppliers in improving their operations via a range of techniques, including just-in-time (JIT) inventory, total quality management (TQM), and statistical process control (SPC). In exchange for the closer relationships and long-term commitments, Ford expected yearly price reductions from suppliers. But incremental IT-enabled cost savings weren't as easy to achieve as anticipated; while first tier suppliers had fairly well developed IT capabilities (many interacted with Ford via Electronic Data

Interchange links), they were not able to invest in new technologies at the rate Ford itself could. Also, the IT maturity (understanding and modernity of technology) decreased rapidly in lower tiers of the supply chain. As more cautious members of Takai's staff had often observed, this supply base was different in its nature and complexity from Dell's supply base.

Another major difference between Dell and Ford was organizational. At Dell, purchasing activities reported into the product development organization. At Ford, purchasing was organizationally independent of product development and had been—historically and up to the present—a powerful force within Ford. Because of the sheer volume of materials and services that Ford purchased, a very slim reduction in purchasing cost could result in very significant savings. Consequently, purchasing was closely involved in nearly every product decision. Engineers were counseled to avoid discussing prices in interactions with suppliers, as price negotiation was the sole province of purchasing agents. How this might work in a more virtually integrated system was unclear.

Ford Production System

The Ford 2000 initiative produced five major, corporationwide reengineering projects. One of these was Ford production system (FPS). Modeled roughly on the Toyota production system, FPS involved a multiyear project that drew on internal and external expertise worldwide. FPS was an integrated system aimed at making Ford manufacturing operations leaner, more responsive, and more efficient. It focused on key attributes of the production process, aspiring to level production and move to a more pull-based system, with synchronized production, continuous flow, and stability throughout the process. One important part of FPS was "Synchronous Material Flow" (SMF), which Ford defined as "a process or system that produces a continuous flow of material and products driven by a fixed, sequenced, and leveled vehicle schedule, utilizing flexibility and lean manufacturing concepts." One key to SMF was "in-line vehicle sequencing" (ILVS), a system that used vehicle in-process storage devices (such as banks and ASRSs[2]) and computer software to ensure that vehicles were assembled in order sequence. By ensuring assembly in order sequence, Ford could tell suppliers exactly when and where certain components would be needed days in advance, and buffer stocks could be dramatically reduced. If such sequenced assembly could be kept level, and if it was well-forecasted, the benefits would be felt throughout the supply chain. The vision was of trucks constantly in motion throughout their lives, in continuous circuits between suppliers and Ford, stopping only to refuel or change drivers, feeding a process that worked like a finely tuned and smoothly running precision instrument.

Order to Delivery

Another key process of Ford's reengineering initiative was order to delivery (OTD). The purpose of the OTD project was to reduce to 15 days the time from a customer's order to delivery of the finished product—a significant reduction on the present performance of 45–65 days. Ford took a holistic approach to the reengineering. Pilot studies in 1997 and 1998 identified bottlenecks throughout Ford's supply chain, including its marketing, material planning, vehicle production, and transportation processes. Ford's approach to implementing an improved OTD process relied on several elements: (1) ongoing forecasting of customer demand from dealers—before OTD Ford had never officially involved dealers in forecasting

[2] A "bank" is a storage area into which partially assembled vehicles can be directed, for the purpose of removing them in a different order than the order in which they entered (i.e., resequencing). An "ASRS" or "Automated Storage and Retrieval System" is essentially a multilevel bank (vehicles are literally stored on top of each other); whereas an ordinary bank provides some resequencing flexibility, an ASRS provides the ability to access any vehicle in the bank at any time. As might be imagined, to hold a large number of vehicles and allow them to be accessed randomly, an ASRS must be very large (roughly the size of a several-story building).

EXHIBIT 1 Dell and Ford Compared

Source: Dell 1998 Financial Report, Ford 1997 Annual Report. *The Wall Street Journal Interactive.*

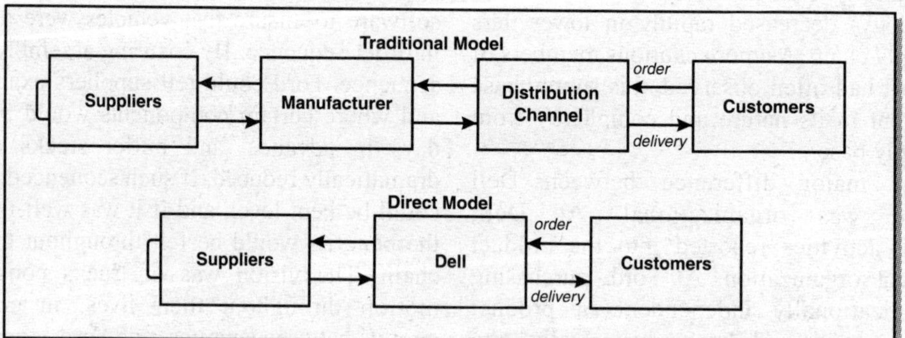

Comparative Metrics (latest fiscal year)

	Dell	Ford Automotive	Ford Fin. Services
Employees	16,100	363,892	
Assets ($millions)	4,300	85,100	194,000
Revenue ($millions)	12,300	122,900	30,700
Net income ($millions)	944	4,700	2,200
Return on sales	7.7%	3.8%	7.2%
Cash ($millions)	320	14,500	2,200
Manufacturing facilities	3 (Texas, Ireland, Malaysia)	180 (in North and South America, Europe, Asia, Australia)	
Market capitalization ($millions)	58,469	66,886	
P/E	60	10*	
5-Year Average revenue growth	55% per year	6% per year	
5-Year Average stock price growth	133% per year	33.4% per year	

*Excludes earnings from Associates spin-off.

demand; (2) a minimum of 15 days of vehicles in each assembly plant's order bank to increase manufacturing stability; gaps in the order bank are filled with "suggested" dealer orders based on historical buying patterns; (3) regional "mixing centers" that optimize schedules and deliveries of finished vehicles via rail transportation; and (4) a robust order amendment process to allow vehicles to be amended for minor color and trim variations without having to submit new orders. The OTD vision was to create a lean, flexible, and predictable process that harmonized the efforts of all of Ford's components to enable it to provide consumers with the right products in the right place at the right time. Ford believed that success in achieving this vision would provide better quality, higher customer satisfaction, improved customer selection, better plant productivity, stability for its supply base, and lower dealer and company costs.

Ford Retail Network

On July 1, 1998, Ford launched the first of its Ford retail network (FRN) ventures in Tulsa, Oklahoma, under the newly formed Ford Investment Enterprises Company (FIECo). Ford Investment Enterprises was formed to take

EXHIBIT 1 Dell and Ford Compared (*Continued*)

Enterprise Model Comparison

A high-level comparison of the Dell and Ford Motor enterprise models is shown below. Besides the lack of a dealer distribution channel, other key differences are Dell's ownership of assembly plants only—all component/subassembly manufacturing is done by its supply base—and the more integrated nature of Dell's sales, R&D, and manufacturing operations. All of the operating principles that underlie Dell's success have counterparts in Ford's breakthrough objectives and key business plan initiatives.

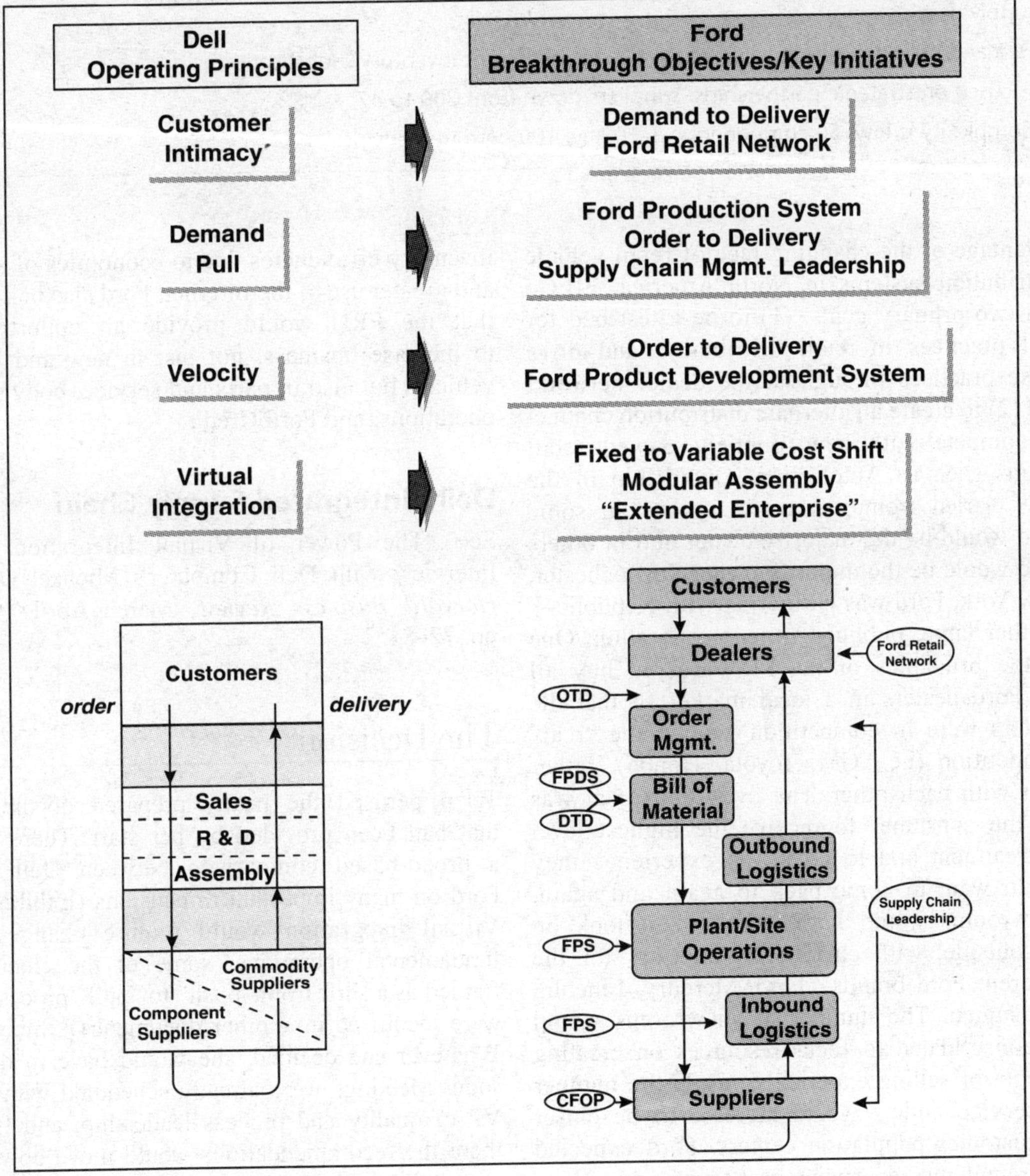

EXHIBIT 1 Food and Dell Compared (*Continued*)

Dell Processes	Ford
Suppliers own inventory until it is used in production	
Suppliers maintain nearby ship points, delivery time 15 minutes to 1 hour	
External logistics supplier used to manage inbound supply chain	
Customers frequently steered to PCs with high availability to balance supply and demand	
Demand forecasting is critical—changes are shared immediately within Dell and with supply base	
Demand pull throughout value chain—"information for inventory" substitution	
Focused on strategic partnerships: suppliers down from 200 to 47	
Complexity is low: 50 components, 8–10 key, 100 permutations	

advantage of the changing face of retail vehicle distribution systems in North America. FIECo had two primary goals: (1) to be a test bed for best practices in retail distribution and drive those practices throughout the dealer network; and (2) to create an alternate distribution channel to compete with new, publicly owned retail chains such as AutoNation. Ownership in the FRN varied from market to market; in some Ford would be the majority owner and in others Ford would be the minority owner. In Rochester, New York, Ford was partnering with Republic—another large, publicly owned corporation. One of the principles of the FRN was to buy all the Ford dealers in a local market so that the dealers were in competition against the "real" competition (i.e., GM, Toyota, Honda), rather than with each other. The overriding goal was for the consumer to receive the highest level of treatment and to create an experience they would want to come back to again and again. Showrooms would have a consistent look on the outside, with customized interiors for the different Ford brands—Ford, Mercury, Lincoln, and Jaguar. The number of showrooms would be consolidated to focus resources on creating a superior selling experience, while the number of service outlets would increase to be closer to customer population centers. Ford expected personnel and advertising cost savings as well as inventory efficiencies due to economies of scale and greater use of the Internet. Ford also believed that the FRN would provide an opportunity to increase business, not just in new and used vehicles but also in parts and service, body shop operations, and Ford Credit.

Dell's Integrated Supply Chain

See "The Power of Virtual Integration: An Interview with Dell Computer's Michael Dell," *Harvard Business Review*, March–April 1998, pp. 72–84.

The Decision

Takai perused the neatly prepared documents that had been provided by her staff. There was a broad-based comparison between Dell and Ford on many important dimensions (Exhibit 1). Virtual integration would require changes in fundamental operations; some of the changes, framed as a shift from "push" to "pull" processes, were identified in another document (Exhibit 2). Whatever she decided, she would have to do it soon. Meetings were already scheduled with the VP of quality and process leadership, and from there the recommendations would move upward, eventually to Nasser.

EXHIBIT 2 Moving from Push to Pull

	Process	Push	Pull
Design	Design strategy	Please everyone	Mainstream customer wants
Marketing	Vehicle combinations	More is better	Minimal
	Pricing strategy	Budget-driven	Market-driven
	Vehicle purchase incentives	Higher	Lower
Manufacturing and Supply	Capacity planning	Multiple material/capacity constraints, driven by program budget	Market-driven (no constraints, FPV/CPV+10% for vehicle, +15% for components
	Schedule and build stability	Maximize production — make whatever you can build	Schedule from customer-driven order bank, build to schedule
Dealer Network	Dealer ordering	Orders based on allocations and capacity constraints	Orders based on customer demand
	Order to delivery times	Longer (60+ days)	Shorter (15 days or less)
	Inventory	High with low turnover	Low with rapid turnover
	Dealership model	Independent dealerships, negotiations with company	Company controlled dealerships (Ford Retail Network)

Reading 2-4

The Power of Virtual Integration: An Interview with Dell Computer's Michael Dell

How do you create a $12 billion company in just 13 years? Michael Dell began in 1984 with a simple business insight: He could bypass the dealer channel through which personal computers were then being sold. Instead, he would sell directly to customers and build products to order. In one swoop, Dell eliminated the reseller's markup and the costs and risks associated with carrying large inventories of finished goods. The formula became known as the *direct business model*, and it gave Dell Computer Corporation a substantial cost advantage.

The direct model turned out to have other benefits that even Michael Dell couldn't have anticipated when he founded his company. "You actually get to have a relationship with the customer," he explains. "And that creates valuable information, which, in turn, allows us to leverage our relationships with both suppliers and customers. Couple that information with technology, and you have the infrastructure to revolutionize the fundamental business models of major global companies."

In this interview with HBR editor-at-large Joan Magretta, Michael Dell describes how his company is using technology and information to blur the traditional boundaries in the value chain among suppliers, manufacturers, and end users. In so doing, Dell Computer is evolving in a direction that Michael Dell calls *virtual integration*. The individual pieces of the strategy—customer focus, supplier partnerships, mass customization, just-in-time manufacturing—may all be familiar. But Michael Dell's insight into how to combine them is highly innovative: Technology is enabling coordination across company boundaries to achieve new levels of efficiency and productivity, as well as extraordinary returns to investors. Virtual integration harnesses the economic benefits of two very different business models. It offers the advantages of a tightly coordinated supply chain that have traditionally come through vertical integration. At the same time, it benefits from the focus and specialization that drive virtual corporations. Virtual integration, as Michael Dell envisions it, has the potential to achieve both coordination and focus. If it delivers on that promise, it may well become a new organizational model for the information age.

How has Dell pioneered a new business model within the computer industry?

If you look back to the industry's inception, the founding companies essentially had to create all the components themselves. They had to manufacture disk drives and memory chips and application software; all the various pieces of the industry had to be vertically integrated within one firm.

So the companies that were the stars 10 years ago, the Digital Equipments of this world, had to build massive structures to produce everything a computer needed. They had no choice but to become expert in a wide array of components, some of which had nothing to do with creating value for the customer.

As the industry grew, more specialized companies developed to produce specific components. That opened up the opportunity to create a business that was far more focused and efficient. As a small start-up, Dell couldn't afford to create every piece of the value chain. But more to the point, why should we want to? We concluded we'd be better off leveraging the investments others have made and focusing on delivering solutions and systems to customers.

Consider a component like a graphics chip. Five or 10 years ago, a whole bunch of companies in the personal computer industry were trying to create their own graphics chips. Now, if you've got a race with 20 players that are all vying to produce the fastest graphics chip in the world, do you want to be the twenty-first horse, or do you want to evaluate the field of 20 and pick the best one?

It's a pretty simple strategy, but at the time it went against the dominant "engineering-centric" view of the industry. The IBMs and Compaqs and HPs subscribed to a "we-have-to-develop-everything" view of the world. If you weren't doing component assembly, you weren't a real computer company. It was like a rite of passage. You somehow proved your manhood by placing small semiconductor chips on printed circuit boards.

And Dell Computer came along and said, "Now wait a second. If I understand this correctly, the companies that do nothing but put chips on motherboards don't actually earn tremendous profit doing it. If we want to earn higher returns, shouldn't we be more selective and put our capital into activities where we can add value for our customers, not just into activities that need to get done?" I'm not saying those activities are unimportant. They need to get done very, very well. But they're not sources of value that Dell is going to create.

When the company started, I don't think we knew how far the direct model could take us. It has provided a consistent underlying strategy for Dell despite a lot of change in our industry. Along the way, we have learned a lot, and the model has evolved. Most important, the direct model has allowed us to leverage our relationships with both suppliers and customers to such an extent that I believe it's fair to think of our companies as being virtually integrated. That allows us to focus on where we add value and to build a much larger firm much more quickly. I don't think we could have created a $12 billion business in 13 years if we had tried to be vertically integrated.

Why can you grow so much faster without all those physical assets?

There are fewer things to manage, fewer things to go wrong. You don't have the drag effect of taking 50,000 people with you. Suppose we have two suppliers building monitors for us, and one of them loses its edge. It's a lot easier for us to get more capacity from the remaining supplier than to set up a new manufacturing plant ourselves. If we had to build our own factories for every single component of the system, growing at 57 percent per year just would not be possible. I would spend 500 percent of my time interviewing prospective vice presidents because the company would have not 15,000 employees but 80,000.

Indirectly, we employ something like that many people today. There are, for example, 10,000 service technicians in the field who service our products, but only a small number of them work for us. They're contracted with other firms. But ask the customer, "Who was that person who just fixed your computer?" The vast majority think that person works for us, which is just great. That's part of virtual integration.

Aren't you just outsourcing your after-sales service? Is what you're describing fundamentally different from outsourcing?

Outsourcing, at least in the IT world, is almost always a way to get rid of a problem a company hasn't been able to solve itself. The classic case is the company with 2,000 people in the IT department. Nobody knows what they do, and nobody knows why they do it. The solution—outsource IT to a service provider, and hopefully they'll fix it. But if you look at what happens five years later, it's not necessarily a pretty picture.

That's not what we're doing at all. We focus on how we can coordinate our activities to create the most value for customers.

With our service providers, we're working to set quality measures and, more important, to build data linkages that let us see in real time how we're doing—when parts are dispatched, for instance, or how long it takes to respond to a request for service. We look at our business and see, for example, that over the next 10 years we are going to be making lots of notebook computers. Dell might need 20 million flat-panel displays, and some years there will be more demand than supply. Other years, there will be more supply than demand. A few companies are currently making multibillion-dollar investments in the manufacture of these displays.

So we cook up a little deal where the supplier agrees to meet 25 percent of our volume requirements for displays, and because of the long-term commitment we make to them, we'll get our displays year in and year out, even when there's more demand than supply. The supplier effectively becomes our partner. They assign their engineers to our design team, and we start to treat them as if they were part of the company. For example, when we launch a new product, their engineers are stationed right in our plants. If a customer calls in with a problem, we'll stop shipping product while they fix design flaws in real time.

Figuring out how many partners we need has been a process of trial and error. You learn when you operate on the cutting edge of technology that things don't always work as planned. The rule we follow is to have as few partners as possible. And they will last as long as they maintain their leadership in technology and quality. This isn't like the automobile business, where you find a tire supplier that you will probably stick with forever. Where the technology is fairly stable—in monitors, for example—we expect our partnerships to last a long time. Others will be more volatile. But regardless of how long these relationships last, virtual integration means you're basically stitching together a business with partners that are treated as if they're inside the company. You're sharing information in a real-time fashion.

We tell our suppliers exactly what our daily production requirements are. So it's not, "Well, every two weeks deliver 5,000 to this warehouse, and we'll put them on the shelf, and then we'll take them off the shelf." It's "Tomorrow morning we need 8,562, and deliver them to door number seven by 7 AM."

You would deal with an internal supplier that way, and you can do so because you share information and plans very freely. Why doesn't the same sharing of information take place across company boundaries? Buyers are often so busy trying to protect themselves that the seller can't really add a lot of value. Government purchasing is the extreme case, with its overly structured procurement system. Protecting the buyer usually ends up disabling the seller—and both lose.

The technology available today really boosts the value of information sharing. We can share design databases and methodologies with supplier-partners in ways that just weren't possible 5 to 10 years ago. This speeds time to market—often dramatically—and creates a lot of value that can be shared between buyer and supplier. So technology enhances the economic incentives to collaborate.

What are the challenges involved in establishing these collaborations?

The key challenge—and the biggest change from business as usual—is changing the focus from how much inventory there is to how fast it's moving. All computer chips carry a four-digit date code. For example, "97–23" means it was built in the twenty-third week of 1997. You can take the cover off any computer and find out how old its parts are, how long it took to make its way through the system. In our industry, if you can get people to think about how fast inventory is moving, then you create real value. Why? Because if I've got 11 days of inventory and my competitor has 80, and Intel comes out with a new 450-megahertz chip, that means I'm going to get to market 69 days sooner.

I think about it this way: Assets collect risks around them in one form or another. Inventory is one risk, and accounts receivable is another risk. In our case—with 70 percent of our sales going to large corporate customers—accounts receivable isn't hard to manage because companies like Goldman Sachs and Microsoft and Oracle tend to be able to pay their bills. But in the computer industry, inventory can actually be a pretty massive risk because if the cost of materials goes down 50 percent a year and you have two or three months of inventory versus 11 days, you've got a big cost disadvantage. And you're vulnerable to product transitions, when you can get stuck with obsolete inventory.

Inventory velocity is one of a handful of key performance measures we watch very closely. It focuses us on working with our suppliers to keep reducing inventory and increasing speed. With a supplier like Sony, which makes very good, reliable monitors, we figure there's no need for us to have any inventory at all. We are confident in putting the Dell name on them, and they work fine. We don't even take these monitors out of the box to test them because we've gotten them to under 1,000 defects per million. So what's the point in having a monitor put on a truck to Austin, Texas, and then taken off the truck and sent on a little tour around the warehouse, only to be put back on another truck? That's just a big waste of time and money, unless we get our jollies from touching monitors, which we don't.

So we went to Sony and said, "Hey, we're going to buy two or three million of these monitors this year. Why don't we just pick them up every day as we need them?" At first, it's a little confusing to the suppliers because you're saying, "Now listen carefully. If you will help us get your product from the end of your line to our customer faster, we won't have any in our warehouse." And the suppliers look at you like you're crazy and not making any sense. They're used to delivering in larger quantities, so at first they think this means you're going to buy less from them. And then the lightbulb goes on, and they realize we'll be buying more because we'll be taking it faster.

So now you have Sony producing a level supply of monitors for you. What happens next?

We tell Airborne Express or UPS to come to Austin and pick up 10,000 computers a day and go over to the Sony factory in Mexico and pick up the corresponding number of monitors. Then while we're all sleeping, they match up the computers and the monitors, and deliver them to the customer.

Of course, this requires sophisticated data exchange. Most people are familiar with the way a company like Black & Decker uses information links with the thousands of retailers that sell its products. When a customer in Omaha buys a drill from his local hardware store, the system immediately tells Black & Decker to send another unit of that particular drill to that particular store. So their system has to replenish supply, unit by unit, to thousands of outlets. From the supplier's point of view, Dell is dramatically simpler. Our orders are typically for thousands of units, and they need to go to only one of three manufacturing centers: Austin, Ireland, and Malaysia. It's almost ideal from a supplier standpoint because we have real-time information on what the demand is, and all the supplier has to do is get the product to us.

And because we build to our customers' order, typically, with just five or six days of lead time, suppliers don't have to worry about sell-through. We only maintain a few days—in some cases a few hours—of raw materials on hand. We communicate inventory levels and replenishment needs regularly—with some vendors, hourly.

The typical case in our industry is the factory building 10,000 units a day, day in and day out. First the machines stack up in the warehouse, and then they stack up in the channel. And all of a sudden, the guy at the end of the chain hollers, "Whoa, hey, we've got too many of these. Everybody stop!" And the order to stop flows back through the chain until it reaches every component supplier. It's literally stop and start, because if you have a 90-day lag between the point of demand and the point of supply, you're going to have a lot of inefficiency in the process. And the more inventory and time you have, the more variability, and the more problems.

In our industry, there's a lot of what I call bad hygiene. Companies stuff the channel to get rid of old inventory and to meet short-term financial objectives. We think our approach is better. We substitute information for inventory and ship only when we have real demand from real end customers.

How does the direct model benefit your suppliers?

We can go to Sony and say, "We're going to be pulling monitors from you in a very consistent, predictable way because the distance between the demand and the source of supply is totally shrunk." The longer that distance, the more intermediary channels you add, the less likely it is you will have good information about demand—so you will end up with more variability, more inventory, higher costs, and more risk.

Another factor that helps keep our demand for computers level is the mix of customers we serve. We don't have any customer that represents more than 1 percent to 2 percent of our revenues. One week Exxon is buying; the next week Shell is buying; the next week Ford is buying. But all companies don't decide in unison, "Well, this week we're going to buy; next week we're not."

You mention your customer mix. Does the direct model imply a particular customer strategy?

If you'd asked me that question 12 years ago, I would have said that we didn't differentiate much between our largest and our smallest customer. Today we do. Our customer strategy is one area where our model has evolved. We've become good at developing what we call "scalable" businesses—that is, those in which we can grow revenues faster than expenses. We really look closely at financial measures like gross margins by customer segment—and we focus on segments we can serve profitably as we achieve scale. People are sometimes surprised to learn that 90 percent of our sales go to institutions—business or government—and 70 percent to very large customers that buy at least $1 million in PCs per year.

When you're trying to target profitable segments, averages obscure a lot, and aggregate financial statements are pretty meaningless. Our approach to segmentation is to take really big numbers and "de-average" them. Until you look inside and understand what's going on by business, by customer, by geography, you don't know anything. This is a lesson we learned the hard way. We incorrectly entered the retail business in 1989, thinking that our direct business wouldn't grow enough, and went into computer superstores and warehouse clubs. But when we really started to understand the segment's profitability, we realized we'd made a mistake, and so we exited.

For years, we didn't actively pursue the consumer market because we couldn't reach our profit objectives. So we let our competitors introduce machines with rock-bottom prices and zero margins. We figured they could be the ones to teach consumers about PCs while we focused our efforts on more profitable segments. And then, because we're direct and can see who is buying what, we noticed something interesting. The industry's average selling price to consumers was going down, but ours was going up. Consumers who were now buying their second or third machines—who wanted the most powerful machines and needed less hand-holding—were coming to us. And without focusing on it in a significant way, we had a billion-dollar consumer business that was profitable. So we decided in 1997 that it was time to dedicate a group to serving that segment.

So, over time, you cut the market into finer and finer segments?

Yes, for a lot of reasons. One is to identify unique opportunities and economics. The other is purely a managerial issue: You can't possibly manage something well if it's too big. Segmentation gives us better attention and focus (see Exhibit 1).

Each segment has its own issues. In education, for instance, how do you get tech support to a classroom when the teacher doesn't have a telephone? You need a totally different approach. Segmenting lets you tailor your programs to the customers' needs. If you just lump diverse customers together, you can be sure that some of them will come last on some manager's list, and

EXHIBIT 1 **Fast-Cycle Segmentation**

Dell's rapid growth in recent years has been accompanied by ever finer cuts at customer segmentation. This is an important element of Dell's virtual integration with customers. The finer the segmentation, the better able Dell is to forecast what its customers are going to need and when. Dell then coordinates the flow of that strategic information all the way back to its suppliers, effectively substituting information for inventory.

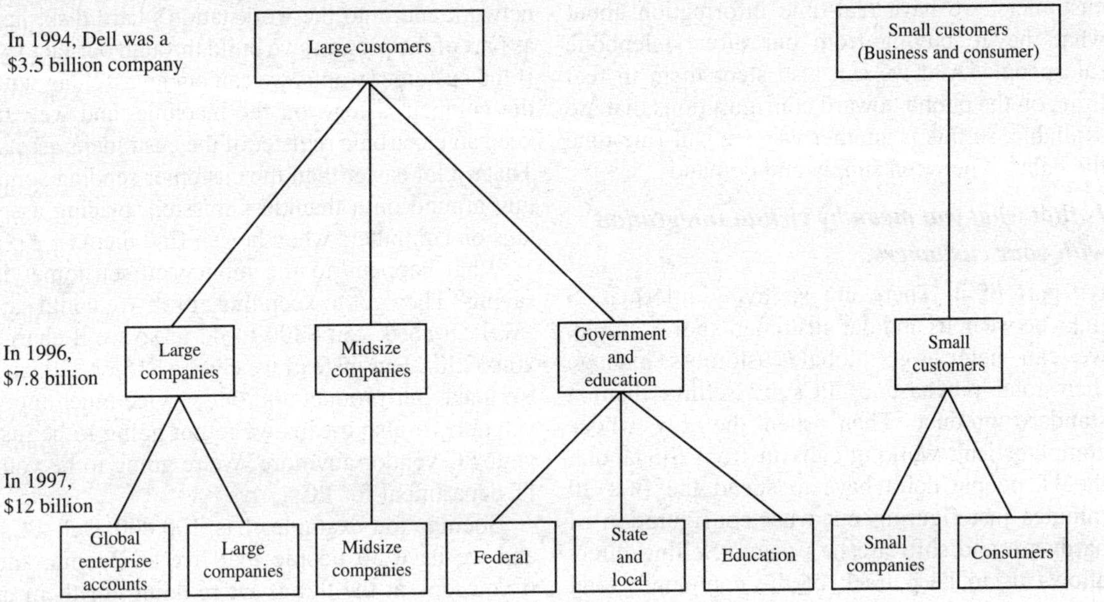

he may never get around to solving their problems. That's why we make serving one segment the manager's only job.

Do you get other benefits from segmenting your customers?

Segmentation gets us closer to them. It allows us to understand their needs in a really deep way. This closeness gives us access to information that's absolutely critical to our strategy. It helps us forecast what they're going to need and when. And good forecasts are the key to keeping our costs down.

We turn our inventory over 30 times per year. If you look at the complexity and the diversity of our product line, there's no way we could do that unless we had credible information about what the customer is actually buying. It's a key part of why rivals have had great difficulty competing with Dell. It's not just that we sell direct; it's also our ability to forecast demand—it's both the design of the product and the way the information from the customer flows all the way through manufacturing to our suppliers. If you don't have that tight linkage—the kind of coordination of information that used to be possible only in vertically integrated companies—then trying to manage to 11 days of inventory would be insane. We simply couldn't do it without customers who work with us as partners.

Could you describe how you forecast demand?

We see forecasting as a critical sales skill. We teach our sales-account managers to lead customers through a discussion of their future PC needs. We'll walk a customer through every department of his company, asking him to designate which needs are certain and which are contingent. And when they're contingent on some event, the salesperson will know what that event is so he can follow up. We can do this with our large accounts, which make up the bulk of our business. With smaller customers, we have real-time information about what they're buying from our direct telephone salespeople. And we can also steer them in real time, on the phone, toward configurations that are available, so this is another way we can fine-tune the balance between supply and demand.

Is that what you mean by virtual integration with your customers?

It's part of it. There are so many information links between us and our customers. For example, we can help large global customers manage their total purchase of PCs by selling them a standard product. Then when the guy whose computer isn't working calls in from Singapore, the IT people don't have to spend the first 30 minutes just figuring out what configuration of hardware and software he's using. Selling direct allows us to keep track of the company's total PC purchases, country by country—and that's valuable information we can feed back to them. We sometimes know more about a customer's operations than they do themselves.

Close customer relationships have allowed us to dramatically extend the value we deliver to our customers. Today we routinely load the customer's software in our factory. Eastman Chemical, for example, has their own unique mix of software, some of it licensed from Microsoft, some of it they've written themselves, some of it having to do with the way their network works. Normally, they would get their PCs, take them out of the box, and then some guy carrying a walkie-talkie and diskettes and CD-ROMs would come to each employee's desk to hook the system up and load all that software. Typically, this takes an hour or two—and costs \$200 to \$300—and it's a nuisance.

Our solution was to create a massive network in our factory with high-speed, 100-megabit Ethernet. We'll load Eastman Chemical's software onto a huge Dell server. Then when a machine comes down the assembly line and says, "I'm an Eastman Chemical analyst workstation, configuration number 14," all of a sudden a few hundred megabytes of data come rushing through the network and onto the workstation's hard disk, just as part of the progressive build through our factory. If the customer wants, we can put an asset tag with the company's logo on the machine, and we can keep an electronic register of the customer's assets. That's a lot easier than the customer sending some guy around on a thankless mission, placing asset tags on computers when he can find them.

What happens to the money our customer is saving? They get to keep most of it. We could say, "Well, it costs you \$300 to do it, so we'll charge you \$250." But instead we charge \$15 or \$20, and we make our product and our service much more valuable. It also means we're not going to be just your PC vendor anymore. We're going to be your IT department for PCs.

Boeing, for example, has 100,000 Dell PCs, and we have 30 people that live at Boeing, and if you look at the things we're doing for them or for other customers, we don't look like a supplier; we look more like Boeing's PC department. We become intimately involved in planning their PC needs and the configuration of their network.

It's not that we make these decisions by ourselves. They're certainly using their own people to get the best answer for the company. But the people working on PCs together, both from Dell and Boeing, understand the needs in a very intimate way. They're right there living it and breathing it, as opposed to the typical vendor who says, "Here are your computers. See you later."

We've always visited clients, but now some of our accounts are large enough to justify a dedicated on-site team. Remember, a lot of companies have far more complex problems to deal with than PC purchasing and servicing. They can't wait to get somebody else to take care of that so they can worry about more strategic issues.

So some of your coordination with customers is made possible through technology, but there's still a good measure of old-fashioned, face-to-face human contact?

Yes, that's right. The idea is to use technology to free people up to solve more complicated problems. For example, a customer like MCI can access our internal support tools online in the same way our own technical-support teams do, saving time and money on both sides. They simply go to www.dell.com, enter some information about their system, and they have immediate access to the same information that we use at Dell to help customers. These tools are used by internal help-desk groups at large companies as well as by individuals.

We've developed customized intranet sites called Premier Pages for well over 200 of our largest global customers. These exist securely within the customers' firewalls, and they give them direct access to purchasing and technical information about the specific configurations they buy from us. One of our customers, for example, allows its 50,000 employees to view and select products online. They use the Premier Page as an interactive catalog of all the configurations the company authorizes; employees can then price and order the PC they want. They are happy to have some choice, and Dell and the customer are both happy to eliminate the paperwork and sales time normally associated with corporate purchasing. That frees our salespeople to play a more consultative role.

We also have developed tools to help customers set up their own customized versions of dell.com. There are about 7,000 of these to date.

How else do you stay close to your customers?

In a direct business like ours, you have, by definition, a relationship with customers. But beyond the mechanisms we have for sales and support, we have set up a number of forums to ensure the free flow of information with the customer on a constant basis. Our Platinum Councils, for example, are regional meetings—in Asia-Pacific, Japan, the United States, and Europe—of our largest customers. They meet every six to nine months; in the larger regions, there's one for the information executives—the CIO types—and then there's one for the technical types.

In these meetings, our senior technologists share their views on where the technology is heading and lay out road maps of product plans over the next two years. There are also breakout sessions and working groups in which our engineering teams focus on specific product areas and talk about how to solve problems that may not necessarily have anything to do with the commercial relationship with Dell. For example, Is leasing better than buying? or How do you manage the transition to Windows NT? or How do you manage a field force of notebook computers?

People in businesses as dissimilar as Unilever and ICI can learn from each other because, amazingly, they have very similar problems when it comes to PCs. And we send not only our top technologists and engineers but also the real engineers, the people who usually don't get out to talk to customers because they're too busy developing products. All of our senior executives from around the company participate, spending time with the customer, listening to how we're doing. The ratio is about one Dell person to one customer. At our last session, we had about 100 customers.

The councils are another way we're able to play more of an advisory role, trying to help our customers understand what the flow of new technology really means, how it will translate into specific products. We try to help the customer anticipate what's happening and be ready. And that helps us, as well, with our own demand forecasting. So we're helping each other in important ways. We hire a lot of people from other companies in the industry, and they tell us that these meetings are unique.

Do you spend a significant amount of your time at these meetings?

I spend three days at each of them. They're great events. In the normal course of our business, I have lots of opportunity to talk to customers one on one, but there is something much more powerful about this kind of forum. Customers tend to speak more openly when they're with their peers and they know we're there and we're listening.

At every Platinum Council, we review what they told us last time and what we did about it. We keep an ongoing record of the issues. Let me give you a concrete example: A few years ago, the engineers responsible for our desktops were operating on the theory that customers really wanted performance from these products—the faster the better. But what the customers actually said at the Platinum Councils was, "Yeah, performance, that's okay. But what I really want is a stable product that doesn't change. Because if I'm trying to run a bank or an airline, I don't care if it's 2 percent faster or 3 percent slower. What really matters is stability." So our engineers thought one thing; the customers thought another thing. It took the direct feedback from the Platinum Councils to spotlight this failure to communicate. We responded by building product with intergenerational consistency over many years. The same feedback has helped shape the creation of our brands. For both our desktop and notebook businesses, we created different brands designed to deliver greater stability to corporate customers, as opposed to the fast technology changes that consumers demand.

As I think back to some of those council meetings, things that would seem fairly small at the time have often turned out three or four years later to become the basis for billions of dollars of revenue—notebooks with longer-life batteries, for example, or loading customers' software for them in our plants.

As your customer strategy has evolved, has the Dell brand changed as well?

A big piece of our brand is being the most efficient and effective way for customers to buy Intel or Microsoft technologies. But beyond that, we're evolving into a technology selector, or navigator. We often talk to customers about "relevant technology." Intel and Microsoft tend to launch into a massive variety of things, some of which are speculative and aimed at exploring new technologies. We think it's our job to help our customers sort out the technology relevant to today's needs from the bleeding edge.

How does that strategy affect your own R&D function? What role does R&D play in your company?

At Dell, we believe the customer is in control, and our job is to take all the technology that's out there and apply it in a useful way to meet the customer's needs. We're not trying to invent new architecture ourselves, but we'll spend a quarter of a billion dollars this year and employ some 1,500 people to improve the whole user experience—that means delivering the latest relevant technology, making it easy to use, and keeping costs down. And in addition to selecting appropriate technology, our R&D group focuses on process and quality improvements in manufacturing.

Before industry standards came into play, the proprietary computing environment bred a kind of technical arrogance that, fortunately, won't fly anymore. Once standards were established, the customer started to define what was going to be successful, and it didn't matter what you invented or how good it was or how fast it was. Increasingly, what matters is what the customers want and whether it works with all their other stuff.

That means we have to stay on top of our customers' needs, and we have to monitor and understand the innovations in the material science world—everything from semiconductors to polymers to liquid crystal displays. You need to track anything having to do with the flow of electrons, and you need to keep asking how these marvelous developments might be useful to customers. The customer doesn't come to you and say, "Boy, I really like lithium ion batteries. I can't wait to get my hands on some lithium ion." The customer says, "I want a notebook computer that lasts the whole day. I don't want it to run out when I'm on the plane."

I was about to leave a meeting at Sony in Tokyo in January of 1993 when someone ran up to me

EXHIBIT 2 The Evolution of a Faster Business Model

The dominant model in the personal computer industry—a value chain with arms-length transactions from one layer to the next:

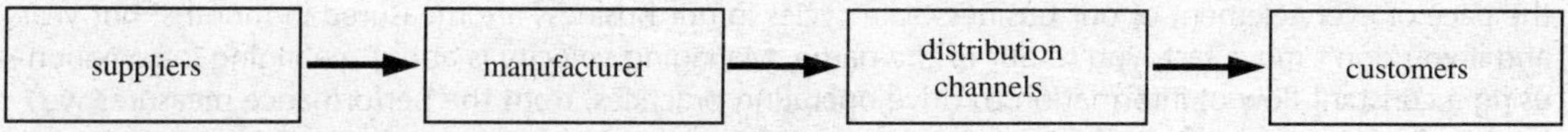

Dell's direct model eliminates the time and cost of third-party distribution:

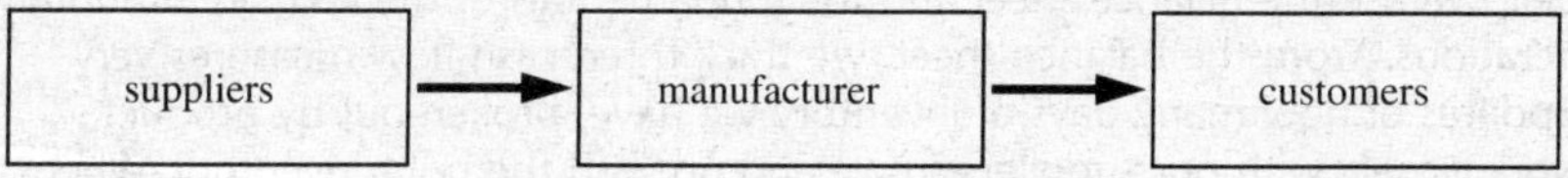

Virtual integration works even faster by blurring the traditional boundaries and roles in the value chain:

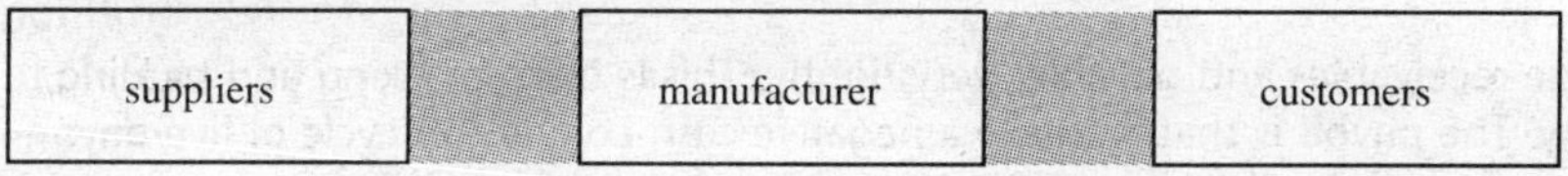

and said, "Oh, Mr. Dell, please wait one minute. I'm from Sony's power technology company. We have a new power-system technology we want to explain to you." And I remember thinking, Is this guy going to try to sell me a power plant? He starts showing me chart after chart about the performance of lithium ion batteries. This is wonderful, I tell him. And if it's true, we're going to put this in every notebook computer we make.

We then sent a team over to check it out, and a year and a half later we were the first computer company to have a notebook that lasted five-and-a-half, six hours. We tested it with American Airlines, handing out the notebooks to passengers at the start of flights from New York to Los Angeles. By the end, the notebooks were still running.

How are the challenges of leadership in a virtually integrated organization different from those you would encounter running a corporation with more traditional boundaries?

The whole idea behind virtual integration is that it lets you meet customers' needs faster and more efficiently than any other model (see Exhibit 2). With vertical integration, you can be an efficient producer—as long as the world isn't changing very much. But virtual integration lets you be efficient and responsive to change at the same time—at least, that's what we're trying to do. We think about Internet commerce as a logical extension of our direct model—and within our first year, we reached a run rate of $2 million a day. It's now about $3 million a day, and during the peak of the Christmas buying season we saw several $6 million days. I'm only half joking when I say that the only thing better than the Internet would be mental telepathy. Because what we're all about is shrinking the time and the resources it takes to meet customers' needs. And we're trying to do that in a world where those needs are changing.

To lead in that kind of environment, you have to be on the lookout for shifts in value, and if the customer decides, "Hey, I don't care about that anymore; now I care about this," we may have to develop new capabilities rather quickly. One of the biggest challenges we face today is finding managers who can sense and respond to rapid shifts, people who can process new information very quickly and make decisions in real time. It's a problem for the computer industry as a whole—and not just for Dell—that the industry's growth has outpaced its ability to create managers. We tell prospective hires, "If you want an environment that is never going to change, don't come here. This is not the place for you."

EXHIBIT 3 Using Information to Speed Execution

by Kevin Rollins

Most of the managerial challenges at Dell Computer have to do with what we call *velocity*—speeding the pace of every element of our business. Life cycles in our business are measured in months, not years, and if you don't move fast, you're out of the game. Managing velocity is about managing information—using a constant flow of information to drive operating practices, from the performance measures we track to how we work with our suppliers.

Performance Metrics. At Dell, we use the balance sheet and the fundamentals of the P&L on a monthly basis as tools to manage operations. From the balance sheet, we track three cash-flow measures very closely. We look at weekly updates of how many days of inventory we have, broken out by product component. We can then work closely with our suppliers so we end up with the right inventory. When it's not quite right, we can use our direct-sales model to steer customers toward comparable products that we do have. So we use inventory information to work both the front and back ends at the same time.

We also track and manage receivables and payables very tightly. This is basic blocking and tackling, but we give it a high priority. The payoff is that we have a negative cash-conversion cycle of five days—that is, we get paid before we have to pay our suppliers. Since our competitors usually have to support their resellers by offering them credit, the direct model gives us an inherent cost advantage. And the more we can shorten our cash-collection cycle, the greater our advantage.

The real-time performance measures in the P&L that we regard as the best indicators of the company's health are our margins, our average selling price, and the overhead associated with selling. We split the P&L into these core elements by customer segment, by product, and by country. These metrics can alert us instantly to problems, for example, with the mix of products being sold in any particular country.

Working with Suppliers. The greatest challenge in working with suppliers is getting them in sync with the fast pace we have to maintain. The key to making it work is information. The right information flows allow us to work with our partners in ways that enhance speed, either directly by improving logistics or indirectly by improving quality.

Take our service strategy, for example. Customers pay us for service and support, and we contract with third-party maintainers (TPMs) to make the service calls. Customers call us when they have problems, and that initial call will trigger two electronic dispatches—one to ship the needed parts directly from Dell to the customers' sites and one to dispatch the TPMs to the customers. Our role as information broker facilitates the TPMs' work by making sure the necessary parts will be on-site when they arrive.

But our role doesn't stop there. Because poor quality creates friction in the system, which slows us down, we want to capture information that can be used to fix problems so they won't happen again. So we take back the bad part to diagnose what went wrong, and we feed that information back to our suppliers so they can redesign the component. Clearly, we couldn't operate that way if we were dealing with hundreds of suppliers. So for us, working with a handful of partners is one of the keys to improving quality—and therefore speed—in our system.

Kevin Rollins is vice chairman of Dell Computer Corporation.

Our goal is to be one or two steps ahead of the change, and in fact to be creating or shaping it, to some extent. That's why we spend so much time with our customers. It's why I personally spend about 40 percent of my time with customers. Often it's a lead customer that says, "Hey, can you put an asset tag on my PC?" And the first reaction is, "Gee, we've never done that before, but why not? Let's give it a try." And then you do it for one customer, then for 10, then for a hundred, and eventually it becomes a standard offering. Putting asset tags on computers isn't by itself a major value shift, but what happens is that we get a series of seemingly small innovations that over time add up to a huge improvement. That's not a bad description of the way we get into businesses. We don't come at it the other way around, with a consulting study that says, "That's an attractive business. Let's go." Nor do we sit around and say, "What do we suppose our customers would like? If we were customers, what would we be thinking?"

So looking for value shifts is probably the most important dimension of leadership. Then there's the question of managing such a tightly coordinated value chain—and there it's all about execution. If you look at Dell's P&L structure, I think you'd be hard-pressed to find companies that deliver the kind of value-added we do with such a small markup. My theory is that if we can continue to keep our markup as low as it is today, we're going to be able to capture most of the opportunities available to us. But that means we cannot get complacent about our growth and get careless about execution.

Sometimes, I'm taken aback when I talk to people who've been in the company for six months or a year and who talk about "the model" as if it were an all-powerful being that will take care of everything. It's scary because I know that nothing is ever 100 percent constant, and the last thing we should do is assume that we're always going to be doing well. But for now, it's working. The direct system really delivers value to the customer all the way from distribution back through manufacturing and design. If you tried to divide Dell up into a manufacturer and a channel, you'd destroy the company's unique value. It's something completely new that nobody in our industry has ever done before. (see Exhibit 3).

Strategic Outsourcing at Bharti Airtel, Ltd.

Faced with exponential growth and a competitive telecom environment, Bharti Airtel is looking for ways to better manage its capital expenditures for telecommunications and information technology. One option is to delegate management of its telecommunications and IT networks to its vendors. The case explores the pros and cons of such an outsourcing arrangement for a company in an industry where technological superiority is considered an essential element in competitive strategy. The case presents an innovative approach to gaining competitive advantage through outsourcing. It offers opportunities to analyze the decision to outsource and the design of the contracts, controls, relationships, and systems that enable successful implementation. As you read the case, consider these questions: What must Bharti do to succeed well in the Indian mobile phone market and what are its core competencies? What do you see as advantages and disadvantages of the outsourcing agreements outlined by Gupta? How do the different outsourcing agreements work towards building these core competencies? If you were Bharti, what major concerns would you have about entering an outsourcing agreement with IBM? With Ericsson, Nokia, or Siemens? How would you structure the agreements to address your concerns and capture any advantages you have identified?

Case 2-5

Strategic Outsourcing at Bharti Airtel Limited

> Budgeting for capital expenditures was a nightmare. Every time we had a change in the network plan we were forced to go back to the vendor and start over. . . . We would have three or four reviews per year. . . . It showed a real conflict of interest between the operator and the vendor.
>
> *Akhil Gupta, June 2005*

Akhil Gupta, joint managing director of Bharti Airtel Limited (the Indian telecommunications firm formerly known as Bharti Tele-Ventures Limited), dropped a newly penned purchase agreement with network suppliers into his inbox, but Gupta did not feel like celebrating. It was early 2004, and the deal had taken three months and a quarter of his time to finalize. Bharti's customer base was growing 100 percent per year, and it was a huge challenge to keep pace with network expansion. Very soon Bharti Airtel would be back at the negotiating table for the fourth time in 12 months. "Budgeting and the tendering[1] process for network expansion is taking up a tremendous amount of management time and bandwidth—bandwidth that is needed elsewhere," said Gupta.

Managing the firm's IT capital expenditures was another challenge. As Gupta explained:

> Our CIO would come to me with a budget, reflecting that the equipment we bought in the last couple of years was no longer of much use; the new software wouldn't run on it. This was painful because we realized that we spent $15 to $20 million and there was already talk of throwing it away because its only use was as a mail server. That's a heck of an expensive mail server!

Professors F. Asís Martínez-Jerez and V. G. Narayanan and Research Associate Michele Jurgens prepared this case as the basis for class discussion rather than to illustrate effective or ineffective management.

[1] Soliciting vendors' bids for contracts.

In the midst of these wildly unpredictable expenditures, Gupta felt that Bharti badly needed a lean and predictable cost model:

> We want to exploit the potential of 300–400 million Indian phone customers. Their purchasing power is relatively low compared to the United States and Europe—there is no way our average customer will pay $10 a month for this service. We need a lot of customers with $4 and $5 revenues per month. If we had a reliable, predictable usage-linked cost structure then we could become the lowest-cost producer of minutes not only in India but perhaps in the world.

From the inbox, Gupta's eye strayed over to the opposite side of his desk. There in the corner was the plan that he and his team hoped would solve his capital expenditures nightmares. This plan consisted of two outsourcing proposals: one to Bharti's key telecom network equipment vendors, Ericsson, Nokia, and Siemens; and the other to its IT equipment vendor, IBM. The documents proposed completely handing over the buildup and management of Bharti's telecom and IT network to these vendors. Gupta explained:

> For the first time in telecom history, perhaps anywhere in the world, the network equipment vendor and the operator would be on the same side of the table. Right now, the equipment vendors make more money when they sell more boxes to us, whereas we needed to ensure that we buy fewer boxes but get maximum capacity and coverage to stay competitive. This [caused] an inherent conflict of interest between the two of us. I felt that we needed a completely different equation.

Although Sunil Mittal, the company's chairman and managing director, had given Gupta free rein to investigate the idea with his colleagues and vendors, thus far he had encountered either stunned silence or outright resistance. "They reacted as if I had suggested giving the family jewels to outsiders," said Gupta. The vendors, on the other hand, were worried about taking on additional risk. He wondered whether he would be able to overcome the objections of his colleagues and the vendors and make this idea work.

[2] IBM Web site, www.ibm.com/news/us/en/2005/05/Business_Leadership_Forum.html, accessed May 10, 2006.

Bharti History and Background

Mittal founded Bharti in 1995 with $900 in start-up capital.[2] Mittal was an entrepreneur who had created and successfully managed several businesses, including a bicycle components business, a portable generator import business, and a venture with Siemens to produce telephone equipment. His goal in creating Bharti Airtel Limited was to take advantage of the liberalization of the Indian telecom market and to bid for a government license to operate the first private mobile telecom service in the Delhi area. Bharti won the government tender and immediately launched its service, known as "Airtel," using the GSM (Global System for Mobile communications technology).

In the first eight years of its existence, Bharti grew by having what Mittal called "a single-minded devotion to the project and the industry." As he also put it, "Our business is telecom and nothing else."[3] Bharti was the first private provider on the market in Delhi and, in 1998, was India's first private provider to turn a profit.[4]

As part of its drive for continuous expansion, Bharti aggressively pursued the acquisition of licenses for mobile operations in other geographic regions, or "circles."[5] This strategy required ever-greater capital inflows. In 1999, Bharti sold a 20 percent equity interest to the private equity firm Warburg Pincus. Soon after, New York Life Insurance Fund, the Asian Infrastructure Group, the International Finance Corporation (IFC), and SingTel[6] all acquired equity interests in Bharti. In 2002, Bharti went public on the Indian National Stock Exchange, the Mumbai (Bombay) Exchange, and the Delhi Stock Exchange, raising

[3] Krishna Palepu, Tarun Khanna, and Ingrid Vargas, "Bharti Tele-Ventures," HBS No. 704-426 (Boston: Harvard Business School Publishing, 2003). Original source: Sunil Mittal quoted in Chakravarti, "Tour de Telecom."

[4] Ibid.

[5] Telecom service in India was divided into geographical areas, called circles, for the purpose of awarding mobile and fixed-line telephone licenses.

[6] SingTel: Singapore Telecommunications Limited, a large Singapore-based telecommunications group.

EXHIBIT 1 Highlights—Bharti's Financial Situation at Year-end 2003 and 2004

Source: Audited consolidated financial statements as per U.S. GAAP for the years ended March 31, 2003, 2004, 2005. Excel file available on the company's Web site, www.bhartiairtel.in. Note US$ to INR exchange rate of 47.53 for the year ended March 31, 2003, and 43.40 for the year ended March 31, 2004.

	Year-end March 31, 2004		Year-end March 31, 2003	
Key Indicators	**Rupees Million**	**$ Millions**	**Rupees Million**	**$ Millions**
Sales	48,320	1,113.4	24,170	509
Net income	5,076	116.9	(2,018)	(42)
Earnings per share	INR 2.76	0.06	(INR 1.10)	(0.02)
Total assets	119,021	2,742.4	88,659	1,865
Total liabilities	73,105	1,684.5	47,981	1,009
Long-term debt (net of current portion)	36,965	851.7	22,736	478
Operating margin	16.9%	16.9%	–2.3%	–2.3%
Profit margin	10.5%	10.5%	–8.3%	–8.3%

$172 million in its initial public offering (IPO). In total, Bharti raised over $1 billion through foreign direct investments by the end of 2002.[7]

The capital inflow allowed Bharti to finance its next stage of growth. In 2001–2002, it obtained mobile licenses for 15 out of India's 23 total circles and also obtained fixed-line licenses for six of them. In addition, leveraging its arrangements with SingTel, Bharti subsequently obtained licenses to become the first private telecommunications service provider in India to launch national and international long-distance service.

By 2003, Bharti was present in all of the major economic and industrial centers—representing 91 percent of all mobile users in India (see Exhibit 9). It was also targeting growth in the remaining eight circles, even those in the most remote regions. Mittal and his team anticipated achieving full coverage of India by 2005.

From a financial perspective, Bharti's position had significantly improved. March 2004 year-end results showed revenues of $1,113.4 million, a 100 percent increase over 2003. Able to take advantage of the economies of scale due to its larger network, Bharti improved its operating margins from negative (–2.25%) in 2003 to positive (16.9%) in 2004. And while it had suffered a net loss in 2003, the next year saw a net income of $117 million. Return on equity in 2004 was nearly 12 percent. (Highlights of Bharti's year-end financial statements in March 2004 are shown in Exhibits 1 and 2.)

Bharti Management and Organization

Bharti, like many of the large Indian industrials, was practically a family-run business. Sunil Mittal was chairman and group managing director of Bharti Airtel Limited. His brother Rakesh Mittal was a board director; Rajan Mittal, another brother, was the joint managing director, overseeing the functional directors of marketing, business development, corporate affairs, and corporate development.

Gupta had known the Mittals for many years and was with Bharti Airtel from its inception. A chartered accountant with a degree from Delhi University, he was CFO from 1995 to 2000, becoming joint managing director in 2001. As joint managing director and CFO, Gupta had responsibility for overseeing the functional directors of finance, information technology, special projects, and regulatory and secretarial concerns. (Bharti's organization chart as of February 2004 is shown in Exhibit 3.)

[7] The equity funds received by Bharti were classified as foreign direct investment and required approval from the Foreign Investment Promotion Board (FIPB) and the Reserve Bank of India (RBI), two of the bodies governing the inflow and outflow of funds in India.

EXHIBIT 2 Bharti's Balance Sheet and Income Statements for 2004

Source: Audited consolidated financial statements as per U.S. GAAP for the years ended March 31, 2003, 2004, 2005. Excel file available on the company's Web site, www.bhartiairtel.in. Note US$ to INR exchange rate of 43.40 for the year ended March 31, 2004.

Bharti's Balance Sheet at Year-end March 31, 2004, in $ millions

Assets	
Total current assets	$ 371,960
Property and equipment, net	1,465,050
Other assets	905,422
Total assets	$2,742,432
Liabilities & Equity	
Total current liabilities	682,561
Long-term debt, net of current portion	851,717
Other liabilities	150,177
Total liabilities	$1,684,455
Common stock, par value Rs. 10 per share	427,043
Additional paid-in-capital	1,108,659
Deferred stock-based compensation	(3,238)
Treasury stock	(12,879)
Retained earnings/(deficit)	(461,608)
Total Liabilities and Shareholders' Equity	$2,742,432

Bharti's Income Statement for the Year Ending March 31, 2004, in $ millions

Revenues	$1,113,363
Operating Expenses	925,611
Cost of goods and services[a]	(743,607)
Selling, general and administrative expenses[b]	(182,004)
Operating Income	187,752
Interest expense (net)	(54,833)
Other income (loss)[c]	4,782
Income before income taxes	137,701
Income tax expense	(20,751)
Net Income	116,950

[a]Including cost of equipment sales.
[b]Including share of profits/(losses) in joint ventures and nonoperating expenses.
[c]Including preoperating costs.

EXHIBIT 3 Bharti's Organization Chart

Source: Company documents.

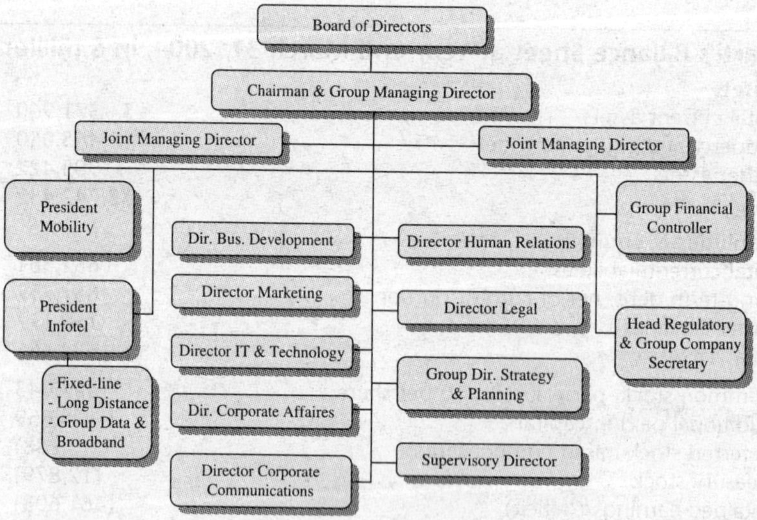

Indian Market for Telecommunications

Prior to the 1990s, the Indian telecommunications environment showed very little change from the 1950s. It took several months, sometimes years, to install a telephone in a home or business, and mobile phones were a foreign luxury. "Even up to 1995, the biggest favor anyone could do for you in India was to get you a phone," said Gupta.[8]

In 1991, India embarked on a policy of economic liberalization, opening up the sector to private competition and foreign investment. Private telecom firms could tender for licenses to operate in each of 23 designated circles. In 1989, before liberalization, there were 4.2 million telephone subscribers; by 2003, telephone subscriptions numbered 54 million, and India's telecom network had become the eighth largest in the world.[9] Total Indian telecom revenue for 2003 was $8.5 billion and was growing at 17 percent per annum.[10]

Wireless services contributed about 18 percent of the $8.5 billion in telecom revenues (see Exhibit 4 for breakdown).[11] Estimates for the wireless market through 2008 showed the market growing from $1.5 billion to $10.9 billion.[12]

Most Indian mobile operators had adopted one of the 2G (2nd generation) technologies—ether GSM or CDMA. By 2003, it appeared that India would soon jump to 3G technologies, or at least to 2.5G technologies.[13] Value-added services—including data transmission, short message service

[8] Interviews with Ahkil Gupta, June 2005.

[9] PricewaterhouseCoopers, "Telecommunication," India Brand Equity Foundation, 2004, www.ibef.org. "Current Issue and Trend in Indian Mobile Market," Report # 04025.

[10] JM Morgan Stanley Equity Research Asia-Pacific, Bharti Tele-Ventures Ltd., June 9, 2005.

[11] Ibid.

[12] Ibid.

[13] 3G mobile technology for mobile telephony is analogous to broadband technology for fixed line in that it provides a similar level of enhanced service—rapid data transfer and the capacity to manage all manner of communication (video, voice, data, multimedia). 2.5G technologies are improvements to 2G technologies that provide many of the same advantages as the 3G technologies.

EXHIBIT 4 Percent Contribution to Indian Telecom Service Revenue, Fiscal Year 2003

Source: Compiled by casewriter based on data from JM Morgan Stanley Equity Research Asia-Pacific, Bharti Tele-Ventures Ltd., June 9, 2005.

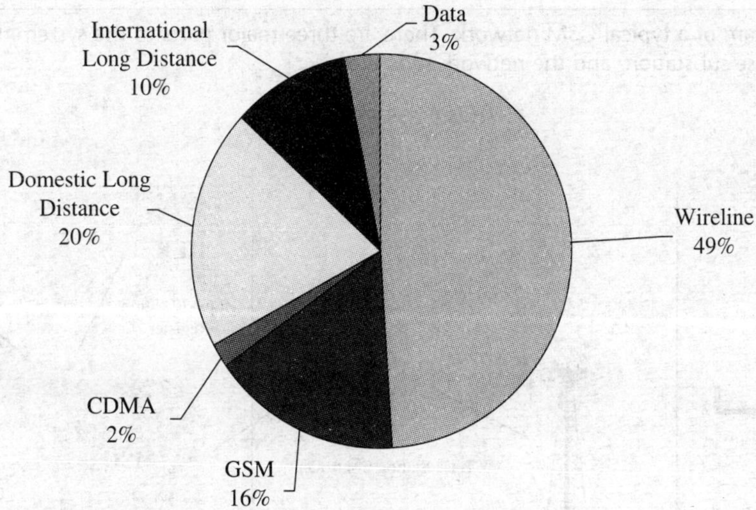

(SMS), games, ring tones, and ring-back tones (different kinds of music that the caller would hear)—were already being offered in urban areas.

Aside from the growth in 3G, huge potential remained in the development of basic phone services. The number of telephone connections (fixed and mobile) per 100 inhabitants in India in 2003 was fewer than six, whereas among all but four OECD countries it was over 100.[14] Customer demand for telecom connections increased daily, and many were bypassing fixed lines and going straight to cell phones. In 2003, over 1.5 million people were signing up for cell phones every month.[15]

Unlike European and American operators, Indian operators chose to sell mobile phones and mobile telephone services separately. As a result, there was no handset subsidies burden on the operator. Mobile services were sold either on a postpaid or prepaid basis. About 60 percent of the business was prepaid—cards allowing the customer to recharge his telephone with telephone time were sold in kiosks, drugstores, and small convenience stores. The remaining 40 percent of the business was postpaid, for businesspeople or business customers who were billed for their telephone use on a monthly basis.[16] Exhibit 5 describes the typical mobile or cellular network architecture.

Market Competition

By 2002–2003, the Indian market had grown highly competitive. Mobile rates were as low as three to four U.S. cents per minute, and ARPU—the average monthly revenue per customer unit—had fallen by 50 percent in three years as telecom providers fought to capture new subscribers.[17] The top competitors were able to lower their unit costs as their market shares increased through acquisitions or bankruptcy of smaller competitors.

[14] OECD Factbook 2006—Economic, Environmental and Social Statistics. Published by Source OECD, http://caliban.sourceoecd.org/vl=4373012/cl=20/nw=1/rpsv/factbook/06-03-02.htm, accessed August 2, 2006.

[15] "Current Issue and Trend in Indian Mobile Market," Report # 04025. Research on Asia Group 2003.

[16] Ibid.

[17] Ibid.

EXHIBIT 5 Typical Mobile Network Architecture

Source: Various Web sites as noted.

Below is a diagram of a typical GSM network. There are three major parts to the system: the mobile handset, the base substation, and the network subsystem.[a]

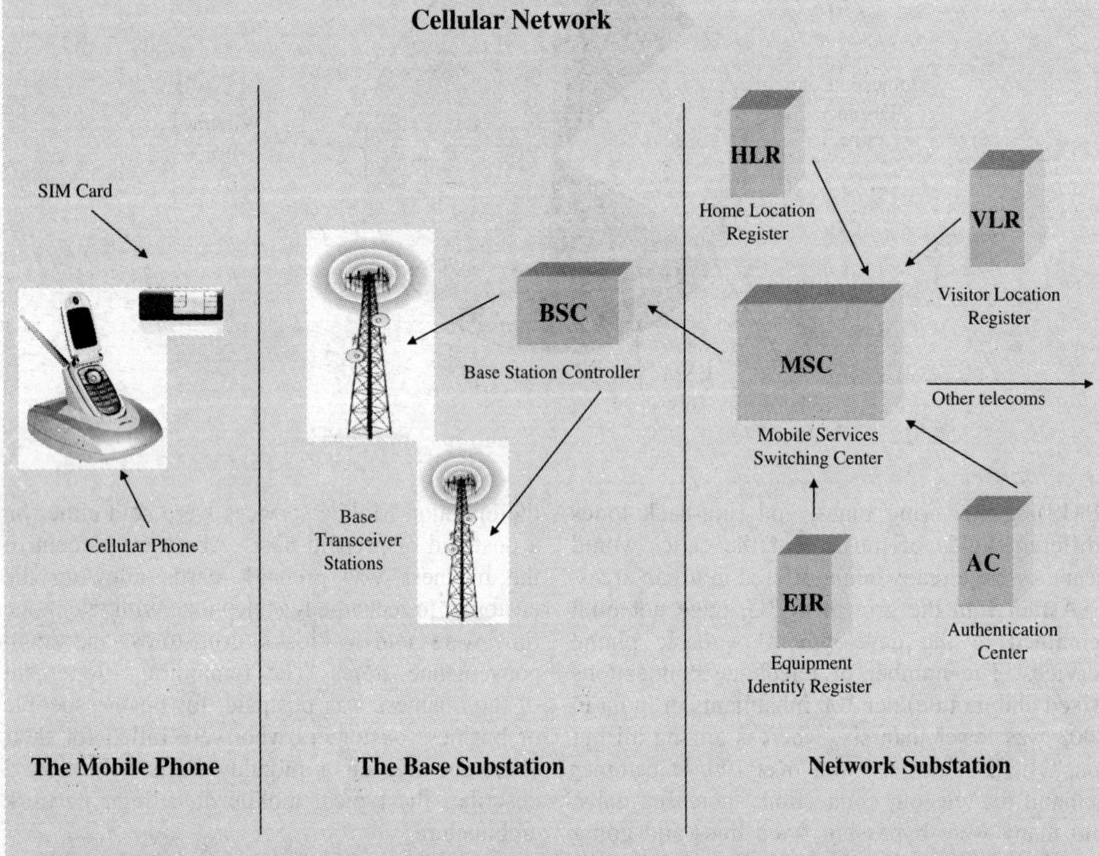

- **The mobile phone**: The mobile phone consists of two parts, the phone itself and the SIM card. SIM stands for subscriber identity module. The SIM card is inserted into the phone and is basically a memory chip or a "smart card" with the user's identity codes and some specific user information such as frequently called numbers or ring tones. The SIM card also allows the user to switch phones without completely reprogramming his handset.
- **The base substation**: This is the first link in the connection between the mobile set and the telephone network. There are two parts to the base substation. The first, the base transceiver station, is really just a big tower with antennas on top. There are always at least two towers—one for inbound and one for outbound transmission.

  The second part to the base substation, the base station controller, manages communication and transmissions between the base transceiver stations and the rest of the network, notably the switching station. One base station can manage up to several hundred base transceiver stations. A base transceiver station can cover an area of 30 to 40 square kms, but if it is located in a congested area, the coverage is much smaller.

EXHIBIT 5 Typical Mobile Network Architecture (*Continued*)

Cellular networks get their name for the pattern in which base transceiver stations are distributed around the base controller station and the pattern by which the network is added to as the user requirements increase. Cellular networks take the form of a honeycomb. As can be seen from the diagram below, the transceiver stations are arranged around the controller station with the controller station at three of the points in the honeycomb. If additional coverage is needed, additional antennas are added on the transceiver station. An antenna that previously operated on a 120-degree basis would now only operate on 60 degrees; the new antennas would take over the remaining 60 degrees.[b]

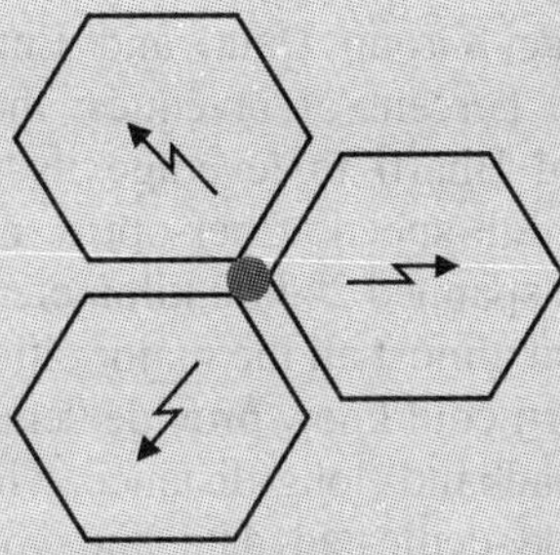

Transceiver in the middle of transmission cells

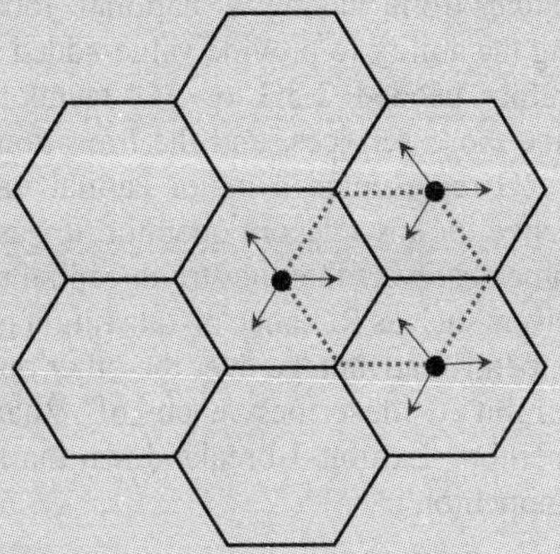

Three transceivers within a cellular network

- **The network substation:** Data from the base substation comes into the network substation through the mobile services switching center (MSC). From the switching center information is communicated either to other base substations in the network, to other mobile systems, or to a fixed-line system for connection to the intended party.

  The mobile services switching center has several databases at its disposal that provide information and validate identities of the caller before passing the communication on. They include:

  - Home location register (HLR)—a database with information about subscribers including their identity and service profile.
  - Visitor location register (VLR)—a database also containing information about subscribers, but with more specific data concerning their whereabouts. During a call it provides information on where to find a subscriber.
  - Authentication center (AC)—acts as an interface between the switching center and the HLR and the VLR, allowing the process of user verification and location to be carried out.
  - Equipment identity register (EIR)—a database containing the list of all valid mobile equipment in the network.[c]

[a]Compiled by casewriter based on information from www.coai.in/aboutus-technology.htm, accessed May 20, 2005.
[b]Compiled by casewriter based on information from www.privateline.com/Cellbasics/Cellbasics02.html., accessed January 5, 2006.
[c]Compiled by casewriter based on information from www.privateline.com/PCS/GSMNetworkstructure.html, accessed May 20, 2005.

By 2003, there were seven major national operators in the Indian telecommunications market: Bharti, BSNL, Hutchinson, Reliance, Tata, Idea Cellular, and MTNL. Bharti and three others had operations in both the fixed and mobile segments. The others operated only in the mobile segment. There were also several strong regional mobile operators, such as Spice and BPL.

With industry consolidation, the focus was switching from having a national footprint to having the ability to provide value-added services. Operators needed 2.5G or 3G technologies to provide those services, and the transition upward from 2G represented a major capital investment challenge for any telecom operator. It was thought by some observers that the strong capital resources of players such as Reliance or Tata might give them a competitive advantage over the other operators.

Exhibit 6 describes each of Bharti's top competitors. Exhibit 7 breaks down market share by competitor.

Bharti's Telecommunications Network

By 2003, Bharti had obtained licenses for mobile operations in 15 out of the total 23 circles. It had a 25 percent market share of the total Indian mobile market and 6 million mobile subscribers. In fixed-line services, it had 1 million customers and licenses for six circles. Upcoming regulatory changes would also allow Bharti to expand wire-line services into any of the circles in which it held a wireless license. Growth in both sectors—wire line and wireless—was expected to be exponential over the coming 18 months as Bharti obtained licenses and built up operations to achieve nationwide coverage.

Operations and Service

Bharti's operations were structured into three strategic business units (see Exhibit 8 for a detailed breakdown):

- Mobile Services: Providing 64 percent of Bharti revenues, this unit was where Bharti had achieved the most in terms of market dominance and customer service; in 6 out of 15 regions, Bharti had over 40 percent market share. It focused on providing excellent customer service through "error-free" service (low call drop rates, broad coverage, etc.), cost efficiency, and innovation in new products and services. Bharti offered post-paid or prepaid billing options, Blackberry™ service, conferencing, fax and data transmission, and other services such as jokes, games, news, and even astrology via the mobile phone.
- Long-Distance, Group Data, and Enterprise: Providing 30 percent of revenues, these services allowed Bharti to leverage its recently completed high-speed fiber-optic network. This network spanned 24,000 kilometers (kms) and connected almost all the major cities in the country. Bharti could now provide "end-to-end service," broadband, long-distance, videoconferencing, and dedicated data and voice line services to business customers.
- Broadband and Telephone Services: Providing 16 percent of revenues, this unit provided wire-line-based telephone services in six circles and broadband services in all major economic centers. Broadband-related services included DSL to homes and businesses, WiFi, virtual private network (VPN), and video surveillance.

Ten percent of revenues pertained to intersegment eliminations.

Technology and Development

By March 2004, Bharti's mobile network connected 1,400 towns using GSM technology. By the end of 2007, Bharti expected to have GSM service up and running in all the 5,161 census towns. To meet this objective, an average of 100 towns per month were to be brought into the system.

Bharti had roughly 5,000 base stations at the end of March 2004. In order to accommodate the required demand for service by March 2007, that

EXHIBIT 6 Indian Telecom Competitors

Source: Various Web sites as noted.

Bharti competed with six major operators in the Indian market, as follows:

BSNL

Former monopoly and still a state-owned business. The oldest telecom operator in the country, its fixed-line operations were omnipresent. In 2003, BSNL still had a subscription base representing 86% of the fixed-line market. It was expected that its market share in fixed-line operations would decline to 58% by 2008 but that its market share in mobiles would rise from 16% in 2003 to 22% by 2008. Overall, it would remain a strong player.[a]

MTNL

Set up in 1986 to facilitate the upgrading of telecom services to the metropolitan centers of Delhi and Mumbai (Bombay), this operator was partially state owned (52.25%) and ran a fairly modern network in those cities and the surrounding regions with fixed-line services to 4.4 million subscribers, or 12% of the Indian market, and mobile services to 500,000 customers, or 1.3% of the Indian market. Broadband services were to be introduced in 2003.[b]

Hutch-Essar

Hutchinson's Indian operations represented a joint venture between Hutchinson Whampoa, the Hong Kong-based conglomerate, and the Essar Group, one of India's largest corporate houses. Hutchinson's investment in the Indian telecom market began in 1992; its cooperation with Essar dated back to 1999.

Hutch India had limited itself to the mobile sector of the telecom market—it had no fixed-line operations. Its mobile strategy was to target the premium segment. In 2003, it was present in 13 of the 23 circles and had 4.1 million customers, or 12% of the mobile market.

Tata

Tata Teleservices was the telecom arm of the Tata Group. Partnering with Motorola, Lucent, Ericsson, and ECI Telecom, Tata had 600,000 wireless customers, or just under 2% of the mobile market in 2003. Tata also had a one-third stake in the wireless provider Idea Cellular (see below).

Idea Cellular

A three-way joint venture between Tata, Birla (another large Indian industrial group), and AT&T, the company adopted the name of Idea Cellular in 2002. It was present in seven circles, four of which represented some of the largest economic and industrial centers. With this concentration, it was able to capture a customer base of 3.7 million customers, or 11% of the entire mobile market in 2003.[c]

Reliance

Reliance Infocomm was a subsidiary of the Reliance Group, an Indian family-run $22.6 billion conglomerate. Reliance entered the market in 2002 with both wireless and wire-line services.

Reliance's key strengths lay in its brand new installed fiberglass network with over 60,000 kms of optical cable stretching throughout India; it was integrated (wireless and wire line) and convergent (voice, data, and video). Reliance had introduced broadband applications including Java applications for the Internet, VPN connections for business clients, and global positioning for vehicle tracking.

In wire line, Reliance had 500,000 customers in 2003 but was expected to increase its customer base to over 8 million by 2008. In wireless, Reliance had a 19.5% market share, representing 6.6 million customers. It was expected to reach 21% market share and 31 million customers by 2008.[d]

[a]Compiled by casewriter based on data from JM Morgan Stanley Equity Research Asia-Pacific, Bharti Tele-Ventures Ltd., June 9, 2005.
[b]Data from MTNL Web site, www.mtnl.net.in/about.htm, accessed January 4, 2006.
[c]Cellular Operators Association of India, www.coai.in/archives_statistics_2004_q1.htm, accessed August 3, 2005.
[d]Compiled by casewriter based on data from JM Morgan Stanley Equity Research Asia-Pacific, Bharti Tele-Ventures Ltd., June 9, 2005.

EXHIBIT 7 Indian Market Share for the Top Seven Telecom Operators

Source: Compiled by casewriter based on data from JM Morgan Stanley Equity Research Asia-Pacific, Bharti Tele-Ventures Ltd., June 9, 2005.

Operator	Wireless Market (%)	Wire-Line Market (%)
Bharti	25%	1%
BSNL	16	86
MTNL	1.5	4.6
Hutch-Essar	12	—
Tata	2	—
Idea	11	—
Reliance	19.5	1
Others	13	—

EXHIBIT 8 Breakdown of Bharti's 2003 Revenues by Activity

Source: Audited consolidated financial statements as per U.S. GAAP for the years ended March 31, 2003, 2004, 2005, Excel file available on the company's Web site, www.bhartiairtel.in.

	Full Year Ending March 31, 2004	
	Rs. Million	% of Total Revenues
Mobile Services	30,927	64%
B & T Services	7,692	16
Long Distance	12,050	25
Enterprise Services	2,620	5
Others	(39)	0
Subtotal	53,250	110
Eliminations	(4,930)	−10
Total	48,320	100

number would need to jump to 40,000 and would require the hiring of over 2,000 to 3,000 people to build and maintain them.[18]

Bharti had also begun deploying EDGE, a 2.5G GSM-compatible technology that allowed it to upgrade its services to 3G performance levels. This was first done in Mumbai and would later be introduced elsewhere in the network. (See Exhibit 9 for Bharti's mobile footprint as of mid-2003.)

Bharti's long-distance network used fiber-optic cables around India. It was present in the international carrier business through the group's participation in the i2i undersea cable system—a joint venture with SingTel. Its international capacity had been further enhanced by a joint venture it had entered into with SingTel and 13 other telecom groups for the construction of SEA-ME-WE4, the Singapore-France submarine cable.

Bharti's Relationships with Its Vendors

As Bharti's presence in the Indian market grew, so did the number of relationships it had with network suppliers. Its initial GSM network was set up with the help of Ericsson. By early 2003, Bharti was also working with Nokia and Siemens, among others. Bharti purchased equipment, installation, and maintenance services from each of these suppliers in one or more of the regional circles in which it was present.

Because the GSM technology was a very open standard, Bharti was comfortable working with several suppliers and could change suppliers if the services offered by one proved unsatisfactory. "In today's telecom world, it's very easy, because everything is 'plug and play,'" said Gupta. This also meant that the environment was very competitive between telecom vendors. As Sunil Mittal explained, "Every six months there was a fresh tender for network expansion. There used to be a parade with one vendor playing against another."[19]

Along with the operations teams, Gupta managed the process of tendering, negotiating, and working with the vendors to install the expanded capacity, but he was uncomfortable with the results. "Typically in the industry, these vendors will sell you a list of components, 'boxes'—an MSC [a switching station], a BSC [a base station], etc.," said Gupta.

[18] Shelley Singh and Rajeev Dubey, "The man who gave away his network," by *Business World India*, October 4, 2004, www.businessworldindia.com/oct0404/coverstory01.asp., accessed May 12, 2005.

[19] Company source.

EXHIBIT 9 Bharti's Cellular Operations in 2003

Source: Krishna Palepu, Tarun Khanna, and Ingrid Vargas, "Bharti Tele-Ventures," HBS No. 704-426 (Boston: Harvard Business School Publishing, 2003). Original source: company documents.

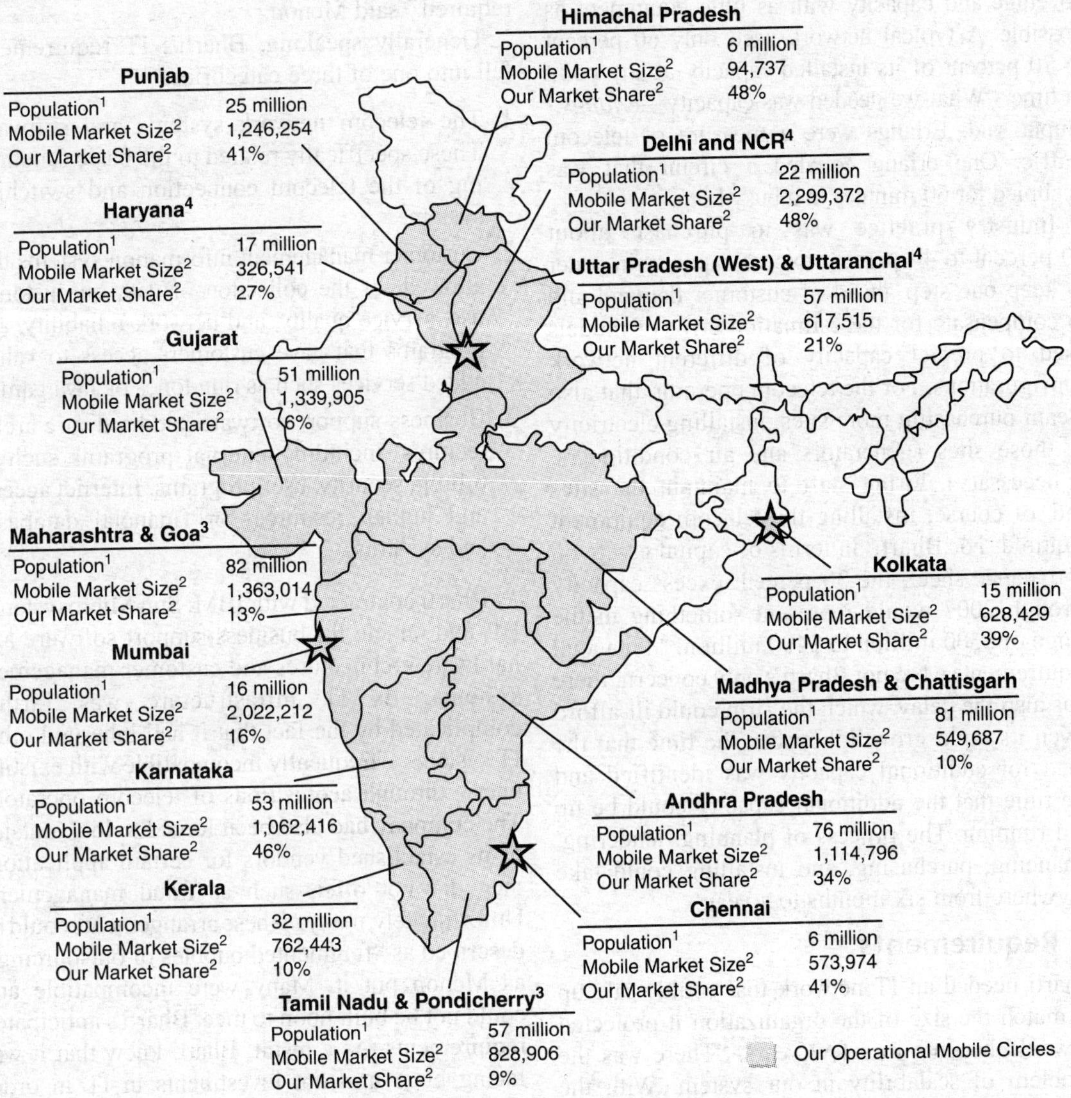

[1]Population estimates are as per National Census, 2001 and are as of March 1, 2001. The population for Uttar Pradesh (West) circle is approximately 37% of the total population for the state of Uttar Pradesh.

[2]Mobile subscriber statistics are as of July 31, 2003 and are based on data released by COAI. Mobile market size comprises the total number of mobile subscribers of all the service providers in a circle.

[3]Demographics of Maharashtra and Tamil Nadu do not include demographics of state capitals (metros) Mumbai and Chennai, respectively.

[4]Demographics of Haryana do not include Faridabad & Gurgaon as they are included in Delhi & NCR. Similarly demographics of Uttar Pradesh (West) & Uttaranchal do not include Noida & Ghaziabad as they are included in Delhi NCR.

There was an inherent conflict of interest in this approach since the vendors always tried to sell more equipment, while the operator wanted maximum coverage and capacity with as little equipment as possible. A typical network used only 60 percent to 70 percent of its installed capacity at any point in time. "What we needed was capacity—*erlangs*," Gupta said. Erlangs were a measure of telecom traffic. One erlang equaled a circuit that was occupied for 60 minutes in a busy hour.

Industry practice was to purchase about 30 percent to 40 percent excess capacity in order to keep one step ahead of customer demand and to compensate for the estimation error of models used to predict capacity of different network configurations. For the telecom operator, that also meant purchasing more sites, installing electricity in those sites (generators and air conditioners, if necessary), hiring staff to maintain the sites and, of course, installing the telecom equipment required. For Bharti, in terms of capital assets on its balance sheet, the 30 percent excess capacity through 2007 would represent something in the range of $300 million to $400 million.[20] Financial requirements were not Bharti's only concern; there was also the delay, which the firm could ill-afford given its rapid growth, between the time that the need for additional capacity was identified and the time that the additional capacity could be up and running. The process of planning, tendering, financing, purchasing, and installing could take anywhere from six months to a year.

IT Requirements

Bharti needed an IT network that could scale up to match the size of the organization it projected it would become in a few years. "There was the problem of scalability in our system. With the very rapid growth, we would soon be making decisions that could not be altered later on and for which we might be sorry," Dr. Jai Menon, group CIO for Bharti, explained.

Bharti looked increasingly to its vendors to provide expertise in integrated systems design. "Our core competency was in operations, not IT design, and thus we could not do much of the architecture software and hardware design we required," said Menon.

Generally speaking, Bharti's IT requirements fell into one of three categories:

1. The telecom network systems and software. These specifically related to the basic functioning of the telecom connection and switching system.
2. Customer management information systems that allowed for the collection of data on customer use, service quality, and network reliability, and programs that gave customers access to value-added services such as ring tones or Java games.
3. Business-support software and hardware architectures, including internal programs such as billing, security, user programs, Internet access, and human resources or financial databases and systems.

Bharti contracted with IBM, Sun Microsystems, HP, and Oracle for business-support software and hardware architectures and customer management systems. Its IT infrastructure was further complicated by the fact that it had inherited other IT systems—frequently incompatible with existing ones—through acquisitions of telecom operators. The company had also been forced to look outside of its established vendors for certain applications they did not offer, such as fraud management. Unfortunately, many of these arrangements could be described as "fragmented bubbles of outsourcing," as Menon put it. Many were incompatible and could not be built upon to meet Bharti's anticipated requirements. As a result, Bharti knew that it was facing huge up-front investments in IT in order to get the right architecture in place and ready to support its growth over the next 10 years. See Exhibit 10 for marketing information on a Bharti service offering.

Human Resources Issue

Related to both IT and network development requirements was the question of human resource scarcity. With constant growth in the market,

[20] Ibid.

Bharti was finding it more and more difficult to hire and retain the best and the brightest. In network development alone, Bharti would need to hire 2,000–3,000 people to accompany network development in 2004. As Gupta put it: "Think of it from the perspective of a talented IT or telecom guy. Would you rather go work for one of the world's top multinational firms, large in size and reputation, or for a local, upcoming operator like us?"

Bharti's Proposed Deal

In the folder on the corner of his desk, Gupta had the proposed outlines of a two-pronged outsourcing structure for Bharti and its vendors. Gupta's strategy included handing over responsibility for the buildup, maintenance, and servicing of the telecom network to equipment vendors. Gupta and his people were talking with Nokia, Siemens, and Ericsson as potential partners. In addition, Gupta was planning to outsource the buildup, maintenance, and servicing of Bharti's core IT infrastructure to IBM. Other vendors besides IBM had been considered, but discussions had gone the farthest with IBM since few IT vendors had experience handling all of the aspects of the proposed deal.

Below are excerpts from each proposal:

Ericsson, Nokia, and Siemens

- The vendor will provide Bharti with network capacity—erlangs—in accordance with Bharti's projected erlang requirements in each of the circles in which Bharti operates and for which they are responsible according to this agreement. In exchange, Bharti agrees to pay the vendor a fee according to the amount of erlang capacity installed. The actual payment for network capacity will be made only when the capacity is up and running and *has been used* by Bharti customers, thereby excluding payment for unused capacity at any point in time.
- Once erlang capacity is installed, ownership of the assets responsible for producing that capacity belongs to Bharti. The responsibility for maintaining the network in good working order, however, rests with the equipment supplier under an operations and management (O & M) agreement.
- In order to ensure the quality of Bharti's service to its end customers, network capacity provided by equipment suppliers will be subject to a number of quality controls specified in service level agreements (SLAs). These are measures of network quality, such as the number of dropped calls and the number of incomplete calls, that will be jointly determined by Bharti and the equipment supplier. [*Penalties and rewards linked to quality achieved were provided.*]
- This agreement is to be for an initial period of three years, subject to renewal by mutual agreement.

IBM

- IBM will provide Bharti with complete and comprehensive end-to-end management service for supplying, installing, and managing all of its hardware and software requirements as concerns the basic IT architecture of the company and all of the applications needed to operate it. The outsourcing includes everything from the computer on the desktop all the way up to the mainframe but excludes all telecom network-specific structures and networks. It includes all internal customer service and all negotiations with external software and hardware suppliers. It also includes the maintenance of all hardware and software, including those provided by other vendors such as security, data warehousing, fraud management, business intelligence, human resource management, financial, and enterprise management systems and software, among various others.
- In order to ensure the quality of Bharti's service to its employees and end customers, IBM services will be subject to a number of quality controls specified in the SLAs, such as hotline customer satisfaction and new application implementation delays. [*In the network proposal, a penalty and reward mechanism was provided for.*]

- In exchange for these services, Bharti agrees to pay IBM a share of its revenues. This agreement is to last for a period of five years, renewable for another five years, for a total of 10 years. The percentage of revenue shared will progressively decline as overall revenue increases.

In discussing the proposals with his vendors, Gupta made it understood that the Bharti personnel presently carrying out tasks that would be taken over by the vendors would be transferred to the vendor in question. A network manager at Bharti today, for example, would become an Ericsson, Nokia, or Siemens employee tomorrow. Should the proposal be accepted by the vendors, around 270 IT staff and 800 network staff could be transferred out of Bharti.

Reactions at Bharti

Don Price, the CTO of Bharti's Mobile Services, was one of the first with whom the new idea was discussed. He had been in the mobile telecommunications business from its inception in the United States with McCaw Communications and was one of the most experienced CTOs in the world. He had never seen such an arrangement before and had expressed serious reservations about handing over network management and operations to the vendors. "The vendors may have access to the world's best technology, but we have the operating expertise," said Price. He grumbled, wondering whether "the financial 'eggs' with no network operations experience thought this one up. Operations . . . it's our bread and butter."

The IT and marketing departments were concerned that software or hardware applications not supported by IBM would no longer be available. Would IBM be willing to work fairly with other vendors, or would the agreement mean that Bharti would no longer have access to certain creative new applications? They were also concerned about the implications the deal would have on the time-to-market of new IT-based services for customers. "OK, give the large fundamental innovation to IBM . . . but keep the quick shots in-house!" was what one senior marketing manager had to say.

Meanwhile, the human resources department was wondering how they would manage the transfer of nearly 1,000 staff members. Some staff might not want to be transferred, or perhaps the vendors might not want to take them. One manager worried: "Bharti is a much smaller company, an Indian company. We have a different way of working with people—India is not a hire-and-fire country. The vendors are much bigger, and they're worldwide companies. The cultures are different. Our staff identifies itself closely with Bharti. How are they going to take being transferred elsewhere?"

Reactions within the company ranks were mild when compared with comments Gupta received after presenting the project to the board of directors. Many were longtime telecom industry practitioners, and to them it was difficult to justify changing from the accepted practices. Gupta had heard one board member comment, "What makes you think that Bharti, an upstart in this industry, could teach the world what to do?" The main concern expressed by all of the board members was the risk of excessive dependence upon the vendors. Gupta recalled the prevailing sentiment of the board: "You will become their slaves." In response to their concerns, SingTel—which was represented on the board—sent a group of experts in to evaluate the project. "Needless to say, the initial reaction of the board was not highly supportive—in fact, the general feeling was negative," explained Gupta.

Vendor Reactions

Initial reactions from vendors were mixed. They liked the opportunity to do more business with a major player—Bharti—but they were concerned with the risks and the need to get "buy-in" from the top levels in their organization. A major concern was that they might be stuck with important investments in network equipment that they made on behalf of Bharti, in the event that Bharti did not use the equipment. If Bharti was transferring the equipment investment risk to the vendors, what was the upside in the deal for them? It

EXHIBIT 10 **An Advertisement for Bharti's Lifetime Service Plan**

Source: Airtel.

was unlikely that they would be able to increase equipment prices to cover all the increased risk.

They were also concerned with absorbing hundreds of Bharti employees. Some of the vendors had very light organizations that would be overwhelmed with such a sudden expansion in the number of employees. Besides the sheer numbers, there was a question of managing the corporate cultural mix. "Our cultures, values, and systems are somewhat different," they fretted.

Of course, there were dangers in *not* signing with Bharti. Bharti would be growing very fast over the next few years. If the vendors turned down this business now, making it look as if they were unwilling to take risks in India, they might later be locked out of lucrative deals not only with Bharti, but perhaps with other operators as well. With the impressive growth projected for the market, most vendors were looking to increase their operations and their market share in India. Nokia, for example, had very little business with Bharti and was behind Ericcson in terms of market share in India. Ericcson, on the other hand, was anxious to lock in its position with Bharti, with which it had been dealing since 1995.

IBM also had concerns about the deal. Although it was keen to develop worldwide partnerships with major clients as per its international "on-demand" strategy, it had until now not even envisaged a revenue share arrangement with a client. If IBM were to take a percentage of Bharti's revenues in exchange for its equipment and services, it would have to forecast Bharti's revenue growth in order to estimate how much it would get paid over the next 5 to 10 years. Yet the investments in IT hardware, software, and people on behalf of Bharti would have to be made by IBM today. To them, it represented a major and unfamiliar risk.

Overall, this meant that IBM needed to be fairly sure of Bharti's future success. Although it knew from experience that there was a strong association between a company's success and the quality of its IT network, IBM could not be certain that its investment in this project today would improve Bharti's chances for success in the future. In fact, IBM's deal with Bharti felt more like betting on a horse in a race. IBM was hoping that the signs were right and that Bharti would gallop to victory.

Cisco Systems, Inc.: Implementing ERP

A young company growing at annual rates that exceed 50 percent needs to replace the failing operational core of its mission critical IT systems. To meet the challenge, the company's managers combine conventional methods and unorthodox choices, fitting their approach to the special circumstances in which they find themselves. This case describes one of the most successful large-scale system implementations ever documented, a project that laid the technological foundation for the creation of an IT-enabled industry giant. As you read the case, consider these questions: What accounted for the success of this project? What were the most important things that Cisco managers did right? What did they do wrong? How did they manage unanticipated problems? Was Cisco smart or lucky with its ERP implementation?

Case 2-6

Cisco Systems, Inc.: Implementing ERP

Pete Solvik, Cisco Systems chief information officer (CIO), considered the last remaining line item of his ERP (Enterprise Resource Planning) implementation budget. Cisco had a history of rewarding performance with cash bonuses, but the amount allocated for rewarding the ERP team, over $200,000, was unprecedented. To be sure, they had delivered a lot in a time frame that no one had believed possible. It had not been easy either. The team members, including Solvik, had taken a risk in joining the project. Rewards should, and would, be generous. The size of the bonus pool, though, made Solvik think: They had done well, but how well? What had gone right? What had gone wrong? Given another project of this magnitude and risk, would they be able to do it again?

Postdoctoral Research Fellow Mark J. Cotteleer prepared this case under the supervision of Professors Robert D. Austin and Richard L. Nolan as the basis for class discussion rather than to illustrate effective or ineffective management.

History of Cisco

Cisco Systems, Inc., was founded by two Stanford computer scientists in 1984 and became publicly traded in 1990. The company's primary product is the "router," the combination of hardware and software that acts as a traffic cop on the complex TCP/IP[1] networks that make up the Internet (as well as corporate "intranets"). With the rise of Internet technologies, demand for Cisco's products boomed and the company soon began to dominate its markets. By 1997, its first year on the Fortune 500, Cisco ranked among the top five companies in return on revenues and return on assets. (See Exhibit 1 for Cisco's financial performance.) Only two other companies, Intel and Microsoft, have ever matched this feat. Perhaps even more impressive, on July 17, 1998, just 14 years after being founded, Cisco's market capitalization passed the $100 billion mark (15 times 1997 sales). Some industry pundits

[1] Transmission Control Protocol and Internet Protocol, together known as TCP/IP, provided a robust standard for routing messages between LANs and created the potential to connect all computers on an ever-larger Wide Area Network (WAN).

EXHIBIT 1 Financials and Other Cisco Statistics

Source: 1998 Annual Report and 1998 10-K form.

Years Ended	July 25, 1998	July 26, 1997	July 28, 1996	July 30, 1995
Net sales	$8,458,777,000	$6,440,171,000	$4,096,007,000	$2,232,652,000
Income before provisions for income taxes	$2,302,466,000	$1,888,872,000	$1,464,825,000	$737,977,000
Net income[a, b, c]	$1,350,072,000	$1,048,679,000	$913,324,000	$456,489,000
Net income per common share (diluted)[d]	$0.84	$0.68	$0.61	$0.32
Shares used in per-share calculation (diluted)	1,608,173,000	1,551,039,000	1,490,078,000	1,425,247,000
Total assets	$8,916,705,000	$5,451,984,000	$3,630,232,000	$1,991,949,000
Stock price the Friday before fiscal year end[e]	$65.167	$35.417	$22.833	$12.458
Number of employees[f]	15,000	11,000	8,782	4,086
Net sales per employee	$563,918	$585,470	$466,409	$546,415
Net income per employee	$90,005	$95,334	$103,999	$111,720

[a] Net income and net income per share in 1998 include purchased research and development expenses of $94 million and realized gains on the sale of a minority stock investment of $5 million. Pro forma net income and diluted net income per share, excluding these nonrecurring items net of tax, would have been $1,878,988,000 and $1.17, respectively.

[b] In 1997, net income and net income per share include purchased research and development expenses of $508 million and realized gains on the sale of a minority stock investment of $153 million. Pro forma net income and diluted net income per share, excluding these nonrecurring items net of tax, would have been $1,413,893,000 and $0.91 respectively.

[c] In 1995, net income and net income per share include purchased research and development expenses of $96 million. Pro forma net income and diluted net income per share, excluding these nonrecurring items net of tax, would have been $515,723,000 and $0.36, respectively.

[d] Reflects the three-for-two stock split effective September 1998.

[e] Stock prices reflect a two-for-one split effective February 1996, a three-for-two split effective November 1997, and a three-for-two split effective September 1998.

[f] Number of employees was taken from respective 10-K forms.

predicted that Cisco would be the third dominant company—joining Microsoft and Intel—to shape the digital revolution.

Don Valentine, partner of Sequoia Capital and vice chairman of the board of Cisco,[2] was the first to invest in Cisco; he took a chance on the young company when other venture capitalists were more cautious. One way Valentine protected his $2.5 million initial investment was by reserving the right to bring in professional management when he deemed it appropriate.

In 1988, Valentine hired John Morgridge as CEO. Morgridge, an experienced executive in the computer industry, immediately began to build a professional management team. This team soon clashed with the founders and, after Cisco's initial public offering in 1990, both founders sold all of their stock and left the company. This departure left Morgridge free to continue his plans to install an extremely disciplined management structure.

Morgridge believed that many Silicon Valley firms decentralized too quickly and did not appreciate the proven ability of the functional organization to grow without sacrificing control. Accordingly, Morgridge maintained a centralized functional organization. While product marketing and R&D were decentralized into three "Lines of

[2] Don Valentine was previously the outside executive chairman of the board of Cisco. Cisco has maintained its chairman of the board as an outside director. Currently, John Morgridge serves as an outside director and chairman of the board.

Business" (Enterprise, Small/Medium Business, and Service Provider), the manufacturing, customer support, finance, human resources, IT, and sales organizations remained centralized.

History of IT at Cisco

Pete Solvik joined Cisco in January 1993 as the company's CIO. At the time, Cisco was a $500 million company running a UNIX-based software package to support its core transaction processing. The functional areas supported by the package included financial, manufacturing, and order entry systems. Cisco was "far and away" the biggest customer of the software vendor that supported the application.[3] Solvik's experience and the company's significant growth prospects convinced him that Cisco needed a change.

> We wanted to grow to $5 billion-plus. The application didn't provide the degree of redundancy, reliability, and maintainability we needed. We weren't able to make changes to the application to meet our business needs anymore. It had become too much spaghetti, too customized. The software vendor did offer [an upgraded version], but when we looked at it we thought "by the time we're done our systems will be more reliable and have higher redundancy but it will still be a package for $300 million companies and we're a $1 billion dollar company."

Solvik's initial inclination was to avoid an ERP solution. Instead, he planned to let each functional area make its own decision regarding the application and timing of its move. Keeping with Cisco's strong tradition of standardization, however, all functional areas would be required to use common architecture and databases. This approach was consistent with the organizational and budgetary structures that Solvik had installed upon his arrival. Solvik felt strongly that budgetary decisions on IT expenditures be made by functional areas while the IT organization reported directly to him. Solvik's objection to ERP solutions was also born out of concerns about the types of "megaprojects" that ERP implementations often became.

[3] Most customers of the software vendors ranged from $50 million to $250 million in revenue.

A Defining Moment

In the following year, little progress was made. Randy Pond, a director in manufacturing[4] and eventual coleader of the project, described the dilemma facing the functional areas in late 1993:

> We knew we were in trouble if we did not do something. Anything we did would just run over the legacy systems we had in place. It turned into an effort to constantly band-aid our existing systems. None of us were individually going to go out and buy a package. . . . The disruption to the business for me to go to the board and say "Okay, manufacturing wants to spend $5 or $6 million to buy a package and by the way it will take a year or more to get in . . ." was too much to justify. None of us was going to throw out the legacies and do something big.

The systems replacement difficulties of functional areas perpetuated the deterioration of Cisco's legacy environment. Incremental modification continued while the company sustained an 80 percent annual growth rate. Systems outages became routine. Product shortcomings exacerbated the difficulties of recovering from outages.

Finally, in January of 1994, Cisco's legacy environment failed so dramatically that the shortcomings of the existing systems could no longer be ignored. An unauthorized method for accessing the core application database—a workaround that was itself motivated by the inability of the system to perform—malfunctioned, corrupting Cisco's central database. As a result, the company was largely shut down for two days.

Cisco's struggle to recover from this major shutdown brought home the fact that the company's systems were on the brink of total failure. Solvik, Pond, and a number of other Cisco managers came to the conclusion that the autonomous approach to systems replacement they had adopted was not going to be sufficient. An alternative approach was needed. Solvik described what they did:

> We said, "we can't wait casually by while Order Entry, Finance, and Manufacturing go out and make three

[4] Subsequent to the implementation, Randy Pond was promoted to the vice president level in manufacturing at Cisco.

> separate decisions." It would take too long to get those applications in place. We needed to take faster action. At that point we got sponsorship from the SVP of Manufacturing, Carl Redfield. He was with Digital before Cisco, in PC manufacturing. He took the lead and said, "OK, let's get on with this. . . . let's start from the manufacturing perspective, and see if we can get the Order Entry and Financial groups in the company interested in doing a single integrated replacement of all the applications, instead of taking a longer time doing separate projects." And so in February, about a month after the [company shutdown], we went about putting together a team to do an investigation to replace the application.

Redfield understood, from previous large-scale implementation experiences at Digital, how "monolithic" IT projects could take on lives of their own. He echoed Solvik's concerns about project size and had strong views about how Cisco should approach a large implementation project.

> I knew we wanted to do this quickly. We were not going to do a phased implementation; we would do it all at once. We were not going to allow a lot of customization either. There is a tendency in MRP systems[5] for people to want the system to mirror their method of operation instead of retraining people to do things the way the system intended them. This takes a lot longer. Also, we wanted to create a schedule that was doable and make it a priority in the company as opposed to a second tier kind of effort.

Selecting an ERP Product

Cisco's management team realized that implementing to meet *business* needs would require heavy involvement from the business community. This could not be an IT-only initiative. It was critically important to get the very best people they could find. Solvik elaborated: "Our orientation in pulling people out of their jobs [to work on the project] was if it was easy then we were picking the wrong people. We pulled people out that the business absolutely did not want to give up."

Consistent with the need for a strong Cisco team, the company would also need strong partners. Solvik and Redfield felt it was particularly important to work with an integration partner that could assist in both the selection and implementation of whichever solution the company chose. Great technical skills and business knowledge were a prerequisite. Solvik explained the choice of KPMG as the integration partner:

> KPMG came in and saw an opportunity to really build a business around putting in these applications. They also saw this as kind of a defining opportunity, to work with us on this project. As opposed to some other firms that wanted to bring in a lot of "greenies," KPMG was building a practice of people that were very experienced in the industry. For instance, the program manager that they put on the job, Mark Lee, had been director of IT for a company in Texas that had put in various parts of an ERP system.

With KPMG on board, the team of about 20 people turned to the software market with a multipronged approach for identifying the best software packages. The team's strategy was to build as much knowledge as possible by leveraging the experiences of others. They asked large corporations and the "Big Six" accounting firms what they knew. They also tapped research sources such as the Gartner Group.[6] By orienting the selection process to what people were actually using and continuing to emphasize decision speed, Cisco narrowed the field to five packages within two days. After a week of evaluating the packages at a high level, the team decided on two prime candidates, Oracle and another major player in the ERP market. Pond recalled that size was an issue in the selection. "We decided that we should not put Cisco's future in the hands of a company that was significantly smaller than we were."

[5] MRP represents a class of systems, often thought of as predecessors of ERP, that focus on planning the material requirements for production. Forecast or actual demand is fed to MRP either manually or from other types of systems. MRP functionality is embedded in the offerings of all leading ERP vendors.

[6] The Gartner Group is a leading industry resource for information on ERP and other information systems and manufacturing related research.

The team spent 10 days writing a request for proposals (RFP) to send to the vendors. Vendors were given two weeks to respond. While vendors prepared their responses, the Cisco team continued its "due diligence" by visiting a series of reference clients offered by each vendor. Following Cisco's analysis of the RFP responses, each vendor was invited in for a three-day software demonstration and asked to show how their package could meet Cisco's information processing requirements. Cisco provided sample data, while vendors illustrated how key requirements were met (or not met) by the software.

Selection of Oracle was based on a variety of factors. Redfield described three of the major decision points:

> First, this project was being driven pretty strongly by manufacturing and Oracle had a better manufacturing capability than the other vendor. Second, they made a number of promises regarding the long-term development of functionality in the package.[7] The other part of it was the flexibility offered by Oracle's being close by.[8]

Cisco also had reason to believe that Oracle was particularly motivated to make the project a success. Pond provided his impression of Oracle's situation: "Oracle wanted this win badly. We ended up getting a super deal. There are, however, a lot of strings attached. We do references, allow site visits and in general talk to many companies that are involved in making this decision." The Cisco project would be the first major implementation of a new release of the Oracle ERP product. Oracle was touting the new version as having major improvements in support of manufacturing. A successful implementation at Cisco would launch the new release on a very favorable trajectory.

From inception to final selection, the Cisco team had spent 75 days. The final choice was team-based. Solvik described how the decision was made and presented to the vendors:

> The team internally made the choice and informed the vendors. There was no major process we had to go through with management to "approve" the selection. We just said "Oracle, you won, [other vendor] you lost." Then we went on to contract negotiations with Oracle and putting a proposal together for our board of directors. The focus immediately turned to issues of how long the project would take, and how much it would cost. The team decided "yes, we will do this and we ought to go forward with the project." So now at the very end of April we were putting the whole plan together.

Going to the Board

Before going to the board for approval, the team needed to answer two very important questions: How much would it cost and how long would it take? They knew their executives were worried that a big project might spin out of control and deliver substandard results. Despite the risks, the team took a pragmatic approach to estimating project requirements. Solvik described the process:

> Our quarters go August to October, November to January, February to April, and May to July.[9] So right here on May 1, beginning of the fourth quarter, we are asking "how long should it take to do a project to replace all of our core systems?" This is truly how it went. We said "you know we can't implement in the fourth quarter. The auditors will have a complete cow." If it takes a year we will be implementing fourth quarter, and that won't work. We thought it really should take 15 months, July or August a year later. Tom Herbert, the program manager, said there's no way we are going to take 15 months to get this done. That's ridiculous. So we started going in the opposite direction and said well can we do it in five months? That just didn't seem right. Understand we did not have a scope yet. In the end we basically settled that we wanted to go live at the beginning of Q3, so we would be completely stable for Q4.

That took care of setting a target date. (See Exhibit 2 for a summary of milestone ERP implementation dates.) Next came the task of estimating a project budget. Once again, Cisco was aggressive: "After we set a date, we estimated budgets. We put this

[7] Redfield later noted that not all of these promises were met in the time frame agreed to during contract negotiations.

[8] Oracle and Cisco world headquarters are both located near San Jose, CA, approximately 20 miles from each other.

[9] Cisco's financial year end is July 31.

EXHIBIT 2 Summary of Milestone ERP Implementation Dates

Source: Cisco ERP Steering Commitee Report, October 20, 1994.

Milestone	Date
Project Kickoff	June 2, 1994
Prototype Setup Complete	July 22, 1994
Implementation Team Training	July 31, 1994
Process, Key Data, Modification Designs Complete	August 31, 1994
Functional Process Approval	September 30, 1994
Hardware Benchmark and Capacity Plan Validated	October 15, 1994
Critical Interfaces, Modifications, and Reports Complete	December 1, 1994
Procedures and End-User Documentation Complete	December 16, 1994
Conference Room Pilot Complete—Go/No Go Decision	December 22, 1994
End-User Training Beings	January 3, 1995
Data Conversion Complete	January 27, 1995
Go Live!	January 30, 1995

whole thing together without really being that far into this program. We just looked at how much it touched" (Pete Solvik). Instead of developing a formal business case (i.e., a financial analysis) to demonstrate the impact that the project would have on the company, the team chose to focus on the issues that had sparked the analysis in the first place. In Solvik's view, Cisco had little choice but to move. He explained his approach to the situation:

> We said that we had this big outage in January. That we were the biggest customer of our current software vendor and that the vendor was being bought by another company. It was unclear who was going to support our existing systems and we needed to do something. The reliability, the scalability, and the modifiability of our current applications would not support our anticipated future growth. We needed either upgrades to the new version of the current application or we needed to replace it. If we replaced it, we could either do it in parts or do it as a whole. We evaluated those three alternatives, talked about the pros and cons of each alternative, and recommended that we replace our systems, big-bang, with one ERP solution. We committed to do it in nine months for $15 million for the whole thing.

Although Cisco was, to some extent, compelled to implement ERP, proceeding without a formal economic justification was also a matter of management philosophy. As Redfield put it:

> You don't approach this kind of thing from a justification perspective. Cost avoidance is not an appropriate way to look at it. You really need to look at it like "Hey, we are going to do business this way." You are institutionalizing a business model for your organization.

At $15 million, the project would constitute the single largest capital project ever approved by the company. (See Exhibit 3 for a breakdown of project costs.) Members of the team prepared, with some trepidation, to take this number to senior management. The first meeting with CEO Morgridge did nothing to alleviate their concerns. Pond described the meeting with Morgridge this way:

> Pete Solvik, Tom Herbert, and I took the proposal to Morgridge and the reaction was pretty interesting. He made the comment "you know, careers are lost over much less money than this." Pete and I were as white as a sheet of paper. We knew that if we failed that we were going to get shot. Failure is not something the business took to well, especially with this kind of money.

But Morgridge okayed taking the project proposal to the board. Unfortunately for Pond and Solvik, the reception was not much warmer there. Pond described what happened:

> Before we even get the first slide up I hear the chairman speaking from the back of the room. He says, "How much?"

EXHIBIT 3 Breakdown of Implementation Costs for Cisco ERP Implementation[a]

Source: Cisco ERP Steering Commitee Report, October 20, 1994.

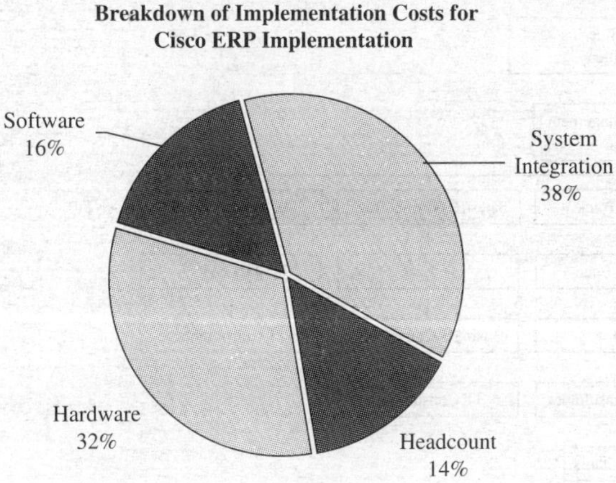

[a] The project budget estimate did not include estimates of the cost of Cisco personnel time beyond some members of the core team.

> I said I was getting to it and he responded: "I hate surprises. Just put the slide up right now." After I put it up he said "Oh my God, there better be a lot of good slides. . . ."[9]

There were and the board ended up approving the project.[10] In the weeks and months following the meeting, Morgridge did his part by making it clear to the rest of Cisco that the ERP project was a priority. The project emerged as one of the company's top seven goals for the year. "Everybody in the company knew this was happening and it was a priority for the business" Pond explained.

Building the Implementation Team

With board approval in hand, the core ERP team lost no time in setting up a structure for the implementation. One of their first acts was to extend Cisco's relationship with KPMG through the end of the implementation. This decision was made based on KPMG's performance through the software selection process, and the firm's continued commitment to staff the project with its most seasoned personnel.

Proceeding with implementation also meant that the team had to expand from its core 20 members to about 100, representing a cross-section of Cisco's business community.[11] Again, the team sought only the very best for inclusion on the project. One of the rules of engagement for those working on the implementation was that it was short term in duration and did not represent a career change for those involved. The effort was framed to those who would work on it as a challenge, a "throw down the gauntlet sort of thing." By this time, getting people to work on the team was not a problem. Elizabeth Fee, an implementation team recruit, describes how the assignment was viewed: "They hand picked the best and the brightest for this team. To each person it was a career advancement possibility. People did it because it was something different, it was THE opportunity."

Team members from across Cisco were placed onto one of five "tracks" (process area teams). Each track had a Cisco information systems leader, a Cisco business leader, business and IT consultants from either KPMG or Oracle, and additional personnel from the business as team members (see Exhibit 4 for a diagram of Cisco's ERP team structure). Tracks were managed from a "Project Management Office" which included Cisco's Business Project manager, Tom Herbert, and Mark Lee, the KPMG Project manager.

Sitting atop the entire project management structure was an Executive Steering Committee comprised of the VP of Manufacturing, the VP of Customer Advocacy, the Corporate Controller, Solvik, Oracle's senior VP of Applications, and the partner-in-charge of West Coast Consulting for KPMG. The presence on the steering committee of such high-level executives from Oracle and KPMG was indicative of the importance these organizations placed on the project's success.

[10] Pond adds that the cause for approval was aided by the fact that the legacy systems crashed on the day of the board meeting. "The day of the meeting [the legacy system] went down. We were able to walk into the board meeting and say, 'It's down again.' It was really a compelling story."

[11] Total employment at Cisco was estimated at the time to be 2,500 people.

EXHIBIT 4 **Cisco ERP Implementation Team Structure**

Source: Company documents.

Cisco ERP Implementation Team Structure

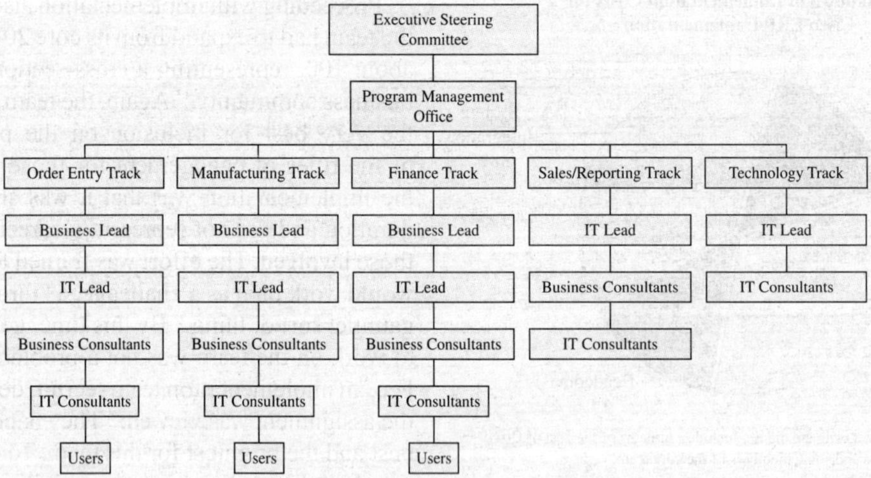

The ERP team's strategy for using the Steering Committee was to empower them in specific ways while relieving them of the need to intervene directly in the management of the project. The committee's role was to provide high-level sponsorship for the project, to ensure visibility, and to motivate the team. The team aimed to make steering committee meetings celebratory events. To ensure this, they focused on addressing steering committee member's questions before meetings.

Implementing Oracle

The team's implementation strategy employed a development technique referred to as "rapid iterative prototyping." Using this approach, team members broke the implementation into a series of phases called "Conference Room Pilots" (CRP). The purpose of each CRP was to build on previous work to develop a deeper understanding of the software and how it functioned within the business environment.

CRP0

The first CRP (CRP0) began with training the implementation team and setting up the technical environment. Here the team worked in two parallel efforts. The first effort focused on getting the team trained on the Oracle applications. Cisco directed Oracle to compress its normal five-day training classes into two 16-hour days. In a two-week period the majority of team members participated in this "immersion" training for the entire application suite. While this was happening, a small "tiger team" was engaged in the second effort, getting the applications up and running.

Following training and setup of the system, the core team met in a session designed to quickly configure the Oracle package. Team members from all areas of the company were "locked" together in an off-site meeting to discuss and decide on the appropriate setting for the hundreds of parameters embedded within the software. Team members were joined by specialists from Oracle and KPMG. Solvik described the experience, its intensity, and results:

> There are all these configurable options on how are you going to run the systems. You set literally hundreds of parameters in these applications. So we went off-site two days, 40 people, and everybody's homework assignment for that off-site meeting, maybe three or four weeks into the project at this stage, was to come in with an 80-20

> recommendation on how to configure the system. We met all day and into the night for two days, going down to the "nth-degree" on how we were going to make this thing run for us. Oracle experts, with KPMG experts, with Cisco business people, Cisco IT people, let's talk about GL, let's talk about Chart of Accounts, talk about this and talk about that. I call it the 1 percent effort that gave us 80 percent accuracy on how we would run this application, as opposed to a typical ERP approach, where you go off for six months, and overanalyze it to death. We had this three to four weeks into the project and we ended up being about 80 percent accurate in terms of how we could do this.

One week after this meeting the team completed CRP0 with a demonstration of the software's capacity to take a Cisco order all the way through the company's business process (Quote-to-Cash).

An important realization coming out of CRP0 was that Cisco would not be able to adhere to one of its early goals for the implementation—to avoid modification of the ERP software. Avoiding modification was important because changes tend to be firm specific and make migration to future application releases difficult and time consuming. The team's experiences during the first phase of the project indicated that without a significant number of changes the software would not be able to effectively support the company. By the time one month had passed, it was clear that some changes would be required. Within two months after that it became clear that some of the changes would be substantial.

CRP1

Building on the lessons learned in CRP0, the implementation team immediately embarked on CRP1. With the team now fully staffed up, the goal of this phase of the project was for each track to make the system work within their specific area. As in earlier work, the emphasis was on getting the system to accommodate Cisco processes without modification. During CRP1, team members generated detailed scripts that documented the purpose for and procedures used to complete a process (see Exhibit 5 for a sample business process script). In order to ensure that all contingencies were accounted for, business process prototype tracking sheets were developed (see Exhibit 6 for a sample prototype tracking sheet). In contrast to CRP0, team members carefully documented the issues they ran across during their modeling. Issues were addressed in weekly three-hour meetings held by the Program Management Office. During these meetings the track leaders from each area worked together to resolve the issues and push the project forward. Modeling during this phase confirmed the concerns about the software. There were huge numbers of business processes that the software could not support.

The implementation team's response to the gaps found in the system was to develop a means for categorizing and evaluating each one individually. "All modification requests were classified as Red, Yellow, or Green. Each one went to the track leads, and anything that was a Red had to go to the Steering Committee for approval." There were few Reds (see Exhibit 7 for list of "Red" modifications). In the end, 30 developers were needed for three months to modify Oracle to support the business.[12] Elizabeth Fee described the process.

> When we realized we were not going to be able to go live "vanilla," we began to work on our modification strategy. The months of July and August were focused on which modifications were we going to do? What's real and what's not. In some cases the user would be saying "you know, the date used to be the first thing you type and in Oracle it's the fourth." In other cases it was the realization that we would have to hire 100 people on the shop floor to open and close work orders if we did not figure out a way to automate it.

[12] When designing the modifications required for the system, Cisco made a concerted effort to stay "out of the core application code." "Core" code is the central programming logic on which application processing is based. Core code modifications are often not supported by the software vendor and can complicate a firm's ability to upgrade existing software with new releases. In Cisco's case, most modifications avoided touching the core code, relying instead on the addition of database fields and technically simple screen changes. In those cases where the core code was altered (usually to bypass certain processing), Cisco personnel worked with Oracle consultants and software engineers to identify appropriate changes. In several cases, Cisco modifications were later incorporated into Oracle's core product.

EXHIBIT 5 Sample Business Process Script

Source: Cisco.

ATP Process

Scope: This process will define how the Available To Promise (ATP) process will work. This process will include how to enter information into the ATP, how to maintain ATP, how to access ATP information, and how the information should be used.

Policy:

All Sales Orders will be assigned as scheduled ship date based upon ATP dates
Master Scheduling will maintain ATP information
Request Date will be left blank if customer did not specify a request date
Schedule date will be entered one week out from today's date

Process for Order Scheduling:

CS Rep

1. Enter Order per Order Entry Process
2. Input Customer Request Date per Order Entry Process
3. If Order is Government Rated or Express complete order line items per Order Entry Process
   Order Entry Process
   a. After Booking of order, Hit Page Down
   b. Choose Order . . . (Order Action Quick Pick)
   c. Choose ATP Inquiry Order
   d. When complete, hit page down again
   e. Choose View Schedule Results
   f. If ATP date matched Scheduled date and no failure reasons are listed below, go to step g. If errors exist, order must be scheduled into Group Available date or have parameters changed in order
   g. Choose page down again and select Choose Order . . .
   h. Choose Demand Order. System will state scheduling complete
4. If order does not follow above, Book the order per the Order Entry Process
   a. Order will be submitted to Demand Interface automatically
   b. If date is available, order will interface
   c. If date is not available order will remain in eligible status after demand interface has run.

Order Scheduler

5. Run Process Exception Report (\Navigate Other Report Run)
   a. Choose Report under Type
   b. Choose Process Exception Report
   c. Choose Demand Interface for Program Name
   d. Choose date range for order rejects
   e. Submit report (F5)
6. Run On-Line ATP process to determine first available date for order to ship
   a. Go into the Order (\Navigate Orders Enter)
   b. Query to bring up order that failed scheduling
   c. Hit page down key
   d. Choose Order . . . (Order Action Quick Pick)
   e. Choose ATP Inquiry Order
   f. Choose View Schedule Results
   g. If ATP date matched Scheduled data and no failure reasons are listed below, go to step h. If errors exist, order must be scheduled into Group Available Date or have parameters changed in order

EXHIBIT 5 Sample Business Process Script (*Continued*)

h. Choose page down again and select Choose Order . . .
i. Choose Demand Order: System will state scheduling complete

ATP System Issues

1. Report for Process Exception currently requires the Demand interface Concurrent Manager ID to be used (due to bug).
2. Table read by Demand Interface is never purged or cleaned up. As a result, records of failure will not be purged after success has occurred. Need to clear the Demand Interface table prior to each run somehow.
3. Process Exception Report will need to sort by Order Request Date
4. Modifications to default promise date from the schedule date after Demand Interface has occurred once. Future changes to schedule date should not affect Request Date.

ATP Process Issues

1. Who will own the decision to use product from another demand class? Under what guidelines?
2. Who will determine which orders will slip out in order to add an order to an ATP date? Under what guidelines?
3. How can we guarantee that when Master Scheduling increases an ATP, that the order that required that date receives it? (Hand-off issues)
4. How will DOA orders work so that they are shipped ASAP?
5. Should Customer Services be allowed to use the Buffer (DO NOT USE) demand class for any reservations?
6. What are exact definitions of promise date, schedule date, and request date? How will they be populated?
7. How to control the use of Master Scheduling? Do Not Use/Buffer Demand Class?

Commentary: Process Issue Number 1
Responsibility for this lies entirely within Customer Service Organization for demand classes that service customer segments. CS not allowed to move available quantity from Non-Revenue demand class without an approval from Master Scheduling (to avoid impacting the revenue plan) or from the Buffer Demand Class.

Commentary: Process Issue Number 2
Open Issue: CS to own resolution on this.

Commentary: Process Issue Number 3
Master Scheduling will change the demand class on the order and online interface of the order if the product is available to avoid confusing communication issues (to be tested in Conference Room pilot).

Commentary: Process Issue Number 5
Elizabeth and Kevin will work on this with Master Scheduling to determine best way to handle.

Commentary: Process Issue Number 6
No.

Commentary: Process Issue Number 7
Request date is customer's requested ship from Cisco date. Promise date is the date that Cisco has committed to ship the order to the customer. Schedule Date is the date used by Manufacturing to assign ATP and to notify CS of changes to the production date once an order has been missed.

EXHIBIT 6 Sample Prototype Tracking Sheet

Source: Cisco.

	A	B	C	D	E	F
1	**Application**	**Type**	**Related**	**Required**	**Comments**	**Status**
2			**Modules**			
3	**Financials & General Ledger**					
4	**System Setup**					
5	Accounting Flexfield Structure	Flexfield	All	Yes	5 segments	Done
6	Value set and values—Company	Flexfield	All	Yes	3 digit	Done
7	Value set and values—Department	Flexfield	All	Yes	6 digit	Done
8	Value set and values—Account	Flexfield	All	Yes	5 digit	Done
9	Value set and values—Project	Flexfield	All	Yes	4 digit	Done
10	Value set and values—Product	Flexfield	All	Yes	3 digit	Done
11	Calendar period types	Accounting	All		4-4-5 calendar	Done
12	Calendar periods	Accounting	All			Done
13	Currencies	Accounting	All		USD	Done
14	Sets of books	Accounting	All		14 sets of books	Done
15	**Functional Setup**					
16	Account Hierarchies and Rollup Groups	Accounting	All			Ongoing
17	Cross validation rules	Accounting	All			
18	Security rules	Accounting	All			
19	Shorthand aliases	Accounting	All			
20	Suspense accounts and Intercompany accounts	Accounting	All			Done
21	Statistical units of measure	Accounting	All			Done
22	Accounting flexfield combination	Accounting	All			
23	Daily conversion rate types	Translation	All			Done
24	Rates	Translation	All			
25	Summary accounts and templates	Summary	GL			
26	JE sources and categories	JE	GL	Yes		Done
27	**Functional Test Cases**					
28	Manual journal entries	JE	GL			
29	Recurring journal entries	JE	GL			
30	Mass Allocation formulae—Rent allocation	JE	GL			
31	Reversing journal entries	JE	GL			
32	Journal import	JE	GL			
33	Online inquiry	Inquiry	GL			
34	Translation	Translation	GL			
35	Define budget and budget organization	Budget	GL			

EXHIBIT 7 Cisco ERP Implementation List of "Red" Modification

Packout:

- Creates a "traveller" (i.e., a list of items to be configured) for build purposes, queues travellers by production cell so that each cell can print its own documentation (and not some other cell's) on demand.
- At the time the carton is being filled, allows barcode scanning to record contents of each box. Assigns a box tracking number and prompts for product serial number entry. Serial numbers are stored for future use and to prevent issuance of duplicates.
- Backflushes inventory from the system when the carton is closed.
- Determines if the box is ready for shipment or waiting for consolidation with other boxes and routes it to correct shipping location. If box is ready for shipment, it is released. If box is ready for consolidation the carton is tracked through its receipt at a consolidation center.
- Identifies last box in a ship set (delivery set) as it is received at a consolidation center and flags personnel to prepare the shipment.

Canada:

- Created a separate installation of the General Ledger and Accounts Payables with a separate set of books and separate currency.
- Allows transfer of data for Cisco General Ledger consolidation.

Product Configurator:

- Enabled Cisco to input "rules" regarding orderability (physical and technical constraints on ordering) in a logical fashion rather than through code.
- Tied to Order Entry—as an order is booked, the order is validated against the configurator.

OE Form:

- Altered process for translating discounts from major order lines to subsidiary lines. Also changes manner in which pricing information is loaded into Oracle.
- Created the ability to allow for landed cost data to be entered on an order.
- Created the ability to allow for multinational orders—where the billing location is in the United States but the shipment is out of the United States.
- Added new fields to capture additional sales order data.
- Added a trigger at bookings to call the configurator.

Net Change Bookings:

- Creates information "synopsis" of the bookings on a daily basis.
- Creates a log of all order activity (plus or minus), which then is used by multiple other systems for reporting.

Discovery of the need to modify Oracle led to some unplanned changes in the project plan and budget. In addition to the identification of required modifications, the implementation team also determined that the Oracle package could not be adequately aligned with the after sales support needs of the company. As a result, the team embarked on a concurrent effort to evaluate and select a service support package. The package was selected and implemented on a schedule that matched the overall implementation schedule. Cisco planned to go live on both packages on the same day.

CRP2 and CRP3

As CRP1 turned into CRP2, and summer turned into fall, the implementation team found itself in the thickest, most difficult part of the implementation. Project scope had expanded to include major modifications and a new after sales support package. One other major scope change also loomed. Because the downstream impacts of the project were much greater than expected, the team decided to tackle some larger technical issues. Whereas before, systems had tended to communicate directly with one another (i.e., "point to point"), a new approach would now be employed in which all data communication would take place via a "data warehouse." Utilization of a data warehouse would allow all of Cisco's applications to access a single source for their information needs.

The scope changes meant further shifts in the utilization of Cisco's resources, especially for the company's 100-person IT department. The technical nature of most of the scope changes meant that this group bore most of the responsibility for the project additions. Solvik described the result:

> Basically all the rest of the IT group started decommitting from their other projects. They said, "we have to spend our time just absorbing the fact that the core systems in the company are changing. We are needing to divert more and more energy, and more and more resources towards the project." IT did nothing else that year. We also decided not to convert any history as part of this project. Instead the data warehouse group created the capability to report historical and future in an integrated data conversion. We renumbered our customers; we renumbered our products; and we changed our bill-of-materials structure. We changed fundamentally all of our underlying data in the company, and the data warehouse became the bridging system that would span history and future together.

By the end of CRP2, the first round of modifications was in place and running. During this time the implementation team continued to deepen its understanding of the Oracle and Service packages and to determine how to best make them work for Cisco. The final goal of CRP2 was to begin testing the system, both hardware and software, to see how well it would stand up to the processing load and transaction volumes required to run Cisco's growing business.

CRP3's focus was on testing the full system and assessing the company's readiness to "go live." A final test was conducted with a full complement of users to see how the system would perform, front to back, with a full transaction load. The implementation team executed these tests by capturing a full day's worth of actual business data and "rerunning" it on a Saturday in January. Team members watched as each track, in turn, executed a simulated day's worth of work. With this test completed to the entire team's satisfaction, everyone felt ready for cutover in February. Pond described the ceremony that concluded CRP3:

> At the end of CRP3 each one of the functional leads presented their piece of the process and said "yes or no" on whether they were ready to go. We did each of them separately and then put everyone in the same room and made them nod their heads and say "we should go." . . . And then we turned the damn thing on. . . .

Cutting Over to the Oracle

> . . . [After cutover] I wouldn't say the company hit the wall, but I would say we had major day to day challenges that needed to be solved quickly to avoid significant impact to the company. For example, our on-time ship, shipping on the date we commit to the customer, fell from 95 percent to about 75 percent; it was still not miserable but it was not good.
>
> *Pete Solvik*

The initial success of Cisco's cutover to Oracle was, to say the least, something less than what was expected. Overall business performance plummeted as users attempted to deal with a new system that proved to be disturbingly unstable. On average, the system went down nearly once a day. The primary problem, as it turned out, was with the hardware architecture and sizing. Ordinarily correcting the deficiency would have required the purchase of additional hardware, thus increasing the total project expenditure. But Cisco had asked for, and gotten, an unusual contract from the hardware vendor. In their contract Cisco purchased equipment based on a promised capability rather than a specific configuration. As a result, the onus for fixing the hardware performance problems fell completely on the hardware vendor.

A second problem had to do with the ability of the software itself to handle the transaction volume required in the Cisco environment. The design of the application exacerbated hardware problems by inefficiently processing common tasks. In retrospect, it was clear where the company had gone wrong in its final testing of the system. As Pond put it: "Some things were seriously broken at big data volumes, . . . and we have a huge database. Our mistake was that we did not test the system with a big enough database attached to it." In testing the system, Cisco had run individual processes sequentially rather than at the same time. In addition, only a partially loaded database was used. After cutover, when all processes were running together over a fully converted database, the system lacked the capacity to process the required load.

The next two months were some of the most trying of the entire implementation. This was particularly true for the IT staff as it tried to grapple with the technical difficulties caused by bringing the new system up. Fee described what it was like at this time:

> It was tough, really stressful. This was a big thing, one of the top company initiatives. There was a lot of focus on getting it done. We were working really long hours; making decisions that would affect the company going forward. . . . We always knew we would make it. It was always a "when," not an "if." There were [many] things you did not like about [the software].

ERP project status became the number one agenda item for weekly executive staff meetings. Strong vendor commitment from Oracle, the hardware vendor, and KPMG led to an eventual stabilization of the software and improved performance. Solvik described the environment:

> So for about 60 days we were in complete SWAT-team mode; get this thing turned around. For example the president of the hardware vendor was our executive sponsor. This vendor probably had 30 people on site at one point. They were all over it. They lost money on this big time. It was great for them to get such a great reference, but it was a tough experience for them. Remember we had bought a capability, so everything they did to add capacity was out of their own pocket.

After Stabilization

The technical problems associated with the Oracle implementation proved to be short-lived. Over the course of the next three months, Cisco and its vendors, working together, stabilized and added capacity to the system. The implementation ordeal concluded with a celebration party for the team and company management. Several members of Cisco's Board of Directors also attended. Expectations were running high that the new information systems would fulfill the promise of supporting the rapid growth that the company had forecasted.

As he signed off on his recommendation for the bonus distribution, Solvik thought about the approach they had taken toward the implementation. "Total systems replacement for \$15 million in nine months—who would have thought we could do it?" He tried to think about the decisions he and the team had made during the course of the implementation. What factors had made the difference between success and failure? Where had they been smart? Where had they been just plain lucky? Could they do it again if they had to?

Module 3

IT Leadership

Deborah L. Soule

In many companies, IT has become fundamental to support, sustain, transform, and grow the business. This pattern has elevated the importance of IT leadership and governance within the company, and dramatically changed the core management and leadership issues in many cases. What kind of leadership is appropriate, given the role that IT plays in the firm? How should IT be organized to best support and enhance business activities? How should IT be governed overall, in order to manage the risk and ensure the value of what is now a strategic and indispensable business asset?

The chapters, article, and cases in this module provide a basis for discussing the high-level management, leadership, and governance activities that set the organizational context for leveraging IT-enabled strategic insight and ensuring IT-driven operational excellence. Chapter 9 explores the concept and practice of IT governance, discussing the connection between IT governance and corporate governance responsibilities, and offering recommendations for initiating and improving IT governance efforts. Chapter 10 presents a contingency framework for considering IT leadership needs and responsibilities, based on the role that IT plays in a company. Acknowledging that the role of IT is shaped by both internal and external factors in organizations and industries, it offers recommendations for practice that account for differences and transitions in the role of IT.

The article and two cases integrate concepts discussed throughout this book. They are intended to help readers explore the dynamics of business strategy, information technology use, and leadership.

Chapter 9

Governance of the IT Function

Governance of a business enterprise or a nonprofit institution is the process of structuring, operating, and controlling the organization with a view to achieving its longterm strategic goals, serving the interests of its various stakeholders, and complying with legal and regulatory requirements. Governance involves establishing chains of responsibility, authority and communication, as well as policies, standards, measurements, and control mechanisms that allow organizational members to carry out their roles and responsibilities. Collectively, these elements serve to define expectations, allocate resources, manage risk, and verify performance for a given domain of responsibility.

Information technology (IT) governance addresses these same issues but with a specific focus on the IT assets and activities within the enterprise. Good IT governance can increase the effectiveness of an enterprise by organizing IT assets so as to optimally enable business goals, protecting enterprise investments in IT, including systems and networks, assuring security and reliability of strategic information, addressing IT-centric business issues such as enterprise resource management, and ensuring appropriate management of enterprise information assets.

The management responsibilities discussed earlier in Module 2—such as project management or investments in information security—are related to IT governance. At one level, the core issues with which managers must grapple are similar: resource allocation choices, risk and return trade-offs, and alignment of goals. What is different is the level at which these issues are addressed. IT governance is the effort to devise an overarching and integrated approach, addressing broad themes such as operating performance, strategic control, risk management, and values alignment. These themes can then be translated into more targeted roles, structures, and procedures at a more tactical and operational level.

This chapter briefly reviews the concept of enterprise governance, before delving into the notion of IT governance more specifically. It explores some of the reasons why IT governance has assumed greater importance for both IT executives and other corporate leaders in recent years. In conclusion, it offers recommendations for approaching and implementing an IT governance effort, based on current best practices and research.

The Essentials of Enterprise Governance

In late 2001, shortly after claiming revenues of $111 billion and having been named "America's Most Innovative Company" for six consecutive years, Enron, an American energy company, filed for bankruptcy. Despite being publicly owned, for years it hid the fact that most of its profits and revenues were derived from deals with special purpose entities, and had managed to avoid reporting debts and losses clearly in its financial statements. During a string of revelations of its irregular accounting procedures the true state of its financial position emerged and its stock price fell from $90 to pennies in a few months.[1] Burgeoning legislation, enacted in response to cases such as Enron's, has pushed senior managers and company boards to attend more carefully to matters of governance.

The need for a system of governance is partially driven by what we refer to as the *agency problem*: the fact that the physical separation between the owners of a company and its managers (or agents) provides those managers the opportunity to act in ways that are advantageous to themselves but detrimental to the interests of the owners.[2] To minimize the agency problem, certain control and monitoring systems are instituted, which attempt to ensure *conformance* to a set of externally defined requirements. Most generally, at the corporate level, these include: (1) a board of directors intended to oversee organizational strategies, structures, and systems on behalf of the shareholders, and (2) an external auditor who should offer insight into the reliability of the company's financial statements.[3] These mechanisms alone are insufficient to ensure effective governance, however. Enron, for instance, was compliant with the New York Stock Exchange requirements yet still failed to ensure effective governance. As a result, in addition to conformance, governance systems also need to address *performance*. We focus on the performance requirement of governance in this chapter.

Governance aims to ensure that managers and employees faithfully translate strategies into operational initiatives throughout the organization, that they protect organizational assets and use them efficiently, and that they comply with laws and regulations. Moreover, and particularly during times of transformative change, governance should also support managers and employees in challenging and validating those strategies. Thus, the objectives of governance include strategic goal satisfaction, operational efficiency, measurement reliability, and compliance.

Governance is the process of establishing lines of responsibility, authority, and communication, as well as policies, standards, measurement, and internal control mechanisms that guide people in fulfilling their roles and responsibilities. These elements can be implemented by management, through different kinds of control systems, to maintain or alter patterns of organizational behavior.

[1] M. Salter, *Innovation Corrupted: The Rise and Fall of Enron,* Harvard Business School Publishing (No. 905-048 and No. 905-049), December 2004.

[2] For more information see M. Jensen and W. Meckling, "Theory of the Firm: Managerial Behavior, Agency Costs, and Ownership Structure." *Journal of Financial Economics* 3: 1976, 305–360.

[3] For a comparative review of corporate governance approaches, see D. F. Larcker and B. Tayan, "Models of Corporate Governance: Who's the Fairest of Them All?" Stanford Graduate School of Business, Ref. CG-11, January 2008.

Traditional operating control systems measure critical performance variables, providing information to diagnose when a system is in control or out of control. However, their focus on outcomes is inadequate in an age where organizations are compelled to continuously learn, innovate, and reinvent themselves—*and* where adaptations in strategy and objectives may be triggered by the insights and efforts of empowered employees rather than by top management.[4] Additional governance mechanisms, especially in knowledge—and information—driven organizations, are needed. Value management systems strengthen and sustain commitment to core organizational values, for instance, by articulating mission statements and vision statements and developing a strong corporate culture. Risk management systems delineate the boundaries between acceptable and unacceptable risks and standards of business conduct. Strategic control systems focus on communicating and implementing the organization's strategy, while encouraging debate about that strategy intended to stimulate learning and growth.[5] Collectively, these sets of controls are intended to achieve the desired balance between innovation and control, and ensure the successful achievement of profit goals and strategies.

The Benefits of Good Enterprise Governance

Good governance, in the form of vigilant board members as well as strong internal control mechanisms, can shape perceptions that, in turn, affect a company's share price or its cost of raising capital. Some international start-up companies deliberately choose to go public by listing on major stock exchanges demanding more robust governance requirements than their home country stock exchange.[6] In addition to gaining global visibility that helps build brand recognition, the ability to meet more demanding listing requirements can confer operational credibility that can translate into long-term lower cost of capital and financial flexibility. Basically, stakeholders view such governance requirements as a quality control mechanism for assuring better defined business processes and efficiency. Private companies and nonprofit organizations, too, can benefit from mechanisms to ensure and demonstrate progress towards stated goals and the efficient and effective use of resources. This is especially important if an organization relies on external resources such as debt-financing or foundation support.

Introducing IT Governance

While many organizations recognize the potential benefits that IT can yield, successful organizations also understand and manage the risks associated with implementing and depending on new technologies. Like enterprise governance, the purpose of IT governance is to ensure that the resources accorded to an initiative are appropriate for the risk and return anticipated from that initiative and that the initiative aligns with organizational goals.

[4] This point is highlighted by Robert Simons, who identifies different control systems (or levers) and their differential impact at various stages of an organization's lifecycle. See R. Simons, *Levers of Control: How Managers Use Innovative Control Systems to Drive Strategic Renewal* (Boston: Harvard Business School Press, 1995).

[5] These categories are based on the work of Simons, who uses the labels: diagnostic control systems; belief systems; boundary systems; and interactive control systems.

[6] See, for example, G. F. Hardymon and A. Leamon, Celtel International B.V.: June 2004 (A), Harvard Business School Publishing (No. 805-120) March 2005.

Malfeasance versus Misfeasance

The Enron events and mismanagement of an IT project, for instance, appear to fall into vastly different categories of behavior, and readers may wonder about the connection between the two. The wrongdoing of some of Enron's senior executives seems to be an example of *malfeasance:* intentional behavior that is legally or morally wrong. It involves dishonesty, illegality, or knowingly exceeding authority for improper reasons. An IT employee who intentionally destroys company data, for example, also commits *malfeasance* although on a different scale to that of Enron. On the other hand, something like project mismanagement is probably more accurately labeled *misfeasance:* behavior that involves commitment of a wrong or error by mistake, negligence or inadvertence. It may indicate incompetence but not intentional wrongdoing. Although they are separate issues, both malfeasance and misfeasance involve poor use of shareholder resources. Therefore, governance (enterprise and IT-level) is concerned with both types of behavior.

Every organization, regardless of its size or profit motive, needs a way to ensure that the IT function supports and advances the strategies and objectives of the overall organization. This implies the need for procedures for cascading strategic goals down into the organization and mechanisms to facilitate the implementation of those strategic goals. Every organization needs a way to ensure that IT effort, skills, and investments are not squandered on low-priority activities while higher-priority needs languish for lack of resources or attention. This implies the need to define criteria for measuring and evaluating IT performance. It further implies the need for procedures to involve relevant stakeholders in critical IT decisions. Briefly, such concerns are the domain of IT governance.

Good IT governance ensures that an organization's IT function achieves its strategic goals, which are set at the higher level of enterprise governance. Further, it does so in an efficient manner via a reliable measurement system and while remaining compliant with relevant laws and regulations.[7]

The Impetus for Better IT Governance

IT governance is not a new phenomenon, but the practice of more formally monitoring and measuring the use of IT assets has received increased attention of late. First, the critical contributions of information and information technology to contemporary organizations have focused attention on ways to better manage potential risks and desired returns in this domain. Second, as companies and other organizations seek to establish and improve general governance, risk management, and compliance practices (GRC), there is increasing attention to the role of IT in enabling these practices.[8]

[7] This characterization is drawn from IBM Redbook: "IBM's IT Governance Approach: Business Performance through IT Execution." Online at www.redbooks.ibm.com/redbooks/pdfs/sg247517.pdf.

[8] Since regulatory compliance and corporate risk management can be addressed through effective IT governance, IT governance, risk management, and compliance (IT GRC) tend to be linked in practice. Further, although particular regulations only affect select subsets of organizations, there is broad-based emphasis on IT-related GRC activities.

These drivers towards better IT governance are discussed under three themes: the business value of IT, the business risk potential of IT, and IT's contribution to corporate regulatory compliance.

The Business Value of IT

A major driver of IT governance is the goal of ensuring that IT creates value for the organization. Spending on IT worldwide has surpassed $2 trillion but many organizations still struggle to prove the payoff from IT. Nicholas Carr's controversial 2003 article (discussed in Module 1), reasoning that the pervasiveness of IT had diminished its value, only aggravated this angst.[9] Many IT leaders found themselves having to refute Carr's logic while justifying their IT budgets and investment requests to their executive teams. Despite understanding intuitively that there can be a profound difference between having technology and using it effectively, they often were ill-prepared to explain how IT contributes to strategic value and productivity gains.

By design, IT governance aims to address such issues. On one level, IT governance includes mechanisms and measures to enhance the day-to-day efficiency and effectiveness of IT, so better governance is expected to improve IT in areas tangible to its business customers such as service quality, cost control, project delivery time, and process improvement. At a more comprehensive level, IT governance should help achieve a central aspiration of many companies: greater alignment of IT with the business.[10]

Better alignment is critical to enable IT to deliver on the expanding technology-related demands from the business. As IT *per se* ceases to be a differentiator, differentiation comes from how IT is leveraged. In the past, most IT managers viewed and justified IT investments in terms of cost-savings such as using IT for automation, efficiency, and cost reduction. But, increasingly, IT is able and expected to drive a more granular level of business model impacts, such as by facilitating more rapid and widespread innovation, underpinning new products and services, or reaching new customers. Making this transition in emphasis from simply using IT to "decrease cost" to using IT to "improve business models" requires both the IT organization and the business to adopt a different approach to IT investment. Furthermore, since initiatives intended to transform a firm's business model tend to exhibit more uncertainty and strategic impact, governance oversight can be especially helpful in ensuring these projects stay on track. Governance practices, such as the establishment of procedures and criteria for evaluating, prioritizing, and monitoring the major IT investments necessary to deliver business value, can help organizations through this transition from a cost-side to a revenue-side perspective of IT.

Recognition of IT Impact

In 2004, after spending more than $300 million on a failed IT pilot, the U.S. Department of Veterans Affairs (VA) shelved a core information systems project.

[9] N. G. Carr, "IT Doesn't Matter," *Harvard Business Review*, May 2003.

[10] According to the IT Governance Global Status Report of 2008, published by PriceWaterhouseCoopers and the IT Governance Institute, in a survey of nearly 750 CIOs/CEOs, nearly 93 percent believe IT is somewhat to very important to the overall corporate strategy but 36 percent report that alignment between IT strategy and corporate strategy is average, poor, or very poor.

In 2005, the budget for another major IT initiative was severely curtailed after an independent study, solicited by the recently recruited CIO, highlighted poor planning and a high risk of failure. In response to years of cost overruns, mismanagement, and lack of accountability, the congressional oversight committee pushed legislation to centralize the department's IT budget under the CIO. Until then, the various VA divisions controlled their own budgets for their major IT projects, and the move towards centralized control was contentious and slow. The following year, the CIO resigned in frustration. Shortly thereafter, the agency received more negative attention due to high-profile losses of equipment that placed citizens' personal information at risk. A short time later, the VA Chief Information Security Officer resigned, complaining that he did not have the authority necessary to do his job properly.

The VA's plight exemplifies another significant driver of interest in IT governance: recognition of the increasing criticality of IT to enterprise viability. In the past, owing to limited technical experience and the complexities of IT, board members and senior executives tended to defer key IT management decisions to IT professionals. These days, however, none can dispute that many critical business activities are thoroughly dependent on information and information systems. At the same time, the interconnectedness of systems, services, and applications, and the volumes of data involved have increased tremendously. These factors substantially affect the complexity of major IT projects, and thus the risk to the organization if such projects get out of control. They even can create an adverse impact from what might appear to be a modest adjustment to an application or data source.

The potential for IT governance efforts to manage and minimize such risks has drawn the attention of shareholders, customers, and senior management alike. The assistant secretary for Information and Technology for the VA, the Honorable Robert T. Howard, notes that the catalyst for the department's IT governance initiative was the series of major IT failures discussed earlier:[11]

> For us it was the Congressional committee—what they saw going on within the Department of Veterans Affairs (VA), the inability to explain where money was going within the IT arena, and . . . a wide variety of ways of operating. A lot of the pressure to reorganize came from Capital Hill, from the oversight committees, primarily from the House of Representatives side. The House Veterans Affairs committee has a subcommittee for oversight. Initially, a lot centered on money and what was going on because of an inability to explain what was going on with the projects and why they never seemed to come to closure.

A theme common to IT governance discussions is that, in order to mitigate the risk to the business, an organization's IT capability can no longer be approached as a "black box." Instead, good governance practices aim to make senior executives and the board accountable for managing the risk and ensuring that stakeholders receive maximum value from IT. As such, governance must involve IT, business customers, and other corporate functions, so as to incorporate diverse viewpoints into key IT decision-making processes, thus shedding some light on the black box.

[11] The Honorable Robert T. Howard, assistant secretary for Information and Technology, U.S. Department of Veterans Affairs, quoted in "IT Governance Roundtable: IT Governance Frameworks," IT Governance Institute (2008).

IT as an Enabler of Corporate Governance and Compliance

Organizations today are subject to an increasing number of regulations governing data retention, information protection, financial accountability, financial risk management, and recovery from disasters. Most countries have regulations regarding the disclosure of business information, with which organizations need to comply. Some industries, such as pharmaceuticals and medical devices, have been heavily regulated for years, while new laws are adding or expanding compliance obligations for many other types of business. Noncompliance can incur business risk in the form of severe penalties such as fines, revocation of business licenses, other constraints on business operations, or even jail time for business representatives.

Two major phenomena, early in the twenty-first century, triggered a series of new regulations impacting businesses and, correspondingly, their IT functions. The first trigger was the devastatingly fatal terrorist attack on September 11, 2001, on the World Trade Center in New York City, and subsequent attacks in Bali, Madrid, and London. Efforts to contain further terrorism included legislation, in the United States and elsewhere, which aimed to track and intercept terrorist funding and communications. Such legislation requires certain organizations to establish and maintain more robust records of transactions, especially financial and communications transactions.

The second trigger, soon afterwards, was a wave of major corporate and accounting scandals in the United States, in which the financial health of affected companies was hidden from current and potential investors, costing them billions of dollars when the share prices ultimately collapsed. In response, the United States enacted the Sarbanes-Oxley Act of 2002, intended to increase internal financial controls in public organizations. Basel II (2004), an international guideline governing banking institutions, was also developed with the intent of minimizing the global impact of similar financial disasters. Both laws have catalyzed a more disciplined approach to IT governance in recent years.

Although IT governance is not a formal requirement specified by the legislation, its effective practice can improve internal controls and accessibility to data that many of these laws demand. (See "IT and Corporate Compliance Requirements" that explores the relationship between IT and a selection of compliance requirements in more detail.)

Since most business processes flow through the IT environment, requests for IT support for compliance may come from many different areas of the business. A significant challenge for the IT function is to align IT assets with the concurrent needs of multiple regulations and to establish coherent and internally consistent responses to multiple requests. Compliance efforts thus draw attention to opportunities for rationalization, standardization, simplification and optimization of enterprise applications, and can prompt a broader reevaluation of business processes.

Benefits of Effective IT Governance

Effective IT governance helps ensure that IT supports business goals, maximizes business investment in IT, and appropriately manages IT-related risks and opportunities.

IT and Corporate Compliance Requirements

Internal Financial Control Probably the most well-known catalyst for better governance is the Sarbanes-Oxley Act, or the Public Company Accounting Reform and Investor Protection Act of 2002. More commonly known as SOX or SARBOX, this U.S. federal law aims to protect investors by improving the accuracy and reliability of corporate disclosures. Other countries and regions, specifically the European Union, have regulations or directives similar to Sarbanes-Oxley, which are designed to enhance disclosure in financial reporting and increase transparency in corporate governance of public corporations.

The Sarbanes-Oxley Act created new standards for corporate accountability as well as new penalties for acts of wrongdoing. Impacting all U.S. public company boards, management, and public accounting firms this law requires firms to, among other things, report more information to the public, maintain stronger independence from their auditors, and report on or have audited their financial internal control procedures. In terms of internal controls, Sarbanes-Oxley formalizes and strengthens demands for internal checks and balances within corporations and requires instituting levels of control and signoff. These controls rely on the ability to document, trace, and audit changes that affect the financial reporting structure.

Since the financial reporting processes of most companies depend on IT systems, IT must, to varying extents, comply with these regulations. First, IT must support enterprise compliance through process controls that ensure that standard processes (e.g., for order processing) exist, are followed, and are accompanied by appropriate approvals. Second, IT must also establish and document controls related to IT activities such as security, application deployment, and change management. For example, any changes that affect financial reporting, such as to an Enterprise Resources System (ERP), must be tested, documented, and approved by appropriate parties before implementation. In addition, Sarbanes-Oxley requires disclosure of significant investments that may affect a company's operating performance. Since large IT projects can fall into this category, there is likely to be more management attention to IT project expenses and deliverables.

Financial Risk Management Basel II is the second of the Basel Accords, recommendations on banking laws and regulations issued by the Basel Committee on Banking Supervision. Established in 2004, Basel II is intended to protect the international financial system from problems that could potentially arise if a major bank or a group of banks collapse. It aims to establish an international standard to guide banking regulators in setting rules regarding the amount of capital reserves banks should hold, depending on their lending and investment practices, in order to sustain their solvency and overall economic stability.

Basel II takes both credit risk and operational risk into account in calculating a bank's minimum capital requirements. Credit risk is that risk associated with nonrepayment of a loan or other line of credit, while operational risk is the potential loss resulting from inadequate or failed internal processes, people, and systems.

As countries implement the Basel II requirements, IT organizations face compliance obligations in ensuring that internal systems are able to measure and report credit and operational risks according to the methodologies defined by Basel II. Moreover, the governance and control of IT activities are even more saliently linked to capital reserve requirements since IT inefficiencies or failures contribute directly to measures of operational risk.

Data Retention The pervasive use of information technology in businesses has generated a torrent of data that must be managed. Management of this volume of data is itself a challenge. In addition, depending on where and with whom they conduct business, organizations need to ensure that critical electronic records of business activities are captured, retained, and maintained in accordance with a variety of regulations worldwide. Many industry laws and regulations, as well as business practices, mandate in very specific terms what information and documentation is to be retained and how long it is retained in an easily accessible form (see Table 9.1). Some laws further require that data be retained in its original business context—for example, if an e-mail references an attachment, then both message and attachment need to be retained and linked. Compliance

TABLE 9.1 Major Global Data Retention and Auditing Regulations

Legislation	Summary of Data Retention Requirements Impacting IT
Sarbanes-Oxley Act of 2002	IT is mostly impacted by Section 404 of the act addressing "management assessment of internal controls." Requires that corporate accountants retain specific records for a minimum of five years.
SEC Regulation 240.17-a	Requires brokers and dealers to retain originals of communication documents, in both paper and electronic formats, and be able to produce or reproduce these records on demand.
Health Insurance Portability and Accountability Act (HIPAA)	Requires health care organizations to retain original medical records for a minimum of five years and often for tens of years.
U.S.A. Patriot Act	Requires financial institutions to provide an audit trail of all monetary transactions for specific periods of time.
Anti-Terrorism, Crime and Security Act of 2001 (U.K.)	Enables the Secretary of State to issue a code of practice for telecommunications providers, specifying the maximum period of time that communications data must be retained.
Personal Information Protection and Electronic Documents Act (Canada)	Requires organizations to institute their own maximum and minimum retention periods for personal information in the private sector. Personal information must be kept accurate and saved only for as long as necessary to satisfy the purposes.
Basel II	Depending on the type of business, national regulatory decisions, and risk parameters, banks must retain at least two and up to seven years' worth of historical data.

Developed by author based on information from following sources: Sun Microsystems, "Challenges of Data Retention Compliance: Simple Solutions for Cost-Effective Information Management" *Business Brief* (2005); J. Lee, "Surviving the Impact of Data Retention Compliance on Mission-Critical Databases," *Princeton Softech Business Brief* (2004).

becomes increasingly complex as critical information is generated and distributed in an increasing variety of disparate forms, including databases, e-mail, instant messaging, voice and integrated messaging systems, video, and unstructured data.

Data retention compliance from the IT perspective involves defining what data must be retained, deciding how long it must be retained, ensuring that it cannot be altered or destroyed prematurely, producing that data or an authentic replication in a timely manner, and securely destroying data at the end of its life.

Information Protection The efficiency of electronic information exchange has propelled its widespread use within and across organizations of all kinds. For example, in the United States, the Health Insurance Portability and Accountability Act (HIPAA) encourages the widespread use of electronic data interchange with the aim of improving the efficiency and effectiveness of the U.S. health care system. At the same time, concerns regarding the confidentiality and appropriate dissemination of certain kinds of information have prompted legislation in this area. Thus, HIPAA legislation includes elements such as the Privacy Rule and the Security Rule, which establish, respectively, regulations for the use and disclosure of "protected health information," and minimum standards for administrative, physical, and technical means for securing "electronic protected health information." Other countries have similar legislation intended to safeguard how certain types of information are electronically disseminated and stored.

From the standpoint of the IT function, information protection involves security measures such as those addressed in Chapter 7 which prevent unauthorized

(*Continued*)

or inappropriate access or modifications to equipment on which protected information is stored. It also requires attention to the security of the software that manages such data and the networks that transmit the data. This may involve a variety of physical, technical, and administrative mechanisms, including establishing authorized users, designing procedures of use, developing mechanisms to prevent inadvertent or intentional misuse, and implementing encryption techniques. Most importantly, the overall information protection effort needs to be coherent, complete, and documented.

Increasing evidence points to the fact that organizations with effective IT governance consistently generate better returns for their shareholders than equivalent organizations with ineffective IT governance.[12] Well-governed companies also exhibit other positive business outcomes, such as cost reductions, improved customer satisfaction, greater security, and enhanced alignment between IT and business.[13]

Furthermore, the maturity of IT GRC practices and capabilities can have a direct positive impact on a range of business performance indicators, such as revenues, profits, and customer retention levels.[14] Companies with more mature IT governance practices are less likely to have customer data stolen or lost, and often face significantly lower financial losses accruing from loss or theft of customer data. Such findings suggest that, as IT governance capabilities mature, organizations end up spending relatively less on regulatory compliance efforts, and their governance, risk management, and compliance capabilities improve. As a result, IT organizations should realize savings from effective IT governance; savings that free up resources and time to investment in innovation and other value-adding ways to grow their businesses.

In practical terms, IT governance is largely about establishing IT quality through its emphasis on and mechanisms for doing the right things and doing things right. As such, it can help to address some of the persistent and pervasive problems in IT, such as outdated technologies, legacy systems, inadequate security, and incomplete documentation, which are largely systemic, rather than technical, problems. (See Table 9.2 for some typical persistent IT-related problems.) With its emphasis on evaluating and communicating risk, setting priorities, justifying expenditures, establishing controls, and assigning accountability, governance contributes a systems approach to problems that cannot be solved by a purely technical approach.

[12] See P. Weill and J. W. Ross, *IT Governance, How Top Performers Manage IT Decisions for Superior Results* (Boston: Harvard Business School Press, 2004). In their book, Weill and Ross report research results showing that companies with better than average IT governance earned at least a 20 percent higher return on assets than organizations with weaker IT governance.

[13] Findings from the IT Governance Global Status Report of 2008, available at http://www.isaca.org.

[14] IT Policy Compliance Group: "2008 Annual Report: IT Governance, Risk and Compliance—Improving Business Results and Mitigating Financial Risk" (2008). Retrieved June 2008 from http://www.itpolicycompliance.com/research_reports/it_governance.

TABLE 9.2 Some IT-Related Problems That Can Be Addressed by Better IT Governance

- A disconnect between IT strategy and business strategy
- IT not meeting or supporting compliance requirements
- High cost of IT with low or unproven return on investment (ROI)
- Serious IT operational incidents
- IT service delivery problems
- Insufficient number of staff
- Staff with inadequate skills
- Problems with outsourcers
- Lack of agility/development problems
- Problems with document content or knowledge management
- Inadequate disaster recovery or business continuity measures (DRP/BCP)
- Electronic archiving or storage problems
- Security and privacy incidents

The Scope and Practice of IT Governance

Conceptually, IT governance can be viewed as the effort to design a system to achieve a set of related objectives:

- Attainment of strategic goals
- Efficient operation
- Reliable measurement
- Compliance management

A high-functioning system continually exchanges feedback among its various elements to ensure that they remain aligned and focused on achieving the goal of the system. The elements of a governance system include leadership roles, organizational structures, business processes, standards, and measures of compliance to these standards. IT governance involves the whole organization, not just IT; therefore, governance requires defining leadership roles and organizational structures involving the business units, the executive team, and board members, as well as IT members. Similarly, it involves designing business processes and standards that may imply obligations of both IT and business unit managers and employees. Collectively, these elements work together to:

- Shape decisions concerning IT use in the organization,
- Determine criteria by which to assess conformance to these decisions, and
- Define mechanisms by which these decisions can be communicated, implemented, and enforced throughout the organization.

Let's consider some prominent, but interrelated, themes of IT governance in further detail.

IT-Business Alignment

A particular objective of IT governance is to ensure that IT strategic goals are met; goals that are, in turn, linked to the overall goals of the enterprise. As the role of IT

IT Governance Research: A Profile of the Work of Weill and Ross

Seminal research on IT governance comes from Peter Weill and Jeanne Ross, of MIT's Center for Information Systems Research, and is based on their studies of 250 enterprises worldwide. Weill and Ross define IT governance as the distribution of IT decision-making rights and responsibilities among enterprise stakeholders, along with the procedures and mechanisms for making and monitoring strategic decisions about IT. They explain that the end-goal of any such framework is to encourage "desirable behavior" by all organizational parties in their use of IT.

Weill and Ross identify five domains of IT decisions:

1. IT principles decisions dictating the role of IT in the enterprise.
2. IT architecture decisions on technical choices and directions.
3. IT infrastructure decisions on the delivery of shared IT services.
4. Business application requirements decisions for each project.
5. IT investment and prioritization decisions.

Their research revealed many types of governance mechanisms and techniques, which they categorize based on what the mechanisms accomplish:

1. Decision-making structures that facilitate decision making (e.g., individual roles, committees, and boards).
2. Alignment processes that ensure alignment between technology and business goals.
3. Communication processes for communicating governance principles and decisions.

Weill and Ross evaluate IT governance based on how well it enables IT to deliver on four objectives: cost-effectiveness, asset utilization, business growth, and business flexibility. Their findings, among others, show that firms with superior IT governance have profits 20 percent higher than similar firms with poor governance pursuing similar strategies. They also find that top performing organizations custom-design IT governance to fit their business strategies. For example, the most profitable companies tend to place strategic emphasis on efficient operations. Accordingly, they aim for more centralization in their IT governance, a design focus that is more suitable for driving the high degree of standardization and high level of shared services, which underpin low business costs. Fast-growing companies, on the other hand, place strategic emphasis on rapid innovation and short time to market. High performers in this category are characterized by decentralized governance approaches, which enhance responsiveness to local customers while still enabling effective prioritization and monitoring of strategic projects.

Their research offers practical contributions to executives by showing how organizations can design and implement a system of decision rights that will transform IT from simply an expense to a profitable investment.

Sources: P. Weill and J. W. Ross, *IT Governance: How Top Performers Manage IT Decision Rights for Superior Results*, Boston: Harvard Business School Press, 2004. P. Weill and J. W. Ross, "A Matrixed Approach to Designing IT Governance," *Sloan Management Review* 46, no. 2 (Winter 2005). J. Ross and P. Weill, "Recipe for Good Governance," CIO.com, June 15, 2004. P. Weill and J. W. Ross, "Ten Principles of IT Governance," *HBS Working Knowledge*, July 4 2004, available at http://hbswk.hbs.edu/archive/4241.html.

shifts from business support to business enablement, there is an increasing need for IT strategy to be developed in parallel with business strategy—rather than in response to it. Thus governance efforts may involve establishing organizational planning and communication processes that connect IT leaders to line-of-business leaders and to the corporate side of the business in tighter discussions of the costs and business impacts of IT initiatives. New organizational structures may include an IT Steering Committee or an IT Strategy Committee, seating both IT and business executives. Such cross-functional structures and processes can ensure that significant changes to the business strategy trigger corresponding adjustments in IT strategy and expenditures and vice versa.

Investment Value

A key goal of governance is to maximize strategic value from major IT investments. Thus, governance efforts should define processes to ensure the involvement of all relevant stakeholders—including IT managers, business unit leaders, functional representatives, and the board—in deciding what kinds of IT investments to pursue. In addition, the board may be directed to review IT budgets and plans on a regular basis. Furthermore, governance efforts might define standard procedures for determining the business worth (both financial and nonfinancial) and risk of IT-enabled business investments, and also specify the criteria for selecting and prioritizing investments.

Consider the Information Technology Division (ITD) of the executive branch of the Massachusetts state government. ITD provides IT services (including Internet access, enterprise applications, wide area network, the official public-facing Web portal www.mass.gov, central e-mail system, and Web and application hosting services) that underpin the efforts of 170+ agencies in the Executive Department to deliver valuable government services to their citizens. In a collaborative arrangement with state agencies, ITD works to obtain and manage funds for large, strategic IT investments. Agencies seeking funds for strategic IT projects must file investment briefs with ITD, justifying the business case for each project in terms of its compliance with the established Business and Technology Principles of the state government. For its part, ITD first engages with the governor and state legislature to file and secure capital funding, and subsequently allocates and manages funding to projects based on their alignment with these principles. The effectiveness of this structured approach to strategic IT investments has prompted emulation by other state governments.

The overall goal is to align IT investments with businesswide priorities, maintain necessary conformance to enterprise-level architecture and infrastructure standards, and manage projects as a portfolio, so as to leverage synergies across business units where possible. The Volkswagen case, later in this module, enables discussion of these issues.

Project Delivery

As IT projects increasingly address business mission-critical activities, a cost-effective project delivery capability becomes increasingly valuable. Governance includes determining responsibilities and accountability (both within IT and within business units and other functions) together with accompanying processes, standards, and measures to ensure that, as far as possible, projects conform to architectural standards, meet business objectives, and deliver on their promised benefits in a cost-effective manner. These efforts may include, for instance, the definition of standard project management processes, the identification of critical project management skills, and the establishment of levels of approval and project milestones to control the disbursement of funding.

An effective project delivery capability also requires attention to the development context, a key part of which is the existence of technical and architectural standards. These, in turn, facilitate the control of costs, faster implementation of new initiatives, as well as subsequent support and maintenance—thus positively influencing both project value delivery and service efficiency. However, since standardization efforts often **confront culture, unique business needs, and legacy situations,** effective governance is necessary to motivate and enforce the necessary standardization. The formation of an IT Architecture Board or committee is frequently the means to achieve stronger central oversight of overall IT architecture.

On one hand, governance efforts aim to systematically reduce project risk by reducing variance in the project implementation process. On the other hand, good governance also allows the right amount of flexibility that will yield more effective results. The AtekPC case, later in this module, explores how one company sought this balance.

Service Delivery

The governance process also addresses the cost-effectiveness of IT services, by specifying structures, roles, and techniques for managing and controlling IT services. Often the cost of funding IT is a hot topic for business customers, largely due to a lack of clarity on their part about how costs are compiled. Mechanisms such as charge-backs and cost transparency help to raise awareness among business users regarding the costs of their visions for IT services, thus allowing for better prioritization and decision making. Service-level agreements (SLAs), for example, also can be developed to define levels of service that are acceptable to each business, and then used as a basis for monitoring services. A governance perspective helps ensure that day-to-day problem fixing and support efforts remain aligned with business needs.

Resource Management

The governance focus on operational efficiency also draws attention to how IT assets and resources, including staff, are utilized. Governance efforts may thus include the formation of organizational structures for overseeing and directing all the organization's IT resources, or the implementation of processes to ensure that IT resource requirements are identified based on business priorities. A future-oriented emphasis on resource management may indicate the need to budget for and perform preventative maintenance or upgrades on essential equipment or applications. Governance efforts may also define structures, criteria, and processes for making decisions regarding the outsourcing of particular skills, technologies, or IT capabilities.

Insufficient IT staff or inadequate skills and expertise among existing IT staff are among the most prominent concerns of contemporary IT organizations.[15] Resource management efforts that recognize these concerns may work to enable more flexible skills-based deployment and establish procedures and timeframes to develop and upgrade internal skills and expertise.

Measurement of IT Performance

A critical part of IT governance involves designing and implementing structures and controls for measuring IT performance reliably and in terms that are valuable to the business and external stakeholders. Often, qualitative measures are more easily available, but governance efforts are likely to gain more buy-in if governance costs and benefits can be quantified. Strategic business value, as viewed by executives, often includes financial measurements and other measures of stakeholder value. Many

[15] Findings from a number of research efforts, including the 2008 PriceWaterhouseCooper survey on IT Governance, the 2008 IBM CIO Leadership survey, and Corporate Executive Board research.

governance initiatives make use of the Balanced Scorecard technique, measuring overall IT performance on a set of different dimensions such as achievement of business goals, user satisfaction, operational excellence, and support for learning and growth.[16]

Risk Management

Risk management is clearly implicit in many of the preceding themes. For example, a focus on investment return should acknowledge the risk that the investment being made in IT fails to provide value for money or is otherwise excessive or wasted. This includes consideration of the overall portfolio of IT investments. A governance focus on project delivery should address project ownership risk, the risk of IT projects failing to meet objectives through lack of accountability and commitment, or perhaps the risk of drawing on inaccurate or incomplete data. Service delivery depends, in a similar fashion, on effective management of a variety of different kinds of risks, as discussed in Module 2. These might include a loss of service, inappropriate access to confidential or sensitive information (access or security risk), or the risk that infrastructure is inadequate to meet the current and future needs of the business in a cost-effective and timely manner.[17] Thus, risk management is central to governance efforts, which may involve identifying various possible sources of risk, as we did above, determining acceptable levels of each type of risk, defining metrics for monitoring and measuring each type of risk, and instituting internal processes and roles to address unacceptable changes in the level of each type of risk.

In conclusion, the scope of IT governance is broad and allows for great variability in how it is defined and implemented. Organizations tend to vary in how they define IT governance—and hence put it into practice—based on which drivers are most salient. For example, in the United States, IT governance efforts are currently largely driven by compliance. In Europe, and especially the United Kingdom, while compliance is still an important component, there is greater emphasis on value and performance.[18] In general, leading-edge organizations view governance from a business value and performance perspective—not just a compliance perspective. The next section examines some implications for IT governance implementation efforts.

Designing IT Governance: Critical Success Factors and Good Practices

Despite general consensus regarding the imperatives and incentives for IT governance, risk management, and compliance (IT GRC), there is great variability in its practice and its effectiveness. Beyond achieving compliance, variability in the practice of IT

[16] For more information, see *IT Balanced Scorecards: End-to-End Performance Measurement of the Corporate IT Function*, Corporate Executive Board, 2003. (A summary is available on the Center for CIO Leadership Web site.) Also see R. S. Kaplan and D. P. Norton, *The Balanced Scorecard: Translating Strategy into Action* (Boston: Harvard Business School Press, 1996).

[17] For a comprehensive perspective on IT risk, see G. Westerman and R. Hunter, *IT Risk: Turning Business Threats into Competitive Advantage* (Boston: Harvard Business School Press, 2007).

[18] P. Williams of PriceWaterhouseCoopers, as quoted in: "IT Governance Roundtable: IT Governance Trends," IT Governance Institute (2007).

GRC is, however, to be expected. After all, any governance initiative should account for the size, industry, strategic goals, organizational culture, and local environment of the enterprise.

At the same time, effective design patterns have been discerned. Thus, although there is no single best model of IT governance, we can identify certain principles that promote effectiveness in designing and implementing an IT governance initiative.

Intentional but Minimalist Design

Every enterprise engages in decision making about IT but enterprises differ in how consistently such decisions are made and in how rigorously these decisions are communicated to affected stakeholders.[19] All companies have various levels of IT control, but many of the processes may be informal or inadequately documented and followed. Many enterprises make IT investments but they vary in how formally such investments are justified and in how rigorously the actual return to the enterprise is monitored and measured.

Often, elements of IT governance that *do* exist have been introduced in piecemeal fashion in response to isolated situations and needs across different applications and business units. These cumulative efforts can result in an incoherent and internally inconsistent patchwork of measures that impedes rather than supports efforts to increase the strategic impact of IT. Intentional design of an IT governance framework can help to bring existing governance mechanisms in line and identify gaps. IT governance design can be based on existing business governance processes, where these exist.

However, it is important not to overdo the effort with elaborate committees, overly complicated procedures, or excessive monitoring and reporting. Governance mechanisms perceived as onerous will trigger resistance and can encourage circumvention of procedures. Governance efforts also shouldn't try to meet all possible goals but should be viewed as a means to highlight and raise discussion about conflicting goals. Since conflicting goals have the potential to create confusion and complexity, they can also frustrate and undermine managers' good governance intentions. Instead, by more clearly linking IT assets and activities to strategic business choices, governance can help organizations prioritize their goals.

Board-Level Leadership

Since governance is the main job of the company board and there is little rationale to govern IT separately from the rest of the business, IT governance should be considered an integral part of overall business governance. This is especially crucial when organizational success depends on the ability of IT to enable achievement of business goals. Thus, boards need to recognize the imperative to exercise the same governance over IT strategies, structures, systems, staff, and standards as they would over any other areas such as finance or marketing. The reading by Nolan and McFarlan, later in this module, expands on this role. As they put it: "A lack of board oversight for IT activities is dangerous; it puts the firm at risk in the same way that failing to audit its books would."[20]

[19] P. Weill and J. W. Ross, "A Matrixed Approach to Designing IT Governance," *Sloan Management Review* 46, no. 2 (Winter 2005), p. 26.

[20] R. Nolan and F. W. McFarlan, "IT and the Board of Directors," *Harvard Business Review,* October 2005.

Yet despite the value of information and information technology assets to most companies, a recent poll suggests that IT governance is far from a priority at board levels.[21] Of the companies surveyed, only 12 percent had implemented board-level oversight mechanisms for IT resources. Further, nearly half the respondents believed that board members did not understand the risks to business operations of information and information systems, particularly the implications of deferred IT maintenance. A relaxed attitude to IT governance may be partly attributed to IT's heritage as a support function, but it also suggests that some boards haven't yet recognized the strategic significance of their IT assets.

Broad-Based Executive Involvement

Beyond the board, executive level commitment to effective IT governance is critical and IT governance initiatives supported by top management have a much stronger chance of success. Although IT governance initiatives are often originally instigated by top management—sometimes impelled, in part, by efforts to improve corporate governance—these initiatives also need to continue as part of the strategic vision. Support for IT governance is expressed by regular engagement, provision of adequate resources, and promotion of good governance practices during conflict situations. Current practice suggests that this high-level support is largely in effect: In the survey for the IT Governance Global Status Report, nearly three-quarters of the respondent organizations indicated a C-level executive (CEO, CFO or CIO) as the champion for IT governance.[22]

More specifically, senior business executives should be actively involved in major IT decisions. Since senior management establishes strategic directions, their involvement can ensure that the management and use of IT remains in line with strategy. When they are not involved, a rift can develop between business objectives and IT capabilities. Broad-based direct senior involvement is associated with stronger IT governance performance, whereas a lack of senior team involvement is a major predictor of ineffective IT governance. The engagement of those in particular executive roles, but especially the CEO, has much greater positive impact than the CIO acting alone.[23]

Clear Ownership but Broad Participation

As a major organizational initiative, IT governance requires an owner with the necessary authority and accountability. Although the board should be ultimately responsible for all governance, they will usually designate an individual or group to be accountable for the design, implementation, and performance of IT governance. Often this is the CIO, but where IT is a fundamental enabler of business, such as in the Financial Services industry, it could be the CEO or COO. In some cases it may be a group such

[21] Findings from IT Governance, a U.K.-based specialist consultancy, training, and publishing company. Retrieved June 2008 from http://www.computerworlduk.com/management/it-business/it-organisation/news/index.cfm?newsid=7335.

[22] See research by Weill and Ross, as well as the 2008 Global Survey on IT Governance, IT Governance Institute.

[23] J. W. Ross and P. Weill, "Recipe for Good Governance," CIO.com, June 15, 2004. Retrieved June 2008 from: http://www.cio.com/article/29162/Recipe_for_Good_Governance.

as an IT Steering Committee. The key is to combine an enterprisewide viewpoint with an understanding of the potential connections between technology and strategy.

At the same time, broad participation is necessary for effective governance implementation. As one CIO puts it, "The real challenge is not the designing of committees, processes, forms, and procedures; it's meeting the challenge of participation. Getting people involved is what IT governance is really about."[24]

A key part of an IT governance leader's role is to gain buy-in to governance and educate colleagues, to ensure access to resources, attention, and support for the governance initiative from business leaders. Business unit managers must be made aware of IT governance mechanisms before they can follow them. Their participation in cross-functional teams to design better IT decision-making processes can help them gain both greater insight into the reasons for particular procedures and a sense of ownership for those procedures. As more managers throughout the organization gain such understanding, they become better positioned to promote effective use of IT as a strategic asset. When business managers can accurately describe how IT governance works, that signals that it is becoming part of the enterprise's management culture and so is more likely to be followed.

Research indicates some variation in putting this principle into practice. In 2004, Weill and Ross reported that "Nearly half of all of the managers in the top 50 percent of governance performers could accurately describe their IT governance, while fewer than 30 percent of the managers could do so in the poorer performers."[25] A 2007 survey of 175 CIOs of large corporations (for which formal governance might be more critical) revealed similar variation. One quarter of respondents believed that less than 20 percent of managers in their companies could accurately describe the decision-making processes governing IT investments and only 46 percent believed that the majority of managers understood the IT decision-making processes. On the brighter side, approximately one-third of respondents believed that 75 percent or more of managers were well-informed as to IT governance.[26]

Enforce Execution but Accommodate Exception

Introducing or improving IT governance requires a well-defined plan. Furthermore, effective governance requires a focus on execution and a willingness to enforce agreed-upon practices. It is important to expect that the implementation of new governance processes, policies, and structures will face resistance at times. The Volkswagen case describes one such situation. For example, efforts to standardize technology, data, and business processes are common to IT governance initiatives because these measures can help to reduce IT and business process costs, increase systems reliability, and enhance security. But measures such as standardization and increased centralization also decrease the relative autonomy that people have had in the past and are magnets for resistance.

[24] L. H. Vogel, "Everyone Gets to Play," CIO.com, September 1, 2006. Retrieved June 2008 from http://www.cio.com/article/24435/Peer_to_Peer_Everyone_Gets_to_Play.

[25] J. W. Ross and P. Weill, "Recipe for Good Governance," CIO.com, June 15, 2004. Retrieved June 2008 from: http://www.cio.com/article/29162/Recipe_for_Good_Governance.

[26] CIO Leadership Survey (2007), conducted by IBM in collaboration with Harvard Business School and Center for Information Systems Research (CISR) at MIT Sloan School of Management.

As a result, despite the need for enforcing standards, the governance process should also allow for exceptions when standard policies block the achievement of agreed-upon shared business goals. The exception process should be a structured, clearly documented, and efficient process that enables different stakeholders (e.g., project sponsors or business unit management) to state their case for requests for variance from the standards and agreed practices. A transparent exception handling process is psychologically valuable because it provides a forum for well-intentioned managers to explain why they feel the standards are limiting business success. More importantly, exception handing also provides a mechanism by which the organization can learn and refine governance policies and practices because it prompts reevaluation of governance controls at periodic intervals.

Define Benefits and Target Expectations

Given that the primary purpose of IT governance is to increase business value and reduce risk, governance design should incorporate a clear and compelling business case for benefits and costs in terms of IT and business goals. Since IT governance often encompasses mandatory compliance activities, a simple ROI metric is neither feasible nor justified.

Instead, organizations should aim to identify a reasonable set of key performance indicators that are meaningful for both IT and the business, and are linked to business and IT goals. These should also be related to the drivers—such as business value, risk management, and compliance—that prompted the IT governance initiative. Weill and Ross suggest a general measure of IT governance effectiveness that evaluates governance efforts in terms of how well it enables IT to deliver on four objectives: cost effectiveness, asset utilization, business growth, and business flexibility, each of which is weighted according to its importance to the organization. It is helpful to institute performance tracking of IT governance metrics from the beginning of the initiative; otherwise, it may easily be experienced as just another layer of regulations and overhead, which triggers staff and business resistance.

Well-chosen metrics satisfy the following criteria:[27]

- They are easy to measure and not confused with targets.
- They offer a high insight-to-effort ratio (i.e., insight into performance and the achievement of goals versus the effort to capture them).
- They are comparable internally (e.g., percent against a base or numbers over time).
- They are comparable externally irrespective of enterprise size or industry.

Aim for Evolution Not Revolution in Implementation

A new governance framework requires individuals to take on new roles and participate in new structures. As discussed, it may impact culturally ingrained norms and can imply substantial changes in procedures such as more formal metrics, less discretionary power, or greater centralization. These changes take time to implement

[27] Adapted from Control Objectives for Information and related Technology (CoBIT) 4.0 reference manual and other sources.

and be absorbed by the organization, often requiring that old ways of doing things be unlearned before new ways can gain traction. Pushing too much too fast can result in an ineffective governance implementation that consumes resources, obscures value, and causes stakeholder dissatisfaction.

A good but simple way to start is to link IT governance to key business objectives, such as cost reduction, innovation, agility, simplification, customer satisfaction, and compliance. If the IT function can communicate in terms of value to the business, the business side is more likely to appreciate and support IT governance initiatives. Many organizations then focus on the basics of IT governance such as installing the right governance bodies, assigning accountability, and establishing channels of communication between business and IT.

Since issues of unlearning and relearning also impact changes to the design of governance, these should be made rarely. Any changes should be primarily driven by significant changes in organization strategy that demand significantly different behaviors in relation to IT assets. Large organizational changes, such as a merger or acquisition, a new outsourcing contract, or a large-scale corporate project, can also provide the impetus for the organization to be more receptive to and ready for other kinds of change. A good practice then is to take advantage of events such as these to review and upgrade the governance practices currently in place.

Summary

This chapter explored the concept of IT governance as a framework of roles, organizational structures, processes, standards, and measures, within which organizational members make decisions and take actions in ways that deliver IT value to the business. This chapter profiled some of the key drivers of more formalized IT governance, and some key goals of IT governance, such as strategic alignment, return on IT investment, and value delivery. The chapter closed by summarizing effective implementation principles from recent practice and research. In particular, the chapter highlighted the relationship between enterprise governance and IT governance, and emphasized the critical roles of not just IT leaders, but corporate leaders and the board of directors in ensuring effective IT governance.

Executives can consider the following questions to assess whether they are adequately addressing the need for IT governance:

1. Do you know how IT is governed in your organization? Can you describe how your organization ensures that IT supports and enables the overall strategic goals and objectives of the business?
2. Do you understand how IT investment decisions are made and monitored? How projects are evaluated and controlled? Can you explain how these processes acknowledge and adjust to strategic business needs?
3. What kinds of metrics do you rely on to ascertain whether IT is effective or not? Are these measures reliable?
4. Does your company have an IT governance owner or group? Is it successful in enlisting senior managers in IT governance discussions?
5. What is the current role of the board of directors in IT governance? Should it be more prominent?

Chapter 10

Leadership of the IT Function

Information technology (IT) has become essential to manage transactions, process information, and capture and disseminate knowledge; tasks that enable and sustain both economic and social activities. In many organizations, IT is fundamental to support, sustain, transform, and grow the business. In this chapter, we discuss how the leadership of IT should be related to its role within the business. We first characterize the broad roles that IT can play within a company or business unit and then consider how and why the role of IT changes over time. We subsequently discuss how particular aspects and responsibilities of IT leadership should be aligned to the role that IT is expected to fill in the business. As the role of IT changes, so should leadership approaches to a firm's IT assets and focal activities. The magnitude of these leadership changes, in terms of style, expertise, and priorities, can often dictate the need for a completely new person in the IT leadership role.

By understanding the role of IT in their organizations, executives can evaluate their IT leadership approach and, on a broader scale, can benchmark their company's IT capabilities against other firms in their industry or across industries.

Understanding the Role of IT in the Firm

The role that IT plays in an organization should strongly influence the approach used to identify opportunities, design, and implement IT-enabled business initiatives, and organize and manage IT resources and professionals. Two key dimensions should be assessed: (1) the business implications of the IT application portfolio; and (2) the business implications of the IT project portfolio.[1] The first dimension describes the extent to which existing IT systems and applications are critical for sustaining enterprise operations and, thus, draws attention to the need for IT excellence in execution. The second dimension assesses the extent to which IT is critical to growing the enterprise

[1] This perspective on IT leadership is based on the "IT strategic impact grid," conceived by F. Warren McFarlan. See F. W. McFarlan, "Information Technology Changes the Way You Compete," *Harvard Business Review*, May 1984.

by shaping future business strategy and capabilities; it highlights the importance of IT innovation efforts. Simultaneous consideration of these two dimensions reveals four broad roles for IT, which frame the decisions executives face in organizing, managing, and governing IT (see Figure 10.1).

Support

In the *Support* quadrant of Figure 10.1, the role of IT in sustaining current business operations and in shaping future business operations or strategy is relatively limited. Despite even widespread and constant use of IT, firms may not be operationally dependent on IT nor approach it as a means to reposition themselves vis-à-vis their markets, suppliers, or competitors. Until fairly recently, support was the typical role of IT in many professional services firms (e.g., law firms and consulting firms). For example, despite one consulting company spending $30 million in the early 1990s to equip each of its 2,000 consultants with laptop computers, consultants in the firm were able to continue serving their clients during a major IT failure of over 24 hours. In addition, the IT project portfolio had few implications for the firm's future business practices.

Factory

In the *Factory* quadrant, IT systems are absolutely critical to current business operations. Think about firms like the Nasdaq Stock Exchange or PSA (previously called the Port of Singapore Authority, prior to its privatization), where reliable, zero-defect operation of IT is essential for performing core activities within the organization and across the extended business network of customers, suppliers, and partners. In Nasdaq's case, system failure, for even a few seconds, can bring the entire securities industry to its knees. In PSA's case, IT failures can halt or seriously hinder global shipping, affecting—not just PSA's operations—but also those of global shippers, freight forwarders, carriers, and customers. In each firm, a significant portion of investments and resources is directed toward projects and initiatives that ensure improved quality, functionality, and 99.999 percent reliability of the IT-enabled operating core.

Turnaround

Firms in the *Turnaround* quadrant view IT as a means for business transformation. While they are not currently operationally dependent on IT, their IT projects and innovations are intended to exploit emerging strategic opportunities or transform business capabilities, raising IT's visibility within the firm. Sometimes, just a single effort to implement a novel technology or new application may position a firm in the *Turnaround* quadrant. Consider the case of Medtronic, a medical technology company providing lifelong solutions to people with chronic disease.[2] Its core operations address the research, design, and manufacture of medical devices, activities for which IT filled a largely supportive role in the past. However, finding itself facing strong competition in its core cardiac pacing business, Medtronic sought to differentiate itself by offering an IT-enabled service: remote monitoring for certain pacemaker models. This initiative,

[2] See L. M. Applegate, Medtronic Vision 2010, Harvard Business School Publishing (No. 807-052), Revised April 2008. Also see the Medtronic 2007 Annual Report and the company Web site www.medtronic.com for more information on Medtronic.

FIGURE 10.1
Analyzing the Role of IT in an Organization

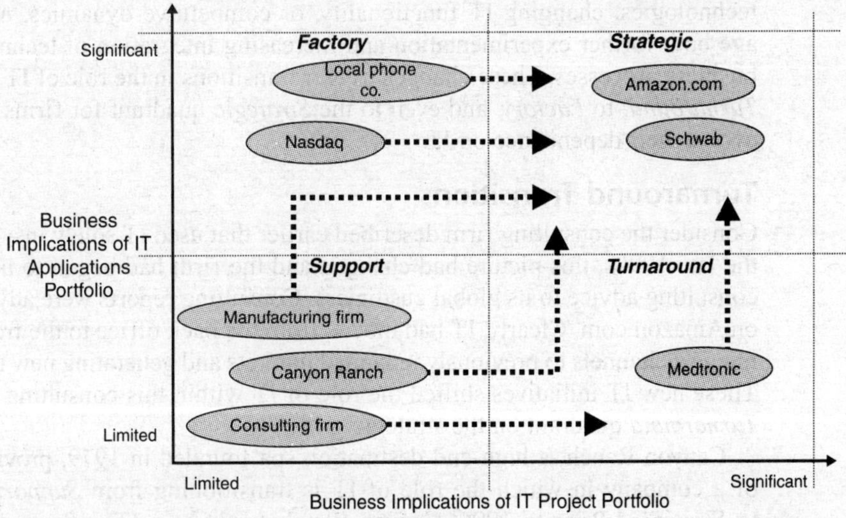

involving the development of new technology and information capabilities, signaled a turnaround in Medtronic's business profile as it leveraged this first experience to launch remote monitoring service offerings for a range of diseases and devices.

Strategic

Firms in the *Strategic* quadrant rely intensely on IT to sustain current business operations *and* enable their future transformation. A firm such as Charles Schwab, a discount brokerage firm, provides an example. At Charles Schwab, a steady stream of technology innovations drove strategy evolution through much of the company's existence, and IT development activities were inextricably linked to defining the company's strategic positioning vis-à-vis competitors. In companies like Charles Schwab, IT and business strategy are not just aligned; they are intertwined, and IT leadership, governance, and investment decisions are made in the boardroom by those charged with assuring business success and survival. In fact, David Pottruck, CEO and chairman of Schwab during the 1990s, publicly stated that he considered Schwab "an IT firm that happens to be in the financial services business."[3]

Recognizing Transitions in the Role of IT

Some firms, like Charles Schwab, Amazon.com, and Google, are incarnated with IT at the core of company strategy and operations. Other firms, such as Nasdaq and PSA, began by using IT to underpin core business operations then evolved from the *Factory* to *Strategic* quadrants over time. Most firms start out using IT in a support role and some can remain in this pattern of use for a long time. Yet internal and external factors, such as increasing organizational familiarity and expertise with core

[3] See L. M. Applegate, et al., Charles Schwab in 2002, Harvard Business School Publishing (No. 803-070), November 2002.

technologies, changing IT functionality, or competitive dynamics, naturally encourage both further experimentation and increasing integration of technology with core business processes. These changes trigger transitions in the role of IT from *Support* to *Turnaround*, to *Factory,* and even to the *Strategic* quadrant for firms that continue to evolve their dependence on IT.

Turnaround Transitions

Consider the consulting firm described earlier that used IT solely in a support role. By the late 1990s, this picture had changed and the firm had begun to use IT to provide consulting advice to its global customers. Consulting reports were advertised and sold on Amazon.com. Clearly, IT had moved from the back office to the front office, offering new channels to previously untapped markets and generating new revenue streams. These new IT initiatives shifted the role of IT within this consulting firm toward the *Turnaround* quadrant on the strategic grid.

Canyon Ranch, a high-end destination spa founded in 1979, provides an example of a company in which the role of IT is transitioning from *Support* to *Turnaround* to *Strategic*.[4] Prior to 1996, Canyon Ranch's only core IT system was its Computer Lodging System, which was primarily used to automate routine back-office accounting, payroll, and reservation activities. The system was programmed by Canyon Ranch accounting personnel in 1986 using the BASIC programming language and was maintained by a single programmer and two technical-support personnel working in the accounting department. But within the context of increasing competition in the hospitality sector and dramatic changes in IT functionality, a change in senior leadership in the mid-1990s triggered drastic changes in the role IT would play in the company in the future. In 1996, senior executives began to explore ways to drive customer loyalty and sought to use real-time business information and analytics to improve the decision making it entailed. Thus began the transition in the role of IT from *Support* to *Turnaround*. With this shift in IT focus, executives began to search for a new IT leader able to drive the IT and business turnaround. Over time, it was expected that the role of IT at Canyon Ranch would continue to transition from *Turnaround* to *Strategy.*

It should be noted that *Turnaround* is an unstable role for IT. Sooner or later, a company will need to ramp up its IT operations to sustain and build on the transformational opportunities created by successful new IT developments and projects; that is, the role of IT gradually assumes a factory-like or strategic role in the company. There may be the rare situation in which a company remains in the *Turnaround* quadrant: perhaps, for example, if a company displays "incubator-like" behavior, in which IT development efforts germinate new strategic offerings that are repeatedly spun out into separate companies. This pattern may, however, signal leadership shortcomings rather than an intentional outcome.

Factory Transitions

A growing number of firms now rely on the factory-like role of their IT systems, and even a few minutes of system downtime can cause major organizational disruption

[4] See L. M. Applegate and G. Piccoli, "Canyon Ranch," Harvard Business School Publishing (No. 805-027), November 2004 (in Module 1).

that, in turn, generates customer dissatisfaction and significant financial problems. Nevertheless, the operational significance of IT can sometimes still be lost on senior leaders. The CEO of an investment bank, for example, only became fully aware of the high level of operational dependence of his firm on IT when a flood above the data center brought all securities trading to a halt. Failure to provision an alternative off-site data center crippled the bank's trading operations and caused massive financial losses. The CEO's new appreciation for the importance of IT in running critical areas of business operations led to the construction of a redundant data center shortly after the incident. The devastation caused at the World Trade Center on September 11, 2001, and the subsequent operating challenges faced by many IT-enabled financial services firms with operations at the WTC, brought global attention to the importance of IT availability and reliability for organizational success and survival.

A small manufacturing firm highlights the shift in IT role from *Support* to *Factory* to *Strategic*. Until the 1990s, the role of IT in this small manufacturing company was strictly support—important for ensuring efficiency of back-office activities like payroll and budgeting, but not absolutely vital to the company's success and survival. As in Canyon Ranch, the IT assets of the company were managed by a technical professional and a small team of technical staff. These individuals interacted with managers and clerks in the payroll and budgeting office but had little interaction with plant personnel and never interacted with senior executives of the company.

In the mid-1990s, however, the company began to expand its product line and entered new markets, domestically and abroad. As the complexity of the business increased, so too did the cost of coordinating operations. As a result, executives in the firm decided to purchase an Enterprise Resource Planning (ERP) system designed to streamline, integrate, and coordinate all aspects of company operations, including how supplies were ordered, products were manufactured and sold, and orders were fulfilled. The new system was intended to enable executives and local business managers to gain better control of the company's operations as it launched new products and rapidly expanded into multiple international locations. Initially, executives did not consider the business impact of the new systems and the need for change in business processes and high level business sponsorship. But as the project faltered, adjustments and key decisions were made. The company hired an experienced team of ERP specialists, appointed an IT manager with both manufacturing operations and technology expertise, and created an IT Council that included vice presidents of manufacturing, sales, accounting, purchasing, and logistics. These decisions signaled recognition of the changing role of IT in the company from *Support* to *Factory*.

Strategic Transitions

But the transition did not stop there. By 2002, business executives began asking for more detailed and timely information from the ERP system to enable them to more closely manage the rapidly growing and increasingly complex company. At the same time, they authorized investment in a new IT application that would collect, and make available, real-time customer information that could then be integrated with information from over 60 plants and two customer service call centers. As the value of IT to strategic decision making increased, the role of IT continued its transition from *Factory* to *Strategic*. **As it did, a senior business leader was appointed as Chief Information**

Officer (CIO), reporting to the CEO, and an IT Executive Steering Committee was formed. By 2006, the company's board of directors was actively involved in the decision of the company to partner with leading customers on the launch of a new state-of-the-art factory focused on custom-fabricated components, for which IT-driven embedded intelligence controlled all aspects of the design and manufacture of products as well as related remote monitoring services.

A local phone service provider offers another example of a firm transitioning, in the role of IT, from *Factory* to *Strategic*. Facing stiff competition from cable operators offering bundled services (e.g., combining voice, television, and high-speed data services) in its traditional markets, it sought to expand its portfolio of services through innovative collaborations with partners. IT development efforts, addressing the company's business services systems, were critical to its ability to seamlessly integrate new products and services and offer them at a price point which would deliver value to its existing customers and draw in new customers. IT-led developments also underpinned the frequent and rapid rollouts of product enhancements (e.g., combined billing; combined wire-line and wireless voice mail) that offered new sources of incremental revenue.

As we advance into the twenty-first century, many banks and other financial services firms, insurance companies, communications and media companies, auto manufacturers, and major retail chains, for instance, are evolving more fully into the *strategic* realm, embedding IT in both their core operations and their core strategy.

These types of evolutions in the role of IT are to be expected, driven by both internal and external conditions. Yet many executives fail to recognize the shift in their expectations of IT, and, as a result, they fail to appropriately transition the management and organization of IT assets. In the remainder of this chapter, we first describe organizational tensions associated with the changing role of IT, and then highlight some critical domains of activity where leadership approaches must change in parallel with IT role changes.

Managing Tensions in the Changing Role of IT

The dimensions of the strategic grid frame some fundamental tensions that must be addressed by a firm's leadership, particularly when the role of IT shifts. The first tension is between execution and innovation, between control and creativity, between stability and change. Another tension lies in the IT function-business unit relationship, as IT transitions from being a support to the business to being an enabler of the business.

Managing the Execution-Innovation Tension

Innovation is becoming an increasingly high priority for many firms and the promise of IT-enabled innovation, explored in Module 1, is immense.[5] Nevertheless, the emphasis a firm should place on aggressive IT innovation also depends on a broad

[5] Seventy percent of senior executives responding to the McKinsey Study on Leadership and Innovation (2007) point to innovation as one of the top three drivers of future growth. In addition, nearly 80 percent of respondents to IBM's Global CEO study (2006) rated business and technology integration of great importance for furthering innovative activities.

assessment of the potential operational impact of IT on a firm and on management's willingness to take risks. If IT can greatly help a firm achieve its strategic objectives and managers are not too risk-averse, a significantly greater investment in innovation may be called for than would be the case if IT was considered merely helpful (i.e., IT fills a *support* role) or if managers wanted to avoid unnecessary risks (i.e., IT fills a *factory* role). At the same time, when rapid innovation is required, leaders must ensure that policies aimed at delivering high operational dependability do not interfere with experimentation and learning.

Managing the IT-Business Relationship

Since its earliest days, IT has involved process analysis and redesign. As a result, in many firms, IT professionals are the "business process" specialists, accustomed to examining business activities as elements of processes intended to achieve certain outputs and looking for opportunities for greater efficiency or effectiveness. Since many systems are designed to interconnect different parts of the business, IT professionals have also become key integrators who can help identify areas of potential interconnection between the needs of different business and functional groups. Because of their end-to-end view of the business, they're well positioned to facilitate the development of integrated business solutions and accustomed to taking the lead in IT-centric business projects. At the same time, however, the IT function's professional concern with issues such as long-term IT architectural coherence, technology mastery, and shared IT services integration can put it at odds with business customers' short-term needs.

On the other hand, business groups, experiencing elevated technological sophistication as well as access to a broader range of IT services options, are often keen to take greater control of their technological requirements. Moreover, the line between consumer technologies and enterprise technologies is blurring, encouraging increased user autonomy and undermining the ability of a centralized IT function to dictate choices and uses of technology in the organization. Web 2.0 technologies, such as blogs, wikis, RSS feeds, and mashups, further promote bottom-up interaction and collaborative creativity, feeding users' perceived self-sufficiency in regards to IT knowledge and use. As a result, IT departments are increasingly challenged to provide communication and computing tools on a par with those to which users are accustomed in their personal lives. Individual employees, especially those whose responsibilities require high levels of mobility, often believe they are more productive using their own technology toolset and may feel justified in circumventing IT standards and guidelines.

Although business groups may be willing to fund particular technology assets and operations essential to their business activities, leadership concerns, such as investment decision rights, budgetary control, *and* subsequent support responsibilities, still need to be addressed to ensure the future viability and flexibility of today's technological choices. Thus, as technologies and business opportunities evolve, boundary management implies a delicate balancing act as both the IT department and business groups adapt their roles and relationships in the pursuit of IT-enabled business solutions.

The appropriate balance between these competing orientations should guide policies for organizing and allocating IT resources to develop, deploy, and manage IT systems. In the next section we discuss ways and means to address these tensions in particular situations.

Leadership Approaches to the Role of IT

The leadership approaches needed to introduce new technologies into a company can be quite different from those needed to maintain established technologies and existing systems. So, as the role of IT in an organization evolves, so too should approaches to IT organization and management change. Most importantly, as firms achieve strategic dependence on IT, the leadership of IT must also become deeply embedded in the leadership of the business. In this section, we elaborate on some of the leadership implications of the role of IT. These are summarized in Appendix 10A.

Support: Organizing for Low-Cost Stability and Incremental Improvement

When IT fulfills a support role, the IT assets of a company usually can be adequately managed by a technical professional and a team of technical staff. Members of the IT function, which can be managed as a cost center, may interact with managers and clerks in some functional areas, such as Operations or Finance, but are unlikely to need to interact directly with senior executives of the company.

The supportive IT function should balance the need for operational stability with that of gaining and leveraging new IT experiences—but at a relatively low cost. Since IT operations are not vital to business continuity, new investments in this area, such as for maintenance, are justified on a cost basis. IT-led innovation priorities tend to be targeted toward incremental, operational improvements, such as increased process automation. These may improve a firm's cost profile but do relatively little to change its position or power in its industry or business network. Such projects can be designed, implemented, and managed by IT specialists with the help of business users.

Decentralized business unit-driven innovation that offers low-risk occasions for the organization to learn about new technological opportunities also can be usefully leveraged. For example, a division of a large consumer products company made a substantial investment in desktop services with modest up-front cost justification. The IT department encouraged managers and administrative support personnel to "use" desktop systems, in concurrence with its own learning curve. In the first year, a number of uncoordinated projects emerged, including several sales force support applications and a number of spreadsheet applications, as business customers gained confidence and pursued new programs with enthusiasm. This approach ultimately caused significant business applications fragmentation, requiring a major effort to develop IT support programs retroactively. Nevertheless, company leaders still deemed this approach more valuable than an IT-led project because it encouraged business customers to embrace the new technology and triggered pursuit of more productive work patterns.

Supportive IT departments, with their relatively modest organizational goals and resources, may find it difficult to attract and retain highly skilled IT professionals or gain access to current technologies. They may benefit from targeting IT generalists who are willing to apply their skills and expertise in a variety of different areas. In addition, an outsourcing arrangement may present a viable and cost-effective solution to ensure operational stability. Outsourcing can offer firms in the *Support* quadrant access to higher IT professionalism, access to more current technologies, and reduce the risk of perpetuating inappropriate IT architecture.

Factory: Organizing for Factory-like Efficiency and Reliability

Firms in the *Factory* quadrant are critically dependent on their IT systems for business continuity, and thus, their leadership approach should focus on ensuring the utmost availability and reliability of these critical assets. At this stage, the IT function should ideally be led by someone who channels both technical and industry knowledge into a strong operations focus and who can enforce a highly disciplined approach to operations and development.

As IT has assumed a critical role in business operations, a key part of the IT department's mission is ensuring the ongoing and day-to-day viability of current systems and applications. Centralized management and control of operations is the most effective means to ensure the necessary degree of systems security, reliability, and availability and to coordinate imperative but preferably unobtrusive maintenance and upgrades to infrastructure and systems. Standardization of computing infrastructure also pays dividends by reducing the complexity and cost of maintaining a firm's IT capabilities. Outsourcing may be a good option for these firms too, unless the company is large and well-managed. An outsourcing arrangement can offer economies of scale for small and midsize enterprises, higher-quality service and maintenance, and the increased technical specialization necessary to build and deploy IT solutions on an international scale.

Factory firms are wise to focus their IT investments on ensuring cost-effective totally reliable operations and on consolidating the infrastructure. Investments should also address the build-out of operational capacity to sustain business growth and improve asset efficiency. In addition, development and investment attention should be given to IT factors necessary to compete in a more competitive industry environment—such as the achievement of industry certifications, security efforts, or support for a broader product portfolio.

IT developments and projects should be designed, implemented, and managed by business unit executives in partnership with IT executives to ensure future business needs are met in conjunction with process continuity. An IT council of business leaders is a useful organizational structure to review and monitor IT goals and objectives for their sufficiency and compatibility with business goals. A centralized approach to new developments can promote adherence to company standards of software, computing platforms, and communication networks, which can simplify subsequent maintenance. A centralized IT group usually has a better chance of producing realistic systems development and deployment estimates than do decentralized business-based groups; their greater experience leads them to be less optimistic and to take account of possible complications that could add overhead time and cost to the project. However, this is not always the case since estimation is often difficult and poorly done, even in the best conditions. Central development control also can improve the chances that new applications are deployed in an orderly fashion without negatively impacting other mission-critical applications.

If factory-like controls and discipline are well-established in an organization, these are more likely to persist even after countervailing organizational changes. For example, a major textile company invested heavily in e-commerce and supply chain management, executing a few very large, centrally managed projects. The new systems, which adhered to corporate IT standards, were well received by all parties. A few years later, management moved IT development activity from the central IT department to the divisions, with the goal of aligning the development of new applications more quickly and effectively with the needs of senior divisional management. With IT standardization problems largely solved, the company was able to install a new organizational structure that enabled the divisions to innovate more rapidly around individual agendas. The results, since the reorganization, suggest that it has been extremely effective. IT standards have endured, while the company's subsequent intranet and extranet projects have been a great success.

Turnaround: Organizing for Experimentation and Rapid Exploitation

Firms in the *Turnaround* quadrant look to their IT function as a catalyst to transform organizational capabilities and reveal new strategic avenues. New IT initiatives are often defined, implemented, and managed at the top levels of the corporation, and the leadership of IT should have direct relationships with the firm's senior executive team. An IT leader with an entrepreneurial approach to getting things done will be a good fit at this stage. This person should have expertise in turning technology-centric ideas into business opportunities and be skilled at collaborating to leverage the cross-functional expertise and resources of different parties.

Since neither IT execution nor IT innovation has previously been critical for these firms, they may initially lack the necessary skills and expertise to implement their project goals. An outsourcing relationship may be a possible way to gain access to project management skills, technology applications, and IT staff not available internally. However, this approach could also imply an unnecessary and perhaps unacceptable delegation of competitiveness in the future. For example, skills, technological capabilities, and related expertise must be continuously enhanced to keep a firm ahead of the curve as its competitors start to imitate its efforts; an inappropriate outsourcing arrangement could jeopardize control in this area. Outsourcing is also less viable when low-structured projects are involved, as is frequent in *Turnaround* situations. In low-structured projects, the ultimate deliverables and processes are subject to significant flux as the true project goals are discovered in an iterative design process. In lieu of outsourcing, a more flexible approach to designing, implementing, and managing IT-enabled initiatives could involve partnerships between business development groups and emerging technologies groups inside an organization or with technology partner firms.

Opportunities for experimentation and learning, as well as speed of deployment, are high priorities in *Turnaround* settings. Although turnaround efforts sometimes emphasize experimentation, learning, and quick results without immediate concern for how they might integrate with the larger organization, they still can be instrumental in ultimately driving the organization to a more strategic position. Consider a large South African retail chain that installed a point-of-sale (POS) inventory tracking system in each of its 50-plus stores. Inventory is a retailer's most significant asset, so management efforts to better balance having too little (i.e., incurring stock-outs) and too much (i.e., incurring excess and waste) can have a big effect on its cost structure and profitability. The project's original purpose was to use accumulated daily sales totals inside individual stores to trigger more precise inventory replenishment. This successful project built new organizational capability and quickly generated significant cost savings.

Later, senior business managers realized that, by linking store POS systems with central systems at corporate headquarters, they could measure product performance across stores (with the potential to adjust product mix to local markets) and help manage warehouse inventory levels throughout the retail chain. Since the communication protocols used by the POS systems were incompatible with the protocols in use by central IT systems, this follow-up effort was expensive. But senior management didn't attribute this to deficient planning.

On the contrary, they recognized that a planning process that explored all possible future uses of POS data would have taken too long and delayed inventory savings in individual stores. Furthermore, planning stage estimates of the benefits of linking POS and corporate systems would have been highly speculative (if they could have been identified at all). The excess time necessary to link corporate systems might have weakened the cost/benefit case to the point where ~~the~~ original project might have been canceled. Instead, the success of the first system set a baseline for future systems. The firm built on the POS-to-corporate network to implement a customer loyalty card and gain a detailed and valuable understanding of the individual buying habits of its key customers.

Strategic: Organizing for Operational Discipline and Business Agility

In firms in the *Strategic* quadrant, both current IT operations and future IT-enabled activities have assumed major importance. In these organizations, the CIO is expected to drive business value by using IT to scale the business and increase market share, expand quickly into new markets and products, and build emerging IT-based businesses. This person needs to possess both technical and general management expertise and have a strong focus on execution and growth.

Within strategically IT-dependent firms, IT executives tend to be members of the executive committee. In some firms, the head of the IT function is a member of the board of directors. As senior executives increasingly recognize IT as central to innovation (and thus future growth and competitive advantage) as well as execution, many more CIOs and senior IT leaders are gaining a prominent seat at the executive table and are expected to play an active role in strategic business decisions.[6]

In the *Strategic* quadrant, where IT remains a critical role in business operations, centralized management of infrastructure and operations continues to be appropriate in supporting ongoing and day-to-day dependability of current systems and applications. A centralized policy-based approach to both virtual and physical resources also can further the simplification, standardization, consolidation, and integration of IT services in common use across businesses and regions. At the same time, the ability to easily reuse and reconfigure IT capabilities and assets provides a robust but agile infrastructure platform for rapid future business growth. Similarly, centralization of data management ensures coordination and synchronization of consolidated or physically distributed databases, so that business users, regardless of their location, can access data as needed.

[6] Findings from the CIO Leadership Survey (2007) conducted by the IBM Center for CIO Leadership, in collaboration with Harvard Business School and MIT Center for Information Systems Research (CISR).

In the *Strategic* quadrant, IT investments focus on initiatives to accelerate and sustain the growth of the business, initiatives that are often defined, implemented, and managed at senior business levels. These include acquisitions that add novel technological capability as well as those that aim to replace or supplement legacy environments, especially where these inhibit rapid scaling of IT infrastructure or operations apace with business needs.

Decentralizing the management of development projects and IT development professionals to business divisions can align the development of new IT applications more quickly and effectively with the needs of senior divisional management. Moreover, infusing the technical expertise and judgment of IT professionals with a stronger business perspective and exposure to the daily minutiae of business can also germinate more powerful insights regarding potential IT-enabled business solutions. Specifically, selected development initiatives are likely to be more technically feasible as well as more commercially viable. Development efforts also have a strong learning focus in the *Strategic* quadrant so, ideally, projects should be shorter in duration, frequently as short as three months. More rapid project turnarounds can support firms in building a pattern of incremental rollouts guided by repeated feedback.

An important part of the *Strategic* IT function's mission is to scan leading-edge technologies, inform potential business users of their existence and possibilities, and initiate explorations of their use to solve business problems or address opportunities. In particular, the IT function's perspective on the information assets of the organization (including information about customers, products, markets, competitors, etc.) should be leveraged in service of legal and regulatory compliance, speed to market, and differentiation of product and service offerings. For example, forward-looking firms in this quadrant are turning to high-performance, self-tuning database accelerators for their ability to perform complex analyses on terabytes of data in real time. Use of these technologies eliminates layers of data warehouse complexity while providing powerful prediction, optimization, and search capabilities that yield accurate information for timely response to critical events. As organizations become increasingly information-intensive, the real costs and benefits of information quality become especially valuable. Available and accurate information confers substantial cost savings in activities such as electronic delivery, direct client access, and distribution patterns based on customer value. Furthermore, it can yield significant new sources of revenue through reducing time to market and supporting targeted cross-selling. Conversely, by preventing and reducing incorrect or insecure information, firms avoid tremendous financial and reputational costs associated with situations such as internal rework, privacy breaches, financial restatements, and revenue leakage.[7]

Strategic IT performance is increasingly measured by business metrics of success, rather than simply meeting deadlines and budgets. Thus, leadership of IT should attend to the achievement of concrete and substantial cost savings for current businesses or to increased revenue or profitability as driven by new IT-enabled products and services or by IT-enabled channels to new markets. At the same time, they must recognize that

[7] P. S. Barth, of NewVantage Partners, presentation to the Advanced Practices Council of the Society for Information Management, May 2008. For more information, see www.NewVantage.com.

perceptions of IT's performance increasingly depend on how well IT managers and professionals communicate and collaborate with their business group colleagues, and nurture the "soft skills" necessary for effectiveness in this domain.

Summary

This chapter focused on key issues surrounding the organization and leadership of IT activities. We argued that good leadership corresponds to the role that IT plays in the firm. Changes in recommended practice are driven by the adoption and integration of new technologies into the business, which offer the potential for different types of services to be delivered in a wide variety of ways, and by the accumulation of managerial and organizational IT-experience.

Determining the best approach to the distribution of IT resources and activities within an organization is a complex task. Leaders must seek an appropriate balance between innovation and control while attempting to optimally engage the perspectives of IT specialists and those of business users. The way a general manager manages the tensions involved depends substantially on many non-IT aspects of the corporate environment. The leadership style of the CEO, and his or her view of the company's future, provides important guidance to the ultimate role that IT will play in the organization. Corporate organizational structure and culture also matter, as does the geographic dispersion of business units.

Executives can consider the following questions to assess whether they are adequately addressing issues of leadership and organization of IT activities and assets, according to the actual or intended roles for IT in their organizations:

1. Can you recognize the role of IT in your organization? How critical is IT to sustaining the enterprise? How critical is IT to growing the enterprise? Do your IT budgets and organizational structures reinforce an appropriate balance between robust execution and flexible innovation?
2. What strategic initiatives has executive management taken to manage IT's criticality relative to maintenance and growth of the enterprise, and are they appropriate?
3. Are your IT investments and performance metrics a good fit with the role that IT plays in your organization? Do your performance metrics effectively describe and monitor IT's contribution to the business?
4. To what degree is the success of your company's business driven by factors local to geographies or business units? Conversely, to what extent is success driven by common factors across geographies and business units? Does the organization of your IT operations fit well with the nature of your business? The organization of your IT development initiatives?
5. Do you understand the need for data sharing and common applications in your organization? Are there standards and processes in place to assure efficient data exchange between business units regardless of the distribution of IT resources now or in the future?
6. How would you characterize the skills and expertise of your IT leader? Is s/he the right person to lead IT given its current role in the company? Are your IT talent management and personnel development initiatives consistent with the current and future role of IT?

Appendix **10A**

Leadership Implications of the Role of IT

	Support	Factory	Turnaround	Strategic
Time horizons	• Short-term vision • Low levels of urgency and longer cycle times	• Medium-term vision • High levels of urgency	• Medium-term vision • Short-term targets	• Long-term vision • Short-term targets and cycle times
Business Focus of IT	• Support core business • Incremental process improvement	• Defend and extend core business in changing competitive environment • Increase productivity and profit contribution	• Identify IT disruptors and industry trends • Analyze IT opportunities and prioritize investments in promising new ventures • Experiment to reduce risk and uncertainty	• Build emerging IT-based businesses • Use IT to scale business and increase market share • Use IT to expand quickly into new products and markets
Key Business Challenges	• Achievement of cost plans	• Achievement of revenue and profit plans • Finding new revenue and profit growth for the immediate future through operating efficiencies and shared services and infrastructure	• Effectiveness of opportunity identification approaches, such as research projects, prototypes, test markets, alliances, and initial investments • Targets cannot be set with precision	• Build the business and scale quickly • Manage rapid growth and complexity • Boundary management and integration across businesses and functions
Key Technical Challenges	• Potential for isolated/ standalone applications and fragmentation • Customer support and application maintenance	• Infrastructure complexity • Adherence to IT standards • System maintainability • Technical coordination across business units and functions	• Speed of deployment • Options value of developments	• Long-term architectural coherence and companywide data standards • Infrastructure dependability • Maintenance of shared IT services
Organization and Management Approach	• Centralized control of IT operations and development group; some business-driven development • Focus on system stability and cost-effectiveness • Annual budgets and plans • Outsource to obtain more current or comprehensive technology and skills • Cost-justification of projects • Incremental modifications	• Strong centralized infrastructure and operations management • Focus on systems availability and reliability • Annual budgets and plans • Outsource to gain economies of scale, better service quality, and geographical scalability • Centralized oversight of new initiatives and developments; few large, centrally managed projects • Thorough planning and operational risk assessment • Enforce standards and orderly deployment	• Identify opportunities closely aligned with or driven by business needs • Partner with technology firms or emerging technology groups internally to pursue projects • New venture financing • Use project-based metrics and timelines • Emphasize learning and experimentation • Consider options value of developments	• Executive level CIO • Centralized management of operations and infrastructure • Decentralized development and projects organization, closely aligned with business needs • Adopt business-building strategies: investment budgets; detailed business plans for new ventures; identify product and market expansion

	Support	Factory	Turnaround	Strategic
Profit Impact of IT Function	• Invest to reduce costs or sustain growth locally	• Invest to consolidate infrastructure and ensure cost-effective highly reliable operations • Evaluate to replace or complement outdated IT infrastructure	• Invest to transform capabilities, reduce costs, and generate immediate-term cash flow • Invest to create future high-growth IT-enabled businesses	• Invest to accelerate and sustain growth, and improve asset efficiency • Substantial profits may be a few years in the future
IT Leader Attributes	Generalists: • Flexible skills and expertise • Consistent execution • Task orientation	Operators: • Deep technical and industry expertise • Strong drive to consistently meet short-term plans • Disciplined execution • Cooperative orientation	Entrepreneurs: • Expertise in turning ideas into opportunities into businesses • Motivated to create new businesses • Able to tolerate risk and ambiguity • Combine creativity with discipline • Collaborative orientation	Business Builders: • General management expertise • Deep technical expertise • Motivated to grow and scale • Top-line focus • Execute to short- and medium-term plans • Performance orientation
Managerial Talent Approach	• Use projects as training opportunities for junior managers	• Create personal consequences for near-term performance including clear penalties for underperformance • Impose "no excuses" management style	• Offer opportunity to build and leave a legacy • Provide psychological rewards: recognition of ideas, freedom to experiment and explore • Provide career advantage: opportunity to satisfy intellectual curiosity	• Provide accountability and authority and reward growth • Opportunity to increase personal wealth through cash bonuses and equity participation
Corporate Involvement	• Limited • Delegate review and monitoring to IT function	• Council of Business Leaders • Review and monitor goals and objectives	• Executive leadership of new venture unit • Set and monitor aggressive targets • Identify IT-enabled opportunities, provide teams and funding • Support experiments and learning in IT	• IT Executive Steering Committee • Invest in IT-enabled business growth • Address problems in scaling IT infrastructure and operations
Selection of Performance Measures	• Traditional budgets and controls • Costs • Quality improvement or effectiveness	• Traditional budgets and controls • Costs • Profits • Asset leverage • Infrastructure reliability, security and availability indicators • Productivity or efficiency	• Project-based milestones • Speed of deployment • Learning and insights • Cost savings • Future options value • Rate of conversion of ideas to opportunities to business launch • Number of development initiatives and success in moving through innovation stages	• Capital efficient profitable growth • Asset leverage • Market share gains • New customer acquisitions • Capital investment efficiency • Expected net present value

Reading 3-1

Information Technology and the Board of Directors

Richard Nolan and F. Warren McFarlan

Ever since the Y2K scare, boards have grown increasingly nervous about corporate dependence on information technology. Since then, computer crashes, denial of service attacks, competitive pressures, and the need to automate compliance with government regulations have heightened board sensitivity to IT risk. Unfortunately, most boards remain largely in the dark when it comes to IT spending and strategy. Despite the fact that corporate information assets can account for more than 50 percent of capital spending, most boards fall into the default mode of applying a set of tacit or explicit rules cobbled together from the best practices of other firms. Few understand the full degree of their operational dependence on computer systems or the extent to which IT plays a role in shaping their firms' strategies.

This state of affairs may seem excusable because to date there have been no standards for IT governance. Certainly, board committees understand their roles with regard to other areas of corporate control. In the United States, the audit committee's task, for example, is codified in a set of Generally Accepted Accounting Principles and processes and underscored by regulations such as those of the New York Stock Exchange and Securities and Exchange Commission. Likewise, the compensation committee acts according to generally understood principles, employing compensation consulting firms to verify its findings and help explain its decisions to shareholders. The governance committee, too, has a clear mission: to look at the composition of the board and recommend improvements to its processes. To be sure, boards often fail to reach set standards, but at least there are standards.

Because there has been no comparable body of knowledge and best practice, IT governance doesn't exist per se. Indeed, board members frequently lack the fundamental knowledge needed to ask intelligent questions about not only IT risk and expense but also competitive risk. This leaves the CIOs, who manage critical corporate information assets, pretty much on their own. A lack of board oversight for IT activities is dangerous; it puts the firm at risk in the same way that failing to audit its books would.

Understanding this, a small group of companies has taken matters into its own hands and established rigorous IT governance committees. Mellon Financial, Novell, Home Depot, Procter & Gamble, Wal-Mart, and FedEx, among others, have taken this step, creating board-level IT committees that are on a par with their audit, compensation, and governance committees. When the IT governance committee in one of these companies assists the CEO, the CIO, senior management, and the board in driving technology decisions, costly projects tend to remain under control, and the firm can carve out competitive advantage.

The question is no longer whether the board should be involved in IT decisions; the question is How? Having observed the ever-changing IT strategies of hundreds of firms for over 40 years, we've found that there is no one-size-fits-all model for board supervision of a company's IT operations. The correct IT approach depends on a host of factors, including a company's history, industry, competitive situation, financial position, and quality of IT management. A strategy that

Richard Nolan (rnolan@hbs.edu) is an emeritus professor of business at Harvard Business School in Boston and a professor of management and organization at the University of Washington Business School in Seattle. F. Warren McFarlan (fmcfarlan@hbs.edu) is a Baker Foundation Professor and the Albert H. Gordon Professor of Business Administration emeritus at Harvard Business School.

Reprinted by permission of Harvard Business Review.

works well for a clothing retailer is not appropriate for a large airline; the strategy that works for eBay can't work for a cement company. Creating a board-level committee is not, however, a best practice all companies should adopt. For many firms—consulting firms, small retailers, and book publishers, for instance—it would be a waste of time.

In this article, we show board members how to recognize their firms' positions and decide whether they should take a more aggressive stance. We illustrate the conditions under which boards should be less or more involved in IT decisions. We delineate what an IT governance committee should look like in terms of charter, membership, duties, and overall agenda. We offer recommendations for developing IT governance policies that take into account an organization's operational and strategic needs, as well as suggest what to do when those needs change. As we demonstrate in the following pages, appropriate board governance can go a long way toward helping a company avoid unnecessary risk and improve its competitive position.

The Four Modes

We've found it helpful to define the board's involvement according to two strategic issues: The first is how much the company relies on cost-effective, uninterrupted, secure, smoothly operating technology systems (what we refer to as "defensive" IT). The second is how much the company relies on IT for its competitive edge through systems that provide new value-added services and products or high responsiveness to customers ("offensive" IT). Depending on where companies locate themselves on a matrix we call "The IT Strategic Impact Grid" (see Exhibit 1), technology governance may be a routine matter best handled by the existing audit committee or a vital asset that requires intense board-level scrutiny and assistance.

Defensive IT is about operational reliability. Keeping IT systems up and running is more important in the company's current incarnation than leapfrogging the competition through the clever use of emerging technology. One famously defensive firm is American Airlines, which developed the SABRE reservation system in the late 1960s. Once a source of innovation and strategic advantage, the SABRE system is now the absolute backbone of American's operations: When the system goes down, the airline grinds to a complete halt. Boards of firms like this need assurance that the technology systems are totally protected against potential operational disasters—computer bugs, power interruptions, hacking, and so on—and that costs remain under control.

Offensive IT places strategic issues either over or on the same level as reliability. Offensive IT projects tend to be ambitious and risky because they often involve substantial organizational change. An offensive stance is called for when a company needs to alter its technology strategy to compete more effectively or to raise the firm to a position of industry leadership. Because of the resources required to take an offensive position, financially and competitively strong companies usually have to be intensively involved in IT on all levels. Wal-Mart, for example, is replacing bar codes with radio frequency identification (RFID) technology, which effectively drives the supply chain directly from the supplier to the warehouse without the need for scanning by associates.

Firms can be either defensive or offensive in their strategic approach to IT—approaches we call "modes." Let's look at each mode in turn.

Support Mode (Defensive)

Firms in this mode have both a relatively low need for reliability and a low need for strategic IT; technology fundamentally exists to support employees' activities. The Spanish clothier Zara, which began as a small retail shop, is a good example; the company keeps strict control over its supply chain operations by designing, producing, and distributing its own clothing. Though IT is used in these areas, the company won't suffer terribly if a system goes down. (For more on Zara, see Kasra Ferdows, Michael A. Lewis, and Jose A.D. Machuca, "Rapid-Fire Fulfillment,"

EXHIBIT 1 The IT Strategic Impact Grid

How a board goes about governing IT activities generally depends on a company's size, industry, and competitive landscape. Companies in support mode are least dependent on IT; those in factory mode are much more dependent on it but are relatively unambitious when it comes to strategic use. Firms in turnaround mode expect that new systems will change their business; those in strategic mode require dependable systems as well as emerging technologies to hold or advance their competitive positions.

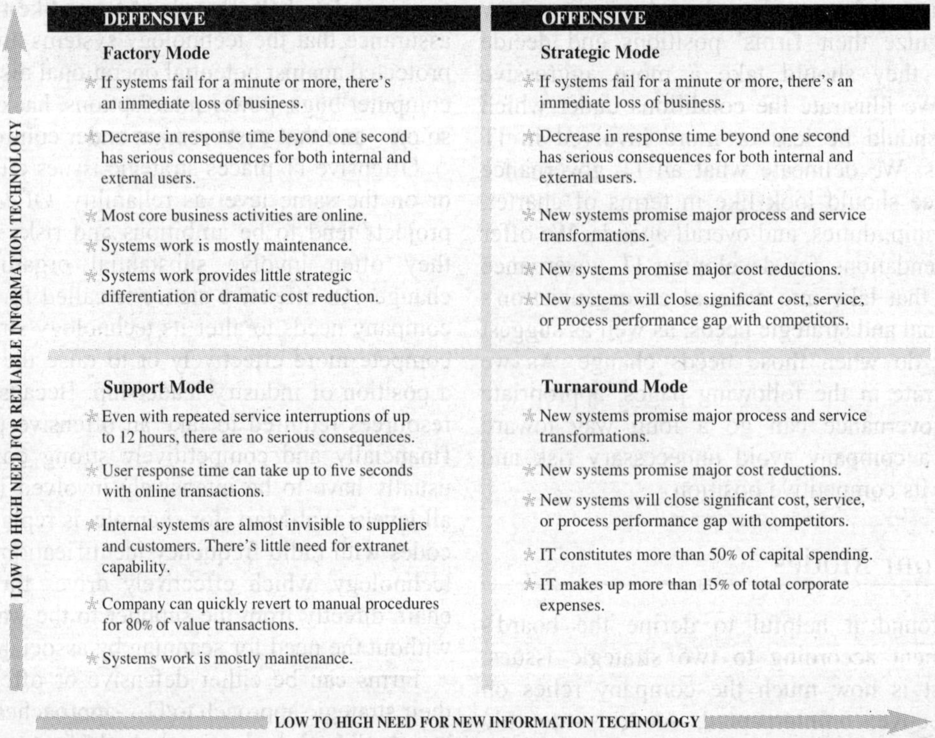

HBR November 2004.) Core business systems are generally run on a batch cycle; most error correction and backup work is done manually. Customers and suppliers don't have access to internal systems. Companies in support mode can suffer repeated service interruptions of up to 12 hours without serious bottom-line consequences, and high-speed Internet response time isn't critical.

For such firms, the audit committee can review IT operations. The most critical questions for members to ask are: "Should we remain in support mode, or should we change our IT strategy to keep up with or surpass the competition?" and "Are we spending money wisely and not just chasing after new technology fads?" (In this mode, the spending mantra is "Don't waste money." For a list of questions appropriate to each mode, see Exhibit 2.)

Factory Mode (Defensive)

Companies in this mode need highly reliable systems but don't really require state-of-the-art computing. They resemble manufacturing plants; if the conveyor belts fail, production stops. (Airlines and other businesses that depend on fast, secure,

EXHIBIT 2 Asking the Tough Questions

What board members need to know about IT depends on the company's strategic position. Firms in support and factory mode should have their audit committees, with the help of an IT expert, query management. Organizations in turnaround and strategic mode will want the assistance of a full-fledged IT committee in getting answers to their questions.

If your company is in **Support Mode,** ask the questions in set **A**.
If your company is in **Factory Mode,** ask the questions in sets **A** and **B**.
If your company is in **Turnaround Mode,** ask the questions in sets **A** and **C**.
If your company is in **Strategic Mode,** ask the questions in sets **A, B,** and **C**.

A

- Has the strategic importance of our IT changed?
- What are our current and potential competitors doing in the area of IT?
- Are we following best practices in asset management?
- Is the company getting adequate ROI from information resources?
- Do we have the appropriate IT infrastructure and applications to exploit the development of our intellectual assets?

B

- Has anything changed in disaster recovery and security that will affect our business's continuity planning?
- Do we have in place management practices that will prevent our hardware, software, and legacy applications from becoming obsolete?
- Do we have adequate protection against denial of service attacks and hackers?
- Are there fast-response processes in place in the event of an attack?
- Do we have management processes in place to ensure 24/7 service levels, including tested backup?
- Are we protected against possible intellectual-property-infringement lawsuits?
- Are there any possible IT-based surprises lurking out there?

C

- Are our strategic IT development plans proceeding as required?
- Is our applications portfolio sufficient to deal with a competitive threat or to meet a potential opportunity?
- Do we have processes in place that will enable us to discover and execute any strategic IT opportunities?
- Do we have processes in place to guard against IT risk?
- Do we regularly benchmark to maintain our competitive cost structure?

real-time data response fall into this group.) These companies are much more dependent on the smooth operation of their technology, since most of their core business systems are online. They suffer an immediate loss of business if systems fail even for a minute; a reversion to manual procedures is difficult, if not impossible. Factory-mode firms generally depend on their extranets to communicate with customers and suppliers. Typically, factory-mode organizations are not interested in being the first to implement a new technology, but their top management and boards need to be aware of leading-edge practice and monitor the competitive landscape for any change that would require a more aggressive use of IT.

Because business continuity in IT operations is critical for these firms, the board needs to make sure that disaster recovery and security procedures are in place. The audit committee for a large East Coast medical center, for example, recently authorized a full disaster recovery, security, and operational environment review simply to ensure that appropriate safeguards were there. The study was expensive but completely necessary because, in the event of a failure, patients' lives would be at risk. (In this mode, the spending mantra is "Don't cut corners.")

Turnaround Mode (Offensive)

Companies in the midst of strategic transformation frequently bet the farm on new technology. In this mode, technology typically accounts for more than 50 percent of capital expenditures and more than 15 percent of corporate costs. New systems promise major process and service improvements, cost reductions, and a competitive edge. At the same time, companies in this mode have a comparatively low need for reliability when it comes to existing business systems; like companies in support mode, they can withstand repeated service interruptions of up to 12 hours without serious consequences, and core business activities remain on a batch cycle. Once the new systems are installed, however, there is no possible reversion to manual systems because all procedures have been captured into databases.

Companies usually enter turnaround mode with a major IT project that requires a big reengineering effort, often accompanied by the decision to outsource or move a substantial portion of their operations offshore. Most firms don't spend a long time in turnaround mode; once the change is made, they move into either factory mode or strategic mode. American Airlines functioned in turnaround mode when it created the SABRE system; now it lives in factory mode. Similarly, the Canadian company St. Marys Cement operated in support mode until it began equipping its trucks with GPS devices, which pushed it into temporary turnaround mode.

Board oversight is critical for companies in turnaround mode; strategic IT plans must proceed on schedule and on budget, particularly when competitive advantage is at stake. (Here, the spending mantra is "Don't screw it up.")

Strategic Mode (Offensive)

For some companies, total innovation is the name of the game. New technology informs not only the way they approach the marketplace but also the way they carry out daily operations. Strategic-mode firms need as much reliability as factory-mode firms do, but they also aggressively pursue process and service opportunities, cost reductions, and competitive advantages. Like turnaround firms, their IT expenditures are large.

Not every firm wants or needs to be in this mode; some are forced into it by competitive pressures. Consider Boeing, a company that dominated the commercial-airline-manufacturing industry until Airbus took the lead. Now convinced that its future rests on the successful design, marketing, and delivery of a new commercial plane, Boeing has embarked on an ambitious technology project that it hopes will return the company to industry dominance. Its new 787 plane, due in 2008, will be equipped with a new lightweight carbon composite skin. Since carbon composite skin is a relatively new material to be used so extensively in a commercial airplane, a neural network will be embedded in the fuselage and wings to constantly monitor load factors and make adjustments as changing conditions warrant. The 787 will be manufactured and assembled through the world's largest project management system, which will simultaneously coordinate thousands of computers and automate an integrated supply chain comprising hundreds of global partners. Each supplier will send components via specially equipped 747s to Boeing's site in Everett, Washington, where the 787 will be assembled in a mere three days, ensuring low costs and fast delivery. The 787 is like a jigsaw puzzle whose pieces must fall into perfect alignment at once, making Boeing both operationally and strategically dependent on IT.

As is the case for firms in turnaround mode, board-level IT governance is critical in strategic mode. Organizations require a fully formed IT oversight committee with at least one IT expert as a member. (The mantra for strategic-mode companies is "Spend what it takes, and monitor results like crazy.")

As we said at the outset, the specific action a company should take with respect to IT oversight depends on which mode it's in. Regardless of its business, it behooves any company to take an in-depth look at its current business through the IT lens. In doing so, a company gains a much firmer grasp of what it needs to be successful.

How to Conduct IT Oversight

Having identified which mode they currently inhabit, companies then need to decide what kind of IT expertise they need on the board. Firms that require a high level of reliability need to focus on managing IT risk. The job of these boards is to assure the completeness, quality, security, reliability, and maintenance of existing IT investments that support day-to-day business processes. Rarely will such companies want a separate IT committee. Instead, the audit committee must do double duty as the IT governance team and delve deeply into the quality of the company's IT systems.

On the other hand, companies that need to go beyond defensive mode require an independent IT governance committee, rather than just having an IT expert serve on the audit committee. The IT governance committee's job is to keep the board apprised of what other organizations—particularly competitors—are doing with technology. Below, we outline the general duties of boards according to their modes.

Inventory the assets (all modes)

A board needs to understand the overall architecture of its company's IT applications portfolio as well as its asset management strategy. The first step is to find out what kinds of hardware, software, and information the company owns so as to determine whether it's getting adequate return from its IT investments.

Physical IT assets—counted as computer hardware—are relatively easy to inventory; intangible assets are not. Despite the fact that intangible assets have largely been ignored by the accounting field, most companies are increasingly reliant on them. Companies have huge investments in applications software, ranging from customer and HR databases to integrated supply chains. The board must ensure that management knows what information resources are out there, what condition they are in, and what role they play in generating revenue. One rule of thumb in determining intangible assets is to first measure the hardware inventory—including all mainframes, servers, and PCs—and then multiply that by 10. This renders a rough notion of what the software inventory will be (including off-the-shelf and proprietary software). The next step is to assure that the IT organization sorts the wheat from the chaff by determining the number and location of aging and legacy programs, and then decide which should be upgraded or maintained.

The board will also want to ensure that its company has the right IT infrastructure and applications in place to develop intellectual assets such as customer feedback about products and services. It needs to know how well employees can use IT systems to analyze customer feedback and develop or improve products and services.

Assure security and reliability (factory and strategic modes)

Ideally, boards of companies in factory and strategic modes should conduct regular reviews of their security and reliability measures so that any interruption of service doesn't send a company into a tailspin. Unfortunately, and all too often, oversight takes place following a crisis.

With the development of highly integrated IT networks within and outside the company, proper security has become paramount. An attack by a hacker or a virus can reduce profits by millions of dollars. An attack on Amazon, for example, would cost the company $600,000 an hour in revenue. If Cisco's systems were down for a day, the company would lose $70 million in revenues. Thus, the board needs to ensure that management is continually evaluating the company's networks for security breaches. (Some companies actually work with would-be hackers to test vulnerability to threats.)

A board will also want to make sure that service outages don't occur in the case of power failures or natural disasters. IT services are analogous to electrical power; an outage of days can trigger the demise of a company, particularly one in defensive mode. For this reason, backup systems must be continually tested to make sure that they actually work. IT also needs to ensure that service continues even while maintenance is under way, so proper detours and backups need to be in place. Many companies use diesel generators to keep backup systems running but, as the gigantic power outage that struck the East Coast of the United States in August 2003 demonstrated, the diesel can run out if the backup systems are in continuous use. In such cases, companies must take special steps. (Following the 2003 blackout, Delta Air Lines arranged for generator fuel to arrive by helicopter in the event of another shortage.)

Avoid surprises (factory, turnaround, and strategic modes)

No board wants to be taken unawares, and the most frequent source of IT-related surprises is from lax or ineffective project management. The larger the IT project, the higher the risk. Consider what happened to candy maker Hershey's when an expansion of its brand new ERP system blew up in the company's face. By the time Halloween rolled around, the company still could not keep track of orders, revenues, and inventory. Best estimates are that this cost the company $151 million.

Even companies that are supposed to be technology experts can botch a project, as EDS proved when it lost $2 billion on a contract to build an intranet for the U.S. Navy. Because EDS didn't fully understand the scope of the strategically important Navy initiative, the project suffered from unexpected delays and technical setbacks, costing EDS massive write-downs that ultimately drove its debt to junk bond status. To avoid such unwanted surprises, boards must ensure that appropriate project management systems are in place and that key decision points along the way are elevated to the appropriate level so that management can decide whether the project is still worth doing.

Companies can also be caught unawares if they don't have adequate service level agreements (SLAs) with vendors or clients, particularly when they choose to outsource their IT activities. A solid, well-thought-out SLA that makes explicit specific terms, deliverables, and responsibilities can help firms avoid serious project management problems. The agreement should guarantee that the needs of all the diverse groups within the company—such as marketing, sales, call center operations, and bad debt collection—are met under the terms of the agreement.

Additionally, legacy systems can present unwanted surprises because companies are so dependent on them, as the Y2K problem demonstrated. Rather than replace those systems, companies tend to build on top of them. And firms running batch-oriented systems often overlay them with new online user interfaces. This can create serious problems for accounting departments: A user of an online query system, for example, may believe that the answer he or she receives is up-to-the-minute; but if, in fact, data files are updated in batch mode, the information could be many hours out of date. Having to sort through such misinformation might require accounting departments to hire additional staff to ensure that financial reporting is done on time. To avoid such problems, the governance committee needs to decide whether it is more economical to maintain legacy hardware, software, and applications or to replace them. It's relatively easy for IT departments to determine when computer hardware needs upgrading. But when it comes to intangible assets such as legacy databases, the question of maintenance versus replacement becomes trickier; it's not uncommon to find maintenance taking up 90 percent of IT programming expenditures.

Watch out for legal problems (turnaround and strategic modes)

Companies can be subject to legal problems if they don't tread carefully around the intellectual property issues relating to IT. The advent of the Linux operating system, for example, has been a boon to many companies; at the same time, making free use of associated patented intellectual property has exposed them to legal risks. Consider SCO's $3 billion lawsuit against IBM, in which SCO alleges that IBM illegally incorporated SCO's intellectual property to the code base of the Linux operating system. Cases like this have made it clear that organizations need to stay alert for possible problems and avoid the expensive distraction of an intellectual property dispute involving IT. The board needs to watch out for such risks and be ready to bring in appropriate legal counsel when necessary to keep the senior management team from being distracted.

Keep an eye out for fresh threats and opportunities (turnaround and strategic modes)

It's a good idea for committee members to interrogate the CIO and line management about new products they may have seen or heard about at technology trade shows or industry conferences. It is also good practice to monitor firms in other industries that have a reputation for making effective use of leading-edge technology applications.

The committee must be on the lookout for technology-based competitive threats that could place a company in what we call "strategic jeopardy," which occurs when executive management is asleep at the switch vis-à-vis the competition. For example, the board can hire, or ask management to hire, a consulting company to gather intelligence, do benchmarking, and develop a scenario of possible threats from competitors, as well as outline opportunities. IT committees should also be sure that management has created a good customer feedback system that allows customers to offer opinions about competitors' products and services. In addition, it's important to monitor companies that may have the means and inclination to become competitors. Had supermarket chains been apprised of what Wal-Mart was up to with RFID, they might not have found themselves blindsided by the retail giant's aggressive supply-chain advances in the grocery business.

Finally, boards of firms in offensive modes must constantly scan for opportunities as technologies advance and the cost of computing drops. Anything that has been performed manually, for example, presents an opportunity not only to automate but also to raise the bar for products or services. Otis Elevator, for instance, dramatically improved its product delivery cycle by intelligently using IT to replace a paper-based tracking and fulfillment system. Once a contract for an elevator, escalator, or walkway is signed, a program called eLogistics sends project information directly from the field via nearly 1,000 local area networks and 1,000 global wide-area networks to contract logistics centers. The result has been a huge drop in inventory and a fivefold improvement in delivery time.

Building the IT Governance Committee

How do you set up an IT governance committee? A company that decides it needs board-level IT oversight must do three things: Select the appropriate members and the chairman, determine the group's relationship to the audit committee, and prepare the charter. The first two are especially important.

We recommend that the IT governance group be made up of independent directors, as is the case with audit and compensation committees. Chairmanship is also critical. For firms in support, factory, or turnaround modes, the chairperson need not be an IT expert but should certainly be a tough-minded, IT-savvy business executive—either a CEO or a top manager who has overseen the use of IT to gain strategic advantage in another organization.

In any case, at least one person on the committee should be an IT expert who should operate as a peer at the senior management and board level. The expert's job is to challenge entrenched in-house thinking. He or she should not think ill of technology-averse cultures and must be a skilled communicator who does not hide behind technology jargon or talk down to board members. The expert should help the committee avoid dwelling on the difficulties of the work and emphasize instead the opportunities. The focus should be on the big picture: Conversations about IT strategy are hard and can be discouraging if the committee gets dragged down in technical details. (In fact, when looking for someone who fits these criteria, boards may find that many talented CIOs and CTOs drop off the list of potential IT committee members.) The IT expert must have not only a solid grounding in the firm's overall business needs but also a holistic view of the organization and its systems architecture. This is particularly important if the firm chooses to outsource its functions and connect multiple vendors across a network. The expert must also thoroughly understand the underlying dynamics governing changes in technology and their potential to alter the business's economic outlook.

Generally speaking, the IT expert serves much the same function as the certified financial expert on an audit committee. A CIO or CTO with solid experience in the management of IT qualifies; for example, the IT oversight committee chairman for the Great Atlantic & Pacific Tea Company (A&P) was previously CEO of an extremely successful supermarket chain on the West Coast, where he achieved impressive business results through effective IT system implementation and management. As chair of the IT committee, he helps balance his company's short-term business needs with long-term IT investments.

Unfortunately, skilled, business-oriented technology strategists are in short supply. In the absence of such a person within a company, an IT consultant who can help sort out technology issues can fit the bill, as might a divisional CEO or COO who is actively managing IT. Alternatively, a manager who has served in an influential technology company such as Microsoft or Oracle can help a firm determine its place on the strategic impact grid, begin to embrace emerging technologies, and locate other experts who can serve on the committee.

Businesses in strategic mode should have an IT oversight committee chaired by an IT expert. In this mode, it's even more important to get the membership right. For example, the chairman of the IT committee for Novell—a company in strategic mode—founded a major IT-strategy-consulting company, sold it to one of the then Big Six accounting firms, and continued as a senior partner in that firm's IT consulting business. Two other members of Novell's IT committee previously served as CIOs in major Fortune 100 companies; they also serve on Novell's audit committee.

We recommend that the relationship of the IT governance committee to the audit committee be very close, because IT issues can affect economic and regulatory matters such as Sarbanes-Oxley compliance. For this reason, it's a good idea to have one audit committee member serve on the IT oversight committee. The charter of the IT committee should explicitly describe its relationship to the audit group, as well as its organization, purpose, oversight responsibilities, and meeting schedule (see Exhibit 3).

Regardless of a company's position, top-level commitment is critical if the board is to engage in IT governance. Board members and senior

EXHIBIT 3 An IT Governance Committee Calendar

To be successful, an IT oversight committee must ensure that its discussions with senior management are deep and ongoing. The committee can help management visualize IT's impact on the firm. We recommend that it develop a to-do calendar of the defensive, offensive, and administrative oversight tasks it needs to carry out over the year. Here's a sample calendar.

Defensive Governance	**Frequency**
IT Projects/Architecture	
Receive update of strategic projects.	Quarterly
Receive update of technical architecture and critique it.	As Needed
Ensure update of applications architecture and critique it.	As Needed
Receive and review update of project investments.	Annual
IT Security	
Critique IT security practices.	Annual
Review and appraise IT disaster-recovery capabilities.	Annual
Review security-related audit findings.	As Needed
Review current developments in security practices, standards, and new security-related technology strategies.	Annual
Internal Controls	
Review IT internal control practices.	Annual
Review IT-related audit findings.	As Needed
Send reports to audit committee regarding IT systems and processes affecting internal controls.	Annual

Offensive Governance	**Frequency**
Advisory Role	
Advise senior IT management team.	As Needed
Stay informed of, assess, and advise the company's senior IT management team about new technologies, applications, and systems that relate to or affect the company's IT strategy or programs.	As Needed
Receive update of IT strategy and critique it.	Annual
Review and critique business plan (annual and three-year).	Annual
Review internal IT assessment measurements and critique action plan.	Annual
Hold private session with CFO.	Quarterly
Strategic Technology Scanning	
Visit other companies to observe technology approaches and strategies.	Annual
Engage outside experts as required to provide third-party opinions about the company's technology strategy.	As Needed
Report to the board on matters within the scope of the committee, as well as on any special issues that merit the board's attention.	Quarterly
Perform other duties as appropriate to ensure that the company's IT programs effectively support the company's business objectives and strategies.	As Needed

(*Continued*)

EXHIBIT 3 **An IT Governance Committee Calendar (*Continued*)**

Administrative	Frequency
Review and assess the adequacy of the IT oversight charter and recommend proposed changes to the board.	As Needed
Evaluate IT oversight committee's effectiveness (self-assessment).	Annual
Approve minutes of prior meetings.	Quarterly
Present report to board regarding the IT oversight committee's activities.	Annual
Hold executive session with committee members.	As Needed
Approve IT committee meeting planner for the upcoming year, and approve mutual expectations with management.	Annual

managers must identify and carefully gauge their current positions on the IT impact grid and decide whether setting up an IT oversight committee is necessary, given the company's current situation. If the need is not clearly understood, or if general buy-in for establishing such a committee—which necessarily includes an IT expert among its members—doesn't exist, then the company shouldn't do it. Any effort to do so will be a waste of time, and failure will sour the chances of establishing such a committee later.

That said, it's clear that as more and more companies in support and factory modes change tactics, and as other firms choose to adopt new technologies to stay ahead of the game, board-level technology governance will become increasingly important. This is good news, for when top managers understand the degree to which they must be accountable for technology, for project expenditures, and for monitoring return on investment from IT, they will do a better job of ensuring that critical systems function as promised. One thing is certain: Given the dizzying pace of change in the world of technology, and the changes IT can force upon a business, there is no such thing as too much accountability.

Volkswagen of America: Managing IT Priorities

Volkswagen's U.S. subsidiary has launched a new process for allocating scarce IT budgets across a portfolio of project requests, in an effort to align IT activities better with corporate strategy. Now that they have used the process for the first time, though, and arrived at a list of approved projects, no one seems happy with the outcome. This case provides an opportunity to discuss the difficult governance issues that arise in making IT investment decisions. As you read the case, consider these questions: What is your assessment of the new process for managing priorities at Volkswagen? Are the criticisms justified? Is it an improvement over the old process? Who controls the budgets from which IT projects are funded at Volkswagen of America? Who should control these budgets? How should Matulovic respond to his fellow executives who are calling to ask him for special treatment outside the new priority management system?

Case 3-2

Volkswagen of America: Managing IT Priorities

Dr. Uwe Matulovic, chief information officer (CIO) of Volkswagen of America (VWoA), placed the telephone in its cradle and leaned back in his chair, replaying the just-completed conversation with one of his peers from the Executive Leadership Team (ELT). The call, Matulovic mused, had been similar to three others he had participated in that week, each with a different ELT member. The results of a new prioritization process—a list of IT projects that would be funded in 2004—had been unveiled only a few days earlier. But already a storm was gathering.

The phone calls from other executives had common themes. All the callers had expressed concern that high priorities for their areas of the company had not been funded. Some had repeated views expressed during the prioritization process by people who worked for them about supposed categorization mistakes that penalized their business units. And each of the calls had concluded with an informal request to insert an unfunded project (or two) into the IT department's work plans. "We don't have to reopen the process," the most recent caller had said, "but perhaps spare capacity might be applied to make some progress on this project in 2004—we've done this before, and it would mean a lot to our area and to the company's growth plans."

The 10 business units that made up VWoA had proposed more than 40 projects, with funding requirements totaling \$210 million (US). A budget of only \$60 million (an amount capped by Volkswagen Group (VWAG), the parent company of VWoA) made some degree of disappointment inevitable. But the intensity of pushback against the new process was surprising. The ELT had endorsed the idea of improving upon the old way these decisions were made, via unstructured debate among executive sponsors. The new process, it was agreed, would make trade-offs explicit and link projects and the core business processes they impacted with VWoA corporate goals. An orderly, rational process would replace what, in the past, had sometimes been haphazard.

But now, questions were being raised about whether the new process was right for VWoA.

Professor Robert D. Austin, Dr. Warren Ritchie, and Greggory Garrett prepared this case as the basis for class discussion rather than to illustrate effective or ineffective management. Certain details have been disguised.

EXHIBIT 1 **The "Himalayas Chart"**

Source: Company documents.

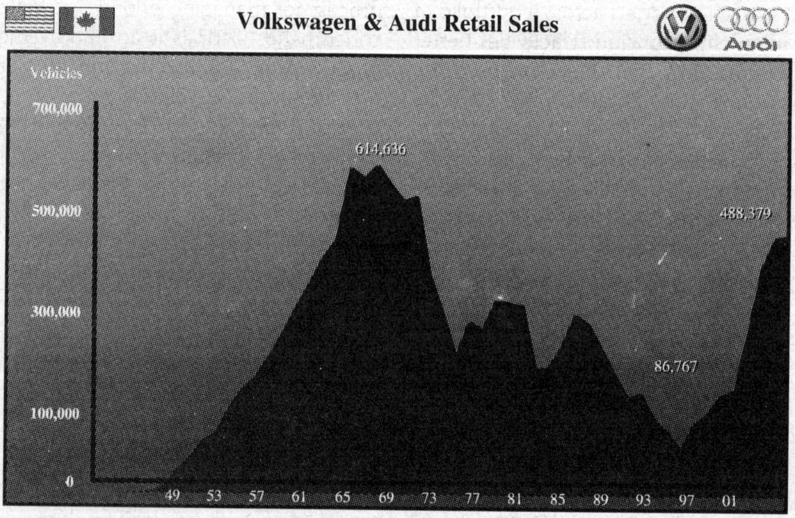

Some business units had seen none of their projects funded. Whispers throughout the company suggested that the process was "too theoretical" and noted that IT infrastructure projects had been treated separately, not forced through the same process, which many considered unfair.

As Matulovic peered through the window into an overcast sky, he wondered whether he should order exceptions to the process. If a project was small and just below the line of funded projects, maybe IT should figure out a way to get it done. Or maybe he should stand his ground and defend the new process. Matulovic did not work *for* the other members of the ELT, but he did have to work *with* them. Whatever he decided could certainly affect working relationships, so he would need to consider his options carefully.

Background—Volkswagen of America

Ferdinand Porsche designed the first Volkswagen automobiles during the 1930s in Germany. The original vehicles, targeted at the mass market ("Volkswagen" means, literally, "people's car"), were intended to transport a family of five at highway speeds, use modest amounts of fuel, and remain within financial reach of most people. The company's signature platform by the late 1940s was the Beetle, which, with its rounded styling and reliable air-cooled engine, became internationally popular. For about 20 years, sales of the Beetle hurtled skyward, propelling the company's total worldwide vehicle sales past a million in 1955 and to a high point in 1969. Although popularity of the Beetle declined throughout the 1970s and its importation was discontinued in the United States, late in that decade, production of Beetles in Latin America continued into the 1990s. It remains the best-selling car of all time.[1]

After peaking in the late 1960s, the pattern of sales for the North American subsidiary of Volkswagen settled into a trying cycle of ups and downs that became known, due to its jagged contours, as the "Himalayas Chart" (see Exhibit 1).

[1] Other marketing nameplates have sold more units, but these nameplates were not the same vehicle in different geographies, nor did they retain as much consistency in core design as the classic Beetle.

Sales fell precipitously until the introduction of the Rabbit in 1977, then recovered briefly before dropping sharply again. This time the introduction of the Jetta prompted another short-lived recovery, followed by a several-year descent to a new low point in the early 1990s known informally within the company as the "Valley of Despair."

It seemed to some that midlevel managers within VWoA had fallen into an unhealthy habit of waiting for the next round of new models to rescue them from present difficulties. Executives wanted to break the cyclical pattern of sales. Through concerted efforts to develop more proactive tendencies and a series of more rapid model introductions (New Golf, New Jetta, New Passat, and New Beetle), sales rose encouragingly into the twenty-first century. New brand positioning and effective advertising helped move the firm into competition with other more upscale brands.

Globally within VWAG in the early 2000s, senior executives began to broaden their view of the traditional VW Group portfolio of vehicles. Upon his arrival in 2001 as VW Group chairman, Dr. Bernd Pischetsrieder initiated a strategy of diversifying the product offerings from VW Group companies. He observed that, globally, the VW Group brands were overrepresented in small-car and lower-priced segments but that much of the industry growth during the previous five years had been in midsized vehicles and emerging segments, such as sport utility and special-purpose vehicles. The new diversification strategy would create a portfolio that matched the global demand for vehicles, not just focus on segments in which the VW Group had traditionally produced.

Simultaneously, Pischetsrieder initiated a consolidation of the VW Group automotive brands into two groups, each with different positioning directions. In these brand groups, one dominant brand represented the *tower*, which was partnered with two smaller-volume brands. For example, in the VW Brand Group, the VW brand served as the dominant brand and was partnered with Bentley and Skoda. These brands were to be positioned as "classic" brands. The other brand group was the Audi Brand Group, which consisted of Audi, SEAT, and Lamborghini; this group was positioned as "sporty." The purpose of consolidating brands into groups was to force some alignment among brands to help determine their requirements for future models in new segments. The result of these changes was that both brand groups proposed a number of new models to be developed and launched over the period from 2004 through 2008.

VWoA's CEO, Gerd Klauss, could see that the implications of the product-diversification strategy being developed in Germany would have a dramatic impact on the U.S. and Canadian importer operations. If all models proposed in 2002 were ultimately approved and produced, VWoA would grow from importing nine models in 2002 to over 22 models by 2008 (see Exhibit 2). This sort of growth in product offering was unprecedented in VWoA history. In order to prepare for this escalation and the associated sales and service expansion, Klauss instituted an organizational readiness program called "Next Round of Growth" (NRG) and made it the key leadership focus (see Exhibit 3). The aims of the NRG program were to define the goals, functions, and organizational changes required at VWoA to support and enable the new global product diversification strategy. Klauss intuitively understood that some of the things that the company was currently engaged in must stop, some new things must start, and other existing activities must be enhanced. The question really became: Which activities belonged in which categories?

VWoA organized itself around core processes that enabled sales and marketing, logistics of vehicle distribution, and after-sales service (see Exhibit 4). These functions would need to be robust as the VW and Audi brands' product variety increased. Plans also called for a continued push to reposition Audi as a tier-one premium brand. Central to the NRG program were a set of ranked high-level business goals, such as "Build Brand

EXHIBIT 2 Potential New Model Introductions, 2003–2007

Source: Company documents.

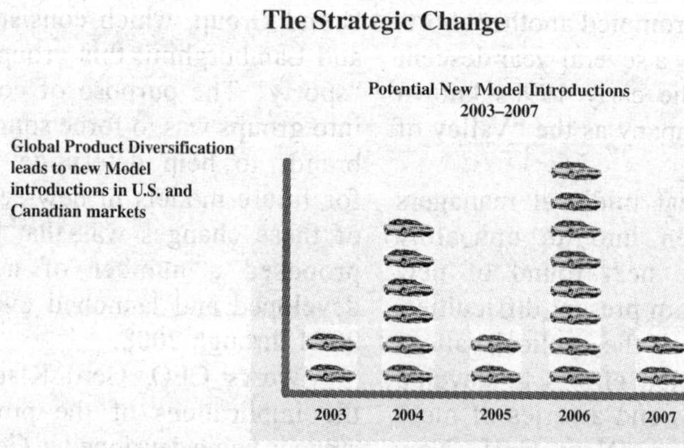

Customer Loyalty" (number one) and "Improve Vehicle Value" (number two). (A list of these goals, with their ranks, is shown in Exhibit 5.)[2]

By 2003, sales had leveled off slightly but at a higher level (though still not at late-1960s levels). Repositioning of brands generated higher margins. The Touareg, the company's foray into the lucrative sport utility vehicle space, had garnered favorable reviews and was poised for market success. New versions of Passat and other models were planned for near-term launch. Overall, prospects for VWoA seemed favorable, despite worldwide auto industry overcapacity, unfavorable currency exchange rates, and high oil prices.

Information Technology at VWoA (1992–2002)

During the 10 years from 1992 through 2002, VWoA executives focused on turning the VW and Audi brands around in the U.S. market. Marketing and selling activities were the funding priority. Information technology was considered a source of overhead to be kept at subsistence levels so that all available funds could be used in the market.

In 1992, in order to reduce short-term IT costs, VWoA entered into a 10-year agreement with Perot Systems, an IT services provider. Perot assumed responsibility for the maintenance, repair, and operation of the IT production environment. After this outsourcing contract was signed, VWoA dramatically reduced its internal IT staff to fewer than 10 people and, in doing so, eliminated much

EXHIBIT 3 Next Round of Growth Enterprise Goal Areas

Source: Company documents.

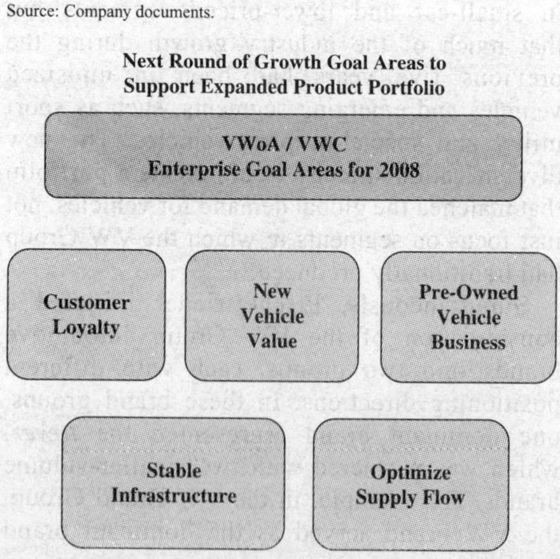

[2] These goal rankings were arrived at in 2002 by a high-level executive group within VWoA.

EXHIBIT 4 VWoA Core Processes and Major Organizational Functions

Source: Company documents.

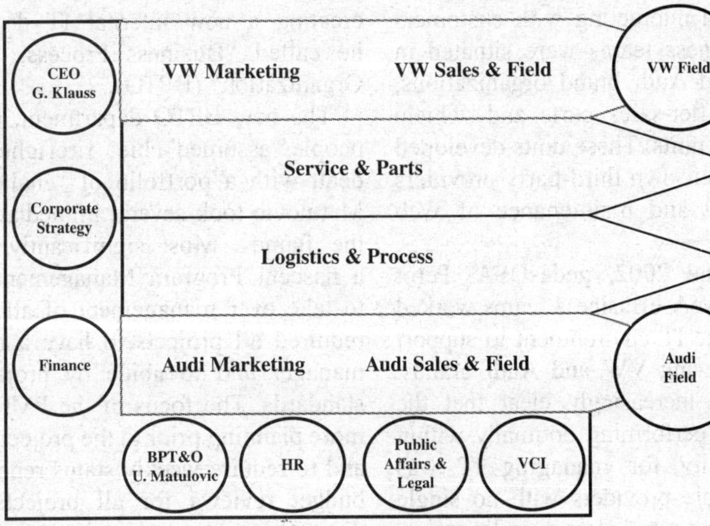

of the knowledge of IT within the company. Over the next few years it became apparent that VWoA had probably cut too deeply. There was insufficient IT knowledge within VWoA even to administer the outsourcing contract. Over the next seven years, VWoA progressively added staff to its internal IT department and built it back to 28 employees.

In 1999, a new Volkswagen Group (VWAG) company was created in the United States, gedasUSA Inc. GedasUSA was the U.S. subsidiary of gedas AG, the consolidator of IT operations within the global Volkswagen group of companies. Although gedas was a wholly owned subsidiary of VWAG, it was established with a mandate to charge external market rates in providing services to other VW-owned companies. GedasUSA assumed responsibility for administering the outsourcing contract with Perot Systems and would assume responsibility for IT operations at the expiration of the Perot contract in 2002. GedasUSA would also undertake development project work for VWoA, using a formal contracting process. To speed the start-up of gedasUSA, all 28 employees of the VWoA internal IT department were transferred to gedasUSA. Again, VWoA was left with no real IT knowledge, having transferred IT capability to gedasUSA. Although the IT knowledge stayed within the VW Group, the arms-length relationship between gedasUSA and VWoA made it appear that the knowledge was barely within VWOA's reach.

During the same period, other organizational entities were also emerging within VWoA and influencing the IT environment. The late 1990s was a period of dramatic growth in the use of the

EXHIBIT 5 Executive's Ranking of Enterprise Goals for VWoA

Source: Company documents.

Enterprise Goal Ranking for Project Prioritization

Enterprise Goal Area	Rank
Customer Loyalty	1
New Vehicle Value	2
Stable Business Infrastructure	3
Pre-Owned Vehicle Business	4
Optimize the Supply Flow	5

Internet to support automotive sales and marketing activities. In 1999, VWoA set up "eBusiness teams" for the purpose of creating digital-marketing assets and interacting with customers in new ways. eBusiness teams were situated in each of the VW and Audi brand organizations, as well as in the after-sales parts and vehicle distribution business units. These units developed relationships with their own third-party providers for the development and maintenance of Web applications.

Between 1999 and 2002, gedasUSA, Perot Systems, and the VWoA eBusiness teams worked together to rebuild the IT environment to support the now rapidly growing VW and Audi brands. However, it became increasingly clear that the IT function was not performing optimally within VWoA. Responsibility for managing IT was shared among multiple providers with no single organizational entity in control of the overall process. Furthermore, the business units within VWoA were increasingly concerned that IT expenses were on the rise and that IT projects seemed to be plagued with schedule and cost overruns.

In 2002, the ELT at VWoA, in conjunction with the global IT organization, decided that a new business unit was required within VWoA, one that could become the single point of governance for all IT issues. That new organization would consolidate the technical elements of the eBusiness teams and act as a point of contact for gedasUSA, which would in turn act as VWoA's lead IT delivery partner. The new internal IT department would be VWoA's third attempt to create such a function in the past decade. It was considered imperative to achieve a stable organizational solution this time. To accomplish this, Matulovic was moved from VWAG headquarters in Wolfsburg, Germany, to the United States to design, establish, and then lead the new organization.

Matulovic was not an information technologist by training or experience. Within VWAG, he had been the leader of process development. Before that he had managed the paint shop in VWAG's largest factory in Wolfsburg. In Matulovic's mind, the major issues at VWoA were not related to technology but rather to the ambiguity that surrounded governance and development processes. Upon his arrival, Matulovic set about creating a new internal IT department, which he called "Business Process, Technology and Organization" (BPTO).

The new BPTO department, composed of 23 people, assumed chief firefighter roles as they dealt with a portfolio of "challenged" projects. Matulovic took several immediate steps to douse the flames. Most significantly, he empowered a nascent Program Management Office (PMO) to take over management of all IT projects and required all projects to have a qualified project manager and to abide by project management standards. The focus of the PMO was to require more planning prior to the project execution phase and to require weekly status reports and monthly budget reviews for all projects. During 2002 these changes were implemented, and gradually, on-schedule and on-budget projects became the norm. Matulovic, satisfied that VWoA had built a capability to do projects right, turned his attention to a different question: Are we doing the right projects?

Choosing the Right Projects to Fund

To implement the NRG program, members of the BPTO and corporate strategy groups at VWoA, in partnership with strategy consultants from gedasUSA, created a high-level business architecture (BA, see Exhibit 6). This architecture explicitly depicted the key resources of the enterprise in an organized way to answer the basic interrogative questions: why, how, who, what, where, and when. It helped strategists understand the relationships among these different elements and included:

- A hierarchical and prioritized view of all major goals (56) across the enterprise
- An enterprisewide function model that displayed all major activities in the corporation
- An enterprisewide information inventory

EXHIBIT 6 **Relationship among Strategy, Business Architecture, and Performance**

Source: Company documents.

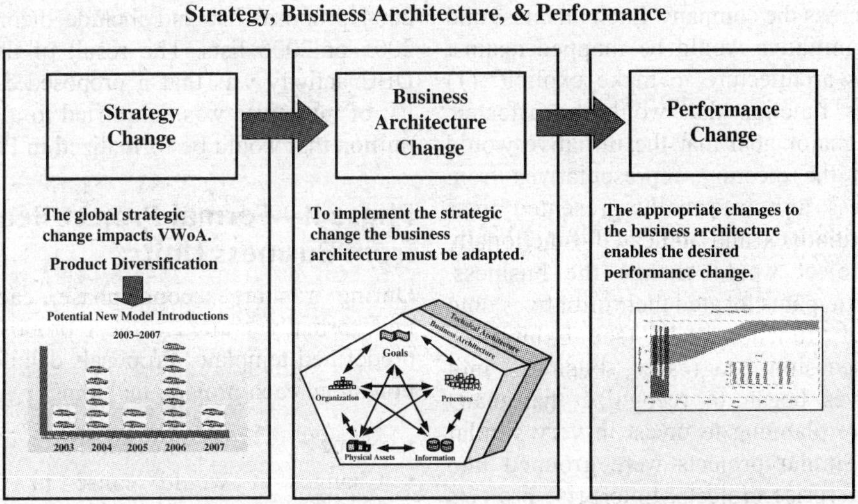

- An organization model mapped to the functions
- A current-state systems inventory mapped to the major functions of the enterprise

The business architecture output was termed a *blueprint* and was expected to play an important role in formalizing governance and prioritization processes because it provided a means of categorizing organizational activity (including IT projects) and relating them in a logical way to the company's strategy and ability to execute strategy.

Several organizational entities would play a role in creating and managing a new process for managing priorities at VWoA. The ELT, of course, had primary responsibility for executing the NRG program, of which the new IT governance processes were a part. An IT steering committee (ITSC), composed of senior business and IT representatives, would guide and approve the process of IT project selection and prioritization. The PMO subsection of BPTO, which had done so much to tame difficulties with out-of-control projects, would administer the IT project-proposal and approval process. The PMO worked with the team that had developed the business architecture to arrive at a detailed process for moving projects through selection and prioritization. And the Digital Business Council (DBC), composed of representatives from the eBusiness teams within each business unit, would do the difficult work—categorizing projects, assessing their business impact, discerning their alignment with goals, and making trade-off decisions—required to reach a final list of projects for which funding was recommended. The entire process was expected to play out in three phases spanning three months, from July through September.

Phase I—Calling for Projects, Communicating Process, and Identifying Dependencies

To start the process, PMO put out a formal call for projects with due dates for proposals. In July, before business unit requests were required to be filed with PMO, the corporate strategy team, working with gedas strategy consultants, facilitated a workshop with members of the DBC. This workshop conveyed to DBC members that project funding would, this year, involve them to a much greater extent and expose them to much more information about proposed initiatives across the company. Each business and technology initiative would be mapped against the business architecture to make explicit: (1) the business function that would be affected, and (2) the major goal that the initiative would advance. At the meeting, representatives from each business unit informally presented their proposed initiatives and indicated functionally how the project would change the business. Meeting participants located their initiatives onto an oversized "function wall" (see Exhibit 7). As the discussion progressed, business unit representatives began to recognize that many of them were planning to invest in very similar initiatives. Similar projects were grouped into common enterprise projects. Enterprise projects were removed from individual business unit lists and added to an enterprise portfolio.

In discussing individual initiatives, the DBC also identified dependencies among projects. It became clear that many projects would affect other projects. Most importantly, some projects could not be started until other projects had been completed. This realization caused business unit representatives to remove initiatives from their 2004 proposal list and include them instead on 2005 or 2006 lists. The result of this phase of DBC activity was that a proposed $210 million list of initiatives was simplified to a list of $170 million that would be formalized in Phase II.

Phase II—Formal Project Requests from Business Units

During a short second phase, each business unit formally crafted project proposals using a predefined template. Proposals detailed information about each project, including:

- Name
- Changes it would cause in the current environment
- A financial model
- The enterprise function that was being improved/affected (as determined in Phase I)
- The enterprise goal that the project would advance

EXHIBIT 7 "Buckets" for Categorizing Project Functionality

Source: Company documents.

Bucket Inititives Based on Functionality

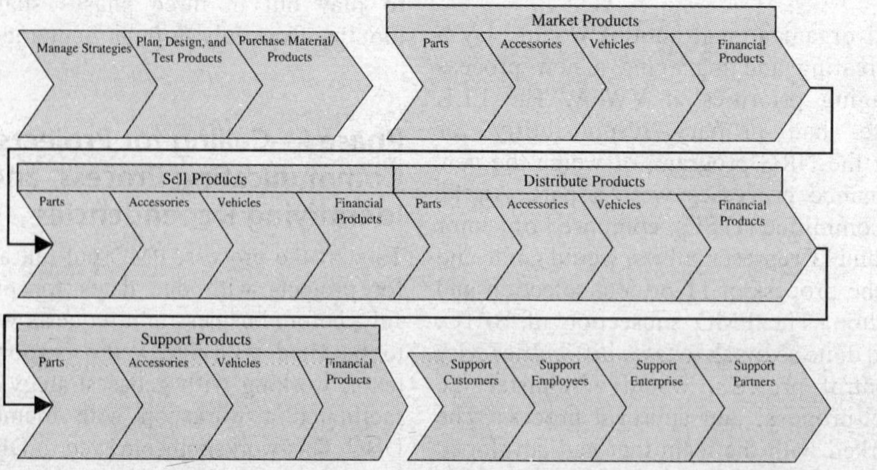

In addition, proposals categorized projects in terms of (1) the type of investment they represented and (2) the type of technological application that would be involved.

Three different investment types were recognized:

Stay in business (SIB)—An action that was required for legislative reasons, to maintain business continuity, or was overtly mandated by the parent organization. Examples of these investments included customer privacy efforts (legislated) or disaster recovery (business continuity).

Return on investment (ROI)—An action that had predictable cost savings, productivity gain, and/or revenue-generating results. This needed to sufficiently exceed the investment, which included the initial setup investments and the ongoing maintenance and operations. For example, you might install a new system because its annual maintenance costs would be 50 percent lower than those of the existing system.

Option-creating investment (OCI)—Similar to ROI, but with less certainty about the cost savings and/or revenue-generating results. These were risky actions taken in anticipation of discovering a new idea or execution that led to a competitive advantage. Frequently, these would be prototypes that, if successful, would evolve into larger implementations that could be justified via ROI criteria.

Three different technological application types were recognized:

Base-enterprise IT platform—Infrastructure services and tools, or common utilities and externally developed applications used across the company (data warehouses, Internet-based communications, desktop productivity tools).

Enterprise applications—Company-specific systems that provided broad functionality across the enterprise or that produced information used throughout the enterprise.

Customized point solutions—Systems and solutions useful in targeted application but not recognized as useful across the enterprise.

The investment and application type would influence how particular investments under consideration would be treated in the selection and prioritization process.

Once proposals were prepared for each project, each business unit's leadership ranked them by priority. Business unit managers assumed that, as in past years, they would at a minimum gain approval for their most highly prioritized projects.

Some business units were uncomfortable, as they associated projects with enterprise goals. The leader of each business unit was an ELT member and thus realized that assigning projects to NRG goals implicitly ranked them in their importance to VWoA. By associating a project with an enterprise goal, they knew they were strengthening or weakening the enterprise-level case for the project. There was a temptation to think of ways to associate projects considered important with a goal important to the company to improve chances of funding.

Initiatives that had been grouped in Phase I as having significant synergies were again called out as potential enterprise projects. They remained in business units' individual portfolios with a special note dictating removal from the business unit portfolio if the enterprise project was approved. Thus, another way to get a project approved was to gain its inclusion in an enterprise project that had a good chance of approval.

Phase III—Transforming Business Unit Requests into Enterprise Goal Portfolios

With all official requests submitted, in September the DBC met for a two-day off-site to convert the emerging business-unit-focused project portfolio into an enterprise-focused portfolio. Prior to the meeting, the corporate strategy and PMO teams used the dependencies and enterprise project groupings from Phase I to create a high-level schedule of all projects. Because many projects depended upon others completing (or starting), many of the 2004 proposed projects clearly could not be started until 2005 or later. Also, some business unit project proposals were officially combined to form enterprise project proposals.

As the overall project list changed due to dependencies and the creation of enterprise projects, DBC representatives reshuffled the projects still on their lists for 2004. Now some of a business unit's most important projects were officially not viable until 2005 or later; others would be considered as corporate projects. So business unit representatives needed to reprioritize their proposals for 2004. The group agreed that each business unit would identify the three most important projects still on the 2004 list. In a flurry of real-time cell phone consultations with business unit managers not on the DBC, each unit arrived, by the end of day one, at a final list of its top three projects.

DBC members returned for a second day to discover their work was far from over. Overnight, the corporate strategy and PMO teams had regrouped the top three picks for each business unit into five goal portfolios, each one corresponding to one of the major enterprise goals from the NRG program (see Exhibit 8). DBC members quickly familiarized themselves with this new representation of the enterprise portfolio and quietly took note of how their business units' submissions related to VWoA goals.

The second day's decision making began with a discussion about the accuracy of the project-to-goal associations proposed by individual business units in their proposal documents. Several projects that had been associated with the most critical NRG goals were reclassified, which dealt a blow to their prospects of being funded. The discussion grew heated. Eventually the team agreed, and the final goal portfolios were determined.

Near the end of the day, the group began to speculate about the amount of the total IT project budget. Of the roughly $60 million available overall, $16 million had been set aside to fund "stay in business" initiatives, most of them infrastructure projects under the discretion of CIO Matulovic; another $30 million would fund enterprise projects, which left about $14 million for the highest-priority business unit projects. These back-of-the-envelope calculations told them immediately that the funding requirements for all the top three projects exceeded the budget. It was not clear how to solve this gap between funding requirements and the budget. They wondered what they should recommend to Matulovic and the ITSC:

- Should they drop the lowest-ranked goal portfolio in its entirety? (If they did this, several business units would not gain approval for any IT projects in 2004.)
- Should they apply an equal percentage of funds to each goal portfolio?
- Should they cut apart each portfolio and fund more projects associated with the most critical goals and fewer projects associated with the less important goals?
- Should they recommend that the importance of business unit priorities be revisited relative to the enterprise priorities from the NRG (perhaps reallocating some enterprise funds to business unit projects)?

Members of the DBC recognized that they had far more information to make this decision than ever before. But the complexity of the surfaced trade-offs was greater also. Without a doubt, this process resulted in a different view of prioritization than simply presenting each business unit's top three initiatives independently (see Exhibit 9 for a summary of the overall process).

Through the lenses of the business architecture and the new process, it appeared that several projects favored by business units did not have sufficient enterprise value to make the funding cut. This outcome seemed to present business unit executives with two options: (1) They could acknowledge that projects from other areas might be more important to achieving enterprise goals, and that the projects they had advocated were not, upon further examination, as important; or (2) they could challenge the merit of the

EXHIBIT 8 Transforming Project Lists into Goal Portfolios

Source: Company documents.

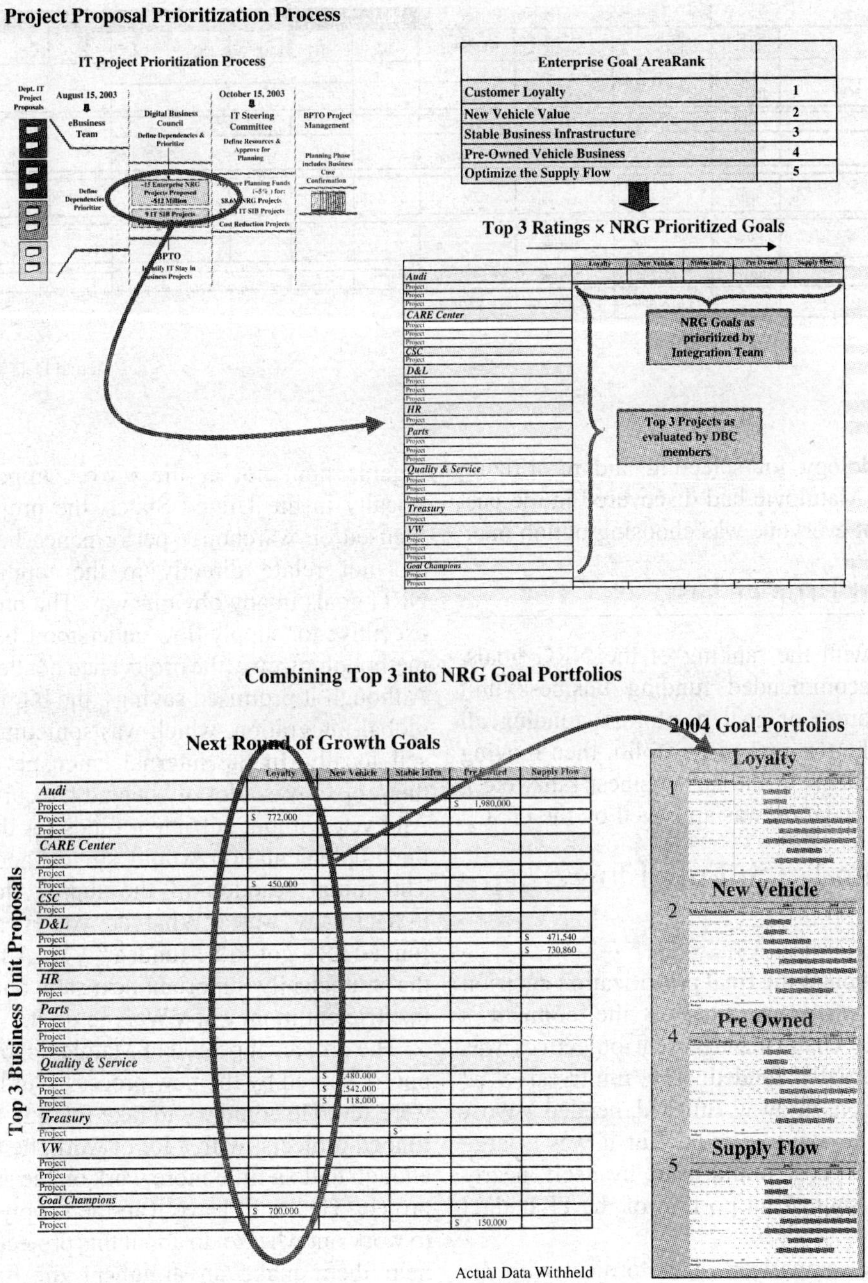

EXHIBIT 8 Transforming Project: Lists into Goal Portfolios (*Continued*)

2004 Customer Loyalty IT Project Portfolio

		2004 Costs ($USD)			2003	2004				2005		
Name	**Submitted By**	**2004 Exp: Business**	**2004 Exp: IT Portion**	**2004 Capital**	**Q3**	**Q1**	**Q2**	**Q3**	**Q4**	**Q1**	**Q2**	**Q3**
Loyalty Project 1	**Audi**	**720,000**	**$0**	**$0**								
Stable Data Infrastructure	*BPTO*	*0*	*420,000*	*0*								
Loyalty Project 2	**Audi**	**223,000**	**704,000**	**264,000**								
Customer Interface Standardization	*BPTO*	*0*	*$250,000*	*50,000*								
Loyalty 3	**VW**	**75,000**	**300,000**	**0**								
Loyalty Project 4	**VW**	**0**	**150,000**	**0**								
Loyalty Project 5	**BPTO**	**300,000**	**150,000**	**0**								
Total		***1,318,000***	***$1,974,000***	***$314,000***								

Actual Data Withheld

new methodology for selecting and prioritizing projects. As Matulovic had discovered in the past few days, not everyone was choosing option one.

The Final Project List

In keeping with the ranking of the NRG goals, the DBC recommended funding business unit projects in order of goal portfolios (funding all projects in the top-ranked portfolio, then moving to the portfolio with the next highest rank, etc.). The recommendation was approved by the ITSC.

The Unfunded Supply Flow Project

One implication of the final prioritization decision was that a project critical to the company's global supply chain management objectives was left only partially funded. The multiyear SAP implementation, midway finished, needed VWoA full funding to stay on track. But it was a large project; its full cost would have, by itself, nearly wiped out a significant portion of the IT budget for 2004.

A cursory comparison of the project with the prioritization process revealed immediately why the project did not get funding. Much of its value would be recognized at the global level of the organization, not at the VWoA importer level. Locally in the United States, the project's value focused on warehouse performance benefits that did not relate directly to the topmost-ranked NRG goals in any obvious way. The business unit executive for supply flow understood, based on the methodology, why the project had not been funded. Although it promised savings, the big impact was global integration, which was sometimes a tough sell locally. In the internal language of VWoA, the project was a lot of "behind the curtain" stuff. And yet, without sufficient funds for this project, the implementation would stretch another year. The initial reaction of the supply flow people in Germany was: "What do you mean it's not funded? It's got to be funded." VWoA had to take the strategically important next step, but there was insufficient money at VWoA to do it.

The project appeared to Matulovic to have been poorly served by the new process. But his options were few. He could try to take funding from other funded projects; with a lot of work, he might find enough to do a little more work on the supply flow project. He could leave it to the supply flow area to work out what to do about this project. He could help them make an argument for funding the project from alternative sources. He could even use this project as a wedge to drive into the new prioritization process and reopen it. Matulovic

EXHIBIT 9 **Summary of Overall Project Prioritization Process**

Source: Company documents.

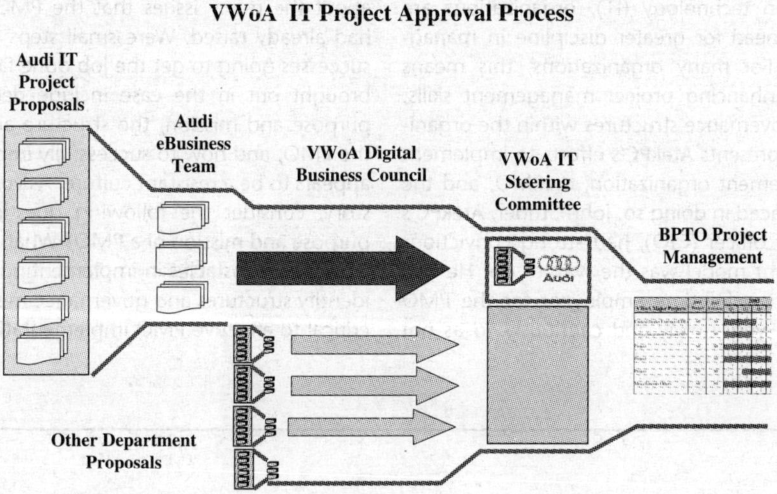

knew the loss of funding would constitute a major setback for globalization initiatives based in Germany.

Matulovic's Decision

Corporate strategy was clear. The difficulty was one of strategy implementation. Most would agree that strategy should drive IT operations, but legacy IT architecture and financial constraints imposed limits on what could be done to enact strategy. Business decisions about IT deployment made in the 1990s, when the company was in survival mode, created a need in the early 2000s for substantial IT investment. But most members of the ELT were either not around during the mid-1990s or had forgotten about decisions to withhold IT investment to support market incentives. Matulovic knew this caused some of his peers to view IT as an expensive item that usually fell short of what they needed from it. From some of the recent phone conversations, he gathered that some also thought this new process amounted to an attempt by the IT department to drive business strategy. It was a difficult situation, as Matulovic observed:

> Setting priorities is one of the hardest things managers do. You try to involve everyone in the process and make it transparent, so that everyone owns the outcomes. But there is always room to second-guess the process, or decisions made in the process. People have a tendency to forget why decisions were made, or that we all agreed on the decision when it was made. What they see is "my project didn't get funded, and this is keeping me from doing my job." IT looks like an obstacle. If there's one thing I'd like to turn around, it's the idea that IT is an obstacle.

The AtekPC Project Management Office

With the ever-increasing challenge of successfully managing information technology (IT), organizations are recognizing the need for greater discipline in managing IT projects. For many organizations, this means establishing or enhancing project management skills, processes, and governance structures within the organization. The case presents AtekPC's efforts to implement a project management organization, or PMO, and the challenges they faced in doing so. John Strider, AtekPC's chief information officer (CIO), had strong convictions that the PMO-light model was the way to go. He had held back on hiring full-time employees for the PMO and was moving very slowly and cautiously so as not to violate AtekPC's culture. He was also concerned about the many issues that the PMO implementation had already raised. Were small steps building on small successes going to get the job done fast enough? Issues brought out in the case include defining the PMO's purpose and mission, the structure and governance of the PMO, and how to successfully implement it in what appears to be a resistant culture. As you read the AtekPC story, consider the following questions: What is the purpose and mission of a PMO? What are the main challenges and obstacles in implementing a PMO? Can you identify structures and governance mechanisms that are critical to effective PMO implementation?

Case 3-3

The AtekPC Project Management Office

A rain had started in the early evening of March 3, 2007, and the streets of Metropolis were cold and grey where the AtekPC headquarters were located. As John Strider, CIO for AtekPC, packed up his briefcase at the end of the day, his thoughts returned to the new Project Management Office (PMO) that he had approved several months ago. During his tenure of over 20 years at AtekPC, Strider had never witnessed the kinds of pressures that were now facing the personal computer (PC) industry. Strider recognized that the industry was in transition and that his information technology (IT) organization would be involved in some critically important projects in the days ahead, as AtekPC sought to take a leadership role in these changes. It was that thought which brought to mind the PMO initiative. If it were implemented right, this PMO could be a big help to AtekPC, but Strider had concerns about what might happen if they tried to push too hard with this idea. Instead of a help, it could become another item on his growing list of problems. There were so many questions on his mind:

> How much PM is enough PM? How much PMO support is enough PMO support? When do you get to the point that the PMO structure and process is enabling productivity and contributes to a more successful outcome with fewer mistakes and a higher quality result—whatever you define success to be at the beginning? And when does PM involvement become administration for its own purposes? When do you cross the line?

Strider thought that he understood what this PMO could do for AtekPC, but the initiative was still in its infancy. It needed time to prove itself. On the one hand, his management team had hired some experienced people with real talent to spearhead the PMO program. On the

Professor F. Warren McFarlan, Professor Mark Keil of Georgia State University, and John Hupp (MSIS 2007) prepared this case as the basis for class discussion rather than to illustrate effective or ineffective management. Certain details have been disguised.

other, they were new to the PC business and to AtekPC. They didn't understand how powerful the culture was here, he thought. As Strider expressed it, the PMO had to become a part of the AtekPC culture, and that required small changes over a long period of time. If the PMO found itself fighting against the culture, it would definitely fail. As CIO, he was keenly aware of the many initiatives and responsibilities that he had to cover with his limited resources, and he knew the PMO was only one of these. He couldn't let things drop just to build up this new PMO. It all had to be done together. Strider knew that his people who were working on the PMO were frustrated that they could not move faster. He, too, was tempted by the thought of rapidly loading up the PMO with more resources and knocking out projects. But in his opinion, that would be a bold and short-lived initiative—too much, too soon, too fast.

Strider closed his briefcase and headed for the elevator. His IT senior management team had been with him many years. He felt confident that he could lead them on the right path without dampening their enthusiasm for this new PMO. But would that be enough? To Strider the payoff was about alignment—aligning strategic business directions with IT resources, and that was the essence of the PMO. There was little margin for mistakes at AtekPC in these changing times.

Industry Background

The PC industry was experiencing tremendous cost pressure and was undergoing a period of consolidation. As profit margins fell, PC makers were launching cost reduction strategies aimed at further improving the efficiency of their supply chains, while lowering the cost of distribution. According to a recent newspaper article:

> The latest financial results for PC makers show a slow down in both sales and profitability. Both corporations and consumers are holding on to their PCs for a longer period of time to avoid the cost and hassles associated with upgrading their equipment. As a result, purchases are being deferred and PC makers are looking at new markets for growth opportunities. The industry appears to be undergoing a wave of consolidation as cost control and scale become more important than ever before.[1]

In 2007, a major news magazine ran a cover article entitled "Whither the PC?" The threats reported in their analysis were worldwide and stemmed from a variety of factors including the growing popularity of mobile phones, PDAs, and Web-based application software.

> For most people, e-mail is the most important application that they use. For a long period of time, sending and receiving e-mail necessitated having a full-fledged PC. Nowadays, though, businesspeople and consumers want to reap the benefit of being able to access e-mail from anywhere, 24-7, without the inconvenience of carrying a notebook computer around with them. Mobile phones and PDAs now provide this functionality, causing many people to question the need for carrying a full-fledged computer. In the boom days of the PC, the market was boundless, but growth has slowed considerably. Moreover, with the growing popularity of Web-based applications, both businesses and consumers are purchasing less expensive machines that can access and run Web-based applications and do not require massive amounts of local processing power or storage. Having ignored reality for years, PC makers are at last doing something. In order to cut costs, they are already streamlining their operations through the use of information technology and looking at new products and new markets to maintain revenue growth and boost profitability.[2]

AtekPC

Founded in 1984, AtekPC had grown to become a mid-sized U.S. PC maker with 2006 sales of $1.9 billion. AtekPC employed 2,100 full-time workers and an additional 200 part-time workers. In spite of rapid growth in the 1990s, AtekPC found itself struggling alongside the world's other PC makers

[1] David Smith, "PC Makers Face Increased Price Competition and Industry Consolidation," *Metropolitan News Journal*, February 17, 2007, p. B7.

[2] "Whither the PC?," *Global News*, March 20, 2007, p. 9.

EXHIBIT 1 AtekPC Information Technology Organizational Chart

Source: AtekPC.

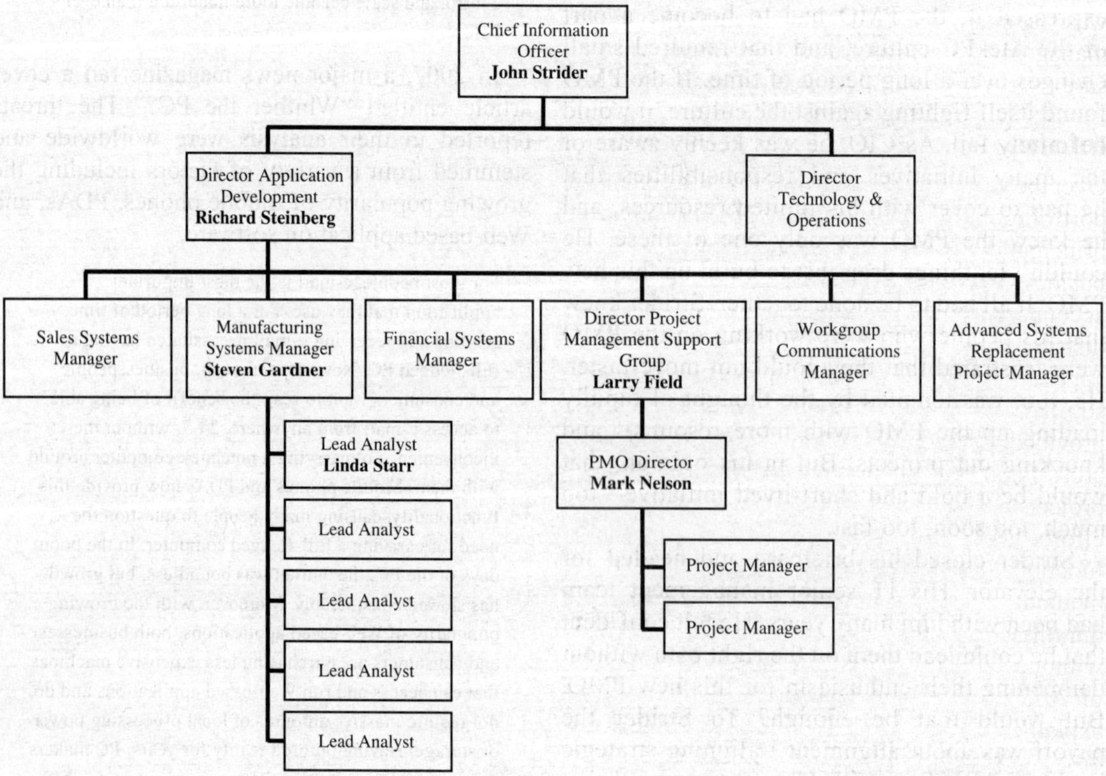

as they grappled with the transition from a growth industry to that of a maturing industry. Strider explained:

> The PC industry has changed and will continue to change at an accelerating pace. At one point, the PC industry enjoyed tremendous growth rates and good profit margins. As a result, we tended not to be as careful as we should have been about controlling costs and dealing with competitive threats. Now, of course, the picture has changed and we are facing increasing competition from Asian PC makers that have transitioned from contract manufacturing to marketing their own branded PCs.
>
> The PC industry is going through some consolidation as larger players acquire smaller players in order to achieve greater scale. So that is the backdrop of our industry today. We have a stronger need than ever before to be aggressive and to move quickly so that we can reduce costs and tap new markets. We need to become a much more agile company so that our capabilities are more consistent with what our name implies. In the future, we are also going to have to be much more savvy in terms of our use of IT, or we will risk either becoming unprofitable or becoming the target of a hostile takeover.

By the fall of 2006, AtekPC had already begun several initiatives aimed at positioning the organization for the future. One of these was the establishment of a Strategic Planning Office whose responsibilities were to propose business changes. Under the auspices of the Strategic Planning Office, the initial PMO effort which was focused on IT projects would one day become an enterprise PMO. AtekPC recognized that they would have to be able to manage projects more efficiently and effectively in order for the proposals of the Planning Office to succeed. By

March 2007, both the Strategic Planning Office and the initial PMO had only been in operation for a few months. According to Strider, AtekPC was facing increasing price competition, and management was under a lot of pressure to make sure every action had a visible payback.

Information Technology at AtekPC

Over the years, AtekPC had developed an extensive portfolio of applications. These applications were principally focused at the operational level for business functions typical of a PC maker, such as accounting, sourcing, manufacturing, sales, and distribution. Architectural integration of these application systems was only moderately achieved, so that, by 2007, functional areas were often provided discrete information services with little cross-functional integration. Information systems projects were typically operational or maintenance efforts undertaken at the request of a particular functional area. They were generally small to medium-sized projects in terms of both size and duration, and they were managed informally without standardized practices. As the director of Application Development, Richard Steinberg explained:

> Historically, we had always just done our own thing. We had a lot of operational projects going on and a lot of enhancements going on, but we had very few enterprise applications going on. . . . Over the years, there were certain people throughout the company that recognized that the quality of the work that we did on projects could be improved. As we began to take a look at what we needed to do in the future, we realized that we had to really hone our skills to be able to move more aggressively and sure-footedly through projects and to be able to handle multiple projects at one time. So I put together a plan for a PMO, essentially a project management methodology for all my areas.

The changing environment that AtekPC faced created a number of challenges which they were planning to address with projects of a large, complex scale. The new PMO was being introduced in order to provide standardization in managing these projects and to gain improvements in the planning and performance of the initiatives. Although AtekPC had undertaken a few large projects in the past that had employed some formal practices, these projects had not resulted in lasting formalization of practices. Steinberg explained:

> You can go back over the years, to Y2K, to the conversion of our order management system; on those major projects they used a project management approach. They didn't realize it. They got everyone together; they talked about what it's going to take to get this done, and they got it done. Everyone handed out awards and said, "That was done well. So now that we're through with that, we've got to get back to doing projects normally." They didn't realize that that is the way to do it. All of a sudden when those major things go away, when that disappears, then you go back to trying to do things out of your back pocket again.

In 2007, IT projects were typically managed by adding PM responsibilities to one of the development staff who were assigned to specific functional areas. For example, the Lead Analyst assigned to Manufacturing would also play the role of project manager. Lead Analysts supervised workgroups of analysts and programmers of varying skill levels, and they were responsible for satisfying the requests of the functional areas as well as the performance of their workgroups. Using an informal project initiation process, users requested IT services through the Lead Analyst who then managed the project with the support of the resources within their workgroup. The manager, in this case the Manufacturing Systems Manager, resolved any issues and conflicts, if needed; otherwise, the request was received, executed, and delivered through the Lead Analyst. Project methods, documentation, practices, and tools were individualized by the Lead Analyst with little or no consistency across IT groups or business areas.

AtekPC had realized many benefits from this informal approach to projects. Lead Analysts often had long tenures in their areas and developed a deep knowledge of the business activities, needs, and people. As a result of their informal approach, they provided rapid response to user requests and were able to address emergent critical needs within their workgroups with few conflicts. Because of this record of responsive delivery, considerable trust was developed between the functional area and their Lead Analyst. The trust-based relationship was highly personalized to the individual employee, and loyalties arose from both sides. The openness of these relationships enabled the Lead Analyst to gather and quickly assess the requirements and to reach consensus on a schedule and delivery date. Linda Star, a Lead Analyst for Manufacturing, described her work in this role:

> In my world I have a variety of users that I talk to. They would say, "I need this." Some would say, "I really need this. Can I get this? This is an emergency, and I have to have it." I would come back, and I would look at what my people are working on and say "I need you to switch gears. I need you to give me two hours, two days, or whatever it takes. We need to get this little piece done.". . . I do a schedule based on what everybody in my group is doing and what I know after talking with them.

This informal approach to project management had traditionally been the norm at AtekPC. Historically, the prevailing view was that IT was peripheral to the core business activities at AtekPC. As a result, IT had been seen as an order-taker, expected to provide service on demand. During the past decade, projects had become increasingly focused on operations and maintenance in an overriding effort to improve efficiencies within the business functions. The development of cross-functional integration systems and the use of Internet technologies were only two of many emerging needs as AtekPC struggled with radical changes in its industry and marketplace. The required new projects were larger, more complex, and they involved multiple functional areas and multiple technological areas, unlike the tightly focused projects that were performed in the past by a single workgroup. The demands of these new initiatives and projects were expected to overtax the current informal project management methods. The AtekPC PMO was being implemented to provide more consistent and better practices for both business and IT projects. However, implementing a PMO at AtekPC was itself a challenge which required skillful management to be successful. A difficult balance had to be maintained, both between maintenance and new development as well as between resources that went into development activities versus resources that went into project management activities under the new PMO. Strider described the challenge:

> We don't have it all figured out. That's better than thinking you do when you don't. In the IT department we have to be better able to manage the conflicts between new business-critical initiatives and operations with incremental changes to existing systems. We cannot sacrifice one for the other. The history is that we've only done operational maintenance, and now we've got to have a culture of doing both.

PMO Mission

The mission of the AtekPC PMO had been gradually evolving since its inception in late 2006. As of Spring 2007, there was not a complete consensus regarding its purpose, its responsibilities, and its authority. While formal documentation and plans for the PMO did not exist, the immediate goal was to establish the office and to prove its value. The general consensus was that the purpose of the PMO was to realize the benefits derived from consistent project practices. Although not clearly specified or measurable at this time, these benefits were expressed in a variety of terms ranging from IT improvements in project performance, efficiency, and resource utilization to enterprise improvements in cost management and corporate capability to launch products. Steinberg explained from the enterprise perspective:

> If I think about the PC industry and its challenges, I think about two things that could be driving for a PMO. One might be cost reduction. We cannot afford to be careless. Frankly, we have to be a lot more cautious about how we use our resources. Another motivation to get better on projects would be that we have to get more creative, adaptive, and agile in launching new products. And in order to launch new products, what would you say is driving those initiatives but project management?

The responsibilities of the PMO were not so clear, however. At present the responsibilities of the PMO were limited to IT projects, although there was ongoing discussion about expanding its scope to an enterprise level PMO that would include business projects in the future. The specific duties of a PMO were typically divided into two categories: project-focused and enterprise-oriented. Project-focused responsibilities such as consulting, mentoring, and training were services that enabled the success of individual projects. On the other hand, enterprise responsibilities addressed services that might improve all projects, such as portfolio management, PM standards, methods, and tools, and project performance archives. Clarification of the responsibilities of the PMO was continuously evolving as AtekPC attempted to gain support and to reach agreement on its mission and charter.

At AtekPC, project-focused responsibilities were the primary means used to prove the merits of their PMO. The plan was to create acceptance by consulting and mentoring on individual projects. Mark Nelson, the new PMO Manager, talked about this effort:

> What I've been doing since October 2006 has been providing mentoring and support for project management with key projects that have been identified by the IT executives. For the immediate future, until we get rolling, the plan is to have me work with a person from a project planning standpoint—regular meetings with the teams, status reporting, maintenance issues, and managing risks.

To that end, the PMO continued to build support from the functional areas and IT personnel involved in these projects. One of the major limitations was the shortage of PMO expert resources available to support these projects; in addition to Nelson, there were three other project managers assigned to the PMO and these were contract employees. Using PMO staff to directly manage projects was done infrequently. However, Nelson had assigned one of his project managers to a critical project involving the launch of a new notebook computer.

Enterprise-oriented responsibilities for the new PMO were slow to develop at AtekPC. The new PMO had been developing some standard project processes and procedures. Steven Gardner, Manufacturing Systems Manager, commented on a project chartering process that the PMO had introduced:

> Nelson helped us develop what we call an "idea form" where we try to eliminate a lot of random calls that are coming to us. We are trying to better prioritize what we work on, and using this "idea form" leads us toward building a business understanding of whatever the idea is that comes along. This forces some thinking up front on our side but also on the requester's side. It helps them think through about usage and all. Why are we going to get savings here? What's the reason for doing this? Is it worth doing this project at the expense of another one? Now, how do I prioritize it? So it is helping us get our arms around the things that we're working on.

The enterprise-focused services developed by Nelson's PMO team were being well received. While progress in this area was constrained by the limited PMO resources, there was a clear agreement even at the CIO level that the PMO was responsible for establishing, publishing, and disseminating project practices, standards, and tools. On the other hand, portfolio management (the change from managing one-off projects to the establishment of techniques for managing continuous streams of projects) and archiving responsibilities (the establishment of archival records of projects for knowledge sharing) were not being addressed. Nelson hoped to be able to include those duties in the PMO's mission as it developed but, without additional resources, this was not achievable in the short term. He also realized that additional resources could only come by taking them from other critical responsibilities, and this might compromise their ability to maintain operational effectiveness. It was a tough balance.

The final area of concern with respect to the mission of the PMO was the issue of authority. Strider recognized that enforcement of these new project practices required formal authority, and he was prepared to provide that only when the PMO had proven itself to the business and IT. For the early development efforts, Nelson was working under the benefit of an implied authority that came from a general awareness of changing management directions. However, the PMO also had the support of the senior vice-president. Mid-level managers who'd witnessed a meandering PMO trying to find its feet could attest to the

EXHIBIT 2 AtekPC "Idea Form"

Source: AtekPC.

IDEA DEVELOPMENT FORM

Section A. *(Requestor completes this section)*	**Project Name:**
Requestor Name: **Date Request Submitted:** **System Name** (if known): **Date needed by:**	
Section B. *(Reviewer completes this section)* Idea Reviewer: Date Reviewed: Project ID:	☐ Approved ☐ Not Approved - Reason for non-approval:

Section C. **Work Type** *(Reviewer completes this section)*

☐ **Enhancement** ☐ **Emergency** ☐ **Fix**

Section D. *(Requestor completes this section)*

1. Provide a Description *(What is it?)*:

2. Why should we do this? *(Explain the business value and select the appropriate benefit type)* Explanation:

Benefit Type *(more than one type can apply)* ***Estimate if possible***

- ☐ Creates Revenue — Estimated annual revenue: ______
- ☐ Cost Avoidance — Estimated cost avoidance: ______
- ☐ Cost Savings — Estimated annual savings: ______
- ☐ Operational Reliability
- ☐ Customer Service Enhancement
- ☐ Quality Improvement

3. Scope *(Describe what it includes and excludes.)*
•

4. Deliverables *(Report changes, new screen, data entry, etc.)*
•

5. Impacted Departments / Customers
•

6. Assumptions
•

7. Related projects
•

8. Risk/Impact of not doing project
•

significance of such high-level affirmation. Larry Field, director of the Project Management Support Group, was a key member of the PMO initiative from its beginning, and he explained: "For us to be effective, we have to have support from the top. And we have that support from the senior vice-president through John Strider and on down. That is the first and most critical thing to make this work."

However, because not all of the senior executives were equally enthused about the PMO concept, authority was primarily being developed bottom-up through the value of the PMO services. Even this was limited to those functional areas and IT areas actively engaging the PMO. There was no current plan to enforce usage at the enterprise level. Nelson summed up this approach with these remarks:

> The big thing is the mentoring that is going on and actually managing the projects. We are being patient right now so that we can get some good concrete examples that we can show them. We can say "look what this is doing

> for you. This project that would have taken a year and a half before, we're doing in three or four months now because we have put these practices in place." And that's the key because it lets us show our worth. That has to be the approach for now.

PMO Organization

Two organizational models were under consideration for the PMO. These were referred to as PMO-heavy and PMO-light, and represented two ends of a spectrum of PMO organizational approaches. At the one extreme, PMO-heavy was characterized by a full staff of project managers who assumed responsibility for the management of all IT projects. This model focused on the acquisition of project management experts, either from internal or external sources, and used these resources to manage projects under the direction of the PMO. In the extreme version of PMO-heavy, no project would operate outside the management and direct control of the PMO. At the other end of the spectrum, PMO-light was characterized by a minimal staff of experts who worked through internal project managers to perform the responsibilities of the PMO. This model focused on the development of the skills of internal project managers who were not formally connected with the PMO. In the extreme version of PMO-light, all projects operated outside of the PMO under existing organizational controls, and the ownership of projects resided within the functional area and IT group charged with execution of the project. The issue of where the PMO should be situated along the spectrum from PMO-heavy to PMO-light was generating a lot of discussion and little agreement. Strider spoke about this controversy:

> Right now, it's four people full-time. . . . Given the speed with which we as a company want to move—we as an industry need to move—I think four permanent people is too small. I see these people assigned to major projects to assist, but the diversity of application is too broad. I don't see all of the management moving into this group. There's kind of a difference of opinion between me and the PMO at this point about that. We're going to have to find some middle ground, . . . I'm fairly convinced it should be light. That doesn't mean I don't question it, because there are a lot of people in this department that are constantly challenging me on that. Which is fine, I mean, I don't ever need a bunch of "yes-men" around.

While Nelson was agreeable to working with a small team at the start, he felt that the delays from this approach might compromise their ability to provide PMO services and to demonstrate its worth to the functional areas of the business. However, he and the other managers recognized that resources were not free, and they had to come from someplace, which meant reducing the capabilities of someone else's work to advance his own. Strider struggled with this challenge, and the current four PMO resources were acquired at the expense of other operational teams. Even as Nelson was working within these limitations, he was hoping to get more help. As he explained:

> If I had no constraints I would like to be able to bring on the team of people consisting of project analysts, as well as managers, very quickly. Bring in a group of people up front. Most of them could be new to get started. Then as you go on, you could pull in from the rest of the organization. They would all be part of the PMO. So we would have varying degrees of experience ranging from senior PM's to people who were junior. We could achieve a lot by just taking this one step.

Steinberg was concerned about the resources required and how the functional areas might perceive adding more people at this time. He explained: "What is the implication of a sponsor in Sales trying to initiate a project that gets approval from the PMO? They don't literally understand what the PMO is. They think it's sort of a road block and an obstacle to progress—a bureaucratic thing."

Steinberg's concern about how people might view the PMO was shared by Strider. Although Strider was convinced that the PMO was the right way to go for AtekPC, he knew that he also had to ensure that IT kept its balance and got the work done. As Strider explained:

> Now, if you add people, where do you add them? The fact that you can add them at all is a breakthrough. Do you add them in this PMO, or do you add them somewhere else? . . . The question is how you get to go where you

need to go, but not violate the culture so much that you cause a big red flag. . . . Because the PMO cannot get the project done. They're not going to write code; they're not going to install servers; they're not going to meet with users who understand functional requirements; they're not going to meet with customers.

On the front lines, Star was getting some information through the grapevine about this new PMO, and she tried to make sense of what she was hearing so that she would be ready to adapt to any new changes. She was certainly hoping for more help, especially with what she viewed as the *administrative things* on a project. As a Lead Analyst, she had dealt with many of the problems of project management, and she was keenly aware of the opportunity that the PMO created for her. She looked forward to learning to be more effective as a project manager, but she wasn't quite certain what was really happening. She described her understanding of the PMO:

> I thought it would be a great idea because I thought at the time that this was going to be a group that was going to head up different projects, and they would be the lead project manager. And then we would be their team. I was assuming that what would happen is that I would still be the person in charge—the lead—for that project, for my group that was working. But I would be, in essence, reporting to this project manager who had the skills and the knowledge and the training and the tools to help us go forward. This was because my background in project management is my own self-created processes and tools that I've made myself in order to create and do the analysis and keeping track and all that. So I thought, they're coming in with all these tools, and eventually they'll be teaching us; and eventually we will be project managers that can stand on our own.

Star's manager, Gardner had the expectation that the PMO model would be more heavy than light. He was already convinced of the merits of the PMO from his group's use of the "idea form" to capture new project requests. In his understanding, the PMO would provide a project manager resource pool. He spoke about his view of the organizational model:

> They are moving from just helping us with methodology types of things to managing projects. . . . They are thinking of a pool of project managers. You might have one such project, and you could borrow that one person for a while. And your project would report to them. I think it's the understanding that they have project managers to which you assign the various projects throughout the department. For instance, we're using one now for this new launch project in addition to the projects we have now. She is starting to take over the role of planning the timeline, scheduling, getting the right folks on board, and making sure everybody's informed—the typical project manager type tasks. . . . As far as project management goes, the project is her responsibility. It's her job.

In Gardner's view, he would maintain control of the project, and for its duration the assigned project manager from the PMO staff would follow his directions. Resources would be assigned in a matrix structure for the duration of the project. This was what Gardner was doing with the current PMO project manager who was assigned to one of his projects, and in Gardner's opinion, this was a big help because he had too few people and a large stack of projects to get done. Gardner was expecting the PMO to furnish his group with project managers in a manner similar to a PMO-heavy.

On the other hand, Field recognized that the problem of PMO structure was not only about IT staffing:

> The problem with a PMO-heavy isn't just bringing on the project managers and analysts. It's also the business resources. Today, we have line managers who are working on multiple projects in addition to their regular jobs, and they can't take on any more. What really drives a lot of the projects in any company is the availability of the business resources to work on those projects. Having the business resources available is already becoming a problem for us. With a PMO-light we are lined up better with the business side in terms of the number of resources, and it's a better balance.

Nelson favored PMO-heavy as the best model for AtekPC, but he recognized that he would not be able to gain acceptance immediately for this approach. The demand for resources was great throughout AtekPC, and the PMO would need to prove itself in order to earn the resources he wanted. He intended to build support for the PMO-heavy model through project successes.

As the PMO gained acceptance, he wanted to implement a PMO-heavy approach, furnishing project managers to the various groups. As he said:

> I don't think there's enough education about project management to know the difference between PMO-light and PMO-heavy. There have been organizational structures that have been discussed . . . But because of the overall change that the company is going through, they are not ready to make any type of decision . . . With these processes and procedures that we're developing we'll establish project planning, tracking, initiation, and closure. All the project managers will help get the IT house in order.

As AtekPC sought to find the right organizational model, the PMO team worked to deliver the services that were slowly building their credibility and proving their value to AtekPC. Finding the right place for the PMO along the spectrum between heavy and light organizational models was an ongoing source of tension that would have to be relieved sooner or later. With more resources, Nelson believed that his team could provide more support faster and move more rapidly ahead with critical projects and standards. On the other hand, Strider reminded Nelson that the PMO was but one of many responsibilities within AtekPC's IT organization. There were other needs for resources, with their own justifications and paybacks. Thus, the issue of PMO heavy versus PMO light was not a simple or easy decision.

Implementation and Culture

AtekPC found itself in a particularly challenging situation as it tried to implement standard methods in an organization that was unaccustomed to consistent, disciplined processes and standardization. IT management realized that in the future they would depend on standards and consistent processes to manage their projects and drive them forward. Nonetheless, implementing a PMO in a non-PM environment was challenging because it went against the grain of the organizational culture. Many people within AtekPC viewed project management as just administrative overhead—something that would inevitably get in the way of doing "real work." Field described the cultural challenge facing the new PMO:

> We are moving from a company that had really no formal project management to a company that would like to be very formal. We are going to be somewhere in the middle. We can't be so rigid about project management. This culture is not going to let us do that. You have to mix the culture in with the methods and the processes. If we go too rigid, it will fail. We have to be a little fluid and dynamic at times, and that upsets some PMO folks, but we have to do it that way here. To succeed we have to develop an organization that will be flexible and will be accurate in its reporting. So that's my struggle—having project management fit into a culture that is changing but is not quite over here yet.

The forces opposing the PMO seemed overwhelming at times to those involved. Strider wondered how willing the IT organization itself was toward changing their processes and adapting to new project management practices. This was a key cultural issue in his mind. Many of the staff, including managers, had little or no experience with formal project management practices. Very few knew how to use any of the software tools available, such as Microsoft Project. In addition to these knowledge barriers, the informality of the current practices was seen as highly attractive by many. The functional areas enjoyed working with IT people who were responsive to their needs and made things happen quickly. The IT staff also found the informality appealing since there was no cost tracking nor were any performance records kept on the projects. The functional areas were not accountable for measuring the benefits resulting from their projects, and the IT project staff was not working within an assigned project budget. Another source of resistance was the lack of understanding, at all levels, of the value of formal project management. Altogether these sources of resistance to a PMO created formidable cultural barriers to its success, which management and the PMO team had to address.

Strider understood many of these cultural barriers and recognized that he would have to find ways of working through them if the PMO were to survive. In a recent discussion around his office table, he had summed up the situation: "My opinion is that I have two choices. I can conform to the culture and survive; or I can fight the culture and fail . . . You can only swim up stream so far and so long, regardless of how good and smart you are. But, if you fight the culture at every turn, you will lose."

For now, the PMO implementation strategy at AtekPC was to work within the culture and to develop forces that would promote the PMO and overcome cultural resistance. Promotional forces included the mentoring, coaching, and training that were being provided by the PMO team. The company was clearly under pressure to change the way it did business, but there was no consensus among senior management concerning the degree to which the PMO was integral to the change process. In Strider's opinion, it was too soon to apply formal authority without evidence of value and without more widespread support for the PMO concept. He believed that more buy-in was needed from the functional areas first. One of the chief cultural issues in his mind was how quickly the functional areas (i.e., the customers of IT) would be willing to adapt to a more formal process. They would have to be willing to prioritize projects and make the tough choices and trade-offs. In some cases, in order to move a project forward, they would have to be willing to help justify additional resources.

Nelson was working to create buy-in from the functional areas by using his team to provide mentoring and direct project management for key projects. He recognized that this implementation strategy was slow work and required considerable patience. For him, the struggle was about creating and delivering proven success. He expressed the challenge as he saw it:

> I can't call it bottom up (his implementation approach) because we got approval at the top for us to come in. But it's like it is almost at the top but not quite there . . . It's viewed as bureaucratic, or it's viewed as having the potential of being bureaucratic. And that's because of the industry itself and its time frame—get the products out, get the orders in. One of the things we've heard from the top is "just don't let this project management and process management slow things down. These are all great things, and we want to see them work; but don't let them get in my way."

As director of Applications Development, Steinberg was one of the early sponsors of the PMO, and he saw some progress in breaking through these cultural barriers. When Steinberg first came to AtekPC, he was given the task of implementing a standard software development methodology. That early methodology effort failed, in his opinion, because the culture was not right for a disciplined approach. Now, he was fully supporting this PMO effort, and he brought to it a deep understanding of the AtekPC culture and its challenges. In his view, only by working with business groups, one at a time, could he get their buy-in to the PMO. He explained his approach:

> The selling of the PMO outside of IT is an issue. As hard as I've tried to push this to get some visibility outside of this department, I've not been able to get any official visibility. What happened is that we began to get our PM people involved in projects and sent them down to the users involved in it. Manufacturing was one of the first areas. The person who is the spokesperson for the IT project in Manufacturing said, "What is this PMO going to do?" When we told her all about it she jumped on it. The same thing happened in Sales.
>
> It's not so well received in certain groups, but fortunately it is in some areas . . . Manufacturing is on board, and Sales is starting to come on board. But I'm not sure that the other functional areas are totally on board with this concept yet.

With some functional areas in support, the PMO team continued their implementation efforts. As Nelson remarked, their advancement to date had been in "*baby steps*." The frustration of such tedious progress tempted them to consider an alternative approach—force the change with top-down mandates and hired experts. Several managers, including those directly involved with the PMO, recognized the need for a larger staff of experts to build standards and methods quickly, and they advocated a rapid, more resource intensive implementation strategy. Such an approach would allow the PMO to prove its value by actively managing more projects and helping AtekPC to achieve better and more consistent project performance. IT management was concerned that such an approach would fail because they couldn't force radical change on AtekPC. Thus, the senior IT managers encouraged a slow, incremental strategy that would allow the PMO concept to prove itself with small victories won through mentoring one project at a time.

Governance

The issue of PMO governance was not widely discussed, but already of some importance. At present, there were no roadmaps or timelines for its maturation, so there was no way to measure PMO performance other than through the subjective opinions of those involved. There was a sense that AtekPC would know whether the PMO was working if the projects were getting done and the company was getting what it needed. Field acknowledged that there were few measures in place for projects or the PMO. He explained:

> How do we measure ourselves? How does a project organization measure success? One of the worries has been will project management, because of its bureaucracy, slow things down. There is still some worry about that. We are trying to say that we will actually speed things up and get things done quicker with less rework. So how do we measure ourselves to say that we are succeeding? We haven't really put those metrics together yet.

Determining how to prove the PMO's value was a major challenge for Nelson: "Proving its value is the only way it's going to work. And this is going to be tough because there hasn't been any collection of data before. But even if it is anecdotal, we can show them that . . . we have to be able to show progress."

Given this approach to measuring PMO performance through subjective consensus and anecdotal data, the next governance issue was figuring out to whom the PMO was accountable. For the moment, it reported to Steinberg as director of Applications Development which, in his opinion, was because of his experience with methodologies and standards. He explained some of the current governance options:

> It currently reports to me in application development, but I really think it should be elsewhere . . . The key is that I've been tapped as the person to get it started. I think at some point down the road, it more correctly should report somewhere else—if not the CIO, somewhere else in the organization . . . I think there's a possibility it could report either to the senior vice-president, or if we institute this new Planning Office, then maybe in the Planning Office.

Strider recognized that the current governance model was only temporary, and explained his views:

> The only reason we can get a PMO established is because there is a Planning Office for the company, and the senior vice-president is committed to a more planned, rigorous, project management approach. I could not drive this internally within IT unless I had that support . . . Right now, it reports to the head of Application Development. Steinberg and I have talked that over time, probably, the PMO will report to me directly. But frankly, I just don't have time right now . . .There's also the Planning Office that doesn't report to me but to the senior vice-president, and that's a possibility.

Understanding this close interaction between the new Planning Office and the PMO, Steinberg shared his overriding concern about it remaining within IT.

> I think as long as it remains an element, a division apart within IT, there will still be this 'us-them' kind of a thing, and the feeling that we're in there to get our way, and it's our axe to grind, and it's to make us look better . . . We've done some work with group applications, and they've been successful. People want more of them. So my hope is that we will have enough breathing room here to get started with the PMO and to show the benefit of it. That will sell it to other areas and allow it to continue to live.

Deciding How Best to Move Forward

The PC industry was changing, and AtekPC was dealing with dramatic pressure from larger competitors such as HP, Dell, and Lenovo. To compete in a changing industry in which consolidation was occurring, AtekPC had implemented a corporate Planning Office. Recognizing the role that IT would likely play in enabling AtekPC to respond to the industry pressures, the senior vice-president had supported the creation of a PMO within IT. The role of the PMO might be expanded to include non-IT projects if it proved to be successful. At the same time, there was a possibility that the PMO might fail due to the challenge of implementing such a measured and disciplined approach to projects in an environment where that was viewed as foreign to the culture. After all, AtekPC was an organization that was used to people rushing around doing whatever it took to build and ship products each and every day.

The PMO implementation had already raised several issues, some of which had proven too controversial to resolve immediately. AtekPC was therefore feeling its way along with the PMO effort. As they tried to hammer out agreement on basic PMO issues, everyone in the IT organization was acutely aware of the challenges they faced and the risk associated with failure. Projects were piling up quickly. Success would depend entirely on their decisions and their efforts, and that was a cause for worry to each of them.

The traffic was at a standstill as Strider drove along the interstate trying to get out of Metropolis and home to his family that evening. It gave him time to reflect again about the PMO. He had guided his management team to this implementation strategy. He had strong convictions that the PMO-light model was the way to go. He had held back on hiring more full-time employees for the PMO. He was concerned about the many issues that the PMO implementation had already raised. Were small steps building on small successes going to get the job done fast enough? He thought to himself as he waited for the traffic to move: "How can I get where we need to go without violating the culture so much that it causes a big red flag? . . . I feel that I've got to do it the way I'm doing it, rather than load up a big PMO and say, 'Here's my PMO.'"

Concluding Thoughts

Prediction is hard, especially of the future.

Yogi Berra, Hall of Fame baseball player and manager

In 1943, Thomas Watson, the venerable chairman of the IBM Corporation, predicted that there would be a world market for "maybe five computers." Today there are hundreds of millions of computers worldwide. The magnitude of error in this "expert's" forecast stands as a reminder that it is difficult to see far into the future. A quick glance backward reinforces the point. In 1992, there were no Web browsers. Before 1995 Amazon.com was but a glimmer in Jeff Bezos's eye. Much has changed very quickly, and nothing has happened to suggest that the IT industry is on the verge of slowing down its pace of evolution and change. There is surely more excitement ahead.

The objective of this book has been to provide its readers with a better understanding of the influence of twenty-first century technologies on executive decisions. While this kind of understanding may help sharpen predictions, our aim has not been to arm you for prediction's sake alone. Instead, we have focused on providing analytic frameworks, and an overview of the issues involved in using those frameworks, to identify opportunities, design and deploy new technology-based businesses, and create business value. These frameworks are based on concepts and theory that have withstood the test of time and remain relevant despite radical changes in the business and technology environment. We have dealt with enduring practical questions from the point of view of the executives who are grappling with them. Not long ago, many predicted the death of traditional economic and management principles. The subsequent fall in technology market stocks suggests that we should not be too quick to throw out fundamental management principles, even as we embrace the new.

Markets and models, capabilities and organization, networked infrastructure and operations, and leadership of the IT organization are core subject areas that can be used to organize the management issues discussed in this book.

As we have demonstrated, the effect of new technologies on markets and industries will be to alter competitive positions and frame new strategic imperatives requiring new capabilities. The new technologies have enabled new business models and improved the viability of old ones; executives in established firms that do not seize the opportunities presented by new technologies will find their market positions threatened.

New networked infrastructures interweave complex business-technical issues that general managers dread, but which ultimately make the difference between a rigid and constraining IT capability and a flexible and dynamic one. These infrastructures involve varying technologies, relationships, and risk management processes.

Finally, there are the challenges of executing technology-based strategic initiatives, an area that many companies cannot seem to master. The projects grow larger and harder, decisions must be made ever more quickly, and leadership and governance issues abound. Most executives express concern that this relentless pace of change is occurring much too fast to enable them (and their organizations) to learn. Yet this is an area that must be mastered if disasters are to be averted and returns from IT investments are to be realized.

We conclude this book with an integrative case that enables an analysis of issues discussed throughout the book. As you review this final case, consider the many opportunities and challenges that confronted these executives and the approaches they used to address them. Return to the questions we asked during the introduction to the book and identify insights you have gained on how to address those questions.

1. How important is IT to our success and survival? Are we missing opportunities that, if properly executed, would enable us to transform our company or industry?
2. Are we prioritizing IT investments and targeting our development efforts in the right areas? Are we spending money efficiently and effectively?
3. Are our IT and business leaders capable of defining and executing IT-enabled strategies? Have we opened an effective dialogue among business executives, IT executives, users, and partners?
4. Does our IT platform enable our business to be both lean and agile? What percentage of our IT-related activities are devoted to operating and maintaining "legacy" applications versus enabling business growth and strategy execution?
5. Are we managing IT assets and infrastructure efficiently and effectively? Is leadership of IT activities appropriately delegated? Do we have the right business and IT leaders, given our goals for its use?
6. Are we organized to identify, evaluate, and assimilate IT-enabled business innovations? Are we missing windows of opportunity to exploit emerging technologies and business models?
7. Is our IT infrastructure sufficiently insulated against the risks of a major operational disaster? Are the appropriate security, privacy, and risk management systems in place to ensure "always on" and "always up" service?

Case C-1

The ITC eChoupal Initiative

On the Challenge of Inclusive Growth

It is now universally acknowledged that no long-term economic growth agenda for India can be feasible without including in its fold the agricultural sector, which is home to 72 percent of the population and 60 percent of the nation's workforce. The challenge lies in sustaining high rates of economic growth with equity over many years in order to convert the world's largest pool of economically disadvantaged people into viable consumers, thereby translating development into economic freedom.

On ITC's Purpose

ITC consciously exercises the strategic choice of contributing to and securing the competitiveness of the entire value chain of which it is a part. This philosophy has shaped the vision for your company, the vision I have referred to in earlier years as "A Commitment Beyond the Market." Creative use of information technology through the eChoupal initiative has enabled your company to bring together diverse agencies, each with specialized competencies, in a bid to empower the Indian farmer.

Excerpts from speech by Chairman Shri Y. C. Deveshwar, ITC Annual General Meeting, 2003

Choupal: A Time-Honored Tradition

The village of Dahod appeared to be an unlikely setting for a technological revolution. Located 25 kilometers south of Bhopal in India's central state of Madhya Pradesh, Dahod was dominated by soybean farmers who made their living as their ancestors did, harvesting their crop and selling it in the local market yard. Kamal Chand Jain was one such soybean farmer. Jain had spent 40 years cultivating a reputation as a trustworthy unofficial leader in this quiet community of 3,000 people. He lived in a simple concrete home that opened onto a dusty crossroads, providing both a physical and social center to the village. For years, his fellow villagers had gathered in the cool cement front room of Jain's home on their way in from the fields or a trip to town to chat, gossip, or share stories and news from the day. This evening gathering was a traditional staple of Indian farm life, not only in Bhopal but all over Madhya Pradesh. In Hindi, the word for this meeting place was *choupal*. The *choupal* constituted an informal assembly, a forum that villagers could call their own, a place where knowledge could be shared and captured.

Meanwhile, in the corporate offices of ITC Limited's International Business Division (IBD) in Hyderabad, Chief Executive S. Sivakumar pondered the *choupal* concept. IBD was the agricultural commodities export division of ITC, and, by March 1999, it was clear that it was lagging behind the other divisions of the company. In 1998, IBD had grossed Rs. 450 crore[1] ($100 million) in agricultural commodities sales, a marginal addition to the total Rs. 7701 crore ($2 billion) in sales generated by ITC's other divisions, which included tobacco, paperboard, retail, hospitality, and foods, among others.

The soybean and its derivatives comprised two-thirds of ITC's agricultural export business.[2] ITC sourced soybeans from farmers

Professor David M. Upton and Research Associate Virginia A. Fuller prepared this case as the basis for class discussion rather than to illustrate effective or ineffective management.

[1] One crore equals 10 million and one lakh equals 100,000. Case uses exchange rate of 1USD=45.23INR (2003).

[2] Soybeans represent IBD's oil seeds, grains, and pulses (OGP) group and comprise approximately 65 percent of the company's gross agricultural exports. IBD's other product groups include coffee and spices, seafood, and value-added horticultural products.

located throughout rural Madhya Pradesh. Madhya Pradesh (MP) had been dubbed India's "soyabowl," as its farmers contributed 4 million of India's 5 million tons of soybean crop. ITC had had a 100-year relationship with farmers (based originally on the tobacco industry)[3] that gave it an integrated presence along the entire value chain, from procuring soybeans from farmers and processing the beans in exclusively hired processing plants, to exporting the processed soymeal via vessel loads and container shipments. When soybeans were processed, about 80 percent of the crushed bean was turned into soymeal, a high-protein extract that was added to poultry and cattle feed. ITC exported soymeal to countries such as China, Pakistan, Bangladesh, and the United Arab Emirates, as well as other parts of Southeast Asia.[4] The remaining 20 percent of the soybean material became edible oil, highly valued for its nutritional content and a very popular cooking medium in the domestic market.

ITC had been successful in selling soybean oil domestically and processed soymeal internationally, but both the input and output sides of the agricultural supply chain in India were still far from efficient. The limited technological resources in India had constrained the dissemination of know-how in rural farming communities. Farmers did not have access to quality inputs, such as sowing seeds, herbicides, and pesticides, or information, such as accurate weather reports, that would help them improve their crop quality as well as the process of bringing it to market. They did not reap financial benefits from any profits made off the valuable soybean-derived materials. In fact, farmers were losing 60–70 percent of the potential value of their crop, with agricultural yields only a third to a quarter of global standards. Similarly, on the output side, middlemen clogged the supply chain, reducing profit margins for both farmers and buyers such as ITC. Unfair practices affected the way the farmers were paid, the weighing of the produce, and the amount of time taken by the process. This drastically increased transaction costs, slashing potential profits for the farmer.

Both farmers and soybean processors were locked in an unproductive cycle. Farmers had limited capacity for risk and therefore tended to minimize their investment in crops, lest inclement weather or pests destroy their investment. This, however, meant a lower-value crop, which translated into slim margins for both the processor and the farmer. With such risk aversion, farmers were also loath to experiment with new farming methods. Since this meant that few new sources of value were found, the cycle continued unabated.

A Seed Is Planted

In March 1999, Sivakumar was challenged by ITC Chairman Y. C. Deveshwar to generate a new business plan for the International Business Division that would bring it up to speed, both in ITC's realm as well as in the global commodities exporting market. But Sivakumar knew that a host of factors—fragmented farms, overdependence on monsoons, and lack of sophisticated inputs and farming practices—undermined the competitiveness of Indian agriculture and, in turn, ITC.

Noting that many of the challenges for both ITC and farmers arose from the ineffective supply chain for agricultural goods, Sivakumar pondered Deveshwar's credo: "What can we do to secure the competitiveness of the entire value chain, so that this business achieves its full potential? On the other hand, how could a small business think of investing large sums towards such a goal?" he thought. Deveshwar suggested exploring the digital technologies that were changing so many of the companies around them. Sivakumar began to rethink the soybean supply chain. He studied the farmers' villages

[3] See www.itcportal.com for more information about ITC Limited.

[4] www.itcibd.com/feedhis.asp.

and market yards to identify pieces of the supply chain that could be improved, so that IBD might reach its goal of Rs. 2,000 crore ($442.6 million) in revenue by the year 2005.

Stunted Growth: From Field to Factory

Farmers in Madhya Pradesh made their living in much the same style as their predecessors 50 years earlier. The process of getting crops to market began with farmers harvesting the soybeans and loading them onto tractors and bullock carts. Farms varied in size from under five acres for a small farmer to greater than 12 acres for a large farmer.[5] An average farmer, with about nine acres of farmland, could expect an annual net income of approximately Rs. 20,000 ($443) from soybeans and wheat together.[6] After the harvest, farmers hauled their loads of produce 30–50 kilometers to the closest *mandi*[7] and then waited for the crop to be auctioned. The auction began when a government-appointed bidder valued the produce and set the initial bid. From here, government-licensed buyers called commission agents (CAs) bid upwards until the crop was sold.

ITC contracted with a specific CA in each *mandi* to bid on behalf of the company. Prices were authorized by ITC's office in Bhopal, MP. Here ITC employed a team of traders who followed the global market. Although the CA knew what price ITC would pay, nothing prevented him from buying from the farmer at a much lower price, selling to ITC at market price, and pocketing the difference.

Once a CA won an auction, the farmer brought his tractor to that CA's shop in the *mandi* and waited for the produce to be weighed on a manually operated balance scale that accommodated only small increments of the lot. The actual weight of the crop was often manipulated at this point because of the inaccuracy of the crude beam scales. For example, if the farmer brought 20 quintals[8] of loose soybeans to the *mandi*, he could expect to lose about 10 kilograms total during the transactions, or 0.5 percent of his original lot. This translated to a loss of about 100 Rs. ($2.22) per lot. After the weighing process, the product was bagged and the farmer was paid. According to the law, CAs were supposed to pay the farmer immediately, but, in smaller *mandis*,[9] farmers were often paid after an unofficial credit period. The CA would simply tell the farmer to return after a few days for the money.

On any given day, at least 1,000 farmers[10] could be found trying to file into the market to sell their produce. Some had to wait for two or three days just to get into the crowded marketplace. Once inside the *mandi*, the farmer was faced with further challenges of the chaos and pressure that characterized the market yard. The Bhopal *mandi*, hosting an average of 1,700 farmers a day and the sole destination for farmers in Dahod, was a dusty yard with a perimeter of booths belonging to the various CAs. It teemed with adolescent boys who ran through the crowd, kicking up dust and eating beans off the farmers' carts. Laughing, joking men loitered and watched the auctioneers.

Farmers suffered as a result of the time it took to sell produce in the *mandi*, for they were dependent on timely cash flow for subsistence. Thus, when harvest time arrived, they all descended upon the *mandi* at once. The crop had to go to market immediately, and, more importantly, it had to be sold. Farmers were stuck in the position of not being able to turn down a CA's offer; in many

[5] For comparison, the average American farm is about 450 acres.

[6] Farmers typically raised more than one type of crop to take advantage of the varying seasons. The soybean season, for example, was from June to September. From October to May, most soybean farmers grew wheat.

[7] Hindi word meaning market yard. Madhya Pradesh had 308 *mandis*, 175 of which were soybean dominated.

[8] A quintal = 100 kilograms. Twenty quintals (two metric tons) was a typical lot size.

[9] Containing two to three commission agents. Larger *mandis* contained 25–30 CAs.

[10] More than 4,000 per day visit larger *mandis*, 1,500 visit medium-size *mandis*, and 1,000 visit smaller *mandis*.

cases it had taken him all day to reach the *mandi* from his village, and to return with a full cart of unsold produce would be a waste of time and money. Farmers rarely had access to adequate storage facilities in which to hold the crop if it was not sold. If a farmer were able to store the soybeans, and sell before or after harvest, without the time pressures associated with a perishable product,[11] he would have more leverage over their value. This was impossible, however, under the prevailing system where the farmer did not have other options.

Once a transaction had taken place, the CA brought the produce to an ITC processing facility. There, ITC paid him for the cost of the soybeans. This was effectively a reimbursement, since the CA had paid the farmer in the *mandi* from his own resources at the time of the sale.

The farmers' isolation from one another and lack of telecommunications meant they had no way of knowing ahead of time what price would be offered the day they arrived at the *mandi* other than word of mouth. As a result, price discovery occurred only at the end of their growing and selling process.

The Seed Is Cultivated

In May 1999, Sivakumar anchored a brainstorming session of the ITC management team in Patancheru, near Hyderabad. The team knew that, in order to reduce costs and inefficiencies incurred along the current supply chain, the "village A → *mandi* B → factory C" cycle had to be broken. Deveshwar's idea of digital technologies came in handy. Indeed, the team worked to develop a business model that incorporated "e" into the age-old tradition of village *choupals* to facilitate a reorganization of the channel. Sivakumar believed that the team had to work with the cultural infrastructure that had evolved in the villages rather than owning or controlling the entire value chain from top to bottom.

[11] Soybeans would perish if allowed to get wet after harvest; thus, ill-timed rains could ruin a stockpiled product.

Knowledge shared and captured in the traditional *choupal* could be extraordinarily useful to farmers, but it had traditionally been limited to verbal communication. In the absence of telecommunications, and even electricity in some places, news from the closest city could take days to reach an outlying farming village. The uncertainty surrounding cash flow prevented the farmers from creating a sound financial base; instead, they had become locked into subsistence living. As D. V. R. Kumar, manager of trading in ITC's Bhopal office, said:

> "We know we can't predict the market, and no one expects to, but some guidance would certainly serve the farmers well. Under the 'old' system, they remained completely in the dark, with no reference points for pricing other than word-of-mouth reports of yesterday's numbers."

Sivakumar and his team knew that the price trends of soybeans and their derivative products could be forecasted. Prices of Indian soybeans generally followed the agriculture futures market on the Chicago Board of Trade and the Kuala Lumpur Commodity Exchange.

Given the volatility of the spot market, and the fact that the value of agricultural commodities was based on largely uncontrollable factors such as weather, disease, and pest infestation, farmers needed to be aware of market activity. They needed to understand their product in its global context, so that they could plan their activities with more confidence.

The eChoupal

At the May 1999 meeting, Sivakumar and his team conceived ITC's eChoupal initiative. The eChoupal was based on the knowledge sharing found in the traditional *choupal* model, but took the concept one step further. ITC supplied a computer kit to each village with the following components:

1. A PC with a Windows/Intel platform, multimedia kit, and connectivity interface
2. Connection lines, either telephone (with bit rate between 28.8 and 36 Kbps) or, more

EXHIBIT 1 www.soyachoupal.com Welcome Page

Source: Company Web site.

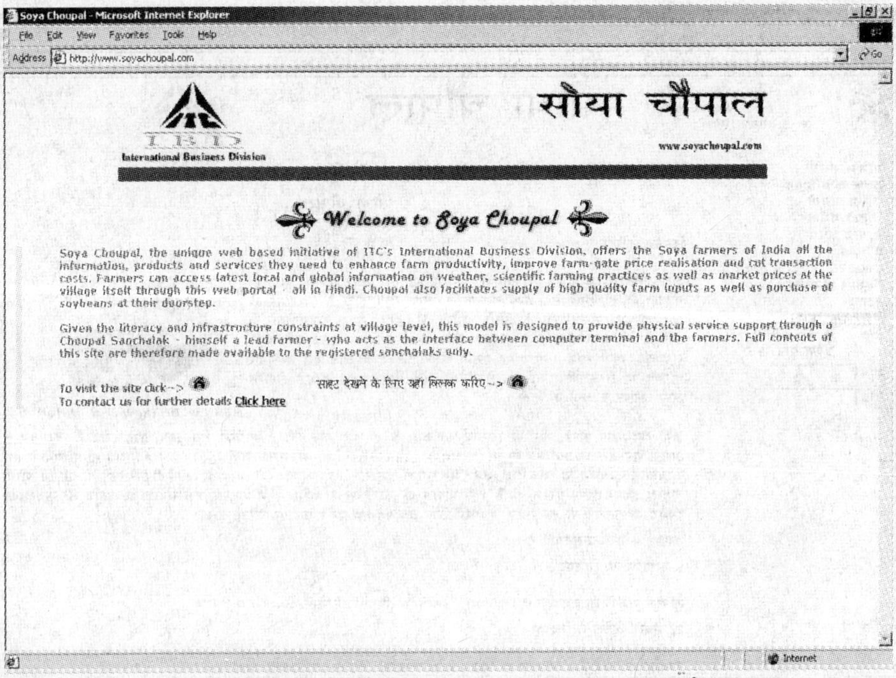

A first-time visitor to www.soyachoupal.com finds this page. Farmers are invited to enter the site via the link (written in Hindi) in the center of the page.

commonly, VSAT[12] (in 75 percent of eChoupals; average 2003 usage 64 Kbps inbound, 1 Mbps outbound)

3. A power supply consisting of UPS[13] and solar-powered battery backup
4. A dot-matrix printer

The total setup cost to ITC was Rs. 170,000 ($3,762) per *choupal*. Another Rs. 100,000 ($2,213) was spent on people, travel, communication, software, and training.[14] With the arrival of these components, nightly *choupals* at the home of Kamal Chand Jain were no longer limited to stories and gossip of the village. Farmers were instead accessing the World Wide Web through a site dedicated specifically to them, ITC's www.soyachoupal.com.

This Web site was updated by the ITC Bhopal office (see Exhibit 1). The data uplink (which provided the source information for the site), however, took place in Bangalore, home of ITC

[12] Very Small Aperture Terminal. Traditionally, VSATs had a few disadvantages; VSAT bandwidth was not very high and restricted to a few hundrend Kbps. There was also a certain amount of latency (the time between initiating a request for data and the beginning of the actual data transfer) between nodes. But these limitations have been overcome to a large extent due to advancement in technology. VSAT providers in India offered up to 52.5 Mbps outroute (from hub to VSAT) and 307.2 Kbps inroute (from VSAT to hub) data rates, with 270 millisecond latency (Network Magazine India).

[13] Uninterruptible power supply.

[14] The company believed it would be able to recover the cost and make a profit within three years of the initial eChoupal rollout.

EXHIBIT 2 Screenshot of Farmer Sign-In Page

Source: Company Web site.

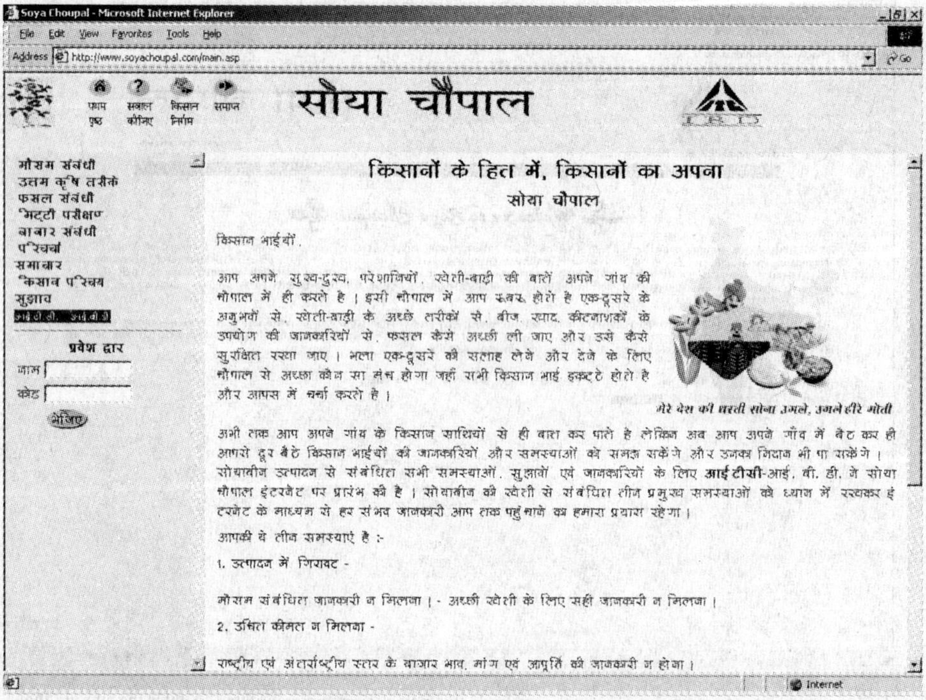

This page invites farmers into the community of the eChoupal, though the Sanchalak must first type in his assigned user name and password (left column). The links on the left address the following categories:

- Districtwide weather information for Madhya Pradesh
- Best practices for soybean farming
- Districtwide crop information for Madhya Pradesh
- Market information
- FAQs
- News
- Feedback
- Company information

Infotech India Ltd., ITC's own information technology subsidiary responsible for developing the software. The site contained much useful information that was previously unavailable to farmers in Madhya Pradesh.

The site opened up by welcoming farmers into the "community" of the eChoupal (see Exhibit 2). On the left side of the screen, there were eight links to the areas of key information that comprised the eChoupal: weather, best practices, crop information, market information, FAQs, news, feedback, and information about ITC. The feature set had been developed progressively with full involvement of the farmers using the system.

EXHIBIT 3 **Screenshot of Weather Page**

Source: Company Web site.

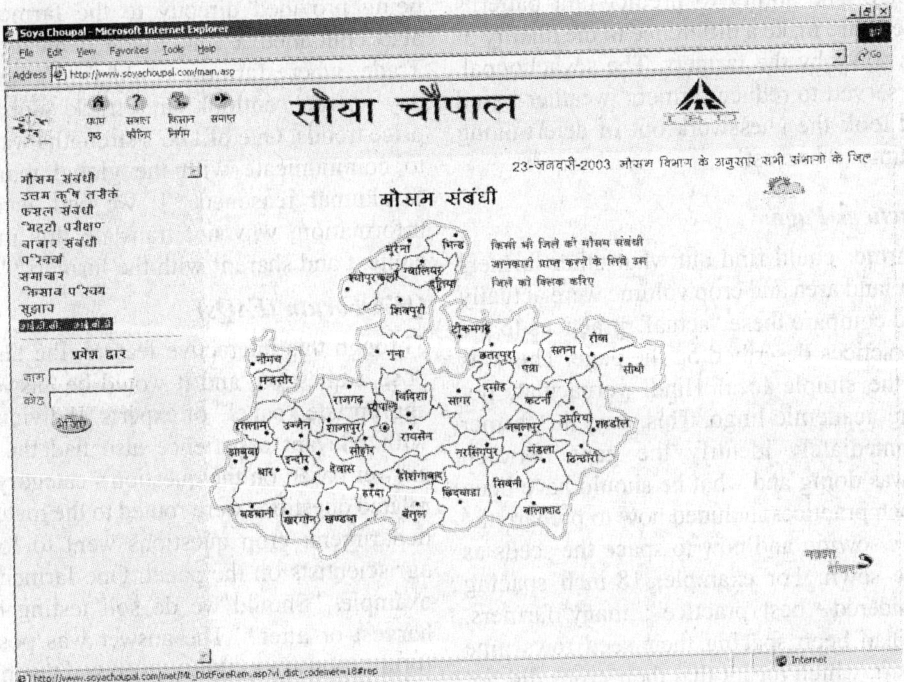

This page features a map of the districts of Madhya Pradesh. Each district is "clickable," and leads the Sanchalak to his localized weather forecast. The day's general weather forecast for the state runs as a marquee along the top of the screen.

Weather Page

India had no private weather service; the government was the only provider of weather information. Before the eChoupal, weather forecasts were rarely communicated to the remote villages of the rural farmers. When they did reach the villages, they were too generalized and did not accurately cover the 30.75 million hectares of Madhya Pradesh. Farmers needed to know their regional weather in order to accurately expect the rains. ITC negotiated with the Indian Meteorological Department, the national weather service, to get localized forecasts for district pockets of 70–80 square kilometers within MP. The result was that, on the soyachoupal weather page, a farmer could click on his home district to see his localized forecast (see Exhibit 3). This knowledge made a lot of difference in the timing of various farm operations such as the application of herbicides and fertilizers.

Furthermore, the difference between harvesting before or after a big rainfall drastically affected the quality of the crop. Ill-timed rains reduced the value of a soybean crop irrespective of the amount of money that was put into it at sowing time. "Farmer A," for example, might spend 8,000 Rs. ($177)/hectare on inputs in the hopes of getting 15,000 Rs. ($332) in return. Similarly, "Farmer B" could put in 5,000 Rs. ($110)/hectare and get about 10,000 Rs. ($221) in return. Poor rains, however, would reduce the value of both A's and B's crops to a 6,000 Rs. (US$ 133) return. Without reasonable knowledge of weather trends, there was reduced incentive for a farmer to spend additional money to produce a higher-quality crop from higher-quality seed. Without an accurate weather forecast, farmers tended to err on the side of frugality. The ability to predict rain patterns would therefore make a difference to the quality of soybeans sown by the farmers. The soyachoupal.com site served to reduce farmers' weather-based risks and took the guesswork out of determining the best time to harvest.

Best Practices Page

Here a farmer could find out what other farmers of similar land area and crop volume were actually doing and compare these "actual" practices to the "ideal" practices described on the page. This was done in the simple local Hindi vernacular, not in obscure academic lingo. This way, the farmer could immediately identify the gaps between what he was doing and what he should have been doing. Such practices included how to prepare the soil before sowing and how to space the seeds as they were sown. For example, 18-inch spacing was considered "best practice"; many farmers, however, had been spacing their seed rows nine inches apart, which meant that their crops did not receive proper ventilation or light. Such conditions led to an undernourished crop.

Crop Information Page

This section contained instructional material such as "How to take a good soil sample" and information as to why soil testing was required. It also provided suggestions for further actions to be taken based on soil-test results.

Market Information

Four links on this page (see Exhibit 4) gave the farmer the options of exploring world demand, world production, *mandi* trading volume, and *mandi* price lists. This way the farmer became involved in the context of his livelihood. He was given knowledge about the *mandi*: the prices (lows and highs), as well as the number of bags that had arrived at the *mandi* to date, and the estimated daily arrivals (usually about 40,000 tons/day in the peak season). The farmer could thus assess the demand for his produce at a particular *mandi*.

This information used to be available only from research institutions or corporations. Now it was being provided directly to the farmer. The site also contained a link to the Chicago Board of Trade, where farmers could find a seven-to-ten-day market outlook and track global soybean price trends. One of ITC's strengths was its ability to communicate with the global markets daily. Sivakumar reasoned, "If we had access to this information, why not translate this into another context and share it with the farmers?"

Q+A Forum (FAQs)

Through this interactive feature, the farmer could pose a question, and it would be answered by an appropriate "panel" of experts. Individual farmers with relevant experience also had the chance to answer based on the question's category. Weather-related questions were routed to the meteorological department; crop questions went to four or five agriscientists on the panel. One farmer asked, for example, "Should we do soil testing before soy harvest or after?" The answer was posted to the forum soon after: "You can do soil testing any time but preferably before the rains." (And to find out when the rains were due, the farmer could check the weather page on the soyachoupal site.)

Another farmer wanted to know why the U.S. soybean crop was "so big" in the world. The answer was a photograph of an American soybean field, with special notation on how much space was provided between plants. This way, farmers in India could compare their methods with those of other countries.

The questions from all of the currently operating eChoupals were stored in a central database so farmers in other locations would be able to access and use the information. The computer's storage ability presented a significant advantage over television or radio, both of which had been considered as other options for this kind of knowledge dissemination.

News Page

This contained excerpts of relevant news items, such as the government's decisions on subsidies or minimum support prices (MSPs), and innovations

EXHIBIT 4 Screenshot of Market Information Page

Source: Company Web site.

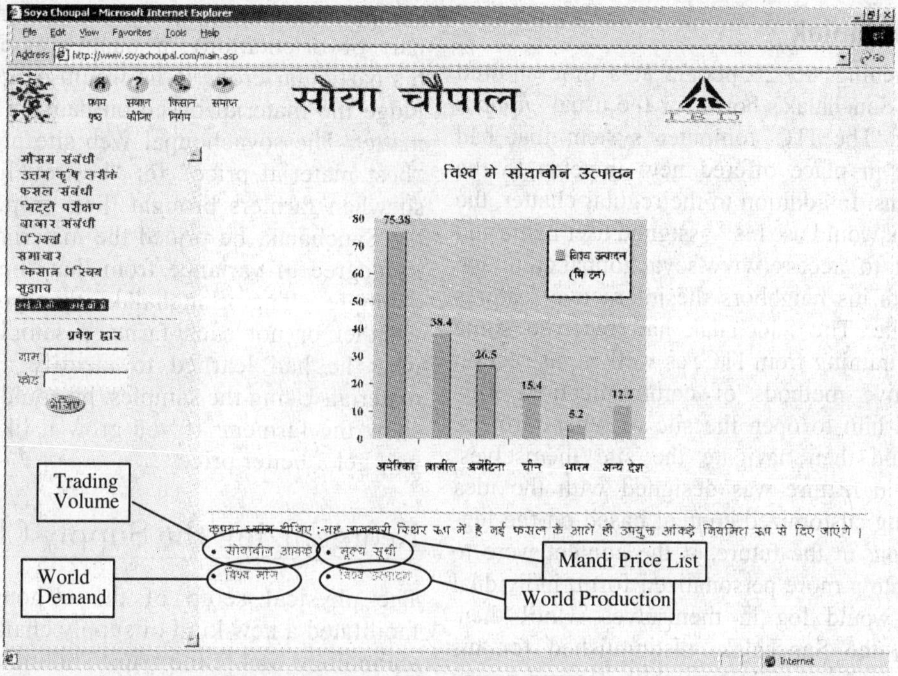

This page shows world soybean production in metric tons. From left to right, the countries' volumes listed are the United States (75.38 mt), Brazil (38.4 mt), Argentina (26.5 mt), China (15.4 mt), India (5.2 mt), and other countries (12.2 mt).

Below the graph are links to other pages on the site related to the soybean market.

in other countries' farming systems. If a farmer did something that was particularly successful or innovative, that was posted to the news section as well. This recognition provided incentive for the farmers, who would otherwise not have the chance to be heard, to try new things.

Lastly, www.soyachoupal.com had a place for suggestions. One of the advantages of the system was that the soyachoupal.com site could be continually tailored to the needs of the farmers. ITC had relied on farmers' input since the start of the project, and, in an effort to keep the site's content dynamic and relevant, it was important that the farmers could continue to be involved in its improvement.

The eChoupal served different purposes over the changing seasons. At harvest time, for example, farmers were more concerned about prices; at sowing time they were more concerned about weather forecasts.

The eChoupal initiative was based on the belief that the farmer needed an alternative to the *mandi* system. By participating in the eChoupal network, farmers were offered new channels through which they could sell directly to ITC, thus eliminating the cost inflation and cheating that occurred through the middlemen. ITC selected a lead farmer in the village to become the caretaker of this equipment and a liaison between ITC and the farmers. This lead farmer, designated *Sanchalak*, was ideally someone like Kamal Chand Jain, someone who was well-known in the village and whose home had already been a natural *choupal* platform for years. The Sanchalak had to be someone whom people felt comfortable visiting and someone who, in turn, welcomed such gatherings in his or her home.

The Sanchalak

In the evening, 15–20 people at a time showed up at the Sanchalak's home for the usual *choupal* gathering. The ITC computer system that had been put in place offered new impetus to the discussions. In addition to the regular chatter, the Sanchalak would use his[15] assigned user name and password to access www.soyachoupal.com and share with his neighbors the interactive features of the site. The Sanchalak had received some basic IT training from ITC, as well as instruction in effective methods of communication. This qualified him to open the site to other farmers, who could then navigate the site themselves. The log-in feature was designed with the idea of offering customized content based on the log-in location; in the future, if the content were to evolve into a more personalized form, individual farmers would log in themselves. Until then, however, the Sanchalak, distinguished for his literacy and communication skills, served as the liaison between ITC and the farmers.

Weather forecasts and *mandi* transactions were printed out and posted on a notice board in the Sanchalak's house. This way, the Sanchalak did not need to open the Web site with the arrival of every visitor. Farmers could stop in and read the printed information at any time throughout the day. If a farmer was unable to read, he only had to ask the Sanchalak's advice. It was in the Sanchalak's best interest to advise the farmer *correctly*, for better-quality produce from each farmer would fetch a higher price from ITC, and this meant a greater commission for the Sanchalak as well as supporting his reputation as an honest broker.

Farmers brought samples of their soybean crop to the Sanchalak's home, where he was equipped by ITC with moisture meters and other tools used to assess the quality of the beans. The company provided "control samples" with which the Sanchalak could perform a quality comparison. Each Sanchalak was trained (as part of orientation) in quality assessment of his particular crop, so he would be qualified to judge the material based on damage or foreign matter. The soyachoupal Web site provided the "best material price" for "best-quality" beans, so when farmers brought their crop sample to the Sanchalak, he priced the material based on its degree of variance from that "best-quality" example. The Sanchalak then determined whether or not each farmer's sample matched what he had learned to identify as the best material. Using the samples, he could physically show the farmers: If you grow it like *this*, you will get a better price.

[15] While most Sanchalaks were men, there were also women who had taken on the role.

Reorganizing the Supply Chain

The physical setup of the eChoupal kiosks facilitated a new kind of supply chain, of which technology was at the crux. Trading outside the *mandi*, for example, was very difficult before the eChoupal. First, the *mandi* provided the only means for price discovery, and farmers reasonably assumed they would fare best in open auction. Second, transactions outside the *mandi* were officially prohibited by the Agricultural Produce Marketing Act. The government had confined agricultural transactions to the *mandis* to protect the farmers from exploitation by unscrupulous buyers. Open auctions were considered the best safeguard against this. At the conception of the eChoupal, however, ITC was able to convince the government of the potential benefits to the farmers and the economy, and the government amended the act to legalize purchases of beans (and other agricultural commodities) outside the *mandi*. The transparency of the eChoupal—the fact that the Web site was accessible to anyone, including the government, to cross-check ITC's prices at any time—facilitated the government's acceptance of the initiative.

The Web technology brought price discovery to the village level. This changed the way farmers did business. First, empowered with the knowledge of what price he would get at an ITC hub, as well as the reports on prices at nearby *mandis*, the farmer was able to make an informed decision about where to go to sell his beans. This knowledge was important, given the costs associated with traveling to the *mandi* with the beans. By learning about prices in the village itself, the farmer could determine how his revenue would compare to the cost of transportation. If he felt he could get a better deal at the *mandi* through the open auction process, he could choose to go there. But given the uncertainty of the *mandi* versus the set published prices offered by ITC's hubs, in addition to the perk of being reimbursed for transport cost, farmers began regularly defecting from the *mandis* and choosing ITC.

Second, by following the real-time prices on the Web site, the farmers could decide *when* to sell. Knowing the price in advance meant that the farmer could go to an ITC hub (assuming he was happy with ITC's price) on his own schedule, even if there were no other reasonable bids on the beans at the *mandi*.

A third feature distinguishing the eChoupal was its transparency. It is arguable that prices could be communicated to farmers by other means, such as telephone or radio broadcast. These methods, however, still relied upon spoken word. The ability to actually see prices being offered, in writing, on the computer screen (in spite of the illiteracy of some of the farmers), was instrumental in establishing the trustworthiness that made the eChoupal effective. The Web model was also more scalable, since one kiosk could be used by hundreds of farmers.

Without price discovery via the Web portal in the villages, selling to ITC hubs directly might be little different than going to the *mandi*. In fact, the *mandi* might be more attractive because the farmers would have the opportunity to sell in an open auction. But with the eChoupal, the farmer was able to make his own informed choice. ITC worked to make its hubs attractive destinations for farmers. In addition to competitive pricing, the hubs contained multiple amenities that were not available to farmers in the *mandis*.

The ITC Hubs

ITC had five processing units in Madhya Pradesh and 39 warehouses, making a total of 44 points to which a farmer could bring his soybeans. This compared to 51 large soybean-based *mandis* in the state. The farmers traveled an average of 20 kilometers to reach a hub, the range being five to 30 kilometers. ITC had 1,695 eChoupals in MP, covering 8,400 villages and reaching 80 percent of soybean- and wheat-growing areas in the state. The physical architecture of the eChoupal model called for a Web kiosk within walking distance (less than five kilometers) and a hub within driving distance (less than 30 kilometers) of every targeted farmer. To make sure this was fulfilled, ITC added three processing hubs and 36 warehouses in MP after the eChoupal project got under way. The distance between farms and hubs was about the same as what a farmer would travel to get to a *mandi*.

Once the farmer arrived at one of ITC's hubs, his beans were weighed on a computerized weighbridge, and the weight was multiplied by ITC's published price. The farmer then received cash on delivery. ITC maintained enough cash in a secure kiosk at the processing plant so that the farmer was fairly and immediately paid. In addition, the farmer was reimbursed for the cost incurred transporting his material to the factory. Depending on how far the farmer had traveled, ITC repaid him based on fixed freight-cost parameters, and that sum was added to the payment for the produce.

Simple amenities at the ITC processing plant made the experience considerably more pleasant than at the *mandi* alternative. After the soybeans had been weighed, a tented seating area provided the farmer with a shaded spot for him to sit and await payment. Restroom facilities were available. None of these existed at the traditional *mandi*. In addition, there were 15-liter jugs of soybean oil available for purchase. ITC made a point of saying, "This is your oil; this was made from your beans." When the farmer bought soybean oil directly from ITC, he skipped four or five people in *that* supply chain, keeping his own purchasing costs to a minimum. The oil was pure and unadulterated because it came directly from the ITC factory.

As an added convenience, the processing facility included a soil-testing lab on the premises, where scientists offered recommendations for fertilizers or additives based on the chemical composition of the farmer's sample. This took three days, while the alternative—going to a government lab—would take longer. Scientists employed by ITC made recommendations on the nutrient dosages that the soil needed based on its properties. They did not recommend any specific brand of fertilizer; they just gave the farmer the soil properties, and then the farmer could choose his own brand of fertilizer based on his soil composition. Freedom of choice was an important principle of the eChoupal concept. Trading manager Kumar said,

> Visiting the eChoupal is not an extra job; this is part of [the farmer's] routine. Their routine is their agriculture. Before, if they wanted information, they had to go to town and ask somebody. Now, we are bringing the information into the village, into the home. It's natural for them.

For his involvement in the ITC procurement process, ITC paid the Sanchalak a 0.5 percent commission on the sale of soybeans. He was, after all, effectively doing ITC's buying—buying that would otherwise have taken place at the *mandi*. The eChoupal system effectively turned the Sanchalak into an entrepreneur, for he also had the opportunity to earn a 2–3 percent commission on orders placed for input items, such as herbicides, sowing seeds, and fertilizers, provided through ITC. Instant-glow gas lanterns and edible oil were also popular sells. With the help of commission from edible soybean oil sales, Dahod Sanchalak Jain earned about Rs. 35,000 ($775) over the three to four months of the 2002 soybean season. "That's a good amount of money for him," said Kumar.

Samyojak

ITC benefited because of the increase in turnover resulting from Sanchalaks organizing and mobilizing farmers to sell to the company. The farmers were happy to have a better-defined channel through which to sell. But what of the middlemen, the commission agents of *mandi* life? All of ITC's CAs were kept, albeit with a new title: *Samyojak*. In this role, former CAs were given additional money-making opportunities within the eChoupal system. ITC mandated that its CAs become Samyojaks if an eChoupal was being set up in their geographic area. In most cases the transformation was achieved by convincing CAs of the potential revenue to be gained through the transactions in the eChoupal. The Samyojak role comprised three major areas of responsibility: (1) setting up the eChoupals; (2) facilitating ITC's purchasing transactions; and (3) helping with ITC's selling transactions.

In the establishment of new eChoupals, the Samyojak assisted ITC teams in village surveys to lay the groundwork. This meant assisting in the selection of the Sanchalak, acting as a liaison between villagers and ITC, and helping villagers understand the potential for the new system to be more efficient and profitable for all parties.

Samyojaks also managed warehousing hubs attached to the processing facilities that stored bought soybeans. They assisted in the logistics of the cash disbursements to farmers arriving at the processing facility. They also helped facilitate transportation links for farmers who could not reach the ITC processing facility themselves.

ITC's selling transactions comprised the "one-stop-shop" feature of the eChoupal. Farmers could buy herbicides, sowing seeds, gas lanterns, fertilizers, and soybean oil among other sundries directly from the company. While the Sanchalak had the responsibility of aggregating the orders in his village, the Samyojak would assist in actually moving the goods from ITC's manufacturing units to the eChoupals and/or warehousing hubs.

Three systems enabled ITC to sell and deliver goods to farmers through the eChoupal. The first was at the village level, where the Sanchalak aggregated demand for products through orders placed by his fellow farmers. This was done during the traditional *choupal* time. The Sanchalak then e-mailed the order to ITC, and the items were either (a) picked up by the Sanchalak at the ITC warehousing hub, or (b) delivered by the Samyojak to the villages. In either case the Sanchalak collected cash payments from his neighbors and remitted them to ITC. Seeds and fertilizers were sold in this way.

The second system did not involve any prior orders. Instead, the Sanchalak bought products based on estimated demand and stocked them in his home. Products sold this way were again procured by either Sanchalak pickup or Samyojak delivery. This system was most effective for consumer goods such as salt, matchboxes, soybean oil, and confectionary items. These were all ITC products, and both the company and the Sanchalak earned a fee from any sales.

The third system for selling additional goods through the eChoupal was "shopping" for the products at the ITC processing facility. When Sanchalaks and farmers visited the ITC facility to sell their produce, they also had the opportunity to peruse the warehousing hubs for items on which they might like to spend their freshly earned cash. Samyojaks managed these warehouses, assisting ITC in creating retail storefronts in the setup for 2003.

This interactive feature of the eChoupal system created an opportunity for ITC, the Sanchalak, and the Samyojak to turn profits that were simply not possible under the traditional system. The Sanchalak's job of arranging and mobilizing the farmers to take their soybeans directly to the ITC processing facility meant greater revenue for the company and commission for the Sanchalak. It was estimated that ITC saved $5/ton on freight cost; from those savings, ITC would reimburse the farmer for the time it took to travel to the ITC facility. The farmer, in turn, earned an average increase of $8/ton. Chairman Y. C. Deveshwar said:

> By creatively reorganizing the roles of traditional intermediaries who deliver critical value in tasks like logistic management at very low costs in a weak infrastructure economy like India, the eChoupal ploughs back a larger share of consumer price to the farmer. Besides providing an alternative marketing channel, this model engenders efficiency in the functioning of *mandis* through competition and serves to conserve public resources that would otherwise be needed to upgrade the *mandi* infrastructure to handle higher volumes of agri output.

For the Samyojak, income potential in the eChoupal system exceeded that of a CA in a *mandi*. ITC paid 1 percent of the transaction value to the CA when buying through the *mandi*. The typical CA turned his cash three times in a month during October to December (the time of peak activity), meaning that his gross return came to 3 percent per month for three months. Thereafter, money lay idle for the most part, except during May and June, when wheat and pulses were harvested. For an ITC Samyojak, there were more frequent opportunities to earn commission off farm inputs and other products being sold through the eChoupal. Commissions ranged from 2 percent to 5 percent per transaction, depending on the product. Samyojaks who assisted ITC in cash disbursements at processing units earned a fee of 1 percent of the transaction. The advantage of this was that the Samyojak now had the potential to earn from his working capital year-round.

The eChoupal leveraged the physical capabilities of the current middlemen while removing them from the flow of information and market signals. CAs-turned-Samyojaks had good terrain knowledge as well as long-standing relationships with villagers, which ITC also hoped to leverage. Samyojaks continued to operate out of *mandis* as hub points, allowing the eChoupal system to coexist with *mandis*.

In fact, ITC continued to buy from the *mandis* even as the eChoupal gathered steam. By 2003, ITC was procuring about 50 percent of its soybeans from the *mandis* and 50 percent from the eChoupal. The company hoped to shift the ratio to about 20 percent *mandi*, 80 percent eChoupal, as new hubs were added to the eChoupal system. The hubs had limited capacity, and, at certain points in the season, when market prices for soybeans were particularly low, ITC benefited from buying from the *mandi* as well as the eChoupal in order to maximize procurement. Furthermore, the *mandi* provided a source of "market intelligence" for ITC, as Samyojaks continued to operate there as well. Samyojaks still got a significant amount of income from their work in *mandis*; they could not yet afford to work solely for ITC.

Principles of the eChoupal

The eChoupal depended strongly on trust. The Web site was simply a medium for the more important human element, the interaction. Interaction was, after all, the initial driver of the *choupal* concept. No contract bound farmers to sell to ITC once they used the Web site. ITC did not ask for commitment; the farmer was free to do as he wished. In fact, the farmer could use all of the eChoupal's facilities, soak in all the information, and still choose to take his crop to the *mandi*.

The bet was that, once given these tools, farmers would realize on their own that selling directly to ITC was the best alternative to the *mandi*. Rajnikant Rai, vice president of trading in IBD Hyderabad, commented:

> We feel that this is how we can win people in the long run, by giving them the tools. Communication and information are developing; mobile phones are here; the Internet is here; we must use these things for education, and let there be no question of hiding information. We let the farmers understand and let them decide who is best in an open, competitive market scenario. Let them decide. They are the judges.

To ensure the Sanchalak's integrity in the process, when he received the computer equipment he took an oath that connected him to ITC. At this oath-taking event, the Sanchalak pledged, before the entire village, to uphold ITC's high standards; not to use the computer for "wrongful" purposes; and to maintain the ethics, image, and concept that ITC has created through the soyachoupal.com site. In addition, the ITC logo was painted on the front of the Sanchalak's home. This vibrant green and yellow mural stretched across the wall from floor to ceiling, identifying the Sanchalak as a liaison of ITC. Through these steps, ITC created a sense of pride and responsibility that infused the Sanchalak nominations. The Sanchalak became a highly visible figure after the ITC overhaul; as a result, potentially unscrupulous Sanchalaks were deterred from taking advantage of the system. If a Sanchalak were to act dishonestly at any point, it would create uproar throughout the village, and ITC would be able to take immediate action. Because the role was viewed as an honor, however, Sanchalaks usually treated their duties with the utmost pride and seriousness.

There were many benefits realized by ITC when the company found a way to buy directly from farmers. First, ITC had more control over the quality of the product it sourced. Direct contact with the farmer enabled knowledge sharing in terms of best practice for sowing, irrigation, and harvesting; therefore, ITC had some additional leverage over what was available to them for purchase. Higher-quality produce, of course, enabled more competitive pricing in the international market. Furthermore, buying directly from the farmer reduced the chance of the produce being adulterated with impurities (which often happened with middlemen). Deveshwar said,

> ITC has demonstrated that it is possible, nay, most crucial to combine the need for creating shareholder value with the superordinate goal of creating national value.

Hunting for Growth

The imperative for growth promulgated by Deveshwar had naturally prompted Sivakumar to seek additional applications of the eChoupal concept. Sivakumar was anxious to see the success of the soybean eChoupal model leveraged into IBD's three other product groups: coffee and spices, aqua food, and value-added horticultural products. Sivakumar thought hard about other commodities. While the basic character of agriculture was the same across India, value chains of different crops had their own intricate dynamics, as did the socioeconomic conditions of each region.

Soon after soybeans started showing promise, ITC had set up pilot eChoupals in three other crops in three different regions of India that were as diverse from one another as possible and representative of all crops in ITC's product portfolio: coffee in Karnataka, aqua (seafood) in Andhra Pradesh, and wheat in Uttar Pradesh. Learnings from these pilots were expected to help the company scale up on a national level. Each of these projects shared a common management approach with respect to their scale and scope: First, pilot-test the concept in a small number of villages; second, make changes based on the learning from the pilot phase and validate them in a larger number of villages; and third, grow the project to reach as many villages as possible and saturate the region. ITC called this approach "Roll Out, Fix It, Scale Up."

Other Commodities

As seen with soybeans, margins could be generated in many other commodities through logistics cost savings between the farm and the factory, where non-value-added activities were eliminated. While these savings could be instantly realized, Sivakumar wondered if they were sustainable over a period of time, as the savings were benchmarked against the current inefficient market. And the market was bound to become more efficient. He reasoned that ITC could potentially generate value via three other primary mechanisms: traceability (i.e., accountability for the quality of the product vis-à-vis its source), ability to match farmer production to consumer demand, and facilitation of an electronic marketplace. The three new eChoupal models were essentially a validation of these mechanisms.

With aqua products, or seafood, traceability provided an opportunity for ITC to generate value (and additional revenue) through the eChoupal. Global consumers of India's seafood would pay premium prices for shrimp that could be traced back to its source. If ITC were able to tell customers not only where a given commodity came from but also how it was produced (e.g., with antibiotics or not), significant gains would be possible. By controlling the source, ITC could guarantee the safety and sanitation of the product and thus receive higher prices.

Similarly, when ITC had greater knowledge of just *what* it was purchasing when procuring crops from rural farmers, value increased for both the company and the farmer. The wheat market was an example of this. Wheat varied greatly in both chemical composition and physical appearance, and, through the eChoupal, farmers learned to recognize which physical characteristics represented certain chemical qualities, such as gluten, protein, or starch content. Customers placed orders based on these chemical qualities. When ITC became able to analyze the crop *before* purchase, at the farm level, and then purchase and store it by chemical-composition category, there was an opportunity for cost savings, as it was expensive to separate wheat after it had been purchased and aggregated at the *mandi*. The farmer, too, benefited from this education. By identifying his high- and low-quality wheat, he could then price the varieties appropriately. He could command a higher price for the high-quality wheat and offer low-quality wheat at a reasonable price to customers who might need it, say, for animal feed. This way, he did not have to charge one *low* price for an amalgamation of wheat of disparate quality.

Coffee presented a new challenge to ITC. Coffee was an estate crop, grown by a large number of small-scale farmers. ITC had a deep knowledge of coffee farm practices; much research had already been done on the industry. The price volatility of coffee was high; variance from base price could reach 40 percent (compared with 20 percent volatility in the soybean market), and buyers would routinely renege on contracts if prices altered beyond tolerance. Market participants were savvy speculators. The importance of an agent in coffee transactions was paramount, and effective price discovery was often the critical part of a deal. With its electronic-trading platform, called Tradersnet, ITC improved real-time price discovery by hosting anonymous trades and letting the prevailing selling prices be known. Information sharing carried over to ITC's customers as well.

"The task of adapting the eChoupal concept for different crops and regions continues to test ITC's entrepreneurial capabilities," said Chairman Deveshwar.

eChoupal as a Marketing Channel

As Sivakumar pondered the relative potential for eChoupal in each of the four commodities, he also turned his eye to the long-term future of a wired rural India. As he clicked through the constantly changing pages of the eChoupal's Web site, he wondered if marketing and distribution to the 60 percent of India's workforce living in rural areas might be the real growth engine for ITC.

ITC's vision for marketing via the eChoupal involved three features: superior product and distinctive functional benefits, process benefits (simplified transactions between buyer and seller), and relationship benefits (farmers' willingness to identify themselves and reveal their purchasing behavior). ITC had conceived ideas for various input items that could be developed for new business given this framework. The company believed that these products could be made available to farmers through the eChoupal, thus increasing the value of the farmer's product as well as generating additional revenue for ITC. Deveshwar called this philosophy a "commitment beyond the market."

> **Fertilizers** Farmers spent an average of Rs. 26,000 crore ($5.7 billion) annually on urea, diammonium phosphate (DAP), and muriate of potash (MOP). Still, farmers could not easily access the fertilizers they needed. Thirty-five percent of DAP and 100 percent of MOP were imported. Logistics had proved to be complicated for most companies. They were unable to access many rural markets because of fragmented, or nonexistent, distribution channels.
>
> **Agrichemicals** Farmers also spent Rs. 3,500 crore ($774.5 million)/year on insecticides, herbicides, and fungicides. The agrichemical market was highly fragmented and consolidated by multinational corporations such as Dupont, Novartis, and Cyanamid. New chemicals were introduced frequently; however, their life cycles in the market were only two or three years. Given the short product cycle, big companies needed immediate market access. Farmers, too, suffered when they could not access these products. High costs of labor, for example, hurt soybean and wheat farmers whose fields could have been covered with herbicides, instead of weeding workers, at a lower cost.
>
> **Seeds** This was a relatively small, fragmented market of Rs. 3,000 crore ($663.9 million)/ year, but only 4 percent of farms used commercial seed. Government-promoted seed corporations made different types of seeds available though cooperatives, and large multinational companies had entered the market with better-quality material. Still, there were lead times of up to three years to make seed varieties available to rural farmers.
>
> **Insurance** Currently, Indians were collectively paying Rs. 50,000 crore ($11 billion) in yearly life insurance premiums, and that market was expected to reach Rs. 150,000 crore ($33 billion) by 2010.[16] Life Insurance Corporation (LIC) was a government-run insurance provider that had already taken a shine to rural markets. Even in the relatively poor states of West Bengal and Bihar, 6 million rural farmers had taken out policies. In 2000, private insurance companies were allowed to enter the market, and, as a result, at least 12 new companies were seeking to expand their business into rural India to compete with LIC. By 2003, rural business comprised 16 percent of LIC's portfolio, but only 9 percent of private companies' portfolios. These markets were largely untapped because of a lack of trustworthy intermediaries. ITC believed that it could create a relationship of trust and help

[16] Company information.

farmers understand the rules and benefits of insurance plans. Eventually, ITC envisioned Sanchalaks being able to offer the eChoupal infrastructure to LIC agents for a fee or to set up its own insurance brokerage company.

An opportunity also existed for other types of insurance policies, covering fire, marine, motor, and workmen's compensation. Insurers, however, had been biased toward larger accounts, leaving less prosperous farmers unable to participate. Insurers lacked quality data on risks and parameters of farm life and were hesitant to insure rural customers. With ITC as a liaison, however, data on rural farmers could be delivered to insurance companies, thus demystifying and uncovering the rural market.

Credit A national survey in 2001 had shown that Indians were saving about 30 percent of their annual income, though not through financial institutions. Both private- and public-sector banks lacked a customer-friendly approach and were often avoided by rural farmers. One of the main reasons that farmers avoided saving through banks was that they were often linked to a loan.[17] If a farmer had savings in the same bank he had borrowed from, the bank could demand that he use those savings to pay back the loan. Oftentimes farmers would rather defer the loan and simply save their cash in their homes, unbeknownst to the bank.

ITC believed that a system of trust engendered through the Sanchalak would facilitate financial transactions. It could channel rural farmers into the mutual fund arena and earn a commission from banks on farmers' investments, using the technology introduced in the eChoupal. *Choupal* discussions would create data on likelihood to invest, and the results would be stored in a data warehouse for future campaigns.

Sustaining Success

Sivakumar wanted to know how to evaluate these new business opportunities for ITC. He knew that the eChoupal could not be everything to everyone, and he wanted to allocate ITC resources constructively. Once the sourcing of their core commodities was sufficiently strengthened, and cost-effective supply chains were running efficiently through the eChoupal, other business opportunities would develop. The poor and fragmented rural consumers were traditionally underserved, but the demand was growing with rising aspiration levels triggered by, for example, broader advertising. Deveshwar said,

> The pioneering eChoupal business model contributes to creating the market through improved farm incomes, whilst placing ITC in a unique position to reap benefits through its closeness to the potential consumer.

Sivakumar also needed to consider the sustainability of the existing eChoupal network and its success to date. Many nonprofit organizations had tried to introduce technology to rural India, but had not been able to sustain their initiatives. Computer equipment was expensive and had a finite lifespan. After a few years it would have to be replaced. Should (and could) ITC bear the cost of continually replacing IT equipment?

ITC was convinced that as more farmers bought products through the upstream channel, many other marketers would follow. But how should ITC best jump-start its upstream commerce initiative to ensure its long-term success?

[17] Total crop loans in 2001 came to Rs. 33,000 crore ($7 billion).

Annotated Bibliography

IT and Business Advantage Bookshelf: Resources to help you learn how IT is both driving and enabling business strategy, capabilities, and value creation.

Applegate, Lynda M. *Crafting Business Models.* Boston: Harvard Business School Publishing (#808-705), 2008 (DVD). Use this online tutorial and the associated toolkit to analyze an established company's business model or to develop the business plan for a new opportunity or venture. You can also use the frameworks and tools to analyze cases in this book.

Austin, Robert D. and Stephen P. Bradley. *The Broadband Explosion*. Boston: Harvard Business School Press, 2004. A collection of essays focusing on the new potential and problems posed by the explosion of broadband.

Benko, Cathleen and F. Warren McFarlan. *Connecting the Dots: Aligning Projects with Objectives in Unpredictable Times*. Boston: Harvard Business School Press, 2003. A hands-on book on how to do a better job of aligning an IT portfolio with corporate strategy.

Bradley, Stephen P. and Richard L. Nolan, eds. *Sense and Respond: Capturing the Value in the Network Era*. Boston: Harvard Business School Press, 1998. This book captures the tremendous shift in the adaptiveness of management control systems and organizations in an information-mediated world.

Brynjolfsson, Erik and Brian Kahin, eds. *Understanding the Digital Economy: Data, Tools and Research*. Cambridge, MA: MIT Press, 2000. Learn the latest research tools for collecting and analyzing the economic impact of the Internet and electronic commerce in the United States and internationally. Main areas of discussion include market structure, competition, and organizational change.

Carr, Nicholas G. *Does IT Matter: Information Technology and the Erosion of Competitive Advantage*. Boston: Harvard Business School Press, 2004. A controversial book that suggests that IT's role as a source of competitive advantage in the past may no longer exist.

Chandler, Alfred D., and James W. Cortada, eds. *A Nation Transformed by Information: How Information Has Shaped the United States from Colonial Times to the Present*. New York: Oxford University Press, 2000. A 250-year history of the information revolution. Provides one of the most comprehensive and thoughtful descriptions of the roots of the information economy.

Chesbrough, Henry. *Open Business Models: How to Thrive in the New Innovation Landscape*. Boston: Harvard Business School Press, 2006. Chesbrough offers diagnostic tools, compelling examples, and other frameworks to help assess your company's current business model and identify ways to create a more open model.

Christensen, Clayton M. and Michael E. Raynor. *The Innovator's Solution: Creating and Sustaining Successful Growth*. Boston: Harvard Business School Press, 2003. Explores the process through which innovations are packaged and shaped within companies and strategies for how companies can shape powerful business plans to create their own disruptive growth.

Davenport, Thomas H. and John C. Beck. *The Attention Economy: Understanding the New Currency of Business*. Boston: Harvard Business School Press, 2001. A thoughtful book that captures the importance of knowledge management in an information-overloaded world.

Drucker, Peter. *Managing in Turbulent Times*. New York: Harper and Row, 1980. This classic book discusses how a firm can draw on the fundamentals of leadership to both protect from threats and take advantage of unexpected opportunities during times of turbulence and disruption.

Friedman, Thomas L. *The World is Flat 3.0: A Brief History of the Twenty-first Century*. New York: Picador, 2007. Explores how exponential technical advances of the digital revolution are "flattening" the world, making it possible to interact and do business through instantaneous connections around the world. Emphasizing that "globalization 3.0" is driven not by major companies or giant trade organizations but by individual freelancers and innovative startups now positioned to compete and win globally, Friedman

offers specific recommendations about the technical and creative skills required to succeed in these new circumstances.

Gladwell, Malcolm. *The Tipping Point.* Boston: Little Brown & Company, 2000. This book persuasively describes the multiple sources that suddenly lead to a massive adaptation of a technology in a short period of time.

Leonard, Dorothy A. *Wellsprings of Knowledge: Building and Sustaining the Sources of Innovation.* Boston: Harvard Business School Press, 1998. Focuses on the knowledge-creating activities and behaviors that managers guide, control, and inspire: developing problem-solving skills, experimenting to build for the future, integrating information across internal project and functional boundaries, and importing expertise from outside the firm.

McKenney, James L., Duncan C. Copeland, and Richard O. Mason. *Waves of Change: Business Evolution through Information Technology.* Boston: Harvard Business School Press, 1995. This book captures the long-term dynamics of an evolving information architecture as it traces more than 30 years of the history of information technology in four organizations.

Nolan, R. L. *Dot Vertigo: Doing Business in a Permeable World.* New York: John Wiley & Sons, 2001. Discussions of the different kinds of organization structure challenges that have been created in an information-enabled world, where the boundaries of an organization are no longer clear.

Schwartz, Evan. *Juice: The Creative Fuel that Drives World Class Inventors,* Boston: Harvard Business School Press, 2004. This book aims to distill common principles in the approaches of great inventors.

Shapiro, Carl and Hal R. Varian. *Information Rules: A Strategic Guide to the Network Economy.* Boston: Harvard Business School Press, 1998. The first book to distill the economics of information and networks into practical business strategies.

Tapscott, Donald, David Ticoll, and Alex Lowy. *Digital Capital: Harnessing the Power of Business Webs.* Boston: Harvard Business School Press, 2000. A book on the implications of a digitized, totally wired world.

Yoffie, David B., ed. *Competing in the Age of Digital Convergence.* Boston: Harvard Business School Press, 1997. An important set of essays on the implications for corporate strategy of computing in a digitized world.

The Business of IT Bookshelf: Resources to help you transform your deployment and management of IT assets in a networked world.

Austin, Robert A., and Lee Devin. *Artful Making: What Managers Need to Know about How Artists Work.* Upper Saddle River, NJ: Prentice Hall, 2003. A thoughtful book that compares the issues involved in developing software with those of producing a play and finds a surprising number of commonalities.

Austin, Robert D., Richard L. Nolan, and Shannon O'Donnell. *Adventures of an IT Leader.* Boston: Harvard Business School Press, 2009. This engaging novel follows the development of a newly appointed CIO, Jim Barton, as he spends a difficult year learning IT leadership, side-stepping the pitfalls that make the CIO job the most volatile, high turnover job in business. Readers can "walk in the shoes" of Barton as they explore the various IT situations, issues, and challenges raised in each chapter. The foundation of a new approach to teaching IT Management, this book is surprisingly difficult to put down!

Baldwin, Carliss Y. and Kim Clark. *Design Rules: The Power of Modularity.* Cambridge, MA: MIT Press, 2000. Argues that the computer industry experienced previously unimaginable levels of innovation and growth because it embraced the concept of modularity, building complex products from small subsystems that could be designed independently yet function together as a whole.

Beck, Kent. *Extreme Programming: Embrace Change.* Reading, MA: Addison-Wesley, 1999. Provides an intriguing high-level overview of the author's Extreme Programming (XP) software development methodology, a controversial approach to software development which challenges the notion that the cost of changing a piece of software must rise dramatically over the course of time.

Brooks, Frederick. *The Mythical Man-Month: Essays on Software Engineering.* Reading, MA: Addison-Wesley, 1995. One of the classics in the field of program management. The author draws on his experience as the head of operating systems development for IBM's famous 360 mainframe computer and distills his wisdom in an easily accessible form.

Chesbrough, Henry. *Open Innovation: The New Imperative for Creating and Profiting from Technology.* Boston: Harvard Business School Press, 2006. This

book describes how principals of open innovation are driving new approaches to developing and leading with IT.

DeMarco, Tom and Timothy Lister. ***Peopleware: Productive Projects and Teams.*** **New York: Dorset House, 1999. Using a conversational and straightforward style, the authors assert that most projects fail because of failures within the teams running them.**

DeMarco,Tom, Peter Hruschka, Tim Lister, Suzanne Robertson, James Robertson, and Steve McMenamin. ***Adrenaline Junkies and Template Zombies: Understanding Patterns of Project Behavior.*** **New York: Dorset House, 2008. This is a highly readable and useful guide to archetypal behaviors—both valuable and detrimental—that emerge in project work and project teams. The authors identify and label, in a humorous and memorable fashion, about 80 behavioral patterns and the reasoning behind them, and offer suggestions for corrective behavior.**

Feghi, Jalal, Jalil Feghi, and Peter Williams. ***Digital Certificates: Applied Internet Security.*** **Reading, MA: Addison-Wesley, 1999. An excellent reference on the subject of encryption and digital certificates.**

Forcht, Karen A. ***Computer Security Management.*** **Danvers, MA: Boyd & Fraser, 1994. A practical book that describes the multiple aspects of computer security and the steps to be taken to gain good results.**

Freiberger, Paul and Michael Swaine. ***Fire in the Valley: The Making of the Personal Computer.*** **New York: McGraw-Hill, 2000. This book explores the origins of the personal computer, focusing especially on the brilliant engineers and programmers that formed the foundation of what would become great computer companies.**

Highsmith, James III. ***Adaptive Software Development: A Collaborative Approach to Managing Complex Systems.*** **New York: Dorset House, 1999. Provides a series of frameworks to help an organization employ adaptive principles, establish collaboration, and provide a path toward using an adaptive approach on large projects.**

Hoch, Detlev J., Cyriac R. Roeding, Gert Purkett, and Sandro K. Lindner. ***Secrets of Software Success: Management Insights from 100 Software Firms around the World.*** **Boston: Harvard Business School Press, 1999. A practical book that focuses on the issues that must be resolved for a successful software implementation.**

Perrow, Charles. ***Normal Accidents: Living with High Risk Technologies.*** **Princeton, NJ: Princeton University Press, 1999. Looking at an array of real and potential technological mishaps—including the Bhopal chemical plant accident of 1984, the Challenger explosion of 1986, and the possible disruptions of Y2K and genetic engineering—Perrow concludes that as our technologies become more complex, the odds of tragic results increase.**

Raymond, Eric S. and Bob Young. ***The Cathedral and the Bazaar: Musings on Linux and Open Source by an Accidental Revolutionary.*** **Sebastapol, CA: O'Reilly and Associates, 2001. A text defining the open source revolution in computing, discussing the advantages of open source computing with such technologies as Perl, Linux, and Apache. Offers a glimpse into the future of these types of technologies and their uses in the digital age.**

Ross, Jeanne and Peter Weill. ***Enterprise Architecture as Strategy: Creating a Foundation for Business Execution.*** **Boston: Harvard Business School Press, 2006. This book makes the case that a firm's enterprise architecture provides the foundation for executing its business strategy. The authors show that an effective enterprise architecture—an IT infrastructure and digitized business processes that automate and support a company's core capabilities—can enhance its profitability, speed time to market, improve strategy execution, and even lower IT costs. They provide practical guidance on the decisions and actions necessary to implement an enterprise architecture aligned with the firm's operating model.**

Smith, H. Jeff. ***Managing Privacy Information Technology and Corporate America.*** **Chapel Hill: University of North Carolina Press, 1994. A very practical book that talks about information technology privacy, current practices, and issues for the future.**

Upton, David. ***Designing, Managing, and Improving Operations.*** **Upper Saddle River, NJ: Prentice-Hall, 1998. An example of Upton's writings on the benefits of incremental improvement strategies and especially the need to design operational infrastructures so that they can be improved incrementally.**

Utterback, James. ***Mastering the Dynamics of Innovation: How Companies Can Seize Opportunities in the Face of Technological Change.*** **Boston: Harvard Business School Press, 1994. An analysis of the forces to manage in developing new products and processes as a strategic force.**

Von Hippel, Eric. *Democratizing Innovation.* Cambridge, MA: MIT Press, 2006. An insightful analysis of how and why things like open source software development work, and a discussion of the promise they hold for the future.

Wheelwright, Steven C. and Kim B. Clark. *Leading Product Development.* New York: Free Press, 1995. A focused view on senior management's role in shaping strategy based on continuous product development as a competitive means. Time from concept to market is the critical success factor.

The IT Leadership Bookshelf: Resources to help you develop the leadership and governance skills needed to lead IT as a business executive or CIO.

Broadbent, Marianne and Ellen Kitzis. *The New CIO Leader: Setting the Agenda and Delivering Results.* Boston: Harvard Business School Press, 2004. This book offers practical advice and frameworks to help CIOs assume the larger, more strategic role that is commensurate with the increasing criticality of information technology in today's organizations.

Ciampa, Dan. *Taking Advice: How Leaders Get Good Advice and Use it Wisely.* Boston: Harvard Business School Press, 2006. Today's leaders have access to many sources of advice from which they could benefit in dealing with high-stakes, unfamiliar situations. Categorizing both types of advice, and types of advisors, Ciampa offers guidance on how a leader can most effectively leverage advice from others.

Kirkeby, Ole Fogh. *The Virtue of Leadership.* Copenhagen: Copenhagen Business School, 2008. A substantive discussion of a philosophy of leadership that draws impressively on thinkers all the way back to the Greeks.

Maister, David H., Charles H. Green, and Robert M. Galford. *The Trusted Advisor.* Free Press, 2001. This book, focused on how professionals develop value-creating trusted relationships with their clients, can be valuable to CIOs who aspire to build credibility and IT thought-leadership among their executive peers.

Stenzel, Joe, Gary Cokins, Bill Flemming, Anthony Hill, Michael Hugos, Paul R. Niven, Karl D. Schubert, and Alan Stratton. *CIO Best Practices: Enabling Strategic Value with Information Technology.* Wiley and SAS Business Series, 2007. This is a compilation of real-world practices used by CIOs and other IT specialists who have successfully mastered the blend of business and IT responsibilities. It offers valuable insight into how to build and exercise strategic IT leadership.

Wageman, Ruth, J. Richard Hackman, Debra A. Nunes, and James A. Burruss. *Senior Leadership Teams: What it Takes to Make Them Great.* Harvard Business School Press, 2008. Turbulent times make demands that outstrip the capabilities of any one person—no matter how talented. This book provides practical guidance on how to leverage diverse senior leadership talents to good effect.

Watkins, Michael. *The First 90 Days: Critical Success Strategies for New Leaders at All Levels.* Boston: Harvard Business School Press, 2003. Offers practical guidance for IT leaders as they transition into a more strategic and business-centric role.

Weill, Peter and Jeanne Ross. *IT Governance: How Top Performers Manage IT Decision Rights for Superior Results.* Boston: Harvard Business School Press, 2004. Just as corporate governance aims to ensure quality decisions about all corporate assets, IT governance links IT decisions with company objectives and monitors performance and accountability. The authors show that firms with superior IT governance produce significantly higher profit margins than firms with poor governance given the same strategic objectives. They offer practical advice on how to design and implement a system of decision rights that enables IT to better deliver on four objectives: cost-effectiveness, asset utilization, business growth, and business flexibility.

Westerman, George and Richard Hunter. *IT Risk: Turning Business Threats into Competitive Advantage.* Boston: Harvard Business School Press, 2007. Outlines a new model for integrated risk management that can help companies focus on their most pressing IT risks while still taking advantage of profit opportunities. Written for a broad base of senior executives, this book offers tools and practices that general managers can understand and use.

Wren, J. Thomas, Douglas A. Hicks, and Terry L. Price, eds. *The International Library of Leadership.* Cheltenham, UK: Edward Elgar, 2004. This three volume set, which begins with ancient Greek philosophers and extends to the work of specialized modern day scientists, is perhaps the most comprehensive (and expensive!) collection of thoughts about leadership available anywhere. The editors have made excellent selections and provide expert annotations and framing discussions of what it means to be the leader.

Index

Page numbers with n. indicate footnotes.

B

N